Frommer's®

4th
Edition

FRUGAL   TRAVELER'S   GUIDES

Costa Rica & Belize
FROM $35 A DAY

by Eliot Greenspan

with Karl Samson & Jane Aukshunas

Macmillan • USA

ABOUT THE AUTHOR

Eliot Greenspan is a poet, journalist, and travel writer. He took his backpack and typewriter the length of Mesoamerica before settling in Costa Rica in 1992. Since then he has worked steadily for the *Tico Times* and continued his travels in the region. He is also the author of *Frommer's Costa Rica '97*.

ACKNOWLEDGMENTS

The author would like to thank Anne Becher and Joe Richey, as well as Teresa Rodríguez, who aided throughout the process—on the road and on the phone: "¿qué más?"

MACMILLAN TRAVEL

A Simon & Schuster Macmillan Company
1633 Broadway
New York, NY 10019

Find us online at **http://www.mgr.com/travel** or
on America Online at Keyword: **Frommer's**.

ISBN 0-02-861103-9
ISSN 1051-6859

Editor: Erica Spaberg
Production Editor: Lori Cates
Page Creation by Debbie Cathcart, Natalie Hollifield, Pete Lippincott, Kevin MacDonald, Candyce McCreary, Tom Missler, Angel Perez, Linda Quigley, and Bryan Towse
Design by Michele Laseau
Digital Cartography by Ortelius Design and Peter Bogaty

SPECIAL SALES

Bulk purchases (10+ copies) of Frommer's and selected Macmillan travel guides are available to corporations, organizations, mail-order catalogs, institutions, and charities at special discounts, and can be customized to suit individual needs. For more information write to: Special Sales, Macmillan General Reference, 1633 Broadway, New York, NY 10019.

Contents

List of Maps

AN INVITATION TO THE READER

In researching this book, I discovered many wonderful places—hotels, restaurants, shops, and more. We're sure you'll find others. Please tell us about them, so we can share the information with your fellow travelers in upcoming editions. If you were disappointed with a recommendation, we'd love to know that, too. Please write to:

Eliot Greenspan
c/o *Frommer's Costa Rica & Belize from $35 a Day,* 4th Edition
Macmillan Travel
1633 Broadway
New York, NY 10019

AN ADDITIONAL NOTE

Please be advised that travel information is subject to change at any time—and this is especially true of prices. We therefore suggest that you write or call ahead for confirmation when making your travel plans. The authors, editors, and Publisher cannot be held responsible for the experiences of readers while traveling. Your safety is important to us, however, so we encourage you to stay alert and be aware of your surroundings. Keep a close eye on cameras, purses, and wallets, all favorite targets of thieves and pickpockets.

WHAT THE SYMBOLS MEAN

✪ **Frommer's Favorites**

Hotels, restaurants, attractions, and entertainment you should not miss.

The following abbreviations are used for credit and charge cards:
AE   American Express   MC   MasterCard
DISC   Discover   V   Visa

The Best of Costa Rica & Belize for the Frugal Traveler

first visited Belize on my way south from Mexico. I traveled with a backpack, camped on Caye Caulker, and spent my days snorkeling and fishing the barrier reef from a small wooden sloop with tattered sails. At night, Gamusa—my dreadlocked captain and host—would make a spicy stew of fresh coconut milk, roots, plantains, and the day's catch. We poured rum into freshly opened green coconuts and ate around an open-air fire. It was hard to leave, but eventually I continued south, via the great Mayan city of Tikal, and landed in San José, Costa Rica, where I've settled. Despite some half-hearted attempts, I seem unable to tear myself away from Mesoamerica. I'm drawn to the desolate beaches that stretch on for miles, the primary lowland rain forests with towering trees and squawking scarlet macaws, the wild white-water rivers, and the snorkeling and diving—some of the best in this hemisphere. I hope this guidebook reflects my five steady years of poking around the parks, beaches, jungles, and hills of both Costa Rica and Belize—as well as the wide-ranging experience of the previous authors, travel writers Karl Samson and Jane Aukshunas—and that it helps you to plan and enjoy your time here. Most of you won't choose to settle down, but many of you will decide to come back.

For decades, Costa Rica and Belize were the well-kept secrets of a handful of biologists, backpackers, anglers, and scuba divers. Gradually, the word leaked out. Although Costa Rica is now one of the most expensive countries in Central America (and Belize isn't far behind), both countries still offer the frugal traveler a lot of options. Room rates have been escalating rapidly in the past few years, but there are still great bargains to be had. Meal costs continue to be low. As far as transportation goes, you'll find it very cheap to get around by bus. Even if you choose to fly, you'll find that airfares, though no longer the incredible bargain they were a few years ago, are still a good deal.

Neither country has a well-developed infrastructure nor many luxury resorts (although Costa Rica is moving in this direction). What they do have in abundance are small inns and hotels, pristine beaches and coral reefs, and thousands of acres of protected forests: rain forests, cloud forests, mangrove forests, and even tropical dry forests. Each country has enough exotic avian species to keep an avid birdwatcher busy for a lifetime. In the case of Belize, you'll find several impressive archeological sites from the classic and post-classic Mayan periods to explore as well. And as you're probably well aware, both have become popular playgrounds for the adventure-travel set: it's possible to white-water raft a jungle river or dive the barrier reef, and a whole lot more in between.

Below I've chosen the very best of what these two countries have to offer, with a particular eye toward frugal, adventurous travelers. Most are covered in greater detail elsewhere in this book; this chapter is merely meant to whet your appetite and give you an overview of some highlights so you can start planning your trip.

1 The Best Natural Wonders

- **Rincón de la Vieja National Park** (northeast of Liberia in Guanacaste, Costa Rica): This is an area of rugged beauty and intense volcanic activity with hot springs, mud baths, and cool jungle swimming holes. Hire a guide and a horse for a day of exploration. As you make your way on horseback, you'll pass through pastureland, scrub savannah, and moist secondary forest, seeing any number of species of birds. Set on a working dairy farm, **Santa Clara Lodge** (☎ 506/223-7141 or 506-666-0473; fax 506/666-0475) makes a great base for exploring this area. See chapter 7.
- **Arenal Volcano/Tabacón Hot Springs** (near La Fortuna, northwest of San José, Costa Rica): When the skies are clear and the lava is flowing, Arenal Volcano provides a thrilling light show accompanied by an earthshaking rumble that defies description. All this can be more than a bit exciting, which is why it's nice to have a natural hot springs to soak in immediately afterward. To really get that one-two punch going, you can sit in the large pool at the **Tabacón Hot Springs Resort** (☎ 506/460-6000) and watch the fireworks at the same time. See chapter 8.
- **The Rio Sarapiquí Region** (north of San José between Guanacaste in the west and the Caribbean Coast in the east, Costa Rica): The area that borders the Sarapiquí river may be the best place for an eco-lodge experience in Costa Rica. Lodges are dotted throughout the protected tropical forests that climb from the Caribbean coastal lowlands into the central mountain range. Many are close to Braulio Carrillo National Park and private nature reserves with excellent birdwatching, including a few that offer accommodation and meal packages that suit a frugal budget. Try **El Gavilán Lodge** (☎ 506/234-9507) for a spot close to the river. See chapter 8.
- **Drake Bay** (The Osa peninsula, Costa Rica): While there are more remote spots in both countries, this is my choice for an isolated getaway. No roads lead directly to Drake Bay, and I hope none ever will. Most visitors take a combination plane, bus, and boat journey to get here, but it's also possible to charter a sea plane that will take you directly to this small, breathtakingly beautiful bay. South of it are miles of deserted beaches, tide pools, spring-fed rivers, waterfalls, and rain-forest trails that run through some of Costa Rica's lushest jungle. While there are some very comfortable eco-lodges in this region, most of them are out of our price range. The alternative is almost as delicious, and certainly more natural: a spacious tent on a raised wooden deck at the **Drake Bay Wilderness Camp** (☎ 506/771-2436 or 506/284-4107; fax 506/771-2436). See chapter 10.
- **Tortuguero Village & the Jungle Canals** (The Caribbean Coast, north of Limón, Costa Rica): Tortuguero Village is a small collection of rustic wooden shacks perched on a narrow spit of land between the Caribbean and a dense maze of jungle canals. It's been called Costa Rica's Venice, but it actually has more in common with the South American Amazon. You can fly from San José into a small airstrip, but it's better to journey in from the interior by boat, slowly plying the Reventazón, Pacuare, or Sarapiquí rivers and connecting canals. On the way, you'll

see a wide variety of herons and other water birds, three types of monkeys, three-toed sloths, and huge American crocodiles. If you come between June and October you may be treated to the awe-inspiring spectacle of a green turtle nesting; tiny Tortuguero beach is the last major nesting site for this endangered species. Most of the lodges here are quite expensive, but **El Manati Lodge** (☎ **506/288-1828**) fits our budget. See chapter 11.

- **The Belizean Barrier Reef** (The Caribbean Coast, Belize): The world's second-longest barrier reef, this intricate coral formation extends for more than 180 miles along the coast of Belize. Teeming with marine life, it is surrounded by crystal-clear waters and is easily visible from many of the cayes. It offers some of the world's most exciting snorkeling, diving, and fishing. The more developed cayes offer various day and overnight trips that explore this lively underwater world. Whether you seek your thrills on it or beneath it, or simply admire its beauty from ashore, Belize's barrier reef is a natural wonder worth beholding. If you want a spot right on the edge of the reef, try **Reef's End Lodge** (☎ **501-5/22419**) on Tobacco Caye, which charges $75 per double per day, including all meals. See chapters 16 and 18.
- **The Cayo district** (Western Belize): This is a rich land of rolling hills, jungle rivers, and pristine rain forest. Canoe on the Macal River with toucans flying overhead, or ride a horse to a Mayan ceremonial cave. This was a prime part of the ancient Mayan empire, and you can still visit the temples and buildings at sites such as Xunantunich, Caracol, and Cahal Pech. **DuPlooy's** (☎ **501-92/3101**) is one of the nicer jungle lodges in the area, but if you opt for one of their shared-bath rooms in the Pink House, you'll be living big, yet within our budget. See chapter 17.
- **The Toledo district** (Southern Belize): Sparsely populated by black Caribs (or Garifuna) along the coast, and by Kekchi and Mopan Maya in the interior, Belize's Toledo district is where you'll find this small country's most untouched rain forests. The pace is slow, but contagious. Watch the village Maya come to market in Punta Gorda, or visit the Garifuna town of Barranco, and feel time losing some of its importance. You may not throw your watch away, but you'll escape its ravages for just a while. With a wide offering of trips, tours, and activities, **Nature's Way Guest House** (☎ **501-7/22119**) remains the adventurers' hub in Punta Gorda. See chapter 18.

2   The Best Adventures & Outings

- **Hooking a Billfish off the Pacific Coast** (Costa Rica): Billfish are plentiful all along Costa Rica's Pacific coast, with boats operating from Playa del Coco to Playa Zancudo. Costa Rican anglers hold world records for their blue marlin and Pacific sailfish catches. Go to Quepos for the best après-fish scene or head to Drake Bay if you want some isolation. **Americana Fishing Services** (☎ **506/223-4331**) can help you find a good charter skipper or specialized fishing lodge. See chapter 3.
- **Rafting the Upper Reventazon River** (near Turrialba, Costa Rica): The class V "Guayabo" section of this popular river offers serious white water. Only experienced and gutsy river runners need apply. If this sounds too hard-core for you, try a two-day float down the Pacuare, a river that passes through primary and secondary forests and a beautiful steep gorge that, sadly, may be dammed soon. **Aventuras Naturales** (☎ **800/308-3394** or 506/225-3939) can arrange either expedition. See chapter 3.
- **Mountain Biking around Lake Arenal** (near Tilarán and Arenal Volcano, Costa Rica): This huge man-made lake, which sits at the base of majestic Arenal Volcano,

has trails that thread along its shores and through neighboring forests and pasture lands. There are a variety of rides for all levels of ability—from novice to expert. The setting is spectacular, and the nearby hot springs at Tabacón offer the promise of a relaxing soak at the end of the day. See chapter 8.

- **Windsurfing Arenal Lake** (near Tilarán and Arenal Volcano, Costa Rica): With steady gale-force winds and stunning scenery, the northern end of Arenal Lake has become a major international windsurfing hot spot. See chapter 8.

- **Hiking Mount Chirripó** (near San Isidro de El General on the Central Pacific Coast, Costa Rica): The highest mountain in Costa Rica is Mount Chirripó, one of the few places in the world where (on a clear day) you can see both the Atlantic and the Pacific at the same time. Hiking to Chirripó's 12,412-foot summit will take you through a number of distinct bioregions, ranging from lowland pastures and a cloud forest to a high-altitude páramo, a tundra-like landscape with stunted trees and morning frosts. See chapter 9.

- **Surfing Pavones** (south of Limón, Costa Rica): Just 8 miles from the Panamanian border, on Costa Rica's Caribbean Coast, is Playa Pavones, reputed to have one of the longest rideable waves in the world—over a kilometer in length. Much more can be said about this experience, but if you're a surfer, you've heard it all before. **Tour Tech International** (☎ 800/882-2636) specializes in surf tours to Costa Rica and will give callers current wave reports. See chapter 10.

- **Sea Kayaking in Belize:** Whether you're cruising along the edge of the barrier reef, languishing in an atoll lagoon, or poking around mangrove estuaries, the calm blue waters off this country's coast are a kayaker's dream come true. **Slickrock Adventures, Inc.** (P.O. Box 1400, Moab, UT 84532; ☎ 801/259-6996) has been leading kayak tours here for years. See chapters 13 and 16.

- **Diving the Blue Hole & Lighthouse Reef** (The Outer Atolls, Belize): A spot first made famous by Jacques Cousteau in the early 1970s, the Blue Hole continues to be one of the ultimate dive sites on the planet. After you finish exploring the steep walls and ledges of this perfectly submerged sinkhole, take a gander at the giant barrel sponges that populate Lighthouse Reef. **The Blue Hole Dive Center** (☎ 501-26/2982) and **M/V Hot Dive** (☎/fax 501-2/34058) both specialize in dive trips. See chapter 16.

- **Spelunking in the Maya Mountains** (Belize): The ancient Maya believed caves were a gateway to the spirit world, and Belize is loaded with caves. Many of them were used as Mayan ceremonial sites. Others are just a great place to admire stalagmites and stalactites. If you're interested in caving, contact **Ian Anderson's Caves Branch** (☎ 501-8/22800). See chapter 13.

- **Taking a Snorkel Trip to Hol Chan Marine Reserve from Caye Caulker** (Belize): Hol Chan is a protected patch of the Belizean barrier reef with some shallow water sections and cuts that are excellent for snorkeling. You'll see giant Jew fish, bright parrot fish, and elegant angelfish. Most trips include a stop at Shark-Ray Alley, where stingrays and nurse sharks congregate. It's safe, but your heart will pound nonetheless. Take a boat from Caye Caulker. You'll make several stops for snorkeling, and have lunch in San Pedro before heading home with the setting sun. See chapter 16.

3 The Best Beaches

With over 750 combined miles of shoreline on its Pacific and Caribbean coasts, Costa Rica offers beachgoers an embarrassment of riches. This can hardly be claimed about Belize. It has but one beach on its coast, but several great beaches on its offshore islands. Nonetheless, whether you want a broad stretch of sand all your own, a lively beach-town with all-night discos, or just a quiet place to leisurely hunt for shells, there's a beach in these two countries just for you.

- **Playa Conchal** (Nicoya peninsula, Costa Rica): A short section of beach consisting entirely of small polished and crushed shells, Playa Conchal isn't great for swimming, but it's a beachcomber's delight. You should have no problem filling your pockets—and a few additional plastic bags—with a wide range of colorful shells and fragments. Better bathing beaches are just a short walk away in either direction. The expected opening of a 300-plus room resort in summer 1996 will certainly change the feel of this once isolated beach, but there are plenty of shells to go around for quite some time. See chapter 7.
- **Playa Montezuma** (Nicoya peninsula, Costa Rica): This tiny beach town at the tip of the Nicoya peninsula has come in and out of vogue, and yet still retains a funky sense of individuality. European backpackers, vegetarian yoga enthusiasts, and UFO seekers choose Montezuma's beach over any other in Costa Rica. Its fabulous 500-foot waterfall is perhaps the primary reason for its popularity, but its phenomenal length is another major draw—the beach seems to stretch on for miles, with plenty of isolated spots for you to plop down a beach towel or mat. See chapter 7.
- **Playa Tamarindo** (Guanacaste, Costa Rica): Not yet overdeveloped, Tamarindo still manages to provide ample lodgings to suit every budget, and excellent restaurants at almost every turn. The beach is long and broad, with sections calm enough for swimmers and others just right for surfers. Located approximately halfway along Guanacaste's coast, Tamarindo makes a good base for exploring other nearby beaches. There are plenty of surfers here, and it hosts one of the most lively nightlife scenes on this coast. See chapter 7.
- **Santa Rosa National Park** (Guanacaste, Costa Rica): If you really want to get away from it all, the beaches in this remote northwestern national park are a good bet. You'll either have to drive (via four-wheel vehicle) or hike 13 kilometers from the park's entrance to reach the closest one. Once there, you'll find only the most basic of camping facilities—outhouse latrines and cold-water showers—but chances are, you'll have the place to yourself. In fact, the only time it gets crowded is in October, when thousands of olive Ridley sea turtles nest in one of their yearly *arribadas* (arrivals). See chapter 7.
- **Manuel Antonio** (Central Pacific Coast, Costa Rica): The first beach destination to become popular in Costa Rica, Manuel Antonio still retains its charms—despite burgeoning crowds and mushrooming hotels. The beaches inside the park are idyllic and the views from the hills upon approach are enchanting. Manuel Antonio is also one of the few remaining habitats for the endangered squirrel monkey. Rooms with views tend to be expensive, but many a satisfied guest will tell you they're well worth it. See chapter 9.
- **Punta Uvita** (Central Pacific Coast, Costa Rica): Part of the Ballena Maritime National Park, this is a wide beach with calm water and plenty of trees for shade. At low tide a sandbar connects the mainland to a small offshore island. Most people visit for the day and stay in nearby Dominical. See chapter 9.
- **Punta Uva** (Southern Caribbean Coast, Costa Rica): Below Puerto Viejo, the beaches of Costa Rica's Atlantic coast take on true Caribbean splendor, with turquoise waters, coral reefs, and palm-lined stretches of nearly deserted white-sand beach. By far the most beautiful is Punta Uva, just a few kilometers south of Puerto Viejo by gravel road. Tall coconut palms line the shore, providing shady respite for those who like to spend a full day on the sand. See chapter 11.

- **Placencia** (Southern Caribbean Coast, Belize): The only true beach in Belize is a nice one. Sixteen miles in length, this beautiful white-sand beach is perfect for a day of sunning. An added benefit is the fun and funky town (see "The Most Scenic Towns & Villages," below). Once you've settled into the slow pace, it's hard to leave. Lots of travelers never do, and you'll find an interesting international community here. One caveat: The last time I visited, there was a noticeable problem with trash, both in and out of the water. See chapter 18.

4 The Best Day Hikes & Nature Walks

- **Lankester Botanical Garden** (Cartago, Costa Rica): If you want a really pleasant, but not overly challenging, day hike, consider a walk among the hundreds of distinct species of flora on display here. **Lankester Garden** (☎ **506/551-9877** or 506/552-3247) is just 17 miles from San José, and its trails meander from areas of open, well-tended garden to shady, natural forest. See chapter 6.
- **Monteverde Biological Cloud Forest Preserve** (northwest of Puntarenas, Costa Rica): Despite its popularity, Monteverde is still a place of incredible natural beauty, and its guides are among the most professional and knowledgeable in the country. Take a tour in the morning to familiarize yourself with the preserve, then spend the late morning or afternoon (your entrance ticket is good for the whole day) exploring it on your own. Once you get off the main trails, Monteverde reveals its rich mysteries with stunning regularity. Walk through the grey mist and look up at the dense tangle of epiphytes and vines. The only noises you'll hear are the rustlings of birds or monkeys, and the occasional distant rumble of Arenal Volcano. All trails are well-marked and regularly tended. See chapter 8.
- **La Fortuna to the Río Fortuna Waterfall** (near Arenal Volcano, Costa Rica): The hike that leads to this waterfall, roughly 3¹/₂ miles outside La Fortuna, is one of my favorites, but it's not for everyone. In fact, it's a bit of a misnomer to call it a hike; it's more of a scramble. Follow the signs out of town along dirt roads and pasture land. Once you reach the lookout, you've got another 20 minutes to go, along a very slippery and muddy path to the base of the falls. The roar of the crashing water is almost deafening. If you want to swim, go just slightly downstream. It's a refreshing rinse, but prepare to get muddy again: You'll have to haul yourself back up those roots and vines you just scrambled down if you want to get back to La Fortuna. See chapter 8.
- **Corcovado National Park** (The Osa peninsula, Costa Rica): This dense, remote swath of lowland rain forest is home to Costa Rica's second-largest population of scarlet macaws. These brilliantly colored birds can be spotted squawking raucously above the park's well-designed network of trails. Most of the jungle lodges in Drake Bay and Puerto Jiménez offer day hikes, but if you want to see the park in a less-touristed fashion, consider hiking in and staying at one of the campgrounds in the interior. This is strenuous hiking, and you'll have to pack in gear and food, but the rewards include some of Costa Rica's most spectacular and unspoiled scenery—much of which can't be seen on a guided tour. On the other hand, because strict limits are placed on the number of visitors allowed into the park each day, you'll feel far from the maddening crowds pretty much regardless of how you choose to experience Corcovado. See chapter 10.
- **Panti Medicine Trail** (Cayo district, Belize): Named after renowned Mayan healer Don Elijio Panti, this is a short, gentle, and well-marked trail through the Belizean jungle that starts on the grounds of Dr. Rosita Arvigo's Ix Chel Farm. Whether you use the book provided or hire a guide, the walk will point out the numerous

medicinal and practical plants and trees found in this small patch of tropical forest, and explain their various uses. At the end of the trail you'll find a replica of the hut Panti used to examine and treat his patients. See chapter 17.

- **Cockscomb Basin Wildlife Sanctuary** (Southern Belize): While sightings of jaguars are rare in this wildlife sanctuary—the only one in the world devoted to preserving these majestic cats—there's something about knowing they're around that raises one's adrenaline level. This pristine rain forest is also home to several other wild species, including the tapir, coati, armadillo, boa constrictor, fer-de-lance, and scarlet macaw. See chapter 18.

5 The Best Bird Watching

Both Costa Rica and Belize offer bird watchers nearly nonstop thrills in protected, pristine habitats that cover a wide range of ecosystems. Coastal islands, mangrove forests, marshy swamps, lowland rain forests, and highland rain and cloud forests all add up to a bounty of excellent opportunities for ornithologists.

- **Parque del Este** (east of San José, Costa Rica): A boon for city birdwatchers, this park hosts oropendula and blue-crowned mot-mot mostly, but other species have been observed here as well. The park rambles on through an eclectic collection of lawns, planted gardens, harvested forest, second-growth scrub, and dense woodland. Take the San Ramón–Parque del Este bus from Avenida 2 between calles 9 and 11 in San José to get here. See chapter 6.
- **The Rio Tempisque Basin** (Northern Costa Rica): At the northern end of the Golfo de Nicoya are some of Costa Rica's most extensive wetlands. Hike in to the Palo Verde Biological Station, or take a boat trip down the Bebedero River with **Guanacaste Tours** (☎ **506/666-0306**) or **Safaris Corobici** (☎ **506/669-1091**). This area is an important breeding ground for gallinules, jacanas, and limpkins, as well as a common habitat for numerous heron and kingfisher species. See chapter 7.
- **Carara Biological Reserve** (near Playa de Jacó on the Central Pacific Coast, Costa Rica): Home to Costa Rica's largest population of scarlet macaws, Carara Biological Reserve is a special place for devoted birdwatchers and recent converts. Macaws are noisy and colorful birds that spend their days in the park, but choose to roost near the coast in the evenings. They arrive like clockwork every morning and then head for the coastal mangroves around dusk. These daily migrations give birders a great chance to see these magnificent birds in flight. See chapter 9.
- **The Cerro de la Muerte** (near San Isidro de El General on the Central Pacific Coast, Costa Rica): This area has recently acquired newfound importance as one of the best places in Costa Rica to see quetzals in the wild. Serious birdwatchers won't want to leave Costa Rica without crossing this spectacular bird off their life lists, and neophytes may be hooked for life after seeing one of these iridescent green wonders fly overhead, flashing its brilliant red breast and trailing two-foot-long tailfeathers. **Albergue de Montaña Tapantí** (☎/fax **506/232-0436**) can almost guarantee a sighting year-round. See chapter 9.
- **Aviarios del Caribe** (near Cahuita on the Caribbean Coast, Costa Rica; ☎ **506/382-1335**): In just a few short years, Aviarios del Caribe has established itself as the premier birdwatching resort on the Caribbean. If it flies along this coast, chances are good for spotting it here. More than 300 species of birds have been seen so far. See chapter 11.
- **Crooked Tree Wildlife Sanctuary** (northwest of Belize City, Belize): The Jabiru is the largest flying bird in the Western hemisphere; it can reach five feet in height,

with a wingspan of up to 12 feet. Jabirus nest in this wildlife refuge in winter. Even if you don't see a Jabiru, you'll see plenty of the more than 70 other species of birds that inhabit the wetlands of this park. See chapter 15.

- **Man-of-War Caye** (Southern Belize): This tiny mangrove caye is only inhabited by hundreds of frigate birds. In the day, they circle the small caye like a permanent, swirling black cloud. During mating season, the males puff out a bright red throat sac the size of a large birthday balloon. Any trip to South Water or Tobacco Caye should include a visit to this small island. See chapter 16.
- **The Ruins of Xunantunich** (Cayo district, Belize): In general, the Cayo district is a rich and rewarding area for birdwatchers. Combine it with a visit to the ancient mounds and semi-restored temples of the ancient Mayan city of Xunantunich, and you've got a great day. On a casual walk around Xunantunich recently, I saw a violaceous trogon, a mess of warblers and fly catchers, a couple of keel-billed toucans, and a roadside hawk. See chapter 17.

6 The Best Offbeat Travel Experiences

- **Studying Spanish, Homestays, and More** (Costa Rica): If you're eager to experience Tico culture in depth, consider enrolling in a two-week Spanish language course, arranging to live with a Costa Rican family for a month or more, or just spending a few of your evenings in a Latin dance studio. San José is home to numerous language institutes that combine intensive classroom work with a pre-arranged homestay, as well as some of the country's best dance academies. For those interested in dabbling in several disciplines simultaneously, the **Costa Rican Language Academy** (☎ **506/233-2070** or 506/223-8938) combines Spanish lessons with classes in Latin dance and Tico cooking. See chapter 5.
- **Volunteering at a National Park** (Costa Rica): The Costa Rican National Parks Service accepts volunteers to work at various parks and bioreserves around the country. A minimum commitment of 45 days is required. Room and board are provided, and in return you are expected to work at ranger stations, maintain trails, and provide upkeep to existing facilities. You may not have much choice in your park assignment. For more information, contact the **Costa Rican National Parks Office** (☎ **506/257-0922**) or **ASVO** (☎ **506/222-6963**). See chapter 3.
- **Observing Olive Ridley Turtles Nesting at Playa Nancite:** This isolated beach in Santa Rosa National Park in the Guanacaste province is the site each October of the massive *arribada* (arrival) of olive Ridley turtles. Tens of thousands of these marine reptiles come ashore *en masse* to lay eggs over a period of just several days. The exact dates remain up to the turtles' discretion, but the beach and month are amazingly consistent. This is a national park, so bring a tent and some supplies and you might just get lucky. See chapter 7.
- **Renting Your Own Caye on the Belizean Barrier Reef** (The Cayes, Belize): This is still a very informal industry (I've never done it myself), but it's possible to rent your own caye for a specified period of time. Most are tiny patches of exposed coral and sand, with a few palm trees and a basic cottage. The owner or a hired water taxi will shuttle you out with your gear and some food supplies and pick you up when you specify. Once you've been dropped off, you're on your own. Ask around in Placencia, Punta Gorda, or Dangriga if you're interested, or call **Glover's Atoll Resort** (☎ **501-5/23048**) and see if they can help you. See chapter 16.
- **Staying in a Mayan Village** (in the Toledo district of Belize): This is a unique chance to step back in time and enter an ancient indigenous culture. The Toledo district is home to numerous Kekchi and Mopan Mayan villages. Many of these

have recently instituted homestay and guesthouse programs that allow visitors to experience the daily life, customs, and diet of the Mayan people. See chapter 18.

7 The Best Views

- **The Summit of Irazú Volcano** (near San José, Costa Rica): From this vantage point, you can see (albeit on a very clear day) both the Pacific and the Caribbean. Even if this experience eludes you, you'll have a view of the volcano's spectacular landscape, the Meseta Central, and the Orosi Valley. See chapter 6.
- **The Montaña de Fuego Inn** (near Arenal Volcano, Costa Rica; ☎ **506/ 479-9106**): From the glass-enclosed front porch of your private wooden cabin, Arenal Volcano seems so close, you'll think you can reach out and touch it. Settle into one of the porch chairs and enjoy the nightly show. When the volcano rumbles and spews, you may have the urge to bolt for cover. See chapter 8.
- **The Restaurant at La Mariposa** (Manuel Antonio, Costa Rica; ☎ **506/ 777-0355**): Couples who choose to dine here arguably have the best view in Manuel Antonio, and that's saying a lot. Come for breakfast or a sunset drink, as dinner can be disappointing. See chapter 9.
- **The Roof of the Casablanca Hotel** (Ambergris Caye, Belize; ☎ **501-26/2327**): From the Casablanca Hotel's rooftop Sunset Bar, you'll have 360° panoramic views of the island, the offshore barrier reef, and the mangroves of the island's west side. The sunsets are spectacular, and there's usually live music. The piano player may not be named Sam, but the Sunset Bar's still a fine place for reminiscing about a lost love. Here's looking at you, Belize. See chapter 16.
- **The Top of El Castillo** (Xunantunich, Cayo district, Belize): You'll be winded after the climb, but it's difficult to find a better place to catch your breath. From the top of this Mayan temple, you'll have a bird's-eye view of the rolling hills that stretch out in every direction. Cars seem like mere specks on the landscape in the nearby border towns of Benque Viejo, Belize, and Melchor de Mencos, Guatemala. After all these years, El Castillo is still the second tallest building in Belize. See chapter 17.
- **The Belize Barrier Reef:** With up to 200 feet of visibility on good days, the waters of Belize are some of the clearest in the world. Whether you're an experienced diver with your own gear or a rank amateur, do not miss the chance to put on a mask, fins and snorkel, or tank and check out the view down below. See chapters 13 and 16.

8 The Best Drives

Driving in both Costa Rica and Belize can be unpleasant, to say the least. Routes are rarely marked, roads resemble bombing ranges, and the famously peaceful Ticos become downright homicidal once they climb behind the wheel of a car. In Belize, once you leave either of the two paved highways, you're in for hours of kidney pounding on either dusty or muddy roads (depending on the season), and oppressively hot tropical temperatures. Nevertheless, a car does provide freedom and independence, and there are some drives that are noteworthy for their scenery.

- **Irazú Volcano and the Orosi Valley** (Central Valley, Costa Rica): A visit to these two places makes an excellent day trip from San José. Start out early to reach the peak of the volcano while the skies are clearest, then spend the afternoon touring the Orosi Valley, with scenic lookouts at both Orosi and Ujarrás. See chapter 6.

- **Braulio Carillo National Park** (northeast of Alajuela, Costa Rica): A trip to the Caribbean coast will take you through this vast national park of mountainous cloud and rain forests. Giant elephant-ear plants line the steep jungle roadside. Broad vistas open up to reveal a number of waterfalls cascading out of the forested mountains. A bridge crosses over the juncture of the clear General river and the sulfuric yellow Río Sucio (Dirty river). Be careful about stopping and don't leave your car parked here for long: Robberies have been reported along this stretch of highway. See chapter 8.

- **La Fortuna–Tiláran–Monteverde** (northern Costa Rica): This route connects two of the country's prime tourist destinations—Arenal Volcano and Monteverde Cloud Forest. Along the way you can marvel at the beauty of Lake Arenal and stop at the wonderful Arenal Botanical Gardens. A four-wheel-drive vehicle is highly recommended for this route, as the section between Tiláran and Monteverde is, to put it mildly, rugged. See chapter 8.

- **The Rocky Coast South of Dominical** (The Pacific Coast, Costa Rica): This stretch of Costa Rica's Pacific coast has often been compared to Big Sur, California. For years, the road along it was the definition of rugged, but recent road work has made it an enjoyable ride. All along, there are informal lookouts where you can pull over and watch the waves crashing on the rocks below. On the inland side of the road are dense lowland rain forests you can enter by side roads that lead to hiking trails and mountain waterfalls. See chapter 9.

- **The Hummingbird Highway** (Central Belize): This highway, really more of a road, is the only truly scenic drive in Belize. It winds its way south from Belmopan through the Maya mountains to Dangriga. Watch out for potholes and washed out sections as you pass through thick rain forest and cross clear jungle rivers. See chapter 17.

9 The Most Scenic Towns & Villages

Earthquakes and isolation have deprived Costa Rica of the architectural splendor found in neighboring nations. Hurricanes have wreaked much the same damage in Belize. Both San José and Belize City are congested and unremarkable cities. Most of the towns and villages in both countries are simple farming and fishing communities, with few attractions for traditional tourists. Still, there are towns and villages both on and off the beaten track that are worth the trip.

- **Cartago** (Central Valley, Costa Rica): Located 15 miles southeast of San José, Cartago was the country's first capital. The city contains the most traces of the country's Spanish-Catholic colonial past. Churches, some still standing, others, in ruins, dominate this small city. The Basilica de Nuestra Señora de los Angeles is the most striking example of an active church and is the site of a massive annual pilgrimage. A public park now occupies what was once the site of a large unfinished church, destroyed in the wake of the 1910 earthquake. And just outside the city are the ruins of the Ujarrás church. Built in 1693, it is the country's oldest church. Cartago makes an easy and interesting day trip out of San José. See chapter 6.

- **Liberia** (Guanacaste, Costa Rica): The capital and commercial hub of the northern province of Guanacaste, Liberia still retains much of its classic Spanish colonial architecture. Walk around the old town and admire the plentiful adobe buildings with ornate wooden doors, heavy beams, central courtyards, and faded, sagging red-tile roofs. Located on a hot and dry lowland savannah that's surrounded by cattle land and distant foothills, Liberia is the only major city in Costa Rica not situated in the temperate Central Valley. It has plenty of lodging options, and makes a great base for exploring the beaches and national parks of Guanacaste. See chapter 7.

- **Golfito** (south of Palmar Norte, Costa Rica): The hub of Costa Rica's southern Pacific zone, Golfito is 210 miles south of San José. Spread out along the winding coastline of the Golfo Dulce (Sweet Gulf), it was once the largest base in the Caribbean for United Fruit Company's banana operations. United Fruit pulled out, but they left behind their unusual company housing. Many of these old wooden homes with gingerbread trim and manicured lawns have since been turned into comfortable budget lodgings. You won't want to stay in Golfito too long (unless you are an avid sportsfisherman or botanical garden fan), but you can easily explore the Osa peninsula from here. See chapter 10.

- **San Ignacio** (Cayo district, Belize): Set in a valley at the juncture of the Mopan and Macal rivers, "San Iggie" (as locals call it) is a quiet town with a frontier feel. It is also the heart of this area's ecotourism industry. The town is connected to its sister city Santa Elena by the single-lane steel suspension bridge, Hawksworth. Just outside of town are jungle rain forests and Mayan ruins. See chapter 17.

- **Dangriga** (near Gales Point, Belize): Located along the central Caribbean coast of Belize, this is the cultural hub of Belize's Garifuna population, a unique people who descended from Carib Indians and free black Americans, and settled on the Belizean coast in the late 18th century. Clapboard houses on stilts are spread around a dense grid of neat dirt roads; chickens scratch around in most front lawns. Two rivers cut through the city and provide shelter for fishing craft and water taxis. There are a number of humble waterfront parks that are nice for a picnic. This is also a great base for exploring some of the outer cayes. See chapter 18.

- **Placencia** (along the Southern Caribbean Coast, Belize): This tiny village is situated on Belize's only beach. Little more than a collection of brightly painted wooden houses on stilts, the lifeline of this town is a narrow sidewalk that runs through its center from north to south. My favorite feature about Placencia is that you're never more than 100 yards from the ocean's edge. See chapter 18.

10 The Best Mayan Ruins & Archeological Sites

- **Guayabo** (Costa Rica): Costa Rica's oldest known city, Guayabo is nestled amid the lush forests of the mountainous Turrialba region of Costa Rica about 45 miles east of San José. Today, it has the distinction of being the country's only major archeological site. While it lacks the ornate majesty of Tikal, it has a wonderful homey lived-in feel. It is believed that its residents were Olmecs fleeing Aztec persecution more than 1000 years before Christ. Today, visitors can experience this Indian past by walking among building foundations, marveling at still-working aqueducts, viewing carved petroglyphs, and touring burial sites. Guayabo is best visited as a day trip from San José. See chapter 6.

- **Caracol** (Belize): An incredibly challenging site to visit, Caracol is the largest Mayan city to be discovered in Belize. Caracol is still not very well excavated, and the roads reaching it are sometimes unpassable, even with a four-wheel-drive vehicle. However, this was once a major classic Mayan center whose people are believed to have defeated Tikal at war in A.D. 562. At 140 feet, the main pyramid is still the tallest man-made structure in Belize. The best way to visit Caracol is to arrange a trip out of San Ignacio or one of the neighboring jungle lodges. See chapter 17.

- **Xunantunich** (Belize): The name of this Mayan ruin translates as "maiden of the rocks." Xunantunich was a thriving city in the classic period, about A.D. 600 to 900. The main pyramid, El Castillo, rises to 127 feet and provides a commanding panoramic vista of the surrounding hills and valleys. The view from the top is amazing. Don't miss it. Xunantunich makes a great day trip out of San Ignacio or one of the nearby jungle lodges. See chapter 17.
- **Lamanai** (Belize): Lamanai, or "submerged crocodile," is one of the more adventurous and offbeat ruins to visit in Belize. Set on the banks of the New river, you'll have to take a boat to get here. Lamanai was occupied from around 1500 B.C. until the Spanish arrived in the 16th century, and it supported non-Mayan populations into the 19th century. In addition to the numerous pyramids and temples, you'll find the ruins of two churches built by the Spanish during the 16th century. Just next to these are the rusting remains of a more recently abandoned sugar mill. The most popular way to visit Lamanai is with an organized tour out of Belize City or Ambergris Caye. See chapter 15.

11   The Best Places to Shop

Neither Costa Rica nor Belize is known for having great shopping. While it's possible to buy indigenous crafts in a few select places, neither country has a very strong crafts or textile tradition. The handcrafts you'll see are mostly imports from nearby Guatemala and other Latin American nations. In most tourist areas, particularly the beach towns, you'll see individual artisans with stands selling handmade jewelry. Buying from these vendors is a bit of a crap shoot; quality and prices vary tremendously. My favorite souvenirs are also among the least expensive items you can buy: coffee in Costa Rica, and Marie Sharp's Hot Sauce in Belize. Below I've listed some of the better stops for frugal-minded shoppers.

- **Central Market** (San José, Costa Rica): No trip to San José is complete without a tour of this indoor labyrinth of shops, stalls, and food stands. Everything from crafts and clothing to freshly butchered meats is sold here, and the surrounding streets host a daily farmers' market. This is the best place to buy freshly roasted whole-bean coffee. See chapter 6.
- **Sarchí** (northwest of San José, Costa Rica): This small city outside of San José has long served as the headquarters for Costa Rica's modest craft industry. Woodworking is the most developed and available craft, with traditional painted oxcarts coming in a wide range of styles and sizes. See chapter 6.
- **Boutique Annemarie** (San José, Costa Rica; ☎ **506/221-6063**): Located in San José's Hotel Don Carlos, this bi-level store sells a broad selection of crafts and clothing. Most items are similar to those you'll see on the streets or in other stores, but here they're all under one roof, and the atmosphere is friendly and relaxed. If you're looking for a clay or silver reproduction of a pre-Columbian figure, this is the place to pick one up. See chapter 6.
- **National Handicraft Center** (Belize City, Belize; ☎ **2/33833**): This one-stop warehouse holds a collection of typical Belizean arts and crafts. Offerings range from modern slate carvings of ancient Mayan glyphs from the Cayo district to carved wooden dolphins and turtles from the cayes. There's plenty of jewelry and knickknacks. Prices are competitive with what you'd pay at the source, and the selection is fairly wide. You can also pick up T-shirts and Marie Sharp's sauces here. See chapter 14.
- **Dangriga** (near Gales Point, Belize): The Garifuna are perhaps the most creative cultural group in Belize. In Dangriga, the center of their community, several

artists have studios you can visit. A walking arts tour might include stops at 32 Tubroose St., where Austin Rodriguez (☎ 5/22308) crafts wooden drums; 22 Magoon St., where Mercy Sabal (no phone) makes traditional Garifuna dolls; and 25 Howard St., the studio of Benjamin Nicholas (☎ 5/22785). Nicholas depicts scenes of Garifuna daily life and religious celebration, as well as Caribbean land-scapes, in his colorful primitivist paintings. See chapter 18.

12 The Best Bargains on Hotels & Bed-and-Breakfasts

Reasonably priced lodgings can be found in both countries, and many are listed throughout this guide. The places mentioned here, however, combine low rates with special perks—everything from unexpected luxury to spectacular scenery to above-average service.

- **Pensión de la Cuesta** (San José, Costa Rica; ☎ **506/255-2896**): This converted home in a residential section of downtown San José was once owned by Costa Rican artist Otto Apuy. In fact, the small barrio here is still populated by some of the country's most active artists. Original art—Apuy's and others'—hangs on al-most every available inch of wall space. The rooms are clean and spacious, and cost $26 for a double, including continental breakfast. See chapter 6.
- **Almost Paradise** (Playa Nosara, Costa Rica; No phone, fax 506/685-5004): The name is appropriate. Sure, you could be right on the beach, instead of 200 meters away and, sure, things could be fancier and more private. But at $36.50 a night for two, including breakfast, this *is* almost paradise. See chapter 7.
- **Amor de Mar** (Playa Montezuma, Costa Rica; ☎ **506/642-0262**): This hotel has brightly varnished woodwork, immaculate rooms, hammocks strung under shady mango trees, a wide grass lawn overlooking the Pacific, and a swimming pool–sized tide pool that's carved into an adjoining rocky shore. The management could, and probably should, charge much more. Get there before they do, and you'll pay $30 for a double with shared bath. See chapter 7.
- **Pensión Flor de Lis** (Santa Elena, Monteverde, Costa Rica; ☎ **506/645-5236**): This new pension is my favorite budget option in Monteverde. Rooms are very simple, but immaculately clean, and the owners make you feel part of the family. They also know and love the area and are eager to share it with guests. A double costs $14. See chapter 8.
- **Casa Verde** (Puerto Viejo, Costa Rica; ☎ **506/798-4244**): If you're traveling on a rock-bottom budget, this may be your best value on the Caribbean coast. It's simple, but the rooms are clean and airy, and all have comfortable beds with mos-quito nets. The friendly owner is quite house-proud, and invariably can be found working in the garden or elsewhere on the grounds. Doubles with a shared bath run $10 to $15. See chapter 11.
- **Jiménez Cabañas** (Caye Caulker, Belize; ☎ **501-22/2175**): These raised palmetto-stick cabins don't come with a sea view, but they're certainly a cut above the competition in their price range on Caye Caulker. For just $24 a night, you'll get a spacious individual cabin with a small porch overlooking a lush, flowering garden; the ocean's only a couple hundred yards away. See chapter 16.
- **Cahal Pech Village** (San Ignacio, Cayo district, Belize; ☎ **501-92/3203** or 501-92/2186): This assortment of new individual cabins and spacious rooms is located on a hill overlooking San Ignacio—just a couple hundred yards from the Mayan ruins of Cahal Pech. Decorated with Guatemalan bedspreads and wall hangings, both cabins and rooms cost just $35 for a double. See chapter 17.

- **DuPlooy's** (San Ignacio, Cayo district, Belize; ☎ **501-92/3101**; fax 501-92/ 3301): As mentioned above, this is one of the more luxurious jungle lodges in the Cayo district. However, the six rooms with shared baths in the Pink House are an excellent value at $40 for a double. The lodge overlooks the Macal River with jungle-covered limestone cliffs opposite. There's a beach on the river, as well as a riverside trail that's great for birdwatching. Horses, canoes, and fishing equipment are all available for rent. See chapter 17.

- **Colton House** (Belize City, Belize; ☎ **501-2/44666**; fax 501-2/30451): It's hard to beat the tropical charm and colonial splendor you'll find here. A lushly planted yard, a wide wrap-around verandah with comfortable chairs, hanging wooden porch swings, hardwood floors, shuttered windows, and big rooms with high ceilings make this a pleasant oasis in the heart of Belize City's historic Fort George district. At $45 for a double, it's a little bit of a splurge, but well worth it. See chapter 14.

13 The Best Affordable Eco-lodges & Wilderness Resorts

The term ecotourism has become so ubiquitous within the travel industry, it's almost become a tired phrase—and it's often trumpeted by tourism operators and hotel owners who do very little in their day-to-day professional lives to combat environmental damage. (Some even contribute to it.)

Generally, outstanding eco-lodges and wilderness resorts are places that have made an ongoing commitment to minimizing their effect on surrounding ecosystems and to supporting the residents of the local communities in which they're located. They should provide guides who are naturalists or biologists, and make additional resources available to satisfy their guests' curiosity. All of the following—which range from tent camps with cold-water showers, communal buffet-style meals, and no electricity to some of the most luxurious accomodations in both Costa Rica and Belize—do. While most lodges are beyond our budget, none exceed it by more than $10 or $15 a night. When you consider the conservation efforts these lodges undertake with their profits, it's nice to know that the extra money you're paying is going toward a good cause.

- **Rara Avis** (near Las Horquetas, Costa Rica; ☎ **506/764-4187**): A pioneer in ecotourism, this eco-resort still provides a premier natural experience in the heart of Costa Rica's central mountain rain forests. Getting to Rara Avis is no longer the kidney-splitting 4-hour ordeal it once was, but you'll still spend plenty of time in a tractor-pulled covered wagon before reaching the isolated yet comfortable Waterfall Lodge ($150 for a double). If you're looking for a more rustic (and economical) nature experience, stay at their El Plastico Lodge, a former penal colony. At $90 for a double, it's still beyond our budget, but as this rate includes all meals, transportation to and from Las Horquetas, and guided tours, it doesn't exceed it by as much as it may seem at first glance. See chapter 8.

- **Drake Bay Wilderness Camp** (Palmar Norte, Osa peninsula, Costa Rica; ☎ **506/ 771-2436** or 506/284-4107): A stay at this premier tent camp is a serious rainforest experience. A lot of it has to do with its location on the Osa peninsula, one of Costa Rica's most isolated and pristine destinations, and its close proximity to Corcovado National Park's dense, lush rain forest. The camp itself is spread over a rocky coastline, where the Agujitas River meets Drake Bay. The tents are on raised slabs, with real beds and electric lights. For $92 a day for two, you get a seaside tent and three square meals. You'll go to sleep to the sound of the waves against the rocky shore and wake to the squawk of scarlet macaws flying overhead. See chapter 10.

- **Aviarios del Caribe** (Cahuita, Costa Rica; ☎ 506/382-1335): Avid birdwatchers cannot help but cross off a large portion of their life lists here. Walk the grounds, sit on the porch, take a boat ride through the mangroves, and check off species after species as your stay unfolds. The rooms are modern and clean; upon arrival, guests are greeted with fresh flowers. A double here will run you $60 including breakfast. See chapter 11.
- **Cabinas Chimuri** (Puerto Viejo, Costa Rica; ☎ 506/798-4244): These Bribri-style A-frame cabins are built out of local materials and are owned and managed by Mauricio Salazar, a local Bribri Indian. The tours, setting, and surroundings make Chimuri the perfect place to get to know the people, customs, and ecology of the Talamanca region. Mauricio will take you to visit the nearby reservation and show you some secrets of jungle herbology and bush medicine. At $20 per double, the accommodations are basic, but you'll have a mosquito net and a porch from which you can easily watch the parade of Caribbean birds pass by. See chapter 11.
- **Banana Bank Ranch** (Belmopan, Belize; ☎ /fax 501-81/2020 or 501-81/23180; This delightful lodge is part of a working cattle ranch located on the bank of the Belize River. Moreover, much of the extensive ranch is still pristine jungle. There are plenty of horses for mounting, trails for hiking, and canoes for plying the river. There's even a small Mayan ruin on the land. At $65 for a double without bath, this is a bit of a splurge, but breakfast is included. See chapter 17.
- **Macal River Tent Camp** (San Ignacio, Cayo district, Belize; ☎ 501-92/2037): This deluxe tent camp is the sister property to one of Belize's premier and longest-running eco-lodges—Chaa Creek Cottages. Here, ten spacious tents are set on raised platforms among the forest trees. The river is down a short path from the campsite, and Ix Chel Farm and Chaa Creek are nearby. At $45 per person including meals, this is quite a savings over a cottage at Chaa Creek ($115 for double, plus meals) and just a little bit of a splurge. Moreover, guests at the tent camp can rent canoes or sign up for any tours offered at Chaa Creek. See chapter 16.
- **Glover's Atoll Resort** (Long Caye, Belize; ☎ 501-5/23048): If you've ever wondered what it might be like to be stranded on your own private desert isle, this may be as close as you'll get. Glover's Atoll Resort is an eco-lodge sitting on a tropical coral reef. Out here on the atolls, the day's activities consist of strapping on a tank or grabbing a snorkel, and hopping into the water. If you want to explore the reef from above, there are sea kayaks available. A week-long stay in a cabin here, including round-trip transportation, is $95 per person. Add an extra $15 per day for meals. See chapter 18.
- **International Zoological Expeditions Lodge at Blue Creek** (Punta Gorda, Belize; ☎ 508/655-1461; fax 508/655-4445 in the U.S.): If you're looking for a deep jungle experience in Belize, this is one of your best bets. Located in rich rain forest near the Mayan village of Blue Creek, about 22 kilometers northwest of Punta Gorda, this is a working research station accommodating hard-core scientists, student groups, armchair biologists, and adventurous travelers. Six comfortable cabins overlook the beautiful Blue Creek river, while the lodge houses the bathrooms and dining area. Although it's a bit out of our price range, the $60 per person per day rates include all your meals. If you want to do some exploring on foot, local guides can be hired for day hikes to the Moho river and other places. See chapter 18.

14 The Best Deals on Dining Out

- **La Cocina de Leña** (San José, Costa Rica; ☎ **506/255-1360** or 506/223-3704): Located in the El Pueblo shopping, dining, and entertainment center, La Cocina de Leña (The Wood Stove) has a rustic feel to it and is slightly overpriced, yet does delicious takes on traditional Costa Rican cooking. The more adventurous dishes include oxtail stew served with yuca and plátano, and *chilasuilas,* or tortillas filled with fried meat. See chapter 6.
- **Bijahua** (San José, Costa Rica; ☎ **506/225-0613**): This restaurant has led the movement toward the creation of a nouvelle Costa Rican cuisine under the careful hand of chef Isabel Campabadal. Traditional ingredients are taken to new heights in such dishes as tiquizque soup, gnocchi ñampi, and shrimp in tamarind butter. Most of the menu is a bit of a splurge for us, but the Bijahua *casado* ($6.50), a meat stew with vegetables, rice, and beans, is well within our range, and a far cry from standard restaurant fare. See chapter 6.
- **Machu Pichu** (San José, Costa Rica; ☎ **506/222-7384**): Come here for the *ceviche* and the mixed-seafood platter—they are among the best served anywhere in the country. The *pisco* sours, potato appetizers, and the animated atmosphere aren't bad either. Those watching their waistlines might want to choose carefully among the fish plates, though: Some are served in heavy cream sauces. See chapter 6.
- **La Piraña** (Playa de Jacó, Costa Rica; ☎ **506/643-3725**): Jacó Beach has been blessed with one of the most innovative restaurants in the country. The menu is an international potpourri—highlights include baked Caribbean red snapper, jerk chicken, blackened steak, and Egyptian pasta Mohammad—and the atmosphere is lively, with a bright primary-colored decor, simple tables, and comfortable seating. Slow-turning ceiling fans augment the gentle cross-breezes. See chapter 9.
- **The Garden** (Puerto Viejo, Costa Rica; no phone): For years, travelers to the Caribbean coast have raved about The Garden, often declaring it their favorite restaurant in Costa Rica. The reasons are as numerous as the many Asian-Caribbean–inspired dishes on the menu. Wonderfully spiced Thai curry, local rundown (a spicy stew made with whatever ingredients the cook can "run down" that day), and Jamaican Jerk chicken are just a few examples. Somehow, all the dishes co-exist effortlessly, and are beautifully presented with a fresh flower and grilled pineapple garnish. See chapter 11.
- **Fort Street Restaurant** (Belize City, Belize; ☎ **501-2/30116**): This casually elegant restaurant is my first choice for dining in Belize City. I often choose to dine outside on the wraparound verandah where there are plastic chairs and sturdy card tables, but the small candle-lit dining room is equally pleasant. Regardless of where you sit, the same chalkboard menu is offered. It changes regularly, but always focuses on fresh seafood. Dinners can be a bit pricey for our budget ($12 to $16), but lunch is a bargain, whether you get the daily special ($4.50) or order à la carte ($4 to $7.50). See chapter 14.
- **G.G.'s Cafe & Patio** (Belize City, Belize; ☎ **501-2/74378**): This casual restaurant is an excellent choice for either lunch or dinner. The small menu features Belizean stewed chicken, pork or beef, spare ribs, and whole snapper. The portions are hearty, and the most expensive item—fresh fish filets—is just $7.50. See chapter 14.
- **Lagoon Restaurant** (Ambergris Caye, Belize; ☎ **501-26/2327**): This is my favorite restaurant in Belize. The frequently changing menu strays far from the

standard Belizean fried-fish fare, and has offered such eclectic dishes as chicken and shrimp satay; orange, onion, and radish salad; chilled cucumber soup; black-bean lasagna; lobster anise; and Cajun shrimp. Don't miss the watermelon granita with blackberry brandy for dessert. This is a bit of a splurge, but well worth it. See chapter 16.

- **Sand Box Restaurant** (Caye Caulker, Belize; ☎ **501-22/2200**): This has long been a favorite dining spot in Caye Caulker. Everything's good, but the curried fish and shrimp served with banana chutney is excellent. The casual service and sand floor remind you that you're in the Tropics. See chapter 16.

15 The Best Nightspots

- **El Cuartel de la Boca del Monte** (San José, Costa Rica; ☎ **506/221-0327**): This is where San José's young, restless, and beautiful come to shake off excess energy. From Wednesday through Saturday the place is jam-packed. Originally a gay and bohemian hangout, it is now overwhelmingly yuppie, although some of the original crowd still make this their evening hangout. See chapter 6.
- **La Esmeralda** (San José, Costa Rica; ☎ **506/221-0530**): This restaurant serves as a meeting place and central dispatch center for scores of local mariachi bands, some of whom even print the restaurant's pay-phone number on their business cards. It's open 24 hours a day. Hire your own combo for a song or two, or just enjoy the cacophony as the bands battle it out through the night. See chapter 6.
- **Salsa 54** (San José, Costa Rica; ☎ **506/221-3220**): This is one of the more serious dance halls in San José, where couples dancing is an art form, not just an evening's diversion. Large, with several separate dance floors, Salsa 54 has plenty of tables with good views of the action for those who just like to watch. There's also a raised stage for those who want to show off their fancy footwork. See chapter 6.
- **San Pedro** (San José, Costa Rica): This is San José's University district, and at night its streets are filled with students milling among a variety of bars and cafes. If you'd like to join them, keep in mind that **La Villa** (☎ **506/225-9612**), **La Maga** (☎ **506/283-5040**), and **Ventanas** (no phone) cater to artists and bohemians, **El Pulpo** (no phone) is popular with young Tico rockers, and **Pizza Caccio** (☎ **506/283-2809**) seems to attract a good share of American students. All of the spots listed above (except La Maga, located 100 meters from the church in San Pedro) are located in the three-block stretch that begins 200 meters east of the church in San Pedro and heads north from there. See chapter 6.
- **Teatro Nacional** (San José, Costa Rica; ☎ **506/221-1329**): This recently restored 100-year-old classical opera house sits like a gem in the center of San José. Catch a show here, admire the classical ceiling mural, and then wander next door for a nightcap at the Gran Hotel's outdoor cafe. Most of the theater and popular concerts are in Spanish, but there are plenty of classical music concerts, dance performances, and other events that cross language barriers. See chapter 6.
- **Harbour Room Bar & Restaurant** (Belize City, Belize; ☎ **501-2/77051**): This unassuming hotel bar turns into one of Belize City's livelier nightspots on weekends, if you get here early enough, you can grab a table in front of one of the open windows that faces Belize Harbour. The company is usually a nice mix of locals, tourists, and yachtsmen. There's even karaoke on some nights. See chapter 14.
- **Tackle Box Bar** (Ambergris Caye, Belize; no phone): Maybe I'm just a party pooper, but the two raging discos here in San Pedro just don't do it for me. If you

like a packed dance floor, pounding bass riffs and multi-colored strobe lights, head over to Tarzan's Club or Big Daddy's. But if you'd like to sip a quiet drink on an outdoor deck, with the Caribbean sea lapping underneath and a starry sky above, come here. See chapter 16.

- **Kulcha Shack** (Seine Bight Village, Belize; ☎ **501-6/22015**): It may not be Broadway or the Royal Court, but it is possible to do "dinner and a show" in Belize. Seine Bight is a Garifuna village just north of Placencia. The Kulcha Shack is a local restaurant that also puts on traditional Garifuna drumming and dance performances. The menu includes several local specialties such as *hudut*, fish stewed in coconut milk and herbs; *tapow*, a similar stew made with vegetables and served with rice and cassava bread; and *bundegah*, which is similar to tapow but is prepared with patties made from grated bananas. Dinner and a show will cost between $20 and $25 per person. See chapter 18.

Saving Money in Costa Rica & Belize

The premise of this book is that it's possible to fully enjoy Costa Rica and Belize on a budget beginning at $35 dollars per day, per person, for meals and hotels. This is based on two people traveling together and sharing the cost of lodging, and doesn't include transportation expenses, tours, admission fees for attractions, or shopping. If you're willing to stay in the lowest-priced accommodations listed in this book (a double room that costs well under $40 a night), you should be able to include all of your transportation expenses and many other costs into your $35 a day. However, there are some areas where most hotel room rates have risen above this range. In places like these, you may want to consider either splurging, visiting in the off-season, or just skipping them altogether. When deciding where to stay, bear in mind that the exact prices quoted in this book do not include hotel taxes. At the time of writing, Costa Rica's hotel tax is a whopping 18.45%. In Belize, it is 7%, although there's talk of lowering the tax in Costa Rica to 15%, and raising it to 15% in Belize. To be safe, ask what you'll be charged when you reserve your room, and remember to factor the tax into your daily budget.

This is roughly how I break down daily costs: $18 per person (based on double occupancy) for a room, $3 for breakfast, $5 for lunch, and $9 for dinner. While not luxurious, this budget should allow you to live comfortably. For those with more financial flexibility, this guide shows you how to cut corners—without sacrificing comfort or quality—and points out experiences and activities that are worth a splurge.

1 50 Money-Saving Tips

AIR TRAVEL

1. Fly off-season. During the off-season (which runs roughly from Easter to Thanksgiving), airlines often offer discounted fares. Sometimes these discounted fares are unadvertised, so always ask when making a reservation.
2. Fly mid-week. It's almost always cheaper to depart between Monday and Thursday, as opposed to during the weekend.

ACCOMMODATIONS

Also see the "Finding an Affordable Place to Stay" sections of chapters 5 and 13 for details about hotel packages and other options.

3. Both Costa Rica and Belize are actively promoting tourism during the rainy season. In Costa Rica, this coincides with the off-season; but in Belize, it follows the off-season (May through November in Costa Rica, June through October in Belize). If you choose to visit during this time, you can take advantage of substantially discounted room rates.

4. Because many hotels don't like to advertise the fact that they'll give a "green season" discount, ask when you book your reservations.

5. If you're going to stay in one spot for a week or more, look into a room or apartment with a kitchenette. You'll save a lot of money on dining costs if you cook some meals yourself.

6. No matter what time of year you travel, if you're going to spend some time in any one spot, be sure to ask the management for a weekly or long-term discount.

7. In the high season, the popular budget hotels fill up fast. If you're going to be traveling to any of the hot spots in this book, definitely try to reserve your room well in advance, or you could get stuck with what's left, which are usually the more expensive rooms.

8. Rooms with shared bathrooms will always save you money—between 20% and 50% in most cases. If you're willing to flexible, you'll find that this brings many attractive small hotels and bed-and-breakfasts into your price range.

9. If you're traveling alone, it's always a good idea to team up with other travelers to cut costs on rooms. See "For Singles," under "Tips for Travelers with Special Needs," in chapters 5 and 13.

10. At Chaa Creek Cottages and DuPlooy's in Belize's Cayo district, you can live in the lap of luxury at budget prices by staying in the former's Tent Camp or the latter's Pink House.

11. You'll always pay more for air-conditioning, although you won't always need it. Even on the coasts, where it gets hot and humid, a good fan is often enough to cool you off.

12. Hotels on the ocean are always more expensive than those just a block or two away from the water. Decide how much time you plan to spend at your hotel, and opt for a room without a view if you want to cut costs.

13. In Belize, you'll save money on a visit to the Cayes if you avoid Ambergris and try Caye Caulker or Tobacco Caye.

14. If you're a diver, you can save a lot of money by purchasing a package that includes your lodging and daily dive trips. Most of the accommodations on Belize's Cayes offer such deals.

15. In the low season, you won't need a reservation in either Belize or Costa Rica. If you arrive at your destination early, you can shop around. Budget hotels are opening all the time and this is a good way to find the best new deals.

16. Camping is an excellent option in both countries, but only during the dry season. Stick to established campsites and national parks, though.

DINING

17. In Costa Rica, eat in small diners or *sodas*. Meals are inexpensive and often quite tasty.

18. In both Costa Rica and Belize, rice and beans are cheap staples, and a good source of protein and carbohydrates.

19. The best deal in Costa Rica is the *casado*, a type of "blue plate special," featuring rice, beans, salad, vegetables, plantains, a fried egg, and either meat or chicken.

20. In Costa Rica, a 10% service charge is always included in your restaurant bill. This

is your tip. Ticos generally do not tip extra. However, at tourist destinations, an additional tip is often expected. You should add an extra 5% to 10% according to the level of service.

21. Although not standardized, at some restaurants in Belize, a service charge is automatically added to your bill. Always check first before tipping.

22. In both Belize and Costa Rica, keep your eye out for a daily special or *plato del día*. This is a great way to economize.

23. If you're really trying to save money on dining, eat a big lunch and a light dinner, or just skip it altogether, in favor of a light snack.

24. In Costa Rica, most bars serve appetizers, or *bocas*, with every drink. Depending on the bar, bocas sometimes border on meal-sized portions.

25. Even if you don't have a kitchenette, visit the local markets and pick up fresh fruit and baked goods. Pretty soon you won't be buying breakfasts.

26. Both Costa Rica and Belize produce national beers and liquors that are very good and less expensive than foreign brands. Stick to the local brands.

LOCAL TRANSPORTATION

27. Bus service in both Costa Rica and Belize is regular, efficient, inexpensive, and relatively comfortable. Although in-country flights are affordable, your transportation costs will be almost negligible if you travel by bus.

28. Taxis are an inexpensive and efficient means of getting around in San José. By law, every taxi must be equipped with and use a meter, or *marea*. However, taxi drivers often try to gouge tourists. Insist that your driver use and abide by the *marea*.

29. In Costa Rica, taxi fares go up an additional 20% after 10pm. Some meters are programmed to include this extra percentage in the displayed fare. Sometimes, taxi drivers will try to get away with using the nighttime setting during the day. Always check to see the setting of your meter at the start of your trip.

30. Taxis in Belize are not metered. Fares are usually standardized. Before heading out for a trip, ask at your hotel how much a certain trip should cost.

31. You'll always save money on taxi fares by getting a small group together to share the cost.

32. In both countries, taxis become quite expensive in rural areas. If at all possible, use buses in the countryside. If not, be sure to negotiate a fixed price before setting out in a cab.

33. If you're going to rent a car in either Costa Rica or Belize, it's almost always considerably cheaper to book in advance from your home country with an international agency such as Avis, Budget, Hertz, or National.

34. In both countries, four-wheel-drive vehicles are the war horses of the rental fleet. Nevertheless, depending on where you're headed, particularly during the dry season, you may only need a two-wheel-drive vehicle, which will save you a considerable amount of money.

35. If using airlines for in-country travel in Belize, fly out of municipal airports. Fares are slightly cheaper and a cab from downtown is usually only B$5 ($2.50) instead of the B$30 ($15) it'll cost to get into town from an outlying airport.

SHOPPING

36. Neither Costa Rica nor Belize has a bargaining culture. You'll almost never be able to bargain a price down in a shop, but if you're buying crafts, jewelry, or souvenirs on the street, you should definitely try to haggle. You'll have to work for it, but you can usually bargain the price down some.

37. Make sure to bring plenty of insect repellent and sunscreen with you. Both of these products are much more expensive to purchase once you arrive in Belize or Costa Rica.
38. Bring all the film you plan to use, as well as a spare battery for your camera. Wait until you get home to develop your pictures.
39. Your best buy in Belize is Marie Sharp's Hot Sauce. Buy plenty of it. It comes in different strengths—from mild to hot—as well as various sizes. It makes a great gift, and be sure to buy some for yourself.
40. In Costa Rica, buy coffee. You can pick up well-packaged export-grade coffee in any supermarket, or buy freshly roasted whole beans at Central Market.

TOURS & ATTRACTIONS

41. If you plan on doing any snorkeling or diving, bring along your own mask, fins, and snorkel. You'll save $5 to $10 per day on the rental fee, and be assured of a good fit.
42. In Costa Rica, if all you want to do is lie on a beach and sunbathe, avoid national parks beaches like Cahuita and Manuel Antonio, where you'll have to pay the $6 daily admission fee for the privilege.
43. In Costa Rica, both new and established tour agencies often advertise discounted tours in the *Tico Times.*
44. Before going on any organized tour, it's worth getting a group together first and trying to bargain a bit.
45. In the Cayo district in Belize, make sure Eva's Restaurant in San Ignacio is your first stop. Check the walls for information on various tours, and then speak to Bob behind the counter about getting together with other like-minded folks.
46. In San José, check out the Centro Nacional de Arte y Cultura (National Arts Center), located on Calle 13 between avenidas 3 and 5. Admission is free.

MONEY MATTERS

47. If you have to make an overseas call, you'll save a lot of money by using an AT&T, Sprint, or MCI operator. Each of these companies has direct-dial service from both Belize and Costa Rica. See "Fast Facts," in chapter 5 for information about calling in Costa Rica; and "Fast Facts," in chapter 13 for information about calling in Belize.
48. Do not exchange money on the streets in San José. You are just asking to be robbed—either directly, with counterfeit bills, or by an elaborate miscalculation scheme. Go to a bank, hotel, or reputable storefront currency-exchange operation.
49. In both Costa Rica and Belize, hotels and restaurants often add a 3% to 10% surcharge to credit-card purchases. Always ask in advance if you plan to make a credit-card purchase.
50. In Belize, avoid exchanging traveler's checks or U.S. dollars in banks. They take out a small percentage. Instead, try to pay for your room with U.S. dollars or traveler's checks. You'll be given a straight 2-to-1 exchange rate, with your change in Belize dollars.

2 How This Guide Can Save You Money

Traveling in Central America isn't the cut-rate bargain it once was. However, conditions have improved and the variety of opportunities has vastly expanded. Both

Costa Rica and Belize are developing large tourism sectors aimed at the active and adventure traveler. There are a host of nature and jungle lodges in each country, and it's still possible to spend some relaxing time on a nearly deserted beach or tiny Caribbean caye.

The following itineraries are intended to serve as guidelines and should allow you to travel around either Costa Rica or Belize, enjoying the best experiences each has to offer, while staying within our budget of $35 per person per day for meals and lodgings. All of the following suggestions are taken from lodgings and restaurants described in greater detail in the individual city and regional chapters of this guide. Remember, these itineraries are just suggestions and your own travel plans will probably require more flexibility. Stay an extra day or two at a destination that really captivates you. Eliminate others. The choices are all yours.

IF YOU HAVE 7 DAYS IN COSTA RICA

Days 1 and 2 (San José)   Unless you're just dying to get to the beach or jungle, spend a couple of days in San José. It's a good way to acclimatize yourself to Costa Rica. Make Pension de la Cuesta your base. This cozy converted home is centrally located and costs just $26 for a double, including continental breakfast. Spend your days visiting the downtown museums, shopping in the Central Market, or on day trips to the nearby Irazú or Poás volcanoes. For an economical lunch, try a *casado* (the local blue plate special) at any soda, or have the *plato del día* (plate of the day) at Manolo's Restaurant for just $2.75. For your dinners you can afford a bit of a splurge, so try some ceviche and seafood at Machu Pichu one night ($9 to $15 per person) and then go to town at Bijahua on your second night ($10 to $20 per person). Take in a show at the National Theater, listen to mariachis at La Esmeralda, or go dancing at one of the salsa salons to round out your evenings.

Day 3 (Arenal Volcano)   As you enter the small town of La Fortuna, the massive volcano looms large before you. Keep heading straight toward it until you come to Montaña del Fuego Inn, where a double will run you just $30 a night. Each of the individual cabins has an unobstructed view of the volcano, which begins rising up just a stone's throw away. During the day you can watch the volcano, birdwatch, or hike to the La Fortuna waterfall. At some point, you must soak in the natural hot springs fed by this smoldering mountain. There are both free and very inexpensive ($2.10) spots to soak in the soothing waters, but I recommend splurging on the $14 entrance fee to enter Tabacón Hot Springs Resort. Dining options are very limited in La Fortuna and around the volcano. Most travelers take their meals in their hotel, but since Montaña del Fuego doesn't have a restaurant yet, you will have to head back to town. The most dependable small *soda* in La Fortuna is El Jardín (on the main road in the center of town). It's standard Tico fare—rice and beans, casados, and sandwiches—and very inexpensive. Another popular local restaurant, with a similar menu, is La Vaca Muca (on the main road, just out of La Fortuna on the road towards Tabacón). You'll have to work on it to spend more than $5 on a meal (not including beer or wine) at either one of these places. For between $8 and $12 per person you can have a slightly more formal meal at the restaurants at Tabacón Hot Springs Resort or at the Arenal Observatory Lodge.

Days 4 and 5 (Monteverde)   Your first day will be mostly taken up with traveling. If you're getting around by bus, you'll want to catch the 8am bus for Tilarán, which will get you there in time to have lunch at a local soda and make the 1pm bus to Santa Elena (Monteverde). If you have a rental car, you'll have much more flexibility. As you circle Lake Arenal, stop now and again to take in the impressive vistas and be sure to get out and visit the Arenal Botanical Gardens. For lunch, try Restaurant Lajas in the small town of Nuevo Arenal. Settle in to your hotel in Monteverde. At $55 for a double, the Hotel Belmar is a bit of a splurge, but has one of the best settings in town, with gorgeous sunset views across the Golfo de Nicoya. On the budget end, a $14 double at Pensión Flor de Lis is certainly basic, but more than acceptable by backpacker standards. Spend the day hiking through either the Monteverde or Santa Elena cloud-forest reserves. Visit the Hummingbird Gallery (it's free) and/or the Butterfly Garden ($5). For lunch you can eat à la carte, or put together something to go at Stella's Bakery for around $5. Then in the evening, treat yourself to some creative international fare at El Sapo Dorado for around $10 per person.

Days 6 and 7 (Montezuma)   There are too many beach choices in Costa Rica to do them justice in this section. Read through the regional chapters to find the one just right for you. That said, you can't go wrong in Montezuma. Amor de Mar ($30 for a double, with shared bath) has one of the most spectacular settings in town. Set on a grassy plot of land that slopes down to the sea, you may never want to leave one of the many hammocks that hang between the mango trees. If you do, there's a natural tide pool carved in the rocks that's great for a cooling dip and the trail to Montezuma's principal waterfall is just across the street. More adventurous types can head to the Cabo Blanco Absolute Nature Preserve or ride a horse to the other waterfall 8 kilometers away. Have breakfast at Amor de Mar, where the fresh fruit and granola plate is massive and the homemade pancakes with bananas are earning local renown. For lunch have the daily special or one of the vegetarian sandwiches at El Sano Banano for under $5. Dine outdoors by the light of oil lamps at Playa de los Artistas, where a plate of fresh grouper in a black-pepper sauce with rich home-baked bread for soaking up the sauce is just $9. You can sample some of the other restaurant offerings in town, but you'll just as likely find yourself repeating the above choices, with no qualms or complaints.

IF YOU HAVE 7 DAYS IN BELIZE

Day 1 (Belize City)   You'll start your vacation in style at Colton House, where a double will run you $45 a night. A wonderfully maintained colonial-era home in the historic Fort George section of town, Colton House makes a great base for a walking tour of Belize City. If the complimentary fruit and coffee are not enough to tide you over, have a full breakfast of eggs, beans, and fry jacks at Big Daddy's for $3. Have your midday meal on the verandah at the Fort Street Restaurant, where the daily lunch special is just $4.50. For dinner, try G.G.'s Cafe and Patio. Although the stewed chicken and beef are both excellent, opt for the fresh broiled fish filet for $7.50. After dinner, walk around the block for at nightcap and some lively conversation at the Harbour Room Bar at the Bellevue Hotel.

Day 2 (Cahal Pech)   Take a morning bus out of Belize City to San Ignacio. Start your stay in the Cayo district at Cahal Pech Village, perched on a hill overlooking "San Iggie" and just a couple hundred yards from the Cahal Pech Mayan ruins. A spacious individual cabin here costs just $35 dollars for two. Have a breakfast of eggs and beans with fresh tortillas and coffee for around $3 in the hotel's restaurant. Spend the morning exploring the neighboring ruins and then head on into town for lunch. Eva's is a must for lunch. The daily special will run you $4.50 and might feature a local specialty like *escabeche* (pickled chicken or fish) or *chilemole* (a traditional spicy Mayan soup with chicken, vegetables, and a hardboiled egg). After lunch, peruse the tour and adventure information tacked all over the walls, then talk to Bob Jones, the owner, and see if there are any tours you want to line up. You might want to go horseback riding for the afternoon, take a canoe out on the Macal river, hop a bus out to the Xunantunich ruins, or just walk around this rustic little town. For dinner, head to Hantley Pieris' Serendib Restaurant. A hefty plate of beef or chicken curry Sri Lankan–style, with rice and salad, is just $4.75. This comes in at around $30 per person, well under our budget, which is good, because we're going to splurge just a little tomorrow.

Day 3 (The Cayo district)   A stay in the Cayo district wouldn't be complete without at least one night at a jungle lodge on either the Macal or Mopan rivers. The Macal River Tent Camp has deluxe and spacious tents on raised platforms set in the forest above the Macal River. Each tent comes equipped with a gas lantern (which is lit for you at dusk), two canvas camp cots with air matresses, and a small deck area with two wooden chairs. Hearty meals are served in the communal eating area. Showers and composting toilets are located in separate buildings, a short walk away from the center of the camp. The gentle sound of the river will put you to sleep, and the raucous songs of many birds will wake you up. Spend the day canoeing on the river, and definitely visit the neighboring Ix Chel Farm and Panti Medicine Trail. An all-inclusive price of $45 per person will get you one night and three solid meals here.

If you prefer a real bed, you can get a similar experience just up the river at DuPlooy's. Although DuPlooy's has made its name as a luxurious jungle lodge, there are six rooms in the Pink House that go for just $40 a double. These rooms all share a couple of common bathrooms, but everything is well-maintained and immaculate. There's nothing else around, so you'll be taking all your meals here, which should run between $20 and $25 per person per day. Meals are served in a common screened-in dining room. Spend your day hiking around the surrounding gardens and forest, paddling on the river, birdwatching, or just lazing around. But you'll also want to spend plenty of time on the open deck that looks out over the river to the limestone cliffs on the far bank.

Day 4 (en route to Placencia)   Although it's not incredibly attractive, Dangriga breaks up the trip conveniently between the Cayo district and Placencia, allowing you time to stop at Blue Hole National Park and St. Herman's Cave on the way. For dependable budget accommodations, try a second-floor room in the new building at Pal's Guest House. At $30 for a double, these come with a private bath, cable TV, and a balcony that looks out over the Caribbean. But be forewarned: Even in these rooms, the feel is decidedly Spartan, with linoleum floors and bare cement shower stalls. For a nicer room in Dangriga, spend a bit more for a night at the Pelican Beach Resort, where a double will run you between $60 and $80. Start your day at Pola's Kitchen where a full breakfast of eggs, beans, juice, and coffee, served with freshly baked bread or johnny cakes, is $4. For lunch try a plate of stewed chicken, rice, and beans at the River Cafe for another $4. During the afternoon, stroll around town, visit some of the local artisans' studios, cop a bench at one of the seaside parks in town, and then head back to Pola's for a dinner of the Garifuna specialty *hudut*—a fish stew cooked in coconut milk and served with mashed plantains—for $8.

Day 5   At this point, you deserve some beach time. For that, it's off to one of Costa Rica's many beaches. Check out the "Best Beaches" section in Chapter 1 and individual beach descriptions in Chapters 7, 9, and 11 to choose a beach that best suits your needs.

The new double rooms at the Seaspray go for $25. They lack any sense of style, but they are clean, spacious and very close to the beach. For breakfast, head next door to Da Tatch, where a massive omelet or fresh pancakes with coffee will run you around $3. Spend your day catching rays, reading a book, and taking the occasional dip in the Caribbean. For lunch, head down the Sidewalk—the town's main thoroughfare—to Omar's Fast Food Stop, where a fish or conch burrito and fresh fruit drink will cost you less than $5. Head back to the beach. After sunset and a shower, grab an outdoor table at Brenda's and enjoy a spicy shrimp dinner or fresh fish filet in Creole seasonings for between $10 and $15.

Days 6 and 7 (Caye Caulker)   To complete the perfect 7 days in Belize, you must visit Caye Caulker. What you sacrifice in foregoing an ocean view, you make up for in ambience and savings at Jimenez Cabañas. At just $24 per double, these individual palmetto cabins set among flowering gardens are a great base for a couple of relaxing days in Caye Caulker. Have breakfast at Glenda's—it's a tradition, and the cinnamon rolls (50¢ a piece) and fresh orange juice (75¢ a glass) are delicious. For lunch, try the conch fajitas ($6.50) at the Rainbow Restaurant, and for dinner head on over to the Sand Box, where a lobster dinner (in season) is just $12. During the day, take a snorkeling trip to the nearby reef, or a full-day excursion to Hol Chan Marine Reserve or Geoff's Caye. For your second dinner here, check out The Castaways Restaurant, which has some wonderfully spicy Indian and Thai chicken dishes for around $8. Whether you fly directly from Caye Caulker to the international airport, or take an early morning water taxi and then a regular cab, you should be able to make your flight home from Belize with time to spare.

Bird Watching, Diving & Other Active Vacations in Costa Rica & Belize

3

Although it's possible to come to either of these countries and stay clean and dry, most visitors want to spend some time getting their feet muddy and their hair wet, exploring the rain and cloud forests, the coral reefs, and the exquisitely clear and warm turquoise blue water.

As awareness of the value of these still largely undeveloped tropical environments and interest in visiting them has grown, dozens of lodges and tour companies have sprung up to cater to travelers interested in enjoying the natural beauties of Costa Rica and Belize. These lodges are usually situated in out-of-the-way locations, sometimes deep in the heart of a forest, and sometimes on a farm with only a tiny bit of natural forest. However, they all have one thing in common: They cater to environmentally aware people with an interest in nature. Bird watching, rafting, kayaking, horseback riding, and hiking are among the most popular activities offered at these lodges. Belize puts a special twist on the experience by providing lodges on the barrier reef from which guests can scuba dive, snorkel, or fish—all while learning about the unique ecology of the reef.

For detailed listings of these lodges, several of which offer special packages that fit our $35-a-day budget, see the "Where to Stay & Eat" sections of the regional chapters that follow (chapters 7–11 and 15–18).

There are myriad approaches to planning an active vacation here. If adventure travel is one of the prime reasons you've chosen to visit, this chapter lays out your options—from tour operators that run multi-activity package tours (which often include stays at eco-lodges) to the best places to practice particular activities (with listings of specialized tour operators, guides, and outfitters). An overview of Costa Rica's national parks and bioreserves is also included because so many of that country's adventure travel offerings take place in these protected areas. It includes suggestions for how to combine a visit to one or two national parks during your stay. After a few tips on health and safety in the wilderness, the chapter closes with a list of educational and volunteer travel options for those with a little more time on their hands and a passion for learning.

Note: Many of the activities described in this chapter stretch our proposed budget. Most require high-tech equipment and/or specialized guides. Nevertheless, if one or more of the activities listed below is a personal passion, it would be a shame to visit either country without partaking in it. Wherever possible, I mention strategies that might help you to cut costs.

1 Organized Adventure Tours

Since many travelers have limited time and resources, organized ecotourism or adventure travel packages, run by tour operators in the United States or in Costa Rica, are a popular way of combining several activities, such as birdwatching, horseback riding, rafting, and hiking with, say, visits to Mayan ruins.

While it is generally possible to cut costs by custom designing your trip and carefully picking and choosing your adventure options, traveling on a package tour has several advantages over traveling independently: All of your accommodations and transportation are arranged and most (if not all) of your meals are included. You'll proceed to each of your destinations quickly without the snags and long delays that those traveling on their own can face. You'll also have the opportunity of meeting like-minded souls who are interested in nature and active sports. Group size is usually kept small (no more than 10 to 20 people), and tours are almost always escorted by knowledgeable guides who are naturalists or biologists. If you plan on packing adventure experiences into every day of your visit, a complete package is a good way to go.

Most of the U.S.–based tour operators listed below, and some of the Costa Rican and Belizean companies covered in the sections that follow, have toll-free numbers. It always pays to do pre-trip research. Prices and tour offerings vary year to year and according to season. Call around and comparison shop and see which operation has the trip or tour that best suits your needs and budget.

Be sure to ask about difficulty levels when you are choosing a tour. While most companies offer "soft adventure" packages that those in moderately good, but not phenomenal, shape can handle, others focus on more hard-core activities that only seasoned athletes or adventure travelers should take on.

U.S.–BASED ADVENTURE TOUR OPERATORS

These agencies and operators specialize in well-organized and coordinated tours, set up for your entire stay. Many travelers prefer to have everything arranged and confirmed before arriving in either Costa Rica or Belize, and this is a good idea in the high season.

COSTA RICA

International Expeditions, Inc., One Environs Park, Helena, AL 35080 (☎ **800/ 633-4734** or 205/428-1700), specializes in independent programs and 10-day natural history group tours.

Journeys International, Inc., 4011 Jackson Rd., Ann Arbor, MI 48103 (☎ **800/ 255-8735** or 313/665-4407), offers small group (no more than 4–12 people) natural history tours guided by Costa Rican naturalists. Horseback riding is included. 8-day, 10-day, and three-week itineraries.

Mountain Travel•Sobek, 6420 Fairmount Ave., El Cerrito, CA 94530 (☎ **800/ 227-2384** or 510/527-8100), offers natural history tours with naturalist guides. 10-day itineraries can include visits to Corcovado and Tortuguero national parks, Monteverde, and Arenal Volcano; activities include jungle walks, boat rides, snorkeling, and swimming. All accommodations are in lodges, with the exception of the first and last nights of each itinerary—these are spent in hotels in San José.

Wilderness Travel, 801 Allston Way, Berkeley, CA 94710 (☎ **800/368-2794** or 510/548-0420), specializes in natural history and bird watching 14-day group tours that are tier-priced, depending on the number of people who sign up (cost decreases with a larger group). Tours include visits to Corcovado and Tortuguero national parks, Monteverde, Arenal Volcano, and Caño Negro National Wildlife Refuge, among other destinations.

Overseas Adventure Travel, 625 Mount Auburn, Cambridge, MA 02138 (☎ **800/221-0814** or 617/876-0533), specializes in natural history and "soft adventure" 10- and 12-day itineraries, with optional 3-day add-on excursions. Tours are limited to no more than 16 people and are guided by naturalists. All accommodations are in small hotels, lodges, or tent camps. Itineraries include visits to most major national parks and private nature reserves.

Costa Rica Connections, 75 Oso St., San Luis Obispo, CA 93401 (☎ **800/345-7422** or 805/543-8823), specializes in natural history tours of major national parks. There is a complete range of independent packages and scheduled group departures for bird watching, fishing, ecotourism, kayaking/rafting, and dive trips, plus the Costa Rica National Orchid show.

BELIZE

Belize Adventure Tours, 110 Harrison Avenue, San Antonio, TX 78029 (☎/fax **210/828-3758**); **Belize Eco Tours,** 9424 Canton Loop, Anchorage, AK 99515 (☎ **800/349-7830**); **Bivouac Adventure Travel,** 336 South State Street, Ann Arbor, Michigan 48104-2412 (☎ **800/878-8747** or 313/761-8777, fax 313/761-7179); **Ecosummer Expeditions,** 1516 Duranleau Street, Vancouver, BC V6H 3S4, Canada (☎ **800/465-8884** or 800/688-8605 in the U.S.); **Global Travel Club,** 1 Kiln Shaw Langdon Hills, Basildon, Essex SS16 6LE, England (☎ **44/268-541732**, fax 44/268-542275); **Great Trips,** P.O. Box 1320, Detroit Lake, MN 56501 (☎ **800/552-3419** or 612/890-4405); **International Expeditions, Inc.,** One Environs Park, Helena, AL 35080 (☎ **800/633-4734** or 205/428-1700); **Sea & Explore, Inc.,** 1809 Carol Sue Avenue, Suite E, Gretna, LA 70056 (☎ **504/366-9985**, fax 504/366-9986); **Winter Escapes,** P.O. Box 429, Erickson, Manitoba R0J 0P0, Canada (☎ **204/636-2968**, fax 204/636-2557).

COSTA RICAN TOUR AGENCIES

Since many U.S.–based companies subcontract portions of their tours to established Costa Rican companies in the field, some travelers like to set up their tour directly with these companies, therefore cutting out the middle man. There are literally scores of agencies in San José that offer a plethora of adventure options. These agencies can generally arrange everything from white-water rafting and sightseeing at one of the nearby volcanoes to a visit to a butterfly farm. As a rule, the companies listed in this section are your best options for one-day guided trips out of San José or affordably priced packages to popular destinations such as Tortuguero or Corcovado. If you're looking to scuba dive, mountain bike, or river raft, you'll probably do best to go directly to the specialized outfitters listed in the separate sections below.

Tour prices tend to be relatively firm and standardized across the industry. However, competition has become fierce in the past couple of years, and you may be able to save money by shopping around, looking for new agencies, scanning the *Tico Times* for special discounts or promotions, and trying to bargain down the price in person. Costa Rican–based tour agencies are particularly useful when you only plan on taking one or two shorter, organized tours during your stay. They also allow you the flexibility of arranging your tours and schedule according to your needs upon arrival or on a whim. However, be careful: This latter strategy can be hazardous in the high season, when rooms and tour space both book up quickly. Because tours are sometimes held only when there are enough interested people or on set dates, it sometimes pays to contact a few of the companies before you leave the U.S. and find out what they might be doing when you plan to be in Costa Rica.

Adventure Land/Tam Tours, P.O. Box 1864-1000, San José (☎ **506/222-3866** or 506/222-2642, fax 506/222-3724), offers a full gamut of San José–based day tours to such destinations as Arenal Volcano and Tabacón Hot Springs, Carara Biological Reserve, and local national parks. All tours include transportation, entry fees, lunch, and a guide.

Costa Rica Expeditions, Dept. 235, P.O. Box 025216, Miami, FL 33102 (☎ **506/257-0766** or 506/222-0333, fax 506/257-1665), offers 3-day/2-night and 2-day/1-night tours of Monteverde Biological Cloud Forest Preserve, Tortuguero National Park, and Corcovado National Park, as well as 1- to 2-day white-water rafting trips and other excursions. All excursions include transportation, meals, and lodging.

Costa Rica Sun Tours, Apdo. 1195-1250, Escazú (☎ **506/255-3418,** fax 506/255-3529), specializes in multi-day tours that include stays at small country lodges for nature-oriented travelers. Destinations visited include Arenal Volcano (with stays at the Arenal Observatory Lodge); Monteverde Biological Cloud Forest Preserve, with stops in Poás and Sarchi; and Corcovado and Manuel Antonio national parks (with overnight stays at Tiskita Jungle Lodge, Corcovado Tent Camp, Lapa Rios, and Drake Bay Wilderness Lodge, among other accommodations).

Ecole Travel, Calle 7, between Avenidas Central and 1, San José (☎ **506/223-2240**, fax 506/223-4128), offers tours and day trips around the country. Specializes in small group and budget tours to Tortuguero, Arenal Volcano, and the Southern Zone.

Fantasy Tours, Apdo. 962-1000, San José (☎ **506/220-2126** or 506/220-0042, fax 506/220-2393), offers a comprehensive list of full-day tours to destinations that include: Arenal Volcano and Tabacón Hot Springs; Poás and Irazu volcanos; Manuel Antonio National Park; Carara Biological Reserve; and Bosque de Paz, a private biological reserve. White-water rafting expeditions, fishing trips, island cruises, and multi-day tours are also available.

Geotur, Apdo. 469 Y-1011, San José (☎/fax **506/227-4029**), specializes in half-day visits to Braulio Carrillo National Park and full-day trips to Carara Biological Reserve. This latter trip provides excellent opportunities to see scarlet macaws in the wild.

OTEC Viajes, Apdo. 323-1002, San José (☎ **506/256-0633**, fax 506/233-2321), offers a wide range of tour options, with a special focus on student and discount travel. Students and teachers should definitely check in here.

Pura Natura, Apdo. 10923-1000, San José (☎ **506/233-9469** or 506/233-9709, fax 506/223-9200), offers 1- to 5-day hiking, mountain biking, and horseback-riding trips that are among the most adventurous of any available in Costa Rica. You can hike through Corcovado National Park or up to the peak of Mount Chirripó, among other trips.

BELIZEAN TOUR AGENCIES

If you wait until you get to Belize and then decide you want to get active, you'll probably do best if you go straight to the next section, "Special-Interest Adventure Travel & Active Sports," and look up the activity in which you're most interested, or check the active sports listings in the regional chapters that follow. Even though adventure travel has been popular in Belize for a few years now, the number of tour operators is still rather small. In Belize City, try: **S&L Travel Services and Guided Tours** (☎ **501/2/77593** or 501/2/75145) or **Discovery Expeditions** (☎ **501/2/30748** or 501/2/30749). Both of these are geared towards the soft adventurer.

2 Sports & Activities A to Z

This section is an A-to-Z compendium of the many activities and active sports available in Costa Rica and Belize. Each listing begins by describing the best places to practice a particular sport or activity and then lists tour operators and outfitters you can contact. If you only want to focus on one active sport during your stay, such as river rafting, these companies are your best bets for quality equipment and knowledgeable service.

You will always save money on adventure activities if you bring your own equipment. However, if diving, kayaking, or mountain biking are only a small part of your travel agenda, it may not be worth the hassle of lugging around bulky and heavy gear during your entire stay.

BIKING

Although there are several major regional and international touring races in Costa Rica each year, in general, the major roads are dangerous and inhospitable to cyclists. The roads are narrow, there's usually no shoulder, and most drivers show little care or consideration for those on two wheels.

The options for mountain bikers and off-track riders are much more appealing. Mountain biking is relatively new to Costa Rica, but growing fast. If you plan to do a lot of biking and are very attached to your rig, bring your own. If you only plan on doing a day or two of biking, it's cheaper and less hassle to rent once you arrive. Several companies and bike shops in San José and elsewhere rent bikes, and the quality of the equipment is steadily improving. See the regional chapters for listings of places that rent.

The best place for mountain biking in Costa Rica is around **Lake Arenal and Arenal Volcano.** The scenery's great, with primary forests, waterfalls, and plenty of trails. And nearby **Tabacón Hot Springs** is the perfect place for those with aching muscles to unwind at the end of the day. (See chapter 8.)

There are only two paved highways in Belize and even these have rough patches, so anyone attempting a bike tour in Belize needs to use sturdy mountain bikes with fat tires. Most of the country is flat, hot, and humid. There are no places for heavy-duty technical riding, so most riders who are comfortable spending long hours on a bike shouldn't have problems. The best place to mountain bike and tour is in the Cayo district. Here you'll find a combination of rolling hills, forests, and Mayan ruins all accessible by dirt road. **Chaa Creek Cottages** (see chapter 17) maintains a fleet of modern mountain bikes and has a very knowledgeable staff. Ask, and they'll recommend a good ride or two.

OUTFITTERS FOR COSTA RICA

Coast To Coast Adventures, Apdo. 2135-1002, San José (☎ **506/225-6055**), prides itself on its two-week tour by horse, raft, mountain bike, and foot (no motorized vehicles are used). Other trips are also available.

EcoTreks Adventure Company, Dept. 262, P.O. Box 025216, Miami, FL 33102 (☎ **506/228-4029** or 800/328-2288 in the U.S., fax 506/289-8191), specializes in mountain biking trips, among other active sports.

Experience Plus/Specialty Tours, Inc., 1925 Wallenburg Drive, Ft. Collins, CO 80526 (☎ **800/685-4565**), offers self-guided and assisted bike tours across the country.

Rio Escondido Mountain Bikes, c/o Rock River Lodge, Apdo. 95, Tilarán (☎ **506/695-5644** or 800/678-2252 in the U.S.), offers bike rentals and tours around the Lake Arenal area.

Serendipity Adventures, Apdo. 64200, Naranjo (☎/fax **506/450-0328** or 800/635-2325 in the U.S.), offers mountain-biking trips, among other expeditions.

OUTFITTERS FOR BELIZE

The following U.S.–based operators offer organized biking trips to Belize: **Bivouac Adventure Travel,** 336 South State Street, Ann Arbor, MI 48104-2412 (☎ **800/878-8747** or 313/761-8777, fax 313/761-7179); **Paradise Bicycle Tours,** P.O. Box 1726, Evergreen, CO 80439 (☎ **800/245-2229** or 303/674-2816); and **Slickrock Adventures, Inc.,** P.O. Box 1400, Moab, UT 84532 (☎/fax **801/259-6996**).

BIRD WATCHING

As one of the world's foremost ecotravel destinations, Costa Rica is visited by thousands of avid bird watchers each year. Lodges with the best bird watching opportunities include: **Albergue de Montaña Savegre** and **Albergue de Montaña Tapantí**, both on the road to San Isidro de El General (they can almost guarantee sightings of resplendent quetzals); **La Paloma Lodge** in Drake Bay (where you can sit on the porch of your cabin as the avian parade goes by); **Villa Blanca** in San Ramón (on the edge of a cloud-forest reserve where quetzals are often seen); **Selva Verde Lodge,** Chilamate (the rooms overlook some woods and the rain forest is just across the river); **Avarios del Caribe** just north of Cahuita; and **D'Galah Hotel** in San José (the University of Costa Rica, an oasis of greenery in the city, is directly across the street).

Some of the best parks and preserves to visit include: **Monteverde Biological Cloud Forest Preserve** (resplendent quetzals and hummingbirds); **Corcovado National Park** (scarlet macaws); **Caño Negro Wildlife Refuge** (wading birds, including Jabiru storks); **Guayabo, Negritos, and Pájaros Islands biological reserves** in the Gulf of Nicoya (magnificent frigate birds and brown boobies); **Palo Verde National Park** (ibises, jacanas, storks, roseate spoonbills); **Tortuguero National Park** (great green macaws); and **Rincón de la Vieja National Park** (parakeets, curassows). Some good excursions to consider if bird watching is your passion are rafting float trips down the Corobicí and Bebedero rivers near Liberia; boat trips to or at Tortuguero National Park; and hikes in any cloud forest.

Unless you crave the companionship of fellow ornithologists, the most economical way to bird-watch in Costa Rica is to simply book your lodgings in birding areas that attract a high percentage of birds and take advantage of local and inhouse guides. Guided hikes will generally run you between $10 and $35 per person, and last anywhere from 2 to 4 hours. However, if you're looking for some power-birding, you might want to check out the companies listed below.

Local and visiting ornithologists have identified over 500 species of birds in Belize. With more than 65% of its territory uninhabited by humans, and ecosystems that range from low limestone cayes and mangrove swamps to highland rain and pine forests, Belize is a paradise for both avians and their human admirers.

The **Belize Audubon Society (BAS)** is very active and has succeeded in establishing numerous bird and wildlife sanctuaries. These include the **Crooked Tree Wildlife Sanctuary**, the **Cockscomb Basin Wildlife Sanctuary, Guanacaste National Park**, and **Shipstern Wildlife Reserve.** At present, the BAS is chiefly involved in education, protection, and management of the various preserves and sanctuaries, but they do sponsor a Christmas bird count, and may be able to help with tour suggestions and birding lists. Contact **BAS** at P.O. Box 1001, Belize City (☎ **501-2/35004**).

Where to See the Resplendent Quetzal

Revered by the pre-Columbian cultures throughout Central America, the resplendent quetzal has been called the most beautiful bird on earth. Ancient Aztec and Maya Indians believed the quetzal protected them in battle, and even the bird's brilliant breast plumage has an Indian legend to explain it: When Spanish conquistador Pedro de Alvarado defeated Maya chieftain Tecun Uman in 1524 near what is today the town of Quezaltenango, Guatemala, the Maya chief was mortally wounded in the chest. Tecun Uman's quetzal covered the dying chieftain's body, and when, upon Tecun Uman's death, the quetzal arose, the once white-breasted bird had a blood-red breast. So integral a part of Guatemalan culture is the quetzal that its name is given to that country's currency.

About the size of a robin, the males of this species have brilliant red breasts, iridescent emerald-green heads, backs, and wings, and white tail feathers complemented by a pair of iridescent green tail feathers that are nearly two feet long. These birds live only in the dense cloud forests that cloak the higher slopes of Central America's mountains. Throughout their range, quetzals are endangered, and though many areas of cloud forest have been preserved as habitats for these beautiful birds, researchers have recently discovered that the birds do not spend their entire lives within the cloud forest. After nesting, between March and July, quetzals migrate to lower slopes in search of food. These lower slopes have not been preserved in most cases, and now conservationists are trying to salvage enough lower-elevation forests to help the quetzals survive. Hopefully, enough land will soon be set aside to ensure the perpetuation of this magnificent species of bird.

Though for many years, Monteverde Biological Cloud Forest Preserve was the place to see quetzals, throngs of people crowding the preserve's trails now make it difficult to see any wildlife. Other places where you are more likely to see quetzals are in the Los Angeles Cloud Forest Reserve near San Ramón, on the Cerro de la Muerte between San José and San Isidro de El General, in Tapantí National Wildlife Refuge, and in Chirripó National Park.

In addition to the reserves listed above, the Cayo district is excellent for bird watching. Both **Chaa Creek Cottages** and **DuPlooy's** cater to bird watchers. See chapter 17 for details on these lodgings.

U.S.–BASED TOUR OPERATORS OPERATING IN COSTA RICA

Costa Rica Connections, 958 Higuera St., San Luis Obispo, CA 93401 (☎ **800/ 882-4665** or 305/279-3252), generally offers three bird watching trips a year, including a 12-day "Tropical Birding" tour.

Geostar Travel, 6050 Commerce Blvd., Suite 110, Rohnert Park, CA 94928 (☎ **800/633-6633** or 707/584-9552), has 7-day and 10-day bird watching tours ($1090, 7 day; $1460, 10 day).

Osprey Tours, P.O. Box 030211, Fort Lauderdale, FL 33302 (☎ **305/ 767-4823**), focuses on customized group bird watching tours.

COSTA RICAN TOUR AGENCIES

Quite a few tour agencies in San José specialize in bird watching day trips and multi-day tours. **San José Travel** (Apdo. 889, San José 1007, ☎ **506/221-0593**, fax 506/ 221-5148) offers one-day quetzal tours; and **Jungle Trails** (Apdo. 2413, San

José 1000, ☎ **506/255-3486**, fax 506/255-2782), sponsors one-day birding excursions to Braulio Carrillo and Poás national parks as well as an extensive 15-day tour.

BUNGEE JUMPING

There's nothing particularly unique about bungee jumping in Costa Rica. Nevertheless, the price you'll pay is generally cheaper than in the U.S., and the scenery's certainly more lush. So if you've yet to take the plunge, this is a great place to give it a try. **Tropical Bungee** (☎ **506/233-6455**) will let you jump off a 265-foot bridge for $45; if you want to do it twice, they'll charge you $70.

CAMPING

Heavy rains, difficult access, and limited facilities make camping a real challenge in Costa Rica. Nevertheless, a backpack and a tent will get you far from the crowds and into some of the most pristine and undeveloped nooks and crannies of Costa Rica.

I recommend sticking to the national park system. Unless you are very experienced and an avid survivalist, you do not want to venture off of well-marked trails in the Costa Rican jungles. Camping in national parks will run you $6 per person per day in entrance fees, plus $1.50 per person per day in camping fees. The types of facilities vary, but most spots have showers and outhouses, as well as picnic tables and basic shelters. Camping isn't allowed in all national parks, so read through the write-ups for each park carefully before packing a tent. Some of the national parks' campsites—Corcovado, for example—have small *sodas*, or kitchens, where you can get basic meals of rice and beans. Camping is generally a little less expensive at the private campsites you'll find at various tourist destinations (see the regional chapters). If you plan on packing in your food, you'll be shopping in supermarkets (in San José) and small general stores or *pulperias*. You can get granola, nuts and grains, canned goods, and fresh staples, but if you depend on trail mix and dehydrated food packages, bring them with you. You'll want to pack in bottled water, or have a good water-purification system. It is a bad idea to camp in Costa Rica during the rainy season.

If you'd like to participate in an organized camping trip, contact **Serendipity Adventures** (Apdo. 64200, Naranjo, Costa Rica; ☎/fax **506/450-0328** or 800/635-2325 in the U.S.). In addition to other expeditions, they offer climbing and camping trips.

The best places to pitch a tent on the beach in Costa Rica are **Santa Rosa National Park** and the **Puerto Vargas campsite in Cahuita National Park**. The best camping treks are, without a doubt, through Corcovado National Park or up Mount Chirripó. My favorite private campsite is **Camping Los Malinches** at Playa Junquillal (see chapter 7).

Belize has excellent camping during the dry season. During the rainy season, particularly in the southern zone, camping is not highly recommended, for obvious reasons. Several of the country's wildlife sanctuaries have camping facilities or permit camping, including the **Cockscomb Wildlife Sanctuary** (see chapter 18) and the **Crooked Tree Wildlife Sanctuary** (see chapter 15). The Cayo district is a boon for campers, with excellent campsites and facilities in close proximity to protected forests, jungle rivers, and Mayan ruins. On the way out to the Cayo district from Belize City, you can camp at the **Monkey Bay Wildlife Sanctuary** (☎ **501/8-23180**). Once in Cayo, check out **Clarissa Falls Cottages** (☎ **501/92-3916**) or **Caesar's Place** (☎ **501/92-2341**), which is owned by the same folks who run **Black Rock Jungle River Lodge**. See chapter 17 for more information on all of the above places.

The best camping on the cayes is in the southern cayes. **Glover's Atoll Resort** (☎ **501-5/23048**) has excellent week-long packages for campers, with basic bath, shower, and cooking facilities included. See chapter 16 for more information.

CANOPY TOURS

Canopy tours are taking off in Costa Rica, largely because they are such a unique way to experience tropical rain forests. It is estimated that some two-thirds of a typical rain forest's species live in the canopy, or the uppermost tangle of branches and leaves. From the relative luxury of the Aerial Tram's high-tech funicular, to the rope and climbing-gear rigs of more basic operations, a trip into the canopy will give you a bird's-eye view of a neotropical forest. There are now canopy tour facilities in **Drake Bay** and **Corcovado National Park, Monteverde,** and **Rincón de la Vieja National Park,** as well as on **Tortuga Island.** With the exception of the Aerial Tram, most involve strapping yourself into a climbing harness and being winched up to a platform some 100 feet above the forest floor.

CANOPY TOUR OPERATORS BASED IN COSTA RICA

Aerial Tram, Apdo. 592-2100, San José (☎ **506/257-5961,** fax 506/257-6053), is located 50 minutes from San José. This modern tram takes you on a 2-hour trip through the rain forest canopy. The cost is $47.50, without transportation.

Canopy Tours, Apdo. 751-2350, San José (☎ **506/223-5595,** fax 506/ 257-5149), is a loose grouping of more adventurous canopy tour operators around the country, with sites in Monteverde, on Tortuga Island, and at the Corcovado Tent Camp. At each site, you'll be strapped into a climbing harness and winched up to a platform in the canopy. At some operations you can slide from one platform to another along a network of climbing ropes. The tours vary, but generally last between 2 to 4 hours and cost around $40 per person.

CAVING/SPELUNKING

Heavy rainfall, underground rivers, and the passage of time all add up to caves—lots of them. Many of them, such as **Chechem Ha** (see chapter 17) were used by the ancient Maya for ceremonies and offerings. The most established and extensive operation geared toward the avid spelunker is **Ian Anderson's Caves Branch** (P.O. Box 356, Belmopan, Belize, ☎/fax **501-8/22800**). Caves Branch has a wide range of wet and dry caves on its own property, and leads trips ranging from simple hikes and cave tubing, to overnight cave camping and survival courses. There are also caves in the southern Toledo district. If you're in Punta Gorda and want to go caving, look up **Belize Adventure Travel** at the **Nature's Way Guest House** (☎ **501-7/22119,** fax 501-7/22199).

CRUISING

There aren't as many cruising or boat-chartering opportunities as you might expect in Belize, given the spectacular scenery, protected waters, great diving, and numerous uninhabited cayes. Many of the vessels that ply this trade are geared to live-aboard divers, and are listed under "Diving," below. Still, there are a few options for those who just want to get away from it all and lie around on the deck of a small cruise ship, yacht, or sailboat.

Since Belize has yet to establish a bareboat chartering industry, the fleet tends to be transient. Your best bet for either a bareboat or captained charter is to ask around in **Belize City, Corozal Town, Placencia,** or any of the **cayes,** or contact the **Belize Tourist Board** (☎ **212/563-6011** or 800/624-0686 in the U.S.; fax 212/563-6033) before your departure. What you find may be pricier than you had in mind. Frugal travelers wishing a taste of the cruising life may be happier sticking to the day trips offered on **Caye Caulker** and **Ambergris Caye** (see chapter 16).

One dependable long-term charter boat is the *Stingray*, a 45-foot catamaran run out of the Ramada Royal Reef by **Fanta-Sea Charters,** P.O. Box 768, Belize City, Belize (☎ **501-2/32712** or ☎ /fax 303/226-1193 in the U.S.).

If you have a real romance for the sea, you'll want to check out the *Rembrandt Van Rijn*, a three-masted Baltic schooner based in Belize City. The *Rembrandt Van Rijn* accommodates up to 40 guests on one- or two-week voyages. This is predominantly a vessel for divers, but non-divers are welcome. Contact **Oceanwide Sail Expeditions,** Westfalenstrasse 92, D-58636 Iserlohn, Germany (☎ **800/334-8582** in the U.S.).

Another interesting option is to book passage on one of the small cruise ships that sail Belizean waters. Both **American Canadian Caribbean Line,** 459 Water St., Warren, Rhode Island 02885 (☎ **800/556-7450**) and **Temptress Cruises,** 1606 NW LeJeune, Suite 301, Miami, FL 33126 (☎ **305/871-2663** or 800/336-8423 in the U.S., 506/220-1679 in Costa Rica) offer a variety of cruise packages. Both of these companies have small ships with deluxe and standard staterooms and cabins. Most of their itineraries cover the coast of Belize, with stops in Ambergris Caye, Dangriga, Placencia, Punta Gorda, Puerto Barrios, and Livingston, Guatemala. In many respects you'll think you're on one of the major cruise lines, although there are no swimming pools or onboard shopping malls.

DIVING

This is where Belize excels. The 185-mile barrier reef offers just as many miles of excellent wall, canyon, and coral diving. You'll almost never feel crowded. Even Ambergris Caye, the most developed and crowded of Belize's dive centers, has enough dive sites to spread the riches around. Down in the southern cayes and on the outer atoll islands, you'll have chances to dive in pristine areas, where very few humans have gone before.

Belize is also an excellent place to learn to dive. Most of the dive operations listed below and most of the shops in Ambergris Caye, Caye Caulker, and Placencia offer introductory resort and open-water certification courses. A full PADI or NAUI certification course runs around $300 or $350 per person including all equipment, class time, and several open-water dives. This is generally cheaper than you can do it at home—and the water is warmer and the setting spectacular.

Diving off the shores of Costa Rica pales in comparison with Belize. Despite the many islands, reefs, caves, and rocks off its coastline, visibility varies with season and location. Generally, heavy rainfall tends to swell the rivers and muddy the waters, even well offshore. Banana plantations and their runoff have destroyed most of the Caribbean reefs, although there's still good diving at **Isla Uvita,** just off the coast of Limón. Most divers choose Pacific dive spots such as **Caño Island, Bat Island,** and the **Catalina Islands,** where they're likely to spot manta rays, moray eels, white-tipped sharks, and plenty of smaller fish and coral species.

The ultimate dive trip in Costa Rica has to be a live-aboard package to Coco Island. However, as the ticket for the average booking—10 days, all-inclusive—is a steep $2,700, you may not be signing up for a while yet.

No matter how you look at it, diving is an expensive activity—in either country. Your best bet for saving money in Costa Rica is dealing directly with the operators in Playa Flamingo, Playa Hermosa, and Playa del Coco (see chapter 7). In Belize, local operators urge the cost-conscious to learn to love the off-season. If you can bear the high temperatures and still air, June through August are excellent times to visit Belize and dive; hotels and dive operators often offer discounts, and the sea is much calmer, increasing visibility and making it much easier to get in and out of the water.

Serious divers will want to check into all-inclusive packages at one of the dive resorts or on one of the live-aboard boats. If you want to make two to three tank dives a day, these can often save you a lot of money over paying for individual dives. However, a package does take away from your flexibility; if you're on one, it's hard to sit out a day or two without feeling like you're throwing money away.

In addition to the companies and lodges listed below, check the listings under Ambergris Caye, Caye Caulker, South Water Caye, and Placencia in the regional chapters that cover Belize. Also, when making a lodging reservation at any of the above destinations, always ask if your hotel offers a dive package. For more information about diving the Blue Hole and Turneffe Islands, see chapter 16.

DIVING LODGES, LIVE-ABOARD BOATS & OPERATORS IN BELIZE

Belize Aggressor III, P.O. Drawer K, Morgan City, LA 70381, (☎ **800/348-2628** or 504/385-2628, fax 504/384-0817), is a 120-foot luxury yacht with over 10 years of experience along the Belizean reef.

Glover's Atoll Resort, P.O. Box 563, Belize City (☎ **501-5/23048**), is an economical dive resort that offers excellent diving to its guests. See chapter 18 for rates and more information.

M/V Hot Dive, 8 North Park Street, Belize City (☎/fax **501-2/34058**), has several live-aboard options and years of experience.

Oceanwide Sail Expeditions, Westfalenstrasse 92, D-58636 Iserlohn, Germany (☎ **800/334-8582** in the U.S.), runs all-inclusive packages on the three-masted schooner *Rembrandt Van Rijn.*

Out Island Divers, San Pedro, Ambergris Caye, Belize (☎ **501-26/2151** or 303/586-6020 in the U.S.; fax 501-26/2810), specializes in trips to the Blue Hole and Lighthouse Reef.

DIVING OPERATORS IN COSTA RICA

In addition to the companies listed in the regional chapters, the operators below are good sources for information, equipment rental, and San José–based diving tours.

Buzos del Tropico, Apdo. 366-3100, Sto. Domingo de Heredia (☎/fax **506/222-5481**), is a full-service dive center, offering equipment rental, certification classes, and trips.

Escenarios Tropicales, Apdo. 2047-1000, San José (☎ **506/224-2555,** fax 506/234-1554), specializes in live-aboard trips to Caño and Coco islands, including 3-day, 5-day, and 10-day itineraries.

Mundo Aquatico, P.O. Box 7875-1000, San José (☎ **506/224-9729,** fax 506/234-2982), is a San José–based operator that offers equipment rental, certification classes, and dive tours.

EcoTreks Adventure Company, Dept. 262, P.O. Box 025216, Miami, FL 33102 (☎ **506/228-4029** or 800/328-2288 in the U.S., fax 506/289-8191), offers a full-service dive center and maintains a boat at Playa Flamingo.

FISHING

Many of the same superlatives used to describe diving in Belize are enthusiastically espoused by anglers to describe the phenomenal fishing here. Whether it's fly-fishing up a jungle river, battling tarpon and bonefish on the flats, or wrestling blue marlin and sails on the open sea, there are fishing thrills to spare in Belize. As with diving, the months of June through August are an excellent time to get low-season discounts, and the fish seem to like the warmer water.

Costa Rica is also a great place to cast a line—anglers have landed more than 65 world-record catches, including blue marlin, pacific sailfish, dolphin, wahoo, yellowfin tuna, guapote, and snook in the waters here. Those with the best luck tend to charter a fishing boat or stay at a fishing lodge, and unfortunately, neither comes cheap. Boat rentals generally start at around $150 per day for inland lake fishing, and run up to $800 through $1,500 for open-ocean adventures. If you're an avid angler and dyed-in-the-wool do-it-yourselfer, there's nothing to stop you from bringing along your rod and reel and choosing a nice spot for some shore casting or fly-fishing. There are plenty of beaches and mountain streams to choose from. Just make sure you obtain a fishing license first. A one-year license for salt-water fishing will cost you $10. Two-month licenses for fresh-water fishing (inland lake and river) cost $30. Most charter fleets and fishing operators can provide a license with little hassle. Alternately, you'll have to visit the San José offices of the **Ministry of the Environment** (☎ **506/257-0922;** Calle 25 between avenidas 8 and 10), between 8am and 5pm, Monday through Friday.

Fishing Lodges & Operators in Belize

In addition to these listings, you can also charter a boat in **Corozal Town, San Pedro, Caye Caulker, Placencia,** and most of the outer cayes. See chapters 15, 16, and 18 for details.

Belize River Lodge, P.O. Box 459, Belize City (☎ **501-25/2459** or 800/748-3715 in the U.S.) is a small fishing lodge on the Belize River, near the airport. It runs three live-aboard yachts.

El Pescador Lodge, P.O. Box 793, Belize City (☎/fax **501-26/2398** or 800/222-0103 in the U.S.), on Ambergris Caye, caters to fishing enthusiasts.

Fishing Lodges & Operators in Costa Rica

In addition to these listings, many of the Pacific port and beach towns—**Quepos, Puntarenas, Playa del Coco, Tamarindo, Flamingo, Golfito, Drake Bay,** and **Zancudo**—support large charter fleets; see chapters 7, 9, and 10 for recommended boats and captains.

Isla de Pesca Lodge, P.O. Box 7-1880-1000, San José (☎ **506/239-1025** or 305/858-7478 in the U.S., fax 506/239-2405), is a tarpon- and snook-fishing lodge in Barra del Colorado run by the Costa Sol Group. It specializes in 7-day all-inclusive packages for $1,990, which include transportation to and from the lodge, deluxe accommodations, all meals, and daily fishing with a boat and guide. Tackle is also provided.

Rio Colorado Lodge, 2121 West Juneau Avenue, Tampa, FL 33604 (☎ **506/232-4063** or 800/243-9777 in the U.S., fax 813/933-3280), was originally set up by the late, and locally legendary, Archie Fields. Located at Barra del Colorado, Rio Colorado maintains a fleet of 23-foot center console boats for river and offshore fishing.

Silver King Lodge, Rainforest Excursions, 1107 East Lemon St., Tarpon Springs, FL 34689 (☎/fax **506/288-0849**), located at Barra de Colorado, is another lodge that specializes in tarpon and snook fishing.

Americana Fishing Services, Apdo. 6241-1000, San José (☎ **506/223-4331,** fax 506/221-0096), is run by Richard Krug, the fishing columnist for the *Tico Times,* who also has a desk at the Hotel Del Rey. Richard can find you a boat and captain to suit your needs.

Fresh-Water Fishing Adventures, Via Alta, Bello Horizonte, Escazú (☎ **506/ 228-4812** or 800/434-6867 in the U.S), offers guided inland river and lake fishing trips in Costa Rica's northern zone. It specializes in off-the-beaten-track and generally unvisited spots, including many jungle river locations.

J.P. Tours, P.O. Box 66-1100, Tibás (☎ **506/284-7592** or 800/308-3394 in the U.S., fax 506/244-0552), is based at the Punta Leona resort on the Pacific coast, and offers deep-sea fishing aboard its 44-foot yacht for around $150 per person per day. Pickup and drop-off can be arranged from any San José hotel.

HORSEBACK RIDING

As Costa Rica moves away from a primarily agricultural economy, it continues to retain its rural roots. This is perhaps most evident in the continued use of horses for real work and transportation throughout the country. What this means for travelers is that horses are easily available for riding, whether you want to take a sunset trot along the beach, a ride through the cloud forest, or a multi-day trek through the northern zone. Your best bet for finding a good and inexpensive mount is to ask around at your particular destination. Almost anywhere outside San José is fine for climbing into a saddle.

Belize was settled and built by seafarers. There's no real ranch or livestock tradition and very little range to ride. But if horseback riding's your thing, you can find a mount. The Cayo district is your best bet, with several outfitters working in or around San Ignacio (see chapter 17). I recommend **Mountain Equestrian Trails,** Mile 8 Mountain Pine Ridge Road, Central Farm P.O., Cayo district (☎ **501-92/ 3310**). This is a basic eco-lodge and camping facility in the heart of the Mountain Pine Ridge, with over 20 well-maintained horses, that's run by horse lovers. You can also try **Banana Bank Lodge** (Box 48, Belmopan, Belize; ☎/fax **501-8/23180**), an eco-lodge and working farm near Belmopan.

HORSEBACK RIDING OUTFITTERS IN COSTA RICA

Rancho Savegre Horseback Tours, Rancho Savegre, c/o Hotel Sirena, P.O. Box 02592, Miami, FL 33102 (☎/fax **06/777-0528** or 800/355-2389 in the U.S.) offers one- and multi-day horseback tours, based out of Rancho Savegre near Quepos.

SEA KAYAKING

With semi-protected water the length of its fabulous barrier reef, as well as offshore atolls, deserted cayes, and mangrove estuaries, Belize is a wonderland for sea kayakers. Many lodgings on the various cayes have sea kayaks for rent (see chapter 16), and if you're in Punta Gorda, check out **Belize Adventure Travel** at the **Nature's Way Guest House** (☎ **501-7/22119**, fax 501-7/22199).

If you're interested in a more serious, multi-day ocean trek, the following companies frequently organize sea-kayaking tours, often in combination with an inland mountain biking and camping segment.

SEA-KAYAKING OUTFITTERS IN BELIZE

Belize Eco Tours, 9424 Canton Loop, Anchorage, AK 99515 (☎ 800/3497830); **Bivouac Adventure Travel,** 336 South State Street, Ann Arbor, MI 48104-2412 (☎ **800/878-8747** or 313/761-8777, fax 313/761-7179); **Global Adventures,** 4693 55th Street, Delta, British Columbia, V4K 3P6, Canada (☎ 604/940-2220, fax 604/ 940-2233); **Monkey River Expeditions,** 1731 44th Avenue SW, Suite 100, Seattle, WA 98116 (☎ 206/660-7777); **Slickrock Adventures, Inc.,** P.O. Box 1400, Moab, UT 84532 (☎ /fax 801/259-6996).

SURFING

When *Endless Summer II,* the sequel to the all-time surf classic, was filmed, the production crew brought its boards and cameras to Costa Rica. Up and down Costa Rica's immense coastline, there are point and beach breaks that work almost all year-round. **Playas Hermosa and Tamarindo** are becoming mini-Meccas for surfers. Salsa Brava in **Puerto Viejo** has a habit of breaking boards, but the daredevils keep coming back for more. You'll almost never find a crowd, but the less sociable and more adventurous keep finding secret spots all around the Osa and Nicoya peninsulas, and along the northern Guanacaste coast. The most memorable rides are to be had at Playa Pavones, which is reputed to have one of the longest waves in the world.

WATCHING SEA TURTLES NEST

Few places in the world have as many sea turtle nesting sites as Costa Rica. Up and down both coasts, five species of these huge marine reptiles come ashore at specific times of the year to dig nests in the sand and lay their eggs. Sea turtles are endangered throughout the world due to overhunting, accidental deaths in fishing nets, development on beaches formerly used as nesting areas, and the collection and sale (often illegally) of their eggs. International trade in sea turtle products is already prohibited by most countries (including the United States), but sea turtle numbers continue to dwindle.

Among the species of sea turtles that nest on Costa Rica's beaches are olive Ridley (known for their mass egg-laying migrations known as *arribadas*), leatherback, hawksbill, green, and Pacific green turtles. Excursions to see nesting turtles have become common, and though these tours are fascinating, please make sure that you and your guide do not disturb the turtles. Any light source (other than red-tinted flashlights) can confuse female turtles and cause them to return to the sea without laying their eggs. In fact, as more and more development takes place along the Costa Rican coast, the lights created by hotels may cause the number of nesting turtles to drop. Luckily, many of the nesting beaches have been protected as national parks. The following are the main places to see nesting sea turtles: **Santa Rosa National Park** (near Liberia; see chapter 7), **Las Baulas National Marine Park** (near Tamarindo; see chapter 7), **Ostional National Wildlife Refuge** (near Playa Nosara; see chapter 7), and **Tortuguero National Park** (on the northern Caribbean coast; see chapter 11). See the regional chapters cross-referenced above for listings of local tour operators.

WINDSURFING

Windsurfing is still not very popular on the high seas here, where winds are fickle, and rental options are limited—even at beachside hotels. Nonetheless, Lake Arenal is considered one of the top spots in the world for high-wind board sailing. During the winter months many of the regulars from Washington's Columbia River Gorge take up residence around the town of Tilarán. Small boards, water starts, and fancy gibes are the norm. The best time for windsurfing Lake Arenal is between December and March. See chapter 8 for more information.

Windsurfing is still a nascent sport in Belize. It's bound to grow in popularity, at least among beginning- and intermediate-level board sailors, since conditions are ideal. During the winter months, steady trade winds blow and the barrier reef keeps the waters protected and relatively calm. Your best bet for windsurfing is to ask around on Caye Caulker and Ambergris Caye, or to go to Ramon's Village in San Pedro (see chapter 16).

WHITE-WATER RAFTING & KAYAKING

Whether you are a first-time rafter or a world-class kayaker, Costa Rica's got some white water suited to your abilities. Rivers rise and fall with the rainfall, but you can get wet and wild here even in the dry season. If you're just experimenting with river rafting, stick to class II and III rivers, like the **Reventazon, Sarapiquí,** and **Savegre.** If you already know which end of the paddle goes in the water, there are plenty of class IV and V sections to run. The best river ride is still the scenic Pacuare river, which, unfortunately, may be dammed soon.

This is another adventure that does not lend itself particularly well to travelers on a tight budget. If, however, you've decided to splurge on an active sport in Costa Rica, white-water rafting is one of my most highly recommended choices. You just can't beat the combination of tropical scenery, wildlife, and adventure it offers. Prices are fairly standardized across the industry, with a one-day trip costing between $60 and $80 per person. This rate includes 4 hours of paddling, all transportation, breakfast, and lunch.

WHITE-WATER RAFTING & KAYAKING OUTFITTERS IN COSTA RICA

Aventuras Naturales, P.O. Box 107360-1000, San José, Costa Rica (☎ 506/225-3939 or 800/308-3394 in the U.S., fax 506/253-6934); **Costa Rica White Water,** Dept. 235, P.O. Box 025216, Miami, FL 33102 (☎ 506/257-0766 or 506/222-0333, fax 506/257-1665); **Costa Sol Rafting,** P.O. Box 8-4390-1000, San José, Costa Rica (☎ 506/293-2151 or 800/245-8420 in the U.S., fax 506/293-2155 or 305/858-7478 in the U.S.); **Escondido Trex,** Apdo. 9, Puerto Jiménez, Osa peninsula, Costa Rica (☎/fax 506/735-5210); **Iguana Tours,** Apdo. 207, Quepos, Costa Rica (☎/fax 506/777-1262 or 506/777-0574); **Rancho Leona Kayak Tours,** Rancho Leona, La Virgen de Sarapiquí, Heredia, Costa Rica (☎ 506/761-1019); and **Rios Tropicales,** Apdo. 472-1200, Pavas, Costa Rica (☎ 506/233-6455, fax 506/255-4354).

3 Costa Rica's National Parks & Bioreserves

Costa Rica has 31 national parks protecting over 11% of the country. The parks range in size from the 530-acre Guayabo National Monument to the 474,240-acre La Amistad National Park. Many of these national parks are undeveloped tropical forests, with few services or facilities available for tourists. Others, however, offer well-maintained trail systems, information centers, and a wealth of natural wonders for visitors to explore and enjoy.

ADMISSION FEES

In 1995, the government of Costa Rica drastically raised admission fees to its national parks, with a two-tiered fee system for residents and foreign visitors. Guess who got to pay more? Following an initial backlash, the government backed down slightly and instituted a confusing system of varied park fees, combined with advanced-purchase discounts. Tourists, tour operators, and hotel owners all complained about the Rube Goldberg lunacy of the situation. Apparently, the government and park system were befuddled as well. In April of 1996, the government instituted its fourth national-park pricing scheme in two years, settling on a flat $6 per person per day fee for any foreigner visiting any national park. No advance purchases are necessary. Costa Ricans and foreign residents continue to pay just $1; children under 12 are admitted free. At parks where camping is allowed, there is an additional charge of $1.50 per person per day.

Costa Rica's National Parks & Bioreserves

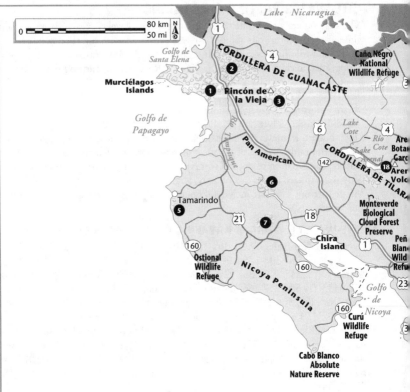

Lake Nicaragua

0 — 80 km / 50 mi — N

Golfo de Santa Elena

CORDILLERA DE GUANACASTE

Caño Negro National Wildlife Refuge

Murciélagos Islands

Rincón de la Vieja

Golfo de Papagayo

Río Tempisque

Pan American

Lake Cote

Río Cote

CORDILLERA DE TILARÁN

Arenal Botanical Garden

Arenal Volcano

Tamarindo

Monteverde Biological Cloud Forest Preserve

Chira Island

Peñas Blancas Wildlife Refuge

160

Ostional Wildlife Refuge

Nicoya Peninsula

Golfo de Nicoya

Curú Wildlife Refuge

Cabo Blanco Absolute Nature Reserve

Pacific Ocean

Coco Island

LEGEND
✈ Airport

Arenal National Park ⑱
Ballena Marine National Park ⑫
Barra Honda National Park ⑦
Braulio Carrillo National Park ⑨
Cahuita National Park ⑮
Carara Biological Reserve ㉑
Chirripó National Park ⑬
Coco Island National Park ⑳
Corcovado National Park ⑯
Guanacaste National Park ②
Guayabo National Monument ㉒

Irazú Volcano National Park ⑩
Juan Castro Blanco National Park ⑰
La Amistad National Park ⑭
Las Baulas Marine National Park ⑤
Manuel Antonio National Park ⑪
Palo Verde National Park ⑥
Poás Volcano National Park ⑧
Rincón de la Vieja National Park ③
Santa Rosa National Park ①
Tapantí National Wildlife Refuge ⑲
Tortuguero National Park ④

2360

NICARAGUA

Barra del Colorado
National Wildlife
Refuge

Caribbean

Sea

Río
Colorado

Río Sarapiquí

④

④

Puerto Viejo
de Sarapiquí

140

⑦

④ ⑨

CORDILLERA CENTRAL

Barva
Volcano

141

⑧

135

1

es/Virilla

✈ ★ SAN
JOSÉ

⑩

⑤

⑧

209

Río Pacuare

Río Reventazón

Río

② ② Turrialba
Volcano

⑫ 32

Cartago
Lankester
Botanical Garden

2

⑲

Limón

36

Hitoy-
Cerere
Biological
Reserve

⑮

Punta
Uva

Gandoca-
Manzanillo
Wildlife
Refuge

Cerro de
la Muerte

34

Río Telire

⑬ Cerro
Chirripó

CORDILLERA DE TALAMANCA

⑪

San
Isidro

Cerro
Dúrika

⑭

Cerro
Kámuk

PANAMA

⑫

Pan American Hwy.

*Coronado
Bay*

34

Río Sierpe

2

San
Vito

Caño Island
Biological
Reserve

Drake
Bay

*Golfo
Dulce*

Golfito

Wilson
Botanical
Garden

Osa Peninsula

⑯

Puerto
Jiménez

Pacific

Ocean

43

The section that follows is not a complete listing of all of Costa Rica's national parks and protected areas, but rather a selective list of just those parks that are of greatest interest and accessibility. They're popular, but they're also among the best. For more information on the national parks, call the national parks office at 506/257-0922 from the U.S., or by dialing 192 from inside Costa Rica. Or you can stop by the **National Parks Foundation** office (☎ **506/257-2239**) in San José, which is located between Calle 23 and Avenida 15. It's open from 8am to 5pm.

THE MOST POPULAR PARKS AND BIORESERVES—FROM A–Z

Below are brief descriptions of Costa Rica's best and most popular national parks and bioreserves. You'll find detailed information about food and lodging options near some of the individual parks in the regional chapters that follow. As you'll see, Costa Rica's national parks vary greatly in terms of attractions, facilities, and accessibility.

In many cases a visit to a national park is a secondary consideration or side-benefit of itineraries based on other criteria. For example, most travelers head to Guanacaste for pure beach time, yet a side trip to **Barra Honda** or **Palo Verde** national parks can break up the monotony of sand and surf.

If you're looking for a camping adventure or an extended stay in one of the national parks, I would recommend **Santa Rosa, Rincón de la Vieja, Chirripó,** or **Corcovado.** Most of the other parks are better suited for day trips or in combination with your travels around the country.

In the case of **Irazú** and **Poás** national parks, you might consider an organized tour (see above under "Costa Rican Tour Agencies" and chapter 5), especially if you don't plan on renting a car. Because it is so remote, package tours are frequently the best way to visit **Tortuguero.** Some of the better parks for do-it-yourself exploration include **Manuel Antonio, Cahuita,** and **Guayabo,** where you'll find well-marked and maintained trails that yield up the parks' natural beauty to the most casual naturalist and hiker.

Since the entrance fees are still relatively steep for budget travelers, it makes sense to plan ahead and try to pick a park (or parks) that fits your needs and interests.

ARENAL NATIONAL PARK

A new park, created to protect the ecosystem that surrounds Arenal Volcano, Arenal has few services or attractions. Basically, the government has set up a toll booth on the access road one must drive to get close to the volcano's lava flows. Most people choose to forego a visit to the park itself in favor of watching the volcano from spots along the dirt road leading to the Arenal Observatory Lodge. From there, you are only approximately one kilometer away, and still plenty close to the volcano. Location: 80 miles northwest of San José. See chapter 8.

BARRA HONDA NATIONAL PARK

Costa Rica's only underground national park, Barra Honda features a series of limestone caves that were once part of a coral reef, some 60 million years ago. Today the caves are home to millions of bats and impressive stalactite and stalagmite formations. There is a camping area, restrooms, and an information center here. Location: 208 miles northwest of San José. See chapter 7.

BRAULIO CARRILLO NATIONAL PARK

This park occupies a large area of the nation's central mountain range. If you're planning to drive from San José to the Caribbean coast, you'll have to pass through it on your way. A deep rain forest, Braulio Carrillo receives an average of 177 inches of rain per year. There are beautiful rivers and majestic waterfalls, and over 6,500 species of plants and animals. The park has an information center, picnic tables, restrooms, and hiking trails. Camping is allowed. Be careful here—make sure you park your car and base your explorations from the park's main entrance and not from just anywhere along the highway. Several robberies and attacks against tourists have been reported at trailheads just off the highway and away from the main entrance. This park also seems to have the highest incidence of lost hikers. Location: 14 miles north of San José. See chapter 8.

CAHUITA NATIONAL PARK

A combination land and marine park, Cahuita National Park protects one of the few remaining living coral reefs in the country. The topography here is lush lowland tropical rain forest. Monkeys and numerous bird species are common. Camping is permitted and there are basic facilities at the Puerto Vargas entrance to the park. Otherwise, you can enter either at the Puerto Vargas entrance or from Cahuita. Location: On the Caribbean coast, 26 miles south of Limón. See chapter 11.

CAÑO NEGRO NATIONAL WILDLIFE REFUGE

A lowland swamp and drainage basin for several northern rivers, Caño Negro is excellent for bird watching. This wildlife refuge makes a good day trip from the La Fortuna/Arenal area. Location: 12.5 miles south of Los Chiles, near the Nicaraguan border. See chapter 8.

CHIRRIPÓ NATIONAL PARK

Home to Costa Rica's tallest peak, 12,536-foot Mount Chirripó, Chirripó National Park is quite a hike, but it has unparalleled views of the Pacific Ocean and the Caribbean Sea from its summit. There is camping and a number of interesting climbing trails. Location: 94 miles southeast of San José. See chapter 9.

COCO ISLAND NATIONAL PARK

A large uninhabited island located 360 miles off Costa Rica's Pacific coast, Coco Island National Park is beautiful, with many endemic species of flora and fauna. The diving here is world-renowned. Unfortunately, this is an exceedingly expensive place to visit. Because there are no overnight facilities on the island, you must visit by boat on a tour. And the average live-aboard boat tour (10 days in duration) runs around $2,700 per person.

CORCOVADO NATIONAL PARK

The largest single block of virgin lowland rain forest in Central America, Corcovado National Park receives over 200 inches of rain per year. One of Costa Rica's increasingly more popular national parks, it is still largely a remote area (it has no roads, and only dirt tracks lead into it). Scarlet macaws live here, as do countless other neotropical species, including two of the country's largest cats, the endangered puma and jaguar. There are camping facilities and trails throughout the park. Location: 208 miles south of San José, on the Osa peninsula. See chapter 10.

GUAYABO NATIONAL MONUMENT

The country's only significant pre-Colombian archeological site, it is believed that Guayabo once supported a population of approximately 10,000 people, some 1,000 years before Christ. Location: 12 miles northeast of Turrialba. See chapter 6.

IRAZÚ VOLCANO NATIONAL PARK

Irazú Volcano is one of Costa Rica's four active volcanoes, and a popular day trip from San José. At 11,260 feet, it is the country's highest volcano. A paved road leads

Monkey Business

No trip to Costa Rica would be complete without at least one monkey sighting. Home to four distinct species of primates, which inhabit the forests along both coasts, as well as those in between, Costa Rica offers the opportunity for one of the world's most gratifying wildlife-watching experiences. You'll need a good guide to see your first few families, but in no time you'll be spotting them on your own. The deep guttural call of a howler, or the rustling of leaves overhead on a jungle trail, are your cues.

Costa Rica's most commonly spotted monkey is the white-faced or **capuchin monkey** (*mono cara blanca* in Spanish). You may recognize this monkey as the infamous culprit from the film *Outbreak*. Contrary to the film's plot, however, these monkeys are endemic to the New World Tropics, and do not exist in Africa. Capuchins are agile, medium-sized monkeys that make good use of their long prehensile tails. They inhabit a diverse collection of habitats, ranging from the high-altitude cloud forests of the central region to the lowland mangroves of the Osa peninsula. It's almost impossible not to spot capuchins at Manuel Antonio (see chapter 9), where the resident white-faced monkeys have become a little too dependent on fruit and junk-food feedings by tourists. Please do not feed wild monkeys, and boycott establishments that try to attract both monkeys and tourists with daily feedings.

Howler monkeys (*mono congo* in Spanish) are named for their distinct and eerie call. Large, and mostly black, these monkeys can seem ferocious because of their physical appearance and deep, resonant howls that can carry for over a mile—even in dense rain forest. (To make these guttural noises, the throat sacs of male howlers vibrate. When a male howler howls, biologists believe he is marking the boundaries of his territory.) Among humans, however, howlers are in fact a little timid, and tend to stay higher up in the canopy than their white-faced cousins. Howlers are fairly common and easy to spot in the dry tropical forests of coastal Guanacaste and the Nicoya Peninsula (see chapter 7).

Even more elusive are **spider monkeys** (*mono araña* in Spanish). These long, slender monkeys are dark brown to black and prefer the high canopies of primary rain forests. Spiders are very adept with their prehensile tails, but actually travel through the canopy with a hand-over-hand motion frequently imitated by their less graceful human cousins on playground "monkey bars" around the world. I've had my best luck spotting spiders along the edges of Tortuguero's jungle canals (see chapter 11), where howlers are also quite common.

The rarest and most endangered of Costa Rica's monkeys is the tiny **squirrel monkey** (*mono titi* in Spanish). These small brown monkeys have dark eyes surrounded by large white rings, white ears, white chests, and very long tails. In Costa Rica, squirrel monkeys can only be found in Manuel Antonio (see chapter 9), and the Osa peninsula (see chapter 10). These seemingly hyperactive monkeys are predominantly fruit eaters and often feed on banana and other fruit trees near hotels in both of the above-mentioned regions. Despite being endangered, squirrels usually travel in large bands, so if you do see them, you'll likely see quite a few.

right up to the crater, and the lookout also allegedly allows you a view of both oceans on a clear day. The volcano last erupted in 1963—the same day President John F. Kennedy visited the country. There is an information center, picnic tables, restrooms, and a parking area here. Location: 34 miles east of San José. See chapter 6.

MANUEL ANTONIO NATIONAL PARK

The grand dame of Costa Rican national parks, Manuel Antonio supports the largest number of hotels and resorts of any national park at its edge. This lowland rain forest is home to a healthy monkey population, including the endangered squirrel monkey. The park is best known for its splendid beaches. However, at $6 per person per day, you may want to think about finding another place to sunbathe and beachcomb, especially if you're traveling in a large group. Location: 80 miles south of San José. See chapter 9.

PALO VERDE NATIONAL PARK

A must for nature lovers and birdwatchers, Palo Verde National Park is one of Costa Rica's best-kept secrets. Part of the Tempisque river lowlands, this park supports a population of more than 50,000 waterfowl and forest birds. The various ecosystems include mangroves, savannah brush lands, and evergreen forests. There are camping facilities, an information center, and a scientific research station. Location: 125 miles northwest of San José.

POÁS VOLCANO NATIONAL PARK

Poás is the other active volcano close to San José. The main crater is more than one mile wide and is constantly active with fumaroles and hot geysers. The area around the volcano is lush, but much of the growth is stunted due to the gasses and acid rain. The park sometimes closes when the gasses get too feisty. There are nature trails, picnic tables, restrooms, and an information center. Location: 23 miles northwest of San José. See chapter 6.

RINCÓN DE LA VIEJA NATIONAL PARK

Rincón de la Vieja National Park is a large tract of parkland of high volcanic activity. There are numerous fumaroles and geysers, as well as hot springs, cold pools, and mud pots. You should hire a guide for any hot spring or mud bath expeditions, because inexperienced visitors have been burned. Literally. Camping is permitted; other facilities include an information center, picnic area, and restrooms. Location: 165 miles northwest of San José. See chapter 7.

SANTA ROSA NATIONAL PARK

Occupying a large part of Costa Rica's northwestern Guanacaste province, Santa Rosa National Park contains the country's biggest tropical dry forest, as well as important turtle nesting sites and the historically significant La Casona monument, where Costa Rican forces routed the American mercenary soldier William Walker. There are caves for exploring. The beaches are pristine and some have basic camping facilities. An information center, picnic area, and restrooms are located at the main campsite and entrance. Location: 160 miles northwest of San José. See chapter 7.

TORTUGUERO NATIONAL PARK

Tortuguero National Park (and its eponymous village) has been called the Venice of Costa Rica because of the maze of jungle canals that meander through this dense lowland rain forest. Small boats, launches, and canoes carry visitors through these waterways, where caiman, manatee, and numerous bird and mammal species are common. The extremely endangered great green macaw lives here. On the beaches, green sea turtles nest every year between June and October. At the park entrance, you'll find a helpful information stand and some well-marked trails. Location: 160 miles from San José. See chapter 11.

4 Tips on Health, Safety & Etiquette in the Wilderness

Much of what is discussed below is common sense. For more detailed information, see "Health & Insurance," in chapters 5 and 13.

HEALTH & SAFETY

While most tours and activities in either country are extremely safe, there are risks involved in any adventurous activity. Know and respect your physical limits before undertaking any strenuous activity. Be prepared for extremes in weather. A sunny morning hike can quickly become a cold and wet ordeal, so when hiking in the rain forest, it's usually a good idea to carry along some form of rain gear, or have a dry change of clothing waiting at the end of the trail. While the Belizean lowlands are usually uniformly hot, be prepared for a dip in temperature when hiking in the Maya mountains or Cayo district. Make sure to bring along plenty of sunscreen when you're not going to be covered by the forest canopy.

If you do any backcountry packing or camping, remember, it really is a jungle out there. Don't go poking under rocks or fallen branches. Snake bites are very rare, but don't do anything to increase the odds of getting bitten. If you do encounter a snake, stay calm, don't make any sudden movements, and *do not* try to handle it. Also, avoid swimming in a major river unless a guide or local operator can vouch for its safety. Though mountainous and white-water sections are generally pretty safe, most mangrove canals and river mouths in Costa Rica support healthy crocodile and caiman populations.

Bugs and bug bites will probably be your greatest health concern in the wilderness. Mostly, bugs are an inconvenience, although mosquitoes can carry malaria or dengue (see chapters 5 and 13 for more information). A strong insect repellent and proper clothing will minimize both the danger and inconvenience of a bite. On the cayes and beaches, you run the risk of getting bitten by sand fleas. These nearly invisible insects leave an irritating welt. Try not to scratch, as this can lead to open sores and infections. Sand fleas are most active at sunrise and sunset, so you might want to cover up or avoid the beaches at these times.

ETIQUETTE

Here's where common sense and some consideration come in handy. Whenever you enter and enjoy nature you should tread lightly and try not to disturb the natural environment. If you must take home a souvenir, take photos. Do not cut or uproot plants or flowers. Pack out everything you pack in, and *please* do not litter. On the reef it is imperative that you do not break, touch, or stand on the coral. Coral reefs are incredibly delicate and slow-growing ecosystems, and even small damage can take decades to heal.

5 Ecologically Oriented Volunteer & Study Programs

Below are some institutions and organizations that are working on ecology and sustainable development projects in Costa Rica and Belize. Contact them if you are interested in studying or volunteering with them. *Note:* Many of these projects are ongoing and ask that volunteers devote more than a week of their time. These are great opportunities for those who have chosen to retire, regardless of their age.

IN COSTA RICA

Global Volunteers. 375 Little Canada Rd., St. Paul, MN 55117. ☎ **800/487-1074** or 612/482-0295.

This unique organization, based in the U.S., offers the opportunity of a lifetime to travelers who've always wanted to have a Peace Corps–like experience but felt they couldn't make a two-year commitment. For two to three weeks, you can join one of their working vacations in Costa Rica. A certain set of skills, such as engineering or agricultural knowledge, is helpful, but by no means necessary. Each trip is undertaken at a particular community's request to complete a project that has been requested by them.

Institute for Central American Development Studies (ICADS). Apdo. 3-2070 Sabanilla, San José. ☎ **506/225-0508.** Fax 506/234-1337.

This organization offers internship and research opportunities in Costa Rica in the areas of environment, agriculture, human rights, and women's studies. They also offer an intensive Spanish-language program. Their address in the United States is Dept. 826, P.O. Box 025216, Miami, FL 33102-5216.

Organization for Tropical Studies (OTS). Apdo. 676, San José. ☎ **506/240-6696.**

The OTS represents several Costa Rican and U.S. universities. Its mission is to promote research, education, and the wise use of natural resources in the Tropics. Research facilities include La Selva Biological Station near Braulio Carrillo National Park and the Wilson Botanical Gardens near San Vito. They periodically offer courses that are open to the general public. Call for details.

Costa Rica's National Park Service Volunteer Program (ASVO). Apdo. 10104-1000, San José, Costa Rica. ☎ **506/222-6963.** Fax 506/223-6963.

It is possible to volunteer with the Costa Rican national park service. A minimum commitment of 45 days is required. You'll assist in trail and park maintenance and will be lodged nearby. Three meals a day are available for an extra supplement of $7 per day. Volunteers with specific skills—biologists, naturalists, etc.—will be given tasks to complement their experiences. You may not have a lot of choice in park selection, but generally a 45-day stay is broken up into two-week stints at different parks.

IN BELIZE

Earthwatch. 680 Mt. Auburn St., Box 403Z, Watertown, MA 02272. ☎ **800/776-0188.** Fax 617/926-8532.

This international organization works at placing volunteers with advanced researchers in the biological and social sciences. Earthwatch runs almost a dozen trips to Belize every year in the areas of marine biology and archeological research. Volunteers pay for their share of room and board (usually around $1,500 for a two-week stint, not including airfare), and in return, work very closely with the researcher to whom they've been assigned. Groups are usually no more than 5 to 10 people, and volunteers are generally entrusted with data collection and tabulation chores.

Institute for Central American Development Studies (ICADS). Apdo. 3-2070 Sabanilla, San José. ☎ **506/225-0508.** Fax 506/234-1337.

This Costa Rica–based organization sometimes offers internship and research opportunities in Belize dealing with environmental and agricultural issues, human rights, and women's studies. Their U.S. address is Dept. 826, P.O. Box 025216, Miami, FL 33102-5216.

Programme for Belize. #2 South Park Street, P.O. Box 749, Belize City, Belize. ☎ **501-2/75616.** Fax 501-2/75635.

This Belizean non-profit organization runs a variety of environmental and ecologically sound programs. At their Rio Bravo Research Station, in the northwestern wilds of Belize, visitors can get a feel for life on a working research station. Rates are $80 per person per day for a private cabin; and $65 per person per day for a bunk in the dormitory. Either way, all your meals and two daily activities are included. These activities range from guided nature hikes and field lectures on tropical biology, to archeological expeditions to the nearby La Milpa Mayan site.

Getting to Know Costa Rica

In Spanish, Costa Rica means "rich coast," which, in retrospect, was a peculiarly hopeful choice for the arriving Spaniards to have selected nearly 500 years ago, since they found very little of what they were looking for: gold, silver, or Indians to convert and enslave. What they found instead was a land of rugged volcanic peaks blanketed with dense forests. Costa Rica was ignored by travelers for centuries, and it wasn't until an intrepid few ventured forth rather recently that Costa Rica began to live up to its name. They discovered some of the most beautiful beaches in Central America along its Pacific and Caribbean coasts, and fascinating varieties of plants, birds, and other wildlife in its dense rain and cloud forests and along its rugged mountain ranges.

After hundreds of thousands of acres of undisturbed forests were set aside as national parks and bioreserves as part of an arrangement to lower the country's national debt, travel to these areas only increased—no doubt because of the curiosity travelers and concerned biologists have about these fast-disappearing areas.

Bordered by the troubled nations of Nicaragua and Panama, Costa Rica is a relative sea of tranquillity in a region of turmoil—a key to its popularity. For more than 100 years, the country has enjoyed a stable democracy; in fact, there isn't even a standing army, a fact of which Costa Ricans are very proud. In addition, former president Oscar Arias Sánchez was awarded the Nobel Peace Prize for his work in implementing a Central American peace plan.

In recent years, Costa Rica has become acutely aware of the riches it has to offer tourists and, as a result, the country is undergoing phenomenal tourist-related growth, which is putting great strains on Costa Rica's natural resources. Though the nation has one of the world's best records in conservation, its forests are still being deforested at an alarming rate and stretches of its coastline are being developed into massive mega-resorts with little regard for the impact such developments will have on the local environment or adjacent towns and villages. However, Costa Rica should remain for many years one of the more fascinating natural destinations in the Americas, largely due to the efforts being made by American and Costa Rican–based ecological organizations to keep it that way for as long as possible.

Costa Rica

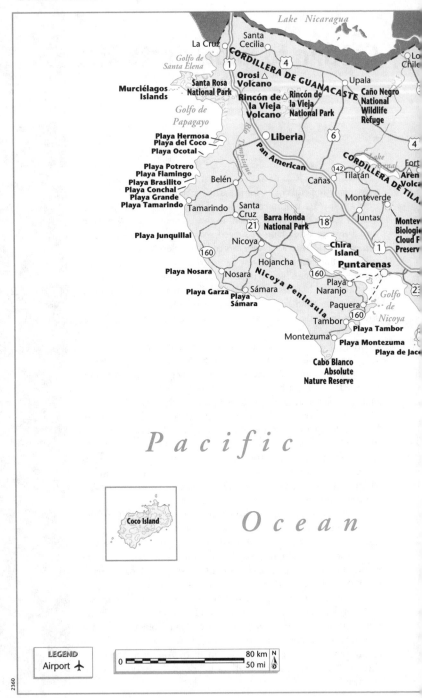

Lake Nicaragua

La Cruz
Santa Cecilia

Golfo de
Santa Elena

CORDILLERA DE GUANACASTE

4

Orosi △
Volcano
Upala

Murciélagos
Islands

Santa Rosa
National Park

Rincón de △
la Vieja
Volcano
Rincón de
la Vieja
National Park

Caño Negro
National
Wildlife
Refuge

Golfo de
Papagayo

Liberia

6

4

Playa Hermosa
Playa del Coco
Playa Ocotal

Pan American

CORDILLERA DE TILA

Fort

Playa Potrero
Playa Flamingo
Playa Brasilito
Playa Conchal
Playa Grande
Playa Tamarindo

Belén

Cañas

142

Tilarán

Aren
Volca

Monteverde

Tamarindo

Santa
Cruz

Barra Honda
National Park

18

Juntas

Montev
Biologi
Cloud F
Preserv

21

Playa Junquillal

Nicoya

160

Hojancha

Chira
Island

1

Puntarenas

Playa Nosara

Nosara

Nicoya Peninsula

160

Playa
Naranjo

Golfo

2

Playa Garza

Playa
Sámara

Sámara

Paquera

de
Nicoya

Tambor

160

Playa Tambor

Montezuma

Playa Montezuma

Playa de Jace

Cabo Blanco
Absolute
Nature Reserve

P a c i f i c

Coco Island

O c e a n

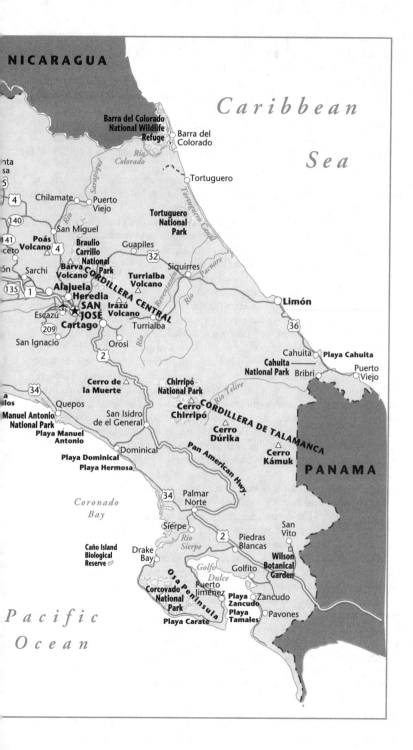

NICARAGUA

Caribbean

Sea

Barra del Colorado
National Wildlife
Refuge
○ Barra del
Colorado

Río
Colorado

○ Tortuguero

nta
sa
5)

4️⃣ Chilamate ○—○ Puerto
Viejo

140

Río
Sarapiquí

Tortuguero
National
Park

141
cero

Poás
Volcano 4️⃣

San Miguel ○

Braulio
Carrillo
National
Park

Guapiles ○

ón Sarchi ○

Barva
Volcano

32

Siquirres ○

CORDILLERA CENTRAL

135 1️⃣ ○ Alajuela

Turrialba
Volcano △

○ Heredia

★ SAN Irazú
JOSÉ Volcano

Limón ●

Tortuguera Canal

Río Pacuare

Escazú ○

Cartago ○

Turrialba ○

Río Reventazón

36

209

Río

San Ignacio ○

2️⃣

Orosi ○

Cahuita ○——○ Playa Cahuita

Cahuita
National Park

Puerto
○ Viejo

Bribri

a
los

34

Cerro de △
la Muerte

Quepos ○

Chirripó
National Park

Río Telire

Manuel Antonio
National Park

San Isidro
de el General ○

Cerro
Chirripó △

CORDILLERA DE TALAMANCA

Playa Manuel
Antonio

Cerro
Dúrika △

Dominical ○

Playa Dominical

Pan American Hwy.

Cerro
Kámuk △

Playa Hermosa

PANAMA

Coronado
Bay

34

Palmar
○ Norte

Síerpe ○

2️⃣

San
Vito ○

Caño Island
Biological
Reserve ▱

Drake
Bay ○

Río
Sierpe

Piedras
Blancas ○

Wilson
Botanical
Garden 🏛

Golfo
Dulce

○ Golfito

Osa Península

Corcovado
National
Park

Puerto
○ Jiménez

Playa ○ Zancudo
Zancudo
Playa
Tamales ○ Pavones

Playa Carate

Pacific

Ocean

1 The Natural Environment

Costa Rica occupies a central spot in the land bridge that joins North and South America. For millennia this land bridge served as a migratory thoroughfare and mating ground for species native to the once separate continents. It was also the meeting place of Mesoamerican and Andean pre-Colombian indigenous cultures.

The country comprises only 0.01% of the earth's land mass, yet is home to 5% of the planet's biodiversity. There are over 10,000 identified species of plants, 850 species of birds, 800 species of butterflies, and 500 species of mammals, reptiles, and amphibians, combined.

The key to this biological richness lies in the many distinct life-zones and ecosystems that can be found in Costa Rica. It may all seem like one big mass of green to the untrained eye, but the differences are profound.

In any one spot in Costa Rica, temperatures remain relatively constant year-round. However, they vary dramatically according to altitude, from uncomfortably hot and steamy along the coasts to below freezing at the highest elevations.

Costa Rica's lowland rain forests are true tropical jungles. Rainfall in them can be well over 200 inches per year and their climate is hot and humid. Trees grow tall and fast, fighting for sunlight in the upper reaches. In fact, life and foliage on the forest floor are surprisingly sparse. The action is typically 100 feet above in the canopy, where long vines stream down, lianas climb up, and bromeliads grow on the branches and trunks of towering hardwood trees. You can find these lowland rain forests along the southern Pacific coast and the Osa peninsula, as well as along the Caribbean coast.

At higher altitudes you'll find Costa Rica's famed cloud forests. Here the steady flow of moist air meets the mountains and creates a nearly constant mist. Epiphytes, or "air plants," which live cooperatively on the branches and trunks of other trees, are both abundant and resourceful in cloud forests, where they must literally extract moisture and nutrients from the air to survive. Since cloud forests are found in generally steep, mountainous terrain, the canopy here is lower and less uniform than in lowland rain forests, providing better chances for viewing elusive fauna. Costa Rica's most spectacular cloud forest is in Guanacaste province: Monteverde Biological Cloud Forest Preserve.

At the highest reaches, the cloud forests give way to elfin forests and *páramo*. More commonly associated with the South American Andes, a páramo is characterized by a variety of tundra-like shrubs and grasses, with a scattering of twisted, windblown trees. Reptiles, rodents, and raptors are the most common residents here. The best place for exploring this unique tundra is Mount Chirripó.

In a few protected areas of Guanacaste, you will still find examples of the otherwise vanishing tropical dry forest. During the long and pronounced dry season (it lasts half the year from November to March), almost no rain relieves the unabating heat. Then, during the rainy season, this deciduous forest is transformed into a lush and verdant landscape. In an effort to conserve much-needed water, the trees drop their leaves but bloom in a riot of color: purple jacaranda, scarlet poró, and brilliantly orange flame-of-the-forest are just a few examples. Because the foliage is not so dense, the dry forests are also excellent places to view a wide variety of wildlife.

Along the coasts, primarily where river mouths meet the ocean, you will find extensive mangrove forests and swamps. Around these seemingly monotonous tangles of roots exists one of the most diverse and rich ecosystems in the country. All sorts of fish and crustaceans live in the brackish tidal waters. Caiman and crocodiles cruise the maze of rivers and unmarked canals, and hundreds of herons and marsh birds nest and feed along the silty banks. Mangrove swamps are often havens

---

Air Plants

Long before Michael Jordan ever won a slam-dunk contest, epiphytes were dazzling biologists and rain-forest trekkers with their acrobatic flights of fancy, far above the forest floor. For this reason, epiphytes, which set no roots in solid ground, have been dubbed *air plants*. Unlike parasites, epiphytes co-exist with—but do not kill—their hosts. Epiphytes are found in everything from temperate northern rain forests, like those found on the Olympic peninsula in Washington state, to tropical rain forests, such as Monteverde, Corcovado, and Braulio Carrillo National Park in Costa Rica. They reach their tallest heights in lowland tropical rain forests and middle-elevation cloud forests, where up to one quarter of all plant species in any given area may be epiphytes. Just look up, you can't miss them.

The diversity of epiphytic plants is immense. There are mosses, ferns and lichen, cacti and orchids, and grand bromeliads, with sharp, radiant leaves. Since their roots cannot burrow into the earth in search of water and nutrients, epiphytes have developed a series of complex processes to meet their needs. Some, by trapping particles of organic matter in the rich canopy environment, create their own miniature patches of soil or mats on tree branches. Others, like bromeliads, have leaf structures that fan out to collect and store water in natural cisterns. Many of these cisterns are used by other forest species as homes, drinking sources, and nesting sites.

---

for waterbirds—cormorants, frigate birds, pelicans, and herons. The larger birds tend to nest up high in the canopy while the smaller ones nestle in the underbrush. The Gulf of Nicoya is a particularly popular nesting spot for frigate birds.

Over the last few years, Costa Rica has taken great strides toward protecting its rich biodiversity. Whereas 30 years ago it was difficult to find a protected area anywhere, now over 11% of the country is protected within the national park system. Another 10% to 15% of the land enjoys some form of protection in private and public reserves and wildlife refuges. Still, Costa Rica's precious tropical hardwoods continue to be harvested at an alarming rate, often illegally, while other primary forests are clear-cut for short-term agricultural gain. Many experts predict that Costa Rica's unprotected forests will be gone by the early part of the 21st century.

This is also a land of high volcanic and seismic activity. There are three major volcanic mountain ranges in Costa Rica, many of which are still active, allowing visitors to experience the awe-inspiring sight of steaming fumaroles and intense lava flows during their stay. Two volcanoes near the capital—Poás and Irazú—are currently active, although relatively quiet. The best places to see volcanic activity are farther north in Rincón de la Vieja National Park and at Arenal Volcano.

Costa Rica's last major earthquake shook the city of Límon on April 22, 1991. Tremors and aftershocks were felt as far away as San José. It's unlikely you will experience a major quake during your visit, but small tremors are relatively common. The first rule of thumb in an earthquake is not to panic. The best place to stand is underneath a doorway—if you can get there in time. Most tremors will have already come and gone by the time you can get yourself into position.

ENYOYING COSTA RICA'S BIODIVERSITY

It's hard not to enjoy Costa Rica's varied natural landscape, but keeping a few pointers in mind can make your visit even more pleasurable.

Remember, animals in the forests are predominantly nocturnal. When they are active in the daytime, they are usually elusive and on the watch for predators. Although the idea of visiting a rain forest may seem like the ultimate tropical fantasy, in reality rain forests are so dense and dark that it's extremely hard for the casual visitor to pick anything out. Birds are much easier to spot in clearings or secondary forests than they are in primary forests. Unless you have lots of experience in the Tropics, a trained and knowledgeable guide is your best bet for enjoying a walk through the jungle, and a good pair of rubber boots (usually provided on a guided tour) is essential.

2 The Regions in Brief

Costa Rica rightfully should be called "Costas Ricas" since it has two coasts, one on the Pacific and one on the Caribbean. These two coasts are as different as the Atlantic and Pacific coasts of North America. The Pacific coast, which can be divided into three distinct regions (Guanacaste and the Nicoya Peninsula, the Central Coast, and the Southern Coast) is characterized by a rugged, though mostly accessible, coastline where mountains often meet the sea to create spectacular stretches of coastline. It varies from the dry sunny climate of the northwest to the hot humid rain forests of the south. The Caribbean coast can be divided into two roughly equal stretches, half of which is accessible only by boat or small plane. This remote coastline is a vast flat plain laced with rivers and covered with rain forests. Farther south, along the stretch of coast accessible by car, there are uncrowded beaches and even a bit of coral reef.

Bordered by Nicaragua in the north and Panama in the southeast, Costa Rica (19,530 square miles) is only slightly larger than Vermont and New Hampshire combined. Much of the country is mountainous, with three major ranges running northwest to southeast. Among these mountains are several active volcanos. Between the mountain ranges are fertile valleys, the largest and most populated of which is the Central Valley. With the exception of the dry Guanacaste region, much of Costa Rica's coastal area is hot and humid and covered with dense rain forests.

The Central Valley The Central Valley is characterized by rolling green hills between 3,000 and 4,000 feet above sea level, where the climate is mild and springlike year-round. It is Costa Rica's primary agricultural region, with coffee farms making up the majority of landholdings. The rich volcanic soil of this region makes it ideal for growing almost anything. The country's earliest settlements were in this area, and today the Central Valley is a densely populated area with relatively good roads and lots of small towns. Surrounding the Central Valley are high mountains, among which are four volcanic peaks. Two of these, Poás and Irazú, are still active and have caused extensive damage during cycles of activity in the past two centuries. Much of the mountainous regions to the north and to the south of the capital of San José have been declared national parks to protect their virgin rain forests from logging. Here you can enjoy the unusual experience of exploring a high-altitude cloud forest, usually shrouded in mist.

Guanacaste and the Nicoya Peninsula With about 65 inches of rain a year, this region is by far the driest in the country and, as such, has been likened to west Texas. Guanacaste province sits at the border of Nicaragua and the Pacific and is named after the shady trees that still shelter the herds of cattle that roam the dusty savannah here. In addition to cattle ranches, Guanacaste boasts semi-active volcanos, several lakes, and one of the last remnants of tropical dry forest left in Central America (dry forest once stretched all the way from Costa Rica to the Mexican state of Chiapas).

The Nicoya peninsula is the site of many of Costa Rica's sunniest and most popular beaches. Because in large part many Americans have chosen to build beach houses and retirement homes here, Nicoya is experiencing quite a bit of new development. While Cancun-style high-rise hotels are far from the norm, condos, luxury resorts, and golf courses are springing up with alacrity.

The Northern Zone   This region lies to the north of San José and includes rain forests, cloud forests, the country's two most active volcanos (Arenal and Rincón de la Vieja), Braulio Carillo National Park, and numerous remote lodges. Because this is one of the few regions of Costa Rica without any beaches, it primarily attracts people interested in nature and active sports. Arenal Lake boasts some of the best windsurfing in the world, and several good mountain-biking trails thread along its shores.

The Central Pacific Coast   The central Pacific coast is the most easily accessible coastline in Costa Rica, and consequently boasts the greatest number of beach resorts and hotels. Playa de Jacó is primarily a charter-company destination attracting Canadian and German tourists, while Manuel Antonio caters to people seeking a bit more tranquillity and beauty. This region is also the site of the highest peak in Costa Rica—Mount Chirripó—where frost is common, even in summer.

The Caribbean Coast   Most of the Caribbean coast is a wide, steamy lowland laced with rivers and blanketed with rain forests and banana plantations. The culture here is predominantly black, with many residents speaking English or Caribbean patois. The northern section of this coast is accessible only by boat or small plane and is the site of Tortuguero National Park, which is known for its nesting sea turtles and riverboat trips. The southern half of the Caribbean coast has several beautiful beaches, and as of yet few large hotels.

The South Pacific Coast   This is one of Costa Rica's most remote and undeveloped regions. Much of the area is protected in Corcovado and La Amistad national parks. A hot, humid region, it is characterized by dense rain forests and rugged coastlines.

3 Costa Rica Today

Modern Costa Rica is a nation of contrasts. On one hand, it is the most technologically advanced and economically stable nation in Central America. Even the smallest towns have electricity, the water is safe to drink, and the phone system is excellent; there isn't a huge gulf between rich and poor, and politically, the nation possesses the most stable democracy in Central America. Since Costa Rica received independence from Spain in 1821, only a handful of its presidents have come from the military (which was disbanded completely in 1948), and it has had even fewer leaders who could be called dictators. (The country's most recent elections in 1990 were so peaceful that crowd control at some polling places was handled by schoolchildren.)

Costa Rica has a population of just under three million, over half of whom live in the Central Valley and are classified as urban. The people are ethnically the most homogeneous of Central America: nearly 96% of the population is of European or Spanish descent, and it is not at all surprising to see blond Costa Ricans. This is largely because the indigenous population in place when the first Spaniards arrived was small and therefore soon reduced by wars and disease until they became a minority. Some indigenous peoples do remain, however, living primarily on reservations around the country. In addition, on the Caribbean coast there is a substantial population of English-speaking black Créoles who came over from the Antilles to work on banana plantations and construct the railroad.

In general, Costa Ricans (who call themselves *Ticos,* a practice that stems from their tendency to add a diminutive, either "tico" or "ito," to the ends of words to connote familiarity or affection) are a friendly and outgoing people. In conversation and interaction with tourists, they are open and helpful. They believe their country to be a classless society where anyone through hard work and intelligence can improve his or her lot in life, and while the average family is wealthy by Latin American standards, the median household income is only $3000 U.S. per year. With high levels of literacy (93%) and education, it is not uncommon to find Costa Ricans who speak English. In a region plagued by internal strife and civil wars, Costa Ricans are proud of their peaceful history, political stability, and relatively high level of development.

On the other hand, Costa Rica currently finds itself mired in economic crisis. The country's per-capita debt ranks among the world's worst. Four years ago, inflation reached a high point of 25%. In an attempt to come to terms with decades of trade deficits and pay back its debt, a more austere economic course was taken, causing the country's vast network of social services, as well as its health care system and its educational institutions, to be overburdened and underfunded. Goaded by the World Bank and the International Monetary Fund, recent administrations have begun the process of privatizing state institutions in order to raise funds and reduce bureaucracy. In the short term, this has led to increased unemployment, lower wages, and more expensive goods and services.

Tourism has surpassed cattle ranching and coffee and banana exports to the point of becoming the nation's top source of income. Ticos whose fathers and grandfathers were farmers find themselves hotel owners, tour guides, and waiters. While most have adapted gracefully and regard the industry favorably as a source for jobs and opportunities for economic advancement, restaurant and hotel staff can seem gruff or disinterested at times, especially in rural areas. And, unfortunately, with greater numbers of tourists have also come increases in crime, prostitution, and drug trafficking. Common sense and street savvy are required in San José and Limón, and it never hurts to be cautious and alert wherever you travel in the country, but only if you're reckless are you likely to have trouble.

There's one final quirk of the Costa Rican character of which you ought to be aware. Time has relative meaning for Ticos. While most tour companies and other establishments operate efficiently, don't expect punctuality. This is a land where most things are better left until *mañana* (tomorrow), and where *ahora* (now) can mean sometime in the next hour or two, or never.

4   History 101

Dateline

- **13,000 B.C.** Earliest record of human inhabitants in Costa Rica.
- **1,000 B.C.** Olmec people from Mexico arrive in Costa Rica searching for rare blue jade.

continues

EARLY HISTORY

Little is known of Costa Rica's history prior to its colonization by Spanish settlers. The pre-Columbian Indians who made their home in this region of Central America never developed the large cities or advanced culture that flowered farther north in what would become Guatemala, Belize, and Mexico. However, from scattered excavations around the country, primarily at Guayabo in the northwest, ancient artifacts have been unearthed that indicate a strong sense of aesthetics. Beautiful gold and jade jewelry, intricately carved grinding stones, and artistically painted terra-cotta ware point toward a highly skilled, if not large, population. The most enigmatic of these ancient relics are carved stone balls, some measuring several yards across and weighing many tons, that have been found along the southern Pacific coast. The purpose of these stone spheres remains a mystery: Some archeologists say that they may have been boundary markers; others think that they were celestial references. Still other scientists now claim that they are not man-made at all, but rather natural geological formations. (Examples of many of these artifacts are on display at several museums in San José, particularly the Jade and Gold Museums.)

In 1502, on his fourth and last voyage to the New World, Christopher Columbus anchored just offshore from present-day Limón. Whether it was he who gave the country its name is open to discussion, but it was not long before the inappropriate name took hold. The earliest Spanish settlers found that the native population of Costa Rica was unwilling to submit to slavery. Despite their small numbers, scattered villages, and tribal differences, they fought back against the Spanish. However, the superior Spanish firepower and the European diseases that had helped to subjugate populations farther north conquered the natives here as well. Yet, when the fighting was finished, the Spanish found very few Indians left that could be pressed into servitude. The Spanish settlers were forced to till their own lands, an exercise unheard of in other parts of Central America. Few pioneers headed this way because they could settle in Guatemala, where there was a large native workforce. Costa Rica was nearly forgotten as the Spanish crown looked elsewhere for riches to plunder and souls to convert.

It didn't take long for Costa Rica's few Spanish settlers to head for the hills, where they found rich volcanic soil and a climate that was less oppressive than in the lowlands. Cartago, the colony's first capital, was founded in 1563, but it wasn't until the 1700s that more cities were founded in this agriculturally rich region. While some haciendas with central courtyards and red-tile roofs can still be seen in Cartago (as well as in Liberia in Guanacaste), Costa Rica lacks much of the splendid Spanish-colonial architecture that can be found farther north in Nicaragua, Guatemala, and Mexico. Numerous earthquakes over the centuries have destroyed what little the Spanish did

- **1,000 B.C.–A.D. 1400** City of Guayabo is inhabited by as many as 10,000 people.
- **1502** Columbus discovers Costa Rica in September, landing at what is now Limón.
- **1519–1561** Spanish explore and colonize Costa Rica.
- **1563** City of Cartago is founded in Central Valley.
- **1737** San José is founded.
- **Late 1700s** Coffee is introduced as a cash crop.
- **1821** On September 15, Costa Rica, with the rest of Central America, gains independence from Spain.
- **1823** Capital is moved to San José.
- **1848** Costa Rica is proclaimed an independent republic.
- **1856** Battle of Santa Rosa; Costa Ricans defeat the United States, which backed pro-slavery advocate William Walker.
- **1870s** First banana plantations are formed.
- **1889** First election is won by an opposition party, establishing democratic process in Costa Rica.
- **1899** The United Fruit Company is founded by railroad builder Minor Keith.
- **1948** After aborted revolution, Costa Rican army is abolished.
- **1987** President Oscar Arias Sánchez is awarded the Nobel Peace Prize for orchestrating the Central American Peace Plan.
- **1994** President Rafael Angel Calderón hands over the reigns of government to José María Figueres, in a peaceful replay of their fathers' less amenable and democratic transfer of power in 1948.

build. (In addition to the above cities, notable examples of mission-style churches, including some now in ruins, can be found near the village of Ujarrás in the Orosi Valley, and on the central plaza in Heredia.)

In the late 18th century, the first coffee plants were introduced, and because these plants thrived in the highlands, Costa Rica began to develop its first cash crop. Yet, transporting the coffee to the Caribbean coast and then on to Europe where the demand for coffee was growing, was time consuming and labor intensive.

FROM INDEPENDENCE TO THE PRESENT

In 1821, Spain granted independence to its colonies in Central America. Costa Rica joined with its neighbors to form the Central American Federation, but in 1838 it withdrew to form a new nation and pursue its own interests, which differed considerably from those of the other Central American nations. By the mid-1800s, coffee was the country's main export. Land was given free to anyone willing to plant coffee on it, and plantation owners soon grew wealthy and powerful, creating Costa Rica's first elite class. Coffee plantation owners were powerful enough to elect their own representatives to the presidency.

This was a stormy period in Costa Rican history, and in 1856 the country was invaded by William Walker, a soldier of fortune from Tennessee who had grandiose dreams of presiding over a slave state in Central America. Prior to his invasion of Costa Rica, he had invaded Baja California and Nicaragua. The people of Central America were outraged by the actions of this man, who had backing from U.S. president James Buchanan. But it was the Costa Ricans, led by their president, Juan Rafael Mora, who marched against Walker and chased him back to Nicaragua. Walker eventually surrendered to a U.S. warship in 1857, but in 1860 he attacked Honduras, claiming to be the president of that country. The Hondurans, who had had enough of Walker's shenanigans, promptly executed him.

Until 1890 coffee growers had to transport their coffee either by ox cart to the Pacific port of Puntarenas or by boat down the Río Sarapiquí to the Caribbean. In the 1870s, a progressive president proposed a railway from San José to the Caribbean coast to facilitate the transport of coffee to European markets. It took nearly 20 years for this plan to reach fruition and more than 4,000 workers lost their lives constructing the railway, which passed through dense jungles and rugged mountains on its journey from the Central Valley to the coast. Part way through the project, as funds were dwindling, the second chief engineer, Minor Keith, proposed an idea that not only enhanced his fortunes, but changed the course of Central American history. Banana plantations would be developed along the railway right-of-way (land on either side of the tracks). The export of this crop would help to finance the railway, and in exchange Keith would get a 99-year lease on 800,000 acres of land with a 20-year tax deferment. The Costa Rican government gave its consent, and in 1878 the first bananas were shipped from the country. In 1899 Keith and a partner formed the United Fruit Company, a business that would eventually become the largest landholder in Central America and cause political disputes and wars throughout the region.

In 1889 Costa Rica held what is considered the first free election in Central American history. The opposition candidate won the election, and control of the government passed from the hands of one political party to another without bloodshed or hostilities. Thus Costa Rica established itself as the region's only true democracy. In 1948 this democratic process was challenged by a former president (from 1940 to 1944), Rafael Angel Calderón, who lost a bid at a second term in office by a narrow margin. Calderón, who had the backing of Communist labor unions and the Catholic church, refused to yield the country's leadership to the rightfully elected president Otillio Ulate, and a revolution ensued. Calderón was eventually defeated by José "Pepe" Figueres. In the wake of this crisis, a new constitution was drafted; among other changes, it abolished Costa Rica's army so that such a revolution could never happen again.

Peace and democracy have become of tantamount importance to Costa Ricans since the revolution of 1948. When Oscar Arias Sánchez was elected president in 1986, his primary goal was to seek a solution to the ongoing war in Nicaragua, and one of his first actions was to close down Contra bases inside Costa Rica and enforce Costa Rica's position of neutrality. In 1987 Sánchez won the Nobel Peace Prize for initiating a Central American peace plan aimed at settling the war in Nicaragua.

In 1994, history seemed to repeat itself, peacefully this time, when José María Figueres took the reigns of government from another son of a former president, Rafael Angel Calderón.

Costa Rica's 100 years of nearly uninterrupted democracy have helped to make it the most stable economy in Central America. This stability and adherence to a democratic process are a source of great pride to Costa Ricans. They like to think of their country as the "Switzerland of Central America," not only because of its herds of dairy cows but also because of its staunch position of neutrality in a region that has been torn by nearly constant civil wars and revolutions for more than 200 years.

5 The Church & Soccer: Costa Rica's Two Religions

Costa Ricans, on the whole, are outwardly devout Roman Catholics. Over 90% of the population defines itself as being Roman Catholic, yet there are small but visible evangelical Christian, Protestant, and Jewish communities, and freedom of religion is a constitutionally guaranteed right. The patron saint of Costa Rica is Nuestra Señora de Los Angeles (Our Lady of the Angels), who has a Byzantine-style church dedicated to her in Cartago. In the church is a shrine that contains a tiny figure of La Negrita, the Black Virgin, to whom miraculous healing powers have been attributed. The walls of the shrine are covered with a fascinating array of tiny silver images, left behind as tokens of gratitude by the faithful for cures of illnesses or other calamities she is believed to have effected. August 2 is the day dedicated to her, when thousands of people make a pilgrimage from San José to Cartago on foot to express their devotion. Another vestige of the Spanish-Catholic tradition in Costa Rica you're bound to encounter among Ticos is the fatalistic streak many of them have. It causes them not to question the accepted order of things, and is best expressed by their nearly constant qualification: "si Dios quiere," which translates as "if God wills."

Soccer is the national sport of Costa Rica and many accord it a level of devotion that far exceeds that granted the church. Although a poor performer in World Cup matches, Costa Rica is a regional powerhouse. The national soccer league season runs from September through June. Perhaps the longest-running rivalry is that between "El Monstro" (the Monster) of Saprissa and "La Liga" (the League, or the Team) of Alajuela, although most major cities and provinces have their own teams. Ticos literally take their soccer loyalties to the street. On game days, you'll see plenty of colored banners—purple and white for Saprissa, red and black for La Liga—streaming from car windows as fans head to or from the stadium. Jubilant followers of the winning team like to celebrate by cruising the city streets, rhythmically beating out their team's name on the car horn.

These two Costa Rican passions are joined by one of the more interesting local legends in the country. It seems that the team from Cartago has not won a national championship since 1940. At that time the team made a pre-game pilgrimage to the basilica to ask for the Virgin's help in the championship match and promised all sorts of devotion and praise should they win. Well, win they did, but instead of getting down on their knees and offering humble thanks, the happy team got sloppy drunk and forgot to honor their vows. Legend has it the Virgin was not pleased and that the Cartago soccer team is perpetually cursed. Residents of Cartago are resigned to the fact, and—unlike *Ligistas* or *Saprissistas*—local fans never get hypercritical of their team, knowing that it's useless to fight divine vengeance.

6 Gallo Pinto, Ceviche & Frescos: Costa Rican Food & Drink

Like other Central American cuisines, Costa Rican food is not especially memorable. Perhaps that's why there's so much international food available throughout the country. However, if you really want to save money, you'll find that Costa Rican food is always the cheapest food available. It's primarily served in *sodas*, Costa Rica's equivalent of diners.

MEALS & DINING CUSTOMS

Rice and beans are the basis of Costa Rican meals. Mixed together and generally served at breakfast, they're called *gallo pinto* and come with everything from eggs and steak to seafood. At lunch or dinner, rice and beans are an integral part of a *casado* (which also means "married"). A casado usually comes with cabbage-and-tomato salad, fried plantains, and a meat dish of some sort.

Dining hours in Costa Rica are flexible: Some downtown restaurants in San José are open 24 hours. Expensive restaurants tend to open for lunch between 11am and 2pm and for dinner between 6 and 11pm.

Appetizers *Bocas* are served with drinks in most bars. Often the bocas are free, but even if they aren't, they're very inexpensive. Popular bocas include *gallos* (tortillas piled with meat, chicken, beans, or cheese), *ceviche* (a sort of marinated seafood salad), and *tamales*.

Soups Black-bean soup, or *sopa negra*, is a watery soup that's served with a poached or boiled egg floating on top. It's one of Costa Rica's most popular soups and shows up on many menus. *Olla de carne* is a delicious soup made with large chunks of beef and several local vegetables, including chayote, ayote, yuca, and plantains, all of which have textures and flavors similar to winter squashes. A soup that's not universally loved, but is certainly distinctive and authentically Tico, is *sopa de mondongo*, which is made from tripe, the stomach of a cow. Some find it delicious, others disgusting. *Picadillos* are vegetable purees made of potato, chayote, or plantains with a little bit of meat. They are often served as a side dish with a *casado,* or as *bocas*.

Sandwiches & Snacks Ticos love to snack, and there are a large variety of tasty little sandwiches and snacks available on the street, at snack bars, and in sodas. *Arreglados* are tiny meat-filled sandwiches, as are *tortas*, which are served on small rolls with a bit of salad tucked into them. *Gallos*, mentioned above, are tortillas piled high with meat, beans, or cheese, usually served with a small salad of shredded cabbage with a few slices of tomato or cucumber. Tacos, tamales, and empanadas also are quite common.

Meat Costa Rica is beef country, one of many tropical nations that chose to convert much of its rain-forest land to pastures for raising beef cattle in the early days before preservation. Consequently, beef is cheap and plentiful, although it may be a bit tougher than that to which you're accustomed. Spit-roasted chicken is also very popular here, and is surprisingly tender.

Seafood Costa Rica has two coasts, and as you would expect, there's plenty of seafood available throughout the country. *Corvina* (sea bass) is the most commonly served fish, and it is prepared innumerable ways, including as *ceviche,* a sort of marinated salad. Be careful: In many cheaper restaurants, particularly in San José, shark meat is often sold as corvina. Rather surprisingly, shrimp and lobster are very expensive, with shrimp often pricier than lobster. This is because both shellfish are a major export.

Vegetables On the whole, vegetables rarely accompany main dishes in Costa Rica. The standard vegetable served with a meal is a little pile of shredded cabbage topped with a slice or two of tomato. For a much more satisfying and filling salad, order *palmito* (hearts of palm salad). Hearts of palm is considered a delicacy in most places because an entire palm tree (albeit a very small one) must be cut down to extract the "heart," or trunk of the tree. This is then peeled, boiled, and chopped into large round discs and served with other fresh vegetables, along with salad dressing. Even here, where palm trees are plentiful, palmito is relatively expensive. Another option is *picadillo,* a stew or puree of vegetables with a bit of meat in it. Most people have a hard time thinking of *plátanos* (plantains) as vegetables, but they are. This giant relative of the banana requires cooking before it can be eaten. Green plantains have a very starchy flavor and consistency, but become as sweet as candy once ripe. Fried plátanos is one of my favorite dishes. *Yuca* (manioc root) is another starchy staple vegetable of Costa Rica.

One more vegetable worth mentioning is the *pejibaye,* a form of palm fruit that looks like a miniature orange coconut. Boiled pejibayes are frequently sold from carts on the streets of San José. When cut in half, a pejibaye reveals a large seed surrounded by soft, fibrous flesh and looks a bit like an avocado. You can eat it like an avocado, too, by just scooping the flesh out.

Fruits Costa Rica has a wealth of delicious tropical fruits. The most common are mangoes (the season begins in April), papayas, pineapples, and bananas. Other less well-known fruits include the *marañon,* which is the fruit of the cashew tree, and has orange or yellow glossy skin; the *granadilla* or *granada* (passion fruit); the *mamón chino,* which Asian travelers will immediately recognize as the rambutan; and the *carambola* (star fruit). When ordering *ensalada de fruita* (fruit salad) in a restaurant, make sure to specify just fresh fruit, since a bowl of canned fruit covered with Jell-O cubes and three scoops of ice cream is what will be brought to your table otherwise!

Desserts *Queque seco,* which literally translates as "dry cake," is a pound cake. *Très leches* cake, on the other hand, is so moist you almost need to eat it with a spoon. *Flan de coco* is a sweet coconut flan. There are many other sweets available, many of which are made with condensed milk and raw sugar (rich and sweet).

BEVERAGES

Frescos, which taste a bit like milkshakes, are my favorite drinks in Costa Rica. They are usually made with fresh fruit and milk or water. Among the more common fruits used are mangoes, papayas, blackberries (*moras*), and pineapples. You will also come across *maracuya* (a type of passion fruit) and *carambola* (star fruit). Some of the more unusual frescos are *horchata* (made with rice flour and a lot of cinnamon) and *chan* (made with the seed of a plant found mostly in Guanacaste—definitely an acquired taste). The former is wonderful; the latter requires an open mind. Order *un fresco de leche sin hielo* if you are trying to avoid untreated water.

Water & Soft Drinks   Although water in most of Costa Rica is said to be safe to drink, visitors often become ill shortly after arriving in Costa Rica. Play it safe and stick to bottled water, which is readily available. *Aqua mineral*, or simply *soda*, is sparkling water in Costa Rica. It's inexpensive and refreshing. Most major brands of soft drinks are also available.

Beer, Wine & Liquor   The German presence in Costa Rica over the years has produced several fine beers, all of which are fairly inexpensive. Licensed local versions of Heineken and Rock Ice are also available. Costa Rica distills a wide variety of liquors, and you'll save money by ordering these rather than imported brands. Imported wines are available at reasonable prices in the better restaurants throughout the country. You can save money by ordering a South American wine, such as a Chilean merlot, instead of a Californian or French one. Café Rica and Salicsa are two coffee liqueurs made in Costa Rica; the former is very similar to Kahlua, and the latter is a cream coffee liqueur. Both are delicious.

Planning a Trip to Costa Rica

5

This chapter answers all your pre-trip questions, including: When is the best time to go to Costa Rica? The cheapest time? How should I get around inside the country? Should I rent a car and what will it cost? Where should I go in Costa Rica? What are the hotels like? How much should I budget for my trip?

1 Visitor Information & Entry Requirements

VISITOR INFORMATION

In the United States, you can get information on Costa Rica by contacting the **Costa Rica Brochure Service** (☎ **800/327-7033**), a representative of the Costa Rican Tourist Board (ICT, or Instituto Costarricense de Turismo) in the United States.

ENTRY REQUIREMENTS

Documents   Citizens of the United States, Canada, Great Britain, and most European nations may visit Costa Rica for a maximum of 90 days. No visa is necessary, but you must have a valid passport. Citizens of Australia and New Zealand can enter the country without a visa and stay for 30 days. Citizens of the Republic of Ireland need a visa, valid passport, and a round-trip ticket in order to enter.

If you overstay your visa or entry stamp, you will have to pay $45 for an exit visa and a nominal fee for each extra month you've stayed. If you need to get an exit visa, talk to a travel agent in San José. They can usually get the exit visa for you for a small fee and save you the hassle of dealing with Immigration yourself. If you want to stay longer than your entry stamp or visa is valid, the easist thing to do is cross the border into Panama or Nicaragua for 72 hours and then re-enter Costa Rica on a new entry stamp or visa. However, be careful. In late 1995, the Costa Rican government began cracking down on "perpetual tourists"; if they notice a continued pattern of exits and entries, they may deny you re-entry.

If you need a visa or have other questions about Costa Rica, you can contact any of the following **Costa Rican embassies:** in the United States, 2112 S St. NW, Washington, DC 20008 (☎ 202/234-2945); in Canada, 135 York St., Suite 208, Ottawa, Ontario K1N 5T4 (☎ 613/562-2855); in Great Britain, 14 Lancaster Gate,

---

Costa Rica Online

If you have a computer and access to the World Wide Web, you'll be able to find a wealth of information on Costa Rica just by sitting at your terminal. You can run a specific search, or try one of these websites: **"Costa Rica Homepage"** (http://www.cr), a central clearinghouse of Costa Rica–related information with sections on Costa Rican art, sports, government, and biodiversity, as well as links to related news and tourism sites (some pages in Spanish); **"Costa Rica's TravelWeb"** (http://www.magi.com/crica), a well-rounded site with tourism and hotel information, news links, an online reservation service, real estate information, and the homepages of the Costa Rican-American Chamber of Commerce; **"Costa Rica's TravelNet"** (http://www.catalog.com/calypso), an extensive tourism site, with hotel and tour listings as well as an online reservation system and links to Temptress Cruises, Rios Tropicales, and Calypso Tours; or **"Tico Net"** (http://www.ticonet.co.cr), a rather rudimentary business and tourism site.

London, England W2 3LH (☎ 71-706-8844). In the United States, Costa Rica also maintains consulates in Atlanta, New Orleans, Chicago, Denver, and Miami.

Lost Documents   If you lose your passport, immediately contact your embassy or consulate, listed in "Fast Facts: Costa Rica," below. Most embassies can replace your passport and help you get an exit visa in about 24 hours. If your embassy won't get your exit visa for you, see a local travel agent or OTEC Viajes, Edificio Ferencz, 2nd floor, Calle 3 between avenidas 1 and 3, 275 meters north of the National Theater (☎ 256-0633). If you try to deal with Immigration yourself, you'll face long lines, long waits, and endless frustration. Local travel agents and agencies regularly deal with Immigration and will charge you about $5 to $10 for the service. If you ticket with them, they'll do it for free.

Customs   Visitors entering Costa Rica are officially allowed to bring in one-half kilo of tobacco products, three liters of wine or liquor, two cameras, two kilos of sweets or chocolates, and up to $100 dollars worth of merchandise. In effect, you can usually bring in any goods and equipment that you will reasonably use during your stay: cameras, film, personal stereo devices, surfing or fishing equipment, even a personal computer. However, Costa Rica has high duties on most electronics and luxury items, and if it appears you are bringing in merchandise to sell (TVs, fax machines, computers, blenders, etc.), you will be assessed a stiff duty at customs.

2 Money

CASH & CURRENCY

The unit of currency in Costa Rica is the colón (¢). In early 1996, there were approximately 200 colónes to the American dollar, but because the colón has been in a constant state of devaluation, expect this rate to have changed somewhat by the time you arrive. Because of this devaluation and accompanying inflation, this book lists prices in U.S. dollars only.

The colón is divided into 100 centimos. There are coins of 50 and 100 centimos and 1, 2, 5, 10, and 20 colónes, however, because of their evaporating value, you will rarely see or have to handle centimos. There are paper notes in denominations of 50, 100, 500, 1,000, and 5,000 colónes. You might also encounter a special-issue 5-colón bill that is a popular gift and tourist souvenir. It is valid currency, although it sells

The Colón, the U.S. Dollar & the British Pound

In early 1996, there were approximately 198 colónes to the American dollar, or 299 colónes to the British pound. However, because the colón has been in a constant state of devaluation, expect this rate to have changed somewhat by the time you arrive. Because of this devaluation and the accompanying inflation, this book lists Costa Rican prices in U.S. dollars only.

Colónes	U.S. $	U.K. £
1	.025	0.017
5	.05	0.033
25	125.00	0.084
50	25.00	0.167
75	375.00	0.25
100	50.00	0.33
200	1.00	0.66
300	1.50	1.00
400	2.00	1.34
500	2.50	1.67
750	3.75	2.51
1,000	5.00	3.34
5,000	25.00	16.72
10,000	50.00	33.44
25,000	125.00	83.61
50,000	250.00	167.22
75,000	375.00	250.84
100,000	500.00	334.45
200,000	1,000.00	668.90
300,000	1,500.00	1,003.34
500,000	2,500.00	1,672.24
1,000,000	5,000.00	3,344.48

for much more than its face value. You may hear people refer to a *roja* or *toucan,* which are slang terms for the 1,000 and 5,000 colón bills, respectively. One hundred colón denominations are called *tejas,* so *cinco tejas* would be 500 colónes.

In recent years forged bills have become increasingly common. When receiving change in colónes it is a good idea to check the larger denomination bills, which should have protective bands or hidden images that appear when held up to the light.

EXCHANGING MONEY

You can exchange money at state-owned banks and most hotels; however, the service at these banks is so slow and cumbersome that this simple transaction can take over an hour and cause unnecessary confusion and anxiety. I don't recommend it. Most hotels and some private banks provide faster service but will shave a few colónes off the exchange rate. Costa Rica recently passed a law opening up the state's banking system. Accordingly, by late 1996, private banks will be able to perform many of the functions previously reserved for state institutions, including exchanging money

What Things Cost in San José	U.S. $
Taxi from the airport to the city center	$12.50
Local telephone call	.05
Double at Hotel Parque del Lago (expensive)	$95.00
Double at Hotel Grano de Oro (moderate)	$70.00
Double at Hotel Bienvenido (inexpensive)	$19.00
Lunch for one at CAFE de Teatro Nacional (moderate)	$9.50
Lunch for one at Soda La Central (inexpensive)	$2.50
Dinner for one, without wine, at Bijahua (expensive)	$17.50
Dinner for one, without wine, at La Cocina de Leña (moderate)	$10.00
Dinner for one, without wine, at Restaurante Campesino (inexpensive)	$5.20
Bottle of beer	.85
Coca-Cola	.85
Cup of coffee	.50
Roll of ASA 100 Kodacolor film, 24 exposures	$6.85
Admission to the Jade Museum	$2.00
Admission to the Gold Museum	$5.00
Movie ticket	$2.50
Ticket at Teatro Melico Salazar	$3.50–$15.00

and cashing traveler's checks. It's expected that the level of service offered by all banks will improve dramatically as a result.

Be very careful about exchanging money on the streets; it is extremely risky. In addition to forged bills and short counts, street money changers frequently work in teams that can leave you holding neither colónes nor dollars.

TRAVELER'S CHECKS

Traveler's checks can be readily cashed at hotels and banks. The exchange rate at banks is sometimes higher than at hotels, but it can take a very long time to cash a traveler's check or exchange money at a bank. If time is an issue, cash your traveler's checks at your hotel. Just be advised that the exchange rate you receive may not be as favorable.

CREDIT CARDS & ATMS

Major international credit cards accepted readily at hotels throughout Costa Rica include American Express, MasterCard, and VISA. Less expensive hotels tend to take cash only. Many restaurants and stores also accept credit cards. Before paying for a hotel with your credit card, check to see if you will be charged extra. Some hotels will charge a surcharge of 5% to 10% for credit-card transactions.

I've heard it's possible to get cash from local ATM machines, but so far I've been unable to verify this rumor, so it's best to come prepared with plenty of cash and traveler's checks. Banks can give you cash advances on your credit card, but expect to be assessed a service charge and spend a lot of time dealing with bureaucracy.

WIRING FUNDS

If you need cash in a hurry, **Western Union** (☎ 506/283-6336) is on Calle 9 between avenidas 2 and 4 in San José. Money can be electronically wired from any Western Union office in the United States to the central office listed above. Once you've arranged for the money to be wired, either pick it up at the central office, or call them to make arrangements for picking up your money at any one of 30 Western Union offices in Costa Rica. The process doesn't come cheap, though. A $100 wire will cost your friends back home $22, and a $1,000 wire, $99.

3 When to Go

Costa Rica's high season runs from late November to late April, which coincides almost perfectly with northern winters and major holiday travel periods. It also coincides perfectly with the Costa Rican dry season. If you want some unadulterated time on a tropical beach and a little less rain on your rain-forest experience, this is the time to come. During this period, however, prices are higher, attractions are more crowded, and you'll need to make your reservations further in advance.

In recent years, local tourism operators have begun calling the tropical rainy season (from May through November) the "green season." The adjective is appropriate. Even brown and barren Guanacaste province becomes lush and verdant. I love traveling around Costa Rica during the rainy season. It's easy to find and bargain for reduced rates, there are far fewer tourists, and the rain is often limited to a few hours each afternoon.

CLIMATE

As a tropical country, Costa Rica has distinct wet and dry seasons. However, some regions are rainy all year and others are very dry and sunny for most of the year. Temperatures vary primarily with elevation, not with season. On the coasts it is hot all year, while up in the mountains, it can be cool at night any time of year. In the highest elevations (10,000 to 12,000 feet), frost is common.

Average Monthly Temperatures and Rainfall in San José

	Jan	Feb	Mar	Apr	May	June	July	Aug	Sept	Oct	Nov	Dec
Temp (°F)	66	66	69	71	71	71	70	70	71	69	68	67
Temp (°C)	19	19	20.5	21.5	21.5	21.5	21	21	21.5	20.5	20	19.5
Days of Rain	1	0	1	4	17	20	18	19	20	22	14	4

Generally speaking, the rainy season is from May to mid-November. Costa Ricans call this wet time of year their winter. The dry season, considered summer by Costa Ricans, is from mid-November through April. In Guanacaste, the dry northwestern province, the dry season lasts several weeks longer than in other places. Even in the rainy season, days often start sunny, with rain falling in the afternoon and evening. On the Caribbean coast, especially south of Limón, you can count on rain all year round, although this area gets less rain in September and October than the rest of the country. The best time of year to visit is in December and January, when everything is still green from the rains, but the sky is clear. However, as mentioned above, advantages to traveling to Costa Rica in the rainy season include lower prices, a lusher landscape, and fewer tourists. Rain doesn't usually fall all day long, and when it does, it's a good opportunity to climb into a hammock and catch up on your reading.

HOLIDAYS

Because Costa Rica is a Roman Catholic country, most of its holidays and celebrations are church-related. The major celebrations of the year are Christmas, New Year's, and Easter, which are all celebrated for several days. Keep in mind that Holy Week (Easter Week) is the biggest holiday time in Costa Rica and many families head for the beach at this time (it's the last holiday before school starts). Also, there is no public transportation on Holy Thursday or Good Friday. Government offices and banks are closed on official holidays, transportation services are reduced, and stores and markets may also close.

Official holidays in Costa Rica include: January 1 (New Year's Day), March 19 (St. Joseph's Day), Thursday and Friday of Holy Week, April 11 (Juan Santamaría's Day), May 1 (Labor Day), June 29 (Saints Peter and Paul's Day), July 25 (annexation of the province of Guanacaste), August 2 (Virgin of Los Angeles' Day), August 15 (Mother's Day), September 15 (Independence Day), October 12 (Discovery of America/Día de la Raza), December 8 (Immaculate Conception of the Virgin Mary), December 24 and 25 (Christmas), December 31 (New Year's Eve).

COSTA RICA CALENDAR OF EVENTS

January
- **Fiesta of Santa Cruz,** Santa Cruz, Guanacaste. A religious celebration honoring the Black Christ of Esquipulas (a famous Guatemalan statue) that features folk dancing, marimba music, and bullfights. Mid–January.

February
- ✪ **Fiesta of the Diablitos,** Rey Curré village near San Isidro de El General. Boruca Indians wearing wooden devil and bull masks perform dances representative of the Spanish conquest of Central America. Fireworks displays, Indian handcrafts market. Date varies. Call the Costa Rican Tourist Board (☎ 800-327-7033) for current dates.

March
- **Día del Boyero** (Ox Cart Drivers' Day), San Antonio de Escazú. Colorfully painted ox carts parade through this suburb of San José, and local priests bless the oxen. Second Sunday.

April
- **Holy Week** (week before Easter). Religious processions are held in cities and towns throughout the country. Dates vary from year to year (between late March and early April).
- **Juan Santamaría Day,** Alajuela. Costa Rica's national hero is honored with parades, concerts, and dances. April 11.

May
- **Carrera de San Juan.** The country's biggest marathon runs through the mountains, from the outskirts of Cartago to the outskirts of San José. May 17.

July
- ✪ **Fiesta of the Virgin of the Sea,** Puntarenas. A regatta of colorfully decorated boats carry a statue of Puntarenas's patron saint. A similar event is held at Playa de Coco. Saturday closest to July 16.
- **Annexation of Guanacaste Day,** Liberia. Tico-style bullfights, folk dancing, horseback parades, rodeos, concerts, and other events celebrate the day when this region became part of Costa Rica. July 24.

August

- **Día de San Ramon,** San Ramon. More than two dozen statues of saints from various towns are brought to San Ramon where they are paraded through the streets. August 31.
- ✪ **Fiesta of the Virgin of Los Angeles,** Cartago. This is the annual pilgrimage day of the patron saint of Costa Rica. Many people walk from San José to the basilica in Cartago. August 2.

September

- **Costa Rica's Independence Day.** Celebrated all over the country. Most distinctive are the nighttime parades of children. September 15.

October

- **Fiesta del Maiz, Upala.** A celebration of corn, with local beauty queens wearing outfits made from corn plants. October 12.
- ✪ **Limón Carnival/Día de la Raza,** Limón. A smaller version of Mardi Gras complete with floats and dancing in the streets. Commemorates Columbus' arrival in Costa Rica. Week of October 12.

December

- ✪ **Festejos Populares,** San José. Bullfights, a horseback parade (El Tope), a carnival with street dancing and floats, and an amusement park all take place at the fairgrounds in Zapote. On New Year's Eve, there's a dance in the Parque Central. Last week of December.
- **Día de la Polvora,** San Antonio de Belen and Jesus Maria de San Mateo. Fireworks displays to honor Our Lady of the Immaculate Conception. December 8.
- **Fiesta de la Yeguita,** Nicoya. A statue of the Virgin of Guadalupe is paraded through the streets accompanied by traditional music and dancing. December 12.
- **Fiesta de los Negritos,** Boruca. Boruca Indians celebrate the feast day of their patron saint, the Virgin of the Immaculate Conception, with costumed dances and traditional music. December 8.
- **Las Posadas.** A country-wide celebration during which children and carolers go door-to-door seeking lodging to re-enact Joseph and Mary's search for a place to stay. Starts December 15.

4 Learning Vacations

Many travelers these days want to participate more actively in the cultural life of their chosen destination, and learn a little to boot. Costa Rica offers numerous Spanish-language programs and Latin-dancing schools. If you've already got some background in either of these areas, a week or two of classes will put some polish on your skills. It's a good idea to reserve your place in a Spanish class or program before you depart for Costa Rica, whereas dance classes can be arranged upon arrival. If you want to pick up as much Spanish as possible and you've never studied the language before, it's best to choose a month-long course with a homestay. Most schools are located in San José, but others have begun to pop up in more scenic spots.

SPANISH LANGUAGE PROGRAMS   As more and more people travel to Costa Rica with the intention of learning Spanish, the number of options increase. Courses are of varying lengths and intensiveness, and often include cultural activities and day excursions. Most Spanish schools can also arrange for homestays with a middle-class Tico family for a total immersion experience. Classes are intensive and often one-on-one. Listed below are some of the larger and more established Spanish-language schools, with approximate costs. Contact the schools for the most current price information.

Central American Institute for International Affairs (ICAI), Apdo. 10302, San José (☎ **506/233-8571;** fax 506/221-5238), offers a four-week Spanish-language immersion program, along with a homestay, for $962. They also offer courses in Central American studies and other topics. In the United States, contact the Language Studies Enrollment Center, P.O. Box 5095, Anaheim, CA 92814 (☎ **714/ 527-2918;** fax 714/826-8752).

Centro Cultural Costarricense Norteamericano, Apdo. 14489-1000, San José (☎ **506/225-9433;** fax 506/224-1480), is an extension of the U.S. embassy in Costa Rica. Its facilities are the most extensive of any language school in the country. Classes cost $245 for a week (20 hours of instruction). Homestays are also available.

Centro Lingüístico Conversa, Apdo. 17-1007, Centro Colón, San José (☎ **800/354-5036,** or 506/221-7649 in Costa Rica; fax 506/233-2418), provides an attractive environment for studying Spanish at its El Pedregal farm 10 miles west of San José. A four-week course, including room and board with a Costa Rican family, costs $1,650 for one person.

Costa Rica Spanish Institute (COSI), Apdo. 1366-2050, San Pedro (☎ /fax **506/ 253-2117**), offers small classes in the San Pedro neighborhood of San José as well as a program at the Pacific beach of Playa Ballena. Cost is $390 per week, with a homestay in San José; $450 at the beach.

Costa Rican Language Academy and More, Avenida Central across from Calle 25B and the Nicaraguan Embassy (Apdo. 233-2070), San José (☎ **506/233-2070** or 506/223-8938; fax 506/233-8670), offers 3, 4, or 5 hours of daily Spanish instruction in one- to four-week packages. Four hours per day for four weeks costs $900, including a homestay. The school also offers classes in Latin dance and Costa Rican cooking.

Forester Instituto Internacional, Apdo. 6945-1000, San José (☎ **506/ 225-3155,** 506/225-0135 or 506/225-1649; fax 506/225-9236), is located 75 meters south of the Automercado in the Los Yoses district of San José. The cost of a four-week language course with a homestay and excursions is approximately $1300.

Instituto Interamericano de Idiomas (Intensa), Calle 33 between avenidas 5 and 7 (Apdo. 8110-1000), San José (☎ **506/224-6353;** fax 506/253-4337), offers two- to four-week programs. A four-week program with 4 hours of instruction daily and a homestay costs $975.

La Escuela Idiomas D'Amore, Apdo. 67, Quepos (☎ **213/912-0600** in the U.S., or 506/777-1143 in Costa Rica; fax 414/781-3151 in the U.S., or 506/777-0543 in Costa Rica) is situated in the lush surroundings of Manuel Antonio National Park. Four weeks of classes, with 4 hours of instruction a day, costs $1,040; with a homestay, the cost rises to $1,290. Part of your tuition is donated to the World Wildlife Fund.

Pura Vida Instituto, Avenida 3 between calles 8 and 10 (Apdo. 890-3000), Heredia (☎ **506/237-0387** or 506/260-6269). For $280, you receive 5 days of classroom instruction, and 6 nights of lodging with a Costa Rican family (all meals included).

LATIN DANCE CLASSES   If you are interested in learning or polishing up your salsa, merengue, or mambo skills, San José is a good place to do it. It may take years to get all the moves and spins down, but even an introductory class or two can give the most terminal wallflowers the confidence to get out on the dance floor. When you feel confident enough, you can try out what you've learned at some of the area nightclubs. The schools listed below all have ongoing classes. Most allow casual drop-in attendance, but some like to start beginning classes at specific times, so call in advance to see when an appropriate class is being offered. Prices range from around $5 for a single-hour class to $50 per month for bi-weekly crash courses. Listed below are several of the dance schools in the San José area.

Costa Rican Language Academy and More, Avenida Central across from Calle 25B and the Nicaraguan Embassy (☎ **506/233-2070** or 506/223-8938); **Malecon,** Calle 17 between avenidas 2 and 4 (☎ **506/222-3214**); Merecumbe (☎ **506/ 224-3531**), with locations in San José, San Pedro, Sabanilla, and Tibas; and Danza Viva, 75 meters south of the Higueron, in San Pedro (☎ **506/253-3110**).

5 Organized Tours & Packages

Instead of paying for your airfare and accommodations separately, you'll usually save money if you purchase an all-inclusive tour or airfare-and-accommodations package. This is especially true when airfares are high or if you're planning to travel with a companion. There are a multitude of both tour operators and packagers, with various specialties, so it's best to work with a travel agent to select the tour or package that's right for you. When you're working with an agent, there are a few questions to keep in mind. Are all entrance and guide fees included? What about meals? Can special dietary requests (vegetarian, low-fat, etc.) be accommodated? Will your hotel selections and reservations be confirmed for you in advance of departure? If a rental car is included in the package, is pickup/delivery included? Do you have unlimited mileage? If all of these things are included in your package, chances are you'll save money.

A few reputable companies that specialize in general-interest tours and packages to Costa Rica include: **Costa Rica Experts,** 3166 North Lincoln Ave., Chicago, IL 60657 (☎ **800/827-9046** or 312/935-1009); **Tourtech** International, 17780 Fitch St., Suite 110, Irvine, CA 92714 (☎ **800/882-2636**); and **Holbrook Travel,** 3540 NW 13th St., Gainsville, FL 32609 (☎ **800/451-7111** or 904/377-7111). One Canadian company specializing in tours to Costa Rica is **Mony Tours,** 5540 Cote des Neiges, Montreal, H3T 1V9 (☎ **514/733-8277**). In addition, quite a few U.S.–and Costa Rican–based tour operators offer natural-history and "soft adventure" tours and packages that can include stays at remote nature lodges; you'll find a comprehensive listing of these organizations in chapter 3.

6 Health & Insurance

STAYING HEALTHY

Staying healthy on a trip to Costa Rica is predominantly a matter of being a little cautious about what you eat and drink, and using common sense. Know your physical limits and don't overexert yourself in the ocean, on hikes, or in athletic activities. Respect and protect yourself from the tropical sun. Try not to eat in seedy dives where cockroaches outnumber fellow diners. I recommend buying and drinking bottled water or soft drinks, but the water in San José and in most of the heavily traveled tourist spots is safe to drink. The sections below will deal with some specific health concerns of which you should be aware.

Vaccinations   No vaccinations are required for a visit to Costa Rica, unless you are coming from an area where yellow fever exists. However, because sanitation is generally not as good as it is in developed countries, you may be exposed to diseases for which you may wish to get vaccinations: typhoid, polio, tetanus, and infectious hepatitis (gamma globulin). If you are planning to stay in major cities, you stand little risk of encountering any of these diseases, but if you venture out into remote regions of the country, you stand a higher risk.

Tropical Diseases   Your chances of contracting any serious tropical disease in Costa Rica are slim, especially if you stick to the beaches or traditional tourist spots. However, **malaria, dengue fever,** and **leptospirosis** all exist in Costa Rica, so it's a good idea to have an idea of what they are.

Malaria is found in the lowlands on both coasts and in the northern zone. Although it is rarely found in urban areas, it is still a problem in remote wooded regions, and along the Atlantic coast. Malaria prophylaxes are available, but several have side effects and others are of questionable effectiveness. Consult your doctor as to what is currently considered the best preventative treatment for malaria before you depart. Be sure to ask whether a recommended drug will cause you to be hypersensitive to the sun. It would be a shame to come down here for the beaches and then never be able to go out in the sun. Because malaria-carrying mosquitoes come out only at night, you should do as much as possible to avoid being bitten by mosquitoes after dark. If you are in a malarial area, wear long pants and long sleeves, use insect repellent, and sleep under a mosquito net or burn mosquito coils (similar to incense, but with a pesticide).

Of greater concern may be dengue fever, which has had periodic outbreaks since 1993. Dengue fever is similar to malaria, and is spread by an aggressive daytime mosquito. This mosquito seems to be most common in lowland urban areas, and Liberia and Limón have been the worst-hit cities in Costa Rica. Dengue is also known as "bone-break fever," because it is usually accompanied by severe body aches. The first infection with dengue fever will make you very sick, but should cause no serious damage. However, a second infection with a different strain of the dengue virus can lead to internal hemorrhaging and may be life threatening.

Many people are convinced that taking B-complex vitamins daily will help prevent mosquitoes from biting you.

One final tropical fever you should know about is leptospirosis. There are over 200 strains of leptospiri, which are animal-borne bacteria transmitted to humans via contact with drinking, swimming, or bathing water. This bacterial infection is easily treated with antibiotics; however, it can quickly cause very high fever and chills, and should be treated promptly.

If you should develop a high fever accompanied by severe body aches, nausea, diarrhea, or vomiting during or shortly after a visit to Costa Rica, it's a good idea to consult a physician as soon as possible.

Costa Rica has been relatively free from the cholera epidemic that has spread through much of Latin America in recent years. This is largely due to an extensive public awareness campaign that has promoted good hygiene and increased sanitation. Your chances of contracting cholera while you're here are very slight. However, it is still advisable to avoid *ceviche,* a raw seafood salad, if it has any shellfish in it. Shellfish are known carriers of cholera.

Riptides   Many of Costa Rica's beaches, particularly on the Pacific coast, have riptides, strong currents that can drag swimmers out to sea. A riptide occurs when water that has been dumped on the shore by strong waves forms a channel back out to open water. These channels have strong currents. If you get caught in a riptide, you can't escape the current by swimming toward shore; that is the equivalent of swimming upstream in a river. To break free of the current, swim parallel to shore, and use the energy of the waves to help you get back to the beach.

Bees & Snakes   Although Costa Rica has Africanized bees and several species of venomous snakes, your chances of being bitten are minimal, especially if you refrain from sticking your hands under rocks in the forest and into hives. If you know that you are allergic to bee stings, consult your doctor before traveling. Your best bet for seeing a fer-de-lance or eyelash viper is a visit to San José's Serpentarium (see chapter 6).

INSURANCE

Before leaving on your trip, contact your health-insurance provider and find out whether your insurance will cover you while you are away. If not, contact a travel agent and ask about travel health-insurance policies. A travel agent can also tell you about trip insurance to cover cancellations or loss of baggage. If you have homeowner's or renter's insurance, you may be covered against theft and loss even while you are on vacation. Be sure to check this before taking out additional insurance. Some credit cards provide trip insurance when you charge an airline ticket, but be sure to check with your credit-card company before assuming you have it. If you decide that your current insurance is inadequate, you can contact your travel agent for information on various types of travel insurance, including insurance against cancellation of a prepaid tour should this become necessary.

The following companies offer various types of travel insurance: **Teletrip** (Mutual of Omaha), P.O. Box 31685, Omaha, NE 68131 (☎ **800/228-9792**); **Wallach and Co., Inc.,** P.O. Box 480, Middleburg, VA 22117-0480 (☎ **800/237-6615**); and **Access America, Inc.,** P.O. Box 90315, Richmond, VA 23286-4991 (☎ **800/424-3391** or 800/284-8300).

7 Tips for Travelers with Special Needs

FOR SENIORS

Many airlines now offer senior-citizen discounts, so be sure to ask about these when making reservations. Due to its temperate climate, stable government, low cost of living, and friendly pensionado program, Costa Rica is popular with retirees from North America. There are excellent medical facilities in San José, and plenty of community organizations to help retirees feel at home. If you would like to learn more about retiring in Costa Rica and applying for residency, contact the **Association of Residents of Costa Rica** in San José (☎ **506/233-8068** or 506/221-2053).

Elderhostel, 75 Federal St., Boston, MA 02110 (☎ **617/426-7788**), offers very popular study tours to Costa Rica. To participate in an Elderhostel program, either you or your spouse must be at least 60 years old. Great birdwatching trips and lectures on Costa Rican culture and history are some of the more interesting aspects of these trips.

FOR SINGLES

You'll pay the same penalty here that you would elsewhere: Rooms are more expensive if you aren't traveling in a pair. If you are looking for someone to travel with, **Travel Companions Exchange,** P.O. Box 833, Amityville, NY 11701-0833 (☎ **516/454-0880**), provides listings of possible travel companions categorized under such headings as special interests, age, education, and location. It costs a minimum of $99 for an eight-month membership and subscription to the service. It is also possible to subscribe to the organization's bi-monthly newsletter without becoming a member. The newsletter costs $24 for a six-month subscription.

FOR FAMILIES

Hotels in Costa Rica occasionally give discounts for children under 12 years old, and usually children under 3 or 4 years are allowed to stay for free. Ask when you book your reservation. However, don't look for the same type of discounts as in the United States.

FOR GAY & LESBIAN TRAVELERS

Costa Rica is a conservative, *macho* country and public displays of same-sex affection are considered rare and shocking. However, gay and lesbian travelers are generally treated with respect and should not experience any harassment.

The **International Gay and Lesbian Association** (☎ **506/234-2411**) can provide helpful information and tips. **Casa Yemaya,** located in the nearby suburb of Moravia (☎ **506/223-3652** or 506/257-8529), is a feminist center and guest lodge that organizes classes, activities, and tours exclusively for women.

FOR STUDENTS

Costa Rica is the only country in Central America with a network of hostels that are affiliated with the International Youth Hostel Federation. Ask at the **Toruma Youth Hostel,** Avenida Central between calles 29 and 31, San José (☎ **506/224-4085**) for information on hostels at Rara Avis, La Fortuna, Lake Arenal, San Isidro, Jacó Beach, Liberia, and Rincón de la Vieja National Park. In San José, there's also a student travel agency: **OTEC,** Edificio Ferencz, 2nd floor, Calle 3 between avenidas 1 and 3, 275 meters north of the National Theater (☎ **506/256-0633**). If you already have an international student identity card, you can use your card to get discounts on airfares, hostels, national and international tours and excursions, car rentals, and store purchases. If you don't have one, stop by the OTEC office with a passport or other piece of identification that shows you are under 35 years old, proof of student status, and two passport photos; for about $10, they'll prepare an ID card for you.

Students interested in a working vacation in Costa Rica should contact the **Council on International Educational Exchange (CIEE),** 205 E. 42nd St., New York, NY 10017 (☎ **212/661-1414** or 212/661-1450). This organization also issues official student identity cards and has offices all over the United States. It recently published *Smart Vacations: The Traveler's Guide to Learning Adventures Abroad* (St. Martin's Press, 1993), a directory of companies, organizations, and schools offering educational travel programs.

FOR TRAVELERS WITH DISABILITIES

Although facilities are beginning to be adapted for those with disabilities, in general, there are few handicapped-accessible buildings in Costa Rica. In San José, sidewalks are crowded and uneven. Few hotels offer handicapped-accessible accommodations, and there are neither public buses nor private vans for transporting disabled individuals. It is difficult for a person with disabilities to get around in Costa Rica.

Kosta Roda, P.O. Box 1312-1100, San Juan de Tibás (☎ **506/236-5185**) is a Costa Rican organization dedicated to bringing about successful travel experiences for persons with disabilities. They can provide you with a list of hotels, museums, tours, and attractions that are wheelchair accessible.

Mobility International USA, P.O. Box 10767, Eugene, OR 97440 (☎ **541/343-1284**), is a membership organization that promotes international educational exchanges for people of all disabilities and ages. In the past, they have sponsored trips to Costa Rica, and may again in the future. For a $25 membership fee, you'll receive their quarterly newsletter and access to their referral service.

8 Getting There

BY PLANE

It takes between 3 and 7 hours to fly to Costa Rica from most U.S. cities, and as Costa Rica becomes more and more popular with North American travelers, more flights are made into San José's Juan Santamaría International Airport. There are several car-rental agencies at the airport. Driving in Costa Rica is not for everyone, however. See "Getting Around" later in this chapter for further information and tips.

THE MAJOR AIRLINES

The following airlines currently serve Costa Rica from the United States, using the gateway cities listed. **American Airlines** (☎ 800/433-7300) has daily flights from Miami and Dallas/Fort Worth. Aviateca, the Guatemalan national airline (☎ 800/327-9832), flies daily from Los Angeles and Miami, and three times weekly from Houston. **Continental** (☎ 800/231-0856) offers flights daily from Houston. **Lacsa,** Costa Rica's national airline (☎ 800/225-2272), has service from New York, Miami, Orlando, New Orleans, Los Angeles, and San Francisco. **Mexicana** (☎ 800/531-7921), has flights from New York, Denver, Miami, Dallas/Fort Worth, San Antonio, San Jose (California), and San Francisco, although with these flights it's necessary to transfer and spend a night in Mexico City. If you travel from Chicago and Los Angeles on Mexicana, you can get to San José in one day. **Taca,** El Salvador's national airline (☎ 800/535-8780), offers flights from Los Angeles, San Francisco, Houston, New Orleans, Miami, and Washington. **United Air Lines** (☎ 800/241-6522) has daily flights from Los Angeles and Washington, with one stop either in Mexico or El Salvador. **Aero Costa Rica** (☎ 800/237-6274) has flights from Atlanta, Orlando, and Miami.

From Europe, you can take any major carrier to a hub city such as Miami or New York and then make connections to Costa Rica. Alternately, **Iberia** (☎ 800/772-4642) from Spain, and **LTU International Airways** (☎ 800/888-0200) from Germany, have established routes to San José that stop first in Miami.

REGULAR AIRFARES

In recent years airfares have been very unstable and price wars have flared up unexpectedly. Fares also vary seasonally. Such instability makes it very difficult to quote an airline ticket price. **APEX (advance-purchase excursion) fares** are often similar from airline to airline, but the cost of a first-class ticket can vary greatly. At press time, an APEX or a coach ticket from New York to San José was running between $649 and $789; from Los Angeles, between $590 and $802. First class from New York starts at about $1,850; from Los Angeles, $2,400. On rare occasions, special fares may be offered at rock-bottom prices, but don't count on it. Regardless of how much the cheapest ticket costs when you decide to fly, you can bet it will have some restrictions. It will almost certainly be non-refundable, and you may have to pay for it within 24 hours of making a reservation. You'll probably have to purchase it anywhere from one week to 30 days in advance, and you're also likely to have to stay over a weekend.

TICKET BROKERS/CONSOLIDATORS

You can shave a little bit off the price you pay by purchasing an airline ticket from what is known as a ticket broker or consolidator. These ticketing agencies sell discounted airfares on major airlines; although the tickets have as many, and sometimes more, restrictions than an APEX ticket, they can help you save money. You'll find ticket brokers' listings—usually just a column of destinations with prices beside them—in the Sunday travel sections of major-city newspapers. You'll almost never get the ticket for the advertised price, but you will probably get it for less than the airline would sell it to you. If you'd like to shop around, try **Cheap Tickets, Inc.** (☎ **800/377-1000**) or **World Travel Consultants** (☎ **800/318-8802**).

BY BUS

Bus service runs regularly from both Panama City, Panama, and Managua, Nicaragua. From Panama City it is a 20-hour, 900-kilometer trip; buses leave Panama City daily at noon. The one-way fare is $20. Call the **Tica Bus Company** (☎ **506/221-8954**) for further information. From Managua, it is 11 hours and 450 kilometers to San José. Buses leave Managua daily at 6am; the one-way fare is between $10 and $15. For more information, call the Tica Bus Company or **Sirca Company** (☎ **506/222-5541** or 223-1464).

Neither of these bus companies will reserve a seat by telephone, so buy your ticket in advance, preferably several days before you plan to travel, especially on weekends or over holidays.

BY CAR

It's possible to travel to Costa Rica by car, but it can be difficult, especially for U.S. citizens. The Interamerican Highway (also known as the Panamerican Highway) passes through Guatemala, El Salvador, Honduras, and Nicaragua after leaving Mexico and before reaching Costa Rica. All of these countries can be problematic for travelers for a variety of reasons, including internal violence, crime, and visa formalities. If you do decide to undertake this adventure, take the gulf-coast route from the border crossing at Brownsville, Texas, as it involves traveling the least number of miles through Mexico. Along the way, it's best not to drive at night because of the danger of being robbed by bandits.

A good resource for those planning this journey is *Driving the Pan-Am Highway to Mexico and Central America* by Audrey and Raymond Pritchard, available through **Interlink 209,** P.O. Box 526770, Miami, FL 33152. To purchase a copy, send $19.95 plus $3 for shipping and handling to the above address.

Car Documents   You'll need a current driver's license, as well as your vehicle's registration and a copy of its title, in order to enter the country.

Central American Auto Insurance   Contact **Sanborn's Insurance Company,** 2009 S. 10th St., McAllen, TX 78505 (☎ **800/222-0158** or 210/686-0711), located about 1¹/₂ hours from Brownsville, Texas. They can supply you with trip insurance for Mexico and Central America—insurance is not available after you have left the United States— and an itinerary. Sanborn's also has branches at other U.S./Mexico border crossings.

BY CRUISE SHIP

More than 200 cruise ships stop each year in Costa Rica, calling at Limón on the Caribbean coast and at Puerto Caldera on the Pacific coast. Cruise lines that offer stops in Costa Rica include Cunard, Royal Caribbean, Holland American, Princess, Regency, and Royal Cruise Line. Contact these companies directly or visit a travel agent to find out more information about cruising to Costa Rica. Most cruise travel is wholesaled, and the best bargains can usually be obtained from such wholesalers and consolidators as **Cruise World** (☎ **800/588-7447**), **Cruises, Inc.** (☎ **800/596-5529**), and **Forever Cruising** (☎ **800/338-8005**).

9 Getting Around

BY PLANE

Flying is one of the best ways to get around Costa Rica. Because the country is quite small, flights are short and not too expensive. The domestic airlines of Costa Rica are **Sansa,** Calle 24 between Avenida Central and Avenida 1 (☎ **506/233-0397,** 506/233-3258, or 506/233-5330), which offers a free shuttle bus from its downtown office to the airport, and **Travelair** (☎ **506/232-7883** or 506/220-3054), which charges more for flights to the same destinations, but is popular because it's more reliable. Flights last between 20 and 50 minutes. Travelair operates from Pavas Airport, 4 miles from San José, and Sansa operates from San José's Juan Santamaría International Airport.

In the high season (December to May), be sure to book reservations well in advance. If you plan to return to San José, buy a round-trip ticket as they tend to be less expensive than two one-way tickets.

BY BUS

This is by far the best way to visit most of Costa Rica. Buses are inexpensive, relatively well maintained, and they go nearly everywhere. There are three types of buses. Local buses are the cheapest and slowest; they stop frequently and are generally a bit dilapidated. Express buses run between San José and most beach towns and major cities; they sometimes only operate on weekends and holidays. A few luxury buses and minibuses drive to destinations frequented by foreign tourists. For details on how to get to various destinations from San José, see the "Getting There" sections of the regional chapters that follow.

BY CAR

Renting a car in Costa Rica is not something to be entered into lightly. The roads are in terrible shape, most rural intersections are unmarked, and for some reason, sitting behind the wheel of a car seems to turn peaceful Ticos into homicidal maniacs. In addition, since all rental cars in Costa Rica bear special license plates, they are readily identifiable to thieves. Nothing is ever safe in a car in Costa Rica, although parking in guarded parking lots helps. The tourist plates also signal police that they can extort money from unwary tourist motorists. Never pay money directly to a police officer who stops you for any traffic violation. Before driving off with a rental car, be sure that you inspect the exterior and point out to the rental company representative every tiny scratch, dent, tear, or any other damage. It is a common practice with many Costa Rican car-rental companies to claim that you owe payment for damages the company finds when you return the car.

On the other hand, renting a car allows you much greater freedom to explore remote areas of the country. Several people have written to me to say that they feel visitors should always rent four-wheel-drive vehicles. I have always rented a regular car during the dry season, and though there are roads I can't drive down, I have managed to get around just fine (including to Monteverde). During the rainy season and on the Nicoya peninsula, four-wheel-drive vehicles are recommended. If, after weighing the alternatives, you decide you want to rent a car, read on.

Avis, Budget, Hertz, National, and **Thrifty** all have offices in Costa Rica. You will save somewhere between $35 and $75 per week on a car rental if you make a reservation in your home country at least one week before you need the car. For example, at press time, the least-expensive Avis car rents for $276 per week, plus insurance (for a total of $374) in San José, but if you book this same car in advance from the United States, you can get it for $198 per week, plus insurance (for a total of $296). To rent a car in Costa Rica, you must be at least 21 years old and have a valid driver's license and a major credit card in your name. See the "Getting Around" section of chapter 6 for details on renting a car in San José. Cars can also be rented in Quepos, Jacó, Liberia, and Limón.

Gasoline   Regular leaded gasoline is what is most readily available in Costa Rica. Most rental cars take regular. However, some of the newer models run on unleaded, which is sold as "super." Ask your rental agent what type of gas your car takes. When going off to remote places, try to leave with a full tank of gas since gas stations can be very hard to find. If you need to gas up in a small town, you can sometimes get gasoline from enterprising families who sell it by the liter from their houses. Look for hand-lettered signs that say "gasolina."

Road Conditions   Roads in Costa Rica are appallingly bad, largely due to neglect and years of corruption in the Transportation Ministry. In 1995, conditions had deteriorated to such a point that local newspapers ran contests to find the largest potholes. There was no lack of contenders. Unfortunately, little relief or repair work is in sight. If possible, before you rent a vehicle, research the conditions of the roads you plan to travel to see if it's necessary to have a four-wheel-drive vehicle to get to your destination. Some paved roads are still badly potholed, so stay alert. Road conditions get especially tricky during the rainy season, when heavy rains and runoff can destroy a stretch of pavement in the blink of an eye. Route numbers are rarely used on road signs in Costa Rica, though there are frequent signs listing the number of kilometers to various towns or cities.

Maps   Car-rental agencies and the ICT information centers (see "Information & Entry Requirements," at the beginning of this chapter) at the airport and in downtown San José have adequate road maps. For a listing of where to where find maps in San José, see "Maps," under "Fast Facts: San José," in chapter 6.

Driving Rules   A foreign driver's license is valid for the first three months you are in Costa Rica. Seat belts are required for the driver and front-seat passengers. Motorcyclists must wear a helmet. Highway police use radar, so keep to the speed limit if you don't want to get pulled over. Speeding tickets can be charged to your credit card for up to a year after you leave the country if they are not paid before departure.

Breakdowns   If your car breaks down and you're unable to get off the road, check to see if there are reflecting triangles in the trunk. If there are, line them up along the road at least 100 feet in front of your car, as a warning to approaching traffic. If not, try to create a similar warning marker using a pile of leaves or branches.

BY FERRY

There are four different ferries operating across the Gulf of Nicoya. Three are car ferries: one across the Río Tempisque; one from Puntarenas to Playa Naranjo; and one from Puntarenas to Paquera. The fourth is a passenger ferry which runs from Puntarenas to Paquera. For more detailed information, see chapters 7 and 9.

HITCHHIKING

Although buses go to most places in Costa Rica, they can be infrequent in the remote regions, and consequently, local people often hitchhike to get to their destinations sooner. If you are driving a car, people will frequently ask you for a ride. In rural areas, a hitchhiker carrying a machete is not necessarily a great danger, but use your judgement. Hitchhiking is not recommended on major roadways or in urban areas.

In rural areas, it's usually pretty safe. However, women should be extremely cautious about hitchhiking anywhere in Costa Rica. If you choose to hitchhike, keep in mind that if a bus doesn't go to your destination, there probably aren't too many cars going there either. Good luck.

LOCATING ADDRESSES

While there are some street addresses in Costa Rica, they are almost never used. Addresses are usually given as a set of coordinates, such as "Calle 3 between Avenida Central and Avenida 1." Many addresses include additional information such as the number of meters or *varas* (an old Spanish measurement roughly equal to a yard) from a specified intersection or some other well-known landmark. Often the additional information is confusing to visitors, but essential for taxi drivers. In San José, many addresses use distances from the Coca-Cola bottling plant that once stood near the market. The bottling plant is long gone, but the address descriptions remain. In outlying neighborhoods, addresses can become long directions such as "50 meters south of the old church, then 100 meters east, then 20 meters south." Luckily for the visitor, these directions are often precise.

FAST FACTS: Costa Rica

American Express   American Express (☎ **506/257-1792**) has a counter in San José at the Banco de San José on Calle Central between avenidas 3 and 5. It's open Monday through Friday from 8am to 7pm, and Saturday 9am to 1pm. To report a lost or stolen card from inside Costa Rica, call toll-free 001-800-528-2121.

Business Hours   **Banks** are usually open Monday through Friday from 9am to 3pm, though many have begun to offer extended hours. **Offices** are open Monday through Friday from 8am to 5pm (but closed for 2 hours at lunch). **Stores** are generally open Monday through Saturday from 9am to 7pm (many close for an hour at lunch). **Bars** are open until 1 or 2am.

Climate   See "When to Go," earlier in this chapter.

Currency   See "Money," earlier in this chapter.

Customs   You can bring in one-half kilo of tobacco products, three liters of liquor, and two cameras duty-free. Laptops, videocameras, and personal CD- and tape players are also allowed.

Driving Rules   See "Getting Around," earlier in this chapter.

Drug Laws   Drug laws in Costa Rica are strict, so stay away from marijuana and cocaine. Many prescription drugs are sold over the counter here, but often the names are different than in the United States and Europe. It's always best to travel with a doctor's prescription if you take regular medication.

Drugstores   A drugstore in Costa Rica is a *farmacia*. You'll find at least one in nearly every town.

Electricity   The standard in Costa Rica is the same as in the United States: 110 volts. However, three-pronged outlets can be scarce, so it's helpful to bring along an adapter.

Embassies/Consulates   The following embassies and consulates are located in San José: United States Embassy, in front of Centro Commercial, on the road to Pavas (☎ 506/220-3939); Canadian Consulate, Calle 3 and Avenida 1 (☎ 506/255-3522); British Embassy, Paseo Colón between calles 38 and 40 (☎ 506/221-5566).

Emergencies In case of **emergencies,** dial 911; for an **ambulance,** call 128; to report a **fire,** call 118; to contact the **police,** call 221-1365 or 221-5337.

Holidays See "When to Go," earlier in this chapter.

Information See "Visitor Information & Entry Requirements," earlier in this chapter. Also see individual city sections for local information offices.

Language Spanish is the official language of Costa Rica. *Berlitz Latin-American Spanish Phrasebook and Dictionary* (Berlitz Guides, 1992) is probably the best phrasebook to bring with you.

Laundry Laundromats are few and far between in Costa Rica; much more common are expensive hotel laundry services. For listings of laundromats, see individual city and town sections.

Liquor Laws Alcoholic beverages are sold every day of the week throughout the year, with the exception of the two days before Easter, and the two days before and after a presidential election.

Lost or Stolen Credit & Charge Cards If you lose your credit- or charge card, it's best to call the Costa Rican office of the company that issued the card immediately: American Express, ☎ 001-800-528-2121; MasterCard, ☎ 506/223-8855; VISA, ☎ 506/252-2155.

Mail Mail to the United States usually takes a little over one week to reach its destination. Postage for a postcard is 25¢; for a letter, 35¢. A post office is called a *correo* in Spanish. You can get stamps at the post office, and at gift shops in large hotels. If you are sending mail to Costa Rica, it can take as long as a month to get to the more remote corners of the country. Plan ahead. Also, many hotels and eco-lodges have mailing addresses in the United States. Always use this address when writing from North America or Europe. Never send cash, checks, or valuables through the Costa Rican mail system.

Maps The Costa Rican Tourist Board (ICT) can usually provide you with good maps of both Costa Rica and San José. For listings of sources for maps in San José, see "Maps," under "Fast Facts: San José," in chapter 6.

Newspapers/Magazines There are three Spanish-language dailies in Costa Rica and one English-language weekly, the *Tico Times.* There is also a bilingual tourist weekly, *Costa Rica Today.* In addition, you can get *Time, Newsweek,* and several U.S. newspapers at hotel gift shops and a few bookstores in San José.

Passports See "Visitor Information & Entry Requirements," earlier in this chapter.

Pets If you want to bring your pet to Costa Rica, make sure it's been vaccinated against rabies and distemper in the last year, and you have the documentation to prove it. In addition, it's best to check with where you plan to stay before assuming your furry companion is welcome.

Police The Judicial Police (*Organismo de Investigacion Judicial*), which handles all robberies, muggings, and other cases of assault, can be reached at 506/221-1365 or 506/221-5337. The Traffic Police (*Policia de Transito*) is at 506/222-9330 or 506/222-9245.

Radio/TV There are 10 local TV channels, and cable TV from the United States is common. There are more than 100 radio stations on the AM and FM dials.

Restrooms These are known as *sanitarios* or *servicios sanitarios.* They are marked *mujeres* or *damas* for women, and *hombres* or *caballeros* for men.

Safety Though most of Costa Rica is safe, crime has become much more common in recent years. San José is known for its pickpockets. It's best to avoid carrying a wallet in your back pocket or in a daypack on your back. If you're carrying a purse or a handbag, keep it tucked under an arm. Be sure not to leave valuables in your hotel room.

If you're driving, don't park your car on the street in Costa Rica, especially in San José; there are plenty of public parking lots around the city. Because all rental cars have special plates, they're easily spotted by thieves who know that such cars are likely to be full of expensive camera equipment, money, and other valuables. Don't leave anything of value in a car parked on the street, not even for a moment. Public intercity buses are also frequent targets of stealthy thieves. Never check your bags into the hold of a bus if you can avoid it. If this cannot be avoided, keep your eye on what leaves the hold every time the bus stops. If you put your bags onto an overhead rack, be sure you can see them at all times.

Taxes All hotels charge 18.45% tax. Restaurants charge 15% tax and also add on a 10% service charge, for a total of 25% more on your bill. There's an airport departure tax of $16.50.

Taxis Taxis are common and inexpensive in San José, but harder to find and more expensive in rural areas. In San José taxis are supposed to charge metered fares. Outside of the city and on longer rides, be sure to agree upon a price beforehand.

Telephones & Faxes Costa Rica has an excellent phone system, with a dial tone similar to that heard in the United States. All phone numbers in Costa Rica have seven digits. For information, dial 113. A pay phone costs 10 colónes (5¢) and most phones take 5-, 10-, or 20-colón coins, though some take 5- or 10-colón coins only.

For making calling-card and collect calls, you can reach an AT&T operator by dialing 0-800-011-4114, MCI by dialing 0-800-012-2222, Sprint by dialing 0-800-013-0123, Canada Bell by dialing 0-800-015-1162, and a Costa Rican international operator by dialing 116 (pay phones may sometimes require a coin deposit). The Costa Rican telephone system allows direct international dialing, but it's expensive. To get an international line, dial 00, the country code, and the number.

To call Costa Rica from the United States, dial 011 followed by the country code 506, then the local number.

You can make **international phone calls,** as well as send fax**es,** from the **ICE office,** Avenida 2 between calles 1 and 3, in San José. The office is open daily from 7am to 10pm. Faxes cost between $4 and $5 per page. (Many hotels will also offer the same service for a fee.) Radiográfica (☎ **506/287-0087**) at Calle 1 and Avenida 5 in San José also has fax service.

Time Costa Rica is on central standard time, 6 ours behind Greenwich mean time.

Tipping Tipping isn't necessary in restaurants, where a 10% service charge is always added to your bill (along with a 15% tax). If service was particularly good, you can leave a little extra at your own discretion. Porters and bellhops get around 75¢ bag. You don't need to tip a taxi driver unless the service has been superior—a tip generally isn't expected.

Visas See "Visitor Information & Entry Requirements," earlier in this chapter.

Water Though the water in San José is said to be safe to drink, outside of the city water quality varies. I recommend playing it safe and sticking to bottled drinks as much as possible, and avoiding ice.

6 San José

At first blush, San José may seem little more than a chaotic jumble of cars, buses, buildings, and people. The central downtown section of San José is an urban planner's nightmare. The once quiet streets are now overburdened by traffic and in a near-constant state of gridlock. Leaded fuels and a lack of emission controls have given San José a brown cloud. The city bustles, but is not particularly hospitable to tourists. Sidewalks are poorly maintained and claustrophobic, and street crime is on the rise. Most visitors quickly seek the sanctuary of their hotel rooms and the first chance to escape the city.

Still, San José is the most cosmopolitan city in Central America. Costa Rica's stable government and the Central Valley's climate have, over the years, attracted people from all over the world. There is a large diplomatic and international business presence here. One result has been the amazing variety of cuisines available in the city's restaurants. Another more recent result has been the proliferation of small hotels in renovated historic buildings. Together these restaurants and hotels provide visitors with a greater variety of options than are to be found anywhere between Mexico City and Bogotá.

San José is a city built on coffee. This is not to say that the city runs on bottomless pots of java. No, San José was built on the profits of the coffee-export business. Between the airport and downtown you pass by coffee farms, and glancing up from almost any street in the city you can see, on the volcanic mountains that surround San José, a patchwork quilt of farm fields, most of which are planted with the *grano de oro* (golden bean), as it is known here. San José was a forgotten backwater of the Spanish empire until the first shipments of the local beans made their way to sleepy souls in Europe late in the 19th century. Soon, San José was riding high on this vegetable gold. Coffee planters, newly rich and craving culture, imposed a tax on themselves in order to build the Teatro Nacional, San José's most beautiful building. Coffee profits also built the city a university. Today, you can smell the coffee roasting as you wander the streets near the central market, and in any cafe or restaurant you can get a hot cup of sweet, milky *cafe con leche* to remind you of the bean that built San José.

Why does coffee grow so well around San José? It's the climate. The Central Valley, in which the city sits, has a perfect climate. At 3,750 feet above sea level, San José enjoys springlike temperatures year-round. It is this pleasant climate and the beautiful views of lush green mountainsides that make San José a memorable city to visit. All you have to do is glance up at those mountains to know that this is one of the most beautiful capital cities in Central America. And if a glance isn't enough for you, you'll find that it's extremely easy to get out into the countryside from San José. Within an hour or two, you can climb a volcano, go white-water rafting, hike through a cloud forest, and stroll through a butterfly garden, among many other activities.

1   Deals & Discounts

San José is chock-full of museums. While they aren't uniformly world-class, none of them charges much for admission, and most offer discounts to children and students with valid ID. The Museum of Contemporary Art and Design at the National Arts Center is excellent, and admission is free. The National Museum and the Jade Museum charge just $1 and $2 per person, respectively. The elaborate Gold Museum and the new Children's Museum have the priciest tickets at $5 a head.

Public buses are one of San José's great bargains—one-way fares are only 10¢–30¢ per person. The Sabana–Cemeterio bus circumnavigates the downtown area, and provides a nice tour of the city for just 15¢. Taxis are also quite inexpensive, although you must insist on the use of the meter (*maría*) or agree on a price before you get in.

When it comes to dining, your best bet for saving money is a soda, which serves inexpensive Costa Rican–style meals. But no visit to San José would be complete without at least one meal or cup of coffee at the Gran Hotel's patio restaurant overlooking the National Theater and all the activity of Plaza de la Cultura.

By all means splurge and buy a ticket for a performance at the National Theater (*Teatro Nacional*). Although you can get a seat for as little as $2 or $3, live it up and spring for an orchestra seat. At most, it'll cost you $10 or $15 to hear the national symphony or see a touring opera company. You'll be hobnobbing with the elite of Costa Rica, so be sure to dress the part.

Afterward, head over to La Esmeralda and have a nightcap or a cup of coffee. Eavesdrop on the constant (and sometimes competing) serenades of the resident mariachi bands. There's no cover charge. If you want a private concert, the going rate is $3 to $7 per song.

Movies are also a great bargain in San José. First-run Hollywood productions (in English, with Spanish subtitles) usually arrive three months after their U.S. release. A ticket will only cost you $2.50. Try the Cine Variedades, Cine Rex, or Cine Magaly to remind yourself what movie theaters were like before the multiplex. For Latin American and European art films (often in their original language, with Spanish subtitles), head down Paseo Colón to the Sala Garbo.

On the streets of San José, you're likely to be bombarded with offers to take this tour or that excursion. Most of them can be replicated just as easily and at a fraction of the cost on public transport. Others are worth splurging on. If you've never been white-water rafting, you won't find a better place to try a one-day excursion than San José. If you dream of spending a day exploring remote islands surrounded by turquoise waters, take one of the day-long cruises around the Gulf of Nicoya (*Golfo de Nicoya*). Another excursion you might want to spring for is a trip to Tortuguero National Park, which combines a bus ride through Braulio Carrillo National Park with a boat ride along jungle canals, and affords a chance to see nesting sea turtles.

2   Orientation

ARRIVING

By Plane   Juan Santamaría International Airport (☎ **506/443-2942** for 24-hour airport information) is located near the city of Alajuela, about 20 minutes from downtown San José. You'll find a taxi stand upstairs to your left, just after you clear

San José

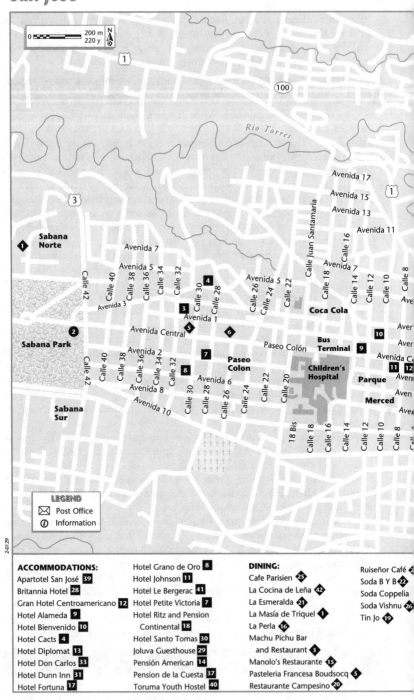

2-0129

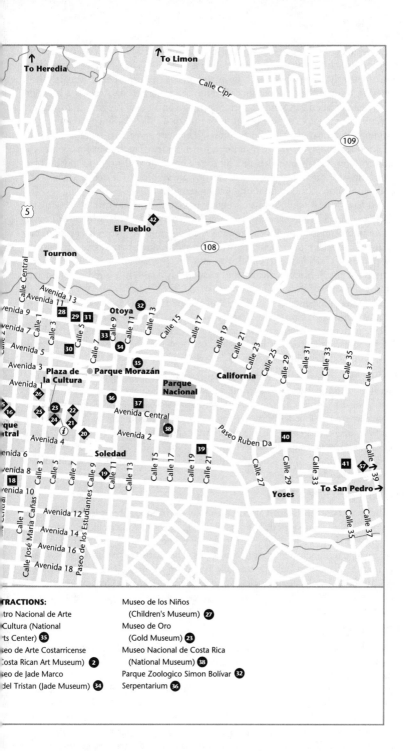

RACTIONS:

tro Nacional de Arte
Cultura (National
ts Center) **35**

seo de Arte Costarricense
Costa Rican Art Museum) **2**

seo de Jade Marco
del Tristan (Jade Museum) **34**

Museo de los Niños
(Children's Museum) **27**

Museo de Oro
(Gold Museum) **23**

Museo Nacional de Costa Rica
(National Museum) **38**

Parque Zoologico Simon Bolívar **32**

Serpentarium **36**

Customs. (A cab ride to downtown San José costs around $12.50.) A cheaper option is the bus, since the one-way fare to San José is only 45¢. The Alajuela–San José bus runs frequently, and stops to pick up passengers at the airport approximately 100 meters in front of the main terminal. It drops off passengers on Avenida 2 between Calle 12 and Calle 14 in San José. Before you hop on a bus at the airport, make sure to ask if it's going to San José or you may end up in Alajuela, since the route isn't prominently displayed on any of the buses. There are several car-rental agencies at the airport, although if you're planning to spend a few days in San José, a car is a liability. However, if you're heading off to the beach immediately, it's much easier to pick up your car at the airport than at a downtown office. Car-rental agencies are located on a little island in front of the main terminal.

You have several options for exchanging money when you arrive at the airport. There's an official state bank inside the main terminal. It's open Monday through Friday from 9am to 4pm. When the bank is closed (and even when it's open), there are usually official money changers (with badges) working both inside and outside the terminal. Outside the terminal, you may be approached by unofficial money changers. Though black-market money changing is illegal, it is quite common and the airport is one of the safer places to try it.

Even though the distance is negligible, and you are certainly welcome to do it yourself, it is common to have a porter carry your bags to a taxi or rental-car agency. Most of these porters wear a uniform identifying them as such, but sometimes moonlighters will try to earn a few dollars here. Either way, make sure you keep an eye on your bags. You should tip the porters about 50¢ per bag.

By Bus   If you arrived in Costa Rica over land and are coming to San José for the first time by bus, where you disembark depends on where you're coming from. Bus companies have offices all over downtown San José. Ask the bus company you've chosen where you'll be let off when you buy your ticket. In general, buses arriving from Nicaragua first enter the city on the west end of town on Paseo Colón. If you are staying here you can ask to be let off before the final stop. Buses entering from Panama pass first through Cartago and San Pedro before letting passengers off in downtown San José.

VISITOR INFORMATION

There is an **ICT (Instituto Costarricense de Turismo)** office at Juan Santamaría International Airport, open daily from 8am to 5pm, where you can pick up maps and brochures before you head into San José. You'll find the office just to the left after you exit the terminal, having cleared customs. The **main tourist information center** is at the Plaza de la Cultura, on Calle 5 between Avenida Central and Avenida 2 (☎ **506/222-1090**), beside the entrance to the underground Gold Museum. The representatives are very helpful. The office is open Monday through Friday from 9am to 5pm and Saturday from 9am to 1pm.

CITY LAYOUT

Main Arteries & Streets   Downtown San José is laid out on a grid. *Avenidas* (avenues) run east and west, while *calles* (streets) run north and south. The center of the city is at Avenida Central and Calle Central. To the north of Avenida Central, the avenidas have odd numbers beginning with Avenida 1; to the south, they have even numbers beginning with Avenida 2. Likewise, calles to the east of Calle Central have odd numbers, and those to the west have even numbers. The main downtown artery is Avenida 2, which merges with Avenida Central on either side of the downtown area. West of downtown, Avenida Central becomes Paseo Colón, which ends at Sabana Park and feeds into the highway to Alajuela, the airport, and the

"I know there's got to be a number here somewhere . . . ": The Arcane Art of Finding an Address in San José

This is one of the most confusing aspects of visiting San José in particular and Costa Rica in general. Though there are often street addresses and building numbers for locations in downtown San José, they are almost never used. Addresses are given as a set of coordinates such as "Calle 3 between Avenida Central and Avenida 1." It is then up to you to locate the building within that block, keeping in mind that the building could be on either side of the street. Many addresses include additional information, such as the number of meters or *varas* (an old Spanish measurement roughly equal to a yard) from a specified intersection or some other well-known landmark. These landmarks are what become truly confusing for visitors to the city because they are often simply restaurants, bars, and shops that would only be familiar to locals. Things get even more confusing when the landmark in question no longer exists. The classic example of this is the Coca-Cola plant, one of the most common landmarks used in addresses in the blocks surrounding San José's main market. It refers to a Coca-Cola bottling plant that once stood in this area. Unfortunately, the edifice is long gone, but the address descriptions remain. You may also try to find someplace near the *antiguo higuerón* (old fig tree) in San Pedro. This tree was felled years ago. In outlying neighborhoods, addresses can become long directions such as "50 meters south of the old church, then 100 meters east, then 20 meters south." Luckily for the visitor, most downtown addresses are straightforward. If you're wondering how mail deliverers manage, you'll be reassured to know that nearly everyone in San José uses a post-office box. This is called the *apartado* system, and is abbreviated Apdo. or A.P. on mailing addresses.

Pacific coast. East of downtown, Avenida Central leads to San Pedro and then to Cartago and the Interamerican Highway heading south. Calle 3 will take you out of town to the north and put you on the road to the Caribbean coast.

NEIGHBORHOODS IN BRIEF

San José is sprawling. Today it is divided into dozens of neighborhoods known as *barrios*. Most of the listings in this chapter fall within the main downtown area, but there are a few outlying neighborhoods you will need to know about.

Downtown   This is San José's busiest area and where you'll find most of the city's museums. There are also many tour companies, restaurants, and hotels. Unfortunately, traffic noise and exhaust fumes make this one of the least pleasant parts of the city. Streets and avenues are usually bustling and crowded with pedestrians and vehicular traffic, and street crime is rampant here.

Barrio Amon/Barrio Otoya   These two neighborhoods, just north and east of downtown, are the site of the greatest concentration of historic buildings in San José. Over the past few years, enterprising entrepreneurs have renovated these old buildings and turned them into hotels. If you're looking for character and don't mind noise and exhaust fumes, this neighborhood makes a good base for exploring the city.

La Sabana/Paseo Colón   Paseo Colón, a wide boulevard west of downtown, is an extension of Avenida Central and ends at La Sabana Park. It has several good, small hotels and numerous excellent restaurants. This is also where many of the city's rental-car agencies have their offices. Because this area is really part of downtown, I have not treated it as a separate area in the hotel and restaurant listings.

San Pedro/Los Yoses Located east of downtown San José, Los Yoses is an upper-middle class neighborhood that is home to many diplomatic missions and embassies. San Pedro is a little farther east and is the site of the University of Costa Rica. There are numerous college bars and clubs all around the edge of the campus and several good restaurants and small hotels in both neighborhoods.

Escazú/Santa Ana Located in the hills west of San José, Escazú and Santa Ana are suburbs with a small-town feel. Although they're only 15 minutes from San José by taxi, they feel much farther away because of their relaxed atmosphere. Many expatriates have settled here, and there are quite a few charming bed-and-breakfasts.

3 Getting Around

By Bus Bus transportation around San José is cheap—the fare is usually somewhere around 15¢. The most important buses are those running east and west along Avenida 2 and Avenida 3. The Sabana–Cementerio bus runs from Sabana Park to downtown and is one of the most convenient buses to use. You'll find a bus stop for the outbound Sabana–Cementerio bus across the street from Costa Rica Expeditions on Avenida 3 near the corner of Calle Central. San Pedro buses leave from the Social Security building on Avenida 2, and will take you out of downtown heading east. Buses are always boarded from the front, and the bus drivers can make change, although they don't like to receive larger bills. Be especially mindful of your wallet, purse, or other valuables, since pickpockets often work the crowded buses.

By Taxi Although taxis in San José have meters (*marías*), drivers sometimes refuse to use them, so occasionally you'll have to negotiate the price. However, always try to get them to use the meter first. The official rate at press time is around 65¢ for the first kilometer and around 25¢ for each additional kilometer. If you have a rough idea of how far it is to your destination, you can estimate how much it should cost from these figures. After 10pm taxis are legally allowed to add a 20% surcharge to the fare. Some of the meters are programmed to automatically include the extra charge. Be careful during the daytime, as some drivers will use the evening setting then as well, or try to charge an extra 20% on top of the higher meter setting. Tipping taxi drivers is not expected. You'll find taxis in front of the Teatro Nacional (high prices) and around the Parque Central at Avenida Central and Calle Central. Taxis in front of hotels and the El Pueblo tourist complex usually charge more than others, although this is technically illegal. You can also get a cab by calling 235-9966, 224-6969, or 226-1366.

On Foot Downtown San José is very compact. Nearly every place you might want to go is within a 15-by-4 block area. Because of the traffic congestion, you'll often find it faster to walk than to take a bus or taxi. Be careful when walking the streets by day or night. Flashy jewelry, loosely held handbags or backpacks, and expensive camera equipment tend to attract thieves. You should also watch your step. Between earthquakes, wear and tear, and negligence, sidewalks in San José have become veritable obstacle courses, and the cause of more than one sprained ankle. Avenida Central is a pedestrians-only street for several blocks around Calle Central toward the Cultural Plaza. At press time they were repaving this section of the avenue to create a pedestrian mall.

By Motorcycle Motorcycles cost approximately the same amount to rent as cars—$35 a day or $210 a week. Due to poor road conditions, they are not recommended unless you are an experienced rider. If you really want to rent a motorcyle in the San

José area, try **Heat Rent A Moto,** Avenida 2 between calles 11 and 13 (☎ **506/ 221-6671**).

By Car   It will cost you around $40 per day to rent a car in Costa Rica, unless you make a reservation before you leave home. If you do decide to rent a car, and pick it up in downtown San José, be prepared for some very congested streets. The following international companies have desks at Juan Santamaría International Airport, as well as offices downtown: **Avis** (☎ 800/331-1212 in the U.S., 506/442-1321 at the airport, or 506/232-9922 in downtown San José); **Budget** (☎ 800/527-0700 in the U.S., 506/441-4444 at the airport, or 506/223-3284 in downtown San José); **Hertz** (☎ 800/654-3131 in the U.S., 506/221-1818 at the airport, or 506/223-5959 in downtown San José); and **National** (☎ 800/328-4567 in the U.S., 506/441-6533 at the airport, or 506/233-4044 in downtown San José). **Thrifty** has an office in downtown San José (☎ 800/367-2277 in the U.S., or 506/255-4141).

You will save somewhere between $35 and $75 per week on a car rental if you make a reservation in your home country at least one week before you need the car. For example, the least-expensive Avis car available rents for about $276 per week, plus insurance (for a total of around $374) in San José, but if you book this same car in advance from the United States, you can get it for $198 per week, plus insurance (for a total of around $296). Though it is possible at some rental-car agencies to waive the insurance charges, you will have to pay all damages before leaving the country if you are in an accident. Even if you do take the insurance, you will have a deductible of between $500 and $1,250. At some agencies you can buy additional insurance to lower the deductible.

There are dozens of other rental-car agencies in San José, most of which will arrange for airport or hotel pickup or delivery. Some of the more dependable agencies include: **Ada Rent a Car,** 50 meters north of Pizza Hut on Paseo Colón (☎ 506/ 233-7733, or 800/232-7368 in the U.S.); **Adobe Rent a Car,** Calle 7 between avenidas 8 and 10 (☎ 506/221-5425); **American Rent a Car,** 425 meters north of the Toyota dealership on Paseo Colón (☎ 506/221-5353); **Hola! Rent a Car,** west of Hotel Irazú, La Uruca, San José (☎ 506/231-5666); **Elegante Rent A Car,** Calle 10 between avenidas 13 and 15 and Paseo Colón at Calle 34 (☎ 506/221-0066, or 800/582-7432 in the U.S.); and **Tico Rent A Car,** Paseo Colón between calles 24 and 26 (☎ 506/222-8920 or 506/223-9642).

To rent a car in Costa Rica, you must be at least 21 years old, and have a valid driver's license and a major credit card in your name.

FAST FACTS: San José

American Express   American Express (☎ **257-1792**) has a counter in San José at the Banco de San José on Calle Central between avenidas 3 and 5. It's open Monday through Friday from 8am to 7pm, and Saturday 9am to 1pm. To report a lost or stolen card from inside Costa Rica, call 001-800-528-2121.

Airport   See "Arriving," earlier in this chapter.

Babysitting   Ask at the front desk of your hotel. This may or may not be possible to arrange.

Bookstores   Chispas Books, Calle 7 between avenidas 1 and Central (☎ **256-8251**), has a wide range of new and used books in English, with an excellent selection of tropical biology, bird, and flora books; it's open daily from 9am to 7pm. For used books in English, stop by **Book Traders** (☎ **255-0508**), open

Monday through Saturday from 9am to 6pm and Sunday from 10am to 5pm; it's located on Avenida 1 between calles 5 and 7.

Camera Repair   Equipos Fotograficos Canon, Avenida 3 between calles 3 and 5 (☎ 233-0176), specializes in Canon, but may be able to repair other brands.

Car Rentals   See "Getting Around," in this chapter.

Climate   See "When to Go," in chapter 4.

Country Code   The country code for Costa Rica is 506; there are no city or area codes.

Currency Exchange   The best thing to do is to exchange money at your hotel. If they can't do this for you, they can direct you to a private bank where you won't have to stand in line for hours. Avoid exchanging money on the street.

Dentist   If you need a dentist while in San José, your best bet is to call your embassy, which will have a list of recommended dentists. Many bilingual dentists also advertise in the *Tico Times*. Because treatments are so inexpensive in Costa Rica, dental tourism has become a popular option for people needing extensive work.

Doctor   Contact your embassy for information on doctors in San José.

Drugstores   There are countless pharmacies and drugstores in San José. Many of them will deliver at little or no extra cost. **Farmacia Fischel,** Avenida 3 and Calle 2, is across from the main post office (☎ 257-7979). It's open Monday through Saturday from 8am to 7pm.

Embassies/Consulates   See "Fast Facts: Costa Rica," in chapter 4.

Emergencies   In case of **fire,** dial 118; for the **police,** dial 117; for an **ambulance,** dial 128; and for general **emergencies,** dial 911.

Express Mail Services   Many international courier and express mail services have offices in San José, including: **DHL** on Paseo Colón between calles 30 and 32 (☎ 290-3020); **EMS Courier** with desks at the principal metropolitan post offices (☎ 233-2762); and **United Parcel Service,** Avenida 3 between calles 30 and 32 (☎ 257-7447). *Beware:* Despite what you may be told, packages sent overnight to U.S. addresses tend to take 3 to 4 days to reach their destination.

Eyeglasses   Look for the word *optica*. **Optica Jiménez** (☎ 257-4658 or 233-4475) and **Optica Vision** (☎ 255-2266) are two dependable chains, with stores around San José. They can do everything from eye exams to repairs.

Holidays   See "When to Go," in chapter 5.

Hospitals   Clinica Biblica, Avenida 14 between Calle Central and Calle 1 (☎ 257-0466 for emergencies or 257-5252), is conveniently located close to downtown and has several English-speaking doctors.

Laundry/Dry Cleaning   Sixaola, Avenida 2 between calles 7 and 9 (☎ 221-2111), is open Monday through Friday from 7am to 6pm and Saturday from 8am to 1pm; it's a dependable place downtown to get clothes cleaned. Alternatively, ask at your hotel—most offer a laundry service, even though it is often expensive.

Libraries   The Centro Cultural Norteamericano-Costarricense, Calle 35 in Los Yoses (☎ 225-9433) has the most extensive English-language library in town. Tourists can get a temporary library card here for about $20, plus a $25 refundable deposit. The National Library is at the corner of Avenida 3 and Calle 15.

Lost Property   If you lose something in San José, consider it gone.

Luggage Storage/Lockers   Most hotels will store luggage for you while you are traveling around the country. Sometimes there is a charge for this service.

Maps   The Costa Rican Tourist Board (ICT) (see "Visitor Information," earlier in this chapter) can usually provide you with good maps of both Costa Rica and San José. Other sources in San José are **Chispas Books,** Calle 7 between avenidas Central and 1 (☎ 256-8251); Libreria Lehmann, Avenida Central between calles 1 and 3 (☎ 223-1212); and **Jiménez & Tanzi,** Calle 3 between avenidas 1 and 3 (☎ 233-8033).

Newspapers/Magazines   The *Tico Times* is Costa Rica's principal English-language weekly paper and serves both the expatriate community and tourists. You will also see *Costa Rica Today,* a bilingual weekly, geared towards tourists, which has almost no news. You can get the *International Herald Tribune,* the *Miami Herald,* the *New York Times, USA Today, Time,* and *Newsweek* as well as other English-language publications. You'll find these publications in hotel gift shops and in bookstores selling English-language books.

Photographic Needs   Film is expensive in Costa Rica, so bring as much as you will need. In a pinch, you can buy film and other photographic equipment at several places around town. I recommend that you wait to have your film processed at home, but if you must develop your prints down here, try **Fuji Foto,** Avenida Central between Calle 1 and Calle Central (☎ **222-2222**).

Police   Dial 117 for the police.

Post Office   The **main post office** (*correo*) is on Calle 2 between avenidas 1 and 3. It's open Monday through Friday from 7am to 10pm, and Saturday from 8am to noon for purchasing stamps from vending machines. For window service, the hours are Monday through Friday from 8am to 5pm.

Radio/TV   There are about 10 TV channels available in San José, plus local cable and satellite TV from the United States. There are dozens of AM and FM radio stations.

Restrooms   These are known as *sanitarios* or *servicios sanitarios.* They are marked *damas* (women) and *hombres* or *caballeros* (men).

Safety   Never carry anything you value in your pockets or purse. Pickpockets and purse slashers are rife in San José, especially on public buses, in markets, or near a hospital. Leave your passport, money, and other valuables in your hotel safe, and only carry as much as you really need when you go out. It's a good idea to make a photocopy of your passport's opening pages and carry that with you. If you do carry anything valuable with you, keep it in a moneybelt or special passport bag around your neck. Day packs are a prime target of brazen pickpockets throughout the city. Stay away from the red-light district northwest of the Central Market. Also, be advised that the Parque Nacional is not a safe place for a late-night stroll.

   Other precautions include walking around corner vendors, not between the vendor and the building. The tight space between the vendor and the building is a favorite spot for pickpockets. Never park a car on the street, and never leave anything of value in a car, even if it's in a guarded parking lot. Don't even leave your car by the curb in front of a hotel while you dash in to check on your reservation. With these precautions in mind you should have a safe visit to San José. Also see "Safety," in "Fast Facts: Costa Rica," in chapter 5.

Taxes All hotels charge a 18.45% tax. Restaurants charge a 15% tax and also add on a 10% service charge, for a total of 25% more on your bill. There is an airport departure tax of $16.50 per person.

Taxis See "Getting Around," earlier in this chapter.

Telephones Pay phones are not as common in San José as they are in North American cities. When you do find one, whether on the street or in a restaurant or hotel lobby, it may take coins of various denominations or it may take only 5- or 10-colón coins. A call within the city will cost 10 colónes. Pay phones are notoriously unreliable, so it may be better to make calls from your hotel, even though you're likely to be charged around 100 colónes per call.

See "Telephones & Faxes," under "Fast Facts: Costa Rica" in chapter 5 for information about international calling.

Time See "Fact Facts: Costa Rica," in chapter 5.

Useful Telephone Numbers For **directory assistance,** call 113; for international directory assistance, call 124; for the exact **time,** call 112.

Water See "Fast Facts: Costa Rica," in chapter 5.

Weather The weather in San José and the Central Valley is usually temperate, never getting extremely hot or cold. May to November is the rainy season, though the rain usually falls only in the afternoon and evening.

4 Where to Stay

Whereas once hotels were popping up all over downtown San José, in the last few years the hotel boom seems to have stopped. There is, in fact, a glut of hotels in San José. This is a boon for frugal travelers. A healthy degree of competition exists among the hotels, so it pays to shop around and ask if any are offering promotions or special packages when you plan to visit.

Of the many hotels in San José, your choices range from luxury resorts to budget pensions charging only a few dollars a night. However, these two extremes are the exceptions, not the norm. The vast number of accommodations, and the best deals, are to be found in the $30-to-$90 price range. Within this price bracket you'll find restored homes that have been turned into small hotels and bed-and-breakfasts. You will also find modern hotels with swimming pools and exercise rooms, and older downtown business hotels.

When considering where to stay in San José, you should take into consideration how long you plan to stay, what you expect to do while you're here, and whether or not you want to be in the heart of the city or out in the suburbs.

Downtown hotels, many of which are in beautifully restored homes, are convenient to museums, restaurants, and shopping, but are often very noisy. Many people are also bothered by the exhaust fumes that permeate downtown streets. If you want clean air and a peaceful night's sleep, consider staying out in the suburbs. Escazú is quiet and has great views, while Los Yoses is closer to the city, yet still quiet. If you've rented a car, I do not recommend staying at a downtown hotel because parking is often expensive and the traffic congestion trying, to say the least. If you plan to take some day tours, you can just as easily arrange these from a hotel situated outside downtown San José.

The city does have one budget alley, on Avenida 2 between calles 11 and 15. Here you'll find a half-dozen inexpensive *pensiones*, catering to backpackers and budget travelers. I've listed the most dependable of the bunch below, but since there are so many in such a concentrated area, it pays to visit a couple and look to see which is currently offering the best room at the best price.

In the past few years, dozens of bed-and-breakfast inns have opened up around the San José area. Most are in residential neighborhoods that are quieter, though less convenient, than downtown locations. You can find out about many bed-and-breakfasts by contacting the **Costa Rica Bed & Breakfast Group** (☎ **506/ 223-4168** or 506/228-9200).

If you plan to be in town for a while or are traveling with family or several friends, you may want to consider staying in an *apartotel.* As the name implies, these are a cross between an apartment and a hotel. You can rent by the day, week, or month, and you'll get a furnished apartment with a full kitchen, and housekeeping and laundry service.

A word about laundry service at hotels: Laundry is often charged by the piece and prices can be ludicrous. At one hotel, my wife and I did a quick tally of our dirty clothes and came up with something like $75 for a load of laundry. Rinse out your own clothes if possible, or take them to a laundromat.

Please keep in mind that the 18.45% hotel-room tax, which adds quite a bit to the price of a room, is not included in rates listed below. If you have set $40 as your total daily room budget, you will want to look for a hotel charging between $30 and $35 per night before tax.

DOWNTOWN SAN JOSÉ
DOUBLES FOR LESS THAN $25

Gran Hotel Centroamericano. Avenida 2 between calles 6 and 8 (Apdo. 3072-1000), San José. ☎ **506/221-3362.** Fax 506/221-3714. 45 rms (all with bath). TEL. $12 single; $15.30 double; $18.30 triple; $21.40 quad. No credit cards. Parking nearby.

Not to be confused with the nearby landmark Gran Hotel Costa Rica, this lodging is located at the back of a shopping arcade only two blocks from the terminal for airport buses, which makes the hotel a good choice if you will be arriving late in the evening. Rooms are small and dark but generally clean.

Hotel Diplomat. Calle 6 between Avenida Central and Avenida 2 (Apdo. 6606-1000), San José. ☎ **506/221-8133** or 506/221-8744. Fax 506/233-7474. 29 rms (all with bath). TEL. $18.50 single; $23.50–$25.25 double. AE, MC, V. Parking nearby.

It's easy to miss the entrance to this hotel. Watch for it on the east side of the street. The lobby is narrow, and the front door is fairly nondescript. The carpeted rooms are rather small but comfortable nonetheless, and some rooms on the upper floors have nice views of the mountains. The tiled baths are clean, and the water is hot. If you get too claustrophobic in your room, there's a sitting area on each floor. The hotel's restaurant is a very attractive dark room with pink tablecloths, flowers on every table, and pastel walls. For those seeking an intimate place for dinner, try one of the tiny booths for two. Prices range from $2.25 for a sandwich to $15 for a lobster dinner.

✪ **Hotel Bienvenido.** Calle 10 between avenidas 1 and 3 (Apdo. 389-2200), San José. ☎ **506/221-1872.** Fax 506/233-2161. 48 rms (44 with bath). $12 single; $19 double; $23 triple. No credit cards. Parking nearby.

This very basic hotel is one of the most popular in the city with travelers on a tight budget. The rooms are clean, though a bit dark, and there is always ample hot water. There are a few very inexpensive rooms with collective baths for groups of four or more. The property was created from an old movie theater, and there are still a few architectural details remaining from the building's former incarnation. This place fills up by early afternoon in the high season, so call ahead for a reservation and ask for a quiet room in the back.

Hotel Fortuna. Avenida 6 between calles 2 and 4 (Apdo. 7-1570), San José. ☎ **506/ 223-5344.** Fax 506/221-2406. 30 rms (all with bath). TEL. $16.30 single; $20.40 double; $24.50 triple; $29.30 quad. AE, MC, V.

Located only two blocks from the Parque Central, the Fortuna has a vague Chinese theme. The second-floor rooms are sunny and warm, and the first-floor rooms are cooler and darker. The brightness of the rooms makes this place feel much more cheery than other hotels, despite the lack of carpeting. Some of the rooms come with televisions, at no extra charge.

Hotel Johnson. Calle 8 between Avenida Central and Avenida 2 (Apdo. 6638-1000), San José. ☎ **506/223-7633** or 506/223-7827. Fax 506/222-3683. 57 rms, 3 suites (all with bath). TEL. $13.88 single; $15.10 double; $18.80 triple; $16.50–$22.80 suite. AE, DC, MC, V. Parking nearby.

The lobby of this large, centrally located hotel is on the second floor. You'll find the hotel patronized primarily by Costa Rican businesspeople and families, but it's a good choice for any budget traveler. In the lobby, there is a TV and several lounge chairs, and on each of the residence floors above, you'll find a sitting area. The rooms have tile floors and open onto a narrow air shaft that lets in a bit of light and noise from other rooms. Bathrooms are relatively clean and roomy. Most rooms come with twin beds. (You might want to test a few beds if you're picky about mattresses.) Depending on availability, you can pay a little extra for a color TV. There's a bar and a dining room where you can get inexpensive meals. The special of the day goes for $2.25, while à la carte meals run from $3 to $5.50.

Hotel Ritz and Pension Continental. Calle Central between avenidas 8 and 10 (Apdo. 6783-1000), San José. ☎ **506/222-4103.** Fax 506/222-8849. 25 rms (5 with bath). $6.50–$14.70 single without bath, $17.15 single with bath; $12.25–$19.60 double without bath, $23.70 double with bath; $15.50 triple without bath, $27 triple with bath; $18.80 quad without bath, $31 quad with bath. AE, MC, V. Parking nearby.

These adjacent lodgings are under the same management. Rooms vary greatly in size and comfort levels, but tend to be dark and a bit musty. Bathrooms are a bit old and those showers that do have hot water use showerhead heaters that just barely work. If the first room you see isn't to your liking, ask to see another in a different price category. The current owners are Swiss, so you'll probably meet quite a few Swiss travelers if you stay here. There's a travel agency and tour company on the first floor.

Pensión American. Calle 2 between Avenida Central and Avenida 2 (Apdo. 4853-1000), San José. ☎ **506/221-4171** or 506/221-9799. 35 rms (none with private bath). $6 single; $12 double. No credit cards. Parking nearby.

This is an old favorite with Central American backpackers. The rooms are dark, the beds are old and uncomfortable, and the walls are paper thin, but somehow this place is always full of hardy young travelers looking to save a few bucks.

Toruma Youth Hostel. Avenida Central between calles 29 and 31, San José. ☎ **506/ 224-4085.** 105 beds (all with shared bath). $6.50 per person per night with an IYHF card; $8.15 with student ID; $9.80 general public. MC, V. Free parking.

This attractive old building, with its long verandah, is the largest youth hostel in Costa Rica. Although it's possible to find other accommodations in San José in this price range, the rooms aren't likely to be as clean. The atmosphere is convivial and will be familiar to anyone who has hosteled in Europe. The large lounge in the center of the building has a high ceiling and a great deal of light. The dorms have four to six beds per room. The staff can help you arrange stays at other hostels as well as trips around the country, and you can store luggage here for 25¢ per day.

DOUBLES FOR LESS THAN $35

Hotel Alameda. Avenida Central between calles 12 and 14 (Apdo. 680), San José. ☎ **506/223-6333.** Fax 506/222-9673. 52 rms. TV TEL. $27.90 single; $31.80 double; $36.70 triple; $41.35 quad. All rates include breakfast. AE, DC, MC, V. Parking nearby.

This is another of San José's large old hotels, but a remodeled lobby and steady up-keep give it a modern feel. The rooms are of medium size, with carpeting, older furniture, small tiled baths, and plenty of closet space. There are large windows so the rooms are bright, but the windows also let in street noises. There's a large restaurant on the second floor. The menu features international and Costa Rican dishes at prices ranging from about $2.50 to $15. There is also room service and a laundry and dry-cleaning service.

Joluva Guesthouse. 936 Calle 3B between avenidas 9 and 11, San José. ☎ **800/298-2418** in the U.S. or 506/223-7961. Fax 506/257-7668 or 619/294-2418 in the U.S. 8 rms (6 with private bath). TV. $25 single without bath, $30 single with bath; $30 double without bath, $40 double with bath. All rates include breakfast. MC, V. Parking nearby.

Though you can find less expensive lodgings than the Joluva, few offer the same degree of old-fashioned architectural detail. Throughout, there are old tile and hard-wood floors and high ceilings. (One room has beautiful plasterwork on the ceiling.) The one drawback is the small size of the rooms. They're also a bit dark, with windows that open into a covered courtyard. In contrast, the breakfast room has skylights which brighten it considerably. The Joluva caters to a gay clientele, but all guests are welcome.

✪ Pensión de la Cuesta. 1332 Cuesta de Nuñez, Avenida 1 between calles 11 and 15. ☎/fax **506/255-2896.** 9 rms (none with private bath). $18 single; $26 double; $34 triple. All rates include continental breakfast. MC, V. Parking nearby.

If you don't mind a clean collective bathroom down the hall from your room, this little bed-and-breakfast is definitely worth considering. It was once the home of Otto Apuy, a well-known Costa Rican artist, and his original artwork is on display throughout. The building itself is a classic example of a tropical wood-frame home and has been painted an eye-catching pink with blue-and-white trim. The rooms can be a bit dark and are very simply furnished, but there is a very sunny and cheery sunken lounge-court area in the center of the house. You'll find this lodging on the hill leading up to the Parque Nacional.

DOUBLES FOR LESS THAN $45

Hotel Cacts. 2845 Avenida 3 between calles 28 and 30 (Apdo. 379-1005), San José. ☎ **506/221-2928** or 506/221-6546. Fax 506/221-8616. 25 rms (21 with private bath). 31–$40 single; $35–$50 double; $45–$55 triple. All rates include continental breakfast. No credit cards. Free parking.

This is one of the most interesting and unusual lodgings I've ever seen. Housed in an attractive contemporary home built onto a slope on a mixed-use (business and residential) street, it has rooms on several levels. The newer ones have telephones and televisions. My favorite is a huge bi-level room with a high beamed ceiling. Breakfast is served on a third-floor terrace. The staff is very helpful: They'll send and receive mail and faxes, exchange money, and store baggage for guests. There's also a tour desk and gift shop.

✪ Hotel Petite Victoria. Paseo Colón, Frente a la Sala Garbo, San José. ☎ **506/233-1812** or 506/233-1813. Fax 506/233-1812. 15 rms (all with bath). TV. $32.60 single; $44.80 double; $53 triple. AE, MC, V. Free parking.

One of the oldest buildings in San José, this tropical Victorian home once served as campaign headquarters for Oscar Arias Sánchez, Costa Rica's former president. Today, after extensive remodeling and restoration, it is an interesting little hotel that offers a historic setting at inexpensive rates. The big covered patio is perfect for lounging in the warm sun and doubles as the hotel's restaurant. Guest rooms have high ceilings and fans to keep the air cool, and medium-to-large tiled bathrooms. Inside, walls are made of wood, so noise can be a bit of a problem, but this is a small price to pay for such old-fashioned elegance. Tour arrangements and laundry service are also offered.

LONG-TERM STAYS

Apartotel San José. Avenida 2 between calles 17 and 19 (P.O. Box 4192-1000), San José. ☎ **800/575-1253** in the U.S. or 506/265-2191. Fax 506/221-6684. 12 apts. TV TEL. $51 single; $61–$65 double; $71–$75 triple. MC, V. Free parking.

Operated by the same company that runs Amstel hotels, this apartotel is located across the street from the National Museum. The furnishings are a bit dated, but there's plenty of space. The building is on a side street off Avenida 2. Though it is fairly quiet, try to get a room as far from the avenue as possible. There are other apartotels around town, but this is the most centrally located and convenient. Maid, laundry, and valet service are all available.

WORTH A SPLURGE

All of the lodgings listed below exceed our daily budget, but offer a level of hospitality, personal service, and charm that justifies their inclusion here. Each was formerly a home, and most are colonial-era mansions. Whether you're looking for a special treat for a night, or just want a bit more peace and tranquillity in the city, these lodgings are worthy of your consideration.

✪ **Britannia Hotel.** Calle 3 and Avenida 11 (Apdo. 3742-1000), San José. ☎ **800/263-2618** in the U.S. or 506/223-6667. Fax 506/223-6411. 24 rms. TV TEL. $73–$97 single; $85–$108 double. AE, DC, MC, V. Parking nearby.

Of the many hotels that have been created from older restored houses in downtown San José, this is the most luxurious. The big, pink building, with its wraparound verandah, is unmistakable and certainly one of the most attractive buildings in the neighborhood. In the lobby, tile floors, stained-glass clerestory windows, a brass chandelier, and reproduction Victorian decor all help set a tone of tropical luxury. After the renovation of the original structure was complete, the owners built a four-story addition, which is separated from the former by a narrow atrium. Rooms in the original home have hardwood floors and furniture; high ceilings and fans help keep them cool. In the deluxe rooms, you'll find a hair dryer and basket of toiletries in the bathroom. Though the streetside rooms have double-glass windows, light sleepers will want to avoid these rooms. The quietest rooms are those toward the back of the addition. In what was once the wine cellar, you'll find a casual restaurant. A buffet breakfast is served in the adjacent skylit room. Afternoon tea and happy-hour drinks are also served. There is room service, and the hotel has an airport shuttle.

✪ **Hotel Don Carlos.** 779 Calle 9 between avenidas 7 and 9, San José (mailing address in the U.S.: Dept. 1686, P.O. Box 025216, Miami, FL 33102-5216). ☎ **506/221-6707.** Fax 506/255-0828. 36 rms. $40–$50 single; $50–$60 double. All rates include continental breakfast. AE, MC, V. Parking nearby.

If you're looking for a small hotel that is unmistakenly tropical and hints at the days of planters and coffee barons, this is the place for you. Located in an old residential neighborhood only a few blocks from the business district, the Don Carlos is popular with both vacationers and businesspeople. A large pre-Columbian reproduction of a carved-stone human figure stands outside the front door of this gray inn, which was a former president's mansion. Inside you'll find many more pre-Columbian stone reproductions, as well as orchids, ferns, palms, and parrots. The wicker furniture in the lounge and the small courtyard leading to a sunny deck with a bubbling fountain tempt guests to relax in the tropical breezes after a day of exploring the capital. Most of the rooms are quite large, and each is a little different from the others. In case you're interested, the paintings throughout the hotel are for sale. The gift shop is one of the largest in the country, and there's a helpful in-house tour company. Complimentary breakfast and moderately priced meals are served in the Pre-Columbian Lounge. Unfortunately, many people can't tolerate the traffic noises here.

Hotel Dunn Inn. Calle 5 and Avenida 11 (Apdo. 6241-1000), San José. ☎ **506/222-3232** or 506/222-3426. Fax 506/221-4596. 27 rms, 1 suite. TV TEL. $45–$55 single or double; $88.50 suite. All rates include continental breakfast. AE, V. Free parking.

Located in the Barrio Amon historic neighborhood, the Dunn Inn is among the better small hotels in the area, offering quiet sophistication at reasonable rates. Part of it is housed in a century-old mansion, while other rooms are in a new wing. The courtyard of the old mansion has been partially covered and turned into a dining room and bar, which, if you have one of the rooms directly above, can be a bit noisy at night. Orchids and bromeliads hang from the brick walls, and a fountain bubbles away beside a huge philodendron. The new wing has some very nice rooms with exposed brick walls. Although it is quite a bit more expensive, the one suite with a whirlpool bath, minibar, hardwood and carpeted floors, potted bromeliads, dual sinks, a lot of sunshine in the bathroom, and paneled walls is luxurious.

✪ **Hotel Grano de Oro.** 251 Calle 30, between avenidas 2 and 4, 150 meters south of Paseo Colón (Apdo. 1157-1007, Centro Colón), San José (mailing address in the U.S.: SJO 36, P.O. Box 025216, Miami, FL 33102-5216). ☎ **506/255-3322.** Fax 506/221-2782. 35 rms, 3 suites. TV TEL. $65–$87 single; $70–$92 double; $120–$140 suite. AE, MC, V (add 6% surcharge). Free parking.

San José boasts dozens of old homes that have been converted into hotels, but few offer the luxurious accommodations or professional service that can be found at the Grano de Oro. Located on a quiet side street off Paseo Colón, this small hotel offers a variety of room types to fit most budgets and tastes. Personally, I like the patio rooms, which have French doors opening onto private patios. However, if you want plenty of space, ask for one of the deluxe rooms, which have large, modern, tiled baths with big tubs. Throughout all the guest rooms, you'll find attractive hardwood furniture, including old-fashioned wardrobes in some rooms. For additional luxury, you can stay in one of the suites, which have whirlpool tubs. The hotel's patio garden restaurant serves excellent international meals and some of the best desserts in the city, and when it comes time to relax you can soak in a hot tub or have a drink in the rooftop lounge, which has a commanding view of San José.

✪ **Hotel Santo Tomas.** Avenida 7 between calles 3 and 5, San José. ☎ **506/255-0448.** Fax 506/222-3950. 20 rms. TV TEL. $50–$75 single; $55–$85 double; $85–$95 triple (5% discount on entire stay after 3 consecutive days). All rates include continental breakfast. Credit cards accepted to guarantee a room reservation only. Parking nearby.

Even though it's on an otherwise nondescript street, this converted mansion is a real jewel inside. Built approximately 100 years ago by a coffee baron, it was once slated to be bulldozed in order to expand the Aurola Holiday Inn's parking lot. Under the direction of American Thomas Douglas, the old mansion has been restored to its former grandeur. The first thing you'll see when you walk through the front door is the beautifully carved wooden desk that serves as the reception area. Throughout the guest rooms you'll find similar pieces, exquisitely crafted from rare Costa Rican hardwoods. The hardwood floors throughout most of the hotel are original and were made from a type of tree that has long since become almost impossible to find. The rooms vary in size, but most are fairly large and have a small table and chairs. Maps of Costa Rica hang on the walls of all the guest rooms, so you can get acquainted with the country. If light is important to you in the morning, ask for one of the rooms that has a skylight in the bath. There are a couple of patio areas, as well as a TV lounge and combination breakfast room and outdoor bar. Laundry service and a baggage storage room are available. The staff and management are extremely helpful with tour arrangements and any other needs or requests. The Santo Tomas recently acquired the adjacent property, and there's talk of expansion and even a swimming pool.

SMALL HOTELS IN SAN PEDRO/LOS YOSES
DOUBLES FOR LESS THAN $35

D'Galah Hotel. Calle Masis, 100 meters past Calle La Cruz (Apdo. 208-2350), San José. ☎/fax **506/234-1743.** 30 rms. TV TEL. $27.50 single; $33.50–$43.25 double. AE, MC, V. Free parking.

If you want to be close to downtown, but away from the smog and traffic, this affordably priced hotel is a good choice. It sits directly across the street from the University of Costa Rica, an oasis of greenery that attracts many species of birds, especially among the bamboo groves. Rooms are a bit old-fashioned and dark, but if you aren't too demanding, you'll find them quite spacious and acceptable. The largest have kitchenettes and sleeping lofts, and the newest have carpets and tiny private patios. Amenities include a small swimming pool, a sauna, and a breakfast room.

WORTH A SPLURGE

✪ **Hotel Le Bergerac.** 50 S. Calle 35 (Apdo. 1107-1002), San José. ☎ **506/234-7850.** Fax 506/225-9103. 18 rms. TV TEL. $58–$68 single; $68–$78 double. All rates include continental breakfast. Corporate rates are also available. AE, DC, MC, V. Free parking.

With all the sophistication and charm of a small French inn, the Hotel Le Bergerac has ingratiated itself into the hearts of repeat business travelers and members of various diplomatic missions. What won them over was the tranquil environment in a quiet suburban neighborhood, spacious and comfortable accommodations, personal service, and gourmet meals. Between the two of them, the owners have a total of 29 years of hotel experience, which may account for the professionalism with which Le Bergerac is operated. Comprised of three houses with courtyard gardens in between, almost all of the rooms are quite large, and each is a little different. My favorites are those with private patio gardens. Some have king beds, and in one, you'll find a little balcony. In the evening, candlelight and classical music set a relaxing and romantic mood. The innovative chef of Paprika Restaurant has recently set up shop here, and now gourmet French and continental dinners are available for guests and by reservation. The hotel also has a helpful tour desk.

SMALL HOTELS & BED-AND-BREAKFASTS IN ESCAZÚ

This affluent suburb about 15 minutes west of San José is popular with North American retirees and expatriates. Quite a few bed-and-breakfasts have sprung up to cater to the needs of visiting friends. If you're interested in staying here, you might contact the **Costa Rica Bed & Breakfast Group** (☎ **506/223-4168** or 506/228-9200).

DOUBLES FOR LESS THAN $45

Hotel Mirador Pico Blanco. Apdo. 900 Escazú. ☎ **506/289-6197.** Fax 506/289-5189. 23 rms. $35 single; $40 double; $45 triple. AE, MC, V. Free parking.

If you'd like a room with a view but can't afford the rates charged at most mountainside inns around the area, check out this cozy and casual hotel. There's nothing fancy about the rooms here, but there are absolutely fabulous views from most of them, as well as from the dining room and terrace. Some rooms have such high ceilings that an appearance of spaciousness is created, and almost all have balconies (albeit small ones). A pool with an inviting terrace has recently been added. The restaurant is a popular and inexpensive spot, possibly the cheapest with a view in the valley. A taxi from the airport will cost you about $15.

WORTH A SPLURGE

Costa Verde Inn. Apdo. 89, Escazú (mailing address in the U.S.: SJO 1313, Box 025216, Miami, FL 33102). ☎ **506/228-4080** or 506/289-9509. Fax 506/289-8591. 8 rms (6 with private bath). Nov 15–Apr 15: $35 single without bath, $50 single with bath; $50 double without bath, $60 double with bath; $70 triple with bath. Apr 16–Nov 15: lower rates apply. All rates include full breakfast. MC, V (add 8% surcharge). Free parking.

If you're a tennis player or someone who values peace and quiet, the Costa Verde Inn is an excellent choice. This sprawling, modern home incorporates flagstone and stone walls successfully throughout and has a vaguely colonial feel. A large and lush garden, complete with a lighted tennis court, surrounds it. My favorite rooms are the two by the tennis courts, one of which has a sunken stone-floored shower. Other rooms have hardwood floors; all have king-size beds. Common areas include a large living room with a fireplace and a wide tiled patio that overlooks the garden. Throughout, you'll see old black-and-white photos that have been hand-colored. Ask the innkeeper about the photographer who took these pictures. You can also find out about various excursions around the country here, and airport pickups can be easily arranged.

A LODGING NEAR THE AIRPORT

Hampton Airport Inn. Autopista General Cañas (Apdo. 962-1000), San José. ☎ **800/426-7866** in the U.S. or 506/443-0043. Fax 506/442-9539. 100 rms. TV TEL. Dec to March: $65 single, $79 double to quad; Apr to Nov: $54 single; $59 double to quad. All rates include continental breakfast. AE, MC, V. Free parking.

If familiarity, a basic level of comfort, and proximity to the airport are important to you, then the Hampton Airport Inn is your best bet. The rooms are what you'd expect from a budget chain, and since the property is new, they don't show much wear and tear. Amenities include an outdoor swimming pool, airport shuttle, free parking, and free local phone calls. This is a good choice if your plane arrives very late or leaves very early, and you don't plan on spending any time in San José.

5 Where to Eat

For decades, Costa Rican cuisine has been dismissed and disparaged. Rice and beans are served at nearly every meal, the selection is minimal, and Ticos generally don't go for spicy food, or so the criticism goes. In recent years, though, some contemporary and creative chefs have been trying to educate and enlighten the Costa Rican palate, particularly in San José, and the early results are promising. Still, most visitors to the capital city quickly tire of Tico fare, even in its more chi-chi incarnation, and start seeking out the many local restaurants serving international cuisines. They are richly rewarded.

San José has a rather amazing variety of restaurants serving cuisines from all over the world and you'll never pay much even at the best restaurants. In fact, you really have to work at it to spend more than $40 per person for an extravagant six- or seven-course meal (not including liquor). Most restaurants fall into the moderately priced range. However, service can be indifferent at many restaurants, since the gratuity is already tacked on to the check, and tipping is not common among locals.

For a true deal, head to a *soda,* the equivalent of a diner in the United States, where you can get good, cheap, and filling Tico food. Rice and beans are the staples here and show up at breakfast, lunch, and dinner. When mixed together, they're called *gallo pinto,* and are usually served for breakfast, garnished with everything from fried eggs to steak. At lunch and dinner, rice and beans are the main components of a *casado* (which means "married")—the Costa Rican equivalent of a "blue plate special." A casado generally is served with a salad of cabbage and tomatoes, fried bananas, and steak, chicken, or fish. A plate of gallo pinto might cost $2, and a casado might cost $2.75 or $3.

While in Costa Rica, be sure to taste a few *frescos.* A fresco is a bit like a fresh fruit milkshake without ice cream, and when made with mangos, papayas, bananas, or any of the other delicious tropical fruits of Costa Rica, it is pure ambrosia. Frescos can also be made with water (*con agua*), and preferences vary. Certain fruits like *carambola* (star fruit), *maracuya* (a type of passion fruit) and *cas* (you'll just have to try it), are never made with milk, only water. While the water in Costa Rica is generally very safe to drink, those with tender stomachs and intestinal tracts should stick to frescos made with milk.

The most expensive dishes in Costa Rican restaurants are those that contain shrimp or lobster. Other fish or meat dishes are always considerably less expensive. The price categories assigned to the restaurants listed below assume that you'll order one main course and one non-alcoholic drink. If you want to save money on a meal, skip wine, which is almost always imported and expensive. Feel free to indulge in the variety of local beers, however—many are quite good and all are inexpensive. *Note:* The prices stated below are exclusive of both the 15% restaurant tax and the 10% service charge that's tacked on to every meal.

IN DOWNTOWN SAN JOSÉ
MEALS FOR LESS THAN $6

Manolo's Restaurante. Avenida Central between calles Central and 2. ☎ **506/221-2041.** All items $3–$9.15. MC, V. Daily 11:30am–3pm, 6–10:30pm upstairs; 24 hours downstairs. COSTA RICAN.

Spread out over three floors, on a busy corner of Avenida Central, you'll find this roomy restaurant popular with Ticos and tourists alike. You can view the action in the street below, or catch one of the live folk-dance performances that are staged nightly. The open kitchen serves up steaks and fish, but there's also a popular buffet of traditional Costa Rican dishes for $5.50. Downstairs you'll find Manolo's Churreria, a good place for a quick sandwich and an espresso.

La Perla. Avenida 2 and Calle Central. ☎ **506/222-7492.** Reservations not accepted. Main courses $1.75–$6.90. MC, V. Daily 24 hours. INTERNATIONAL.

It's easy to walk right past this place (I did) the first time you try to find it. The entrance is on the corner directly across from the National Cathedral, and the restaurant itself is just below street level. Long on atmosphere it isn't, but the food is good and the portions are large. The house specialty is *paella,* a Spanish rice-and-seafood dish for only $5. Other good choices are *sopa de mariscos,* a seafood soup with mussels and clams in a delicious broth; and *huevos à la ranchera,* prepared a bit differently than in Mexico and a filling meal any time of the night or day. This is a good place to come after a show at the Melico Salazar Theater.

Restaurante Campesino. Calle 7 between avenidas 2 and 4. ☎ **506/255-1356.** Main courses $2.25–$5.50; whole chicken $5; half chicken $2.70. MC, V. Daily 11am–midnight. COSTA RICAN/CHINESE.

This little restaurant serves delicious chicken, so don't even think about ordering any of the Chinese dishes on the menu. The secret of this delectable chicken is in the wood fire over which the chicken is roasted. Depending on how hungry you are, you can get a quarter, half, or full chicken; you might also try the *palmito* (hearts of palm) salad. Eat here, or if you must, take an order to go. You can't miss this place—look for the smoking chimney high above the roof, or the window full of chickens roasting over an open fire at street level.

Soda B Y B. Calle 5 and Avenida Central. ☎ **506/222-7316.** Sandwiches $1.25–$3.50; breakfasts $1.15–$2.50; main courses $1.75–$3.50. DC, MC, V. Daily 8:30am–10pm. COSTA RICAN.

Located on the corner across from the Tourist Information Center on the Plaza de la Cultura, this spot is popular with downtown shoppers and office workers. Service is prompt, prices (and noise level) are low, and the food is surprisingly good for a sandwich shop. Slide into a high-backed wooden booth and order the *chalupa de pollo B Y B*—it's a sort of tostada piled high with chicken salad and drenched with sour cream and guacamole.

Soda Coppelia. Paseo Colón between calles 26 and 28. ☎ **506/223-8013.** Reservations not accepted. Main courses $1.75–$4.50. No credit cards. Mon–Sat 8am–7pm. COSTA RICAN.

If you're looking for a filling, cheap, and quick breakfast or lunch in the Paseo Colón area, I recommend this soda. You'll find it near the Universal movie theater. The wooden booths and a few tables on a covered walkway (noisy) are frequently full of local businesspeople because the meals are so reasonably priced. A thin steak will run you $2.20. The burgers, sandwiches, and baked goods (such as flaky empanadas or carrot bread) are all good choices.

Soda Vishnu. Avenida 1 between calles 1 and 3. ☎ **506/222-2549.** Reservations not accepted. Main courses $1.25–$2.50. No credit cards. Daily 7am–9:30pm. VEGETARIAN.

Vegetarians will most certainly find their way here. There are booths for two or four people and photo murals on the walls. At the cashier's counter you can buy natural cosmetics, honey, and bags of granola. However, most people just come for the filling *plato de dia* that includes soup, salad, veggies, an entrée, and dessert for around $2. There are also bean burgers and cheese sandwiches on whole-wheat bread. There is another Vishnu around the corner on Calle 3 between Avenida Central and Avenida 1.

MEALS FOR LESS THAN $12

Cafe Parisien. Gran Hotel Costa Rica, Avenida 2 between calles 1 and 3. ☎ **506/221-4011.** Sandwiches $2–$3.50; main courses $3–$19.20. AE, MC, V. Daily 24 hours. INTERNATIONAL.

The Gran Hotel Costa Rica is hardly the best hotel in San José, but it does have a picturesque patio cafe right on the Plaza de la Cultura. A wrought-iron railing, white columns, and arches create an Old World atmosphere, and on the plaza in front of the cafe a marimba band performs and vendors sell handcrafts. Open 24 hours a day, it's one of the best spots in town for people-watching. Stop by for the breakfast buffet ($6.50) and fill up as the plaza vendors set up their booths; peruse the *Tico Times* over coffee while you have your shoes polished; or simply bask in the tropical sunshine while you sip a beer. Lunch and dinner buffets are also offered for $7.50.

La Cocina de Leña. El Pueblo. ☎ **506/255-1360** or 506/223-3704. Main dishes $5 –$19.50. AE, DC, MC, V. Daily 11am–11pm. COSTA RICAN.

Located in the unusual El Pueblo shopping, dining, and entertainment center, La Cocina de Leña (The Wood Stove) has a rustic feel to it. There are stacks of firewood on shelves above the booths, long stalks of bananas hanging from pillars, tables suspended by heavy ropes from the ceiling, and most unusual of all—menus printed on paper bags. In many ways this is simply a glorified soda, but if you're adventurous you could try some of the more unusual dishes. Perhaps oxtail stew served with yuca and plátáno might appeal to you; if not, there are plenty of steaks and seafood dishes on the menu. *Chilasuilas* are delicious tortillas filled with fried meat. Black-bean soup with egg is a Costa Rican standard and is well done here, and the corn soup with pork is equally satisfying. For dessert there is *très leches* cake as well as the more distinctive sweetened *chiverre*, which is a type of squash that looks remarkably like a watermelon.

La Esmeralda. Avenida 2 between calles 5 and 7. ☎ **506/221-0530.** Main courses $3.50–$6.50. AE, DC, MC, V. Mon–Sat 11am–5am. COSTA RICAN.

No one should visit San José without stopping in at La Esmeralda at least once, the later at night the better. This is much more than just a restaurant serving Tico food: It is the Grand Central Station of Costa Rican mariachi bands. In fact, mariachis and other bands from throughout Central America and Mexico hang out here every night waiting for work. While they wait they often serenade diners in the cavernous open-air dining hall of the restaurant. Friday and Saturday nights are always the busiest, but you're bound to hear lots of excellent music any night of the week. A personal concert will cost you anywhere from $3 to $7 per song depending on the size of the group, but if you're on a tight budget, you'll still be able to hear just fine eavesdropping on your neighbors. The classic Tico food is quite good. Try the coconut flan for dessert.

Machu Pichu Bar and Restaurant. Calle 32 between avenidas 1 and 3, 150 meters north of the Kentucky Fried Chicken on Paseo Colón. ☎ **506/222-7384.** Main courses $3.50–$11. No credit cards. Daily 11am–3pm and 6–10pm. PERUVIAN/CONTINENTAL.

Located just off Paseo Colón near the Kentucky Fried Chicken, Machu Pichu is an unpretentious little restaurant that has become one of the most popular places in San José. The menu is primarily seafood (especially sea bass), and consequently most dishes tend toward the upper end of the menu's price range. Also, many of these fish dishes come in thick cream sauces. You're better off sticking with the two-person seafood sampler, combined with different appetizers. One of my favorite entrées is *Causa Limeña,* lemon-flavored mashed potatoes stuffed with shrimp. The ceviche here is excellent, as is the *aji de gallina,* a dish of chopped chicken in a fragrant cream sauce, and octopus with garlic butter. Be sure to ask for a *pisco sour,* a Peruvian specialty drink.

Pasteleria Francesa Boudsocq. Calle 30 at Paseo Colón. ☎ **506/222-6732.** Pastries $1.05–$2.75; main courses $3.50–$7.20. MC, V. Mon–Sat 8am–7pm. PASTRIES/FRENCH.

Ticos love their pastries and bakeries, and pastry shops abound all over San José. However, this little place on Paseo Colón is one of the best I've found. They have savory meat-filled pastries that make good lunches, as well as plenty of unusual sweets that are great afternoon snacks. Recently they've begun serving sit-down lunches. You can get a traditional casado, or a daily special with a French flair, like coq au vin. There are only a couple of tables here.

✪ **Ruiseñor Café.** Teatro Nacional, Avenida 2 between calles 3 and 5. ☎ **506/233-4488.** Sandwiches and soups $3.45–$4.50; main courses $4.40–$8. MC, V. Mon–Sat 10:30am–6pm. CONTINENTAL.

This is one of my favorite places to eat in all of San José. Even if there's nothing special at the Teatro Nacional during your visit, you can enjoy a meal or a cup of coffee here and soak up the neoclassical atmosphere. The theater was built in the 1890s from the designs of European architects, and the art nouveau chandeliers, ceiling murals, and marble floors and tables are purely Parisian. There are changing art displays by local artists to complete the très chic cafe atmosphere. The menu includes such continental dishes as quiche, Hungarian goulash soup, and wiener schnitzel, but the main attractions are the specialty cakes and tortes which are displayed in a glass case. Ice cream dishes are raised to a high art form here with names such as Passionate Love and Spaghetti ice cream. The ambience is classic French cafe, but the marimba music drifting in from outside the open window reminds you that you're still in Costa Rica. The owners run restaurants with similar menus at the Contemporary Art Museum in the Sabana Park and on Avenida Central in Los Yoses.

✪ **Tin Jo.** Calle 11 between avenidas 6 and 8. ☎ **506/221-7605.** Main courses $3.75–$10.15. AE, MC, V. Mon–Sat 11:30am–3pm and 5:30–10:30pm; Sun 11:30am–10pm. CHINESE/THAI.

San José has hundreds of Chinese restaurants, but most simply serve up tired takes on chop suey, chow mein, and fried rice. In contrast, Tin Jo has a wide and varied menu, with an assortment of Cantonese and Szechuan staples, as well as a few Thai dishes. The *mu shu* is so good here, you may even forgive the fact that the pancakes are actually thin flour tortillas. Some of the dishes are served in edible rice-noodle bowls, and the pineapple shrimp in coconut-milk curry is served in a hollowed-out half of a fresh pineapple. The bow-tied and vested waiters are helpful, and you'll have real tablecloths and cloth napkins. There's one table set in a small courtyard garden that adds a touch of romance to the meal.

WORTH A SPLURGE

✪ **La Masía De Triquel.** Sabana Norte, 175 meters north and 175 meters west of the Datsun Agency. ☎ **506/296-3528** or 506/232-3584. Reservations recommended on weekends. Main courses $6.50–$20.50. AE, DC, MC, V. Mon–Sat 11:30am–2pm and 6:30–11pm. SPANISH.

Despite the death of founding chef Francisco Triquell, a relocation, and a healthy field of competitors, La Masía de Triquel is still San José's finest Spanish restaurant. Francisco Triquell Jr. has seen to that. Service is extremely formal and the regular clientele includes most of the city's upper crust. Although Costa Rica is known for its beef, here you'll also find wonderfully prepared lamb, quail, and rabbit. Seafood dishes include the usual shrimp and lobster, but also squid and octopus. However, there is really no decision to be made when perusing the menu: Start with a big bowl of gazpacho and then spend the rest of the evening enjoying all the succulent surprises you'll find in a big dish of *paella.*

IN SAN PEDRO/LOS YOSES
MEALS FOR LESS THAN $12

✪ **Il Pirón.** Sabanilla, in front of the UNED, ☎ **506/234-7851.** Reservations recommended on weekends. Main courses $3.75–$12.50. MC, V. Tue–Sat 11am–3pm, 6–11pm; Sun 11am–3pm. ITALIAN.

When fire destroyed its first home, the owners' moved to the other side of the University, in Sabanilla. Service is formal, but not overbearing. Il Pirón feels like a quiet, neighborhood restaurant should—with great food and not much pretense. Toward the rear, the room opens onto a small interior garden with flowering heliconia and hanging orchids. The meat and fish dishes are wonderful, but don't pass on the pasta. Try the *spaghetti creola,* which contains shrimp in a fresh tomato sauce with hints of curry and vodka. The tagliatelle is homemade and the foccacia with rosemary is divine. Whenever I go, it seems the conversation at the tables around me is mostly in Italian—always a good sign.

WORTH A SPLURGE

✪ **Bijahua.** 50 meters west and 300 meters south of Mas X Menos in San Pedro. ☎ **506/ 225-0613.** Reservations recommended. Main courses $6.80–$19.80. AE, MC, V. Mon–Fri noon– 2:30pm, 7–10:30pm; Sat 6:30–11pm. COSTA RICAN.

This restaurant is almost single-handedly seeking to erase Costa Rica's historical culinary infamy. Using traditional ingredients, chef Isabel Campabadal has created an exotic and innovative menu. Instead of potato, the gnocchi are made from ñampi, an indigenous tubor, and the tamale appetizer is made from pejibaye, a diminutive palm nut. Main dishes include red snapper stuffed with green plantain purée and shrimp croquettes topped with a maracuyá sauce. Whatever you do, save room for the passion fruit soufflé. The service and setting are both elegant, and it pays to come for lunch, when the atrium ceiling and an entire wall of orchids can be seen in their full splendor.

IN ESCAZÚ

Muy. One kilometer above the Pico Blanco Inn. ☎ **506/254-6281.** Reservations recommended on weekends. Main courses $3.25–$7.25. MC, V. Mon–Fri 5–11pm; Sat–Sun noon– 11pm. BBQ/TEX MEX.

Located high on a hill above Escazú, this casual restaurant combines great views with classic barbecue and Tex-Mex cooking. The best views are from the small outdoor deck, but you'll be seated on plastic lawn chairs. Inside is less scenic, but more formal. The same menu is served inside and out, and the portions are hefty. Stick to the standards— chicken fajitas or barbeque ribs—and wash it all down with a tangy margarita.

STREET FOOD & LATE-NIGHT BITES

On almost every street corner in downtown San José you'll find a fruit vendor. If you're lucky enough to be in town between April and June you can sample more varieties of mangoes than you ever knew existed. I like buying them already cut up in a little bag. They cost a little more this way but you don't get nearly as messy. Be sure to try a green mango with salt and chili peppers. That's the way they seem to like mangoes best in the steamy Tropics—guaranteed to wake up your taste buds. Another common street food that you might be wondering about is called *pejibaye,* a bright orange palm nut about the size of a small apple. They are boiled in big pots on carts. You eat them in much the same way you would an avocado, and they taste a bit like squash.

If it's 1am and you've just got to grab a bite, you're in luck. San José has quite a few all-night restaurants including La Perla, La Esmeralda, and Cafe Parisien, all of which are described above. Another popular place, which is almost exclusively for men, is the Soda Palace on Avenida 2 and Calle 2 (see "San José After Dark" for more information).

6 Seeing the Sights

Most visitors to Costa Rica try to get out of the city as fast as possible so they can spend more time on the beach or off in the rain forests. Before you join them, take some time to enjoy the country's main metropolis—there are quite a few attractions here to keep you busy for a while. Some of the best and most modern museums in

Central America are in San José, several of which have a wealth of fascinating pre-Columbian artifacts. New additions include a modern and expansive children's museum, as well as a centrally located National Arts Center, with a museum and several performing-arts spaces. There are great things to see and do just outside San José in the Central Valley. If you start doing day trips out of the city, you can spend quite a few days in this region.

THE TOP ATTRACTIONS

☼ Centro Nacional de Arte y Cultura (National Arts Center). Calle 13 between avenidas 3 and 5. ☎ **506/255-2468.** Free admission. Tue–Sun 10am–4:30pm. Bus: Any downtown bus.

Occupying a full city block, this was once the National Liquor Factory (FANAL). Now, it houses the offices of the Cultural Ministry, several performing-arts centers, and the Museum of Contemporary Art and Design. The latter has featured several impressive traveling international exhibits since its inception, including large retrospectives by Mexican painter José Cuevas and Ecuadorean painter Oswaldo Guayasamin. If you're looking for modern dance, experimental theater, or a lecture on Costa Rican video, this is the place to check.

Museo de Arte Costarricense. Calle 42 and Paseo Colón, Parque la Sabana este. ☎ **506/222-7155.** Admission $1.50 adults, children and students free. Tue–Sun 10am–4pm. Bus: Sabana–Cementerio.

This small museum at the end of Paseo Colón in Parque la Sabana was formerly an airport terminal. Today, however, it houses a collection of works in all media by Costa Rica's most celebrated artists. On display are some exceptionally beautiful pieces in a wide range of artistic styles, demonstrating how Costa Rican artists have interpreted and imitated the major European artistic movements over the years. In addition to the permanent collection of sculptures, paintings, and prints, there are regular temporary exhibits. If the second floor is open during your visit, be sure to go up and have a look at the conference room's unusual bas-relief walls, which chronicle the history of Costa Rica from pre-Columbian times to the present with evocative images of the people. On weekends local artists sell their work on the plaza in front of the museum. The Ruiseñor Cafe makes a wonderful pit stop.

☼ Museo de Jade Marco Fidel Tristan (Jade Museum). Avenida 7 between calles 9 and 9B, 11th Floor, INS Building. ☎ **506/223-5800,** ext. 2584. Admission $2 adults, children free. Mon–Fri 8am–4:30pm. Bus: Any downtown bus.

Among the pre-Columbian cultures of Mexico and Central America, jade was the most valuable commodity, worth more than gold. This modern museum displays a huge collection of jade artifacts from throughout Costa Rica's pre-Columbian archeological sites. Most of the jade pieces are large pendants that were parts of necklaces and are primarily human and animal figures. A fascinating display illustrates how the primitive peoples of this region carved this extremely hard stone. Most of the jade pieces date from 330 B.C. to A.D. 700.

There is also an extensive collection of pre-Columbian polychromed terra-cotta vases, bowls, and figurines. Some of these pieces are amazingly modern in design and exhibit a surprisingly advanced technique. Particularly fascinating is a vase that incorporates real human teeth, and a display that shows how jade was embedded in human teeth merely for decorative reasons. Most of the identifying labels and explanations are in Spanish but there are a few in English.

Before you leave be sure to check out the splendid view of San José from the lounge area.

✪ **Museo de Los Niños (Children's Museum).** Calle 4 and Avenida 9. ☎ **506/233-2734.** Admission $5 adults, $2.50 students, $1.50 children under 12. Tues–Sun 9am–5pm. Bus: Any downtown bus.

This museum is located a few blocks north of downtown, on Calle 4. It's within easy walking distance, but you might want to take a cab, as you'll have to walk right through the worst part of the red-light district to get there.

This recently converted prison houses an extensive collection of exhibits designed for the edification and entertainment of children of all ages. Experience a simulated earthquake, or make music by dancing across the floor. Many of the exhibits encourage hands-on play. If you have children with you, you will definitely want to come here, and you may want to visit even if you don't. Be careful: This museum is large and spread out and it's easy to loose track of a family member or friend.

✪ **Museo de Oro Banco Central (Gold Museum).** Calle 5 between Avenida Central and Avenida 2, underneath the Plaza de la Cultura. ☎ **506/223-0528.** Admission $5 adults, $1.50 students, 75¢ children under 12. Tue–Sun 10am–4:30pm. Bus: Any downtown bus.

Located directly beneath the Plaza de la Cultura, this unusual underground museum houses one of the largest collections of pre-Columbian gold in the Americas. On display are more than 20,000 troy ounces of gold in more than 2,000 objects. The sheer number of small pieces can be overwhelming and seem redundant. However, the unusual display cases and complex lighting systems show off every piece to its utmost. This museum also includes a gallery for temporary art exhibits and a numismatic and philatelic museum.

✪ **Museo Nacional de Costa Rica.** Calle 17 between Avenida Central and Avenida 2, on the Plaza de la Democracia. ☎ **506/257-1433.** Admission $1 adults, students and children under 10 free. Tue–Sun 8:30am–4:30pm. Closed Dec 25 and 31. Bus: San Pedro.

Costa Rica's most important historical museum is housed in a former army barracks that was the scene of fighting during the civil war of 1948. You can still see hundreds of bullet holes on the turrets at the corners of the building. Inside this traditional Spanish-style courtyard building, you will find displays on Costa Rican history and culture from pre-Columbian times to the present. In the pre-Columbian rooms, you'll see a 2,500-year-old jade carving that is shaped like a seashell and etched with an image of a hand holding a small animal. Among the most fascinating objects unearthed at Costa Rica's numerous archeological sites are many *metates* or grinding stones. This type of grinding stone is still in use today throughout Central America. However, the ones on display here are more ornately decorated than those that you will see anywhere else. Some of the metates are the size of a small bed and are believed to have been part of funeral rites. A separate vault houses the museum's small collection of pre-Columbian gold jewelry and figurines. In the courtyard, you'll be treated to a wonderful view of the city and see some of Costa Rica's mysterious stone spheres.

Museo Nacional de Ciencias Naturales "La Salle." Across from the southeast corner of Parque la Sabana. ☎ **506/232-1306.** Admission $1 adults, 50¢ children. Mon–Fri 8am–4pm, Sat 8am–noon, Sun 9am–4pm. Bus: Escazú or Pavas from Avenida 1 and Calle 18.

Before heading out to the wilds of the Costa Rican jungles, you might want to stop by this natural-history museum and find out more about the animals you might be seeing. There are stuffed and mounted anteaters, monkeys, tapirs, and many others. The collection includes animals from all over the world, as well. There are 1,200 birds and 12,500 insects on display. A collection of 13,500 seashells is another highlight.

Museo de Entomologia. In the basement of the University of Costa Rica's School of Music, San Pedro. ☎ **506/207-5647.** Admission $1.50. Mon–Fri 1–4pm. Bus: San Pedro from Avenida 2 between calles 5 and 7.

The Tropics have produced the world's greatest concentration and diversity of insects, and here at this small museum you can see more than one million mounted specimens from around the world. The butterfly collection is the star attraction here.

BIRDS, BUTTERFLIES, SNAKES & OTHER CRITTERS

Parque Zoologico Simon Bolívar. Avenida 11 and Calle 7, in Barrio Amón. ☎ **506/233-6701.** Admission $1 adults, children under 10 free. Tue–Fri 8am–3:30pm, Sat–Sun 9am–5pm. Bus: Any downtown bus, then walk.

I don't think I have ever seen a sadder zoo than this little park tucked away beside the polluted Río Torres. It is a shame that a country that has preserved so much of its land in national parks would ignore this zoo. The cages here are only occasionally marked, and many are dirty and small. The collection includes Asian, African, and Costa Rican animals. For many years, there have been plans to build a new zoo with more modern displays; while some minor improvements have been made, there's still a long way to go.

Serpentarium. Avenida 1 between calles 9 and 11. ☎ **506/255-4210.** Admission $2.50 adults, 75¢ children between 6–13. Daily 9am–6pm. Bus: Any downtown bus.

The Tropics abound in reptiles and amphibians, and the Serpentarium is an excellent introduction to all that slithers and hops through the jungles of Costa Rica. The live snakes, lizards, and frogs are kept in beautiful, large terrariums that simulate their natural environments. Poisonous snakes make up a large part of the collection with the dreaded fer-de-lance pit viper eliciting the most gasps from enthralled visitors. Also fascinating to see are the tiny, brilliantly colored poison-arrow frogs. Iguanas and Jesus Christ lizards are two of the more commonly spotted of Costa Rica's reptiles, and both are represented here. Also on display is an Asian import—a giant Burmese python, one of the largest I've ever seen. This little zoological museum is well worth a visit, especially if you plan to go bashing about in the jungles. It will help you identify the numerous poisonous snakes you'll want to avoid. If you show up around 3pm you may catch them feeding the piranhas and perhaps some of the snakes.

Spyrogyra Butterfly Garden. 100 meters east and 100 meters south of El Pueblo Shopping Center. ☎ **506/222-2937.** Admission $5. Daily 8am–3pm. Bus: Calle Blancos bus from Calle 3 and Avenida 5.

Butterflies have been likened to self-propelled flowers, so it comes as no surprise that butterfly gardens are becoming all the rage throughout the Tropics these days. If you'd like to find out why, drop in at Spyrogyra. Though this butterfly garden is smaller and less spectacular than the other two listed below, it's a good introduction to the life cycle of butterflies. You'll find Spyrogyra near El Pueblo, a 20-minute walk from the center of San José.

✪ **Zoo Ave.** La Garita, Alajuela. ☎ **506/433-8989.** Admission $7.50 adults, $1 children under 12. Daily 9am–5pm. Bus: Catch an Alajuela bus on Avenida 2 between calles 12 and 14. In Alajuela, transfer to a bus for Atenas and get off at Zoo Ave before you get to La Garita.

Dozens of scarlet macaws, reclusive owls, majestic raptors, several different species of toucans, and a host of brilliantly colored birds from Costa Rica and around the world make this place an exciting one to visit. Bird watching enthusiasts will be able to get a closer look at birds they may have seen in the wild. There are also large iguana, deer, and monkey exhibits—and look out for the 12-foot-long crocodile! Zoo Ave only houses injured, donated, or confiscated animals.

PARKS & GARDENS

The grand dame of San José's parks is the Parque La Sabana, located at the western edge of town where the Paseo Colón hits the Interamerican Highway. Formerly the country's main airport, La Sabana is the largest and most sprawling of the urban parks. The old terminal building now houses the Museo de Arte Costarricense (Costa Rican Art Museum). Beyond this lie numerous soccer fields, a running track, and basketball courts. There is also a nice lake and several eucalyptus groves.

Downtown San José is loaded with small parks and plazas. None are particularly notable, but most have benches or chairs and provide a nice place to take a break and watch the daily parade pass by. The Plaza de la Democracia (Democracy Plaza) is a large expanse of concrete located behind the National Museum. It's become the site of a block-long street market of stands selling T-shirts, souvenirs, and other trinkets. The Plaza de la Cultura (Cultural Plaza) is another mostly concrete affair, located beside the Teatro Nacional. Here you'll often find marimba bands, street performers, local artists, and a large resident pigeon population.

In front of the high-rise Holiday Inn, you'll find the Parque Morazan, which is one of my favorite places for a quick time out and some light-hearted people-watching.

If you're looking for a more extensive park or garden experience, you'll have to head out of San José a little. Just a few kilometers east of downtown is Parque del Este (Eastern Park), a wide expanse of mixed pastureland and forests, set in the hills overlooking San José. There are picnic and athletic facilities there, as well as some of the city's best bird watching. To get there, take the San Ramón–Parque del Este bus from Avenida 2 between calles 9 and 11.

Even farther afield, just outside the old capital city of Cartago, is the **Lankester Botanical Garden** (☎ 506/551-9877 or 506/552-3247). Created in the 1940s by English naturalist Charles Lankester, the garden is now administered by the University of Costa Rica. Its primary goal is to preserve the local flora, with an emphasis on orchids and bromeliads. There are more than 1,200 varieties of orchids in Costa Rica, and no less than 800 species are on display at this botanical garden in Cartago province. Paved trails wander from open, sunny gardens into shady forests. In each environment, different species of orchids are in bloom. There is an information center, and the trails are well tended and well marked. To get there, take any Cartago bus from San José, then the Paraíso bus from the south side of the Parque Central in Cartago. Admission is $2.50 adults, 25¢ children. Open daily from 8:30am to 3:30pm; closed on all national holidays.

NEARBY ATTRACTIONS

The Butterfly Farm. In front of Los Reyes Country Club, La Guácima de Alajuela. ☎ **506/ 438-0400.** Admission $10 adults, $5 students and children under 12. Daily 9am–3pm. Bus: San Antonio–Ojo de Agua on Avenida 1 between calles 20 and 22.

At any given time, you may see around 30 of the 80 different species of butterflies raised at this butterfly farm south of Alajuela. The butterflies live in a large enclosed garden similar to an aviary, and flutter about the heads of visitors during tours of the gardens. When we visited we saw glittering blue morphos and a butterfly that mimics the eyes of an owl. In the demonstration room you'll see butterfly eggs, caterpillars, and pupae. Among the latter, there are cocoons trimmed in a shimmering gold color and cocoons that mimic a snake's head in order to frighten away predators. The farm also offers a bee tour during which you can observe bees at work in glass observation hives.

Butterfly Paradise. On the road from San Joaquín to Santa Barbara, 1 kilometer north, and 350 meters west, on the right-hand side. ☎ **506/265-6694.** Admission $10 adults, $5 children under 12. Daily 9am–3pm. Bus: First take a bus to Heredia from Calle 1 between avenidas 7 and 9 in San José. In Heredia, transfer to a bus bound for either San Joaquín or Santa Barbara. In San Joaquín, you can get a taxi.

This butterfly garden is similar to the other two and offers the same experience—a guided walk through a screened-in butterfly garden. You'll see dozens of beautiful butterflies and learn all about their feeding, mating, and egg-laying habits. In the museum collection there are more butterflies to marvel over, and many other insects as well.

Cafe Britt Farm. North of Heredia on the road to Barva. ☎ **506/260-2748.** Admission $19–$25 per person, including transportation from downtown San José. Three tours daily 9 and 11am, and 3pm. Tours Nov–Feb during the harvest season; store open daily 8am–5pm all year.

Though bananas are the main export of Costa Rica, people are far more interested in the country's second most important export crop—coffee. Cafe Britt is one of the leading brands of coffee, and the company has put together an interesting tour and stage production at its farm, which is 20 minutes outside of San José. Here, you'll see how coffee is grown. You'll also visit the roasting plant to learn how a coffee "cherry" is turned into a delicious roasted bean. Tasting sessions are offered for the visitor to experience the different qualities of coffee. There is also a store on the premises where you can buy very reasonably priced coffee.

Museo Joyas del Tropico Humedo (Jewels of the Rain Forest). 100 meters east of the cemetery of Santa Domingo de Heredia. ☎ **506/244-5006.** Admission $5 adults, $2.50 children under 12. Mon–Sat 9am–5pm; Sun 10am–6pm. Bus: At Calle 1 between avenidas 7 and 9, take the Heredia–Tibás–Santo Domingo bus, then taxi from Santo Domingo.

Far more than just another bug collection, this exhibit takes the position that insects are works of art, tiny tropical jewels. The displays are artistically arranged and include more than 50,000 arthropods and insects (including thousands of different butterflies) collected from around the world by former Oregon biologist Richard Whitten and his wife Maggie.

7 Outdoor Activities

Due to the smog and pollution, you'll probably want to get out of the city before undertaking any strenuous or aerobic activity. However, there are some options available in and around San José, if you want to brave the natural and man-made elements.

La Sabana Park (at the western end of Paseo Colón), formerly San José's international airport, is the city's center for active sports and recreation. Here you'll find everthing from jogging trails, soccer fields, and a few public tennis courts to the National Stadium. All the facilities are free and open to the public. If you really want to experience the local culture, look for a pickup soccer game you can join here.

For information on horseback riding, hiking, and white-water rafting trips from San José, see "Side Trips from San José," at the end of this chapter.

BIKING

Riding a bike in and around San José is suicidal; I don't recommend it.

GOLF & TENNIS

If you want to play tennis you can try to get one of the public courts at the **Parque La Sabana.** Some of these courts are lit, but the park is decidely not safe after dark.

Your best bet for tennis or golf is the **Cariari Hotel & Country Club** (☎ 506/
239-0022). Guests at the Cariari and Herradura Hotels can play golf for $35 greens
fees, $25 for a cart and $15 equipment rental. Guests at other hotels must call in
advance and may or may not be granted permission, depending on management's
discretion and course availability. Tennis court usage is free for guests of Cariari
and Herradura hotels, and totally off-limits for others. For guests, the courts are open
until 10pm.

JOGGING

If you want to jog, head for La Sabana Park or Parque del Este, east of town in the
foothills above San Pedro. Both are described above. It's never a good idea to jog at
night, on busy streets, or alone. Women should be particularly careful about jogging
alone.

SWIMMING

If you aren't going to get to the beach anytime soon and you're dying to cool off,
check out the new **Agua Mania** (☎ 506/293-2890) on the road to San Antonio de
Belén, near the Hotel Herradura. This modern water theme park has water slides,
tube rides, and a wave pool, as well as miniature golf and go carts. Open Tuesday
through Thursday and Sunday 9:30am to 5:30pm; Saturday until 10pm. Admission
is $7.50 for adults, $5 for children under 12. Buses that pass Agua Mania leave
almost every hour from Avenida 1 between calles 18 and 20.

Alternatively, you can spend an afternoon relaxing in a spring-fed swimming pool:
Head out to **Ojo de Agua** (☎ 506/441-2808), on the same road to San Antonio
de Belén. The crystal-clear waters are cool and refreshing, and even if it seems a bit
chilly in San José, it's always several degrees warmer out here. This place is very popular with Ticos and can get quite crowded on weekends, but you do have to keep an
eye on your valuables. Admission is 75¢. Buses leave almost hourly for Ojo de Agua,
departing from Avenida 1 between calles 18 and 20.

8　Spectator Sports

Ticos take their *fútbol* seriously. Although not up to European or World Cup standards, Costa Rican professional soccer is some of the best in Central America. The
soccer season runs from September through June, with the finals spread out over several weeks in late June and early July. You don't need to buy tickets in advance. Tickets generally run between $2.50 and $12.50. It's worth paying a little extra for *sombra
numerado* (reserved seats in the shade). Other options include *sombra* (general admission in the shade), *palco* and *palco numerado* (general admission and reserved mez-
zanine), and *sol general* (general admission in full sun). The main San José team is
Saprissa (affectionately called *El Monstro*, or The Monster). Saprissa's stadium is in
Tibás (take any Tibás bus from Calle 2 between avenidas 3 and 7). Games are usually held on Sunday at 11am, but occasionally they're scheduled for Saturday afternoon or Wednesday evening. Check the local newspapers for game times and
locations.

The **Vuelta de Costa Rica** is a Central American version of the Tour de France.
Bicycle racers from around the region spend several weeks each December battling
each other up and over the mountains on the roads of Costa Rica. If you're traveling around the country during December, check the local papers for routes and racing
times, and you may be able to watch the pack pass by.

During the first week of January, Costa Rica hosts the **Copa del Cafe** (The Coffee Cup), an important international event on the junior tennis tour. Matches are held at the **Costa Rica Country Club** (☎ **506/228-9333**) in Escazú. Admission is $5; you can buy tickets at the box office.

Although I hesitate to call it a sport, Las Corridas a la Tica (**Costa Rican bullfighting**) is a popular and frequently comic stadium event. Instead of the blood-and-gore/life-and-death confrontation of traditional bullfighting, Ticos just like to tease the bull. In a typical *corrida,* anywhere from 50 to 150 *toreadores improvisados* (literally, improvised bullfighters) stand in the ring waiting for the bull. What follows is a slapstick scramble to safety whenever the bull heads towards a crowd of bullfighters. The braver bullfighters try to slap the bull's backside as the beast chases down one of their buddies. You can see a bullfight during the Festejos Populares in Zapote, a suburb east of San José. The corridas run all day and well into the night during Christmas week and the first week in January. Admission is between $2 and $5. Take the Zapote bus from Calle 1 between avenidas 4 and 6.

9 Shopping

Serious shoppers will be disappointed in Costa Rica. Aside from coffee, there isn't much that is distinctly Costa Rican that you can buy. To compensate for its own relative lack of handcrafts, Costa Rica does a brisk business in selling crafts and clothes imported from Guatemala and Panama. If you're not traveling on to either of these countries, you may want to pick up some of these crafts and textiles. Still, there are are some interesting and unique items to buy, as discussed under "Best Buys," below (see also "The Best Places to Shop," in chapter 1).

Shopping in San José centers around an area marked by the parallel streets of Avenida 1 and Avenida 2, from about Calle 14 in the west to Calle 13 in the east. For several blocks west of the Plaza de la Cultura, Avenida Central is a pedestrians-only street where you'll find store after store of inexpensive clothes for men, women, and children.

Most shops in the downtown district are open Monday through Saturday from about 8am to 6pm. You'll find that some shops close for lunch while others remain open. When you do purchase something, you'll be happy to find that there is no sales tax.

As I've mentioned previously, Costa Rica does not have a tradition of bargaining. You can basically forget about bargaining in gift shops and established stores. In markets and street stalls, you should be able to shave a little off the asking price, but the vendors will make you work for it.

BEST BUYS

Two words of advice—buy coffee. Buy as much as you can carry. Coffee is the best shopping deal in all of Costa Rica. Although the best Costa Rican coffee is supposedly shipped off to North American and European markets, it's hard to beat the coffee that's roasted right in front of you here. Cafe Britt is the big name in Costa Rican coffee. The most expensive brand, it's not necessarily the best. For good flavor and value, visit Cafe Trebol on Calle 8 between Avenida Central and Avenida 1. I highly recommend buying your coffee here. They'll pack the beans for you in whatever size bag you want. Be sure to ask for whole beans; Costa Rican grinds are too fine for standard coffeemakers. Best of all is the price: One pound of coffee sells for about $1.75. It makes a great gift and keeps for a long time in your refrigerator or freezer. If you should happen to buy prepackaged coffee in a supermarket in Costa Rica, be sure the package is marked *puro;* otherwise, it will likely be mixed with a good amount of sugar—the way Ticos like it.

One good coffee-related gift to bring home is a coffee sock and stand. This is the most common mechanism for brewing coffee beans in Costa Rica. It consists of a simple circular stand, made out of wood or wire, which holds a sock. Put the ground beans in the sock, place a pot or cup below, and pour boiling water through. You can find the socks and stands at most supermarkets, and in the Mercado Central. Depending on its construction, a stand will cost you between $1.50 and $5; socks run around 30¢, so buy a few spares.

If your interest is in handcrafts, there are many places for you to visit. As I've said, the quality of Costa Rican handcrafts is generally very low, and the offerings are limited. The most typical items you'll find are handpainted wooden oxcarts. These come in a variety of sizes and the big ones can be shipped to your home for a very reasonable price.

You may also run across carved masks made by the indigenous Boruca people of southern Costa Rica. These full-sized balsa-wood masks come in a variety of styles, both painted and unpainted, and run anywhere from $10 to $70, depending on the quality of workmanship.

International laws prohibit purchasing endangered wildlife—visitors to Costa Rica should not buy any wildlife or plants, even if they are readily for sale. The Audubon Society does not tolerate sales of any kind of sea-turtle products (including jewelry), wild birds, lizard or snake skin, coral, or orchids (except those grown commercially). It's especially hard to capture the subtle shades and colors of the rain and cloud forests, so to avoid getting home only to discover that the photos you took on your trip don't do justice to the beauty of Costa Rica, you might want to buy one of the picture books on Costa Rica.

MARKETS

Bargain hunters and souvenir hounds will find the best deals at markets. There are several markets near downtown, but by far the largest is the **Mercado Central,** which is located between Avenida Central and Avenida 1 and calles 6 and 8. Inside this dark maze of stalls you'll find all manner of vendors. Although this is primarily a food market, you can find vendors selling Costa Rican trinkets, crude leather goods, and musical instruments. Be especially careful about your wallet or purse; this area is frequented by very skillful pickpockets. All the streets surrounding the Mercado Central are jammed with produce vendors selling from small carts or loading and unloading trucks. It's always a hive of activity, with crowds of people jostling for space on the streets. In the hot days of the dry season, the aromas can get quite heady.

There is also a daily **street market** on the west side of the **Plaza de la Democracia.** Here you'll find two long rows of temporary stalls selling T-shirts, Guatemalan handcrafts, small ceramic *ocarinas* (a small musical wind instrument), and handmade jewelry. You may be able to bargain the price down a little bit, but bargaining is not a traditional part of the vendor culture here, so you'll have to work hard to save a few dollars.

SUBURBAN MALLS

In recent years, large suburban malls have been springing up all around San José and its neighboring suburbs. There's **Multiplaza** in Escazú, **Plaza del Sol in Curridabat,** and the unfinished, but already bustling, **Mall San Pedro.** Inside, you'll find food courts and familiar name-brand favorites, from Victoria's Secret lingerie to Bennetton jeans and shirts. Due to high import taxes, prices are substantially higher here than in North America or Europe.

SHOPPING A TO Z
ART GALLERIES

Art is beyond the budget of most frugal travelers; however, Central America (Nicaragua and Costa Rica in particular) is the center of a growing "primitive" painting movement. These simple scenes of country life and wild jungles are done in a bold colorful style, and are often quite a good buy.

Amir Art Gallery. Calle 5 between avenidas 1 and 3. ☎ **506/255-3261.**

This gallery carries original artworks in a variety of mediums featuring Central American themes. Some of it is pretty gaudy, but this is a good place to find Nicaraguan and Costa Rican "primitive" paintings. There's a second location nearby at Avenida 5 between calles 3 and 5.

Galleria Andromeda. Calle 9 at Avenida 9. ☎ **506/223-3529.**

This small, personal gallery features contemporary national artists of good quality. There are usually prints and paintings by several artists on display, and prices are very reasonable.

HANDCRAFTS

Despite Costa Rica's paltry crafts industry, you'll be bombarded with chances to buy handcrafts. Your best bet is either an outdoor market or one of the shops listed below, where a large selection will help you find something that suits your fancy.

The most appealing artisans' market close to San José is the **La Garzas Handicraft Market** in Moravia (see below). If you want to stick to downtown San José, try the outdoor market on the Plaza de la Democracia, though prices here tend to be high and bargaining can be difficult. If you prefer to do your crafts shopping in a flea-market atmosphere, head over to **La Casona** on Calle Central between Avenida Central and Avenida 1. Also be sure to visit the excellent **Annemarie Souvenir Shop** in the lobby of the Hotel Don Carlos.

Several shops around San José sell a wide variety of crafts—from the truly tacky to the divinely inspired. Here are some of the places to look for such items.

Annemarie Souvenir Shop. Calle 9 between avenidas 7 and 9. ☎ **506/221-6063.**

Occupying two floors of the Hotel Don Carlos, this shop has an amazing array of wood products, leather goods, *papier-mâché* figurines, paintings, books, cards, posters, and jewelry. You'll see most of this stuff at other shops, but not in such a relaxed and unpressured environment.

Asociacion Nacional Pro Desarrollo de La Artesania (Anda). Avenida Central between calles 5 and 7. ☎ **506/233-3340.**

If you're looking for Guatemalan clothing and they're asking too much on the Plaza de la Cultura, you might try this shop in the center of town. They also carry Boruca masks, carved gourds, T-shirts, and other souvenir-type items.

Las Garzas Handicraft Market. In Moravia, 100 meters south and 50 meters east from the Red Cross Station. ☎ **506/236-0037.**

This artisans' market is a short ride out of San José, and includes more than 25 shops that sell wood, metal, and ceramic crafts, among a large variety of other items.

Mercado de Artesanos Canapi. Calle 11 and Avenida 1. ☎ **506/221-3342.**

This store carries a wide variety of typical Costa Rican handcrafts, including large, comfortable woven-rope hammocks; reproductions of pre-Columbian gold jewelry and pottery bowls; coffee-wood carvings; and many other carvings from rare Costa Rican hardwoods. In general, the crafts are of low quality.

Suraska. Calle 5 and Avenida 3. ☎ **506/222-0129.**

If you haven't been impressed with the quality of the handcrafts you've seen, save your money for a visit to this store. Among the selections here are ceramics, mobiles, and jewelry. Of particular note are the wood carvings of North American artist Barry Biesanz, who turns out exquisite pieces of finely worked hardwood. Be forewarned, however: These pieces are expensive.

LEATHER GOODS

Malety. Avenida 1 between calles 1 and 3. ☎ **506/221-1670.**

Costa Rican leather goods cost more and are of poorer quality than their North American counterparts. With that caveat, this is one of best outlets in San José for locally produced leather bags, briefcases, purses, wallets, and more. A second store is located on Calle 1 between Avenida Central and Avenida 2.

LIQUOR

Cafe Rica, similar to Kahlua, and **Salicsa,** a cream liqueur, are two delicious liqueurs made from coffee in Costa Rica. You can buy these liqueurs in government liquor stores and tourist shops, but just about the best prices I have seen are at the supermarket chain Mas X Menos. There is a Mas X Menos outlet on Paseo Colón and another on Avenida Central at the east end of town, just below the Museo Nacional de Costa Rica.

10 San José After Dark

With the increased numbers of people visiting Costa Rica, San José has taken strides to meet the nocturnal needs of tourists and residents alike. You'll find plenty of interesting clubs and bars, a wide range of theaters, and some very lively discos.

To find out what's going on in San José while you're in town, pick up a copy of the *Tico Times.* (If you speak Spanish, purchase *La Nación.*) The former is a good place to find out where local expatriates are hanging out; the latter's "Viva" section has extensive listings of everything from discos and movie theaters to live music.

THE PERFORMING ARTS

Theater is very popular in Costa Rica. Downtown San José is studded with small theaters. Since local tastes tend towards the burlesque, the crowd pleasers are almost always simplistic sexual comedies. **The National Theater Company** (☎ 506/257-8305) is one major exception, tackling works from Lope de Vega to Lorca to Mamet. Almost all of the theater offerings are in Spanish, though there are two amateur theater groups that stage works in English periodically. Check the *Tico Times* to see if anything is running during your stay.

Aside from theater, Costa Rica has a surprisingly strong modern dance scene. Both the University of Costa Rica and the National University have **modern dance companies** that perform regularly in San José. Two independent companies—Los Denmedium and Diquis Tiquis—are of excellent calibre. Sadly, however, you're

In case you want to be welcomed there.

We're here to see that you're always welcomed at establishments everywhere. That's why millions of people carry the American Express® Card – for peace of mind, confidence, and security, around the world or just around the corner.

do more

Cards

In case you're running low.

We're here to help with more than 118,000 Express Cash

locations around the world. In order to enroll, just call

American Express before you start your vacation.

do more

Express Cash

And just in case.

We're here with American Express® Travelers Cheques
and Cheques *for Two*.® They're the safest way to carry
money on your vacation and the surest way to get a
refund, practically anywhere, anytime.

Another way we help you...

do more

**Travelers
Cheques**

almost more likely to catch these troupes performing in New York or Caracas than in San José.

The **National Symphony Orchestra** is a respectable orchestra by regional standards, though their repertoire tends to be rather conservative. The symphony season runs from March through November, with concerts roughly every other week at the Teatro Nacional, Avenida 2 between calles 3 and 5 (☎ **506/221-1329**). Tickets cost between $2.50 and $15 and can be purchased at the box office.

Visiting artists also stop in Costa Rica from time to time. Recent concerts have featured Spanish tenor Jose Carreras, romantic crooner Julio Iglesias, and the rock band Jethro Tull. Many of these concerts and guest performances take place in San José's two historic theaters: the **Teatro Nacional** and the **Teatro Melico Salazar,** Avenida 2 between Calle Central and Calle 2 (☎ **506/222-2653**). Prices for international events are relatively comparable to what you might pay in New York or London.

Costa Rica's cultural panorama changes drastically every March, when the country hosts large arts festivals. In odd-numbered years the festival features purely local talent, but in even-numbered years the month-long fete offers up a nightly smorgasbord of dance, theater, music, and monologue from around the world. Most nights of the festival, you'll have between 4 and 10 shows to choose from. Many are free, and the most expensive ticket is $5.

THE CLUB & MUSIC SCENE

If you like to dance, you'll find plenty of places to get down in San José. Salsa and merengue are the main beats that move people here and many of the dance clubs, discos, and salons feature live music on the weekends. However, if you're looking to catch some jazz, rock, or blues in a small club, there's not nearly the selection.

The "Viva" section of the *La Nación* newspaper has weekly performances. A couple of dance bands to watch for are Marfil and Los Brillanticos. Liverpool is a popular rock cover band, and if you're looking for jazz, check out Expresso or pianist Manuel Obregon.

A good place to sample a range of San José's nightlife is **El Pueblo,** a shopping, dining, and entertainment complex done up like an old Spanish village. It's just across the river to the north of town. The best way to get there is by taxi; all the drivers know El Pueblo well. Within the alleyways that wind through El Pueblo are a dozen or more bars, clubs, and discos. There is even a roller-skating rink here. **Cocoloco** (☎ **506/222-8782**) features nightly "fiestas," and **Discoteque Infinito** (☎ **506/ 221-9134**) has three different ambiences under one roof. Across the street you'll find **La Plaza** (☎ **506/222-5143**), one of my favorite dance spots.

LIVE MUSIC

Akelarre. Calle 21 between avenidas 4 and 6. ☎ **506/223-0345.**

This popular club is located in a renovated old house near the Museo Nacional. There are several rooms in which to check out the action, as well as a garden out back. There are frequent live music performances by hot Costa Rican groups.

Casa Matute. Calle 21 and Avenida 10. ☎ **506/222-6806.**

This historic old house just south of the Supreme Court has been converted into a sprawling club complex, with an assortment of theme rooms ranging from a Whiskey Bar to a French Left Bank–style cafe. It's become immensely popular with young

---

Only in the Central Valley: Dining Under the Stars on a Mountain's Edge

While there are myriad unique experiences to be had in Costa Rica, there's just one that can only be experienced in San Jose's Central Valley: dining on the side of a volcanic mountain. These hanging restaurants, called *miradors,* are a resourceful response to San Jose's topography. Because the city is set in a broad valley surrounded on all sides by volcanic mountains, people who live in these mountainous areas on the edges of the valley have no other place to build a roadside cafe, so vertically they build. Many of the roads through these mountains are studded with these hillside hanging restaurants.

While the food at most of these establishments is not usually spectacular, the views often are, particularly at night, when the whole wide valley sparkles in a wash of lights. The town of Aserri, 6 miles south of downtown San José, is the king of miradors, and Mirador Ram Luna (☎ 506/230-3060) is the king of Aserri. Grab a window seat and, if you've got the fortitude, order a plate of *chicharrones* (fried pork rinds). There's often live music, just in case the whole experience makes you feel like dancing. You can hire a cab for around $8 or take the Aserri bus at Avenida 6 between Calle Central and Calle 2. Just ask the driver where to get off.

Ticos. There's almost always live music here, provided by many of the same bands you'd find on another night at Akelarre.

La Esmeralda. Avenida 2 between calles 5 and 7. ☎ **506/233-7386.**

A sort of mariachi Grand Central Station, La Esmeralda is a cavernous open-air restaurant and bar that stays open 24 hours a day. In the evening, mariachi bands park their vans out front and wait to be hired for a moonlight serenade or perhaps a surprise party. While they wait, they often fill the restaurant with loud trumpet blasts and the sound of the big bass guitarón. If you've never been serenaded at your table before, this place is a must. A song will cost you anywhere from $3 to $10, depending on the size of the group you hire.

DISCOS & SALONS

El Tobogan. 200 meters north and 100 meters east of the La Republica main office, off the Guapiles highway. ☎ **506/257-3396.**

The dance floor in this place is about the size of a football field, yet it's always packed. This is where Ticos come with their loved ones for a night out. There's always a live band here, and sometimes they're very good.

Salsa 54. Calle 3 between avenidas 1 and 3. ☎ **506/221-3220.**

This is *the* place to salsa in San José. In addition to the informal instruction you'll soak up just by watching, you might even be able to take a Latin-dance class here.

Las Tunas. Sabana North, 500 meters west of ICE office. ☎ **506/231-1802.**

This happening place serves Mexican food and barbecue, but where it really cooks is in the bar and disco—live Costa Rican pop music is featured weekly.

THE BAR SCENE

San José has an amazingly eclectic bar scene. There are upscale hotel bars, down-and-dirty dives, sports bars, and student hangouts. The one thing that all of them have in common is something called a *boca,* the equivalent of a *tapa* in Spain. It's a little dish of snacks that arrives at your table when you order a drink. In most bars, the bocas are free; but in upscale bars, the bocas are more sophisticated, and you'll have to pay for these delectable treats. Regardless of where you go, you'll find drinks reasonably priced, with beer costing around $1 or $1.50 and mixed drinks around $2 to $3.50.

Charleston. Avenida 4 between calles 7 and 9. ☎ **506/255-3993.**

This relaxed bar has a 1920s theme. Businessmen like to unwind here after a grinding day. Great recorded jazz music plays on the stereo and sometimes there are even live bands.

El Cuartel de La Boca del Monte. Avenida 1 between calles 21 and 23. ☎ **506/221-0327.**

This popular bar began life as an artist and bohemian hangout. Over the years it's become the leading meat market for the young and well-heeled. However, artists still come, as do foreign-exchange students, visiting tourists and, for some reason, many of the river-rafting guides, so there's always a diverse mix. There's usually live music here on Wednesday and Friday nights, and when there is, the place is packed shoulder to shoulder.

Nashville South. Calle 5 between avenidas 1 and 3. ☎ **506/233-1988.**

As its name implies, this is a country-and-western bar. Very popular with homesick expatriates, Nashville has a friendly atmosphere and fun music. The television is usually tuned to a professional sporting event or CNN.

Rio. Avenida Central, Los Yoses. ☎ **506/253-5088.**

This bar and restaurant is close to the University of Costa Rica, and consequently attracts a younger clientele during the day. At night, Rio is overflowing with a well-heeled, hipper-than-thou crowd.

Risa's Bar. Calle 1 between Avenida Central and Avenida 1. ☎ **506/223-2803.**

This second-floor bar is in a beautiful old building in the heart of downtown San José. There's a big dug-out canoe over the bar, but the exposed brick walls and the U.S. rock videos give Risa's a very North American urban atmosphere. The music is loud! At the end of the night, you can either walk back down the stairs, or take the curving slide out.

Shakespeare Bar. Avenida 2 and Calle 28. ☎ **506/257-1288.**

Located next to the Sala Garbo movie theater, this classy little spot is a good place to meet after a movie or a show at the Sala Garbo or Laurence Olivier Theater next door.

Soda Palace. Calle 2 and Avenida 2. ☎ **506/221-3441.**

Mostly a men's hangout, this dingy but brightly lit bar hardly lives up to its name, but is a Costa Rican institution. It opens directly onto busy Avenida 2 and is open 24 hours a day. Men of all ages sit at the tables conversing loudly and watching the world pass by. You never know what might happen at the Palace. Mariachis stroll in, linger for a while, then continue on their way. Legend has it that the revolution of 1948 was planned right here.

HANGING OUT IN SAN PEDRO

The two-block stretch of San Pedro just south of the University of Costa Rica is the closest thing to the Left Bank or the East Village you'll find in Costa Rica. Bars and cafes are mixed in with bookstores and copy shops. It's one of the few places in town where you can sit calmly at an outdoor table or walk the streets, without constantly checking over your shoulder and reaching for your wallet. You can just stroll the strip until someplace strikes your fancy or try:

La Maga. 100 meters east of the Church in San Pedro. ☎ **506/283-5047.**

This artsy cafe is named after a character in Julio Cortázar's novel *Hopscotch*. Inside, you'll find comfortable wooden tables and racks of magazines and newspapers for perusing. La Maga just took over and remodeled the building next door, turning it into a cavernous performing space for Costa Rica's avante-garde and experimental theater and dance troupes.

La Villa. 200 meters east and 100 meters north of the Church in San Pedro. ☎ **506/225-9612.**

This converted Victorian house holds the ghosts of Che Guevarra and Camilo Cienfuegos, or at least you'll see posters of them and other Latin American revolutionaries on the walls. Around the tables you'll find poets and painters mixing with a new generation of student activists, all in a lively atmosphere. There's even a foosball table in the far back.

THE GAY & LESBIAN SCENE

Because Costa Rica is such a conservative and Catholic country, the gay and lesbian communities here are rather discreet. Homosexuality is not generally under attack, but many gay and lesbian organizations jealously guard their privacy, and the club scene is not entirely stable. Women should definitely check in with **Casa Yemaya** (☎ **506/223-3652** or 506/257-8529) for suggestions on clubs and community connections, while both men and women can call the **International Gay and Lesbian Association** (☎ **506/234-2411**).

As of press time, the happening gay and lesbian bars and dance clubs were **Deja Vu,** Calle 2 between avenidas 14 and 16 (no phone) and **La Avispa,** Calle 1 between avenidas 8 and 10 (☎ **506/223-5343**). The former is predominantly a guy's hangout, while the latter is popular with both men and women, although both sometimes set aside certain nights of the week or month for specific communities.

MOVIES & MORE

Most of the movies shown in San José are first-run U.S. productions in English with Spanish subtitles that get here about three months after originally opening in the States. Ticos tend toward action flicks and there's almost always a Schwarzenegger or Van Damme film to choose from. Even if you aren't interested in what's playing, it's worth the $2.50 admission just to see a movie in an old-style theater with a full-sized screen. Try out the **Cine Magaly,** Calle 23 between Avenida Central and Avenida 1 (☎ **506/223-0085**); Cine Rex, Calle Central between avenidas 2 and 4, just off the Parque Central (☎ **506/221-0041**); or **Cine Variedades,** Calle 3 between Avenida Central and Avenida 1 (☎ **506/223-0085**). These theaters even have balconies. Check the "Viva" section of *La Nación* or the *Tico Times* for movie listings and times.

Sala Garbo, 100 meters south of the Pizza Hut on Paseo Colón (☎ **506/222-1034**) shows foreign and art films, usually in Spanish, but sometimes with English subtitles.

CASINOS Gambling is legal in Costa Rica and there are casinos at virtually every major hotel. However, as in Tico bullfighting, there are some idiosyncracies involved in *gambling à la tica*. If blackjack is your game, you'll want to play "rummy." The rules are almost identical, except the house doesn't pay double on blackjack; instead it pays double on any three-of-a-kind, or three-card straight flush. If you're looking for roulette, what you'll find here is a bingo-like spinning cage of numbered balls. The betting is the same, but some of the glamour is lost. You'll also find a version of five-card draw poker, but the rule differences are so complex, I advise you sit down and watch for awhile and then ask some questions before joining in. That's about all you'll find. There are no craps tables or baccarat. Recently, there's been some controversy over slot machines: one-armed bandits are outlawed, but you're able to play electronic slots and poker games. Most of the casinos are quite casual and small by international standards. You may have to dress up slightly at some of the fancier hotels, but most are accustomed to tropical vacation attire.

11 Side Trips from San José

San José makes an excellent base for exploring the beautiful Meseta Central and the surrounding mountains; in fact, it's possible to explore much of the country on day tours from San José. Perhaps the easiest way to do it is on a guided tour, but if you rent a car, you'll have greater independence (and possibly save money). There are also many day trips that can be done by public bus, which is by far the most economical means of getting around. Below I give information on many of the day tours offered by tour companies in San José. These are arranged by type of activity. In addition to the tours listed below, there are many other tours, some of which combine two or three different activities or destinations. Companies offering a wide variety of primarily nature-related day tours out of San José include: **Costa Rica Expeditions** (☎ 506/257-0766 or 506/222-0333); **Costa Rica Sun Tours** (☎ 506/255-3418); **Ecole Travel** (☎ 506/223-2240); **Fantasy Tours** (☎ 506/220-2393); **Geotour** (☎ 506/227-4029); **Otec Tours** (☎ 506/256-0633); and **Swiss Travel Service** (☎ 506/231-4055).

Most of the tour prices are standardized, however, since competition is fierce, it always pays to make a few calls and shop around before settling on a tour company.

As you're conducting your research, find out how much time is spent in transit and eating lunch, in addition to how much time is alloted for the primary activity. I've had complaints about tours that were rushed or spent too much time on secondary activities.

RECREATIONAL DAY TRIPS

BIKING   Narrow mountain roads with spectacular views make for some great, though strenuous, biking in Costa Rica. As yet, though, there are only a few companies offering cycling trips. **Rios Tropicales** (☎ 506/233-6455) offers a day-long mountain-bike trip to Tapantí National Park. Most of the riding on this trip is downhill, and there are numerous opportunities to birdwatch and explore nature trails. The cost of $70 includes transportation, use of biking equipment, breakfast, and lunch. Rios Tropicales also offers multi-day biking and rafting trips.

Other companies offering bicycling trips include **El León Viajero** (☎ 506/233-9398), which has three different tours ranging in price from $70 to $95, and **EcoTreks** (☎ 506/289-8192), which rents mountain bikes and designs custom tours for travelers.

BUNGEE JUMPING   There's nothing truly unique about bungee jumping in Costa Rica, but it's a little bit less expensive than in the U.S. If you've always had the bug, **Tropical Bungee** (☎ 506/233-6455) will let you jump off a 265-foot bridge for $45; they'll charge you $70 if you want to do it twice. Transportation is $7 each way.

CRUISING   Several companies offer cruises to the lovely Tortuga Island in the Gulf of Nicoya, and these excursions include gourmet buffet meals and stops at a deserted (until your boat arrives) beach. Companies offering these trips include **Bay Island Cruises** (☎ **506/296-5551**), **Calypso Tours** (☎ **506/233-3617**), and **Sea Ventures** (☎ **506/257-2904**). The cruises cost around $70 per person and include transportation from San José to Puntarenas and back.

HIKING   If you do not plan to visit Monteverde or one of Costa Rica's other cloud-forest preserves, consider doing a day tour to a cloud forest. Guided hikes through these misty, high-altitude forests provide an opportunity to visit one of the Tropics' most fascinating habitats. Bird watching and a chance to learn about the ecology of a cloud forest are the main attraction of these trips. One of the most popular and highly recommended hiking tours is to the **Los Angeles Cloud Forest Reserve.** This tour is operated by Hotel Villablanca (☎ **506/228-4603**) and includes a 3-hour guided walk through the cloud forest. The cost is $75 per person, including transportation, breakfast, and lunch. Another cloud forest day hike is offered by **Senderos de Iberoamérica** (☎ **506/255-2859**). This trip takes you to the Los Juncos Biological Reserve for a total of 5 hours of guided walks. Transportation, breakfast, and lunch are all included in the $70-per-person cost.

HORSEBACK RIDING   If you enjoy horseback riding, you have your choice of many fascinating locations near San José for day-long trips. The going rate for a day ride out of San José is around $70 per person, including transportation, lunch, and a 4-hour guided ride. **L.A. Tours** (☎ **506/221-4501**) offers rides through pastures and along the beach. **Sacramento Horseback Ride** (☎ **506/237-2116**) offers rides through mountain forests and pastures. **La Paz** (☎ **506/221-3060** or 506/222-5005) offers a trip through the cloud forest on the flank of Poás Volcano; the ride visits two different waterfalls. **El León Viajero** (☎ **506/233-9398**) offers three different horseback-riding tours, each in a different part of the country.

PRE-COLUMBIAN RUINS   Though Costa Rica lacks such massive pre-Columbian archeological sites as can be found in Mexico, Guatemala, or Honduras, it does have Guayabo National Monument, a small excavated town, which today is but a collection of building foundations and cobbled streets. If you have a car, or are an intrepid bus hound, you can do this tour on your own. If not, **Senderos de Iberoamérica** (☎ **506/255-2859**) offers trips to Costa Rica's most extensively excavated pre-Columbian archeological site for $70 per person.

RAFTING, KAYAKING & RIVER TRIPS   Cascading down from Costa Rica's mountain ranges are dozens of tumultuous rivers, several of which have become very popular for white-water rafting and kayaking. For between $65 and $90 per person, you can spend a day rafting through lush tropical forests. Longer trips are also available. Some of the more reliable rafting companies are: **Aventuras Naturales** (☎ **506/225-3939,** or 800/308-3394 in the U.S.); **Costa Rica White Water** (☎ **506/257-0766** or 506/222-0333); **Costa Sol Rafting** (☎ **506/293-2151,** or 800/245-8420 in the U.S.); and **Rios Tropicales** (☎ **506/233-6455**). If I had to choose just one day trip to do out of San José, it would be a white-water rafting trip.

There are also some raft and boat trips on calmer waters. These trips usually focus on the wildlife and scenery along the river. **Sarapiquí Aguas Bravas** (☎ **506/292-2072**) offers tours that include a boat trip down the Sarapiquí River, a quiet river fed by clear mountain streams. The scenery along this river is a combination of rain forest and farms. These tours pass through the lush Braulio Carillo National Park along the way. Sarapiquí Aguas Bravas also runs rougher sections of the same river.

Perhaps the best-known river tours are those that go to Tortuguero National Park. Though it's possible to do this tour as a day trip out of San José, it's a long and expensive day. You're much better off doing it as a 1- or 2-night trip. See Chapter 11, "The Caribbean Coast," for details.

RAIN FOREST AERIAL TRAM   When you first see the **Aerial Tram** (☎ 506/257-5961), you may wonder where the slopes are. Built on a private reserve bordering Braulio Carillo National Park, the tramway is the creation of rain-forest researcher Dr. Donald Perry, whose cable-car system through the forest canopy at Rara Avis helped establish him as an early expert on rain-forest canopies. The tramway takes visitors on a 90-minute ride through the rain-forest tree tops, where they have a chance to glimpse the complex web of life that makes these forests so unique. There are also well-groomed trails and a restaurant on site, so it can easily turn into a full-day trip. The cost for tours, including transportation from San José, is $65 per person. Alternatively, you can pay $47.50 per person and take a bus from Calle 12 between avenidas 7 and 9 in San José. Buses leave every half-hour; a one-way fare costs $2.

VOLCANO TRIPS   Poás, Irazú, and Arenal volcanoes are three of Costa Rica's most popular destinations. For more information on the Arenal Volcano, see chapter 8, and for more information on Poás and Irazú, see below. Numerous tour companies in San José offer trips to all three volcanoes, and though the trips to Poás and Irazú take only half a day, the trips to Arenal take all day. I don't recommend these latter trips because you often arrive when the volcano is hidden by clouds and leave before the night's darkness shows off its glowing eruptions. Tour companies offering trips to Poás and Irazú include **Costa Rica Expeditions** (☎ **506/257-0766** or 506/222-0333); **Costa Rica Sun Tours** (☎ **506/255-3418**); **OTEC Tours,** Edeficio Ferencz, Calle 3 between avenidas 1 and 3, Apdo. 323-1002, San José (☎ **506/256-0633**); **TAM,** Calle Central between Avenida Central and Avenida 1 (☎ **506/256-0203** or 506/222-3866); **Vic-Vic Tours,** Calle 3 between avenidas 5 and 7 (☎ **506/233-3435**); **San Jose Travel,** Calle 11 and Avenida 2 (☎ **506/257-4511**); and **Swiss Travel Service** (☎ **506/232-7188**). Prices range from $25 to $30 for a half-day trip to $50 to $70 for a full-day trip.

CARTAGO, THE OROSI VALLEY & IRAZÚ VOLCANO

Located about 15 miles southeast of San José, Cartago is the former capital of Costa Rica. Founded in 1563, it was Costa Rica's first city—and was in fact its only city for almost 150 years. Irazú Volcano rises up from the edge of town, and although it is quiescent these days, it has not always been so peaceful. Earthquakes have damaged Cartago repeatedly over the years, so that today there are few of the old colonial buildings left standing. In the center of the city a public park winds through the ruins of a large church that was destroyed in 1910, before it was ever finished. Construction was abandoned after the quake, and today the ruins are a neatly manicured park, with quiet paths and plenty of benches.

Cartago's most famous building, however, is the **Basilica de Nuestra Señora de Los Angeles** (the Basilica of Our Lady of the Angels), which is dedicated to the patron saint of Costa Rica and stands on the east side of town. Within the walls of this Byzantine-style church is a shrine containing the tiny figure of La Negrita, the Black Virgin, nearly lost amid its ornate altar. As legend has it, La Negrita first revealed herself on this site to a peasant girl in 1635. Miraculous healing powers have been attributed to La Negrita, and over the years thousands of pilgrims have come to the shrine seeking cures for their illnesses and difficulties. The walls of the shrine are covered with a fascinating array of tiny silver images left as thanks for cures affected by La Negrita. Amid the plethora of diminutive arms and legs, there are also hands, feet, hearts, lungs, kidneys, eyes, torsos, breasts, and—peculiarly—guns, trucks, beds, and planes. There are even dozens of sports trophies which I assume were left in thanks for helping teams win big games. August 2 is the day dedicated to La Negrita. On this day, tens of thousands of people walk to Cartago from San José and around the country in devotion to this powerful saint.

If you'd like to soak in a warm-water swimming pool, head 2.5 miles south of Cartago to Aguas Calientes. A little more than a mile east of Cartago, you'll find **Lankester Botanical Garden** (☎ **506/551-9877**), well-known for its orchid collection. See "Attractions," above, for details.

Buses for Cartago leave San José every 10 minutes from Calle 5 and Avenida 18. The length of the trip is 45 minutes; the fare is about 35¢.

Located 20 miles north of Cartago, 11,260-foot-tall **Irazú Volcano** is one of Costa Rica's more active volcanoes, although at this time it is relatively quiet. It last erupted on March 19, 1963, on the day that President John F. Kennedy arrived in Costa Rica. The eruption showered ash on the Meseta Central for months after, destroying crops and collapsing roofs, but enriching the soil. There is a good paved road right to the rim of the crater, where a desolate expanse of grey sand nurtures few plants and the air smells of sulfur. The landscape is often compared to that of the moon. There are magnificent views of the fertile Meseta Central and Orosi Valley as you drive up from Cartago, and if you're very lucky you may be able to see both the Pacific and the Caribbean at the same time. Clouds usually descend by noon, so schedule your trip up here as early in the day as possible. From the parking area, a short trail leads to the rim of the volcano's two craters, their walls a maze of eroded gullies feeding onto the flat floor far below. This is a national park, so admission is $6 per person (see "Costa Rica's National Parks & Bioreserves," in chapter 3 for more information). Don't forget to wear warm clothes. This may be the Tropics, but it can get cold at the top. On your way back down, stop for breakfast at **Restaurant Linda Vista** (☎ **506/225-5808**). It's on the right as you come down the mountain. Located at an elevation of 10,075 feet, it claims to be the highest restaurant in Central America; there are walls of windows looking out over the valley far below. A hearty Tico breakfast of gallo pinto with ham will cost about $2.50.

Buses leave for Irazú Volcano Saturday, Sunday, and holidays from Avenida 2 between calles 1 and 3 (in front of the Gran Hotel Costa Rica). The fare is $3.90 and the trip takes about 1¹/₂ hours. To make sure the buses are running, call 272-0651. If you are driving, head northeast out of Cartago toward San Rafael, then continue driving uphill toward the volcano, passing the turnoffs for Cot and Tierra Blanca en route.

The **Orosi Valley,** southeast of Cartago and visible from the top of Irazú on a clear day, is called the most beautiful valley in Costa Rica. The Reventazon River meanders through this steep-sided valley until it collects in the lake formed by the Cachí Dam. There are scenic overlooks near the town of Orosi at the head of the valley, and in Ujarrás on the banks of the lake. Near Ujarrás are the ruins of Costa Rica's oldest church (built in 1693), whose tranquil gardens are a great place to sit and gaze at the surrounding mountains. Across the lake is a popular recreation center, called Charrarra, where you'll find a picnic area, swimming pool, and hiking trails. In the town of Orosi there is yet another colonial church built in 1743; a small museum here displays religious artifacts.

It would be difficult to explore this whole area by public bus, since it's not a densely populated region. However, there are buses from Cartago to the town of

Orosi. During the week, these buses run every half-hour and leave from a spot one block east and three blocks south of the church ruins in Cartago. Saturday and Sunday, a bus runs every hour from the same vicinity and will drop you at the Orosi lookout point. The trip takes 30 minutes, and the fare is 30¢. If you are driving, take the road to Paraíso from Cartago, head toward Ujarrás, continue around the lake, then pass through Cachí and on to Orosi. From Orosi, the road leads back to Paraíso.

POÁS VOLCANO

This is another active volcano accessible from San José in a day trip. Just 23 miles from the capital, it's accessed via narrow roads that wind through fertile farmland and dark forests. As at Irazú, there's a paved road to the top. The volcano stands 8,800 feet tall and is located within a national park, which preserves not only the volcano but also dense stands of virgin forest. Poás's crater is over a mile across and is said to be the second-largest in the world. Geysers in the crater sometimes spew steam and muddy water 600 feet into the air, making this the largest geyser in the world. There's an information center where you can see a slide show about the volcano, and marked hiking trails through the cloud forest that rings the crater. About 20 minutes from the parking area, along a forest trail, is an overlook onto beautiful Botos Lake, which has formed in one of the volcano's extinct craters.

Because the sulfur fumes occasionally become dangerously strong at Poás, the park is sometimes closed to the public. This is a national park and admission is $6. For more information, see "Costa Rica's National Parks & Bioreserves," in chapter 3.

There's an excursion bus on Sundays and holidays leaving from Calle 12 and avenidas 2 and 4 at 8:30am and returning at 2:30pm. The fare is $3 roundtrip. The bus is always crowded, so arrive early. Other days, take a bus to Alajuela, then a bus to San Pedro de Poás. From there you will have to hitchhike or take a taxi ($20 roundtrip), which makes this alternative almost as costly as a tour. All the tour companies in San José offer excursions to Poás, although they often don't arrive until after the clouds have closed in. If you're traveling by car, head for Alajuela and continue on the main road through town toward Varablanca. Just before reaching Varablanca, turn left toward Poasito and continue to the rim of the volcano.

HEREDIA, ALAJUELA, GRECIA, SARCHÍ & ZARCERO

All of these cities and towns are northwest of San José and can be combined into a long day trip (if you have a car), perhaps in conjunction with a visit to Poás Volcano. The scenery is rich and verdant, and the small towns and scattered farming communities are truly representative of Costa Rica's agricultural heartland. If you're relying on buses, you'll be able to visit any of the towns listed below, but probably just one per day.

Heredia was founded in 1706. On its central park stands a colonial church dedicated in 1763. The stone facade leaves no questions as to the age of the church, but the altar inside is decorated with neon stars and a crescent moon surrounding a statue of the Virgin Mary. In the middle of the palm-shaded park is a music temple, and across the street, beside several tile-roofed municipal buildings, is the tower of an old Spanish fort. Of all the cities in the Meseta Central, this is the only one with some colonial feeling to it. You'll still see adobe buildings with Spanish tile roofs along narrow streets. Heredia is also the site of the National Autonomous University, so you'll find some nice coffee shops and bookstores near the school. Buses leave for Heredia almost every 5 minutes from Calle 12 and Avenida 2, and from Calle 1 between avenidas 7 and 9. Fare is 30¢.

Alajuela is one of Costa Rica's oldest cities, and is located only 12 miles from San José. Although it is an attractive little city filled with parks, there isn't much to see or do here. The **Juan Santamaría Historical Museum,** Avenida 3 between Calle Central and Calle 2 (☎ **506/442-1838**), commemorates Costa Rica's national hero, who gave his life defending the country against a small army led by William Walker, a U.S. citizen who invaded Costa Rica in 1856. Walker was trying to set up a slave state in Central America. Open Tuesday through Sunday from 10am to 6pm; admission is free. Buses leave for Alajuela every 10 minutes from Avenida 2 between calles 10 and 14. Fare is 45¢.

From Alajuela, a narrow, winding road leads to the town of **Grecia,** which is noteworthy for its unusual metal church, painted a deep red with white gingerbread trim. The road to Sarchí is to the right as you go around the church.

Sarchí is Costa Rica's main artisan town. It is here that the colorfully painted miniature oxcarts you see all over Costa Rica are made. Oxcarts such as these were once used to haul coffee beans to market. Today, though you may occasionally see oxcarts in use, most are purely decorative. However, they remain a well-known symbol of Costa Rica. In addition to miniature oxcarts, many other carved wooden souvenirs are made here with rare hardwoods from the nation's forests. There are dozens of shops in town, and all have similar prices. The other reason to visit Sarchí is to see its unforgettable church. Built between 1950 and 1958, the church is painted pink with aquamarine trim and looks strangely like a child's birthday cake. Buses leave for Sarchí every 25 minutes from Calle 8 between Avenida Central and Avenida 1. Fare is 60¢.

Beyond Sarchí, on picturesque roads lined with cedar trees, you will find the town of **Zarcero.** In a small park in the middle of town is a menagerie of topiary sculptures (sculpted shrubs) that includes a monkey on a motorcycle, people and animals dancing, an ox pulling a cart, a man wearing a top hat, and a large elephant. It's worth the drive to see this park or, better yet, you can stop here on the way to La Fortuna and Arenal Volcano. Buses for Zarcero leave from San José daily at 9:30am and 12:15, 4:15, and 5:15pm from Calle 16 between avenidas 1 and 3. Fare is 75¢.

The road to Heredia turns north off the highway from San José to the airport. To reach Alajuela from Heredia, take the scenic road that heads west through the town of San Joaquín. To continue on to Sarchí, it's best to return to the highway south of Alajuela and drive west toward Puntarenas. Turn north to Grecia and then west to Sarchí.

TURRIALBA

This attractive little town 33 miles east of San José is best known as the starting point and home base for many popular white-water rafting trips. However, it is also worth a visit if you have an interest in pre-Columbian history or tropical botany. Guayabo National Monument is one of Costa Rica's only excavated pre-Columbian sites and is open to the public. It's located 12 miles northeast of Turrialba and preserves a townsite that dates to between 1000 B.C. and A.D. 1400. Archeologists believe that Guayabo may have supported a population of as many as 10,000 people, but there is no clue yet as to why the city was eventually abandoned only shortly before the Spanish arrived in the New World. Excavated ruins at Guayabo consist of paved roads, aqueducts, stone bridges, and house and temple foundations. There are also grave sites and petroglyphs. The monument is open daily from 8am to 4pm. This is a national park, and admission is $6 at the gate. For more information, see "Costa Rica's National Parks & Bioreserves," in chapter 3.

Botanists and gardeners will want to pay a visit to the **Center for Agronomy Research and Development (CATIE),** which is located 5 kilometers southeast of Turrialba on the road to Siquerres. This center is one of the world's foremost facilities for research into tropical agriculture. Among the plants on CATIE's 2,000 acres are hundreds of varieties of cacao and thousands of varieties of coffee. The plants have been collected from all over the world. There are trees, vegetables, and ornamental plants. CATIE is open Monday through Friday from 8am to 4pm. For information on guided tours, call **506/556-6431.**

While you're in the area, don't miss an opportunity to spend a little time at **Turrialtico** (☎ **506/556-1111**), a lively open-air restaurant and small hotel high on a hill overlooking the Turrialba Valley. The view from here is one of the finest in the country, with the lush green valley far below and volcanoes in the distance. Meals are quite inexpensive and a room will cost you only $20 a night. This place is popular with rafting companies who bring groups here for meals and for overnights before, after, and during multi-day rafting trips. You'll find Turrialtico about 6 miles out of Turrialba on the road to Siquierres.

7

Guanacaste & the Nicoya Peninsula

Guanacaste province is Costa Rica's sunniest and driest region. The rainy season starts later and ends earlier here, and overall it is more dependably sunny than in other parts of the country. Combine this climate with a coastline that stretches from the Nicaraguan border to the southern tip of the Nicoya peninsula and you have an equation that yields beach bliss. Beautiful beaches abound along this coastline. Some are pristine and deserted, some are lined with luxury resort hotels, and still others are backed by little villages where you can still get a room for under $30 a night. These beaches vary from long, straight stretches of sand to tiny coves bordered by rocky headlands. Whatever your passion in beaches, you're likely to find something that comes close to perfection.

Guanacaste is also Costa Rica's "wild west," a dry landscape of cattle ranches and cowboys, who are known here as *sabaneros,* a name that derives from the Spanish word for savannah or grassland. This is big country, with big views and big sky. If it weren't for those rain forest–clad volcanoes in the distance, you might swear you were in Texas.

1 Exploring Guanacaste

Like Texas, Guanacaste presents problems for casual touring. By car or bus, the closest beaches are around 5 hours from San José. While two beaches might appear relatively close on the map, the 10 to 20 kilometers of dry, rutted dirt road separating them can try your time, patience, and car's suspension system. Moreover, though there's dependable and daily bus service to most beaches in Guanacaste, direct connections between these beaches are quite rare. During the dry season, the hillsides in Guanacaste turn browner than the chaparral of southern California. Dust from dirt roads blankets the trees in many areas and the vistas are far from tropical. Driving these dirt roads without air-conditioning and hermetically sealed windows can be extremely unpleasant. In the rainy season, those rutted and dusty roads become muddy messes that make a four-wheel-drive vehicle necessary. Still, don't rule out Guanacaste during the rainy season— in fact, it's my favorite time to visit. The hillsides are a beautiful, rich green, and the sun usually shines all morning, giving way to an afternoon shower, when a nice siesta is often in order.

In Guanacaste, getting there is definitely less than half the fun. If you're set on beach hopping and touring the region, rent a four-wheel-drive vehicle; otherwise, pick a spot and plan to spend most of your time there. Once there, prepare to settle in for some serious, and relaxing, beach time.

The beaches aren't the only attraction here, either. At one time this land was covered with a dense, though fairly dry, forest that was cut for lumber to create pasturelands for grazing cattle. Today, that dry tropical forest exists only in remnants preserved in several national parks. Up in the mountains, in Rincón de la Vieja National Park, the landscape changes, so that you not only find lush rain forests and wildlife, but also hot springs and bubbling mudpots similar to those in Yellowstone National Park in the United States.

2 Liberia

232 kilometers NW of San José; 133 kilometers NW of Puntarenas

Founded in 1769, Liberia is the capital of Guanacaste province, and though it can hardly be considered a bustling city, it does have the distinction of having a more colonial atmosphere than almost any other city in the country. Narrow streets are lined with charming old adobe homes, many of which have ornate stone accents on their facades, carved wooden doors, and aged red-tile roofs.

Liberia is best looked upon as a base for exploring this region. From here it is possible to do day trips to nearby beaches and three national parks, although only two of them have facilities for visitors. Several moderately priced hotels are located on the outskirts of Liberia at the intersection of the Interamerican Highway and the road to the Nicoya peninsula and its many beaches. See "Where to Stay," later in this section, for detailed descriptions of the area's lodging options.

ESSENTIALS
GETTING THERE & DEPARTING

By Plane The airstrip in Liberia has finally been cleared to accept commercial international flights. However, at press time, no airlines have instituted regular flights to Liberia. Check with your travel agent, as this is expected to change.

Sansa (☎ **506/233-0397,** 506/233-3258, or 506/233-5330) has flights to Liberia leaving daily at 11:15am from the Juan Santamaría International Airport. This flight stops first in Tambor. The one-way fare is $25.

Travelair (☎ **506/220-3054** or 506/232-7883) has flights daily to Liberia at 12:30pm from San José's Pavas International Airport. This flight stops first in Tamarindo. Fares are $82 one-way; $136 roundtrip.

By Bus Express buses leave San José daily at 7, 9, and 11:30am and 1, 3, 4, 6, and 8pm from Calle 14 between avenidas 1 and 3. The ride is 4 hours. A one-way fare costs $2.80. From Puntarenas, buses leave at 5:30, 7, and 9:30am and noon and 5pm. The ride takes 2¹/₂ hours. A one-way fare costs $1.80.

Buses depart for Monteverde and San José from the Liberia bus station on the edge of town, 200 meters north and 100 meters east of the main intersection on the Interamerican Highway. Express buses for San José leave daily at 4:30, 6, 7:30, and 10am and 12:30, 2, 4, 6, and 8pm. To reach Monteverde, take any Puntarenas or San José bus leaving before 1pm. Get off at the Río Lagarto Bridge and catch the Puntarenas–Santa Elena bus, which departs at approximately 3:15pm. For information on getting to various beaches, see sections below.

By Car Take the Interamerican Highway west from San José, and follow the signs for Nicaragua. It takes approximately 4 hours to get to Liberia.

ORIENTATION

The highway passes slightly to the west of town. At the intersection with the main road into town, there are several hotels and gas stations. If you turn east into town, you will come to the central square in less than a kilometer.

Information There is a small **tourist information center** (☎ 506/666-1606) three blocks south of the modern white church on Liberia's central park. While you're here gathering information, you can quickly tour the center's little museum of Guanacaste culture. The emphasis is on the life of the *sabanero*. The center is open Monday through Saturday from 8am until noon and 1 to 5pm.

EXPLORING RINCÓN DE LA VIEJA NATIONAL PARK

This national park has an area of geothermal activity similar to Yellowstone National Park in the United States. Fumaroles, geysers, and hot pools cover a small area of this park, crating a bizarre, other-worldly landscape. Its main entrance is situated 25 kilometers northeast of Liberia down a badly rutted dirt road. There are several lodges located around the perimeter of the park, and all offer guided hikes and horseback rides into the park. In addition to hot springs and mudpots, there are waterfalls, a lake, and a volcanic crater to be explored. The bird watching here is excellent, and the views out across the pasturelands to the Pacific Ocean are stunning. Entrance **fees** for this park are $6 per person per day, with an additional $1.50 per person per day fee for camping.

NEARBY RAFTING TRIPS

Leisurely raft trips (no white water) are offered by **Safaris Corobicí** (☎ 506/669-1091) about 40 kilometers south of Liberia. They have 2-hour ($35), 3-hour ($43), and half-day ($60) trips that are great for families and birdwatchers. Along the way you may see many of the area's more exotic animal residents—howler monkeys, iguanas, caiman, coatimundis, otters, toucans, parrots, mot-mots, trogons, and many other species of birds. Aside from your binoculars and/or camera, a bathing suit and sunscreen are really the only things you need to bring on these trips.

NEARBY GUIDED BOAT TOURS & HORSEBACK RIDES

If you are staying in Liberia and want to tour the surrounding countryside with a guide, contact **Guanacaste Tours** (☎ 506/666-0306) in nearby Cañas. This company offers boat tours down the Bebedero River to Palo Verde National Park, which is south of Cañas and is best known for its migratory bird populations. They also lead a horseback trip up through the cloud forest on Miravalles Volcano, which is north of Cañas.

EXPLORING SANTA ROSA NATIONAL PARK

Best known for its remote, pristine beaches, reached by several kilometers of hiking trails or four-wheel-drive vehicle, Santa Rosa National Park is a fine place to ramble, watch sea turtles nest, and surf. Located 30 kilometers north of Liberia on the Interamerican Highway, it covers the Santa Elena peninsula and has the distinction of being Costa Rica's first national park. Unlike other national parks, it was founded not to preserve the land but to preserve a building, known as **La Casona,** which played an important role in Costa Rican independence. It was here, in 1856, that Costa Rican forces fought the decisive Battle of Santa Rosa, forcing the U.S.–backed soldier of fortune William Walker and his men to flee into Nicaragua. Inside the

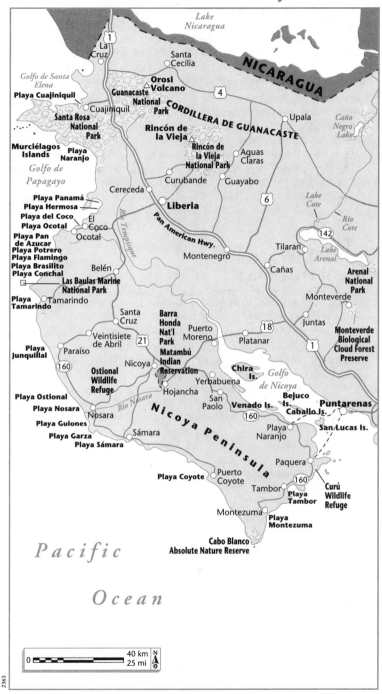

Lake Nicaragua

NICARAGUA

La Cruz

1

Santa Cecilia

Golfo de Santa Elena

Playa Cuajiniquil

Orosi Volcano

Guanacaste National Park

Cuajiniquil

CORDILLERA DE GUANACASTE

4

Upala

Caño Negro Lake

Santa Rosa National Park

Rincón de la Vieja

Rincón de la Vieja National Park

Aguas Claras

Murciélagos Islands

Playa Naranjo

Golfo de Papagayo

Cereceda

Curubande

Guayabo

Liberia

6

Lake Cote

Río Cote

Playa Panamá
Playa Hermosa
Playa del Coco
Playa Ocotal

El Coco
Ocotal

Pan American Hwy.

Montenegro

Tilaran

142

Lake Arenal

Playa Pan de Azucar
Playa Potrero
Playa Flamingo
Playa Brasilito
Playa Conchal

Belén

Cañas

Arenal National Park

Las Baulas Marine National Park

Monteverde

Playa Tamarindo

Tamarindo

Santa Cruz

Barra Honda Nat'l Park

Puerto Moreno

18

Juntas

1

Monteverde Biological Cloud Forest Preserve

Veintisiete de Abril

21

Platanar

Playa Junquillal

Paraíso

Matambú Indian Reservation

Nicoya

160

Ostional Wildlife Refuge

Río Nosara

Chira Is.

Golfo de Nicoya

Yerbabuena

Hojancha

San Paolo

Venado Is.

Bejuco Is.
Caballo Is.

Puntarenas

Playa Ostional

Playa Nosara

Nosara

Nicoya Peninsula

160

San Lucas Is.

Playa Guiones

Sámara

Playa Naranjo

Playa Garza
Playa Sámara

Paquera

Playa Coyote

Puerto Coyote

Tambor

160

Curú Wildlife Refuge

Playa Tambor

Montezuma

Playa Montezuma

Pacific

Cabo Blanco Absolute Nature Reserve

Ocean

0   40 km   N
    25 mi

2363

restored ranch house you'll find relics from and representations of that historic battle. This small museum and monument is open daily from 8am until 4:30pm.

The entrance fee for this park is $6 per person per day. Camping is allowed at several sites within the park for an extra $1.50 per person, but you must reserve a campsite in advance. Call the National Parks Service at 506/257-0922 for more information. There are also several budget lodgings around the village of Caujiniquil.

The Beaches   Eight kilometers west of La Casona down a rugged road that is impassable during the rainy season is Playa Naranjo. Four kilometers north of Playa Naranjo along a hiking trail that follows the beach you'll find Playa Nancite. Playa Blanca is 21 kilometers down a dirt road from Caujiniquil, which itself is 20 kilometers north of the park entrance. Playa Nancite is known for its *arribadas* (mass egg-layings) of olive Ridley sea turtles, which come ashore to nest by the tens of thousands each year in October. Nearby Playa Naranjo is best known for its perfect surfing waves, which break at Witch's Rock just offshore. On the northern side of the peninsula is the even more remote Playa Blanca, which can be reached in the dry season if you have a four-wheel-drive vehicle. This beach is reached by way of the village of Caujiniquil.

WHERE TO STAY IN TOWN
DOUBLES FOR LESS THAN $25

Hotel Bramadero. Carretera Interamericana, Liberia, Guanacaste. ☎ **506/666-0371.** Fax 506/666-0203. 25 rms (all with bath). $13–$18.50 single; $19–$28 double; $23–$32.50 triple; $27–$37 quad (higher prices are for A/C rooms). AE, MC, V.

This roadside motel lacks ambience, but the rates are good and the rooms are generally clean. Rooms without air-conditioning can be a bit musty and most rooms are crammed wall-to-wall with beds, so ask to see a couple rooms before accepting one. Behind the restaurant is the hotel's small pool, which is wonderfully cooling in an area that is the hottest, driest, and dustiest in Costa Rica. Rooms closest to the road and the hotel's attached restaurant and bar can be noisy at night, especially on the weekends, when families from San Josia flee the cool elevations for the warmth of the lowlands. The restaurant is quite popular, despite the fact that it gets a lot of traffic noise and serves mediocre, though filling, meals.

Hotel Guanacaste. 25 meters west and 100 meters south of the bus station, Liberia, Guanacaste. ☎ **506/666-0085.** Fax 506/666-2287. 29 rms (all with private bath). $11.50 single; $14.75 double; $20.50 triple; $23 quad. MC, V.

This very economical little hotel is primarily a hostel-type establishment catering to young travelers on a tight budget. In addition to the simply furnished rooms, there's a basic soda serving cheap Tico meals. The management can help arrange trips to nearby national parks and tell you about other interesting budget accommodations, including campgrounds, in the area. The two newest rooms are doubles with air-conditioning and cost slightly more. You'll find this basic hotel around the corner from Hotel Bramadero.

DOUBLES FOR LESS THAN $45

✪ Nuevo Hotel Boyeros. Apdo. 85, Liberia, Guanacaste. ☎ **506/666-0722** or 506/666-0995. Fax 506/666-2529. 70 rms. A/C TEL. $34 single; $42 double; $54 triple. AE, MC, V.

You'll find this economical lodging just before the main Liberia intersection on the Interamerican Highway, and though it isn't as attractively landscaped as other lodgings in town, it's all right in a pinch. Arches with turned wooden railings and a red-tile roof give this two-story motel-style building a Spanish feel. In the courtyard of the hotel are two pools—one for adults and one for children—as well as a snack bar. All the rooms have a private balcony or patio overlooking the pool. The best and coolest rooms are on the second floor of the east wing. The small restaurant serves meals ranging in price from $3.80 to $7.50. Guests also have access to a gym/fitness center two blocks away.

WORTH A SPLURGE

Hotel El Sitio. Liberia, Guanacaste. ☎ **506/666-1211.** Fax 506/666-2059. 52 rms. A/C TV TEL. $50 single; $65 double; $75 triple; $85 quad. AE, DC, MC, V.

Located about 80 yards west of the fire station on the road to Santa Cruz and the beaches, this hotel has the feel of a traditional Spanish hacienda. Throughout the hotel, there are red-tile floors and original paintings of local Guanacaste scenes on the walls. The rooms have all been remodeled and now have cool tile floors instead of carpeting, and newer air-conditioning units. The pool area is shady (a welcome relief from the strong Guanacaste sun), and there is even one of those famous pre-Columbian stone spheres in the garden. Beside the pool, there is a rancho-style bar/restaurant. Other amenities and services include horseback riding, bike rentals, a children's play area, a whirlpool tub, tour arrangements, and a car-rental desk.

A SPLURGE CHOICE NEAR CAÑAS

✪ **Hotel Hacienda La Pacífica.** Apdo. 8-5700, Cañas, Guanacaste. ☎ **506/669-0266** or 506/669-0050. Fax 506/669-0555. 33 rms. $55 single; $67 double; $77 triple; $87 quad. AE, MC, V.

If you want a central location for exploring the national parks of this region, there are few better choices than the Hacienda La Pacífica. Originally started as a research facility and wild-animal rehabilitation center, the hotel is now a spacious mini-resort with attractive grounds, organized tours and activities, marked trails, and an inviting pool. It's located on the banks of the gentle Corobicí river, which is a good place for bird watching.

Though the hotel is 40 kilometers south of Liberia, it is still convenient for visiting Santa Rosa and Rincón de la Vieja national parks, as well as Palo Verde National Park and the Lomas Barbudal Biological Reserve. Rooms vary in size, though all have tile floors and a patio of some sort. The larger rooms have private sun patios, as well as another patio. These rooms also have sliding-glass doors that make the rooms quite bright; high ceilings keep them cool. The open-air restaurant is shady and cool and serves moderately priced meals. The lodge offers a number of services, including horseback riding ($10 per hour), bike rentals ($3 per hour), guided walks ($10), rafting trips ($35 for 2 hours), and tours to the different national parks. On the grounds, you'll also find a restored 19th-century adobe house, and nearby there is a small, privately owned zoo.

WHERE TO STAY NEAR RINCÓN DE LA VIEJA NATIONAL PARK
DOUBLES FOR LESS THAN $35

Hacienda Lodge Guachepelin. Apdo. 636, Alajuela. ☎ **506/442-2864** or 506/442-2818. Fax 506/442-1910. 6 rms (none with private bath), 2 dorms. $9 per person in dorm; $14 single; $32–$35 double. Meals are an additional $17 per person per day. No credit cards.

Located 23 kilometers northeast of Liberia on the edge of Rincón de la Vieja National Park, this rustic lodge is housed in a 112-year-old ranch house. The rooms are pretty basic, and the dorms are actually the old bunkhouse. The ranch is still in operation today, and in addition to exploring the park, you can ride horses and commune with the pigs, dairy cows, and beef cattle. It isn't easy to get to the lodge and once you arrive you'll need a few days to explore the park, so plan on taking all your meals here and going on a few guided tours. A horseback tour with a bilingual guide will cost around $24 per person for a half-day ride. This is one of the closest lodges to the thermal springs (10 kilometers) and bubbling mudpots (5 kilometers) of Rincón de la Vieja National Park. Horseback rides to the geothermal areas, as well as to various lakes, the top of a nearby dormant volcano, and some beautiful waterfalls can be arranged. If you're driving a car, you'd better have four-wheel-drive or high clearance (though in the dry season it's sometimes passable in a regular car). To reach the lodge, drive about 5 kilometers north of Liberia and turn right on the dirt road to Curubande, which you will pass through in about 12 kilometers. Continue on this road for another 6 kilometers, passing through the ranch's gate, before arriving at the lodge. When you contact the lodge to make a reservation, you can arrange to be picked up in Liberia for $7 per person ($14 round-trip).

Santa Clara Lodge. Apdo. 17-5000, Quebrada Grande de Liberia, Guanacaste. ☎ **506/ 223-7141** or 506/666-0473. Fax 506/666-0475. 7 rms (none with bath), 1 cabin. $15 single without bath; $27–$30 double without bath, $41 double with bath; $32–$35 triple without bath, $45 triple with bath. Meals are an additional $17 per person per day. No credit cards.

Santa Clara Lodge is located in the foothills of Guanacaste's volcanic mountains on a working dairy farm where guests are invited to participate in the morning milking. With shady grounds on the banks of a small river, the setting is quite tranquil. You can sit beneath the palapa sipping a drink and listen to the chickens clucking in the yard or go for a swim in the mineral-water pool. The lodge is well-suited for exploring the region if you have your own car or want to arrange tours. Santa Rosa, Guanacaste, and Rincón de la Vieja national parks are all within an hour's drive. You can also hike through field and forest to four different waterfalls. Guided hikes ($10) and horseback rides ($20 to $50) can be arranged, as well as a trip to the hot springs, which is particularly worthwhile. Rooms are simply furnished, as you might expect on a working ranch, and only the cabin has a private bath. Meals are filling Tico fare, including rice and beans, steaks, chicken and fries, salads, and fruits. It is also possible to camp here. To reach the lodge, head north from Liberia for about 23 kilometers and turn right on the road to Quebrada Grande. In Quebrada Grande, turn right at the soccer field and continue for another 4 kilometers. You can also arrange free transportation from Liberia to the lodge if you phone in advance.

WORTH A SPLURGE

Rincón De La Vieja Mountain Lodge. Apdo. 114-5000, Liberia, Guanacaste. ☎ **506/ 225-1073** or 506/234-8835. Fax 506/234-1676. 27 rms (all with private bath). $38.50 single; $48.40 double; $66 triple; $81.40 quad. AE, MC, V.

This is the closest lodge to the Las Pailas mudpots and the Azufrale hot springs. The rustic lodge is surrounded by grasslands that conjure up images of the African savannah. It's at the end of the road and feels very remote (that is, the road here is really, really bad). The polished-wood main lodge looks like a cross between a ranch hacienda and a mountain cabin. There's a long verandah set with chairs, and inside is a small lounge and dining room with long tables for communal meals. Some of the rooms are quite small, while others have lots of space. Some have hammocks on their verandahs and others back up to a small stream. Meals, which are simple but hearty Tico fare, will cost you $26 to $30 a day. The lodge offers numerous day tours either on foot or horseback. Transportation from Liberia can be arranged at an additional cost. If you are driving, follow the directions to the Hacienda Lodge Guachepelin and continue driving on this dirt road for another 7 kilometers, passing the turnoff for the park entrance.

WHERE TO EAT

You don't have too many choices for dining in Liberia, and even fewer near Rincón de la Vieja, so your hotel dining room is certainly going to be the most convenient. However, most hotels serve standard fare at best. In town, the most popular alternative is **Pizzeria Pronto,** which is located 100 meters west of the tourist information center and serves a wide range of pizzas baked in a clay oven. For meals a cut above what you might expect to find in this cow town, try the following restaurants.

✪ **Restaurante Pókopí.** 100 meters west of the gas station on the road to Santa Cruz. ☎ **506/666-1036.** Main courses $3.15–$10.15. AE, MC, V. Daily 11am–10pm. CONTINENTAL.

It doesn't look like much from the outside, but this tiny restaurant has a surprising amount of class inside. An even more pleasant surprise is the unusual (for rural Costa Rica) variety of continental dishes on the menu. Order one of their delicious daiquiris while your peruse the menu, which is on a wooden cutting board. You have your choice of dolphin (the fish, not the mammal) prepared five different ways, pizza, chicken Cordon Bleu, chicken in wine sauce, and other equally delectable dishes. However, for a real surprise, order the chateaubriand. It comes to your table with great flair, surrounded by succulent fresh vegetables and a tomato stuffed with peas. Be sure to dine early if you want a quiet meal; attached to the restaurant is a disco that swings into action at 9pm, Wednesdays through Sundays. And you thought you were out in the sticks.

Restaurant Rincón Corobicí. Interamerican Highway, 4 kilometers north of Cañas. ☎ **506/669-1234.** Reservations not accepted. Main courses $2.50–$15.50. MC, V. Daily 8am–10pm. COSTA RICAN/INTERNATIONAL.

The food is actually mediocre, but the setting, particularly during the day, more than makes up for it. While there is plenty of covered seating in the main open-air dining room, you'll want to choose a table on the wooden deck, which overlooks a beautiful section of the Corobicí river. The sound of rushing water tumbling over the rocks in the riverbed is soothing accompaniment to the simple-but-filling meals. The whole fried fish is your best choice here, though they also have steaks, lobster, shrimp, and sandwiches. This restaurant makes an ideal lunch stop if you are heading to or from Liberia or have just done a rafting trip on the Corobicí river. Be sure to try the fried yuca chips. You may never go back to french fries.

3 Playa Hermosa & Playa Panamá

258 kilometers NW of San José; 40 kilometers SW of Liberia

Playa Hermosa means "beautiful beach," which is a very appropriate name for this crescent of sand. Surrounded by dry, rocky hills, this curving gray-sand beach is long and wide and rarely crowded, despite the presence of the Condovac La Costa condominium development on the hill at the north end of the beach. Fringing the beach is a swath of trees that stay surprisingly green right through the dry season. The shade provided by these trees is a big part of the beach's appeal. It gets hot here and some shade is always appreciated at the beach. At both ends of the beach rocky headlands jut out into the surf, and at the base of these rocks, you'll find tide pools that are fun to explore.

Beyond Playa Hermosa, you'll find Playa Panamá, which has recently been transformed from one of the most remote and underdeveloped beaches in Guanacaste to the first to host, not one, but two major resort hotels. Since these resorts are located slightly north of Playa Panamá proper, it is still possible to enjoy the quiet beauty of this big, calm beach.

ESSENTIALS
GETTING THERE & DEPARTING

By Plane   The nearest airports with regularly scheduled service are Liberia and Tamarindo. From either of these places you can arrange a taxi to bring you the rest of the way.

By Bus   Express buses leave San José daily at 3:20pm from Calle 12 between avenidas 5 and 7, stopping first at Playa Hermosa and next at Playa Panamá, 3 kilometers farther north. The trip takes 5 hours. One-way fare costs $3.80.

Alternately, you can take a bus from San José to Liberia (see "Liberia," above, for details) and then take a bus from Liberia to Playa Hermosa or Playa Panamá. Buses leave Liberia for these two beaches daily at 7:30 and 11:30am and 3:30, 5:45, and 7pm. The trip lasts 45 minutes. A one-way fare costs $1.

One bus departs for San José daily at 5am from Playa Panamá, with a stop in Playa Hermosa along the way. Buses to Liberia leave Playa Panamá at 5am and 4pm, stopping in Playa Hermosa a few minutes later. Ask at your hotel about where to catch the bus.

By Car   Follow the directions for getting to Liberia, then head west toward Santa Cruz. Just past the village of Comunidad, turn right. In about 11 kilometers you will come to a fork in the road. Take the right fork. These roads are relatively well marked, and a host of prominent hotel billboards should make it easy enough to find the beach. It takes about 5 hours from San José.

ORIENTATION

There are no real towns here, just a few houses and hotels on and near the beach. You will come to Playa Hermosa first, followed by Playa Panamá a few kilometers further along on the same road.

Information & Watersports-Equipment Rental   In the middle of Playa Hermosa, you'll find **Aqua Sport** (☎ **506/670-0353**), the tourist information and watersports equipment–rental center for Playa Hermosa. Kayaks, sailboards, canoes, bicycles, beach umbrellas, snorkel gear, and parasails are all available for rental at fairly reasonable rates. This is also where you'll find the local post office, public phones, and a restaurant (see "Where to Eat," below).

SWIMMING & DIVING

Either beach is usually good for swimming, although Playa Panamá is slightly more protected. If you want to do some diving while you're here, check in at the dive shop at La Costa Hotel & Villas at the north end of the beach. A two-tank dive should run around $60 per person.

GUIDED NATIONAL PARK TOURS

Ecotours (☎ **506/670-0458**) is located just south of Aqua Sport near the middle of Playa Hermosa. This small operation organizes guided tours to most of the national parks and natural attractions in the region.

WHERE TO STAY
DOUBLES FOR LESS THAN $35

Cabinas Playa Hermosa. Apdo. 117, Liberia, Guanacaste. ☎/fax **506/670-0136.** 22 rms (all with bath). $16.30 single; $32.60 double; $40.75 triple; $48.90 quad. No credit cards.

This little hotel, tucked away under shady trees, is a sprawling beachfront spread at the south end of Playa Hermosa. Each large room has a pair of Adirondack chairs on its front porch, and the beach is only a few steps away. Rooms 1 through 4 directly front the ocean, but they are also very close to the restaurant and bar, so can be noisy. The rest are located in several low buildings that run perpendicular to the beach. Even though most of the rooms are rather dark, they are large and have a lot of closet space. Each has two double beds. Horseback riding and boat trips can be arranged. The open-air restaurant has a rustic tropical feel to it, with unfinished tree trunks holding up the roof. Seafood and homemade pasta are the specialties. Menu prices range from $3.75 to $10.50; service can be quite slow and inattentive. To find the hotel, turn left at the first road into Playa Hermosa. The hotel's white archway gate is just after the curve.

WORTH A SPLURGE

✪ **El Velero Hotel.** Playa Hermosa, Guanacaste. ☎ **506/670-0330.** Fax 506/670-0310. 13 rms. $54 single or double; $68 triple; $80 quad. Rates slightly higher during Christmas and Easter, and slightly lower during off-season. AE, MC, V.

This small Canadian-owned hotel is the nicest moderately priced place on Playa Hermosa. It's located right on the beach and has its own small swimming pool beside an open-air bar. White walls and polished tile floors give El Velero a Mediterranean flavor. The guest rooms are large and most have high ceilings. The upper third of each room's walls are screens, so there is plenty of cross-ventilation. Fans also help keep the rooms cool. Bathrooms are small and have showers only. When I last visited, construction had started on eight new rooms. Various tours, horseback riding, and fishing trips can be arranged through the hotel; however, the most popular excursions are the full-day and sunset cruises on the hotel's namesake, a 38' sailboat. The hotel has its own restaurant, which offers a good selection of meat, fish, and shrimp dishes in the $6.50-to-$12.50 range.

WHERE TO EAT

Aqua Sport. On the beach. ☎ **506/670-0353.** Reservations not accepted. Main courses $4.50–$15.50. MC, V. Daily 9am–9pm (noon–9pm in rainy season). CONTINENTAL.

Part of the Aqua Sport market and equipment-rental shop is a small open-air restaurant with tables of polished hardwood. The beach is only steps away, and the atmosphere is very casual. The food, however, is much better than what you would expect from such a place. The focus is on seafood—grilled lobster for $15.50, shrimp à la diabla for $7.50, and huge paella or assorted seafood platters that feed four for $45 and $50 respectively.

4 Playa del Coco & Playa Ocotal

253 kilometers NW of San José; 35 kilometers W of Liberia

Playa del Coco is one of the most easily accessible beaches in Guanacaste, with a paved road right down to the water, and has long been a popular destination with middle-class Ticos from San José. Unfortunately, most of the hotels right in town are quite run-down, and the water is neither very clean or appealing (this is a busy fishing port). The crowds that come here like their music loud and constant, so if you're in search of a quiet retreat, stay away. On the other hand, if you're looking for a beach with a variety of budget hotels and plenty of cheap food and beer close at hand, you may enjoy Playa del Coco.

The beach, which has a grayish brown sand, is quite wide at low tide and almost nonexistent at high tide. In between high and low, it's just right. Trash is a bit of a problem right in town. However, if you walk down the long, curving beach to the north of town, you're bound to find a nice, clean spot to unfold your blanket. Better still, if you have a car, head over to Playa Ocotal, which is a couple of kilometers down a dirt road. This is a tiny pocket of a cove bordered by high bluffs, and is quite beautiful.

ESSENTIALS
GETTING THERE & DEPARTING

By Plane   The nearest airport with regularly scheduled flights is in Liberia. From there you can take a bus or arrange for a taxi to take you to Playa del Coco.

By Bus   An express bus leaves San José at 10am daily from Calle 14 between avenidas 1 and 3, stopping first in Playa del Coco. Allow 5 hours for the trip. A one-way ticket is $2.80. From Liberia, buses leave at 5:30 and 8:15am and 12:30, 2, 4:30, and 6:15pm. The trip takes 45 minutes. A one-way ticket costs $1.10.

One bus departs daily from Playa Ocotal for San José at 9:15am, stopping in Playa del Coco a few minutes later. Buses for Liberia leave at 7 and 9:15am and 2, 3, and 6pm.

By Car   Follow the directions for getting to Liberia and Playa Hermosa, but take the left fork instead. It takes about 5 hours from San José.

ORIENTATION

Playa del Coco is a small but busy beach town. Most of its hotels and restaurants are either on the water or on the road leading into town. Playa Ocotal is south of Playa de Coco on a dirt road that leaves the main road just before the beach. Playa Ocotal is a collection of vacation homes, condos, and hotels, and has one bar on the beach.

FUN ON & OFF THE BEACH

There is not much to do here except lie on the sand, hang out in the sodas and bars, or go to the discos. If you're interested, you might be able to join a soccer match (the soccer field is in the middle of town). Over at nearby Playa Ocotal there are often pickup volleyball games by the soda on the beach. It's also possible to arrange horseback rides; ask your hotel.

Scuba Diving   Scuba diving is the most popular watersport in the area and dive shops abound. **Bill Beard's Diving Safaris** (☎ 506/670-0012), **Mario Vargas Expeditions** (☎ 506/670-0351), and **Rich Coast Diving** (☎ 506/670-0176) all offer equipment rentals and dive trips. A two-tank dive, with equipment, should cost between $60 and $80 per person. Both Mario Vargas and Diving Safaris also offer PADI-certification courses.

Sportfishing   Full- and half-day sportfishing excursions can be arranged through **Papagayo Sportfishing** (☎ 506/670-0354) or the **Hotel Flor de Itabo** (☎ 506/670-0011).

WHERE TO STAY
DOUBLES FOR LESS THAN $25

Cabinas Chale. Playa del Coco, Guanacaste. ☎ **506/670-0036.** Fax 506/670-0303. 25 rms (all with bath). $20.20 single; $23.40 double; $26.85 triple; $30.20 quad. No credit cards.

Located down a dirt road to the right as you are coming into town, this small lodging is quite a bit better than those directly on the beach, and is also much quieter. Your only company as you stroll down to the beach, which is only 150 feet away, may be a herd of grazing cattle. The rooms are simply furnished with double beds, overhead fans, tile floors, and refrigerators, and each comes with a Tico clothes-washing sink called a *pila*. Some larger rooms have just been added and these are a bit nicer than the older rooms. There is a Spartan, screen-walled bar that is open only during the busy season (November to April), and a small pool on a raised patio in back.

La Luna Tica. Playa del Coco, Guanacaste. ☎ **506/670-0279.** 31 rms (all with bath). $12–$17 single; $17–$22 double; $23–$28 triple; $31.50–$36.50 quad. Breakfast is included. No credit cards.

This is a good budget choice if you want to be close to the the beach. It's located just south of the soccer field and its 15 oldest rooms are located right on the beach. These are very basic, have polished concrete floors, and are kept very clean. The newer rooms are in the annex just across the street. Three of these have air-conditioning. The nicest rooms are on the second floor; each has hardwood floors and is flanked by a cool verandah. The Luna Tica also has a traditional *soda* right on the beach, serving inexpensive Tico meals and fish dishes. Considering that the room rates include breakfast, this is the best deal in town.

WORTH A SPLURGE

Hotel La Flor de Itabo Apdo. 32, Playa del Coco, Guanacaste. ☎ **506/670-0292** or 506/670-0011. 16 rms, 8 apts. $31–$50 single; $31–$57 double; $70 apartment for one to four people. AE, DC, MC, V.

This is the most luxurious of the hotels right in Playa del Coco, and though it is not on the beach, the pool is large and the grounds are lushly planted. Toucans and parrots squawk and talk amid the flowers, adding their own bright colors to an already colorful garden. Stone reproductions of pre-Columbian statues provide a touch of the mysterious at this quiet retreat. With fewer than two dozen rooms, the service here is reliably good. The most inexpensive rooms are in four bungalows, with screened-in windows and fans. The standard rooms are more spacious, have air-conditioning, and are attractively decorated with wood carvings and Guatemalan textiles. The apartments are located a little bit away from the main building. While they are larger than the standard and bungalow rooms, have air-conditioning, and include kitchenettes, they tend to feel a bit Spartan. Italian dishes are the specialty of the restaurant, with main courses ranging from $6.10 to $10.15. The bar is decorated with flags from all over the world and is a popular hangout with sport fishermen. There is even a small casino here. In addition to a pool, the hotel has a volleyball court, children's play area, and a small park.

✪ **Hotel Villa Casa Blanca** Apdo. 176-5019, Playa del Coco, Guanacaste. ☎/fax **506/670-0448.** 10 rms, 4 suites. $40–$50 single; $50–$55 double; $60–$65 triple; $80–$85 suites. Breakfast is included. AE, MC, V (add 6% surcharge).

With friendly, helpful owners, beautiful gardens, and attractive rooms, this bed-and-breakfast inn is my favorite spot in the area. The inn is located in a new development about 500 meters from the beach and is built in the style of a Spanish villa. All the guest rooms have their own distinct characters, and though some are a bit cramped, others feel quite roomy. One room has a canopy bed and a beautiful bathroom with a step-up bath. The suites are higher up and have ocean views. My favorite has a secluded patio with lush flowering plants all around. A little rancho serves as an open-air bar and breakfast area, and beside this is a pretty little lap pool with a bridge over it. Villa Blanca also represents several rental houses and condos in the area, so if you plan to stay for a week or more or need lots of room, ask about these.

WHERE TO EAT

There are dozens of cheap open-air restaurants at the traffic circle in the center of El Coco village. These restaurants serve Tico standards, with an emphasis on fried fish. Prices are quite low, and so too is the quality for the most part. For better food try the following two places. For views, you can't beat the restaurant at **El Ocotal Beach Resort** and for desserts, lunch or snacks, there's **San Francisco Treats.**

✪ **Helen's.** 100 meters south of the ice factory. ☎ **506/670-0121.** Reservations not accepted. Main courses $4.85–$12.50. No credit cards. Daily 11am–10pm. COSTA RICAN/SEAFOOD.

This is a local favorite, and because Helen's husband is a fisherman, the seafood is always absolutely fresh. The ceviche comes in a big bowl and is enough for meal. Be sure to try the lobster soup if it's on the menu.

El Rancho de Ocotal. Playa Ocotal. ☎ **506/670-0429.** Reservations not accepted. Pizzas $5–$7.50; main courses $7.50–$15. MC, V. Daily 8am–10pm. INTERNATIONAL.

This open-air restaurant near the beach at Playa Ocotal specializes in wood-oven pizzas, but is also popular for its swimming pool. You can order a meal or just a drink and use the pool for as long as you like. There are also steaks and seafood on the menu.

5 Playas Flamingo, Potrero, Brasilito & Conchal

280 kilometers NW of San José; 66 kilometers SW of Liberia

These beaches were among the first in Costa Rica to attract international attention, and today Playa Flamingo remains the most highly developed beach on this stretch of coast. This isn't surprising when you see the blue water and narrow strand of white sand that is Playa Flamingo. The views from Playa Potrero are beautiful; on Playa Brasilito, budget travelers have a chance at some fun in the sun without spending a fortune; and, until quite recently, Playa Conchal was the exclusive find of a select group of beachcombers. What makes this grouping of beaches so memorable are the little, rocky islands offshore and the long sweeps of beach that are separated by a rugged peninsula.

On **Playa Brasilito** you will find one of the only two real villages in the area. The soccer field is the center of the village, and around its edges you'll find a couple of little *pulperias* (general stores). There's a long stretch of beach, and though it is of gray sand, it still has a quiet, undiscovered feel to it (at least on weekdays). Playa Brasilito is rapidly becoming popular both with Ticos and budget travelers from abroad. There's now a disco here and on weekends it can get pretty crowded and noisy.

Just south of Brasilito is the small, crushed-shell beach of **Conchal.** At press time, finishing touches were being put on a major 300-room resort, which should drastically change the feel of this former beachcomber's secret retreat.

Only a few miles away is the luxury resort beach called **Playa Flamingo.** This is one of Costa Rica's top resort beaches, with luxury hotels, a marina, a private airstrip, retirement and vacation homes, and one of the only white-sand beaches in the area. In fact, the old name for this beach was Playa Blanca, which made plenty of sense. When the developers moved in, they needed a more romantic name than "White Beach," so it became Playa Flamingo, even though there are no flamingos.

You'll probably want to spend plenty of time on this beautiful beach. Playa Flamingo is on a long spit of land that forms part of Potrero Bay, or Bahia Flamingo, as the developers wish it to be known. On the ocean side of the peninsula, there is the long white-sand beach, behind which is a dusty road and then a mangrove swamp. At the end of the sand spit is a fortress-like rock outcropping upon which most of Playa Flamingo's hotels and vacation homes are built. There are great views from this rocky hill. If you are not staying on Playa Flamingo, you should know that there are parking spots all along the beach road where you can park your car for the day. There is, however, little shade on the beach, so be sure to use plenty of sunscreen and bring an umbrella if you can. The bay side of the peninsula is where the marina is located.

If you continue along the road from Brasilito without taking the turn for Playa Flamingo, you will soon come to **Playa Potrero.** The sand here is a brownish gray, but the beach is long, clean, and deserted. You can see the hotels of Playa Flamingo across the bay. Drive a little further and you will find the still underdeveloped **Playa La Penca** and **Sugar Beach.**

ESSENTIALS
GETTING THERE
By Plane   The nearest airport with regularly scheduled flights is in Tamarindo. From there you can arrange for a taxi to drive you to any one of these beaches.

By Bus   Express buses leave San José daily at 8 and 10:30am from the corner of Calle 20 and Avenida 3, stopping at Playas Brasilito, Flamingo, and Potrero, in that order. The ride takes 6 hours. A one-way ticket costs $4.50.

Express buses depart Playa Potrero for San José at 9am and 2pm, stopping a few minutes later in Playa Flamingo and Playa Brasilito. Ask at your hotel where the best place is for catching the bus. Buses to Santa Cruz leave Portrero at 9am and 5pm. If you are heading north toward Liberia, get off the bus at Belén and wait for a bus going north. Buses leave Santa Cruz regularly for San José.

By Car   There are two major routes to these beaches. The most direct route is by way of the Tempisque river ferry. Take the Interamerican Highway west from San José. 47 kilometers past the turnoff for Puntarenas, turn left for the ferry. After crossing the Tempisque river, follow the signs for Nicoya, continuing north to Santa Cruz. About 16 kilometers north of Santa Cruz, just before the village of Belén, take the turnoff for Playas Flamingo, Brasilito, and Potrero. After another 20 kilometers, take the right fork to reach these beaches. The drive takes about 6 hours.

It is often slightly quicker, particularly on Friday and Saturday when beach traffic is heavy, to drive north all the way to Liberia and then come back south, thus avoiding the lines of cars waiting to take the ferry. This also applies if you are heading back to San José on a Sunday. After you reach Liberia, follow the directions for reaching Playa Hermosa, but continue on the main road past the town of Filadelfia, until the village of Belén. Turn right here until you reach Huacas, where there will be signs pointing you toward Playa Flamingo.

ORIENTATION
These beaches are strung out over several miles of dirt roads. Playa Flamingo is by far the most developed. It is located down a side road, while the villages of Brasilito and Potrero are right on the main road.

FUN ON & OFF THE BEACH
Though Playa Flamingo is the prettiest beach in this area, Playa Potrero has the gentlest surf, and therefore is the best swimming beach. Playa Conchal, which is nearly legendary for its crushed pink seashells, is a short walk south of Brasilito, and though it is beautiful, the drop-off is quite steep and known for its dangerous riptides. The water at Playa Brasilito is often fairly calm, which makes it another good swimming choice. However, my favorites are Playas La Penca and Sugar Beach.

Scuba Diving   Scuba diving is quite popular here. The following companies can all take you out for a day of underwater exploration. **The Quicksilver/Holiday Scuba** (☎ 506/654-4010) operates out of the Hotel Aurola Playa Flamingo, **EcoTreks** (☎ 506/654-4141) is based at the Flamingo Marina Hotel and Club, and **Costa Rica Diving** (☎ 506/654-4148) is located on the road to Playa Portrero. All of them offer trips out to the Catalina and Bat Islands for between $60 and $90. Both Quicksilver/Holiday and EcoTreks also offer PADI-certification courses.

Sportfishing   If you want to go sportfishing, you'll have plenty of options here. The **Marina Flamingo Yacht Club** (☎ 506/654-4203) can hook you up with a variety of boats based along its docks. A full-day fishing excursion can cost between $450 and $1,200, depending on the size of the boat. Half-day trips cost between $250 and $550. These prices are for the full boat (between two and eight people depending on size) and usually include lunch and drinks.

Alternatively, you can contact the **Bahia Portrero Resort Hotel & Club** (☎ 506/654-4183), **Flamingo Marina Hotel & Club** (☎ 506/290-1858), **Club Villas Pacífica** (☎ 506/654-4137), or Tom Bradwell at **Blue Marlin Sport Fishing** (☎ 506/654-4043). The choices are many and competition is fierce here, so shop around to find the boat, skipper, and price that best fit your needs.

Horseback Riding   If you'd rather stay on dry land, you can arrange a horseback ride with **Jalisco Tours** (☎ 506/654-4106). They charge approximately $10 per hour for their rides.

Mountain Biking   You can rent a mountain bike from **EcoTreks** (☎ 506/654-4141) at the Flamingo Marina Hotel and Club. Ask the folks at EcoTreks and they'll point you to a ride suited to your ability and conditioning level.

WHERE TO STAY
DOUBLES FOR LESS THAN $25

Cabinas Conchal. Playa Brasilito (Apdo. 185-5150, Santa Cruz), Guanacaste. ☎/fax **506/654-4257.** 8 rms (all with private bath). $19 single or double; $23 triple; $29 quad. No credit cards.

Located on the south edge of Brasilito, Cabinas Conchal consists of several yellow buildings inside a walled compound. The stucco-and-stone construction gives the buildings a bit of character as well as added security. Some rooms have just a double bed, while others have a double and a pair of bunk beds. All are quite clean. Table fans help keep the rooms cool. The beach is about 200 meters away.

DOUBLES FOR LESS THAN $35

✪ **Cabinas Cristina.** Playa Potrero (Apdo. 121, Santa Cruz), Guanacaste. ☎ **506/654-4006.** Fax 506/654-4128. 5 rms (all with bath). $22.50 single; $25.25 double; $28.50 triple; $33.40 quad. No credit cards.

This little place is located on Playa Potrero across the bay from Playa Flamingo and a few kilometers north of Brasilito. Although Cabinas Cristina isn't right on the beach, it's still a great value in this area of high-priced hotels. The rooms are spacious and very clean (they fill up fast), with hot plates, refrigerators, dressers, bars with stools, tiled baths, and double and bunk beds. On the verandah there are large rocking chairs. The friendly owner, Daniel Boldrini, speaks some English. There is a small pool in the middle of a grassy green yard and a thatched-roof palapa. Playa Potrero is just a 5-minute walk down a dirt road.

Hotel Brasilito. Playa Brasilito, Santa Cruz, Guanacaste. ☎ **506/654-4237.** Fax 506/654-4247. 15 rms (all with private bath). $22–$31 single; $28–$36 double. V.

This hotel, right in Brasilito and just across a sand road from the beach, offers basic, small rooms that are generally quite clean. There's also a bar and big open-air restaurant serving economical meals. This is still one of the best values in town, though the building across the street is a disco, which makes it difficult go to bed early on the weekends. The higher prices are for rooms with air-conditioning. Rates also rise during Christmas and Easter. Rooms "A" and "B" have a nice balcony and ocean views. The hotel also rents snorkeling equipment, body boards, and horses, and can arrange a variety of tours.

WORTH A SPLURGE

✪ **Hotel Sugar Beach.** Playa Pan de Azucar (Apdo. 90), Guanacaste. ☎ **506/654-4242** or 307/733-2904 in the U.S. Fax 506/654-4329 or 307/733-1058 in the U.S. 29 rms, 2 suites. $80–$125 single or double; $150–$200 suite. AE, MC, V.

Just as the name implies, the Hotel Sugar Beach is located on a white-sand beach—one of the few in the area and therefore one of the most attractive. So far, this hotel is the only thing out here, giving it strong measure of seclusion and privacy. The beach is on a small cove surrounded by rocky hills. Unfortunately, the hills become very brown and desolate in the dry season (which is when most tourists come to visit), so don't expect the verdant tropics if you come down here in March or April. The hotel itself is perched above the water. Nature lovers will be thrilled to find wild howler monkeys and iguanas almost on their doorsteps. Snorkelers also should be happy here; this cove has some good snorkeling in the dry season. The newest rooms are set back amid the trees and are quite large. Tile floors, wicker furniture, beautiful carved doors, and big bathrooms all add up to first-class comfort. The oldest rooms are the most basic, though they are in an interesting circular building. Hammocks under the trees provide a great way to while away a hot afternoon. The open-air dining room is in a circular building with a panoramic vista of ocean, islands, and hills. There are daily specials with prices from $6 to $15 for entrees. Scuba-diving and snorkeling trips, horseback riding, and fishing-boat charters can be arranged. The hotel rents masks and fins, sea kayaks, and boogie boards.

Hotel Bahia Potrero Beach Resort. Playa Potrero (Apdo. 45-5051, Santa Cruz), Guanacaste. ☎ **506/654-4183.** Fax 506/654-4093. 14 rms (all with bath). $69 single or double; $76 triple. All rates include continental breakfast. AE, MC, V.

This comfortable little beach hotel is on Playa Potrero and, from the beach in front, has a view of Playa Flamingo across the bay. Set in a green garden with a white wooden fence surrounding the property, the Bahia Flamingo feels like a private home in the country. A laid-back atmosphere prevails—with hammocks for dozing, a pool, and miles of nearly deserted beach for strolling and swimming. The rooms are large and cool, though a little dark. They all have refrigerators and a small patio. Fishing and snorkeling trips can be arranged. To find this hotel, watch for the sign pointing down a road to the left a mile or so after you pass the turnoff for Playa Flamingo. The hotel's restaurant is a breezy, high-ceilinged room and has a nice view of the green lawns, white fence, and blue ocean. Meals of fresh seafood and hearty steaks average $5 to $10.

LONG-TERM STAYS & CAMPING

If you plan to be here for a while or are coming down with friends or a large family, you might want to consider renting a condo or house. They rent for anywhere between $100 and $300 per day in the high season (slightly less during the low season). For information and reservations, contact **Sea View Rentals,** Apdo. 77, Santa Cruz, Guanacaste (☎ **506/654-4007;** fax 506/654-4009).

It's possible to camp on Playa Potrero, but there's no camping on the other beaches. Contact **Maiyra's** (☎ 506/654-4213), where sites are available for $2 per person. Maiyra's also has some basic cabins.

WHERE TO EAT

Dining options are not great for the budget traveler in this area. You can find basic sodas in Brasilito, Potrero, and La Penca, but not much else. Most of the restaurants in Flamingo are geared towards the well-heeled set. The one great exception is Marie's (see below).

Amberes. Playa Flamingo near the Flamingo Marina Hotel. ☎ **506/654-4001.** Reservations recommended in high season. Main courses $5.90–$16.50. MC, V. Daily 6:30–10pm. CONTINENTAL.

This is the happening spot in Flamingo, but it's not cheap. Not only is it the most upscale restaurant outside of a hotel, but it also boasts a bar, a disco, and even a tiny casino. So, you can come for dinner and make it an evening. Though the menu changes daily, you'll always find a wide selection of dishes, with the accent on seafood. Fresh fish served either meuniere or provence style are two of the best dishes here. One drawback is that they play their music way too loud at dinner. Thankfully, the open-air disco doesn't start cranking until 10pm. The bar opens at 5pm.

✪ **Marie's.** Playa Flamingo near the Flamingo Marina Hotel. ☎ **506/654-4136.** Reservations not accepted. Sandwiches $2–$5.50; main courses $4–$15. V. Daily 6:30am–9pm.

Right in the middle of all the luxury hotels at Playa Flamingo is a great little place for a snack or a full meal. The menu is primarily sandwiches and other lunch foods, but on the blackboard behind the bar you'll find daily specials such as mahi-mahi (called "dorado" down here) and, from August to December, lobster and conch. You'll also find such Tico favorites as casados and ceviche. Tables in the open-air restaurant are made from slabs of tree trunks. Be sure to try the three-milks cake (*très leches*, a Nicaraguan specialty), which just might be the moistest cake on earth.

6 Playa Tamarindo

295 kilometers NW of San José; 73 kilometers SW of Liberia

Tamarindo is growing rapidly, but so far the development remains a mixture of mostly small hotels in a variety of price ranges and an eclectic array of restaurants. The beach itself is a long, wide swath of white sand that curves gently from one rocky headland to another. Behind the beach are low, dry hills that can be a very dreary brown in the dry season but instantly turn green with the first brief showers of the rainy season. The dust that turns the hills brown can also make the main street through Tamarindo extremely unpleasant to walk along, so stick to the beach.

Though there is only one major resort hotel in town, the abundance of stylish smaller hotels have made Tamarindo one of the most popular beaches on this coast. Fishing boats bob at their moorings at the south end of the beach, and brown pelicans fish just outside the breakers. A sandy islet offshore makes a great destination if you are a strong swimmer; if you're not, it makes a great foreground for sunsets. Tamarindo is popular with surfers, who ply the break right here, or use it as a jumping-off place for Playas Grande, Langosta, Avellana, and Negra.

Nearby Playa Grande is one of the last nesting sites for the giant leatherback turtle, the largest turtle in the world. This beach is usually too rough for swimming, but the beach break is becoming a surfer favorite.

ESSENTIALS
GETTING THERE & DEPARTING

By Plane   Sansa (☎ **506/233-0397,** 506/233-5330, or 506/233-3258 in San José) flies non-stop to Tamarindo from San José's Juan Santamaría International Airport at 7am Monday through Saturday. The flight takes 45 minutes. Sansa also has a daily 11:15am flight that stops first in Tambor and Liberia before touching down in Tamarindo. This takes 1¹/₂ hours. The one-way fare for either flight is $50.

   Travelair (☎ **506/220-3054** or 506/232-7883) flies to Tamarindo daily at 7:40am and 12:30pm from San José's Pavas International Airport. The first flight makes one stop en route, the second is non-stop. Flight durations are 1 hour 15 minutes and 50 minutes, respectively. Fare is $82 one-way, $136 round-trip.

   Sansa flights leave Tamarindo for San José at 7:55am Monday through Saturday and daily at 1pm. Travelair flights leave for San José at 9:05am and 1:30pm daily.

By Bus   Two express buses leave San José daily for Tamarindo. The 3:30pm bus departs from Calle 14 between avenidas 3 and 5 and takes 5¹/₂ hours. The one-way fare is $4.20. The 4pm departure leaves San José from Calle 20 between Avenidas 1 and 3, takes 6 hours, and costs $4.10 for a one-way ticket.

   Alternately, you can catch a bus to Santa Cruz from the Calle 20 station. Buses leave San José for Santa Cruz daily at 7:30 and 10:30am and 2, 4, and 6pm. Duration is 5 hours. One-way fare is $3.50. Buses leave Santa Cruz for Tamarindo daily at 4:30, 6:30, 8:30, and 11:30am and 1 and 8:30pm. Duration is 1¹/₂ hours. One-way fare is $1.40.

   If you are coming from Liberia, you can take a Santa Cruz or Nicoya bus (which run almost hourly), get off in the village of Belén, south of Filadelfia, and wait for the next Tamarindo-bound bus. However, since buses to Tamarindo are infrequent, you may have a long wait. It's generally best to go to Santa Cruz and pick up the Tamarindo-bound bus there.

   A direct bus leaves Tamarindo for San José daily at 5:45am. Buses to Santa Cruz leave at 6, 6:30, 7, and 9am and noon and 3pm. In Santa Cruz you must transfer to a San José bus.

By Car   The most direct route is by way of the Tempisque river ferry. Take the Interamerican Highway west from San José, and 47 kilometers past the turnoff for Puntarenas, turn left toward the ferry. After crossing the Tempisque river, follow the signs for Nicoya, continuing north to Santa Cruz. About 16 kilometers north of Santa Cruz, just before the village of Belén, take the turnoff for Tamarindo. In another 20 kilometers take the left fork for Playa Tamarindo. The drive takes about 6 hours.

   On Fridays and Saturdays, when beach traffic is heavy, it is often quicker to drive all the way north to Liberia and then come back south, thus avoiding the lines of cars waiting to take the ferry. This also applies if you are heading back to San José on a Sunday. See the section "Playas Flamingo, Potrero, Brasilito & Conchal," above for more specific directions.

ORIENTATION

The unpaved road leading into town runs parallel to the beach and dead-ends just past Cabinas Zully Mar. There are a couple of side roads off this main road that lead further on to Playa Langosta, where several of the newer hotels are to be found.

FUN ON & OFF THE BEACH

Tamarindo is a long beach and though it can be great for swimming at times, it is often too rough. You also have to be careful when and where you swim on Tamarindo Beach. There are rocks just offshore in several places, some of which are exposed only at low tide. An encounter with one of these rocks could be nasty, especially if you are bodysurfing. Also, you should avoid swimming near the estuary mouth, where the currents can carry you out away from the beach.

If you want to just laze on the beach, you can pick up beach chairs, umbrellas, and mats at **Tamarindo Tour/Rentals** (☎ **506/654-4078**), located on the right as you come into town. It is open daily, and doubles as the local information center and ICT office.

Snorkeling, Surfing & Sea Kayaking If you want to try any of these watersports while in Tamarindo, **Iguana Surf** (☎ **506/654-4019**) is your one-stop source for equipment. To get there, head up the main road, turning left before the Zully Mar cabins (in the direction of the Hotel Pasatiempo) and then follow this road as it turns right and the shop will be prominently on your left. These folks are open daily and rent snorkeling equipment ($15 per day), boogie boards ($10 per day), sea kayaks ($35 per day), and surfboards ($20 per day). They also have half-day and hourly rates for many of these items.

You can also rent similar equipment at slightly lower rates from **Tamarindo Tour/ Rentals** (☎ **506/654-4078**), open daily, and located on the right as you enter town.

Sportfishing **Papagayo Excursions** (☎ **506/654-4254**), which has its office at the Hotel Tamarindo Diria, offers folks a chance to go after the big ones that abound in the waters offshore. From here it takes only 20 minutes to reach the edge of the continental shelf and the waters preferred by marlin and sailfish. Although fishing is good all year, the peak season for billfish is between mid-April and August. Rates for the boat are $250 to $450 for a half day and $350 to $700 for a full day. Alternatively, you can contact **Tamarindo Sportfishing** (☎ **506/653-0090**), which offers half-day trips for between $250 and $500 and full-day trips for between $350 and $800.

Watching Nesting Sea Turtles On nearby Playa Grande, leatherback sea turtles nest between August and February. One of the best times to see this activity is at night. For optimal viewing, join a night tour—they usually cost $12 per person. Only a few guides are licensed to operate these tours and all groups are required to use only red-light flashlights. No flash photography is allowed because any sort of light can confuse the turtles and prevent them from laying their eggs. Before going on one of these tours, make sure that your guide will be following all precautions aimed at protecting the turtles. Playa Grande is just north of Tamarindo across a small river mouth. The trips simply ferry folks across in small pangas and then you walk 5 to 10 minutes up Playa Grande.

Bicycling, Horseback Riding, and Other Activities Bicycles are available for rent at **Tamarindo Tour/Rentals** (see above for phone and location), and you can arrange to go horseback riding through **Papagayo Excursions** (☎ **506/654-4254**). Rates for horses, with a guide, are $25 for 2 hours. This company also offers 2-hour boat tours of the nearby estuary for $20 per person and full-day trips to Palo Verde National Park for $75. The estuary tours, which head back into the mangrove swamp near Tamarindo, are very popular and are offered by several companies around town. Ask at your hotel, and you should be able to arrange one of these boat trips for under $13.

WHERE TO STAY
DOUBLES FOR LESS THAN $25

In addition to the cabinas and hotel listed below, there are two campgrounds in Tamarindo: a private campground on the beach just before Tamarindo Tour/ Rentals on the outskirts of town; and **Tito's Camping,** out by the Hotel Capitan Suizo on the road toward Playa Langosta. Tito's charges $2 per person.

Cabinas Marielos. Playa Tamarindo, Guanacaste. ☎ **506/653-0041.** 14 rms (all with bath). $16.20 single; $18.80 double; $20.90 triple; $25 quad. No credit cards.

This place is located down a palm-shaded driveway across the road from the beach. Rooms are clean and fairly new, though small and simply furnished. There are tile floors and wooden chairs on the patios. Some of the bathrooms do not have doors, but they are clean. There is even a kitchen that guests can use. The garden provides a bit of shade. The hotel provides a laundry service and can arrange turtle tours.

Cabinas Zully Mar. Tamarindo, Guanacaste. ☎ **506/226-4732.** 27 rms (all with bath). $13.80–$23.90 single; $18.67–$36.58 double; $23.55–$42.55 triple. AE, MC, V.

The Zully Mar has long been a favorite of budget travelers staying in Tamarindo. The newer rooms, which are in a two-story white-stucco building with a wide, curving staircase on the outside, have air-conditioning and are more comfortable. The doors to these guest rooms are particularly interesting; they're hand carved with pre-Columbian motifs. There are also high ceilings with fans, tile floors, a long veran-dah, and large bathrooms. The older rooms are much smaller and more Spartan. Although there are mango trees out front for shade, there is little other landscaping, and the sandy grounds look a bit unkempt. Don't let this bother you: Miles of beach are just across the street, as are a popular restaurant and bar.

Hotel Pozo Azul. Playa Tamarindo, Santa Cruz, Guanacaste. ☎ **506/653-0280** or 506/ 653-0286. 27 rms (all with bath). $22.60–$28.60 double or triple; $35.80 quad. No credit cards.

This is one of the first hotels you'll spot as you drive into Tamarindo proper. It's on the left side of the road and therefore not on the beach. There isn't much shade on the grounds, but there are swimming pools for adults and kids. In the 17 rooms with air-conditioning, there are also hot plates, refrigerators, tables and chairs, large win-dows, and *pilas* (sinks) for washing clothes. Some rooms have covered parking to keep your car out of the blistering heat. There is no restaurant here, so you'll have to either cook your own meals or walk into town to one of the restaurants. In recent years, the Pozo Azul has become a surfer hangout.

WORTH A SPLURGE

✪ **Hotel El Milagro.** Playa Tamarindo (Apdo. 145-5150, Santa Cruz), Guanacaste. ☎ **506/ 653-0042** or 506/441-5102. Fax 506/441-8494. 33 rms. $45 single with fan, $55 single with A/C; $50–$60 double with fan, $60–$70 double with A/C. Additional persons $10. All rates include continental breakfast. AE, MC, V.

This place started out as a restaurant but has expanded into an attractive little hotel on the edge of town. It's located across the road from the beach, and the rooms are lined up in two long rows facing each other behind the restaurant. The front wall of each room is made of louvered doors that can be opened up to give the room plenty of air. These doors open onto small semicircular patios. Rooms are comfortable and have high ceilings. Pretty gardens and some big, old shade trees make El Milagro even more attractive. The restaurant serves excellent continental dishes, and there is a swimming pool with a swim-up bar. There's also a children's pool. Various tours and excursions can be arranged through the hotel.

☼ Sueño del Mar. Playa Tamarindo, Guanacaste. ☎/fax **506/653-0284.** 3 rms, 1 suite. $65–$85 single; $75–$95 double; $95–$165 suite. All rates include breakfast. AE, MC, V.

This place is such a gem I hesitate to let the secret out. Located at the south end of Tamarindo beach on Punta Langosta, it's the little touches and innovative design that set Sueño del Mar apart. The rooms are actually small, but feature four-poster beds made from driftwood, African dolls on the window sills, Kokopeli candle holders and open-air showers with sculpted anglefish, hand-painted tiles, and lush tropical plants. Fabrics are from Bali and Guatemala. Somehow, all this works well together, along with the requisite hammocks nestled under shade trees right on the beach. The suite is a separate small *casita* with its own kitchen, verandah, and sleeping loft. The breakfasts are earning local renown. The beach right out front is rocky and a bit rough, but does reveal some nice quiet tidal pools at low tide.

WHERE TO EAT
MEALS FOR LESS THAN $6

In addition to the places listed below, there's an **unnamed restaurant** in a basic wooden shack, next to the Sunrise Cafe, where I've had some of the freshest fish dinners of my life. The **Soda Natural,** next to Cabinas Marielos, is also a good, inexpensive spot for breakfast and lunch.

Fiesta del Mar. At the end of the main road. No phone. Reservations not accepted. Main courses $3.95–$14. No credit cards. Daily 8am–11pm. STEAK/SEAFOOD.

Located across the circle from the beach, the Fiesta del Mar specializes in steaks and seafood cooked over a wood fire. Try the the whole fried fish for $4.50, or splurge for the grilled steak in garlic sauce for $8. The open-air dining area is edged with greenery and has a thatched roof, so it feels very tropical. There is also live music several nights a week.

Restaurant Zully Mar. At the end of the road. No phone. Most items $3–$12.50. No credit cards. Daily 7am–11pm. COSTA RICAN.

This restaurant, opposite the hotel of the same name, is right on the beach at the end of the road that leads into Tamarindo. It's definitely a step above the average Tico-style open-air restaurant. The food is good, and the view can't be beat. Sit and watch the boats bob in the swells just offshore while you dine on fresh fish sautéed in garlic. The bar is a popular hangout with locals and tourists, and a big bowl of ceviche accompanied by a few drinks is a favorite order. Be forewarned: This place is often mobbed, especially on weekends, when they sometimes set up a huge stereo system and blast dance music.

Panadería Johann. On the road into town. No phone. Reservations not accepted. Most items: $2–$9. No credit cards. Daily 6am–8pm. BAKERY/PIZZA.

There are always fresh-baked goodies at this Belgian-run bakery on the outskirts of Tamarindo, although what you might find on any given day is never certain. Possibilities include buttery croissants, vegetarian pizzas, chocolate eclairs, and different types of bread. A whole pizza goes for around $9. If you are heading out to the beach for the day, be sure to stop by and pick up some bread or pastries. There are a few tables out back where you can eat your pizza. There is also a separate open-air restaurant, **El Cocodrillo,** located next door.

MEALS FOR LESS THAN $12

☼ Coconut Café. On the left as you come into town. No phone. Reservations not accepted. Main courses $6.45–$16.60. No credit cards. Daily 6–10pm. INTERNATIONAL.

This is one of Tamarindo's more atmospheric restaurants. A thatched roof, wicker furniture, and fresh flower arrangements all set on a raised deck add up to a gringo fantasy of the Tropics, but isn't that what you came down here for anyway? The Coconut Cafe serves some of the most imaginative food in town, including such dishes as red chicken curry, mahi-mahi macadamia, shrimp brochettes, and fondue. However, because the menu changes daily, you can expect other equally enticing dishes when you visit. Below the dining room there is a comfortable lounge. The only drawback here is that the very dusty road is only a few feet away.

El Milagro. On the left as you enter town. ☎ **506/653-0042.** Reservations not accepted. Main courses $5.10–$14.50. AE, MC, V. Daily 7am–11pm. CONTINENTAL/COSTA RICAN.

Lush gardens and wide terraces make this the most attractive restaurant in town, and you might even be able to go for a swim in the adjacent pool if you're so inclined. Reproductions of pre-Columbian stone statues stand in the gardens and the bar has carved-wood columns. On those rare occasions when it is raining, you can retreat to one of the indoor dining rooms. Though the emphasis here is on seafood, you'll also find such unexpected offerings as chicken Cordon Bleu, fried Camembert, banana flambé, crêpes with ice cream, and hot fruits in amaretto sauce.

7 Playa Junquillal

30 kilometers W of Santa Cruz; 20 kilometers S of Tamarindo

Playa Junquillal (pronounced "hoon-key-*awl*") is a long, windswept beach that, for most of its length, is backed by grasslands. This gives it a very different feel from other beaches on this coast. There is really no village to speak of here, so if you're heading out this way, plan on getting away from it all. It's not a cliché; Junquillal is truly off the beaten path. Once here, your options for what to do are limited to whatever is on offer at your chosen hotel. However, the long beach is good for strolling and the sunsets are superb.

GETTING THERE & DEPARTING

By Plane   The nearest airport with regularly scheduled flights is in Tamarindo. You can arrange a taxi from the airport to Playa Junquillal.

By Bus   An express bus leaves San José daily at 2pm from the corner of Calle 20 and Avenida 3. Trip duration is 5 hours. One-way fare is $2.40.

Alternatively, you can take a bus to Santa Cruz (see "Playas Flamingo, Potrero, Brasilito & Conchal" for details) and from there, take the 6:30pm bus to Playa Junquillal. The ride takes 1¹/₂ hours and the one-way fare is $1.20.

The one express bus to San José departs Playa Junquillal daily at 5am. There is also a daily bus to Santa Cruz that departs at the same time.

By Car   Take the Interamerican Highway from San José. 47 kilometers past the turnoff for Puntarenas, turn left toward the Tempisque ferry. After crossing the Tempisque river, continue north through Nicoya to Santa Cruz. In Santa Cruz, head west 14 kilometers to the town of 27 de Abril, which is where the pavement ends. From here, it is another 18 rough kilometers to Playa Junquillal.

HITTING THE BEACH

Other than walking on the beach, swimming when the surf isn't too strong, and exploring tide pools, there isn't much to do here, which is just fine with me. This beach is ideal for anyone who just wants to relax without any distractions. Bring a few good books. Actually, the larger hotels here—Antumalal, Iguanazul, and Villa Serena—all offer plenty of activities and facilities, including volleyball, swimming pools, tennis courts, and even a disco at Hotel Antumalal. Sportfishing trips can also be arranged at most hotels. At the Iguanazul, guests can rent bicycles, a good way to get up and down this beach.

WHERE TO STAY & EAT

In addition to the lodgings listed below, **Camping Los Malinches** has wonderful campsites on fluffy grass, amidst manicured gardens, on a bluff above the beach. Camping will run you $7 per tent, but entitles you to bathroom and shower privileges.

DOUBLES FOR LESS THAN $35

El Castillo Divertido. Playa Junquillal, Santa Cruz, Guanacaste. ☎ **506/680-0015.** 7 rms. Dec–Apr $25 single, $30 double; May–Nov $17 single, $23 double. No credit cards.

Quite a few people have moved to Costa Rica from around the world in hopes of living out fantasy lives impossible in their home countries. This fanciful hotel is just such a creation. Built by a young German, the hotel is a tropical rendition of a classic medieval castle (well, sort of). Ramparts and a turret with a rooftop bar certainly grab the attention of passersby. Guest rooms here are fairly small, though rates are also some of the lowest in the area. Ask for an upstairs room with a balcony. The hotel is about 500 meters from the beach.

Hibiscus Hotel. Playa Junquillal (Apdo. 163-5150, Santa Cruz), Guanacaste. ☎ **506/680-0737.** 5 rms (all with private bath). $28 single; $32.50 double; $37 triple. No credit cards.

Though the accommodations here are very simple, the German owner makes sure that everything is always clean and in top shape. The grounds are pleasantly shady and the beach is just across the road. The rooms have cool Mexican tile floors and firm beds.

WORTH A SPLURGE

✪ **Iguanazul Hotel.** Playa Junquillal (Apdo. 130-1550, Santa Cruz), Guanacaste. ☎/fax **506/680-0783** or 506/232-1423. 24 rms. Dec–Apr $47.50–$65 single, $60–$80 double, $70–$85 triple; May–Nov $35–$55 single, $45–$65 double, $52–$70 triple. AE, MC, V.

Though the gravel road leading up to this hotel doesn't make Iguanazul seem too promising, once you step through the entryway and see the resort-like pool, you may well be captivated. Set on a windswept, grassy bluff above a rocky beach, Iguanazul is far from the madding crowd. It is definitely a spot for sun worshippers who like to have a good time, and the clientele tends to be young and active. The pool is large, as is the surrounding patio area. There's a volleyball court, and the bar plays lively classic rock throughout most of the day. Don't, however, expect a tropical setting; grasslands surround the hotel, which gives the area the feel of Cape Cod or the Outer Banks. Guest rooms are beautifully decorated with basket lampshades, wicker furniture, red-tile floors, high ceilings, and blue-and-white tile bathrooms. The higher prices are for air-conditioned rooms.

There are also plenty of things to do around here. You can rent horses, bicycles, and body boards. Captain Gene runs sportfishing charters out of the hotel, and there are board games, dart boards, and table tennis for those who find the sun and sea monotonous. The hotel also maintains a well-stocked gift shop and the food here is excellent.

Hotel Villa Serena. Playa Junquillal (Apdo. 17, Santa Cruz), Guanacaste. ☎/fax **506/680-0573.** 10 rms. $65 single or double; $75 triple; $85 quad. Rates are substantially lower during off-season. AE, MC, V.

Each of these individual bungalows is surrounded by neatly manicured lawns and gardens. The hotel is directly across the street from the beach, which is free of rocks and excellent for swimming most of the time. The hotel's main building houses the second-floor dining room, which serves filling and tasty European-style meals and has an enticing view of the beach. Art nouveau decorations and European art abound throughout the building, giving the hotel a very sophisticated feel for such a remote location. The rooms are quite roomy and have ceiling fans, dressing rooms, and large bathrooms. Each has its own covered patio, and only steps away is the small pool. The German owner is very friendly and helpful, and can arrange horseback riding or fishing tours.

8 Playa Sámara

35 kilometers S of Nicoya; 245 kilometers W of San José

Playa Sámara is a pretty beach on a long horseshoe-shaped bay. Unlike most of the rest of the Pacific coast, the water here is excellent for swimming, since an offshore island and rocky headlands break up most of the surf.

Because Playa Sámara is easily accessible by bus or car, and because there are several cheap cabinas, sodas, and discos here, this beach is popular with young Ticos out for a weekend of beach partying and families seeking a quick and inexpensive getaway. In the wake of this heavy traffic, the beach can get trashed. However, the calm waters and steep cliffs on the far side of the bay make this a very attractive spot, and the beach is long and wide. Directly behind the main beach is a wide, flat valley that stretches inland and to the north.

ESSENTIALS
GETTING THERE & DEPARTING

By Plane Sansa (in San José: ☎ **506/233-0397,** 506/233-3258, or 506/233-5330) flies to Carillo (15 minutes south of Sámara) at 7am Monday through Saturday, and at 11:15am on Sundays, from San José's Juan Santamaría International Airport. The flight makes two stops en route. Duration is 1 hour and 30 minutes. Fare is $50 each way.

Travelair (in San José: ☎ **506/220-3054** or 506/232-7883) flies to Carillo daily at 7:40am from San Jose's Pavas International Airport. Duration is 40 minutes. Fare is $75 one-way, $122 round-trip.

The Sansa flight leaves Carillo for San José at 8:50am Monday through Saturday, and at 1:30pm on Sundays. Travelair flies out of Carillo daily at 9:40am.

By Bus An express bus leaves San José daily at noon from Calle 14 between avenidas 3 and 5. Trip duration is 6 hours. One-way fare is $4.75.

Alternatively, you can take a bus from this same San José station to Nicoya and then catch a second bus from Nicoya to Sámara. Buses leave San José for Nicoya daily at 6, 8, and 10am and noon, 1, 2:30, 3, and 5pm. Duration is 6 hours. Fare is $3.90. Buses leave Nicoya for Sámara and Carillo daily at 8am and 2 and 3pm. Duration is 1½ hours. Fare to Sámara is $1.05; fare to Carillo is $1.25.

The express bus to San José leaves daily at 4am. Buses for Nicoya leave daily at 5:30 and 6:30am. Buses leave Nicoya for San José daily at 4, 7:30, and 9am and noon, 2:30, and 5pm.

By Car Follow the directions for Playa Junquillal above, but in Nicoya, follow the signs south to a road that has recently been paved all the way to the beach. Rumor has it an important government official has a beach house here.

ORIENTATION

Sámara is a busy little town at the bottom of a steep hill. The main road heads straight into town, passing the soccer field before coming to an end at the beach. Just on the edge of town is a road to the left that leads to most of the more expensive hotels here. This road also leads to Playa Carillo and the Guanamar Resort.

FUN ON & OFF THE BEACH

Aside from sitting on the sand and soaking up the sun, the main activities in Playa Sámara seem to be hanging out in the sodas and dancing into the early morning hours. If you stay close to the center of town (by the soccer field), expect to stay up until the disco closes down.

You'll find that the beach is nicer and cleaner down at the south end near Las Brisas del Pacifico hotel. For fewer crowds, head south to **Playa Carillo,** a long, flat beach about 20 minutes from Sámara.

Spelunking Spelunkers will want to head 62 kilometers northeast of Playa Sámara on the road to the Tempisque ferry. Here, at Barra Honda National Park, there is an extensive system of caves. See chapter 3.

WHERE TO STAY & EAT

In addition to the accommodations listed below, you'll find a slew of very inexpensive places to stay along the road into town and around the soccer field. Many of the rooms at these places are less accommodating than your average jail cell. However, you can pitch a tent right by the beach for a few dollars at **Camping Cocos,** where you can also use their basic showers and bathrooms.

DOUBLES FOR LESS THAN $25

Cabinas Belvedere. Playa Sámara, Guanacaste. ☎ **506/685-5004.** 3 rms (all with private bath). $20.40 single; $24.50 double. Rate includes continental breakfast. No credit cards.

This tropical Swiss chalet is located on the hillside across the street from the Hotel Marbella on the inland edge of town. The rooms are rather small, but they are immaculate and have fans and mosquito nets. The clincher for me, though, are the framed velvet paintings on the walls.

DOUBLES FOR LESS THAN $35

✪ **Hotel Giada.** Playa Sámara, Nicoya, Guanacaste. ☎ **506/222-7553** or 506/222-7443. Fax 506/223-5426. 13 rms (all with bath). $20 single; $31 double; $39 triple; $45 quad. All rates include continental breakfast. MC, V.

This new Italian-owned hotel is located on the left-hand side of the main road into town, about 150 meters before the beach. The rooms are all very clean and comfortable and even have a small balcony. Breakfasts are served in a cool, shady central gazebo. The management is very helpful, and can arrange dive or fishing expeditions, and horseback riding trips.

DOUBLES FOR LESS THAN $45

Hotel Marbella. Playa Sámara (Edificio Cristal, Avenida 1a, San José), Guanacaste. ☎/fax **506/233-9980.** 14 rms, 6 apts. Nov–Mar $30 single, $44 double, $57 triple, $63.50 apt; Apr–Oct $25 single, $37 double, $47 triple, $53 apt. Weekly discounts available on apartment rentals. AE, MC, V.

Though it is a bit of a walk to the beach and the immediate surroundings are none too appealing, this small German-run hotel is properly tropical in decor. You'll find the Marbella just around the corner from the road that leads down to the soccer fields and the beach. Guest rooms are fairly large, and have red-tile floors and woven mats for ceilings. There are open closets and modern bathrooms with hot water. The apartments are a good choice for families or long-term stays. There's a small swimming pool in a gravel courtyard and a second-floor dining room with rattan chairs and a bamboo-fronted bar. All the rooms have a small balcony or porch, though not necessarily any sort of a view. You can inquire here about the three A-frame chalets across the street. The dining-room only serves breakfast these days, but you'll also find a bar and snack bar here.

WORTH A SPLURGE

Hotel Las Brisas del Pacífico. Playa Sámara (Apdo. 11917-1000, San José), Guanacaste. ☎/fax **506/656-0076** or 506/233-9840 in San José. 36 rms. Nov–Apr $60–$95 double, $70–$105 triple; May–Oct $45–$75 double or triple. AE, MC, V.

Located on the road out towards Carillo, this hotel is set amid very shady grounds right on a quiet section of the beach and backs up a steep hill. Most of the rooms are up a long and steep flight of stairs at the top of the hill. However, in exchange for climbing the stairs, you do get an excellent view of the bay. These hilltop rooms have large balconies and walls of glass that take in the views. The third-floor rooms are the largest here, but due to the design, the second-floor rooms actually have the best views. At the base of the hill, there are rooms in stucco duplexes with steeply pitched tile roofs and red-tile patios. These rooms have cold-water showers only, but it's never cool enough here to warrant hot showers. Only a few steps from the beach, there is a small pool with a cold-water whirlpool. The main dining room is a breezy open-air restaurant surrounded by lush garden plantings. The menu changes daily, but the emphasis is always on German and European cuisine. Main course prices range from $6.50 to $12.50. There is also a second pool and bar at the top of the hill.

WHERE TO EAT

There are numerous inexpensive sodas in Sámara, and most of the hotels have their own dining rooms. In town, try the following.

Colochos Bar. On the main street through town. ☎ **506/680-0445.** Reservations not accepted. Main courses $4.90–$15.50. No credit cards. Daily 11am–10pm. COSTA RICAN/SEAFOOD.

This open-air rancho restaurant on the main road into town offers a wide selection of seafoods. There are four different types of ceviche, lobster dishes, paella, and plenty of shrimp plates. Prices are very reasonable and portions are large. Though there's a thatched roof over your head, you'll find lace doilies on the tables.

9 Playa Nosara

55 kilometers SW of Nicoya; 266 kilometers W of San José

Playa Nosara is actually several beaches, almost all of which are nearly deserted most of the time. Because the village of Nosara is several kilometers from the beach, and because the land near the beach has been turned into a large, spread-out resort community, Nosara has been spared the sort of ugly, uncontrolled growth characteristic of many other Guanacaste beaches. All of the hotels are spread out and most are tucked away down side roads. There is not the hotels-on-top-of-hotels feeling that you get at Playa Flamingo. In fact, on first arriving here, it's hard to believe there are any hotels around at all. Nosara has long been popular with North American retirees, and they too have made sure that their homes are not crammed cheek-by-jowl in one spot. Their houses are hidden amongst all the trees that make Nosara one of the greenest spots on the Nicoya peninsula. So, if you are looking for reliably sunny weather and a bit of tropical greenery, this is a good bet.

The best way to get to Nosara is to fly; however, with everything so spread out, that makes getting around once you've arrived difficult. The roads to and in Nosara are in horrendous shape, and though there has long been talk of some sections being widened and paved, it will probably still be quite a few years before the blacktop reaches Playa Nosara.

ESSENTIALS
GETTING THERE & DEPARTING

By Plane   **Sansa** (in San José: ☎ **506/233-0397,** 506/233-3258, or 506/233-5330) flies one flight a day to Nosara, departing San José's Juan Santamaría International Airport at 7am. The flight makes one stop en route. Duration is 1 hour and 10 minutes. Fare is $50 each way.

   Travelair (in San José: ☎ **506/220-3054** or 506/232-7883) also makes one flight a day to Nosara. It departs San José's Pavas International Airport at 10:45am, and makes one stop en route. Duration is 1 hour. Fare is $82 one-way, $122 round-trip.

   One Sansa flight a day departs Nosara at 8:25am. Travelair flights take off daily at 11:55am.

By Bus   An express bus leaves San José daily at 6:15am from Calle 14 between avenidas 3 and 5. Trip duration is 7 hours. One-way fare is $4.25.

   You can also take a bus from San José to Nicoya (see "Playa Sámara," above, for details), and then catch a second bus from Nicoya to Nosara. A bus leaves Nicoya for Nosara daily at 1pm. Duration is 3 hours. One-way fare is $1.10.

   The bus to San José leaves daily at 4pm. The bus to Nicoya leaves daily at 6am. Buses leave Nicoya for San José daily at 4, 7:30, and 9am and noon, 2:30, and 4pm.

By Car   Follow the directions above for getting to Playa Sámara, but watch for a fork in the road a few kilometers before you reach that beach. The right-hand fork leads, in another 22 kilometers of terrible road, to Nosara.

ORIENTATION
The village of Nosara is about 5 kilometers inland from the beach; however, most of the hotels listed here are on the beach itself.

FUN ON & OFF THE BEACH
There are several beaches at Nosara, including the long, curving Playa Guiones, Playa Nosara, and, my personal favorite, the diminutive **Playa Peleada.** This latter is a short, white-sand beach lined with sea grasses and mangroves. However, there isn't too much sand at high tide, so you'll want to hit the beach when the tide's out. At either end of the beach there are rocky outcroppings that reveal tide pools at low tide. Surfing and bodysurfing are both good around here. **Playa Guiones** in particular is garnering quite a reputation as a consistent and rideable beach break. Because the village of Nosara is several miles inland, these beaches are very clean, secluded, and quiet.

   When evening rolls around, don't expect a major party scene. Nightlife in Nosara seems to be centered around the two bars located across from each other by the town's soccer field.

Fishing Charters   Most of the hotels in the area can arrange fishing charters for between $250 and $300 for a half-day or $400 and $600 for a full day. These rates are for one to four people. You can also contact **Pesca Bahia Garza** (☎ 506/680-0856) and arrange a half-day or full-day's fishing trip.

Bird- and Sea-Turtle Watching   Bird watchers should explore the mangrove swamps around the estuary mouth of the Río Nosara. Just walk north from Playa Peleada and follow the river bank; explore the paths into the mangroves.

If your timing is right, you can do a night tour to nearby **Playa Ostional** to watch nesting olive Ridley sea turtles. These turtles come ashore by the thousands in a mass egg-laying phenomenon known as an *arribada*. These arribadas take place 4 to 10 times between July and November, with each arribada lasting between 3 and 10 days. Consider yourself very lucky if you should happen to be around during one of these fascinating natural phenomena. Even if it is not turtle-nesting season, you may want to look into going up to Playa Ostional. During the dry season, you can usually get there in a regular car, but during the rainy season, you'll need four-wheel drive. This beach is part of Ostional National Wildlife Refuge. At the northwest end of the refuge is India Point, known for its tidepools and rocky outcrops.

WHERE TO STAY

DOUBLES FOR LESS THAN $20

Cabinas Chorotega. Nosara, Guanacaste. ☎ **506/680-0836.** 8 rms (two with private bath). $6.50–$10 single; $13–$16 double. No credit cards.

Located on the outskirts of Nosara village, Cabinas Chorotega is about 5 kilometers from the beach, so you'll need to have some sort of transportation if you stay here and want to go the beach. The rooms are very basic but clean, and the rooms with private baths are a particularly good value. Some rooms have more windows and are quite a bit brighter than others, so look at a couple of rooms if you can.

DOUBLES FOR LESS THAN $40

✪ **Almost Paradise.** Playa Nosara (Apdo. 15, Bocas de Nosara), Guanacaste. No phone. Fax **506/685-5004.** 6 rms (all with bath). $32 single; $36.50 double. No credit cards. Rate includes breakfast.

Located on the hill above Playa Peleada, this delightful bed-and-breakfast is aptly named. This older wood building is a welcome relief from all the concrete and cinderblock so common in Costa Rican construction. The rooms are simple and clean, and feature colorful local artwork. All have access to an inviting covered verandah, with strung hammocks and an ocean view. The attached restaurant has gone through several incarnations over the years, yet has remained a local favorite.

WORTH A SPLURGE

✪ **Estancia Nosara.** Playa Nosara (Apdo. 37, Bocas de Nosara), Guanacaste. ☎/fax **506/680-0378.** 10 rms. $36–$42 single; $42–$51 double; $50–$59 triple; $58–$67 quad. MC, V.

Although this hotel is a mile or so from the beach, it's set amid shady jungle trees and has a swimming pool and tennis court, which together make Estancia Nosara a good value. There's a man-made waterfall tumbling from a small hill of stones near the pool and reproductions of pre-Columbian stone statues in the lush garden. The guest rooms are in two buildings and have red-tile floors, kitchenettes, high ceilings, overhead fans, showers with hot water, and plenty of closet space. There's a large open-air restaurant serving moderately priced meals. The hotel rents out horses, boogie boards, snorkling equipment, and bikes. A full day of fishing arranged through the hotel will cost $400 for the boat, which can take up to four people.

Hotel Villa Taype. Playa Nosara (Apdo. 8-5233, Bocas de Nosara), Guanacaste. ☎/fax **506/680-0763.** 12 rms, 6 bungalows. $55–$75 single or double; $75–$95 triple. V.

Although a relatively new hotel, this place has already changed its name and management once. Construction is underway on additional bungalows and the gardens still have a few years to go before they fill in the bare spots left over from the initial building. The room decor is very simple, but quite attractive. There are white-tile floors, high ceilings, overhead fans, and well-designed bathrooms. The least expensive rooms are those without air-conditioning. All have patios, but the bungalows have their own little ranchito, with a sitting area and hammock. The dining room, with its wood ceiling and arched windows overlooking the pool, serves moderately priced meals. The swimming pool has a swim-up bar. There is also a tennis court here, and you can rent body boards, surfboards, tennis rackets, and snorkeling gear. Best of all, the beach is only 100 yards away.

WHERE TO EAT

Doña Olga's. On the beach at Playa Peleada. No phone. Reservations not accepted. Main courses $1.75–$16. No credit cards. Daily 6:30am–10pm. COSTA RICAN.

Little more than a roof with some tables under it, Olga's is still one of the most popular restaurants in Nosara. Gringos and Ticos alike hang out here savoring fried-fish casados, sandwiches, and breakfasts that include huge helpings of bacon. On the weekends the cavernous structure beside the restaurant becomes a lively disco.

10 Playa Montezuma

166–184 kilometers W of San José (not including the ferry ride); 36 kilometers SE of Paquera; 54 kilometers S of Naranjo

For years Montezuma has enjoyed near-legendary status amongst backpackers, hippie expatriates, and European budget travelers. This fame and tourist traffic has had its price. The haphazard collection of budget lodgings that sprung up were generally pretty ratty, long-term campers were trashing the beach, and Montezuma earned a nasty reputation for having a sewage problem. In recent years, local businesspeople and hotel owners have joined together, and most of these problems have been addressed. The town has a well-tended feel and there are now lodgings of value and quality in all price ranges. The local community even passed an ordinance shutting down all loud discos in the town center, so it's possible to get a good night's sleep now.

Still, it is the natural beauty, miles of almost abandoned beaches, rich wildlife, and jungle waterfalls that first made Montezuma famous, and they are what keep this one of my favorite beach towns in Costa Rica. The water here is a gorgeous royal blue, and beautiful beaches stretch out along the coast on either side of town. Be careful though: The waves can occasionally be too rough for casual swimming and you need to be aware of stray rocks at your feet. Be sure you know where the rocks and tide are before doing any bodysurfing. The best places to swim are in front of the El Sano Banano Cabinas, or several kilometers further north at Playa Grande.

ESSENTIALS

GETTING THERE & DEPARTING

By Bus and Ferry   If you are traveling from San José by public transportation, it will take you two buses and a ferry ride to get to Montezuma. This can require spending a night in Puntarenas, so don't plan on heading out this way unless you have plenty of time.

Buses leave San José for Puntarenas daily every 30 minutes between 5am and 7pm from the corner of Calle 12 and Avenida 9. Duration is 2 hours. Fare is $2.

From Puntarenas take the *lancha* or **Paquereña** (☎ **506/661-2830**), which leaves from the pier behind the market at 6 and 11am and 3pm. This passenger launch should not be confused with the two car ferries that also leave from Puntarenas, and you should always check the schedule before making plans. Duration is 1¹/₂ hours. Fare is $1.10.

The bus south to Montezuma will be waiting to meet the lancha when it arrives in Paquera. Duration is 1 hour and 45 minutes. Fare is $2.70.

When you're ready to return, the bus for Paquera leaves Montezuma daily at 5:30 and 10am and 2pm and meets the Paquereña ferry, which leaves for Puntarenas at 8am and 12:30 and 5pm. Total trip duration is 4 hours. Total combined bus and ferry fare is $3.80.

The car ferry from Paquera leaves at 6 and 10:30am and 2:30 and 7pm. The car ferry from Naranjo leaves at 5:10 and 8:50am and 12:50 and 5pm.

By Car   Take the Interamerican highway from San José to Puntarenas and catch either the Naranjo ferry or the Paquera ferry.

The Naranjo ferry leaves daily at 3, 7, and 10:50am and 2:50 and 7pm. Duration is 1¹/₂ hours. Fare is $9.50 for cars, $1.40 for adults, and 75¢ for children.

The Naviera Tambor ferry to Paquera leaves daily at 4:15 and 8:45am and 12:30 and 5:30pm. Duration is 1¹/₂ hours. Fare is $11.50 for a car; $1.50 for adults, $4 for adults in first class; $1 for children, $2 for children in first class.

Montezuma is about 1¹/₂ hours south of Paquera and 3 hours south of Naranjo. The road from Paquera to Tambor has been upgraded with the arrival of the resort hotel and taking the Paquera ferry will save you time and some very rough, dusty driving. Beyond Tambor, it's approximately another 50 minutes to Montezuma.

ORIENTATION

The bus stops at the end of the road into the village. From here, hotels are scattered up and down the beach and around the village's few sand streets. You'll be bombarded with opportunities to rent a horse, or take one of the tours to the famous waterfalls.

Information   Before you jump at the first offer, you might want to pay a visit to the **tour-and tourist-information desk** in a little kiosk in the center of the village.

Another good resource is **Monte-aventuras** (☎ **506/642-0025**), which functions as a tour and information clearinghouse. Located in an office at the entrance to the Hotel El Jardin, Monte-aventuras can arrange boat tours and rafting trips, and offers car and motorcycle rentals, international phone and fax service, and currency exchange.

FUN ON & OFF THE BEACH

In Montezuma, mostly you just hang out on the beach, hang out in a restaurant, hang out in a bar, or hang out in a hammock at your hotel. However, if you're interested in more than just hanging out, head for the waterfall just south of town. This waterfall is one of those tropical fantasies where water comes pouring down into a deep pool. It's a popular spot, but it's a bit of a hike up the stream. There are actually a couple of waterfalls up this stream, but the upper falls are by far the more spectacular. You'll find the trail to the falls just over the bridge south of the village (just past Las Cascadas restaurant). At the first major outcropping of rocks the trail disappears and you have to scramble up the rocks and river for a bit. In places a trail will reappear for small sections. Just stick close to the stream and you'll eventually hit the falls.

Horseback Riding & Visiting a Great Tide Pool   Several people around the village rent horses for around $5 to $7 an hour, though most people choose to do a 4-hour horseback tour for $20 to $30. These latter rides usually go to a second waterfall 8 kilometers north of Montezuma. This waterfall cascades straight down into a deep tide pool at the edge of the ocean. The pool here is a delightful mix of fresh and sea water, and you can bathe while gazing out over the sea and rocky coastline. This is one of my favorite swimming holes in all of Costa Rica. You can also ride a horse to Cabo Blanco. Luis, whose rental place is down the road that leads out of town to the left, is a reliable source for horses, as is Roger.

Other Activities   In the center of the village, there are a couple of rental shops where you can rent a bicycle by the day or hour, as well as boogie boards. If you'd like to get out on the water and visit yet another beautiful beach, ask at the information center about boat trips to Tortuga Island. These tours last 5 hours and cost around $25, which is a considerable savings over similar trips offered by companies in San José, although the trips out of San José include a gourmet lunch that isn't a part of trips from Montezuma.

A SIDE TRIP TO CABO BLANCO NATURE RESERVE: PELICANS, HOWLER MONKEYS & BEAUTIFUL BEACHES

As beautiful as the beaches around Montezuma are, the beaches at **Cabo Blanco Absolute Nature Reserve,** 11 kilometers south of the village, are, in many peoples' opinions, even more beautiful. Located at the southernmost tip of the Nicoya peninsula, Cabo Blanco is a national park that preserves a nesting site for brown pelicans, magnificent frigate birds, and brown boobies. The beaches are backed by lush tropical forest that is home to howler monkeys that are often seen (and heard!). You can hike through the preserve's lush forest right down to the deserted, pristine beach. This is Costa Rica's oldest official bioreserve and was set up thanks to the pioneering efforts of conservationists Karen Mogensen and Nicholas Wessberg. Admission is $6. There are usually shared taxis heading out this way from Montezuma in the morning. The fare is around $5 per person.

WHERE TO STAY

Now that camping on the beach is discouraged, campers will have to make do at El Rincón de los Monos, which is near the beach, charges about $3 per tent, and provides showers and bathrooms.

DOUBLES FOR LESS THAN $15

Cabinas El Tucan. Montezuma, Cóbano de Puntarenas. ☎ **506/642-0284.** 9 rms (all with shared bath). $8 single; $10 double. No credit cards.

This small two-story lodging is on the road south to Cabo Blanco and is located just around the corner from the main road into town. Rooms are small and Spartan but generally clean. The second-floor rooms are nicer, with varnished wood walls and floors, and a small verandah overlooking the road.

Hotel Lucy. Montezuma, Cóbano de Puntarenas. ☎/fax **506/642-0273.** 10 rms (all with shared bath). $5 single; $10 double. Rates lower in the low season. No credit cards.

This converted two-story home has the best location of any budget lodging in Montezuma, right on a pretty section of beach a bit south of town, in front of Los Mangos. If you can snag a second-floor room with an ocean view, you'll be in budget heaven. The beach here is a bit rough and rocky for swimming, but the sunbathing and sunsets are beautiful nonetheless.

Hotel Moctezuma. Montezuma, Cóbano de Puntarenas.☎/fax **506/642-0058.** 22 rms (15 with private bath). $5 single without bath, $10 single with bath; $8.50 double without bath, $14.50 double with bath; $16.75 triple with bath; $19 quad with bath. V (add 10% surcharge).

Located right in the center of the village and overlooking the small bay, the Hotel Moctezuma offers basic but clean rooms with fans, in two facing buildings. Some of the rooms are upstairs from the hotel's noisy bar and restaurant. It's noisy here, but you get a verandah with an ocean view. If you like to go to sleep early, try to get a room at the back of the hotel's building across the street instead. The walls here don't go all the way to the ceiling, which is great for air circulation but lousy for privacy.

Pensíon Arenas. Montezuma, Cóbano de Puntarenas. No phone. 14 rms (all with shared bath). $5 single; $10 double. Rates slightly reduced in the low season. No credit cards.

Traditionally, this has been the backpacker's first choice in Montezuma. Rooms are split between an old wooden house and a newer cement building. The end rooms on the second floor are probably the best because they catch the breezes. However, most rooms have fans. This place is about as basic as it gets in Costa Rica. You are right on a small stretch of beach and just 50 yards from the center of town.

DOUBLES FOR LESS THAN $25

Hotel La Aurora. Montezuma, Cóbano de Puntarenas. ☎ **506/642-0051.** Fax 506/642-0025. 8 rms (all with private bath). Dec–Mar $12.25–$24.50 single, $16.30–$24.50 double ($5 each additional person); Apr–Nov $8–$16 single, $8.15–$16.30 double ($3 each additional person). No credit cards.

Just to the left as you enter the village of Montezuma, you'll see this large white house. The rooms are spread around the spacious three-story building, which also features a small library of books, some hammocks and comfortable chairs, and flowering vines growing up the walls. In fact there are vines all over La Aurora, which give it a tropical yet Gothic feel. Most rooms are of average size and have wooden walls that don't go all the way to the ceiling, which improves air circulation but reduces privacy. There are two new rooms up on the third floor, with balconies and an ocean view over the tree tops. Fresh coffee and tea are provided every morning. There is also a kitchen available to guests, and lunch and dinner are served at reasonable prices.

DOUBLES FOR LESS THAN $35

✪ **Amor de Mar.** Montezuma, Cóbano de Puntarenas. ☎/fax **506/642-0262.** 12 rms (8 with private bath). $30 single or double with shared bath; $35–$50 single, double, or triple with private bath. No credit cards.

It would be difficult to imagine a more idyllic spot in this price range. In fact, it's hard to imagine a much more idyllic spot at all. With its wide expanse of neatly trimmed grass sloping down to the sea, tide pools (one of which is as big as a small swimming pool), and hammocks slung from the mango trees, this is the perfect place for anyone who wants to do some serious relaxing. The owners, who have young children, love to have other families as guests and there's always a cheerful family atmosphere. However, couples and individuals will also enjoy a stay at Amor de Mar simply for the stunning location and beautiful hotel building, which abounds in varnished hardwoods. The big porch on the second floor of the main building makes a great place to sit and read or to just gaze out to sea. Only breakfast is served here, with the specialty being homemade whole-wheat French bread.

Los Mangos. Montezuma, Cóbano de Puntarenas. ☎ **506/642-0259** or 506/642-0076. Fax 506/642-0036. 10 rms (6 with private bath), 10 bungalows. Dec–Mar $20 single without bath, $35 single with bath; $25 double or triple without bath, $40 double or triple with bath; $60 bungalow. Rates are slightly lower from April to November. V.

This is still the only hotel in Montezuma to have its own swimming pool. The hotel is across the road from the water south of town near Amor de Mar, and takes its name from the many mango trees under which the bungalows are built (May through June is the heart of mango season). The rooms are fairly basic and, in an older building close to the road, are a good value. However, it is the octagonal bungalows built of Costa Rican hardwoods that are the most attractive accommodations. Each bungalow has a small porch with rocking chairs, a thatched roof, a good amount of space, and ceiling fans for stirring up the air. The swimming pool is built to look like a natural pond and there's even an artificial waterfall flowing into it. Beside the pool is a large rancho-style restaurant and bar serving reasonably priced French and Italian meals.

WORTH A SPLURGE

El Sano Banano. Montezuma, Cóbano de Puntarenas. ☎/fax **506/642-0068.** 3 rms, 12 cabins, 1 apt (all with private bath). Dec–Mar $24.50–$36.70 single room; $28.50–$36.70 double room; $49–$57 cabin; $49–$98 apt. Rates lower during off-season. AE, MC, V (add 10% surcharge).

El Sano Banano is the sort of tropical retreat many travelers dream about. It is located about a 10-minute walk up the beach to the left as you enter the village. From the front porch of your cabin you can sit and listen to the waves crashing on the beach a few feet away. Please do not try to drive up the beach, even if you have a four-wheel-drive vehicle. Seclusion and quiet are the main offerings of this place and cars would ruin the atmosphere. If you don't want to carry all your bags, you can leave some of your stuff at the Sano Banano restaurant in the village, and the hotel will bring them to your room. There are two types of cabins here—octagonal hardwood Polynesian-style buildings and white ferroconcrete geodesic domes that look like igloos—as well as three more standard rooms in the main building. All the rooms are set amid a lush garden planted with lots of banana and elephant-ear plants, and there are big rocks scattered beneath the shady old trees. The rooms and cabins vary in age and style, so have a look at a couple if you can. All have refrigerators, coffee makers, and hot plates, and many guests opt for extended stays. One other thing you should know is that the showers, though private, are outside of the cabins in the trees. This is the Tropics. Why not?

WHERE TO EAT
MEALS FOR LESS THAN $6

El Sano Banano. On the main road into the village. ☎ **506/642-0272.** Reservations not accepted. Main courses $3.25–$6.50. V (with a 10% surcharge). Daily 7am–10pm. VEGETARIAN.

Delicious vegetarian meals including nightly specials, sandwiches, and salads are the specialty of this ever-popular Montezuma restaurant, although fish and chicken dishes are also served. You can even order a sandwich with cheese from the cheese factory in Monteverde. The day's menu specials are posted on a blackboard out front early in the afternoon so you can be savoring the thought of dinner all day. Any time of day or night, the yogurt-fruit shakes are fabulous. El Sano Banano also doubles as the local movie house. They show nightly videos, projected on a large screen, and have a library of more than 300 movies. The movies begin at 7:30pm and require a $2.50 minimum purchase.

Las Cascadas. On the road out of town toward Cabo Blanco. ☎ **506/642-0049.** Reservations not accepted. Main courses $2.80–$9.80. No credit cards. Daily 9am–9pm. COSTA RICAN/SEAFOOD.

This little open-air restaurant is built on the banks of the stream just outside of the village and takes its name from the nearby waterfalls. The short menu sometimes includes fresh fish filets, whole red snapper, or shrimp in salsa ranchera. There are few more enjoyable places in Costa Rica to have a meal. You can sit for hours beneath the thatched roof listening to the stream rushing past.

MEALS FOR LESS THAN $12

✪ **Playa de Los Artistas.** Across from Hotel Los Mangos. No phone. Reservations not accepted. Main courses $4–$12.50. No credit cards. Daily 6–10:30pm. ITALIAN/MEDITERRANEAN.

If you're craving Italian food for dinner, this is the place to find it in Montezuma. The open-air restaurant is beside an old house fronting the beach, and there are only a few tables. Arrive early if you want to be sure of getting a seat; this place is popular. Meals are served in large, broad ceramic bowls, set on wooden-ringed coasters, and come with plenty of fresh bread for soaking up the sauces. The menu changes nightly, but always features several fish dishes. The fresh grouper in a black-pepper sauce is phenomenal.

MONTEZUMA AFTER DARK

Ever since the local bars were required to turn down their music at 10pm, most of Montezuma's raging nightlife has moved to the Kaliolin Disco, 1.5 kilometers south of town. Kaliolin's is open Wednesday, Friday, and Saturday nights, and even provides a free taxi back into town at the end of the evening or, more likely, early the following morning (they're open until 2 or 3am).

If your evening tastes are a bit mellower, one of the restaurants in town, El Sano Banano, also doubles as the local movie house. See their listing under "Where to Eat," above, for more information.

EN ROUTE TO TAMBOR & MONTEZUMA

Oasis Del Pacífico. Playa Naranjo (Apdo. 200-5400), Puntarenas (mailing address in the U.S.: SJO 1552, P.O. Box 025216, Miami, FL 33102-5216). ☎/fax **506/661-1555.** 36 rms. $36.70 double; $49 up to four people. AE, MC, V.

Located just 3 minutes from the Playa Naranjo ferry dock, this casual little resort is a family-run operation that provides a quiet place to relax in the sun. Though the beach here isn't very good for swimming, there is a good-size pool. You'll also find a kiddie pool, a play area, and plenty of lawn for the kids to run around on if you should bring the family. The friendly owners will make sure you feel right at home and introduce you to their various pets—dogs, macaws, and a deer. The guest rooms have tile floors and high ceilings, and vary considerably in size. Along the tiled verandah there are hammocks just waiting for some serious relaxing. You can also try your hand at fishing from the resort's private pier. Meals in the resort's dining room often include exotic dishes prepared by the Singaporean owner. Horseback riding and fishing trips can be arranged. The greatest attraction of this place is that it is very convenient, yet feels remote.

If you're driving, on your way out to Montezuma from Paquera or Naranjo, you will pass the **Curú National Wildlife Refuge.** Located 16 kilometers north of Tambor, Curú makes a wonderful stop for a few hours and has several pretty, secluded beaches, as well as forests and mangrove swamps. This private reserve is extremely rich in wildlife. Howler and white-faced monkeys are often spotted here, as are quite a few species of birds. Admission is $5.

8

The Northern Zone

I f you like your ecotourism rough and gritty, but don't think you can take the heat and humidity of the Osa peninsula, this is the area for you. The northern zone, roughly defined here as the area north of San José and between Guanacaste province on the west and the lowlands of the Caribbean coast on the east, is a naturalist's dream come true. There are rain forests and cloud forests, jungle rivers, and an unbelievable diversity of birds and other wildlife. In addition to its reputation for muddy hiking trails and crocodile-filled rivers, the northern zone also claims one of the best windsurfing spots in the world (on Lake Arenal, which is free of crocodiles, by the way) and Costa Rica's most active volcano. Arenal Volcano, when free of clouds, puts on spectacular nighttime light shows and by day is reflected in the waters of nearby Lake Arenal.

1 Puerto Viejo de Sarapiquí

82 kilometers N of San José; 102 kilometers E of La Fortuna

The Sarapiquí region, named for the river that drains this area, lies at the foot of the Cordillera Central mountain range. To the west is the rain forest of Braulio Carillo National Park, and to the east are Tortuguero National Park and Barra del Colorado National Wildlife Refuge. In between these protected areas lie thousands of acres of banana, pineapple, and palm plantations. It is here that you can see the great contradiction of Costa Rica. On one hand the country is known for its national parks, which preserve some of the largest tracts of rain forest left in Central America, but on the other hand, nearly every acre of land outside of these parks has been clear cut and converted into plantations (and the cutting is still continuing).

Within the remaining rain forests, there are several lodges that attract naturalists (both amateur and professional) who are interested in learning more about the rain forest.

ESSENTIALS
GETTING THERE & DEPARTING

By Bus Express buses leave San José daily at 6:30, 7, 9, and 10am and noon, 1, 3, 3:30, and 4pm from Avenida 11 between Calle Central and Calle 1. If you are heading to La Selva, Rara Avis, or El

The Northern Zone

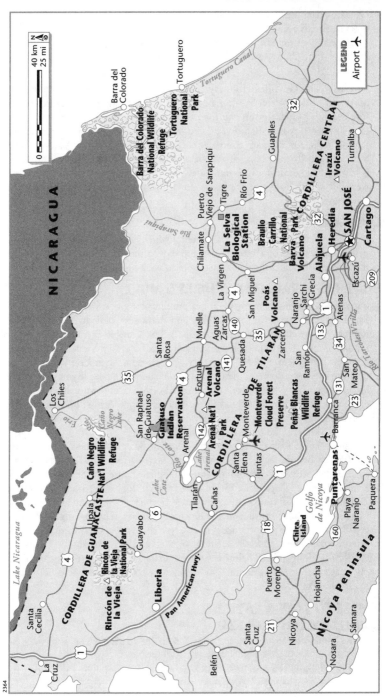

Gavilán lodges, be sure you are on a bus going though Las Horquetas. Duration is 4 hours. Fare is $3.75.

Express buses for San José leave Puerto Viejo daily at 4, 6, 8, and 10:30am and 2, 3, and 4pm. Buses leave Las Horquetas for San José daily at 7 and 11:30am and at 3 and 5:15pm.

By Car   The Guápiles Highway, which leads to the Caribbean coast, heads north out of downtown San José on Calle 3 before heading east. Turn north before reaching Guápiles on the road to Río Frio and continue north through Las Horquetas, passing Rara Avis, La Selva, and El Gavilán lodges, before reaching Puerto Viejo. An alternative route goes through Heredia, Barva, Varablanca, and San Miguel before reaching Puerto Viejo. This is a more scenic route, but the road is in very bad condition in certain stretches. If you want to take this route, head west out of San José and then turn north to Heredia and follow the signs for Varablanca.

ORIENTATION

Puerto Viejo is a small town at the center of which is a soccer field. If you continue past the soccer field on the main road and stay on the paved road, you will come to the Río Sarapiquí and the dock where you can look into arranging a boat trip.

BOAT TRIPS, RAIN-FOREST HIKES & MORE

For the adventurous, Puerto Viejo is a jumping-off point for trips down the Río Sarapiquí to Tortuguero National Park and Barra del Colorado National Wildlife Refuge on the Caribbean coast. Boat trips can be arranged at most hotels in town. A boat for up to ten people will cost you around $100 to Oro Verde Lodge and back, $300 to Tortuguero, and $275 to Barra del Colorado. Alternatively, you can head down to the town dock on the bank of the Sarapiquí and see if you can arrange a less expensive boat trip on your own. Several boatmen in town will take out small groups for a few hours for around $15 to $20 per person. A trip down the Sarapiquí, even if it's only for an hour or two, provides opportunities to spot crocodiles, caiman, monkeys, sloths, and dozens of species of birds.

Another option is to do a kayak trip down the Sarapiquí. These trips are offered by **Rancho Leona,** La Virgen de Sarapiquí, Heredia (☎ **506/761-1019**), a small stained-glass workshop, kayaking center, and guest house on the banks of the Río Sarapiquí in the village of La Virgen. The trips are done as a package that includes 2 nights' lodging in simple, dormitory-style accommodations and an all-day kayak trip with some basic instruction and lunch on the river. The cost for the 2-day trip is $75 per person. No experience is necessary and the river is very calm. Other more extensive trips and trips for experienced kayakers can be arranged.

All of the lodges listed below arrange excursions throughout the region, including boat trips on the Sarapiquí, guided hikes in the rain forest, and horseback or mountain-bike rides.

WHERE TO STAY & EAT
DOUBLES FOR LESS THAN $25

Mi Lindo Sarapiquí. Puerto Viejo, Sarapiquí. ☎ **506/766-6281.** 6 rms (all with private bath). $8.50 single; $16.50 double; $24.80 triple. No credit cards.

This little family-run hotel is in the center of town overlooking the soccer field. The comfortable and clean rooms are on the second floor, above the large restaurant and bar.

WORTH A SPLURGE

✪ **El Gavilán Lodge.** Apdo. 445-2010, Zapote, San José. ☎ **506/234-9507.** Fax 506/253-6556. 15 rms (12 with private bath). $40 single; $50 double; $75 triple. Lower rates during the low season. All rates include breakfast. MC, V.

Located on the banks of the Río Sarapiquí just south of Puerto Viejo on the road to Río Frio, El Gavilán is surrounded by 250 acres of forest reserve (secondary forest) and 25 acres of gardens planted with lots of flowering ginger. Guest rooms are simply furnished, but do have fans and hot water, and there are always fresh flowers. The rooms in the main building are fairly basic, but have huge bathrooms with two sinks. Other rooms are in rustic duplexes with cement floors. There is also a whirlpool spa out in the garden. Tico meals are served buffet style, and there are always plenty of fresh fruits and juices (though no alcohol is served, so bring your own). Lunch and dinner each cost $9. People with an interest in the outdoors and nature are the ones who will most enjoy a stay here. There's a kilometer-long nature trail here at the lodge and various excursions can be arranged. Guided hikes through the forest ($15 per person), horseback rides ($15 per person), and river trips ($20) are all offered.

Oro Verde Station. Apdo. 7043-1000, San José. ☎ **506/233-6613.** Fax 506/223-7479. 14 rms (8 with private bath). $29.50 single; $49.20 double; $64.90 triple. AE (San José office only).

Surrounded by nearly 20,000 acres of private reserve (3,000 acres of which is virgin forest) and bordering the Barra del Colorado National Wildlife Refuge, the Oro Verde Station is primarily a facility for researchers and students but is also open to the public. The nearest road is 30 miles away, so the lodge can only be reached by boat. The lodge's several high-peaked thatched-roof buildings lend a very tropical air to the facilities. Guest rooms are fairly basic, as you might expect at a research facility, and meals are often less than memorable. Both lunch and dinner are in the $5-to-$10 range. There are plenty of hiking trails; river trips and guided hikes can be arranged at additional cost.

✪ **Rara Avis.** Apdo. 8105-1000, San José. ☎/fax **506/764-4187;** ☎ 506/256-4876 and fax 506/253-0844 in San José. 19 rms (10 with private bath). $45 single with shared bath, $85 single with private bath; $90 double with shared bath, $150 double with private bath. All rates include transportation from Las Horquetas, guided hikes, and three meals daily. MC, V.

Once the exclusive stomping grounds of scientists and students, Rara Avis was made famous by the pioneering canopy research of Dr. Donald Perry, who first erected his famous canopy cable-car system in the rain forest here. Since that time, Rara Avis has become a very popular destination for people with a more casual interest in the rain forest. Though Perry's canopy cable car is no longer operating here, the rain forest research facility is still a fascinating place to visit. To get to Rara Avis, you must first travel to the village of Las Horquetas, which is between Guápiles and Puerto Viejo de Sarapiquí. In Las Horquetas, you are met by a tractor that takes 3 hours to cover the 15 kilometers to Rara Avis's lodges (there are two lodges and one cabina here). The road has recently been graded, but the last 3 kilometers are still over a road made of fallen logs and deep, deep mud. The Waterfall Lodge is by far the more comfortable and has rustic rooms and a wraparound porch. The more economical El Plastico Lodge was at one time a penal colony, and though it has been renovated and converted, it is still very Spartan. There is a new cabin a 10-minute walk away from the main lodge, set deep in the forest by a river, with two comfortable rooms for those wanting closer communion with nature. Meals are basic Tico-style dishes with lots of beans and rice. Rara Avis is adjacent to Braulio Carillo National Park and together the two have many miles of trails for you to explore. Birdwatchers take note: More than 320 species of birds have been sighted here. When making reservations, be sure to get directions for getting to Las Horquetas.

2 Arenal Volcano & La Fortuna

140 kilometers NW of San José; 61 kilometers E of Tilarán

If you've never experienced it first hand, the sight and sound of an active volcano erupting should inspire awe and admiration. Until 1937 when the mountain just west of La Fortuna was first scaled, no one ever dreamed that it might be a volcano. Gazing up at the cinder-strewn slopes of Arenal Volcano today, it is hard to believe that people could not have recognized this perfectly cone-shaped volcano for what it is. However, in July of 1968, the volcano, which had lain dormant for hundreds of years, erupted with sudden and unexpected violence. The nearby village of Tabacón was destroyed and nearly 80 of its inhabitants were killed. Since that eruption more than a quarter century ago, 5,358-foot-high Arenal has been Costa Rica's most active volcano. Frequent powerful explosions send cascades of red-hot lava rocks tumbling down the western slope of the volcano. During the day, the lava flows steam and rumble. However, it is at night that the volcano puts on its most mesmerizing show. If you should be lucky enough to be here on a clear night, you will see the night sky turned red by lava spewing from Arenal's crater. In the past few years, the forests to the south of the volcano have been declared Arenal National Park. Eventually this park should stretch all the way to Monteverde Cloud Forest Preserve.

Lying at the eastern foot of this natural spectacle is the tiny farming community of La Fortuna. In recent years, this town has become a center for volcano watchers from around the world. There are several inexpensive cabinas and moderately priced hotels in and near La Fortuna, and it is here that you can arrange night tours to the best volcano-viewing spots, which are 17 kilometers away on the western slope, past the Tabacón Hot Springs.

ESSENTIALS
GETTING THERE & DEPARTING

By Bus   Buses leave San José for La Fortuna daily at 6:15, 8:40, and 11:30am from Calle 16 between avenidas 1 and 3. Duration is 4¹/₂ hours. Fare is $3.35.

Alternatively, you can take a bus to Ciudad Quesada from the same location in San José and then take a local bus from Ciudad Quesada to La Fortuna. Ciudad Quesada buses leave San José daily every hour from 5am to 7:30pm. Duration is 3 hours. Fare is $2. Buses leave Ciudad Quesada for La Fortuna at 6, 7, and 11am and 1, 3, and 6pm. Duration is 1 hour. Fare is $1.10.

Buses depart La Fortuna for San José daily at 5 and 11am and 2:45pm. Buses to Ciudad Quesada leave at 5, 6:30, 7:20, 9:20, 10, and 11:15am and 3:30pm daily. From there you can catch one of the hourly buses to San José. There are also buses to Tilarán, at the northern end of Lake Arenal, daily at 8am and 4pm.

By Car   There are several routes to La Fortuna from San José. The most popular is to head west on the Interamerican Highway and then turn north at Naranjo, continuing north through Zarcero to Ciudad Quesada. From Ciudad Quesada one route goes through Jabillos while the other goes through Muelle. This latter route is the better road. It is, however, a little quicker to go first to Alajuela and then head north to Varablanca before continuing on to San Miguel where you turn west toward Río Cuarto and Aguas Zarcas. From Aguas Zarcas, continue west through Muelle to the turnoff for La Fortuna. Travel time either way is around 3 hours. A new route from San Ramón (west of Naranjo) north through Tigra, though unpaved, is very scenic, and passes the Villablanca and Valle Escondido lodges.

ORIENTATION

La Fortuna is only a few streets wide, with almost all the hotels, restaurants, and shops clustered along the main road that leads out of town towards Tabacón and the volcano. There are several small information and tour-booking offices across the street from the soccer field.

EXPERIENCING THE VOLCANO

The first thing you should know is that you can't climb Arenal Volcano. It is not safe due to the constant activity; several foolish people who have ignored this warning have lost their lives, and others have been severely injured. Watching Arenal's constant eruptions is the main activity in La Fortuna and is best done at night when the orange lava glows against the starry sky. Though it is possible to simply look up from the middle of town and see Arenal erupting, the view is better from the west side of the volcano. If you have a car, you can drive to the west side, but if you have arrived by bus, you will need to take a taxi or tour. Arenal National Park constitutes an area of 2,920 hectares, which include the viewing and parking areas closest to the volcano. The park is open from 8am to 10pm daily and charges $6 admission per person. However, unless you need to actually feel the heat of a lava flow, you will probably find the view of the natural fireworks perfectly acceptable on the dirt road just outside the park entrance.

Night tours are offered through every hotel in town and at several tour offices on the town's main street at a cost of $5 to $10. Almost all of the tours include a stop at one of the hot springs. These tours are a good bargain if you have no car. Alternatively you can take a cab from La Fortuna to Tabacón for around $3.50, and to the park entrance for around $5. If you want to stay a while and watch, make sure you arrange for a ride home before being dropped off. Hitchhiking is common and relatively safe around here, but you don't want to be out on these desolate roads late at night with no sure ride back to your lodgings.

MORE TO SEE & DO

Aside from the impressive volcanic activity, the area around Arenal Volcano is also packed with other natural wonders.

Leading the list of side attractions is the **Río Fortuna waterfall,** which is located about 5^1/$_2$ kilometers outside of town in a lush jungle setting. There is a sign in town to indicate the road that leads out to the falls. You can hike or drive (depending on recent rainfall) to almost within viewing distance of the impressive falls. Once you get to the lookout, it's another 15- to 20-minute hike down a steep path to the pool formed by the waterfall. You can swim here, but stay away from the turbulent water at the base of the fall: Several people have drowned here. Instead, check out and enjoy the calm pool just around the bend. The trail down to the base of the waterfall has recently been upgraded and there is now a $3 per person entrance fee. However, be warned that in one spot you must shimmy down a makeshift ladder carved into a fallen tree trunk, maintaining your balance with a piece of heavy rope.

If this seems like too much exercise, you can rent a horse and guide for transportation. You can arrange this through your hotel or through **Aventuras Arenal** (☎ **506/479-9133**), **Jacamar Tours** (☎ **506/479-9010**), or **Pura Vida** (☎ **506/ 479-9045**). All of these companies also offer most of the tours listed below.

Taking a Soothing Soak in Tabacón Hot Springs

One of the primary fringe benefits that Arenal Volcano has bestowed on the area are several naturally heated thermal springs. Located at the sight of the former village, Tabacón Hot Springs Resort is the most extensive and luxurious spot to soak your tired bones. It is also the most expensive, so if you're really watching your budget, check out one of the other options below. However, if you're looking to pamper yourself, this is worth a splurge. A series of variously sized pools, fed by natural springs, are spread out among lush gardens. At the center is a large pool with a slide, swim-up bar, and perfect view of the volcano. One of the stronger streams flows over a sculpted waterfall, with a rock ledge underneath that provides a perfect place to sit and receive a free hydrologic shoulder massage. The resort also offers professional massages, mud masks, and an excellent restaurant serving local and Italian dishes. Entrance fees are $14 for adults, $7 for children.

Across the street from the resort and down a gravel driveway is another bathing spot fed by the same springs. You'll find several large pools here, but far more basic facilities and no view. Admission is $2.10.

Finally, there is a free public spot located in a densely forested section of the road between Tabacón and the park entrance. This area has some very rudimentary dams set in a section of a warm side stream. To find it, keep going past the Tabacón Hot Springs Resort away from La Fortuna. You'll soon enter the forested section. After a few tight turns, the path leading down to the springs is on your left. There's a small sign and this is a well-known and popular spot, so you'll usually see several cars parked on the side of the road here.

Another good ride is up to Cerro Chato, an extinct side cone on the flank of Arenal. There is a pretty little lake up here. Either of these tours should cost around $15 to $20 per person.

You can also arrange a tour to the **Venado Caverns,** which are a 45-minute drive from La Fortuna. You'll see plenty of stalactites, stalagmites, and other limestone formations, of course, but you'll also see bats and cave fish. Tours here cost between $25 and $30.

La Fortuna is also the best place from which to make a day trip to the **Caño Negro National Wildlife Refuge.** This vast network of marshes and rivers is 100 kilometers north of La Fortuna near the town of Los Chiles. This refuge is best known for its amazing abundance of bird life, including roseate spoonbills, Jabiru storks, herons, and egrets, but you can also see caiman and crocodiles. Birdwatchers should not miss this refuge, though keep in mind that the main lake dries up in the dry season, which reduces the numbers of wading birds to be seen. Full day tours to Caño Negro average between $35 and $45 per person.

You can also go rafting with **Desafio Raft** (☎ 506/479-9464) or **Aguas Brava** (☎ 506/479-9025). Both of these companies offer daily rides of class I-II, III, and IV-V, on different sections of the Sarapiquí River. A full day of rafting costs $60 to $80 per person. Both of the above companies also offer guided mountain-bike rentals and guided tours.

WHERE TO STAY IN LA FORTUNA

In addition to the lodgings listed below, there is **Los Lagos campground** a few minutes west of La Fortuna. It charges $4 per person and has cooking and bathroom facilities, forests, trails, and lakes.

DOUBLES FOR LESS THAN $15

Hotel Fortuna. La Fortuna, San Carlos. ☎ **506/479-9197.** 15 rms (7 with private bath). $6 single or double (shared bath); $10 single or double (private bath); $15 triple (private bath). AE, MC, V.

Located one block south of the gas station, this small hotel is dark and very basic, but the rooms are clean and the prices are great. The second-floor rooms are a bit brighter than those on the ground floor, and have a comfortable shared sitting area. There is an open-air restaurant at the front of the hotel.

DOUBLES FOR LESS THAN $30

Hotel Las Colinas. 150 meters south of the National Bank, La Fortuna, San Carlos. ☎/fax **506/479-9107.** 17 rms (all with private bath). $14.70 single; $26 double; $33.40 triple. Prices significantly reduced in low season. MC, V.

This three-story building in the center of town offers clean but basic rooms. You'll need to be in good shape if you stay in one of the third-floor rooms, which have the best views, since the stairs are very steep. There are a few rooms on the ground floor, but they don't even have windows to the outside and are very dark. My favorite room is number 33, with a private balcony and unobstructed view of Arenal Volcano.

✪ **Hotel San Bosco.** La Fortuna, San Carlos (200 meters north of the gas station). ☎ **506/479-9050.** Fax 506/479-9109. 27 rms. $21.50–$33.40 single; $24.45–$37.49 double; $29.34–$40.75 triple; $48.90 suite. MC, V.

Located a block off La Fortuna's main street, the San Bosco has two styles of rooms. The older, cheaper rooms are small and dark and have cement floors. However, the newer rooms are much more attractive and have stone walls, tile floors, air-conditioning, reading lights, and benches on the verandah in front. The suite features a television set. Up on the top floor of the hotel, there is an observation deck for volcano viewing.

WORTH A SPLURGE

✪ **Las Cabañitas Resort.** Apdo. 5-4417, La Fortuna, San Carlos. ☎ **506/479-9400** or 506/479-9343. Fax 506/479-9408. 30 cabins. Dec–Apr $65 single, $72.50 double; May–Nov $60 single, $65 double. AE, MC, V.

Located one kilometer east of town, these rustic mountain cabins are spacious and immaculate inside. About half of the cabins face the volcano and have little porches where you can sit and enjoy the show by day or night. Each cabin is built of varnished hardwoods and has a beautiful floor, a high ceiling, louvered walls to let in the breezes, a modern tile bathroom down a few steps from the sleeping area, and rocking chairs on the porch. There is a small kidney-shaped swimming pool with a snack bar beside it and also a larger, full-service restaurant. Some of the rooms are wheelchair accessible. Various tours can be arranged through the hotel.

Hotel-Rancho El Corcovado. Apdo. 25, El Tanque de La Fortuna, San Carlos. ☎ **506/479-9300.** Fax 506/479-9090. 25 rms. $37 single; $47 double; $57 triple. MC, V.

This hotel is located 7 kilometers east of La Fortuna. While only the west-facing rooms offer a volcano view (and only from their porches), all rooms are clean and have platform beds. There are good views from the central swimming pool's patio. The hotel has colorful gardens, its own small lake and forest trails, and an inexpensive restaurant serving Tico standards from 6am to 7pm. The owners run an air taxi service for harrowing flights over the volcano and transportation to other destinations. This hotel isn't quite as attractive as Las Cabañitas up the road, but neither is it as expensive.

WHERE TO STAY NEAR THE VOLCANO
DOUBLES FOR LESS THAN $35

Montaña de Fuego Inn. La Palma de la Fortuna, San Carlos. ☎ **506/479-9106.** Fax 506/479-9295. 2 rms, 10 cabinas. $30 single or double; $38 triple. MC, V.

This hotel offers bed-rattling volcano proximity, at prices far below the fancier western-slope lodges. Located 8 kilometers out of La Fortuna on the road to Tabacón, these individual cabinas have wonderful volcano views from their spacious glassed-in porches. Inside, the cabinas are all varnished wood, with sparse but new appointments. The two rooms are in an older, remodeled home, have kitchenettes, no view, and are used primarily by larger groups and families.

WORTH A SPLURGE

✪ **Arenal Observatory Lodge.** Apdo. 1195-1250, Escazú. ☎ **506/257-9489** or 506/257-3273. Fax 506/257-4220. 26 rms. $36–$55.20 single; $40.79–65.20 double; $65.80–$75 triple. AE, MC, V.

This rustic lodge was originally built for the use of volcanologists from the Smithsonian Institution, but is today open to the public as well. The lodge is only $2^1/_2$ miles from the volcano and is built on a high ridge, which gives it the best view of any of the local lodges. Lying in bed at night listening to the eruptions, it is easy to think that the lodge is in imminent danger. The superior rooms feature a floor-to-ceiling window, with a spectacular view of the volcano. The less expensive rooms are less luxurious and don't have their own view, but if you stay here, you're never very far from a good view. Surrounding the lodge is the Arenal National Park, which includes thousands of acres of forest and many kilometers of trails. The lodge offers a number of guided and unguided hiking options, including a free morning trip to a new lava flow. A four-wheel-drive vehicle is recommended for the 9-kilometer dirt road up to the lodge, but two bridges now eliminate the need to ford any major rivers.

ANOTHER SPLURGE CHOICE SOUTH OF LA FORTUNA

Villablanca Hotel. Apdo. 247-1250, San Rafael de Escazú. ☎ **506/228-4603.** Fax 506/228-4004. 5 rms, 54 casitas. $68 single; $89 double; $104 triple; $152 quad casita. AE, MC, V.

Villablanca is certainly out of the way, and perched as it is, high in the cloud forest, it isn't the sort of place people come to when they want to work on their tans. However, if you are interested in birdwatching or exploring the cloud forest, there is no better place in the country. Owned and operated by a former president of Costa Rica, this lodge consists of 54 Tico-style *casitas,* "little houses," surrounded by 2,000 acres of farm and forest. There are also five new rooms in the main building. While the rooms are all up to par, the casitas are what make this lodge special. Each is built of adobe and has traditional tile floors and whitewashed walls with deep blue trim. This is the classic color scheme of 19th-century adobe homes throughout the country. Inside, you'll find a rounded fireplace in one corner, window seats, comfortable hardwood chairs, colorful curtains, and twin beds covered with attractive bedspreads. Rooms also have electric teapots and small refrigerators. Bathrooms are done in beautiful tiles and have tubs that look out through a wall of windows. In the hacienda-like main lodge, you'll find the dining room, where simple-but-filling buffet meals are served. Also in this building are an unusual atrium garden, library, lounge, gift shop, and small bar. Adjacent to the lodge there are 11 kilometers of trails through the Los Angeles Cloud Forest Reserve. Admission to the reserve is $22 per person, and includes a guided hike. You can also rent horses ($10 per hour). Transportation to and from the lodge is $35 each way. Alternatively, you can take a public bus from San José to San Ramón and then take a taxi for around $10. If you are driving, head west out of San José to San Ramón and then head north, following the signs to Villablanca.

3 Tilarán & Lake Arenal

200 kilometers NW of San José; 20 kilometers NW of Monteverde; 70 kilometers SE of Liberia

This remains one of the least-developed tourism regions in Costa Rica, but not for lack of resources or charms. Lake Arenal, a man-made lake with an area of 33 square miles, is the largest lake in Costa Rica and is surrounded by rolling hills that are partly pastured and partly forested. At the opposite (east) end of the lake from Tilarán lies the perfect cone of Arenal Volcano. The volcano's barren slopes are a stunning sight from here, especially when reflected in the waters of the lake. The north side of Lake Arenal is a dry region of rolling hills and pastures, distinctly different from the lusher landscape near La Fortuna.

People around here used to curse the winds, which often come blasting across this end of the lake at 60 knots or greater. However, since the first sailboarders caught wind of Lake Arenal's combination of warm fresh water, steady blows, and spectacular scenery, things have been changing quickly. Although the town of Tilarán is still little more than a quiet farm community, out along the shores of the lake hotels are proliferating. Even if you aren't a fanatical sailboarder, you still might enjoy hanging out by the lake, hiking in the nearby forests, and catching glimpses of Arenal Volcano.

The lake's other claim to fame is its rainbow-bass fishing. These fighting fish are known in their native South America as *guapote* and are large members of the cichlid family. Their sharp teeth and fighting nature make them a real challenge.

ESSENTIALS
GETTING THERE & DEPARTING

By Bus   Express buses leave San José for Tilarán daily at 7:30 and 9:30am and 12:45, 3:45, and 6:30pm from Calle 14 between avenidas 9 and 11. Duration is 4 hours. Fare is $3.

There are also morning and afternoon buses from Puntarenas to Tilarán. Duration is 3 hours. Fare is $2.15.

From Monteverde (Santa Elena), there is a bus daily at 7am. Duration is 3 hours. Fare is $1.25.

Direct buses to San José leave daily at 5, 7, and 7:45am and 2 and 4:45pm. Buses to Puntarenas leave at 6am and 1pm daily. The bus to Santa Elena (Monteverde) leaves daily at 1pm. Buses also leave regularly for Cañas, where you can catch buses north or south along the Interamerican Highway. Buses for La Fortuna, at the south end of Lake Arenal, leave daily at 7am and 1pm.

By Car   From San José, take the Interamerican Highway west toward Puntarenas and then continue north on this road to Cañas. In Cañas, turn east toward Tilarán. The drive takes 4 hours. If you are thinking of heading up this way from La Fortuna, be aware that for several kilometers the road is unpaved and in very bad shape. The road should not be tried in a regular car except during the dry season.

ORIENTATION

Tilarán is about 5 kilometers from Lake Arenal. All roads into town lead to the central park, which is Tilarán's main point of reference for addresses. If you need to exchange money, check at one of the hotels listed here. If you need a **taxi** to get to a lodge on Lake Arenal, call **695-5324**.

WINDSURFING, FISHING & MORE

Windsurfing   If you want to try windsurfing, you can rent equipment from **Tilawa Windsurfing Center** (☎ 506/695-5050), which has its facilities on one of the lake's few accessible beaches about 5 miles from Tilarán on the road around the west end of the lake. Windsurfers rent for $40 to $46 per day and lessons are also available. Over on the other side of the lake, on the way to Nuevo Arenal, you'll find the new **Tico Wind** (fax 506/695-5420, or ☎ 800/678-2252 in the U.S.), which rents equipment for $50 per day or $275 per week between November and April. Working in conjunction with Tico Wind, **Rio Escondido** is a new mountain bike–rental operation. Use of a top-of-the-line bike will run you around $35 per day. If you can't reach the above rental operations, ask at the **Rock River Lodge,** where you will be outfitted.

Fishing   If you want to try your hand at fishing for rainbow bass, contact **J.J.'s Fishing Tours** (☎ 506/695-5825). A half-day fishing trip will cost between $30 and $100 per person depending on the number of people in your party.

Boating   If you'd just like to go for a boat ride on the lake, ask at **Xiloe Lodge** (☎ 506/259-9192).

Horseback Riding & Hiking   If you're looking for another way to get around on dry land, the folks at Tilawa can arrange for you to rent a horse for $15 per hour. If you feel like strapping on your hiking boots, there are some trails for hiking on the far side of Lake Arenal, near the smaller Coter Lake.

Swimming   You can swim in Lake Arenal, but finding a nice beach can be tricky. The water level varies greatly here. When the water level is low, there's plenty of exposed bank, but much of it is either very rocky, or a muddy clay. When the water level is high, the banks are flooded. There's a nice swimming area in front of the Bahía Azul Lake Resort. You can also try swimming at the spot where most windsurfers put in, on a spit of land near the Rock River Lodge.

Up above Lake Arenal on the far side of the lake from Tilarán you'll find the beautiful little heart-shaped **Coter Lake.** This lake is surrounded by forest and has good swimming.

VISITING THE BOTANICAL GARDENS

A taxi to Coter Lake will cost around $12. Continuing south on the road around the lake will bring you to the town of Nuevo Arenal, where the pavement ends. If you continue another 4 kilometers on this road, you will come to the **Arenal Botanical Gardens** (☎ 506/694-4273), which is open daily from 9am to 5pm and charges $4 admission. These private gardens were only started in 1991 but are already quite beautiful and extensive. Not only are there many tropical plants and flowers to be seen, but there are always butterflies and hummingbirds in the gardens.

WHERE TO STAY

DOUBLES FOR LESS THAN $25

Cabinas Mary. On the south side of the park, Tilarán, Guanacaste. ☎ **506/695-5479.** 18 rms (13 with private bath). $10 single with shared bath, $12 single with private bath; $15 double with shared bath, $20 double with private bath. No credit cards.

Located right on Tilarán's large and sunny central park, Cabinas Mary is a very basic, but fairly clean lodging. It's upstairs from the restaurant of the same name and has safe parking in back. Rooms are large and have plenty of windows. You even get hot water here, which is a surprise at this price. The restaurant downstairs is a gringo hangout. It's open daily from 6am to 10pm; meals cost between $3 and $7.

Hotel Naralit. Tilarán, Guanacaste. ☎/fax **506/695-5393**. 20 rms. $11 single; $21 double; $26 triple. V.

This newer budget hotel is a good bet in Tilarán. The rooms are clean and most even have televisions. There are three second-floor rooms that have a nice balcony with a view of the town's church.

Cabinas El Sueño. Tilarán, Guanacaste. ☎ **506/695-5347**. 12 rms (all with private bath). $10 single; $16 double; $20 triple. MC, V.

Right in the middle of this small town, Cabinas El Sueño is a simple two-story accommodation, but it is clean and the management is friendly. There is parking in back and a small courtyard complete with a fountain on the second floor of the building. Downstairs there's a restaurant and bar.

DOUBLES FOR LESS THAN $45

Bahía Azul Lake Resort. Laguna de Arenal, Tilarán, Guanacaste. ☎/fax **506/695-5750**. 15 rms. TV. $25 single; $40 double; $45 triple. MC, V.

Located 5 kilometers from Tilarán on a small bay of Lake Arenal, Bahía Azul is popular both with windsurfers and vacationing Ticos. Most of the rooms are in a two-story white building that sits on a grassy slope overlooking the lake and green hills beyond. However, my favorite rooms are those down closer to the water. The setting is very tranquil during the week, though on weekends it can get a bit noisy with speedboats racing around the lake. The rooms here are a bit run-down, but all have small refrigerators, ceiling fans, and large windows. There is a bar and restaurant where the meal prices range from $4 to $8. The hotel also has fishing gear and water skis for rent, and offers boat trips and trips to Arenal Volcano and Tabacón Hot Springs. A taxi from Tilarán to Bahía Azul will cost you around $5.

✪ Rock River Lodge. Apdo. 95, Tilarán, Guanacaste. ☎/fax **506/695-5644**. 6 rms; 8 bungalows. $35–$55 single or double; $45–$65 triple. MC, V.

Set high on a grassy hill above the lake, this small lodge looks as if it might have been transported from Hawaii. The guest rooms are housed in a long, low lodge set on stilts. Walls and floors are made of hardwood and there are bamboo railings along the verandah. Wind chimes let you know when the winds are up, and there are sling chairs on the porch. Rooms are of medium size and have one double bed and a bunk bed, as well as modern tiled bathrooms. Though fairly simple in style, this is one of the most attractive lodges in the area. The newer bungalows are further up the hill, offer more privacy, and some even have sculpted bathtubs. It's a long walk down to the lake (not to mention the walk back up), so having a car is recommended. Meals will cost you around $25 per person per day, and are served in the spacious open-air restaurant where there's a large stone fireplace. This hotel caters to sailboarders and other active travelers. When the wind isn't up, owner Norman List offers mountain-bike trips.

WORTH A SPLURGE

Hotel Tilawa. Apdo. 92, Tilarán, Guanacaste. ☎ **506/695-5050** or 800/851-8929 in the U.S. Fax 506/695-5766. 28 rms. TEL. $50 single; $65 double; $85 triple. AE, MC, V.

Built to resemble the Palace of Knossos on the island of Crete, the Hotel Tilawa is an avid windsurfer's dream brought to reality. The American owners, who for years have run a windsurfing center on Lake Arenal, opened this hotel to provide wealthier windsurfers with a comfortable place to stay. The hotel sits high on the slopes above the lake and has a sweeping vista down the lake. Unusual colors and antique paint effects make the hotel look as though it has been weathered by the ages (though it is actually only a few years old). Inside there are wall murals and other artistic paint treatments throughout the hotel. Guest rooms have dyed cement floors, Guatemalan bedspreads, and big windows. Some have kitchenettes. Hotel amenities include a swimming pool and tennis court. There is a bar/disco beside the pool, as well as a moderately priced restaurant in the main building. The Tilawa can arrange not only windsurfing but mountain biking, horseback riding, fishing trips, and excursions around the lake.

A BED-AND-BREAKFAST

✪ **Chalet Nicholas.** Apdo. 72-5710, Tilarán, Guanacaste. ☎/fax **506/694-4041.** 3 rms. $39 double. $10 each additional person. All rates include full breakfast. No credit cards.

This friendly, American-owned bed-and-breakfast is located 2 kilometers west of the town of Nuevo Arenal and sits on a hill above the road. There are great views from the garden, and one of the three rooms has a view of Arenal Volcano out the window. The modern home is set on three acres and has pretty flower gardens, an organic vegetable garden, an aviary full of toucans and other colorful birds, and behind the property acres of forest through which you can hike in search of birds, orchids, butterflies, and other tropical beauties. If you don't mind the lack of privacy, the upstairs loft room is the largest. It even has its own private deck. No smoking is allowed in the house or on the grounds. Owners John and Catherine Nichols go out of their way to make their guests feel at home.

WHERE TO EAT

If you are staying in Tilarán, there are numerous inexpensive eateries, including restaurants at Cabinas Mary and Cabinas El Sueño, both of which are mentioned above. Also, around the corner from Cabinas Mary is **El Lugar,** a popular restaurant and bar that is worth checking out. If you are staying outside of town, you'll likely be eating in your hotel's dining room since there are few restaurants around the shores of the lake. Worth mentioning is **Equus BBQ,** a small open-air restaurant in front of Xiloe Lodge. This restaurant specializes in roast chicken and steaks. If you are staying down near Nuevo Arenal, try the following restaurant.

Restaurant Lajas. On the main street through town. ☎ **506/694-4169.** Reservations not accepted. Main courses $2–$3.90. No credit cards. Daily 11am–9pm. COSTA RICAN.

This surprisingly fancy little restaurant is one of the best values in Costa Rica. There are red tablecloths on every table, waiters in bow ties, and a wall of mirrors to make the tiny dining room look larger than it really is, but these are only the incidentals. The real reason to eat here is for good Tico cooking at rock-bottom prices. The deal of the day is always the casado. You won't walk away hungry or poor.

4 Monteverde

167 kilometers NW of San José; 82 kilometers NW of Puntarenas

To be frank, I have a love/hate relationship with Monteverde. Next to Manuel Antonio, this is Costa Rica's most internationally recognized tourist destination. The fame and accompanying traffic have led me to dub it the Monteverde Crowd Forest. Nevertheless, the extensive network of private reserves up here are incredibly rich in biodiversity, and the organization and infrastructure help guarantee a reasonably rewarding experience for first-time eco-adventurers.

Monteverde translates as "Green Mountain," and that is exactly what you will find up here at the end of a long, rutted dirt road that passes through mile after mile of often dry, brown pasture lands. All of those pastures you pass through were once covered with dense forest, but now only small pieces of that original forest remain.

The village of Monteverde was founded in the 1950s by Quakers from the United States who wished to leave behind the constant fear of war and the obligation to support continued militarism through U.S. taxes. They chose Costa Rica because it was committed to a nonmilitaristic economic path. Although Monteverde's founders came here to farm the land, they recognized the need to preserve the rare cloud forest that covered the mountain slopes above their fields, and to that end they dedicated the largest adjacent tract of cloud forest as the Monteverde Biological Cloud Forest Preserve.

Perched on a high mountain ridge, this tiny, scattered village and surrounding cloud forest are well known both among scientific researchers and ecotravelers. Cloud forests are a mountain-top phenomenon. Moist, warm air sweeping in off the nearby ocean is forced upward by mountain slopes, and as the moist air rises it cools, forming clouds. The mountain tops of Costa Rica are almost daily blanketed in dense clouds, and as these clouds cling to the slopes, moisture condenses on forest trees. This constant level of moisture has given rise to an incredible diversity of innovative life forms and a forest in which nearly every square inch of space has some sort of plant growing on it. Within the cloud forest, the branches of huge trees are draped with epiphytic plants—orchids, ferns, bromeliads. This intense botanic competition has created an almost equally diverse poulation of insects, birds, and other wildlife. **Monteverde Biological Cloud Forest Preserve** covers 26,000 acres of forest, including several different life zones that are characterized by different types of plants and animals. Within this small area are more than 2,000 species of plants, 400 bird species, and 100 different species of mammals. It is no wonder that the reserve has been the site of constant scientific investigations since its founding in 1972.

The preserve was originally known only to the handful of researchers who came here to study different aspects of life in the cloud forest. However, as the beauty and biological diversity of the area became known outside of university circles, casual visitors began arriving. For many, the primary goal was a chance to glimpse the rare and elusive quetzal, a bird once revered by the pre-Columbian peoples of the Americas. As the numbers of visitors began to grow, lodges began opening, word spread, more lodges opened, and so on. Today Monteverde is a prime example of too many people chasing after the same little piece of nature. On a much smaller scale, Monteverde is akin to the Yosemite Valley—a place of great and fragile beauty whose very beauty is threatened by its popularity. However, despite the hordes of ecotourists traipsing the trails of Monteverde, it is still a beautiful place and offers a glimpse into the life of one of the world's most threatened ecosystems. I urge you, though, to seriously consider visiting another cloud forest area in an effort to lessen the impact of tourism on Monteverde. Other places you could visit include **Villablanca** and the **Los Angeles Cloud Forest Reserve,** or the **Tapantí National Wildlife Refuge,** which has several nearby lodges. At either of these places you will find far fewer crowds and usually better chances of seeing the famed quetzal.

ESSENTIALS
GETTING THERE & DEPARTING

By Bus   Express buses leave San José daily at 6:30am and 2:30pm, from Calle 12, 75 meters North of avenida 7. Duration is 3^1/$_2$ hours. Fare is $4.75.

There is also a daily bus that departs Puntarenas for Santa Elena, only a few kilometers from Monteverde, at 2:15pm. The bus stop in Puntarenas is across the street from the main bus station. Duration is 2^1/$_2$ hours. Fare is $2.50.

There is a daily bus from Tilarán (Lake Arenal) at 1pm. Duration is 3 hours (40 kilometers!). Fare is $1.10.

One other option is to take **Costa Rica Expeditions' van** (☎ 506/257-0766) from San José. You must have a reservation. Fare is $35 each way.

The express bus departs from Monteverde for San José daily at 6:30am and 2:30pm. The bus from Santa Elena to Puntarenas leaves daily at 6am. If you should be heading to Manuel Antonio, take the 6am Santa Elena–Puntarenas bus and transfer in Puntarenas. To reach Liberia, take the 6am Santa Elena–Puntarenas bus and get off at the Río Lagarto Bridge, where the bus reaches the paved road. You can then flag down a bus bound for Liberia (almost any bus heading north). The Santa Elena–Tilarán bus leaves daily at 7am.

By Car   Take the Interamerican Highway toward Puntarenas and follow the signs for Nicaragua. About 31 kilometers past the turnoff for Puntarenas, watch for the Río Lagarto Bridge. It takes about 2¼ hours to this point. Take the dirt road to the right just before the bridge. From this turnoff, it's another 38 kilometers (1½ to 2 hours) to Monteverde. The going is very slow because the road is so bad. Many people are told that this road is not passable without four-wheel drive, but I have been driving it for years, albeit in the dry season, in regular cars. Just don't try it in the rainy season unless you have four-wheel drive. Be sure you have plenty of gas in the car before starting up to Monteverde. This grueling road eats up fuel, and the one gas station in Monteverde doesn't always have gas.

ORIENTATION

As you approach Santa Elena, take the right fork in the road if you are heading directly to Monteverde. If you continue straight, you will come into the village of Santa Elena, which has a bus stop, health clinic, bank, general store, and a few simple restaurants and budget hotels.

Monteverde, on the other hand, is not a village in the traditional sense of the word. There is no center of town, only dirt lanes leading off from the main road to various farms. This main road has signs for all the hotels and restaurants mentioned here and dead-ends at the reserve entrance.

Getting Around   A **taxi** (☎ 645-5322) between Santa Elena and either the Monteverde Biological Cloud Forest Preserve or the Santa Elena Rainforest Reserve will cost around $7. Count on paying between $4 to $6 for the ride from Santa Elena to your lodge in Monteverde.

Fast Facts   In Santa Elena, you'll find the Puntarenas bus stop, a few general stores, a bank, and a health clinic. There is also a small **information center** (☎ 506/645-5025). It's located across the street from the National Bank and is open Monday through Saturday 9am to noon, and 1 to 6pm.

EXPLORING THE WILDLIFE PRESERVE

Don't expect to see all the plants and animals you've been reading about during your visit because many of them are quite rare or elusive. However, with a guide hired through your hotel or on one of the preserve's official guided 2- to 3-hour hikes, you can see far more than you could on your own. At $15 per person, the preserve's tours may seem expensive, especially after you pay the $6 reserve entrance fee, but I strongly recommend that you go with a guide. I went into the reserve twice in the same morning—once on my own and once with a guide—and with the guide I saw much more and learned much more about cloud forests and their inhabitants. On the other hand, while alone I saw a rare bird, a guan, that I didn't see when walking the trails with a dozen other interested but rather noisy visitors. There is much to be said for walking quietly through the forest on your own.

The preserve is open daily from 7am to 4pm. Because only 100 people are allowed into the preserve at any one time, you may be forced to wait for a while before being allowed in. However, if you go the afternoon before you want to visit, you can usually get tickets for early the next morning. Rubber boots are available at the preserve entrance and rent for $2. The trails can be very muddy depending on the season, so ask at the entrance and these boots may make your hike much more pleasant.

Before venturing into the forest, have a look around the information center. There are several guidebooks available, as well as posters and postcards of some of the preserve's more famous animal inhabitants. Perhaps the most famous resident of the cloud forests of Costa Rica is the quetzal, a robin-sized bird with iridescent-green wings and a ruby-red breast, which has become extremely rare due to habitat destruction. The male quetzal also has two long tail feathers that make it one of the most spectacular birds on earth. The best time to see quetzals is early to midmorning, with February through April (mating season) being the easiest months to spot these magnificent birds.

Other animals that have been seen in Monteverde include jaguars, ocelots, and tapirs. After the quetzal, Monteverde's most beautiful resident was the golden toad (sapo dorado). However, following several years of low precipitation, the golden toad seems to have disappeared from the forest, its only known home in the entire world. There has been speculation that the toad was adversely affected by a natural drought cycle, the disappearing ozone layer, pesticides, or acid rain. Photos of the golden toad abound in Monteverde, and I'm sure you'll be as saddened as I was by the disappearance of such a beautiful creature.

To learn even more about Monteverde, stop in at the **Monteverde Conservation League** (☎ **506/645-5003**) office, which is located across the street from the gas station. This office is open Monday through Friday from 8am to noon and from 1 to 5pm, and from 8am to noon on Saturdays. They also sell informative books, t-shirts and cards here, and proceeds go to help ongoing conservation efforts and to purchase more land for the Bosque Eterno de Los Niños (Children's Eternal Forest).

BIRD WATCHING & HIKING OUTSIDE THE PRESERVE

Ample bird watching and hiking opportunities can also be found outside the preserve boundaries. You can avoid the crowds at Monteverde by heading 5 kilometers north from the village of Santa Elena to the **Santa Elena Forest Reserve.** This 900-acre cloud forest has a maximum elevation of 5,600 feet, which makes it the highest cloud forest in the Monteverde area. There are 8 kilometers of hiking trails as well as an information center. As it borders the Monteverde Preserve, a similar richness of flora and fauna are to be found here. Entry fees at this reserve go directly to support local schools.

The **Bajo Tigre Trail** is a 2-mile-long trail that's home to several different bird species not usually found within the reserve. The trail starts a little past the CASEM artisans' shop and is open daily from 8am to 4pm. The trail has been undergoing some upkeep and improvements, but the Monteverde Conservation League has promised to keep the entrance fee very low.

You can also go on guided 3-hour hikes at the **Reserva Sendero Tranquilo** (☎ **506/645-5010**), which has 200 acres of land, two-thirds of which is in virgin forest. This reserve is located up the hill from the cheese factory, charges $15 for its tours, and is open daily from 5am to 2pm seasonally.

The **Monteverde Eco-Farm** (☎ 506/645-5222) is open daily from 7am to 5pm. More than 100 species of birds have been seen here. There are also good views and two waterfalls. Admission is $5.

CANOPY TOURS, NIGHT TOURS & HORSEBACK RIDING

For an elevated look at the cloud forest, check out the local branch of **Canopy Tours** (☎ 645-5423), which has an office across from Hotel El Tucan. The 2¹/₂ hour tours run three times daily and cost $40 for adults, $25 for children under 12.

Almost all of the area hotels can arrange a variety of other tour and activity options, including night trips to the Arenal Volcano (a grueling 4-hour ride away), guided night tours of the cloud forest, and, of course, horseback riding. The going rate for horseback rides with a guide is between $7 and $10 per person per hour. **Meg's Riding Stables** (☎ 506/645-5052) is one of the more established operators and offers 4-hour guided rides for around $35.

OTHER THINGS TO SEE & DO IN MONTEVERDE

You can glimpse another part of the area's history at **El Trapiche** (☎ 506/645-6054), where the process of making *tapa dulce* is demonstrated on Tuesdays, Thursdays, and Saturdays on an old-fashioned sugar mill. El Trapiche is open Tuesday through Sunday from 11am to 10pm, serves tipico food, and sells homemade sugar products. You'll find El Trapiche 1¹/₂ kilometers north of Santa Elena on the road to Tilarán.

Because the vegetation in the cloud forest is so dense, most of the forest's animal residents are rather difficult to spot. If you were unsatisfied with your sightings, even with a naturalist guide leading you, you might want to consider attending a slide show of photographs taken in the preserve. These slide shows are presented by the **Hummingbird Gallery** (☎ 506/645-5030) daily at 4:30pm. Admission is $3. The Monteverde Lodge presents a similar slide show at 6:15pm on Mondays, and Wednesday through Friday.

You'll find the Hummingbird Gallery just outside the preserve entrance. Hanging from trees around the gallery are several hummingbird feeders that attract more than seven species of these avian jewels. At any given moment, there might be several dozen hummingbirds buzzing and chattering around the building and your head. Inside you will, of course, find a lot of beautiful mounted and unmounted color prints of hummingbirds. There are also many other beautiful photos from Monteverde available in prints or postcards. The gallery is open daily from 9:30am to 5pm.

Birds are not the only colorful fauna in the Monteverde cloud forest. Butterflies abound here, and the Butterfly Garden, located near the Pensión Monteverde Inn, displays many of Costa Rica's most beautiful species. Besides the hundreds of preserved and mounted butterflies, there are also gardens and a greenhouse where you can watch live butterflies. The garden is open daily from 9:30am to 4pm, and the admission is $5 for adults and $2.50 for children, which includes a guided tour and informative lecture on the life cycle of these interesting creatures. The best time to visit is between 11am and 1pm, when the butterflies are most active.

If your taste runs towards the slithery, don't miss the quaint **Serpentarium Santa Elena** (☎ 506/645-5238), which is on the road to the preserve just out of town, open daily from 9am to 4pm, and charges $3 admission.

SHOPPING

If you're in the mood to do some shopping, stop in at CASEM, which is on the right just past Restaurant El Bosque. This crafts cooperative sells embroidered clothing, t-shirts, posters and postcards with photos of the local flora and fauna, locally grown and roasted coffee, and many other items to remind you of your visit to Monteverde. CASEM is open Monday through Saturday from 8am to 5pm, and on Sunday from 10am to 4pm (closed Sundays May through October). Between November and April, you can also visit the Sarah Dowell Watercolor Gallery, which is up the hill from the cheese factory and sells paintings by this local artist.

WHERE TO STAY

When choosing a place to stay in Monteverde, be sure to check whether the rates include meals or not. In the past all the lodges operated on the American plan (three meals a day are included). This practice is on the wane, though, so rates can be misleading if you don't read carefully.

DOUBLES FOR LESS THAN $15

Hotel El Tucan. Santa Elena, Puntarenas. ☎ **506/645-5017.** 14 rms (7 with bath). $5 single without bath, $10 single with bath; $10 double without bath, $20 double with bath. No credit cards.

This very basic hotel is located on the edge of Santa Elena (on the back road from the village's main street to the road to Monteverde) and consequently does not have the rural feel of many of the area's other accommodations. Though the rooms without baths are only slightly larger than closets, they are fairly clean. Rooms with a private bath are slightly larger, with some housed in a separate building across the street. Costa Rican–style meals are served in a very basic dining room on the ground floor. Keep in mind that this hotel is 5 kilometers from the preserve. If you don't have a car, transportation to and from the reserve by taxi is going to add a bit to the cost of the room.

Pensión Flor De Lis. Santa Elena, Monteverde. ☎/fax **506/645-5236.** 8 rms (3 with private bath). $7 single, $14 double, $21 triple (shared bath); $10 single, $20 double, $30 triple (private bath). V.

This new pension is my favorite budget option in Monteverde. Located 75 meters up a dirt road, just out of Santa Elena on the way to the preserve, this hotel has an authentic rural feel. Rooms are very simple, but immaculately clean. The owners will make you feel part of the family. They also know and love the area and are eager to share it with guests. A homecooked breakfast will cost an extra $3.

Pensión Manakin. Apdo. 11-5655, Santa Elena, Monteverde, Puntarenas. ☎/fax **506/ 645-5080.** 15 rms (6 with private bath). $7 single without bath, $20 single with bath; $14 double without bath, $20 double with bath. V.

Though most of the rooms here are merely tiny cubicles with bunk beds and cement floors, the rooms with private baths are a bit better. These rooms have carpeting and clean tile bathrooms. When I last visited, the owners were building a restaurant and were also allowing people to put up tents on their property. You'll find this *pensión* about a third of the way from Santa Elena to the preserve down a short dirt road to your right.

Pensión Monteverde Inn. Apdo 10165-1000, San José. ☎ **506/645-5156.** 10 rms (8 with private bath). $5 per person with shared bath; $8 per person with private bath. No credit cards.

Of the numerous inexpensive lodgings in the area, this one has the most pleasant surroundings. Located just past the Monteverde Butterfly Garden, the Monteverde Inn is a couple of hundred yards off the main road on a small farm. Owner David Savage and his family have operated this simple, rustic lodge for years. The rooms are small and come with two twin beds or a double bed. Hardwood floors keep the rooms from seeming too Spartan. It's a bit of a walk up to the park entrance, but once you reach the main road, you can try hitching a ride. Horse rentals here are $5 per hour. This is a good choice for those who have to watch their colónes. Economical meals are available.

DOUBLES FOR LESS THAN $25

Pensión Flor Mar. Apdo. 10165-1000, San José. ☎ **506/645-5009.** Fax 506/645-5011. 13 rms (3 with bath). $26 per person without bath, $30 per person with bath. All rates include three meals daily. No credit cards.

The Flor Mar was one of the first lodges to open in Monteverde and initially catered almost exclusively to professors and students doing scientific research in the reserve. Study groups are still the bulk of the Flor Mar's business, but casual visitors are also welcome, though the accommodations are very basic (scientists and students don't seem overly concerned with their accommodations). The rooms are very simply furnished, which means bunk beds in some rooms. There are also no views to speak of here. However, this lodge is close to the park entrance, which is a definite plus if you don't have a car. The dining room is large and rather dark, but there is a much more appealing lounge in the lower of the lodge's two main buildings. Note that the rates here include all your meals.

DOUBLES FOR LESS THAN $35

El Establo. Apdo. 549-2050, San Pedro. ☎ **506/645-5110** or 506/645-5033. Fax 506/645-5041. 20 rms. $25 single; $35 double; $40 triple; $45 quad. AE, MC, V.

Horses are an integral part of Costa Rican culture and are a common sight in Monteverde. El Establo, as its name implies, makes use of a stable theme in its architectural design. Though the hotel is next to the road, there are 120 acres of farm behind it, and half of this area is in primary forest. Most of the rooms are situated off a large enclosed porch that contains plenty of comfortable chairs and a fireplace. Guest-room doors look as if they were salvaged from a stable, but inside, the rooms are carpeted and have orthopedic mattresses and modern bathrooms, though with showers only. The end rooms have a bit more light than others. Of course the hotel also has plenty of horses for rent at $7 per hour with a guide. Meals will run you around $21 per person per day.

El Bosque. Apdo. 1165-1000, San José. ☎ **506/645-5129** or 506/645-5158. Fax 506/645-5129. 21 rms. $22 single; $30 double; $36 triple; $40 quad. MC, V.

Hidden down the hill behind El Bosque restaurant (on the main road to the preserve), is one of Monteverde's best values. Though the rooms are very basic, they are clean, fairly large, and have high ceilings, picture windows, and double beds. The cement floors and simple furnishings are what help keep the rates down. The rooms are arranged in a semicircle around a minimally landscaped garden. The setting may not be spectacular, but if you're going to spend all day in the preserve, this shouldn't bother you too much. The hotel also has a camping area ($5 per person per night).

The hotel's restaurant is a hundred yards up a dirt road and down a path that crosses a jungly ravine on a footbridge, which turns going for breakfast into a morning birdwatching trip. Tico standards and international dishes are served here, with prices ranging from $4 to $15.40.

Cabinas El Gran Mirador. Monteverde, Puntarenas. ☎ **506/645-5087.** 4 cabins (none with private bath). $17 per person. All rates include breakfast. No credit cards.

If you're looking for a bit more adventure and rusticity than is offered at any of the lodges in Monteverde or Santa Elena, give these friendly folks a call. The rustic wooden cabins are all very simply furnished and have great views of Arenal Volcano (when it's clear). Sleeping is dormitory style and if you're alone, you probably will be grouped with other travelers. The cabins are a long way from the Monteverde Biological Cloud Forest Preserve, but they are close to the Santa Elena Rainforest Reserve. You can now reach these cabins year-round in a four-wheel-drive vehicle, so it's no longer necessary to be taken in by horseback—although you can still rent horses for $8 per hour.

WORTH A SPLURGE

✪ **Hotel Belmar.** Apdo. 17-5655, Monteverde, Puntarenas. ☎ **506/645-5201.** Fax 506/645-5135. 32 rms. $45 single; $55 double; $65 triple. Discounts are available in low season. No credit cards.

You'll think that you're in the Alps when you stay at this beautiful Swiss chalet–style hotel. Set at the top of a grassy hill, the Belmar has stunning views all the way to the Nicoya Gulf and the Pacific Ocean. Afternoons in the dining room or lounge are idyllic, with bright sunlight streaming in through a west-facing wall of glass that provides a grandstand seat for spectacular sunsets. Most of the guest rooms come with wood paneling, French doors, and little balconies that open onto spendid views. Meals usually live up to the surroundings and run around $21 per person per day. The Belmar is up a road to the left of the gas station as you come into the village of Monteverde.

✪ **El Sapo Dorado.** Apdo. 9-5655, Monteverde, Puntarenas. ☎ **506/645-5010.** Fax 506/645-5180. 20 rms (all with bath). $55.00 single; $65.00 double; $77.00 triple. Sunset Terrace Suites an additional $10. No credit cards.

Located up on a steep hill from the main road between Santa Elena and the preserve, El Sapo Dorado (named for Monteverde's famous "golden toad") offers attractive cabins with good views. The cabins are built of hardwoods both inside and out and are surrounded by a grassy lawn. Big windows let in lots of light, and high ceilings keep the rooms cool during the day. The older cabins also have fireplaces, a welcome feature on chilly nights. The newer rooms all have spacious terraces with sunset views. The hotel's restaurant is open to the public and serves three meals daily. The dinner menu changes nightly, but among the regular offerings are chicken with orange sauce, homemade ravioli, and filet mignon with pepper-cream sauce; there is always a vegetarian item. Prices range from $7 to $12. There is a large patio terrace from which you can watch the sunset while listening to classical music. The bar here stays open until 11pm and is usually fairly quiet. To find the hotel and restaurant, watch for the sign on the main road to the preserve.

WHERE TO EAT

Most lodges in Monteverde have their own dining rooms, and these are the most convenient places to eat. Because most visitors to Monteverde want to get an early start, they usually grab a quick breakfast at their hotel. It is also common for people to have their lodge pack them a bag lunch to take with them to the preserve. However, there are now several inexpensive restaurants scattered along the road between Santa Elena and Monteverde. Two inexpensive places worth mentioning are the **Pizzeria de Johnny** near the Hotel Heliconia and the **Soda Cerro Verde** across from the gas station. If your lodge doesn't offer meals or you've tried the food there and aren't impressed, there are a couple of options. However, keep in mind that since the lodges are scattered across more than 3 miles of road, it can be a long hike to eat a meal if you don't have your own vehicle.

When it comes to lunch, you can get a bag lunch from your hotel as I already mentioned, or you can piece together your own on the way to the preserve. Stop in at **Stella's Bakery** (across the road from the CASEM gift shop) for some fresh bread and a piece of cake or some cookies. Stella's is open daily from 6am to 6pm and also has a small cafe where you can get pizzas, eggplant parmigiana, salads, and deliciously decadent baked goods. Next, stop by the **Monteverde Cheese Factory** and pick up some of the best cheese in Costa Rica (you can even see it being made). The cheese factory is open Monday through Saturday from 7:30am to 4pm and on Sunday from 7:30am to 12:30 pm. And then, there you have it: the ingredients for a great picnic lunch.

El Sapo Dorado. Road to the left as you leave Santa Elena. ☎ **506/645-5010.** Reservations are recommended. Main courses $6.60–$13.50. No credit cards. Daily 7am–9pm. INTERNATIONAL.

Located high on a hill above the main road, El Sapo Dorado provides great sunsets and good food for accompaniment. The menu here is a little bit more imaginative than at most restaurants in Monteverde, which makes it well worth a visit even if you miss the sunset. A recent menu included such dishes as grilled corvina, fettuccini in peanut-squid sauce, and filet mignon in pepper-cream sauce. In addition to a large, formal dining room, there is a patio that's a great spot for lunch or an early dinner. Rounding out the entire scene is taped classical music in the evenings.

The Central Pacific Coast

9

The central Pacific coast offers several of the most easily accessible beaches in Costa Rica. They range from the somewhat seedy Puntarenas and the cut-rate, fun-in-the-sun, Jacó to the jungle-clad hillsides of Manuel Antonio and Dominical. For the most part, this coast is not as spectacular as that of the more rugged Nicoya peninsula, but neither is it as brown and desolate-looking in the dry season. The climate here is considerably more humid than farther north, but not nearly as steamy as along the south Pacific or Caribbean coasts. Jacó and Manuel Antonio are Costa Rica's two most developed beaches, while Puntarenas, a former seaport, offers the most urban beach setting in the country (it's just a short day trip away from San José). If you are looking to get away from it all and spend as little money as possible, Dominical should be your top choice on this coast.

This is also where you'll find some of Costa Rica's most popular and spectacular national parks and biological reserves: namely, Manuel Antonio National Park, home of three-toed sloths and white-faced monkeys; Chirripó National Park, a misty cloud forest that turns to barren páramo at the peak of the mountain that lends its name to the park, Mt. Chirripó; and Carara Biological Reserve, one of the last places in Costa Rica where one can see the disappearing dry forest join the damp, humid forests that extend south down the coast and glimpse an occasional scarlet macaw.

1 Puntarenas

130 kilometers W of San José; 113 kilometers S of Liberia; 60 kilometers N of Playa de Jacó

After decades of decay and neglect, Puntarenas is currently undergoing a major makeover. Plans are in the works to build a modern cruise ship dock that will accommodate up to two of these floating resorts at a time. A 10-mile-long spit of land jutting into the Gulf of Nicoya, Puntarenas was once Costa Rica's busiest port, but that changed several years ago, when the government inaugurated nearby Puerto Caldera, a modern container port facility. After losing its port, the city survived primarily on commercial fishing. Watching the tourist boom bring big bucks to other cities, Puntarenas decided to grab its piece of the pie. To that end, the city built a sewage treatment plant to clean up its water and now has the only beach-cleaning machine in Costa Rica. The town's beachfront Paseo de los Turistas (Tourist Walk), a ten-block promenade of ice cream stands, small restaurants, and arcades will be the next area spruced up. When all the work is finished, Puntarenas should also have a convention and recreation center, a seaside aquarium, a museum, and an artisans row, where visitors will be able to stock up on regional arts and crafts.

With a good highway leading all the way from San José, Puntarenas can be reached in an hour and a half by car, which makes it the closest beach to San José—at least in elapsed time if not in actual mileage. Because Puntarenas is a city, a former port town, and commercial fishing center, this beach has a very different character from any other beach in Costa Rica. The beach itself, a long straight stretch of sand with gentle surf, is backed for most of its length by the Paseo de los Turistas. Across a wide boulevard from the paseo are hotels, restaurants, bars, discos, and shops. It's all very civilized, though the preponderance of cement gives it too much of an urban feel for my taste. The views across the Gulf of Nicoya and the sunsets are quite beautiful, and there is almost always a cooling breeze blowing in off the water. All around town you'll find unusual old buildings, reminders of the important role Puntarenas once played in Costa Rican history. It was from here that much of the Central Valley's coffee crop was once shipped, and while the coffee barons in the highlands were getting rich, so too were the merchants of Puntarenas.

If you're in Costa Rica for only a short time and want to get in some time on the beach, Puntarenas is certainly an option, though bathing here still seems more the exception than the rule. You can even do it in a day trip from San José. Likewise, if you are looking for a base from which to visit national parks up and down the Pacific coast, Puntarenas is a good choice. From here you can head north to the national parks in Guanacaste or south to Carara Biological Reserve. Also, if you are heading out to any of the beaches at the southern end of the Nicoya peninsula, you'll be passing through Puntarenas to catch one of the three ferries. Puntarenas is most popular as a weekend holiday spot for Ticos from San José and is at its liveliest on the weekends.

ESSENTIALS
GETTING THERE & DEPARTING

By Bus   Express buses leave San José daily every 30 minutes between 5am and 7pm from the corner of Calle 12 and Avenida 9. Duration is 2 hours. Fare is $2.

The main Puntarenas bus station is a block east of the Hotel Imperial, which is in front of the old main dock on the Paseo de los Turistas. Buses to San José leave daily every 30 minutes between 5am and 7pm. The bus to Santa Elena leaves daily at 2:15pm from a stop across the railroad tracks from the main bus station. Buses to Quepos (Manuel Antonio) leave daily at 5 and 11am and 2pm. A bus leaves for Liberia daily at 5:30pm.

By Car   Head west out of San José on the Interamerican Highway, passing the airport and Alajuela, and follow the signs to Puntarenas. The drive takes about 1 1/2 hours.

By Ferry   See the "Playa Tambor" or "Playa Montezuma" sections of chapter 7 for information on crossing to Puntarenas from Paquera or Naranjo on the Nicoya peninsula and returning.

ORIENTATION

Puntarenas is built on a long, narrow sand spit that stretches 3 miles out into the Gulf of Nicoya, and marked by only five streets at its widest. The ferry docks for the Nicoya peninsula are near the far (west) end of town as are the bus station and market. The north side of town faces an estuary, while the south side faces the mouth of the gulf. The **Paseo de los Turistas** is on the south side of town, beginning at the pier and extending out to the point. If you need a **taxi,** call **663-2020.** Car rentals are available from **Elegante Rent-a-Car** (☎ **506/661-1958**).

WHAT TO SEE & DO

Take a walk along the Paseo de los Turistas. It's yet to be transformed into a well-maintained boardwalk, but there are numerous small sodas, as well as some arcade games and souvenir stands. The hotels across the street range in style from converted old wooden homes with bright gingerbread trim, to modern concrete monstrosities, to tasteful art-deco relics needing a new coat of paint. If you want to go swimming, the ocean waters are now said to be perfectly safe (pollution was a problem for many years). Alternatively, you can head out to the end of the peninsula to the Balneario Municipal, the public pool. It is huge, has a great view (albeit through a chain-link fence), and is surrounded by lawns and gardens. Entrance is only $1 for adults and 50¢ for children. The pool is open Tuesday through Sunday from 9am to 4pm. If the beach right here in the city doesn't appeal to you, head back down the spit to the Playa Dona Aña, a popular beach park several kilometers south, with picnic tables, bath and changing rooms, and a restaurant.

Puntarenas isn't known as one of Costa Rica's prime sportfishing ports, but there are usually a few charter boats available. Check at your hotel or at the Hotel Colonial. Rates are usually between $250 and $400 for a half-day and between $400 and $600 for a full day. These rates are for up to four people.

The most popular water excursions from Puntarenas are yacht cruises among the tiny uninhabited islands of the Guayabo, Negritos, and Pajaros Islands Biological Reserve. These cruises include a gourmet seafood buffet and a stop at beautiful and undeveloped Tortuga Island, where you can swim, snorkel, and sun. The water is a clear blue, and the sand is bright white. Several San José-based companies offer these excursions, with round-trip transportation from San José, but if you are already in Puntarenas, you may be able to get a discount by boarding here. **Bay Island Cruises** (☎ **296-5551**), **Calypso Tours** (☎ **233-3617**), and **Sea Ventures** (☎ **506/ 257-2904**) are just three of the companies that offer similar tours and will pick you up at your hotel in San José. The price for one of these trips is around $70 per person. Some of these companies also offer sunset cruises with live music, snacks, and a bar.

WHERE TO STAY
DOUBLES FOR LESS THAN $15

Hotel Ayi Con. 50 meters south of the market (Apdo. 358), Puntarenas. ☎ **506/661-0164.** 44 rms (22 with private bath). $7.50 single without bath, $11.85 double without bath; $9.20 single with bath, $16.40 double with bath; $20 double with bath and A/C. No credit cards.

Centrally located near the market and the ferry-boat docks, the Ayi Con is your basic low-budget Tico accommodation. It's above a row of shops in a very busy shopping district of Puntarenas and is frequented primarily by Costa Ricans. Back-packers will find that this is probably the best and the cleanest of the cheap hotels in Puntarenas. If you're just passing through and have to spend a night in town, this place is convenient and acceptable.

Hotel Imperial. Paseo de los Turistas, frente al Muelle (Apdo. 65), Puntarenas. ☎ **506/ 661-0579** or 506/661-0600. 27 rms (10 with private bath). $8.75 single without bath, $12.50 single with bath; $17.50 double without bath, $24 double with bath; $20.50 triple without bath, $27 triple with bath. No credit cards.

The Imperial, despite its name, is as basic as hotels get in Costa Rica and would hardly be worth mentioning if not for its location and atmosphere. Located directly across from the old main dock, the hotel is a weather beaten, green wooden building that certainly must have seen its share of sailors in days past. The architecture is classic tropical colonial, with high ceilings, wide halls, and wooden walls that don't go all the way to the ceiling (to keep the air circulating). In the middle of the large building, there is a narrow courtyard garden that has seen better days. Definitely look at a few rooms here before committing. If you decide to stay, I recommend one of the second-floor rooms with a shared bath that face the beach—these seem to be the lightest, breeziest, and cleanest in the joint.

DOUBLES FOR LESS THAN $25

Cabinas Midey. Calle 15 and Avenida 2, Puntarenas. ☎/fax **506/661-1553.** 12 rms (all with bath). A/C TV. $25 up to four persons; $35 up to eight. MC.

This is a new French-owned establishment catering to budget European travelers and is a good choice for larger groups. The apartment-style rooms all come with full kitchens and at least two separate bedrooms. There's no hot water, but that's usually not a big problem in Puntarenas. There is secured parking. Rooms 4 and 5 have ocean views and a balcony.

DOUBLES FOR LESS THAN $35

Hotel Tioga. Paseo de los Turistas (Apdo. 96-5400), Puntarenas. ☎ **506/661-0271** or 506/255-3115 in San José. Fax 506/661-0127. 46 rms (all with bath). A/C. $24.50–$37 single; $30–$45 double. All rates include breakfast. AE, MC, V. Slightly lower rates in off season.

This 1950s modern-style hotel is Puntarenas's old standard on the Paseo de los Turistas. The beach is right across the street and there are plenty of restaurants within a short walk. When you walk through the front door, you enter a courtyard with a pool that has been painted a brilliant shade of blue. In the middle of the pool, there is even a tiny island with a tree growing on it. The four-story hotel is built around this pleasant setting. Rooms vary in size, and some come with cold-water showers only, so if you must have hot water (not really necessary in these hot regions), be sure to request it. The larger rooms are attractive, with huge closets and modern bathrooms. The smaller, less expensive rooms have louvered, frosted-glass windows to let in lots of light and air while maintaining some privacy. The restaurant and bar are on the second floor and there is a breakfast room and lounge on the fourth floor, so you can look out across the water as you enjoy your complimentary breakfast.

WORTH A SPLURGE

Hotel Las Brisas. Paseo de los Turistas (Apdo. 83-5400), Puntarenas. ☎ **506/661-4040.** Fax 506/661-1487. 19 rms (all with bath). A/C. $30 single; $50 double; $65 triple (discounts in the off-season). AE, MC, V.

Out near the end of the Paseo de los Turistas, you'll find a very clean hotel with large air-conditioned rooms, a small pool out front, and the beach right across the street. All the rooms have tile floors, double or twin beds, and small tables. Large picture windows keep the rooms sunny and bright during the day. The hotel's small open-air dining room serves some of the best food in town with the emphasis on continental dishes. The bouillabaise is excellent, and if you're lucky you might happen on a Greek-style fish special or homemade moussaka. It's worth staying here just to enjoy the food.

Hotel Porto Bello. Apdo. 108, Puntarenas. ☎ **506/661-1322** or 506/661-2122. Fax 506/661-0036. 37 rms. A/C TEL. Dec–Apr $45 single, $55 double, $65 triple; May–Nov $35 single, $45 double, $55 triple. AE, DC, MC, V.

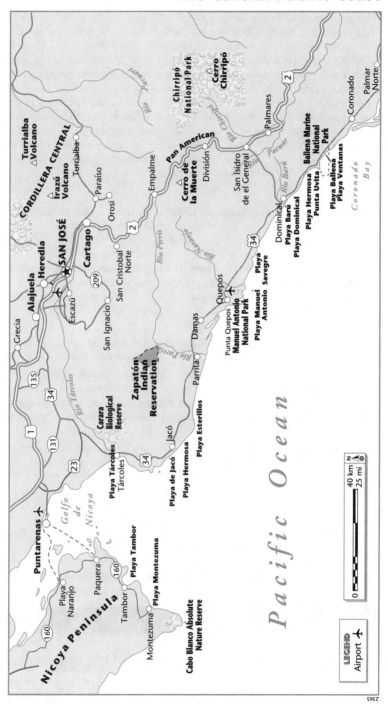

Located about 7 kilometers before downtown Puntarenas, on the narrow spit behind the soccer field, the Porto Bello is a popular weekend escape for wealthy Ticos. The stucco walls of the hotel are almost blindingly white, but are tempered by the lush overgrown gardens that surround the buildings. Most of the rooms have high ceilings, red-tile floors, attractive teak-and-cloth headboards, and balconies or patios that are often hidden by the shrubbery. Watch out: The window unit air conditioners can be loud. Most of the double rooms have televisions, but ask first. There are pools for adults and kids, a poolside bar, and even a small beach. You can hire a water taxi for a spin around the bay or book an all-day cruise of some of the remote and picturesque islands out in the gulf. The open-air restaurant is breezy and cool, with a high ceiling and stucco walls. Grilled meats and seafood are the specialties here—with main courses ranging in price from $6 to $20.

WHERE TO EAT

Since you are in a seaport, you should be sure to try corvina—the national fish dish of Costa Rica—at least once. The most economical option is to pull up a table at one of the many open-air snack bars along the Paseo de los Turistas. They have names such as Soda Rio de Janeiro and Soda Acapulco, and serve everything from sandwiches, drinks, and ice cream to ceviche and whole fish meals. Sandwiches are priced at around a dollar and a fish filet with rice and beans should cost around $3.50. In addition to the restaurants listed below, you might want to try the **Restaurant and Pizzeria La Terraza** (☎ 506/661-3820), housed in a lovely wooden house with gingerbread trim on the Paseo de los Turistas.

Bierstube. Paseo de los Turistas between calles 21 and 23, Paseo de los Turistas. ☎ **506/661-0330.** Reservations not necessary. DC, MC, V. 10am–12pm daily. GERMAN/SEAFOOD.

This German-Tico beer garden also happens to serve excellent seafood. The restaurant is a huge open room with a high ceiling. Louvered windows swing open and provide fresh breezes and a view of the bay. There is beer on tap and good hearty meals. The *filete bierstube* is a fresh piece of corvina in a light tomato sauce, with mushrooms and peppers.

La Caravelle. Paseo de los Turistas between calles 21 and 23, Paseo de los Turistas. ☎ **506/661-2262.** Reservations recommended in high season and on weekends. Main courses $5.50–$15. MC, V. Wed–Sat noon–2:30pm and 6–10pm, Sun noon–10pm. FRENCH.

For more than 16 years, La Caravelle has been serving fine French dinners amid an eclectic cafe atmosphere. The restaurant's walls are decorated with a curious assortment of paintings, as well as a carousel horse, which give La Caravelle a very playful feel. The menu, however, is strictly traditional French, with such flavorful and well-prepared dishes as tenderloin with bourguignonne sauce or a tarragon béarnaise. There are quite a few good seafood dishes, as well as a salade niçoise. There's a modest assortment of both French and Chilean wines to accompany your meal, though prices are a bit high (as they are all over Costa Rica).

2 Playa de Jacó

108 kilometers W of San José; 60 kilometers S of Puntarenas

Playa de Jacó is the closest thing Costa Rica has to Fort Lauderdale during spring break. This long stretch of beach is strung with a dense hodgepodge of hotels in all price categories, cheap souvenir shops, seafood restaurants, pizza joints, and even a miniature golf course. If you're looking for a cheap place to spend a week in the sun that is close to San José, Jacó continues to be the top choice. Charter flights arrive weekly from Montreal and Toronto and consequently many of the hotels here are owned by Canadians, some of whom speak French and Spanish but little English. Jacó is also now gaining popularity with Germans and young Ticos, so if English is your native tongue, you may find yourself in a distinct minority here. This is the most touristy beach in Costa Rica and is a prime example of what happens when rapid growth hits a beach town. However, on the outskirts of town and close to the beach there is still plenty of greenery to offset the excess of cement along the town's main street. In fact, this is the first beach on the Pacific coast that actually has a tropical feel to it. The humidity is palpable and the lushness of the tropical forest is visible on the hillsides surrounding town. In hotel gardens, flowers bloom profusely throughout the year.

ESSENTIALS
GETTING THERE & DEPARTING

By Bus   Express buses leave San José daily at 7:30 and 10:30am and 3:30pm from the "Coca-Cola" Bus terminal at Calle 16 between avenidas 1 and 3. Duration is 3 hours. Fare is $2.20.

Buses from San José to Quepos also stop in Jacó (they let passengers off on the highway about one kilometer from town). These buses leave San José daily at 6, 7, and 10am and noon, 2, 4, 5, and 6pm. Duration is 3 hours. Fare is $1.80.

From Puntarenas, you can catch Quepos-bound buses daily at 5 and 11am and 2pm, and get off in Jacó. Duration is 1 hour. Fare is $1.50.

The Jacó bus station is at the north end of town about 50 yards off the main road near the Hotel El Jardin. Buses for San José leave daily at 5 and 11am and 3pm. Buses bound for Quepos stop in Jacó around 6am, noon, and 4pm. Since schedules can change it is best to ask at your hotel about current times of departures.

By Car   There are two main routes to Jacó. The easier though longer route is to take the Interamerican Highway west out of San José and get off at the Puntarenas exit. From here, head south on the Costanera, the coast road. Alternatively, you can take the narrow and winding, though more scenic, old highway, which turns off the Interamerican Highway just west of Alajuela near the town of Atenas. This highway meets the Costanera a few kilometers west of Orotina.

ORIENTATION

Playa de Jacó is a short distance off the southern highway. One main road runs parallel to the beach and it is off this road that you will find most of the hotels and restaurants.

Getting Around   While almost everything is within walking distance in Jacó, you can rent a bicycle or scooter from several shops on the main street or call a taxi (☎ 643-3030). For longer excursions, you can rent a car from **Ada** (☎ 506/643-3207), **Economy** (☎ 506/643-3280) or **Zuma** (☎ 506/643-3207). Expect to pay approximately $50 for a one-day rental.

Fast Facts   Both the **Banco Nacional** and **Banco de Costa Rica** have branches in town on the main road and are open Monday through Friday 9am to 3pm. Botiquín Garabito, the town's **pharmacy,** is down the street from the Banco Nacional. There is a **gas station** out by El Bosque restaurant at the south end of town. The **health center** and **post office** are at the municipal center at the south end of town, across from El Naranjal restaurant. A **public phone office,** from which you can make international calls, is located in the ICE building on the main road. This office is open Monday through Saturday from 8am to noon and from 1 to 5pm.

The **Solar Laundry** (☎ 506/643-3096) is located a few blocks in from the center of town and is open Monday through Friday 8am to 5pm.

FUN ON & OFF THE BEACH

Unfortunately, the water here has a nasty reputation for riptides, as does most of the water off Costa Rica's Pacific coast, so be careful. Even strong swimmers have been know to drown in the power rips. At times storms far offshore cause huge waves to pound on the beach, making it impossible to go in the water at all. In this case, you'll have to be content with the hotel pool (if your hotel has one).

After you've spent some time on Playa de Jacó, you might want to visit some of the other nearby beaches, of which there are several. **Playa Esterillos,** 22 kilometers southwest of Jacó, is long and wide and almost always nearly deserted. **Playa Hermosa,** 10 kilometers southeast of Jacó, where sea turtles lay eggs from July to December, is also well-known for its great surfing waves. Playa Herradura, about 6¹/₂ kilometers northwest of Jacó, is ringed by lush hillsides and has a campground and a few very basic cabinas. All of these beaches are beautiful and easily reached by car or bicycle (if you've got plenty of energy).

The same waves that often make Playa de Jacó unsafe for swimming make this beach one of the most popular in the country with gringo surfers. In addition, there are a couple of other excellent surfing beaches nearby—Playa Hermosa and **Playa Escondida.** Those who want to challenge the waves can rent surfboards for around $2.50 an hour and boogie boards for $1.50 an hour.

Biking If you would rather stay out of the surf but still want to get some exercise, you can rent a bike for around $8 per day or $1.50 per hour. Both bikes and boards are available from several places along the main road.

Diving Scuba divers can arrange dive trips through **Viajes Jaguar** (☎ 506/ 643-3242), which has its office in an older house next door to the phone office on the main road into town. A two-tank drive is a pricey $80 ($100 with equipment rental). They also rent snorkeling gear for $10 a day.

Sportfishing If you're interested in doing some sportfishing, **Viajes Jaguar** (☎ 506/643-3242) rents boats and other equipment (see above for office location). A half-day fishing trip for four people will cost $325 and a full day will cost $450.

CARARA BIOLOGICAL RESERVE: A FAMOUS NESTING GROUND FOR SCARLET MACAWS & A PLACE TO SEE CROCODILES

Fifteen kilometers north of Jacó is Carara Biological Reserve, a world-renowned nesting ground for scarlet macaws. It has several miles of trails open to visitors. There is a loop trail that takes about an hour and another trail that is open only to tour groups. The macaws migrate daily, spending their days in the park and nights among the coastal mangroves. It is often best to view them in the early morning, when they arrive, or around sunset when they head back to the coast for the evening. Among the other wildlife you might see here are caimans, coatimundis, armadillo, pacas, peccaries, river otters, kinkajous, and, of course, hundreds of species of birds. Be sure to bring along insect repellent, or, better yet, wear light cotton long sleeves and pants. The reserve is open daily from 8am to 4:30pm. This is a national park and admission is $6 per person. There are several companies offering tours to Carara Biological Reserve for around $30 or $35. Check at your hotel or contact **Fantasy Tours** (☎ 506/643-3231 or 506/643-3383) for schedules and more information.

Just north of the entrance into the Carara Biological Reserve is the bridge over the **Tarcoles River.** The muddy banks of this river are home to a healthy population of American crocodiles. This bridge is a prime viewing spot for both the crocodiles and the macaw migrations, and thieves and pickpockets work it regularly. Do not leave your car or valuables unguarded, and be wary if yours is the only car parked here.

ORGANIZED TOURS OF NEARBY SITES

If you will be spending your entire Costa Rican visit in Jacó but would like to see some other parts of the country, you can arrange tours through the local office of **Explorica** (☎ 506/643-3586). This company offers day tours to Poás and Irazú volcanoes, white-water rafting trips, cruises to Tortuga Island, trips to Braulio Carillo and Manuel Antonio national parks, and other places. They also offer overnight trips. Rates range from $55 to $75 for day trips. Horseback-riding tours are also very popular. These trips give you a chance to get away from all the development in Jacó and see a bit of nature. Contact Fantasy Tours, or **Sanchez Madrigal Bros.** (☎ 506/643-3203) to make a reservation. Tours lasting 3 to 4 hours cost around $25 to $30.

WHERE TO STAY IN PLAYA DE JACÓ

Since Playa Leona and Playa Hermosa de Jacó (not to be confused with Playa Hermosa in Guanacaste) are close by, many people choose accommodations in these beach towns as well. Selected listings for these two towns follow this section.

DOUBLES FOR LESS THAN $25

Cabinas Las Palmas. Playa de Jacó, Puntarenas. ☎ **506/643-3005.** Fax 506/643-3512. 23 rms (all with bath). $19.10–$44.85 single; $22.85–$54.60 double; $26.10–$64.40 triple. No credit cards.

Although all of the rooms here are acceptable, the newer ones are a bit nicer. Some rooms come with refrigerators, hot plates, kitchen sinks, laundry sinks, and tables with four chairs, so you can set up housekeeping and stay a while. All have tile floors and very clean bathrooms, and most have two double beds. The three rooms with air-conditioning are the most expensive rooms here and I'm not sure they're worth the extra $20. There are lots of flowers in the garden, and the location down a narrow lane off the main road makes Las Palmas a quiet place. If you're coming from San José, take the Jacó exit from the Costanera and go straight through the first (and only) intersection you come to. Take a right on the narrow lane just past Cabinas Antonio.

Chalet Santa Ana. Playa de Jacó, Puntarenas. ☎ **506/643-3233.** 8 rms (all with bath). $15–$22 single or double; $31 for up to five people. No credit cards.

Located at the quiet south end of the beach across from Hotel Jacófiesta, Chalet Santa Ana is a small two-story building. Though it is rather basic, the guest rooms sleep up to five people and half of them have kitchenettes. There's carpeting in some of the rooms, and walls are of varnished wood. The second-floor rooms have the added advantage of high ceilings and access to a large verandah with chairs. Though the surroundings are not too attractive, this is a good deal for Jacó.

Flamboyant Hotel. Apdo. 18, Playa de Jacó, Puntarenas. ☎ **506/643-3146.** 8 rms. $21–$29 single; $23–$34 double; $25–$36 triple; $27–$38 quad. No credit cards.

The Flamboyant doesn't quite live up to its name, but it is still a good value. The rooms are arranged around a small swimming pool, and only a few steps from the beach. All the rooms are spacious and have kitchenettes, but the furnishings are quite simple. You'll find the Flamboyant down a narrow lane from the Flamboyant Restaurant, which is on the main road in the middle of Jacó.

Hotel Zabamar. Playa de Jacó, Puntarenas. ☎ **506/643-3174.** 20 rms. $20.40 single, $32.60 single with A/C; $24.50 double, $36.70 double with A/C; $32.60 triple, $44.80 triple with A/C. Rates are lower from Apr 15–Dec 15; further rate reductions may be available for longer stays. MC, V.

The Zabamar is set back from the beach in an attractively planted compound. The older rooms have red-tile floors, small refrigerators, ceiling fans, hammocks on their front porches, and showers in enclosed, private patios. There are also 10 newer rooms with air-conditioning. There are even *pilas* (laundry sinks) in little gravel-and-palm gardens behind the older rooms. Some rooms have rustic wooden benches and chairs. The shallow swimming pool stays quite warm. Travelers traveling on tight budgets will appreciate the size of the older, less expensive rooms. A little open-air bar/restaurant serves inexpensive seafood and burgers.

DOUBLES FOR LESS THAN $35

Cabinas Alice. 100 meters south of the Red Cross, Playa de Jacó, Puntarenas. ☎ **506/ 643-3061** or 506/237-1412. 22 rms (all with bath). $20.20 single; $25.35 double; $32.50–$43.95 triple. MC, V.

Cabinas Alice, though a small and modest Tico-run place, is one of the best values in Jacó. The rooms are in the shade of large, old mango trees, and the beach is right outside the gate. Since the rooms vary in age, ask to take a look at a couple before accepting one. The largest rooms have kitchens, and also happen to be closest to the small pool and the beach. The rooms in back each come with a carved wooden headboard and matching nightstand, a tile floor, a large shower, and potted plants. The other rooms are pretty basic, with nothing but a double and a single bed in the room. The road down to Cabinas Alice is across from the Red Cross center. Meals are served in a small dining room where you can get a fish filet fried in garlic and butter for under $5. This place is popular with young Ticos and fills up fast during the high season.

DOUBLES FOR LESS THAN $45

Hotel El Jardin. Playa de Jacó, Puntarenas. ☎/fax **506/643-3050.** 7 rms. Dec–Apr $25 single, $37 double; May–Nov $12 single, $24 double. V.

Though this hotel's namesake garden is nothing to write home about, the El Jardin does offer economical rates, comfortable rooms, and friendly French-speaking management. This combination seems to have made it one of the more popular small hotels in Jacó. The guest rooms are large and clean, and have big bathrooms as well. There is a small pool in the center of the garden. You'll find this hotel at the far north end of the beach near the San José bus stop.

WORTH A SPLURGE

Apartotel Gaviotas. Playa de Jacó, Puntarenas. ☎ **506/643-3092.** Fax 506/643-3092. 12 apts. Dec–Apr $50.50 one to five people; May–Nov $18.50 single, $24.66 double, $28.12 triple, $31.40 quad. AE, DC, MC, V.

Although it's on the inland side of the main road and is a bit of a walk from the beach, this is one of the nicest places in town. These cheerful little apartments are intended for families or groups who plan to stay for a week or more but in the off-season they are a great bargain even for two people. Each apartment has a front wall of windows looking onto the little pool, a cathedral ceiling with clerestory windows, and a fan. Floors are tile, as are the kitchen counters. The living rooms have built-in couches, and in the bedrooms you'll find a double bed and a bunk bed. In each bathroom you'll find an elegant scalloped sink. There is no restaurant on the premises, but there is a small bar beside the pool.

✪ Hotel Club del Mar. Apdo. 107-4023, Playa de Jacó, Puntarenas. ☎/fax **506/643-3194.** Fax 506/643-3194. 18 rms. Nov–Apr $53–$73.50 single or double; May–Oct $30–$55 single or double. MC, V.

Because of its location, friendly owners, and attractively designed new rooms, this is my favorite hotel in Playa de Jacó. The Club del Mar is at the far southern end of the beach where the rocky hills meet the beach. The best rooms are in two newer two-story shell-pink buildings, each of which has eight rooms. Each room has a green-tile floor, pastel bedspreads, fascinating custom-made lampshades, and tile bathroom counters, plus French doors that open onto private patios. Older rooms are almost as attractive and have Guatemalan throw rugs, bamboo furniture, kitchens, and front walls of glass. A small swimming pool is right by the beach and there is a first-class restaurant on the premises. Owner Philip Edwardes oversees the kitchen and at times personally prepares such dishes as lemon chicken and chateaubriand. However, it is the conviviality and helpfulness of Edwardes and his wife, Marilyn, that make a stay here so enjoyable. The Edwardeses also arrange horseback rides, raft trips, and various other tours.

۞ Pochote Grande. Apdo. 42, Playa de Jacó, Puntarenas. ☎ **506/643-3236.** Fax 506/220-4979. 24 rms. Dec–Apr $45 single, $50 double, $55 triple; May–Nov $35 single, $40 double, $50 triple. MC, V.

Named for a huge, old *pochote* tree on the grounds, this very attractive hotel is located right on the beach at the far north end of Jacó. The grounds are shady and lush, and there's a small pool. Guest rooms are large enough to sleep four comfortably and have kitchenettes. All the rooms have white-tile floors and a balcony or patio, and the second-floor rooms are blessed with high ceilings. The restaurant and snack bar serve a mixture of Tico, German, and American meals (the owners are German by way of Africa). Prices for meals range from $3 to $9. There is also a gift shop. This place stays full with charter groups in the high season.

Villas Miramar. Playa de Jacó, Puntarenas. ☎ **506/643-3003.** 12 rms. Dec–Apr $50 single or double, $60 triple; May–Nov $38 single, double, or triple. MC, V.

Located down a narrow lane off the main road through town, the Miramar is about 100 feet from the beach. It has its own small pool surrounded by a terrace and flowing hibiscus. Guest rooms sport a Spanish architectural style with arched doorways, wrought-iron wall lamps, and red-tile floors throughout. There are large patios and all of the rooms have kitchenettes. There are also barbecues in the gardens in case you'd like to grill some fish or steaks. The apartments vary in size; the largest can sleep up to six people.

NEARBY PLACES TO STAY & EAT
DOUBLES FOR LESS THAN $45

Cabinas Las Olas. Playa Hermosa de Jacó, Puntarenas. ☎/fax **506/643-3687.** 3 rms, 3 cabinas. $22.50–$35.50 single; $35.50–$40.75 double; $45 cabina for up to six people. No credit cards.

Playa Hermosa is a renowned surfing beach and this is its prime surfer hotel. The main building is on the hill by the road. Two of the rooms are located upstairs and have two double beds, a verandah with a hammock, and ocean views. Downstairs is a smaller budget room that's fine for a single traveler. The rooms are basic but comfortable. Closer to the beach are three A-frame cabins or *ranchos,* which have a roomy bedroom on the second floor (in the peak of the A-frame), and a single bed, bunk bed, kitchenette, and bathroom on the ground floor. Between the main building and the cabins is a pool with a small stone waterfall. Out by the ocean there is a simple cafe that serves breakfast and lunch, and a thatched palapa strung with hammocks for watching the waves, horseback riders, and sunsets.

WORTH A SPLURGE

Punta Leona Hotel & Club. Apdo. 8592-1000, San José. ☎ **800/554-4398** in the U.S., or 506/231-3131. Fax 506/232-0791. 108 rms, 72 apts. A/C TV. $58–$82 single or double; $92–$150 for four to eight people. AE, DC, MC, V.

This gated resort and residential community 10 kilometers north of Jacó boasts the most impressive grounds of any easily accessible hotel in Costa Rica. Rain forest, white-sand beaches (two of them), and a rocky promontory jutting out into the Pacific all add up to drama rarely encountered in Costa Rican resorts. After passing through the resort's guarded gate, you drive more than a mile down a gravel road that passes through dense primary rain forest before arriving at the grassy lawns that sprawl beneath the huge trees, spared during the construction of the buildings here. The main guest rooms are not as luxurious as one would hope, but that is the small price you must pay for such a setting. The standard hotel rooms are housed in Spanish-style buildings with red-tile roofs and white stucco walls. Inside, you'll find that the beds and bedspreads are a bit dated, but otherwise the rooms are comfortable. In addition to these rooms, there are a variety of different apartment types, including some unusual small chalets. Despite the steep per-room prices, these rooms become a good deal for budget travelers traveling in a group.

Restaurant Léon Marino serves a variety of moderately priced Costa Rican and international dishes. There is also a more informal outdoor restaurant that serves grilled meats and typical meals, as well as two bars and a disco. Sportfishing, sunset cruises, and sail board, jet ski, and horse rentals are all available. Scuba lessons and rental equipment are also offered. Two swimming pools, 4 miles of beach, tennis court, boutique, supermarket, and a conference room round out the facilities.

✪ **Terraza del Pacifico.** Playa Hermosa de Jacó (Apdo. 168), Jacó, Puntarenas. ☎ **506/643-3222** or 506/643-3444; 212/213-2399 or 212/213-1838 in the U.S. Fax 506/643-3424. 43 rms. A/C TV TEL. $66 single or double; $72 triple. AE, MC, V.

It may be a bit out of town, but the Terraza del Pacifico is the best beachfront hotel in the Jacó area. Located just over the hill at the start of Playa Hermosa, this hotel seems to have done everything right. Rooms are built so that they all have ocean views, and in the middle of the hotel complex is a circular pool with a swim-up bar and plenty of chaise lounges for sunbathing and siestas. Red-tile roofs and white walls give the buildings a very Mediterranean look (the management is Italian), while hardwood balcony railings add a touch of the Tropics. The guest rooms all have either a patio or balcony, and the room curtains are hand painted with colorful bird and flower images. The hotel's restaurant is located within a few feet of the high-tide mark and serves good Italian food. During the high season there is also a small casino operating nightly from 6pm until 12am.

CAMPING

There are several campgrounds in or near Playa de Jacó. **Madrigal,** at the south end of town at the foot of some jungly cliffs, is my favorite. The campground is just off the beach and has a bar/restaurant that is open from 7am to 10pm. You can also try **Camping Garibaldi,** which is centrally located, or **El Hicaco,** which is close to the beach, but right next door to an open-air disco, so don't expect to get much sleep if you stay here. Campsites should run between $2 and $3 per night.

WHERE TO EAT

Many of the accommodations in Playa de Jacó and nearby beach towns have good restaurants and quite a few guests choose to eat all their meals at their hotels. Budget travelers who really want to save money on meals can always stay at a hotel that provides kitchenettes for its guests, shop at the local supermercado, and fix their own meals. But even most inexpensive lodgings have small restaurants that serve good, cheap meals.

If you're feeling adventurous and want to eat in town, I recommend the following places. In addition, **The Garden Cafe, Ceviche del Rey,** and **Restaurante Esperanza** are local favorites, and **Pizzeria Verona** has excellent clay-oven pizzas and homemade pastas. Actually, one of the best restaurants in town is the dining room at the **Hotel Cocal,** which is open to the public. The menu includes such dishes as chateaubriand for two, wiener schnitzel, and pepper steak.

MEALS FOR LESS THAN $10

✪ **El Bosque.** 27 yards south of the gas station. ☎ **506/643-3007.** Reservations recommended during high season. Main courses $4.50–$12.80. MC, V. Tues–Sun 10:30am–9:30pm. INTERNATIONAL.

Located on the highway heading south to Manuel Antonio, El Bosque (The Forest) is set amid shady mango trees and flowering gardens. The dining room itself is a small open-air building and the furnishings are heavy colonial reproductions. Shrimp or lobster is a bit pricey at $12.80, but you can get a delicious corvina filet for just over $4. If you are not in the mood for seafood, you can order steak or chicken. There is also a long list of fresh juices and fruit shakes from which to choose. El Bosque makes a great meal stop if you are on your way back from Manuel Antonio, and if you are staying in Jacó, they will provide free transportation to and from the restaurant.

Killer Munchies. 300 meters south of the Hotel Jacó Beach. ☎ **506/643-3354.** Reservations not accepted. Main courses $2.05–$10.75. No credit cards. Mon–Fri 5:30–9pm, Sat–Sun noon–10pm.

The name says it all. This restaurant serves hearty burritos, simple pasta dishes, and a wide array of freshly baked pizzas. With vines covering latticed walls and an abundance of potted palms, the ambience is somewhere between an early '80s fern bar and a college beer hall. Try to get a table on the covered deck, so you can watch the people passing by and the pizzas being made in the outdoor wood-burning oven. My favorite item is the Greek pizza, with olives, feta cheese, and anchovies, but the barbeque-chicken pizza is also delicious.

✪ **La Piraña.** Apdo. 116, Playa de Jacó. ☎ **506/643-3725.** Reservations recommended during high season. Main courses $3.80–$6.50. AE, DC, MC, V. Tues–Sun 6am–2pm and 5pm–11pm. INTERNATIONAL.

This new restaurant adds a welcome dose of pizzazz to Jacó's culinary scene. The menu can vary nightly, and while the selection is always eclectic, the quality is reassuringly consistent. The owners often organize theme nights featuring haute cuisine from one or another corner of the world, with the most popular dishes finding their way onto the permanent menu. Baked Caribbean red snapper, jerk chicken, blackened steak, and Egyptian pasta Mohamad all happily co-exist here, alongside Costa Rican standards prepared with some subtle twists. The restaurant seats 75 in a spacious open room beneath slow-spinning ceiling fans. The colors here mix and match like the dishes—blue-tile floors, yellow walls, red tables, and teal chairs. Note the unusual hours. Breakfasts are equally pleasing, with fresh baked scones and pastries, light and fluffy omelets, and homemade jams.

PLAYA DE JACÓ AFTER DARK

Playa de Jacó is the Central Pacific's party beach town and there are several discos that stay busy every night during the high season and on weekends during the low season. The most popular is the **Disco La Central,** right on the beach near the south end of town. Located in a huge open-air hall, it features the requisite '70s flashing lights and suspended mirrored ball. A garden bar in a thatched-roof building provides a slightly quieter place to have a drink. **Los Tucanes Disco Club** is another happening place and is located one street over from Disco La Central. Both discos charge a nominal cover charge of around $3. On the north end of town, situated on the road that leads to the airport, is **Upé!,** another favorite nightspot, while Los Faroles Restaurant (200 meters north of the Jacó Beach Hotel) also doubles as the **Jacó Rock Cafe** on weekends.

3 Manuel Antonio National Park

140 kilometers SW of San José; 69 kilometers S of Playa de Jacó

No other destination in Costa Rica has received more intentional attention than Manuel Antonio. Many first-time visitors to Costa Rica plan their vacation around seeing it. It's no surprise why: The views from the hills overlooking Manuel Antonio are spectacular, the beaches inside the park are idyllic, and its jungles are crawling with white-faced and squirrel monkeys, among other forms of exotic wildlife. The flipside is that you'll have to pay more dearly to see it and you'll have to share it with far more fellow travelers than you might prefer. Still, this is one of the most beautiful locations in the entire country and it is possible to stay within our proposed budget here.

Gazing down on the blue Pacific from high on the mountainsides of Manuel Antonio, it is almost impossible to hold back a gasp of delight. Offshore rocky islands dot the vast expanse of blue. In the foreground the rich deep green of the rain forest sweeps down to the water. Even cheap Instamatics regularly produce postcard-perfect snapshots. It is this superb view that hotels at Manuel Antonio sell, and this view that keeps people transfixed on decks, patios, and balconies along the 7 kilometers of road between Quepos and the national park entrance.

One of the most popular national parks in the country, it is also one of the smallest, covering fewer than 1,700 acres. Its several nearly perfect small beaches are connected by trails that meander through the rain forest. One of its most striking features is how quickly the mountains surrounding its beaches rise as you head inland from the water. However, Manuel Antonio National Park was created not to preserve its beautiful beaches but its forests—home to endangered squirrel monkeys, three-toed sloths, purple-and-orange crabs, and hundreds of other species of birds, mammals, and plants. Whereas once this entire stretch of coast was a rain forest teeming with wildlife, now just this small rocky outcrop of forests remains.

Unfortunately, the popularity of Manuel Antonio has brought about rampant development and ever-growing crowds of beachgoers. In just the last few years, these factors have turned what was once a peaceful and pristine spot into an area full of hastily built, overpriced hotels, packed parking areas, and noisy crowds. This is not to say that the park is not still beautiful, nor does it mean that there are not good hotel values here. It just means that Manuel Antonio has become completely overburdened with adoring throngs, some of whom have taken to feeding the wild animals, in a dangerous caricature of what ecotourism should be. In addition, the stream that forms the boundary of the park and through which park visitors must wade is often polluted with garbage and human waste. On weekends the beaches are packed with people and the disco blares its music until early morning, drowning out the sounds of crickets and frogs that once lulled visitors to sleep here. A shanty town of snack shacks lines the road just outside the park, which makes this area look more like a slum than a national park. Supposedly the environs on the edge of the park are soon going to be improved, and a major resort complex is planned (which may or may not be an improvement), but as yet nothing has happened.

Those views that are so bewitching also have their own set of drawbacks. If you want a great view, you aren't going to be staying on the beach and, in fact, you probably won't be able to walk easily to the beach. This means that you'll either be driving back and forth, taking a lot of taxis, or riding the public bus a lot. Also keep in mind that it's hot and humid here and it rains a lot. However, the rain is what keeps Manuel Antonio lush and green, and this wouldn't be the Tropics if things were otherwise.

If you're traveling on a budget, you'll likely end up staying in the nearby town of Quepos, which was once a quiet banana port. However, disease wiped out most of the banana plantations, and now the land is planted with oil-palm trees. As you approach Quepos by road, you pass through miles and miles of these oil-palm plantations. Today Quepos is shaping up a bit and you'll find nice boutiques and U.S.–styled coffee bars, yet overall it still has the feel of a low-rent tourist boom town.

Despite these caveats, Manuel Antonio is still a beautiful spot, and if you plan your visit carefully, you can avoid many of the problems that detract from its appeal. If you avoid the peak months from December to March, you will avoid most of the crowds. If you must come during the peak months, try to avoid weekends, when the beach is packed with families from San José. If you visit the park early in the morning, you can leave when the crowds begin to show up at midday.

ESSENTIALS
GETTING THERE & DEPARTING

By Plane **Sansa** (☎ **506/233-0397,** 506/233-3258, or 506/233-5330 in San José) flies to Quepos, the town nearest the park, at 8am and 3pm Monday through Saturday, and at 10am on Sunday. All flights leave from San José's Juan Santamaría International Airport. Duration is 20 minutes. Fare is $30 each way.

Travelair (☎ **506/220-3054,** or 506/232-7883 in San José) also flies to Quepos daily at 8:10 and 11:55am and 3:15pm, but from San José's Pavas International Airport. Duration is 20 minutes. Fare is $45 one way, $72 round-trip.

Alternatively, you can fly Sansa to Palmar Sur or Puerto Jiménez or Travelair to Palmar Sur. From either of these two towns, you can then take a taxi to Manuel Antonio.

When you're ready to depart, Sansa (☎ **506/771-0161** in Quepos) flights to San José leave at 8:35am and 3:35pm Monday through Saturday, and at 10:35am on Sunday.

Travelair flights leave for San José daily at 10:45am and 12:25 and 3:45pm.

When you land at the airport in Quepos, there is a local transportation service that works with both Travelair and Sansa. They meet every plane and charge $4 per person for transport to any hotel in Quepos or Manuel Antonio. You can also arrange hotel pickup for your return flight with them, upon arrival. Alternatively, there are sometimes (but not always) cabs waiting at the airport. These charge between $7.50 and $10 per car for up to four people, depending on which hotel you're staying at and your bargaining abilities.

By Bus Express buses to Manuel Antonio leave San José daily at 6am, noon, and 6pm from Calle 16 between avenidas 1 and 3. Duration is 3¹/₂ hours. Fare $5.10.

Regular buses to Quepos leave San José daily at 7 and 10am and 2 and 4pm. Duration is 5 hours. Fare is $3.20.

Buses leave Puntarenas for Quepos daily at 5 and 11am and 2pm. Duration is 3¹/₂ hours. Fare is $3.

Many of the buses for Quepos stop to unload and pick up passengers in Playa de Jacó. If you're in Jacó, you can try your luck at one of the covered bus stops out on the Interamerican Highway.

From Quepos, buses leave for Manuel Antonio roughly every hour, daily from 6am to 10pm. Fare is 30¢.

When you're ready to depart, the Quepos bus station is next to the market, three blocks east of the water and two blocks north of the road to Manuel Antonio. Express buses to San José (trip duration is 3¹/₂ hours) leave daily at 6am, noon, and 5pm (there is an additional departure at 3pm on Sunday). Local buses to San José (duration is 5 hours) leave at 5 and 8am, noon, and 4pm. In the busy winter months, purchase your ticket several days in advance.

Buses for Puntarenas leave daily at 4:30 and 10:30am and 3pm. Any bus headed for San José or Puntarenas will let you off in Playa de Jacó.

By Car   From San José, take the Interamerican Highway west to the Puntarenas turnoff and head south on the Costanera, the coastal road through Jacó. This is an excellent road until south of Puerto Caldera. From there until south of Jacó, the potholes are killers. Some are so old they've sprouted grass. At Parrita, 44 kilometers past Jacó, the pavement gives out completely and you spend the next 25 kilometers bumping along on potholed, washboarded, muddy gravel road (although this is better than the potholed paved road). Needless to say, the driving is slow.

An alternative is to take the narrow and winding old highway, which turns off the Interamerican Highway just west of Alajuela near the town of Atenas and joins the Costanera near Orotina, just in time to catch the worst of the potholes. You'll still have to drive that rutted road between Jacó and Quepos.

ORIENTATION

Quepos is a dusty little port town at the mouth of the Boca Vieja Estuary. After crossing the bridge into town, take the lower road (to the left of the high road). In four blocks, turn left and you will be on the road to Manuel Antonio. This road winds through town a bit before starting over the hill to all the hotels and the national park.

Getting Around   Taxis here generally ply the main road between Quepos and the national park entrance and charge a flat fee according to the direction they are traveling. A taxi between Quepos, any hotel along the road toward the park, and Manuel Antonio costs around $3. The return trip from the park to your hotel should only cost about 50¢. This is a fixed price, so watch out for drivers who try to charge more. However, if you are going anywhere off the main road, you will be charged more, so make sure to negotiate a price first.

The **bus** from Quepos to Manuel Antonio, and vice versa, takes 15 minutes and runs roughly every hour from 6am to 10pm daily. Fare is 30¢.

You can also rent a car from **Elegante Rent a Car** (☎ **506/777-0115**) for around $50 a day. Their office is in downtown Quepos, next to La Buena Nota gift shop, and they will meet you at the airport with your car if you arrange it in advance. If you choose to rent a car, never leave anything of value in it unless you intend to stay within sight of the car at all times. Car break-ins are commonplace here. There are now children who offer to watch your car for a small price when you leave it outside the park entrance. Take them up on the offer if you want to avoid damage to your car by thieves trying to find out what's in your trunk.

Fast Facts   The new **Laundromat Bati** is located out on the edge of town on the road toward Manuel Antonio. They offer drop-off and self-service, and are open Monday through Friday 8am to noon and 2 to 6pm. There's a **pharmacy** called

Botíca Quepos on the corner of the main street where you make the turn for Manuel Antonio (☎ 777-0038); it's open daily from 7am to 7pm.

EXPLORING THE NATIONAL PARK

Manuel Antonio National Park is a good park for self-exploration. All the trails are well-marked and maintained, and you will be given a small map (albeit in Spanish) when you pay your entrance fee. A quiet walk on any of the trails is sure to reveal an abundance of tropical flora and fauna. There are great lookouts and it's even possible to find a secluded ocean cove. Nevertheless, if you really want to see wildlife and learn about tropical ecosystems, it is best to take a guided tour. Almost any hotel in the area can hook you up with one of the local guides, who generally charge around $15 to $30 per person for a 2-to-3 hour hike. If you are staying in Playa de Jacó, several of the hotels and tour agencies in town offer day trips to Manuel Antonio (for more information, see the section on Playa de Jacó, above.) A 2- or 3-hour guided hike should cost between $25 to $30 per person. Many visitors choose to see the park on an organized tour that may include visits to other national parks and biological reserves. See chapter 5 for listings of U.S. and San José–based tour companies you can contact either before leaving the United States or upon arrival in San José, if this interests you. However, I strongly advise against day trips to Manuel Antonio from San José, as the driving time make these rushed and unenjoyable.

ENTRY POINT, FEES & REGULATIONS

The park entrance is situated on Playa Espadilla, the beach at the end of the road from Quepos. To reach the park station, you must cross a small stream that is little more than ankle deep at low tide but can be knee or even waist deep at high tide. Just after crossing the stream, you'll see the guard station. The park fee is $6 per person per day. This is where you can pick up the small map of the park, mentioned above. The park is closed on Mondays, but open Tuesday through Sunday from 8am to 4pm year-round. Camping is not allowed. The Parks Service only allows 600 visitors to enter each day, which may mean that you won't get in if you arrive in mid-afternoon during the high season. Make sure to keep your entrance stub, as you may want to leave and re-enter the park.

THE BEACHES

Playa Espadilla, the public beach from which you enter the park, is often perfect for board surfing and bodysurfing, but can be a bit rough for casual swimming. There a couple of little shops by the water that rent boogie boards, beach chairs, and beach umbrellas.

Playa Espadilla Sur is the first beach you come to within the park boundaries. This is usually the least crowded beach in the park, and one of the best places to find a quiet shade tree to plant yourself under. If you want to explore farther, you can walk along this soft sand beach or follow a trail through the forest behind the beach. At the far end there is a short connecting trail to Playa Manuel Antonio, which is sometimes clear enough to offer good snorkeling along the rocks at either end. A branch trail from this beach leads up and around Punta Catedral (Cathedral Point), a high promontory bluff, where there are some spectacular views. If you take this trail, wear good shoes. Cathedral Point is one of the best places to spot monkeys, though you are more likely to see a white-faced monkey rather than a rare squirrel monkey. At low tide, Playa Manuel Antonio shows a very interesting relic left by its pre-Columbian residents, a circular stone turtle trap. From Playa Manuel Antonio there is another, slightly longer, trail to the Puerto Escondido where there is a blow-hole that sends up plumes of spray at high tide. Beyond here, at Punta Surrucho, there are some sea caves. Still, be careful when hiking beyond Puerto Escondido: What seems like easy beach hiking at low tide becomes treacherous to impassable at high tide. Two other trails wind their way inland from the trail between Playa Manuel Antonio and Puerto Escondido. It's great to spend hours exploring the steamy jungle and then take a refreshing dip in the ocean.

HORSEBACK RIDING, KAYAKING & OTHER ACTIVE SPORTS

If your tropical fantasy is to ride a horse down a beach between jungle and ocean, contact **Stable Equus** (☎ **506/777-0001**), which charges $30 for a 2-hour ride in Manuel Antonio. This stable allegedly treats its animals more humanely than other stables in the area, and is also concerned with keeping horse droppings off the beaches. Full-day horseback riding excursions to a typical Costa Rican farm are provided by **Rancho Savegre Tours** (☎ **506/777-0528**). Tours cost $60 per person and include hotel transfers, lunch, and several swimming stops.

If you're interested in kayaking among the rocky islets of Manuel Antonio National Park or up the nearby Isla Damas estuary, contact **High Tide Ocean Kayaking** (☎ **506/777-0403**). They charge $60 for a full-day paddle around the estuary (including lunch at La Tortuga restaurant) or through the national park (with a picnic on the beach). **Iguana Tours** (☎ **506/777-1262**) offers all the above tour options, as well as white-water rafting trips on the nearby Naranjo and Savegre rivers ($65 to $70 full day). Large multi-person rafts are used during the rainy season, and single person "duckies" are broken out when the water levels drop. **Amigos del Río** (☎ **506/777-0082**), **Rió Loco White Water Rafting** (☎ **506/777-1170**), and **Rainforest Expeditions & School** (☎ **506/777-1170**) also offer full-day rafting trips for around $65 to $75 per person.

THINGS TO SEE & DO IN QUEPOS

For a closer look at some exotic birds and other assorted wildlife than you may have gotten in the park, check out **Jardin Gaia,** a wildlife rescue center that rehabilitates and breeds injured and confiscated animals, many of them endangered. The center is located on the road between Quepos and Manuel Antonio. Jardin Gaia is open daily from 8am until 4pm and charges $5 per person, which includes a brief, but informative, tour and plenty of print information.

If you're staying in Quepos and don't want to go all the way over the hill to the park, you can swim and lounge at **Nahomi,** Quepos's public swimming pool. You'll find this pool on a tiny peninsula at the end of the road that parallels the water. Admission is around $1 and the pool is open daily from 9am to 7pm. The rocky promontory on which the pool is built feels like an island and is surrounded by the turquoise waters of a small cove. This recreational area has recently been touched up and now features one of the town's most popular evening discos.

Quepos is one of Costa Rica's billfish centers, and sailfish and marlin, as well as tuna, are all common in these waters. If you're into sportfishing and happen to be here between December and April, see what's being offered at **La Buena Nota** (☎ 506/777-0345), or try hooking up with Blue Fin Sportfishing (☎ 506/777-1676), **Costa Rican Dreams** (☎ 506/777-0593), **Marlin Azul** (☎ 506/777-0191), **Sportfishing Costa Rica** (☎ 506/257-3553), **Sportfishing Quepos** (☎ 506/777-0493), or **Sportfishing Karahé** (☎ 506/777-0170). A full day of fishing should cost between $450 and $850, depending on the size of the boat.

If you'd just like to go for a cruise around the area and maybe do a bit of snorkeling, diving, or fishing, see if the *Byblos I* (☎ **506/777-0411**) is making trips while you are there. Full-day cruises including lunch and the use of fishing and snorkeling gear cost $80 per person, while a 3-hour sunset cruise costs $40.

If you're looking for souvenirs, try **La Buena Nota** (☎ **506-777-0345**), on the left just over the bridge as you enter Quepos; they have recently opened a second shop across from the Hotel Karahé on the road to Manuel Antonio. These little shops are jam-packed with all sorts of beach wear, souvenirs, and U.S. magazines and newspapers, and also act as informal information centers for the area. If you'd like to find out about renting a house, this is a good place to ask.

If you're looking for someplace to sit and read the newspaper you just bought at La Buena Nota, check out **Cafe Milagro** next door. One of the few homey coffee houses I've found in Costa Rica, the folks here roast their own beans and also have a mail-order service to keep you in Costa Rican coffee year-round.

WHERE TO STAY

There are very few beachfront hotels in Manuel Antonio, so consequently, if you want to be able to walk out of your room and be on the beach without taking to the road, you're going to have to pay for the privilege.

If you're traveling on a rock-bottom budget, you'll get more for your money by staying in Quepos and taking the bus to the beaches at Manuel Antonio every day. The rooms in Quepos may be small, but they are much cleaner and more appealing than those available in the same price category on the other side of the hill.

DOUBLES FOR LESS THAN $15

Hotel Malinche. Quepos. ☎/fax **506/777-0093.** 28 rms (all with bath). $7.35–$14.70 single; $12.50–$30 double. MC, V.

A good choice for backpackers, the Hotel Malinche is located on the first street to your left as you come into Quepos. You can't miss the hotel's arched brick entrance. Inside you'll find bright rooms with louvered windows but no screens, so be sure to buy some mosquito coils before night falls. (Mosquito-repelling incense coils are available in drugstores and general stores.) The rooms are small but have hardwood floors and clean bathrooms. The more expensive rooms are new and have air-conditioning and carpets.

Hotel Quepos. Apdo. 79, Quepos. ☎ **506/777-0274.** 24 rms (15 with bath). $5 single without bath, $10 double without bath; $10 single with bath, $15 double with bath. No credit cards.

This little budget hotel is both comfortable and clean. There are hardwood floors, ceiling fans, a large sunny TV lounge, even a parking lot and laundry service. The management is very friendly, and downstairs from the second-floor hotel is an interesting souvenir shop and a charter-fishing office. This hotel is across from the soccer field on the way out of town toward Manuel Antonio.

DOUBLES FOR LESS THAN $25

Cabinas Pedro Miguel. Apdo. 17, Manuel Antonio, Quepos. ☎/fax **506/777-0035.** 14 rms (all with bath). $21.20–$36.60 single or double; $43.20 quad. AE, MC, V.

Located a kilometer outside Quepos on the road to Manuel Antonio (across from Hotel Plinio), these cabinas are very basic, with cement floors and cinderblock walls, but at least they're away from the fray and surrounded by forest. The second-floor rooms are newer, cleaner, and have carpeting as well as a glimpse of the water from the verandah. One of them is huge, with a kitchen and a back wall made entirely of screen. From it, guests can look out over a lush stand of trees. During the high season a restaurant serving Costa Rican standards opens, and the owners encourage guests to participate in meal preparation. There's a tiny swimming pool that sometimes has water in it. The management here is very friendly.

Cabinas Piscis. Apdo. 219, Quepos. ☎ **506/777-0046.** 18 rms (6 with private bath). $15 single with shared bath, $25 single with private bath; $20 double with shared bath, $30 double private bath; $5 each additional person. V.

If you want to be within walking distance of the park but out of earshot of the booming speakers of the town's disco, and you don't want to spend a lot of money, this is one of the only choices you have left. The rooms are basic but clean, and the management is very friendly. The 12 newer rooms all have shared baths, whereas each of older rooms has a private bath. The beach is just a hundred yards or so down a forest trail. You find Cabinas Piscis on the beach side of the road just before you reach the bottom of the hill and Manuel Antonio.

Cabinas Ramirez. Playas Manuel Antonio, Quepos. ☎ **506/777-0003.** 17 rms (all with bath). $14.50–$18.70 single; $18.70–$22.80 double. No credit cards.

These basic beachside cabinas are the most popular budget choice near the park, especially among young Ticos. The hotel is next door to the restaurant/bar and disco Mar y Sombra, so evenings can be loud here. The rooms are basic cinderblock affairs, with concrete floors. Some are quite dark and prisonlike, but all are clean. Ask to see several first and you should find a nice one. The owner also allows camping for backpackers with tents, for about $1.

✪ **Cabinas Vela-Bar.** Apdo. 13, Manuel Antonio, Quepos. ☎ **506/777-0413.** Fax 506/777-1071. 9 rms (all with bath), 1 apt, 1 house. $16.30–$23.60 single; $21.20–$31 double; $35–$57.86 triple; $52.20–$73.35 quad. AE, MC, V.

You'll find this unusual little hotel up the dirt road that leads off to the left just before the end of the road to Manuel Antonio National Park. It has a wide variety of room choices. If you're on an exceedingly tight budget, you can stay in a tiny room or, if you have a little more money to spend, you can opt for a spacious one-bedroom house that has tile floors and arched windows. There are double beds and tiled bathrooms in all rooms. The open-air restaurant/bar is deservedly very popular. Check the chalkboard for the day's special. Entrees range in price from $5.10 to $11.50.

DOUBLES FOR LESS THAN $35

La Colina. Apdo. 191, Quepos. ☎/fax **506/777-0231.** 5 rms, 6 suites. Dec–Apr $20.40 single, $32.60 double; $53 suite; May–Nov $12.25 single, $20 double; $36.50 suite. All rates include breakfast. V.

This casual little bed-and-breakfast is operated by a couple of Colorado natives who moved down to Manuel Antonio a few years ago and converted this house into a B&B. Although the rooms are fairly small, they are stylishly decorated. They have black-and-white–tile floors, louvered French doors, and despite the small size of the rooms, a good writing desk. Outside each room there is a patio with a few chairs and a small table. Breakfast is brought to your room, but you'll probably choose to take it on the patio. The six new suites were still under construction when I last visited, but they will all be larger, and have air-conditioning and ocean views. There was also a two-tiered swimming pool in the works, as well as a bar and restaurant.

DOUBLES FOR LESS THAN $45

Cabinas Espadilla. Manuel Antonio, Quepos. ☎/fax **506/777-0416.** 32 cabinas. $35–$45 cabina with fan; $55–$65 cabina with air-conditioning. V.

There isn't much shade around these cabinas, but they are clean and close to the beach. The rooms are spacious and most have kitchenettes. Although there isn't much in the way of decor or closet space in any of them, there are enough beds to sleep up to four people comfortably (a double bed and a bunk bed). High ceilings and fans keep the older rooms cool, and in the newer, more expensive rooms there is air-conditioning. Bars on the windows ensure security. The older rooms here are over-priced, but the newer rooms are fairly reasonable. You'll find these cabinas down the side road that runs perpendicular to the beach in front of Playa Espadilla.

El Lirio. Apdo. 123, Quepos. ☎/fax **506/777-0403.** 9 rms. Dec–Apr $45 single, double, or triple; May–Nov $28.50 single, double, or triple. AE, MC, V. All rates include continental breakfast.

Although the nicest rooms overlook the road and consequently can be a bit noisy, there are some quieter rooms at the back of the grounds near the swimming pool. A Mediterranean style prevails here, with arches, stucco walls, and red-tile floors and roofs. Rooms have a southwestern motif, high ceilings, mosquito nets over the beds, and tiled bathrooms. The grounds are quiet and lush and are planted with many tropical flowers and orchids. There are also some large trees that provide much-needed shade. You'll find El Lirio on the left near the top of the hill as you drive from Quepos to Manuel Antonio. All in all this is a very attractive place and a pretty good deal.

WORTH A SPLURGE

Apartotel El Colibri. Apdo. 94, Manuel Antonio, Quepos. ☎ **506/777-0432.** 10 rms. Dec–Apr $50 single, $60 double, $70 triple, $80 quad; May–Nov $25 single, $30 double, $35 triple, $40 quad. V.

If you have dreams of a secluded retreat where you can laze in a hammock and watch hummingbirds sip nectar from crimson flowers, this hotel is for you. The eight basic rooms are set amid a garden that would have kept Monet or Gauguin happy for years. Narrow paths wind up a hill through lush vegetation that completely hides the rooms from the street. You'll feel as though you have the whole place to yourself in these cozy duplex rooms, each of which has a king-size bed with a Guatemalan bedspread, high ceilings with overhead fans, screen-and-cinderblock walls, red-tile floors, framed posters of Costa Rican wildlife, and French doors that lead to a patio. The spacious patios make the rooms seem much larger than they are and come with hammocks, tables and chairs, and barbecues for grilling any fish you might catch (or buy). There are even rooms with beautiful kitchenettes with blue-and-white–tile counters and coffee makers. True tropical elegance. There is a small pool and a couple of older rooms close to the road that are not nearly as nice as the others.

✪ **Hotel Costa Verde.** Apdo. 106-6350, Quepos. ☎ **506/777-0584** or 506/777-0187. Fax 506/777-0506. 42 rms. Dec–Apr $65–$90 single or double; May–Nov $40–$70 single or double. AE, DC, MC, V.

The guest rooms at Costa Verde have long been some of my favorite in the area. With their screen walls they seem to sum up the sensual climate of the Tropics—no need for walls when they only keep out the breezes. Over the years Costa Verde has continued to add new rooms, and today the original rooms are some of the least expensive, but are still quite pleasant. Most of the rooms have ocean views, kitchenettes, and balconies, and the more expensive rooms have loads of space. When I last visited they were finishing the construction of 16 new deluxe suites that will each have air-conditioning and a jacuzzi. There's a very pretty little pool set into the hillside, and up above the pool is an open-air restaurant that looks into the forest trees, where sloths are sometimes seen. To one side of the dining room is a long bar. Costa Verde is more than halfway down the hill to Manuel Antonio, about a 10-minute walk from Playa Espadilla.

El Dorado Mojado. Apdo. 238-6350, Quepos. ☎ **506/777-0368.** Fax 506/777-1248. 4 rms, 4 villas. A/C. Dec–Apr $40.75 single, $48.90 double, $73.35 villa; May–Nov $32.60 single, $40.75 double, $48.90 villa. All rates include breakfast. MC, V.

The architectural uniqueness of the buildings at this small hotel make it one of the most interesting places to stay in Manuel Antonio. Both the villas, with full kitchens, and the smaller standard rooms are very luxurious. The buildings are set back in the forest and are connected by a raised walkway below which grow lush tropical plants. The buildings resemble modernized banana plantation houses with walls of glass that extend vertically for two stories before angling in to form an atrium effect. Standard rooms are located either upstairs (with hardwood floors and more light) or downstairs (with painted red-tile floors). Other interesting and attractive touches include cane-sided cupboards, open-air showers with walls of glass block, and Guatemalan bedspreads. The villas also have TVs, carved antique headboards, and Murphy beds. Some people might find the forest shade a bit dark, but it is still a beautiful setting. I would request Villa A, which has earned the title "monkey villa" for the frequent visits local primates pay to it, or Villa D, which sits beside a flowing stream and offers the most privacy.

Hotel Plinio. Apdo. 71, Quepos. ☎ **506/777-0055.** Fax 506/777-0558. 6 rms, 6 suites, 1 jungle house. Dec–Apr, $40 single, $60–$70 double, $75 standard suite or house; $90 deluxe suite. May–Nov, lower rates available. All rates include a breakfast buffet. AE, MC, V.

The Plinio was for many years a favorite of budget travelers visiting Manuel Antonio, and although its room rates have crept up over the years, it's still a great value. The hotel is built into a steep hillside, so it's a bit of a climb from the parking lot up to the guest rooms and restaurant (roughly the equivalent of three flights of stairs). Once you are up top, though, you'll think you're in a treehouse. Floors and walls are polished hardwood, and there are even rooms with tree-trunk pillars. The hotel's suites are the best value. These are built on either two or three levels. Both types have sleeping lofts, while the three-story rooms also have rooftop decks. My favorite room is known as the jungle house and is set back in the forest. The restaurant, which is one of the most popular in Manuel Antonio, serves a variety of good Italian food, with entree prices ranging from $4.90 to $9.50. Behind the hotel there's a forest with 5 kilometers of trails, and, at the top of the hill, a 50-foot-tall observation tower with an incredible view. There's also a snack bar near the pool for lunches. A lap pool, kid's pool, and recreation room with library round out the amenities.

✪ **Villas Nicolas.** Apdo. 236, Quepos. ☎ **506/777-0481.** Fax 506/777-0451. 12 rms. $59–$90 single or double; $75–$105 triple; $90–$150 quad. Weekly, monthly, and low-season rates available. No credit cards.

These large "villa-suites" pack a big punch for the buck. Built as terraced units up a steep hill in deep forest, they give a real feeling of being in the jungle. These rooms and suites come in a variety of sizes and shapes, but all are spacious and well appointed, with wood floors, throw rugs, separate living rooms, and large bathrooms. Some rooms even have full kitchenettes, which make longer stays comfortable and feasible. My favorite feature, though, are the huge balconies, with both sitting chairs and a hammock. There's also a small pool. The rooms highest up the hill have views I'd be willing to pay a lot more for.

WHERE TO EAT

For the cheapest meals around, head to one of the dozen or so open-air shacks near the side of the road just before the circle at the entrance to the park. The standard Tico menu prevails with prices in the $2.50-to-$8 range. Though these little places lack atmosphere, they do have a view of the ocean.

In Quepos, both **El Gran Escape** and **La Marquesa** are good bets. If you're staying in Quepos, and you're planning to do your own cooking or just want to pick up a snack, the market (two blocks in from the main road into town) sells lots of delicious fruit and fresh vegetables, among other staples. There are also several all-purpose grocery stores in downtown Quepos.

MEALS FOR LESS THAN $12

✪ **Barba Roja.** Quepos—Manuel Antonio Road. ☎ **506/777-0331.** Reservations not accepted. Sandwiches $2.50–$3.05; main courses $5.10–$11.30. V (with 7% surcharge). Tues–Sun 5am–9:30pm; Monday 4–9:30pm. SEAFOOD/CONTINENTAL.

Perched high on a hill with stunning views over jungle and ocean, the Barba Roja is the kind of restaurant that people discover on the last day of their vacation and wish they had known about the day they arrived. The rustic interior is done with local hardwoods and bamboo, which give the dining room a warm glow. Take a seat at the counter, and you can sit for hours gazing out at the view. If you tire of the view, glance around at some of the original art by local artists. There is even a gallery attached to the restaurant. Best of all, however, is the food. On the blackboard, there are daily specials such as grilled fish steak served with a salad and baked potato. The restaurant is open for breakfast and serves delicious whole-wheat French toast. For lunch, there are a number of different sandwiches, all served on whole-wheat bread. If you are in the mood to hang out and meet interesting people from all over the world, spend some time at the bar sipping piña coladas or margaritas.

Karola's. Quepos—Manuel Antonio Road. ☎ **506/777-0424.** Reservations not accepted. Main courses $3.30–$12.75. No credit cards. Thurs–Tues 7am–10pm. SEAFOOD/CONTINENTAL.

The steep driveway leading down to this open-air restaurant is within a few feet of the Barba Roja parking lot but is easily overlooked. Watch closely when you're up at the top of the hill. The restaurant is across a footbridge from its parking lot and is set against a jungle-covered hillside. Far below you can see the ocean if you are here during the day. Grilled seafoods are the specialty, but they also do peel-and-eat shrimp with a great house sauce. Desserts, such as macadamia pie, are good, and you can order margaritas by the pitcher.

La Tortuga. Isla Damas. No phone. Reservations not accepted. Main dishes $3.40—$10.80. V. Daily 9am—8pm. SEAFOOD.

This is one of the most unusual restaurants in Costa Rica. Even though it only serves basic Tico fare, it is an experience that should not be missed. To reach it, you must first drive north out of town toward Playa de Jacó. Watch for the COMPLEJO TURISTICO sign and turn west for another mile or so. When you reach the water, you'll find a boatman waiting to take you out to the restaurant on a large converted boat. If there is no boatman around, flash your lights and beep your horn; someone will come for you. The menu is primarily fish, and the owner seems to always have the very best catches of the day. The great seafood, exhilarating boat ride, and the view across the estuary to the forested mountains beyond make this place well worth the effort. If the TV is blaring, ask them to turn it down; they'll oblige.

✪ **Plinio Restaurant.** 1 kilometer out of Quepos toward Manuel Antonio. ☎ **506/ 777-0055.** Main courses $4.90–$9.50. AE, MC, V. Daily 7–10am and 5–10pm. ITALIAN/ GERMAN.

This is the most popular restaurant in Manuel Antonio and is located in one of my favorite hotels. The open-air restaurant is a sort of covered deck about three stories above the parking lot, so be prepared to climb some steps before you get to eat. It's worth it, though. The basket of bread that arrives at your table shortly after you sit down is filled with delicious treats, and the menu is also full of tempting dishes. Italian is the primary cuisine here, but you may also encounter nightly German specials. The last time I visited the owner said they might even begin experimenting with dishes from Thailand and India. Some of my favorite dishes here include the spaghetti with pesto and the broccoli-and-cauliflower parmigiana. There's also a great antipasto platter that includes prosciutto, salami, and cheese.

Restaurant Vela-Bar. 100 meters down side road near the park entrance. ☎ **506/777-0413.** Reservations not accepted. Main courses $5.10—$11.50. AE, MC, V. Daily 7–10am, 11:30am–2:30pm, 5:30–11pm. Closed for lunch June–Nov. INTERNATIONAL.

The Vela-Bar is a small and casual place the serves some of the more creative cookery in Manuel Antonio. This is also the best of the restaurants closest to the park entrance. Seafood and vegetarian meals are the specialties here, and the most interesting dishes are almost always the specials posted on the blackboard. A typical day's choice might include fresh fish in sherry or wine sauce and curried vegetables.

MANUEL ANTONIO AFTER DARK

The main evening entertainment at Manuel Antonio is the disco that appears after dark at **Restaurant Mar y Sombra.** You can also hang out at the **Vela-Bar,** which is up the road to the left just before you reach Manuel Antonio and seems to be popular with gay men. The bar at the **Barba Roja** restaurant is another good place to hang out and meet people in the evenings. If you are staying in Quepos, check out the **Disco Arco Iris,** which is across the bridge just before entering town and is built over the water, or the new disco at the Nahomi recreation complex. If you just can't stay away from the gaming tables, the **Hotel Kamuk** in Quepos has a small casino and will even foot your cab bill if you try your luck and lay your money down.

EN ROUTE TO DOMINICAL

Playa Matapalo is a long strand of flat beach that is about midway between Quepos and Dominical. Although it is not as spectacular as either of those two beaches, it does have its charms. Unfortunately, the surf is often too rough to allow much swimming here, although boogie boarding can be good. Foremost among this beach's charms are peace and quiet. With only a few places to stay, there are no crowds here, and Matapalo is still basically a little village. The beach itself is about a kilometer from the village. In addition to the hotel listed here, there is an Italian restaurant that serves economical meals, a Tico cabina with a disco, and other projects in the works.

El Coquito Del Pacífico. Playa Matapalo (Apdo. 6783-1000, San José). ☎ **506/233-1731.** Fax 506/222-8849. 6 cabinas. $36 single or double; $42 triple; $48 quad. No credit cards.

This little collection of cabinas is operated by the same people who run the Hotel Ritz/Pensión Continental, a budget-travelers' standard in San José. The cabinas are all quite large and have white-tile floors, high ceilings, colorful sheets on the beds, and overhead fans. There is a small restaurant/bar, and you can rent mountain bikes and boogie boards. Horseback rides can also be arranged. There are plans to add a swimming pool. This is one of the first places you come to when you hit the beach.

4 Dominical

29 kilometers SW of San Isidro; 42 kilometers S of Quepos; 160 kilometers S of San José

The secret has started to slip out, but Dominical and the coastline south of Dominical remain excellent places to find isolated beaches, spectacular views, remote jungle waterfalls, and abundant budget lodgings. Dominical has both right and left beach breaks, which means there are usually surfers in town, but, so far, this area is generally undeveloped, spread out, and slow paced.

Leaving Manuel Antonio, the road south to Dominical runs by mile after mile of oil-palm plantations. However, just before Dominical, the mountains once again meet the sea. From Dominical south, the coastline is dotted with tide pools, tiny coves, and cliff-side vistas, all of which bring Big Sur, California to mind. Dominical is the largest village in the area and has several small lodges both in town and along the beach to the south. The village enjoys an enviable location on the banks of Río Baru, right where it becomes a wide lagoon before emptying into the ocean. There is good birdwatching along the banks of the river and throughout the surrounding forests.

ESSENTIALS
GETTING THERE & DEPARTING

By Plane   The nearest airport with regular service is in Quepos. From there you can hire a taxi, rent a car, or take the bus.

By Bus   To reach Dominical, you must first go to San Isidro de El General or Quepos. Buses for San Isidro de El General leave San José daily every hour from 5:30am to 5pm from Calle 16 between avenidas 1 and 3. Leave no later than 9:30am if you want to catch the 1:30pm bus to Dominical. Duration is 3 hours. Fare is $2.70.

From San Isidro de El General, buses leave for Dominical at 7am and 1:30 and 3pm. The bus station for Dominical is one block south of the main bus station and two blocks west of the church. Duration is 1 1/2 hours. Fare is $1.50.

From Quepos, buses leave daily at 5:30am and 1:30pm. Duration is 3 1/2 hours. Fare is $3.50.

When you're ready to leave, note that buses only depart Dominical for San Isidro de El General twice daily, at 7:30am and 3pm. If you want to get to San José the same day, you'll have to catch the morning bus. Buses to Quepos leave at approximately 7am and 1:30pm. Buses leave San Isidro for San José every hour from 5:30am to 5pm.

By Car   From San José, head south (toward Cartago) on the Interamerican Highway. Continue on this road all the way to San Isidro de El General, where you turn right and head down toward the coast. The entire drive takes about 5 hours.

ORIENTATION

Dominical is a small village on the banks of Río Baru. The village is to the right after you cross the bridge and centers around the soccer field and general store, where there is a public telephone.

EXPLORING THE BEACHES & BALLENA MARINE NATIONAL PARK

Because the beach in the village of Dominical is unprotected and at the mouth of a river, it is often much too rough for swimming. However, you can go for a swim in the lagoon at the mouth of the Río Baru, or head down the beach a few kilometers to the little sheltered cove at Roca Verde. If you have a car, you should continue driving south, exploring beaches as you go. At the village of Uvita, 16 kilometers south of Dominical, you'll reach the northern end of the Ballena Marine National Park, which protects a coral reef that stretches from Uvita south to Playa Piñuela and includes the little Isla Ballena, which is just offshore. At low tide an exposed sandbar allows you to walk about and explore the island. This park is named for the whales that are sometimes sighted close to shore in the winter months.

HORSEBACK TOURS & RAIN-FOREST HIKES

Although the beaches stretching south from Dominical should be beautiful enough to keep most people content, there are lots of other things to do. Several local farms offer horseback tours through forests and orchards, and at some of these farms you can even spend the night. **Hacienda Baru** (☎ **506/771-1903,** leave message) offers several different hikes and tours, including a walk through mangroves and along the river bank (good bird watching), a rain-forest hike through 200 acres of virgin jungle, an all-day trek from beach to mangrove to jungle that includes a visit to some Indian petroglyphs, an overnight camping trip, and a combination horseback-and-hiking tour. Tour prices range from $15 to $60 if there is only one person. If you're traveling with a group, you'll be charged a lower per-person rate, depending upon the number of people in your group. Note, however, that each tour can only accommodate six people. Hacienda Baru can also help you arrange various hikes and horseback rides on other nearby farms.

Down near Uvita there are several beautiful waterfalls that make wonderful destinations for hikes or horseback rides. Ask at Uvita's Cabinas El Cocotico for Jorge Diaz, who leads people to the **Emerald Pools Falls,** also a great place to go for a swim.

FARM STAYS

Finca Brian y Milena, Apdo. 2-8000, San Isidro de El General (☎ **506/771-1903,** leave message), offers day and overnight trips to their farm in the hills outside of Dominical. Here you can birdwatch, explore the tropical rain forest, and visit a working farm where tropical fruits, nuts, and spices are grown. If you stay for several nights, you can visit the Santo Cristo or Diamante waterfalls by horseback or on foot. At night you can soak in the hot tub. Rates begin at $30 per person per day. Horse rentals and overnight excursions are additional.

WHERE TO STAY

In addition to the places listed here, if you continue south another 16 kilometers, you'll find a campground on Playa Ballena and a couple of basic cabinas in Uvita.

DOUBLES FOR LESS THAN $15

Roca Verde. Dominical. No phone. 12 rms (7 with private bath). $7 single, double, or triple without bath; $10 single with bath, $15 double with bath, $20 triple with bath. No credit cards.

This hotel has a wonderful location a couple of kilometers south of Dominical. The setting is superb—on a little cove with rocks and tide pools at the near end. If you're driving, you'll only be able to take the back road from town at low tide, since the road actually crosses a section of the beach. The cheaper rooms are very basic, with wooden walls, a fan, one small window, and a couple of beds. The shared toilets and showers are comparable to what you might find at a campground. The more expensive cabins have private baths and a decidedly tropical feel. The Roca Verde's open-air restaurant/bar is popular with tourists and Ticos alike and it often doubles as a disco on weekend nights, so be prepared.

DOUBLES FOR LESS THAN $25

✪ Albergue Willdale. Dominical (Selva Mar, Apdo. 215-8000, San Isidro de El General). ☎/fax **506/771-1903.** 7 rms (all with private bath). $20 single; $25 double; $30 triple. No credit cards.

The Albergue Willdale is located directly across from the soccer field and is by far the friendliest place in Dominical. Directly behind the lodge is the river, where you can go swimming, fishing, or paddling around. The owners of this lodge are from Virginia, and they'll gladly fill you in on all there is to do in the area. The rooms are large and have big windows and patios. There are reading lights, fans, hot water, and attractive Mexican bedspreads. If you are interested in staying for a while, the Dales also rent a very comfortable house up in the hills for $120 a night. The house even has its own swimming pool.

DOUBLES FOR LESS THAN $35

Bella Vista. Dominical (Selva Mar, Apdo. 215-8000, San Isidro de El General). ☎/fax **506/771-1903.** 4 cabins. $30 single; $40–$45 double. All rates include continental breakfast. No credit cards.

"Bella Vista" means "beautiful view" and that is exactly what you get when you stay at one of these small rustic cabins high in the hills south of Dominical. This is a very basic sort of place, but the owners are friendly and the location is superb. Transportation between Dominical and Bella Vista is $10 per person each way. Simple meals are served ($4 for breakfast and lunch, $5 to $7 for dinner), though one of the cabins has its own kitchen. The favorite activity of guests is an all-day horseback ride through the rain forest to a beautiful waterfall. The price of $40 per person includes your horse, guide, and lunch.

Cabinas Nayarit. 200 meters west of Rancho Coco, Dominical. ☎ **506/771-1878.** 18 rms (14 with private bath). $28.50 up to three people w/shared bath; $33 up to three people w/private bath. V.

Wedged between the mouth of the Río Baru and the beach, there are several sandy lanes lined with simple houses and some cabinas, which primarily cater to surfers. Of these, Cabinas Nayarit is the best. There are several styles of rooms here including older rooms with fans and lots of beds (crowded), older rooms with air-conditioning, and newer rooms with air-conditioning, skylights, carved wooden headboards, and jalousie windows.

Hotel Río Lindo. Dominical. ☎ **506/771-2009.** Fax 506/771-1725. 10 rms (all with private bath). Dec—Apr $25–36 single, $32–$44 double. Slightly lower rates from May–November. No credit cards.

This two-story hotel is located near the entrance to Dominical just across the bridge where the road turns into the village. Rooms are simple but clean and all have ceiling fans. The upstairs rooms are definitely the better choice. These rooms are larger, have nicer furnishings, and better ventilation. Adjacent to the hotel is the Restaurant Maui, a moderately priced place that seems to keep the stereo blaring all day long.

WORTH A SPLURGE

Punta Dominical. Apdo. 196-8000, San Isidro de El General. ☎ **506/787-0016** or 506/787-0017. 4 cabins. $35 single; $50 double; $62 triple; $74 quad. No credit cards.

Located about 4 kilometers south of Dominical on a rocky point, this place has a stony cove on one side and a sandy beach on the other. The cabins and restaurant are set among shady old trees high above the surf, and have excellent views of both coves. The best views are to be had from the cabins higher up the hill, but all have good views. The cabins, built on stilts and constructed of dark polished hardwood, all have big porches with chairs and hammocks. Screened and louvered walls are designed to catch the breezes. The bathrooms are large and have separate changing areas. The hotel's open-air restaurant, which specializes in seafood, is one of the best in Dominical. Entree prices range from $3.50 to $15.

WHERE TO EAT

Right in town, there's the **Soda Laura,** which serves basic Tico meals and has a nice view of the river mouth. Dishes range in price from $1.75 to $8. Other options include **San Clemente Bar and Grill,** a gringo hangout and sports bar specializing in Mexican-American food, and the **Restaurant Maui,** which is next to the Hotel Río Lindo. These latter two places serve meals that cost between $3.50 and $15. However, if you want to sample the best food in the area, hands down, head south of town to the **Hotel Punta Dominical.**

5 San Isidro de El General: A Base for Exploring Chirripó National Park

120 kilometers SE of San José; 123 kilometers NW of Palmar Norte; 29 kilometers NE of Dominical

San Isidro de El General is the largest town in this region and is located on the Interamerican Highway in the foothills of the Talamanca Mountains. Although there isn't much to do right in town, this is the jumping-off point for trips to Chirripó National Park. This is also the transfer point if you are coming from or going to Dominical, and most buses traveling the Interamerican Highway stop here.

ESSENTIALS
GETTING THERE & DEPARTING

By Bus   Express buses leave San José daily at 5:30am and 5pm from Calle 16 between avenidas 1 and 3. Duration is 3 hours. Fare is $2.70.

Buses from Golfito and Puerto Jiménez will also drop you off in San Isidro (see chapter 10 for schedules).

There are also buses from Quepos to San Isidro daily at 5:30am and 1:30pm. Duration is 3½ hours. Fare is $3.50.

Buses depart San Isidro for San José daily every hour between 5:30am and 5pm. The principal **Musoc** (☎ 771-0414) company bus station is located 200 meters north of the central park. Buses to Dominical leave daily at 7am and 1:30 and 3pm from a separate station 200 meters west of the central park. Buses to Golfito pass through San Isidro at around 10am and 2 and 6pm. Buses to Puerto Jiménez leave daily at 9am and 3pm. It is generally best to catch these latter two buses at the gas station and soda located at the principal intersection of the Interamerican Highway and San Isidro. Alternatively, you can ask at the Musoc station for current bus information.

By Car   It is a long and winding road from San José to San Isidro; this section of the Interamerican Highway is one of the most difficult sections of road in the country. Not only are there the usual car-eating potholes, but you must also contend with driving over the 11,000-foot-high Cerro de la Muerte (Mountain of Death), which the ICT (Costa Rican Tourism Board) would like to rename Buenavista (Beautiful View). This aptly named mountain (in either case) is legendary for its dense afternoon fogs, blindingly torrential downpours, steep drop-offs, constant switchbacks, and breathtaking views. In other words, drive with care. And bring a sweater; it's cold up at the top. It'll take you about 3 hours to get to San Isidro.

ORIENTATION

Downtown San Isidro is just off the Interamerican Highway. The main bus station is two blocks west of the north end of the central park.

EXPLORING CHIRRIPÓ NATIONAL PARK

At 12,412 feet in elevation, Mount Chirripó is the tallest mountain in Costa Rica, and because of the great elevations within the national park named after it, temperatures can even dip below freezing, especially at night. If you are headed up this way, come prepared for chilly weather. The elevation and low temperatures have produced a very different sort of environment for Costa Rica. Above about 10,000 feet only stunted trees and shrubs can survive in regions known as *paramos*. If you are driving the Interamerican Highway between San Isidro and San José, you will pass through a paramo on the **Cerro de la Muerte** (Mountain of Death).

Hiking up to the top of Mount Chirripó is one of Costa Rica's great adventures. On a clear day (usually in the morning), you can see both the Pacific Ocean and the Caribbean Sea from the summit. You can do this trip fairly easily on your own if you have brought gear and are an experienced backpacker. While it is possible to hike from the park entrance to the summit and back down in two days, it is best to allow four days for the trip to give yourself time to enjoy your hike fully and still spend some time on top, since that's were the glacier lakes and paramos are. (There's a simple, but wonderful, lodge near the summit where you can stay overnight.) For much of the way you'll be hiking through cloud forests that are home to the spectacular quetzal, Costa Rica's most beautiful bird. These cloud forests are cold and damp, though, so come prepared for rain and fog.

ENTRY POINT, FEES & REGULATIONS

Although it's not that difficult to get to Chirripó National Park from nearby San Isidro, it's still rather remote. And to see it fully, you have to be prepared to hike. To get to the trailhead, you have two choices: car or bus. If you choose to drive, take the road out of San Isidro, heading north toward San Gerardo de Rivas. The trailhead is 15 kilometers (9 miles) down the road. Otherwise, you can catch a bus in San Isidro that'll take you directly to the trailhead in San Gerardo de Rivas. Buses leave daily at either 5:30am (from the central park) or 2pm (from a station 200 meters south of the park). The fare is $1.05 and the trip takes 1 1/2 hours. Buses return to San Isidro daily at 7am and 4pm. Because the hike to the summit of Mt. Chirripó can take between 6 and 12 hours, depending upon your physical condition, I recommend taking the earlier bus so you can start hiking when the day is still young, or arriving the day before and spending the night in San Gerardo de Rivas (there are a number of inexpensive cabinas there), before setting out early the following morning.

Park admission is $6 per day. If you plan to stay at the lodge near the summit, you must make reservations in advance, since the number of people who can stay there is limited (see "Staying at the Summit Lodge," below). Note that camping is not allowed in the park. Finally, it's possible to have your gear carried up to the summit. Just outside the park entrance in San Gerardo de Rivas you'll find an informal group of guides and pack rats who will haul your gear up for you, charging between $15 and $20 per pack, depending on weight. They use horses in the dry season, but must carry the loads themselves during the rainy season.

STAYING AT THE SUMMIT LODGE

Reservations for the lodge on Mt. Chirripó must be prepaid at the **National Parks office** in San José or San Isidro (☎ **506/771-3155**). The lodge holds only 40 people; 25 of those spaces can be reserved in San José, while 15 are controlled by the San Isidro office. There's no food or bedding at the lodge, so be sure to bring something to eat, a campstove if you want to cook, and a sleeping bag. There is a fee of $2.50 per person per night.

WHERE TO STAY & EAT IN SAN ISIDRO DE EL GENERAL
DOUBLES FOR LESS THAN $15

Hotel Chirripó. South side of church, San Isidro de El General. ☎ **506/771-0529.** 41 rms (20 with private bath). $5 single without bath, $7.50 double without bath; $10 single with bath, $13 double with bath, $19 triple with bath. V.

This budget hotel is about the best you'll find right in San Isidro and is located on the central square within a couple of blocks of all the town's bus stations. Rooms vary considerably. Some have windows (and street noise), and some have no windows (or street noise). Stay away from the rooms in front, since these are the noisiest. There's a large restaurant at the front of the lobby.

EN ROUTE TO SAN JOSÉ: TWO PLACES TO SEE QUETZALS IN THE WILD

Between San Isidro de El General and San José, the Interamerican Highway climbs to its highest point in Costa Rica and crosses over the Cerro de la Muerte. This area has recently acquired a newfound importance as one of the best places in Costa Rica to see quetzals in the wild. March, April, and May are nesting season for the quetzals, and this is usually the best time to see them. However, in this area, it is often possible to see them year-round. On one 2-hour hike here, without a guide, our small group spotted eight of these amazing birds. All of the lodges listed below, along with some new ones, are located along a 20-kilometer stretch of the Interamerican Highway. You'll probably start seeing their billboards and placards with painted quetzals long before you see any birds.

✪ **Albergue De Montaña Savegre.** Kilometer 80 Carretera Interamericana Sur, San Gerardo de Dota (Apdo. 482, Cartago). ☎ **506/771-1732.** 16 cabins. $63 per person. All rates include three meals daily. V.

This working apple and pear farm, which also has over 600 acres of primary forest, has recently acquired quite a reputation as one of the best places in the country to see quetzals. The farm has long been popular as a weekend vacation and picnicking spot for Ticos, but now people from all over the world are searching out the rustic lodge. The rooms here are quite basic, but if you're serious about birdwatching this shouldn't matter. Hearty Tico meals are served, and if you want to try your hand at trout fishing, you might luck into a fish dinner. You'll find this lodge 9 kilometers down a dirt road off the Interamerican Highway.

✪ **Albergue de Montaña Tapantí.** Kilometer 62 Carretera Interamericana Sur, Macho Gaff, Cartago (Apdo. 1237-1000, Pavas). ☎/fax **506/232-0436.** 11 rms. $60 single or double; $75 triple; $85 quad. MC, V.

If you want to hike around in the cloud forest, see quetzals, and then return to a large, comfortable room with a private bath, then this deluxe lodge is what you're looking for in this area. The buildings at Tapantí are built to resemble Swiss chalets, and you may think you're in Switzerland when you feel how cold it gets here at night. The lodge is at 10,000 feet and frost is not uncommon. However, there is a fireplace in the lounge. Most of the guest rooms are actually suites with separate bedrooms and living rooms. Luckily, they also have heaters. The lodge's dining room serves such Swiss specialties as beef fondue and raclette, as well as other continental dishes. Guided hikes, horseback rides, and bird watching walks are all available through the lodge.

The Southern Zone 10

The heat and humidity are more than many people can handle, but this remote southern region of Costa Rica is one of the country's most beautiful and wild areas. Lush forested mountains tumble into the sea, streams still run clear and clean, and scarlet macaws squawk raucously in the treetops. However, this beauty does not come easy; you must have plenty of time or plenty of money (preferably both), plus a desire for a bit of adventure if you want to explore this region. Because there are few roads, most of the most fascinating spots can be reached only by small plane or boat, although hiking and four-wheeling will also get you into some memorable surroundings as well.

Not surprisingly, this region has only very recently opened up to tourism. It is, after all, an 8-hour drive from San José. Despite an increased interest in southern Costa Rica by international travelers and Ticos alike (Corcovado National Park and Caño Island Biological Reserve are here, and a duty-free port just opened in Golfito), there are still relatively few places to stay. It's best to put some forethought into planning a vacation down here.

1 Drake Bay

145 kilometers S of San José; 32 kilometers SW of Palmar

Located on the northern end of the Osa peninsula, Drake Bay is what adventure travel is all about. Little more than a collection of lodges catering to naturalists, anglers, scuba divers, and assorted vacationers, the bay can only be reached by boat or chartered sea plane, which makes it one of the more remote destinations in Costa Rica. Because of the bay's remoteness, there has been little development here. Accommodations vary from tents on wooden platforms and cement-walled cabinas to very comfortable lodges that border on the luxurious. There are few conventional phones and no power lines in Drake Bay, so radio and cellular phones and electrical generators stand in. The village of Drake Bay has its own water system, but it is infamous for its unreliability. If you're headed out this way you may occasionally find yourself without water for a shower, but the problem rarely lasts long.

The bay is named after Sir Francis Drake, who is believed to have anchored here in 1579. Emptying into the bay is the tiny Río Agujitas, which acts as a protected harbor for small boats and is a great place to do a bit of canoeing or swimming. It is here on the Río Agujitas that many of the local lodges dock their boats. Stretching south from Drake Bay are miles and miles of deserted beaches. Adventurous explorers will find tide pools, spring-fed rivers, waterfalls, forest trails, and some of the best birdwatching in all of Costa Rica. If a paradise such as this appeals to you, Drake Bay makes a good base for exploring the peninsula.

South of Drake Bay lie the wilds of the Osa peninsula and **Corcovado National Park.** This is one of Costa Rica's most beautiful regions, yet it is also one of its least accessible. Corcovado National Park covers about half of the peninsula and contains the largest virgin lowland rain forest in Central America. For this reason, Corcovado is well known among naturalists and researchers studying rain-forest ecology. Take note of the operative words here—rain forest. It does, indeed, rain here. In fact, some parts of the peninsula receive more than 250 inches per year. In addition to producing lush forests, this massive amount of rain also produces more than a few disgruntled visitors. If you're of the opinion that rain ruins a vacation, you might want to consider going elsewhere in Costa Rica.

ESSENTIALS

Because Drake Bay is so remote and only accessible by water or chartered plane, it is highly recommended that you have a room reservation before you arrive. The lodges listed here are scattered along several kilometers of coastline.

Although they are always useful to have on hand in Costa Rica, a flashlight and rain gear are essential in Drake Bay.

GETTING THERE

By Plane　The closest airport to Drake Bay is in Palmar Sur, a taxi and boat ride away. **Sansa** (☎ **506/233-0397,** 506/233-3258, or 506/233-5330) flies to Palmar Sur at 9am Monday through Saturday, and at 11:15am on Sundays, from San José's Juan Santamaría International Airport. The former flight stops at Coto 47 and Puerto Jiménez en route, and the latter stops at Puerto Jiménez, Golfito, and Coto 47 en route. Duration is 1 hour and 50 minutes and 2 hours and 20 minutes, respectively. Fare is $50 each way.

Travelair (☎ **506/220-3054** or 506/232-7883) has flights to Palmar Sur that depart daily at 8:10am from San José's Pavas International Airport. This flight stops at Quepos en route. Trip duration is 55 minutes. Fare is $73 one-way, $119 round-trip.

Many hotels in Drake Bay run charter flights to Palmar Sur during the high season (see "Where to Stay," below, for details), and it is even possible to charter a seaplane that will fly you directly to the bay. If this option interests you call **Alas Anfibias de Costa Rica** (☎ **506/232-9567**), but be forewarned: This is an extremely expensive option, costing around $750 each way, for four passengers.

By Bus　Express buses leave San José daily for Palmar Norte at 5, 7, 8:30, and 11am and 1, 2:30, and 6pm from Avenida 18 between calles 2 and 4. Duration is 5 hours. Fare is $3.90.

You can also catch a Golfito-bound bus from this same station and get off in Palmar Norte.

Once in Palmar Norte, ask when the next bus goes out to Sierpe. If it doesn't leave for a while (they aren't frequent), consider taking a taxi (see below).

By Taxi and Boat　Once you arrive at either the Palmar Norte bus station or the Palmar Sur airstrip, you'll most likely need to take a taxi to the village of Sierpe. The

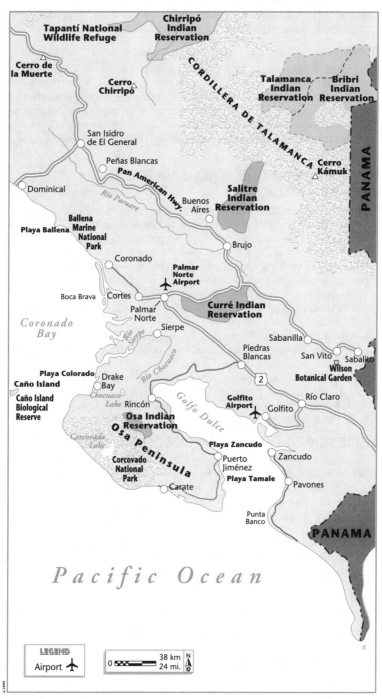

The Southern Zone

Tapantí National
Wildlife Refuge

Chirripó
Indian
Reservation

Cerro de
la Muerte

Cerro
Chirripó

CORDILLERA DE TALAMANCA

Talamanca
Indian
Reservation

Bribri
Indian
Reservation

San Isidro
de El General

PANAMA

Peñas Blancas

Pan American Hwy.

Cerro
Kámuk

Dominical

Río Pacuare

Buenos
Aires

Salitre
Indian
Reservation

Ballena
Marine
National
Park

Playa Ballena

Brujo

Coronado

Palmar
Norte
Airport

Boca Brava

Cortes

Curré Indian
Reservation

Coronado
Bay

Palmar
Norte

Río Sierpe

Sierpe

Sabanilla

Piedras
Blancas

San Vito

Sabalito

Wilson
Botanical Garden

Playa Colorado

Caño Island

Drake
Bay

Río Chocuaco

2

Caño Island
Biological
Reserve

Chocuaco
Lake

Rincón

Golfo Dulce

Río Claro

Golfito
Airport

Golfito

Osa Indian
Reservation

Corcovado
Lake

Osa Peninsula

Playa Zancudo

Zancudo

Corcovado
National
Park

Puerto
Jiménez

Playa Tamale

Pavones

Carate

Punta
Banco

PANAMA

Pacific Ocean

LEGEND

Airport ✈

0 ▭▭▭▭ 38 km
24 mi.

N

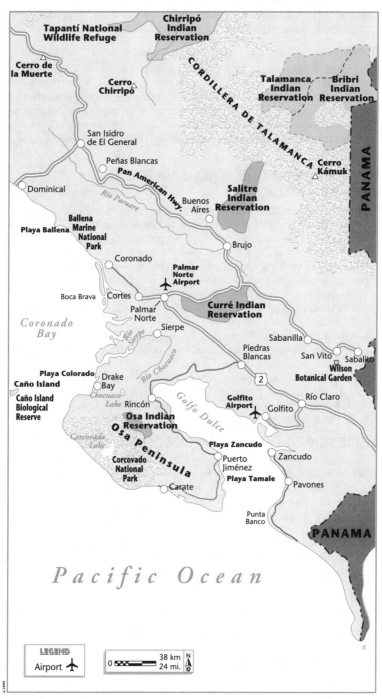

fare should be between $10 and $15. A seat on a boat from Sierpe down river to Drake Bay will cost you another $15.

DEPARTING

Have your lodge arrange a boat trip back to Sierpe for you. Be sure the lodge also arranges for a taxi to meet you in Sierpe for the trip to Palmar Sur or Palmar Norte. (If you're on a budget, you can ask around to see if a late morning public bus is still running from Sierpe to Palmar Norte.) In either of the two Palmars, you can make onward plane and bus connections. At the Palmar Norte bus terminal, almost any bus headed north will take you to San José, and almost any bus headed south will take you to Golfito.

WHAT TO SEE & DO: BEACHES, RAIN FORESTS, WILDLIFE & HIKING

Beaches, forests, wildlife, and solitude are the main attractions of Drake Bay. While Corcovado National Park is the area's star attraction (covered in the next section), there's plenty to soak up in Drake Bay. Osa peninsula is home to an unbelievable variety of plants and animals: more than 140 species of mammals, 267 species of birds, and 117 species of amphibians and reptiles. While you aren't likely to see a high percentage of these animals, you can expect to see quite a few, including several species of monkeys, coatimundis, scarlet macaws, parrots, and hummingbirds. The tallest tree in Costa Rica, a 230-foot-tall silk-cotton tree, is located within Corcovado, as is Costa Rica's largest population of scarlet macaws. Other park inhabitants include jaguars, tapirs, sloths, and crocodiles. If you're lucky, you might even see one of the region's *osas*. Though the word means "bear" in English, in this case it refers to the giant anteaters that live on the peninsula.

Around Drake Bay and within the national park there are many miles of trails through rain forests and swamps, down beaches, and around rock headlands. All of the lodges listed below offer guided excursions into the park. It is also possible to begin a hike around the peninsula from Drake Bay.

A SIDE TRIP TO CAÑO ISLAND BIOLOGICAL RESERVE

One of the most popular excursions from Drake Bay is a trip out to Caño Island and the Caño Island Biological Reserve for a bit of exploring and snorkeling or scuba diving. The island is located about 12 miles offshore from Drake Bay and was once home to a pre-Columbian culture about which little is known. A trip to the island will include a visit to one of this culture's cemeteries, and you'll also be able to see some of the stone spheres that are commonly believed to have been carved by the people who once lived in this area. The island is most unique for its geological isolation: Due to plate tectonics, the island has remained separate from the rest of Central America for more than 40 million years. The dominant tree species is the huge cow or milk tree, which produces a milky sap that can be drunk. Few animals or birds live on the island, but the coral reefs just offshore teem with life and are the main reason most people come here. Most of the lodges listed below offer trips to Caño Island. You can also do some sportfishing while you're in the area. Almost any of the lodges can arrange a charter boat for you.

WHERE TO STAY & EAT

I have chosen to list nightly room rates at the following lodges. However, because all but the least expensive places are all-inclusive, there is some distortion involved. Also, please note that these lodges do most of their business in package trips that include

Costa Rica's Pre-Columbian Past: The Stone Ball Mystery

While Costa Rica lacks the great temples and bas-relief carvings of the Mayan, Aztec, and Olmec cities of northern Mesoamerica, its pre-Colombian residents did leave a legacy that continues to cause archeologists and anthropologists to scratch their heads in wonder. Over a period of several centuries, hundreds of painstakingly carved granite spheres, which appear to have been carefully positioned, were left by the peoples who lived on the Diquis delta along the Terraba river in southern Costa Rica. These "stone balls," which range from the size of a grapefruit to over 7 feet in diameter, can weigh up to 30 tons. Many reach near spherical perfection. But here's where the heart of the mystery lies: These deceptively simple archeological relics have no known relatives in the northern hemisphere.

Archeologists believe that the spheres were created during two defined cultural periods. The first, called the Aguas Buenas period, dates from around A.D. 100–500. Few spheres survive from this time. The second, later phase, during which spheres were created in apparently greater numbers, is called the Chiriquí period, which lasted from approximately A.D. 100–1500. The "balls" believed to have been constructed during this time frame are widely dispersed along the entire length of the lower section of the Terraba river. Many archeologists believe that the spheres were handcarved in a very time-consuming process, using stone tools, perhaps aided by some sort of firing process. However, an alternative theory holds that granite blocks were placed at the bases of powerful waterfalls and the hydraulic beating of the water against stone carved the blocks into their near-perfect spherical shapes. Whichever theory may be right, many of these stone carvings have been found miles from any known source of raw granite, indicating a difficult and lengthy transportation process.

They tend to be located near burial sites, and their size and placement are often interpreted to have both social and celestial significance, although these are still little more than educated guesses. Unfortunately, many of the stone balls have been plundered and currently decorate front yards in the fancier neighborhoods of San José. Some have been shipped out of the country. The National Museum in San José (see chapter 6) has a nice collection, including one massive sphere in the center courtyard. With the city laid out behind you, the ball with its attendant urban backdrop provides a never-fail photo opportunity. You can also see the stone balls in their original placements near the small airport in Palmar Norte or on Caño Island, just 12 miles off the Pacific coast near Drake Bay.

several-nights' lodging, all meals, transportation, and tours. If you intend to spend several nights and do several tours while you are here, be sure to ask about these packages. They could constitute a significant saving for you.

DOUBLES FOR LESS THAN $50

Cabinas Cecilia. Drake Bay, Osa peninsula. ☎ **506/382-3299.** 6 rms (2 with private bath). $25 single; $50 double. All rates include breakfast and dinner.

If cost is a factor to you, this is just about the cheapest place to stay in Drake Bay. Although these cabinas, housed in a cinderblock bunker, are rather stark, they are fronted by a long verandah with a nice view of the bay. Rooms vary in size; some have bunk beds, while others have twin or double beds. Other than the beds, there is no furniture in the rooms. Meals are served in a separate open-air dining room a short distance from the cabinas. The owner also runs a separate bar and restaurant, a short hike up the steep hill above the cabinas.

Cocalito Lodge. Apdo. 63, Palmar Norte, Osa peninsula. No phone in Costa Rica. ☎ **519/ 782-3978** (in Canada). Fax 506/786-6150 (in Costa Rica). 3 rms, 6 cabins (all with private bath). May–Nov $18.50–$35 single, $37–$60 double; Dec–Apr $20–$35 single, $40–$70 double. $7 to put up a tent anytime. MC, V (with a 6% surcharge added).

The owners of this little place right on the beach south of La Paloma Lodge are gringos who have been living here for years. Their choice of this remote alternative lifestyle has translated into a rustic and casual beachfront lodge that attracts primarily a younger crowd. Some of the rooms are a bit dark and cramped, but there are also larger and more expensive cabinas that offer plenty of room. In my opinion, Cocalito's greatest attraction is that it is right on a beautiful little cove bordered on both ends by rocky outcrops. At all of the more expensive lodges here in Drake Bay, you have to do a bit of walking (often down muddy trails) to get to a swimmable beach. So, if having the beach right outside your door is more important than having a large, luxurious room, Cocalito might be for you. The lodge's dining room offers excellent meals, with many ingredients from the owners' organic garden. Meals cost an additional $30 per day. Electricity is provided by a combination of solar and hydraulic sources, but conserved for the most essential appliances and functions. At night, candles and torches provide most of the lighting. A variety of tours are offered including trips to Caño Island ($50 for snorkelers, $110 for scuba divers), guided hikes ($15 to $50), horseback rides ($35), deep-sea fishing ($350 per day for three people), and boat tours of the nearby mangrove swamp ($50).

WORTH A SPLURGE

Drake Bay Wilderness Camp. Apdo. 98-8150, Palmar Norte, Osa peninsula. ☎ **506/ 771-2436** or 506/284-4107. Fax 506/771-2436. 4 tents (all with shared bath), 21 rms. Tents $46 single, $92 double; rooms $68 single, $136 double, $204 triple. All rates include three meals daily. MC, V.

This is one of the most convenient and best-located lodges at Drake Bay. It backs onto the Río Agujitas and fronts the Pacific, but because it's on a rocky spit, there isn't a good swimming beach. The lodge offers a variety of accommodations of different ages and styles. Travelers who want to rough it a bit or economize can opt for a large tent, while those seeking more comfort can ask for one of the newer rooms. These rooms have ceiling fans, verandahs, and good mattresses on the beds. The older rooms, though smaller, are also very clean and comfortable and were recently remodeled. The family-style meals are filling, with an emphasis on fresh seafood and fresh fruits. The lodge provides free use of its canoes, free same-day laundry service, and fax service for guests. Tours offered by Drake Bay Wilderness Camp include hikes within the national park ($55 per person), trips to Caño Island ($55 per person for snorkelers, $90 per person for scuba divers), a horseback riding tour ($35 per person), and sportfishing charters for $250 per day for up to 3 people.

✪ **La Paloma Lodge.** Apdo. 97-4005, San Antonio de Belen, Heredia. ☎/fax **506/ 239-0954** or 506/239-2801 (radio phone at the lodge). 5 rms, 5 cabins. Rooms $85 single, $140 double; cabins $180 double, $210 triple. From May 1–Nov 15, rates are 10% lower. Packages are also available. All rates include three meals daily. V (7% surcharge added).

Birdwatchers will find no better place to stay in Drake Bay. Situated on a hill that can leave the out-of-shape a bit winded, La Paloma offers expansive ocean views. The main lodge building is a huge, open-air, thatched structure with a long verandah. Over in one corner is a sitting area that makes for a pleasant place to meet other lodge guests. All of the cabins are built on stilts, feature large verandahs, and are set among lush foliage facing the Pacific Ocean. The three older cabins are my favorites simply for their spaciousness and seclusion. Four screen walls keep you in touch with nature and let the ocean breezes blow through. However, the newer cabins do provide wonderful ocean views from their main sleeping lofts. The beach is down at the bottom of the hill and there is a new tiled pool with superb sunset views. The electricity is shut off each evening at 9:30pm, which might irritate some late-night bookworms, but if you're like me, you'll want to get up at dawn to watch the early-morning birds. The rooms, though much smaller, are still very attractive and have good views from their verandahs, which, like the cabins, have hammocks. Excursions available include hikes in the park ($65 per person), trips to Caño Island ($65 per person), horseback rides ($50 per person), scuba diving ($100 per person), and sportfishing charters ($450 for up to four people). There are also canoes, kayaks, and snorkeling equipment for rent.

Marenco Biological Reserve. Centro Comercial El Pueblo, Local No. 49-50 (Apdo. 4025-1000), San José. ☎ **506/221-8166.** Fax 506/255-1346. 25 rms. $55–$65 single; $110–$130 double; $165–$195 triple. All rates include three meals daily. No credit cards.

Marenco is located a few kilometers south of Drake Bay, and is consequently one of the closest lodges to Corcovado National Park. The lodge, which is set on a hillside overlooking the ocean, is surrounded by 1,235 acres of private reserve. There are more than 4 kilometers of trails through the reserve and the birdwatching here is often excellent. Accommodations are comfortable, albeit fairly simple. All the rooms have ocean views and porches so you can enjoy the sunsets and even birdwatch right from your room. The newer rooms are larger and more comfortable, but the older ones have a lot of style. Rooms are mostly in duplex cabins around the landscaped grounds, and if you get one of the larger rooms, you can lie in bed and gaze out at the forest through walls of screen. The thatched roofs give the compound the feel of a small village. Meals are served family-style in an open-air dining room that has a great view down the hill to the Pacific. Marenco offers the same sorts of tours available at other lodges and charges similar rates.

Corcovado Adventure Tent Camp. Drake Bay, Osa Peninsula. ☎ **506/284-1679.** 10 tents (all with shared bathrooms). $45 single; $90 double. All rates include three meals daily. No credit cards.

If you don't mind camping, this place, midway between the lodges at Drake Bay and Marenco Biological Reserve, is a good choice in the moderate-price category. The tents are quite large and are set on wooden decks, and a nice swimming beach is only a few yards away. There are plenty of modern showers and toilets. The large dining room serves simple meals with an emphasis on fresh seafood. Various tours are available and there are kayaks and snorkeling gear available for rent. With rates comparable to those of the cheapest places in the village and tents as large as some of the village's least-expensive rooms, this makes a good choice for anyone who prefers a bit more seclusion and more of an adventurous setting. Excursions you can arrange here include guided hikes ($60 per person), trips to Caño Island ($60 per person), horseback rides ($45 per person), and sportfishing charters ($400 for up to four people).

Cabinas Jinetes de Osa. Drake Bay, Osa peninsula. ☎ **506/273-3116** or 506/284-3743. 9 rms (6 with shared bath). $40–$50 single; $80–$100 double. All rates include three meals daily. MC, V (6% surcharge added).

Although the rooms are small and dark, this is still one of the nicer places at the lower end of the scale in Drake Bay. The wooden construction of the building that houses the rooms and the long verandah almost directly above the beach are what give this lodge an edge over moderately priced lodges in Drake Bay. It is also the closest of the less expensive places to the docks on the Río Agujitas, which is nice for those with heavy bags. Basic Tico-style meals are served in a small open-air dining room.

A NEARBY PLACE TO STAY & EAT

Hotel Pargo. Sierpe. ☎/fax **506/788-8032.** 10 rms. A/C. $20 single; $30 double; $40 triple. No credit cards.

This modern two-story hotel is the only hotel in Sierpe, and is located at the dock from which boats leave to head down river to Drake Bay. So, if you are on your way to Drake Bay and expect to arrive in Sierpe late in the day (when no boats are heading downriver), this is where you should spend the night. Rooms are fairly large, though simply furnished, and are clean. The hotel can arrange most of the same tours that are offered at Drake Bay. These become particularly economical if you can organize a group of at least five people. There is an inexpensive open-air restaurant adjacent to the hotel.

2 Puerto Jiménez: Gateway to Corcovado National Park

35 kilometers W of Golfito by water (90 kilometers by road); 85 kilometers S of Palmar Norte.

Despite its small size and languid pace, Puerto Jiménez is a double boom town, where rough jungle gold panners mix with wealthy ecotourists, budget backpackers, and a surprising number of celebrities seeking a small dose of anonymity and escape. Located on the southeastern tip of the Osa peninsula, the town itself is just a couple of gravel streets, with the ubiquitous soccer field, a block of general stores, some inexpensive sodas, a butcher shop, and several bars. Scarlet macaws fly overhead and mealy parrots provide wake-up calls.

On first glance it is hard to imagine anything ever happening here, but looks are often deceiving. Signs in English on walls around town advertise a variety of tours, with most of the excursions being to nearby Corcovado National Park. The national park has its headquarters here, and this town makes an excellent base or embarkation point for exploring this vast wilderness. The budget lodgings listed here are all located in Puerto Jiménez proper, with the more luxurious places farther south on the Osa peninsula from here. As the home base and resupply station for gold miners—most of them panning illegally—seeking to strike it rich in the jungles in and around the park, Puerto Jiménez's streets can get pretty rowdy at night when panners actually cash-in a find—during those times, the bars host some hard drinking that knows few bounds or time limits.

ESSENTIALS

GETTING THERE & DEPARTING

By Plane **Sansa** (☎ **506/233-0397,** 233-3258, or 233-5330) has flights departing Monday through Saturday at 9am to Puerto Jiménez, and Sundays at 11:15am, from San José's Juan Santamaría International Airport. The former flight stops at Coto 47 en route; the latter flight is nonstop. Duration is 45 minutes nonstop; 1 hour and 15 minutes with a stop. Fare is $50 each way.

Travelair (☎ **506/220-3054** or 232-7883) has daily flights to Puerto Jiménez departing at 8:15am. These flights stop first in Golfito. Duration is 1 hour and 20 minutes. Fare is $81 dollars one-way; $136 roundtrip.

By Bus   Express buses leave San José daily at 6am and 12pm from Calle 12 between avenidas 7 and 9. Duration is 9 hours. Fare is $7.

Buses depart Puerto Jiménez for San José daily at 5 and 10:30am.

By Boat   There is daily passenger launch service from Golfito to Puerto Jiménez at 11am. The boat leaves from the municipal dock. Duration is 1 1/2 hours. Fare is $3.

It is also possible to charter a water taxi in Golfito for the trip across to Puerto Jiménez. You'll have to pay around $35 for an entire launch, which can usually hold up to seven people.

One launch a day departs Puerto Jiménez for Golfito from the public dock at 6am.

By Car   Take the Interamerican Highway east out of San José (through San Pedro and Cartago) and continue south on this road. In 3 hours or so, you'll pass through San Isidro de El General. In another 3 hours or so, take the turnoff for La Palma and Puerto Jiménez. This road is paved at first, but at Rincón turns to gravel. The last 35 kilometers are slow and rough, and, if it's the rainy season, too muddy for anything but a four-wheel-drive vehicle.

ORIENTATION

Puerto Jiménez is a dirt-laned town on the southern coast of the Osa peninsula. The public dock is over a bridge past the north end of the soccer field. The bus stop is two blocks east of the center of town. There are several general stores here. Puerto Jiménez is the most popular base for exploring Corcovado National Park.

EXPLORING CORCOVADO NATIONAL PARK

Although a few gringos have, over the years, come to Puerto Jiménez to try their luck at gold panning, the primary reason for coming here these days is to arrange a visit to Corcovado National Park. Within a couple of hours of the town by four-wheel-drive vehicle, there are several entrances to the park. However, there are no roads into the park, so once you reach any of the entrances, you'll have to start hiking. Exploring Corcovado National Park is not something to be undertaken lightly, but neither is it the expedition that some people make it out to be. The biggest problems of overnight backpacking trips through the park are the heat and humidity. Frequent rain storms cause the trails to be quite muddy, and should you choose the alternative of hiking on the beach, you will have to plan your hiking around the tides. Often there is no beach at all at high tide. Remember that you can always book a tour of Corcovado from a tour company in Puerto Jiménez or better yet, through a lodge in Drake Bay (see "Where to Stay & Eat," under "Drake Bay," above) or elsewhere along the Osa peninsula (see "Where to Stay & Eat Around the Osa Peninsula," below)—it's what most visitors do.

GETTING THERE & ENTRY POINTS

There are four primary entrances to the park, which are really just ranger stations reached by dirt tracks. Once you've reached them, you'll have to strap on a backpack and hike. Perhaps the easiest one to reach from Puerto Jiménez is the **La Leona ranger station,** accessible by car, bus, or taxi. If you choose to drive, take the dirt road from Puerto Jiménez to Carate (Carate is at the end of the road). From Carate it is a 3-kilometer hike to La Leona. To travel there by bus, pick up one of the collective buses leaving Puerto Jiménez for Carate daily at 6am and 2:30pm (returning at 8am and 4:30pm). A one-way fare costs $3.15. The bus will pass several campgrounds and small lodges as it approaches the park. Otherwise you can hire a taxi, which will charge approximately $35 dollars each way to Carate.

Alternatively, you can travel to **El Tigre,** about 14 kilometers by dirt road from Puerto Jiménez, where there is another ranger station. But, note that trails from El Tigre go only a short distance into the park. The third entrance is in **Los Patos,** which is reached from the town of La Palma northwest of Puerto Jiménez. From here, there is a 19-kilometer trail through the center of the park to Sirena, a ranger station and research facility (see "Beach Treks & Rain-Forest Hikes," below). Sirena has a landing strip that is used by charter flights. The northern entrance to the park is **San Pedrillo,** which you can reach by hiking from Serena; or by boat from Drake Bay or Sierpe (see "Beach Treks & Rain-Forest Hikes," below). It's 14 kilometers from Drake Bay.

If you're not into hiking in the heat, you can charter a plane in Puerto Jiménez to take you to Carate, Sirena, Drake Bay, or even Tiskita Lodge, which is across the gulf south of Playa Pavones. Contact **Alfa Romeo Aero Taxi** (☎ 775-1515) for details.

FEES & REGULATIONS

Park admission is $6 per person per day. Some of the ranger stations have simple dormitory-style lodgings, cantinas, and campsites, but all must be reserved in advance through the **Parks Service** at their offices in either Puerto Jiménez (☎ 506/735-5036) or San José (☎ 506/257-0922). You'll find the Puerto Jiménez office one block east of the main street at the end of town near the soccer field. Only 35 persons are allowed to camp at each ranger station. For more information about making arrangements while in San José, see chapter 3.

INFORMATION

If you plan to hike the beach trails from La Leona or San Pedrillo, be sure to pick up a tide table at the park headquarters' office in Puerto Jiménez. The tide changes rapidly; when it's high, the trails can be impassable.

BEACH TREKS & RAIN-FOREST HIKES

There are quite a few good hiking trails in the park. Some of the better known ones are the two beach routes, starting at either the La Leona or San Pedrillo ranger station. None of the park's hikes is easy, but the forest route from the Los Patos ranger station to Sirena, while long, is less taxing than either of the beach treks, which can only be completed when the tide is low. The Los Patos–Sirena hike is, as mentioned above, 19 miles through rain forest. It's beautiful and Sirena is a fascinating place to end up: A research facility, as well as ranger station, it's frequented primarily by scientists studying the rain forest. One of the longest hikes, from San Pedrillo to Sirena, can only be done during the dry season. Between any two stations, the hiking is arduous and will take all day, so it's best to rest between hikes, if at all possible. Some distances for reference: It's 16 kilometers from Sirena to La Leona (and vice versa); La Leona is 25 miles along the beach to San Pedrillo; from San Pedrillo, it's another 9 kilometers to Marenco Biological Reserve (see "Where to Stay & Eat" in "Drake Bay," for lodging information).

WHERE TO STAY & EAT IN THE PARK: CAMPSITES, CABINS & CANTINAS

The La Leona ranger station has a campground, some very basic dormitory-style cabins, and a cantina. Reservations are essential at the various ranger stations if you plan on eating or sleeping inside the park. Campsites in the park are $1.50 per person per night. A dorm bed will run you $2.50, and meals are around $13.50 per day. There is camping and a cantina at Los Patos ranger station. Sirena has bunks, a campground, and a cantina. Every ranger station has potable water, but it's advisable to pack in your own; whatever you do, don't drink stream water.

ACTIVE SPORTS OUTSIDE THE PARK

Closer to Puerto Jiménez, kayaking trips around the estuary and up into the mangroves and out into the gulf are popular. Contact **Escondido Trex** (☎ **506/735-5210**), which has an office in the Sodita Carolina restaurant. More adventurous multi-day trips are also available.

If you're interested in doing some billfishing or deep-sea fishing, check around the public dock for notices of people with charter boats. Rates are usually around $400 for a full day or $300 for a half-day.

WHERE TO STAY IN PUERTO JIMÉNEZ
DOUBLES FOR LESS THAN $15

Cabinas Marcelina. Puerto Jiménez. ☎ 506/735-5007. Fax 506/735-5045. 6 rms (all with private bath). $5 single; $10 double; $14.20 triple. No credit cards.

Located at the southern end of Puerto Jiménez's main street, these basic rooms are a good choice for anyone on a shoestring budget. The owner keeps the tile-floored rooms clean and there is surprisingly little mildew (always a problem in cinderblock buildings). Bathrooms are basic but adequate.

Cabinas Puerto Jiménez. 50 meters north of Bar y Restaurant El Rancho, Puerto Jiménez. ☎ **506/735-5090** or 506/735-5152. 10 rms (all with private bath). $6 single; $12 double; $18 triple. No credit cards.

Located right on the waterfront at the north end of the soccer field, this inexpensive accommodation even offers a few rooms with views of the bay. The exterior of the building, with its varnished wood, is probably more appealing than the rooms themselves. Though large, the guest rooms have cement floors and are very basic. However, they are kept very clean and are the best choice in town for travelers on a tight budget.

DOUBLES FOR LESS THAN $35

Agua Luna. In front of the public dock, Puerto Jiménez. ☎ **506/735-5034** or 506/735-5108. 14 rms (all with private bath). A/C TV. $30 single, double, or triple. No credit cards.

These very reasonably priced rooms offer the most luxury of any of the in-town lodgings in Puerto Jiménez. Agua Luna is located right at the foot of the town's public dock and backs up to a mangrove forest. The six older rooms directly face the gulf, across a fenced-in gravel parking area. The most surprising feature in each of these rooms is the huge bathroom, which includes both a shower and a tub facing a picture window that looks into the mangroves. There are two double beds in each room, and on the tiled verandah out front you'll find hammocks for lounging. The newer rooms were still under construction when I last visited. These are located a half-block away, and will be slightly smaller and slightly cheaper than those in the original building.

Hotel Manglares. Apdo. 55-8203, Puerto Jiménez. ☎ **506/735-5002.** Fax 506/735-5121. 10 rms. $25 single; $30 double. MC, V.

This hotel was once the best choice in town, but it's been resting on its laurels for a while now; consequently, the rooms are a bit rundown. Located on the edge of the mangrove forest, some of its rooms can only be reached by an elevated walkway through the mangroves. The trees, and several bird feeders, assure good bird watching. The rooms in front are a bit small and can be musty. The rooms in back are slightly larger and more attractive, and surprisingly don't cost any extra. These latter rooms are surrounded by a small groomed garden, and back up on the mangroves. All the rooms have fans to keep you cool, and there is a restaurant serving inexpensive Tico standards, as well as seafood and pizza.

DOUBLES FOR LESS THAN $45

✪ **Doña Leta's Bungalows.** Apdo. 91, Puerto Jiménez, ☎/fax **506/735-5180.** 8 bungalows. $45 single or double; $55 triple. Discounts in the off-season. No credit cards.

These attractive new cabins are located on a spit of land jutting out into the gulf, just east of town and the airstrip. The smaller cabins are octagonal and have just one double bed, while the larger ones feature a sleeping loft, with a double and single bed above, and a double bed below. All the cabins come with a refrigerator, two-burner stove, private bath, and carved-wood door. There is a large central deck built under and around a large fig tree that is frequented by scarlet macaws. The grounds also include a couple of volleyball nets, a small patch of beach, and a semi-groomed trail through the mangroves.

WHERE TO STAY & EAT AROUND THE OSA PENINSULA

As with most of the lodges in Drake Bay, the accommodations listed in this section include three meals a day in their rates and do a large share of their business in package trips. Per-night rates are listed, but be sure to ask about package rates if you plan to stay a while; they could save you money.

WORTH A SPLURGE

✪ **Bosque del Cabo Wilderness Lodge.** Osa peninsula (mailing address in the U.S.: Interlink 528, P.O. Box 025635, Miami, FL 33152). ☎/fax **506/735-5206.** 6 cabins. $90–$100 single; $140–$160 double; $150 triple. All rates include three meals daily. No credit cards.

This simple yet tasteful lodge is located 500 feet above the water at the southern tip of the Osa peninsula, where the Golfo Dulce meets the Pacific Ocean. It is surrounded by 300 acres of land that the owners purchased to preserve a piece of the rain forest. The thatched-roof cabins are attractively furnished and are set amid beautiful gardens. Meals are well prepared and filling, and usually feature fruits grown here. There's a trail down to a secluded beach that has some tide pools. Surfing is a popular activity here, as are hiking and horseback riding. Trips to the national park or fishing can be arranged. A taxi from Puerto Jiménez is $15.

✪ **Corcovado Lodge Tent Camp.** Costa Rica Expeditions, Apdo. 6941-1000, San José. ☎ **506/257-0766** or 506/222-0333. Fax 506/257-1665. 20 tents. $62.60 single; $110.60 double. All rates include three meals daily. AE, MC, V.

Costa Rica Expeditions' Corcovado Lodge Tent Camp is a pioneer in the growing trend towards "luxury" camping lodges. The 20 spacious tents here are all set in a small compound on a low bluff right above the beach. Each tent has two twin beds, a table, and a couple of folding chairs on the front deck. Toilets and showers are a short walk away. Behind the tent camp, forested mountains rise up, and just a few minutes' walk away is the entrance to Corcovado National Park. To reach this lodge is an adventure in itself. You can either take a five-seater chartered plane to the gravel landing strip at Carate and then walk for 45 minutes to the lodge, or take the lodge's specially designed pontoon boat from Golfito or Puerto Jiménez. If you have a four-wheel-drive vehicle, you can get as far as the landing strip and then walk the remaining 1.5 kilometers. Once you're here, you have a real sense of being away from it all.

Meals are served in a large screen-walled dining room furnished with picnic tables. A separate but similar building is furnished with hammocks, a small bar, and a few board games. Services at the lodge include guided walks and boat excursions both into the national park and out to Caño Island. The newest addition to the lodge is a canopy platform located 120 feet up an ancient Ajo tree. Package rates that include transportation and tours are also available, and are actually the way most people come here.

WHERE TO EAT IN PUERTO JIMÉNEZ

Bar Restaurant Agua Luna. 25 meters north of the public pier. ☎ **506/735-5033.** Reservations not accepted. Main courses $2.50–$8.50. No credit cards. Daily 9am–11pm. COSTA RICAN.

The first restaurant you come to after arriving in Puerto Jiménez by boat is also one of the best restaurants in town. Little more than a collection of tiny thatched ranchos (the equivalent of Mexican *palapas*), set amid shady gardens, Agua Luna has a nice view of the water. The bar is popular and the music is usually loud, so don't expect a quiet, romantic dinner for two. Seafood is plentiful and fresh, and prices for fish dinners are low even for Costa Rica—enjoy.

Sodita Carolina. On the main street. ☎ **506/735-5185.** Reservations not accepted. Most items $2.15–$8. No credit cards. Daily 6am–10 or 11pm. COSTA RICAN.

This is Puerto Jiménez's budget travelers' hangout and also serves as an unofficial information center. The restaurant is in the center of the town's main street. The walls are painted with colorful jungle and wildlife scenes, to whet the appetites of new arrivals and satisfy the needs of armchair travelers. Once again, seafood is the way to go. They've got good fried fish as well as a variety of ceviches. The black-bean soup is usually good, and the casados are filling and cost less than $3. If you need a place to stay, there are five basic rooms with cement floors and private baths behind the restaurant. The rooms cost $5 per person, are located behind the kitchen, and front a pretty unattractive yard.

3 Golfito

87 kilometers S of Palmar Norte; 337 kilometers S of San José

This old banana port is set on the north side of the Golfo Dulce and is at the foot of lush green mountains. The setting alone is beautiful enough to make this one of the most attractive cities in the country, but Golfito also has an undeniable charm all its own. Sure, the area around the municipal park is kind of seedy, but if you go a little bit farther along the bay, you come to the old United Fruit Company housing. Here you'll find well-maintained wooden houses painted bright colors and surrounded by neatly manicured gardens. These old homes are experiencing a sort of renaissance as they become small hotels catering to shoppers visiting the adjacent duty-free shopping center. Golfito is the gateway to several jungle lodges located around the gulf, as well as the main embarkation point for ferries and water taxis to Playa Zancudo, Pavones, and Puerto Jiménez. Golfito is also close to some lovely botanical gardens that you can easily spend a day or more touring—not to mention the great opportunities for bird watching and other activities.

ESSENTIALS
GETTING THERE & DEPARTING

By Plane Sansa (☎ **506/233-0397,** 233-3258, or 233-5330) has flights to Golfito departing Monday through Saturday at 6am; Wednesday through Friday at 1pm; and Sundays at 11:15am from San José's Juan Santamaría International Airport. Duration is 45 minutes. Fare is $50 each way.

Sansa returns to San José Monday through Saturday at 7am; Wednesday through Friday at 2pm; and Sundays at 12:15pm.

Travelair (☎ **506/220-3054** or 232-7883) has flights to Golfito daily at 8:15am from San José's Pavas International Airport. The flight stops in Quepos and Palmar Sur en route. Duration is 1 hour. Fare is $76 one way, $129 round-trip.

Travelair returns to San José daily at 9:45am with a stop at Quepos en route.

By Bus Express buses leave San José daily at 7am and 3pm from Avenida 18 between calles 2 and 4. Duration is 8 hours. Fare is $6.50.

Buses depart Golfito for San José daily at 5am and 1pm from the bus station near the municipal dock.

By Boat A passenger launch leaves Puerto Jiménez, on the Osa peninsula, daily at 6am. Duration is 1¹/₂ hours. Fare is $3.

You may also be able to hire a boat to take you across the Golfo Dulce to Golfito. However, as there are not very many available in Puerto Jiménez, you're likely to have to pay quite bit ($40 to $65 each way) for such a service.

The passenger launch departs Golfito for Puerto Jiménez daily at 11am.

By Car It is a straight shot down the Interamerican Highway south from San José to Golfito. However, it is a long and arduous road. In the 8 hours it takes to drive the 337 kilometers from San José, you'll pass over the Cerro de la Muerte (Mountain of Death), which is infamous for its dense fog and torrential downpours. Also, for almost the entire length of this road, you will have to contend with potholes of gargantuan proportions. Just remember that if the road is suddenly smooth and in great shape, you can bet that around the next bend there will be a bottomless pothole that you can't swerve around. Take it easy.

ORIENTATION

Getting Around If you can't get to your next destination by boat, bus, or car, **Alfa Romeo Aero Taxi** (☎ **775-1515** or 296-5596) runs charters to most of the nearby destinations, including Carate, Drake Bay, Sirena, and Puerto Jiménez. A taxi ride anywhere in town should cost around 75¢ each way.

Fast Facts If you need to **exchange money,** you can do so at the **gas station,** or "La Bomba," in the middle of town. There is a **laundromat** on the upper street of the small downtown that charges $3 for a 5-pound load. If you drop off your clothes in the morning, they'll be ready in the afternoon.

SPORTFISHING

The waters off Golfito offer some of the best sportfishing in Costa Rica, and if you'd like to try hooking into a possible world-record marlin or sailfish, contact Steve Lino at **Golfito Sportfishing** (☎/fax 382-2716). A full-day's fishing trip will cost between $350 and $550. This company operates out of nearby Zancudo Beach and also offers multi-day packages. Other companies to check with are **Leomar Sportfishing & Diving** (☎ 775-0230) and **Roy's Zancudo Lodge** (☎ 775-0515), which offer trips at similar prices.

Several lodgings in Golfito and the surrounding area offer guided fishing trips or special fishing packages. They are also good places for camaraderie or just to share a drink with like-minded folks. In Golfito, check out Las Gaviotas Hotel; outside Golfito, there's Punta Encanto.

KAYAKING

If you want to explore the waters of the Golfo Dulce check out **Yak Yak Kayaks** (☎ 775-1179). These folks offer a variety of tours for everyone from beginners to advanced kayakers. They include paddles to nearby mangroves and an island with a waterfall and a freshwater swimming hole, and overnight tours to Playa Zancudo. Rates are $7 per hour for single kayaks; $10 per hour for two-person kayaks. A half-day tour, including lunch, runs around $50 per person. Yak Yak Kayaks has their "office" on the beach in front of Las Gaviotas Hotel.

TOURING THE BOTANICAL GARDENS

About 30 minutes by boat out of Golfito, you'll find **Casa Orchideas,** a private botanical garden. Two-hour tours of the gardens cost $5 per person with a minimum of four people. Most hotels in the region can organize a tour to the garden; if not, you'll have to hire a boat to get there, which should cost you around $75 for the trip and waiting time.

If you have a serious interest in botanical gardens, consider an excursion to **Wilson Botanical Gardens** (☎ 773-3278 or 240-6696), located in the town of San Vito, about 65 kilometers to the northeast. The gardens are owned by the Organization for Tropical Studies and include more than 2,000 species of tropical plants from around the world. Among the plants grown here are many endangered species, which makes the gardens of interest to botanical researchers. Despite the scientific aspects of the gardens, there are also many beautiful and unusual flowers amid the manicured grounds. A full day in the gardens, including lunch, will cost you $17. A half-day walk around costs $8.

If you'd like to stay the night here, there are rustic rooms and cabins. Rates, including three meals, run between $53 and $71 per person. You need to make reservations beforehand if you wish to spend the night. You'll find the gardens about 6 kilometers before San Vito. To get here from Golfito, drive back out to the Interamerican Highway and continue south toward Panama. In Cuidad Neily, turn north.

EXPLORING THE TOWN

Other than sportfishing or kayaking its waters and exploring nearby botanical gardens, there isn't a whole lot to do in Golfito other than make connections to other places. You can walk or drive through town admiring the United Fruit Company buildings, drop in at one of the souvenir shops, and have a drink overlooking the gulf. However, these simple pursuits may be augmented by more tourist-oriented activities as this area gains in popularity. Check the bulletin boards in restaurants around town to see what sort of tours or activities are available when you arrive.

WHERE TO STAY IN GOLFITO
DOUBLES FOR LESS THAN $15

Cabinas Jardin Cervecero Alamedas. 100 meters south of the Depósito Libre, Golfito. ☎ **506/775-0126.** 6 rms (all with private bath). $12.25–$14 single, double, or triple. AE, MC, V.

These six new rooms have been built across the gravel driveway from one of the more popular restaurants in the area around the free port. The rooms are clean, and each has one double, one single, and one bunk bed. I prefer the upstairs rooms which have wood, instead of concrete, floors and more air circulation.

Casa Blanca Lodge. 300 meters south of the Depósito Libre, Golfito. ☎ **506/775-0124.** 10 rms (all with private bath). $5–$7.50 single; $10–$15 double; $15 triple or quad. No credit cards.

In the old United Fruit Company neighborhood near the airport, there are many pretty, old houses surrounded by attractive, neatly manicured gardens. Several of these old homes have been turned into inexpensive hotels catering to shoppers visiting the free port. This is one of the nicer of the small family-run hotels. The rooms in the new annex are more attractive and more comfortable than those in the main building, which tend to be dark and musty.

DOUBLES FOR LESS THAN $25

Golfo Azul. Barrio Alameda, 300 meters south of the Depósito Libre, Golfito. ☎ **506/775-0871.** Fax 506/775-1849. 24 rms. $18.75 single, double, or triple; $23–$32 single to quad with A/C. MC, V.

Azul offers a quiet location amid the most attractive part of Golfito. Many of the people who stay here are Ticos in town to shop at the nearby Depósito Libre (free port). However, anyone will appreciate the clean rooms. The smallest rooms are cramped, but there are larger rooms, some with high ceilings that make them feel even more spacious. Bathrooms are tiled and have hot water, and rooms have either fans or air-conditioning. The hotel's restaurant is housed in an older building and is brilliantly white inside and out. Meals are quite reasonably priced.

DOUBLES FOR LESS THAN $35

Las Gaviotas Hotel. Apdo. 12-8201, Golfito. ☎ **506/775-0062.** Fax 506/775-0544. 18 rms, 3 cabañas. $30–$35 single or double; $32.50–$45 triple; $70 cabaña. AE, MC, V.

If you want to be right on the water, this is a good option in Golfito. Situated a short taxi ride out of town on the road that leads to the Interamerican Highway, Las Gaviotas has long been the hotel of choice on the Golfo Dulce. There is a long pier that attracts the sailboat and sportfishing crowd. For landlubbers, there's a small pool built out over the water. Guest rooms, which are set amid attractive gardens, all face the ocean, and though they are quite large, they're a bit Spartan and are starting to show their age. There are small tiled patios in front of all the rooms, and the cabañas have little kitchens. The more expensive rooms have air-conditioning. A large open-air restaurant looks over the pool to the gulf, while around the corner there is a large open-air bar. In addition, there's a small gift shop. The waterfront location is this hotel's greatest asset.

WORTH A SPLURGE

Complejo Turístico Samoa del Sur. 100 meters north of the public dock. ☎ **506/775-0233.** Fax 506/775-0573. 14 rms. TV TEL. $40 single to quad. AE, MC, V.

It's hard to miss the two giant thatched spires that house this new hotel's already-established restaurant and bar. The rooms are spacious and clean. Varnished-wood headboards complement two firm and comfortable double beds. There are red-tile floors, modern bathrooms, and carved-wood doors. The rooms all share a long covered verandah that is set perpendicular to the gulf, so there aren't any views to speak of here. If you want to watch the water, you're better off grabbing a table at the restaurant.

✪ **Hotel Sierra.** Apdo. 37, Golfito (Apdo. 5304-1000, San José). ☎ **506/775-0666** or 506/233-9693; 506/224-3300 in San José. Fax 506/775-0087 or 506/224-3399 in San José. 72 rms. A/C TV TEL. $39 single; $46.80 double; $53.30 triple. AE, DC, MC, V.

Located right beside the airstrip, the Hotel Sierra has become the hotel of choice of people flying in and out of Golfito. It offers the most luxurious accommodations in town, with a courtyard swimming pool, aviaries full of squawking macaws, and a big dining room and bar. The building is constructed to be as open and breezy as possible, though the guest rooms also have modern air conditioners. Covered walkways connect the hotel's various buildings, and lots of tropical plants and cages full of birds lend an exotic flavor to the surroundings. The rooms have pale blue–tile floors, and windows on two sides to let in plenty of light. Bathrooms are very large, and there are also safes in all the rooms. The swimming pool is fairly large and even has a swim-up bar. For light meals and snacks, there is a casual restaurant on the far side of the pool. Prices in the main dining room are also fairly moderate, and there are several lobster dishes for around $15. All in all, this place offers very good value.

AN UNFORGETTABLE TROPICAL HIDEAWAY

✪ **Rainbow Adventures.** Apdo. 63, Golfito (mailing address in the U.S.: Michael Medill, 5875 N. Kaiser Rd., Portland, OR 97229). ☎ **506/775-0220,** or 503/690-7750 in the U.S. Fax 503/690-7735 in the U.S. 4 rms, 3 cabins. $125–$143 single; $160–$180 double; $45 each additional person. All rates include three meals daily, plus transportation to and from Golfito. No credit cards.

If your vision of the perfect tropical hideaway is a luxurious little open-walled cabin overlooking a secluded beach backed by tropical jungle, then Rainbow Adventures may just be your pot of gold. This isolated lodge is surrounded by 1,000 acres of rain forest that abuts Corcovado National Park. The grounds immediately surrounding the lodge are neatly manicured gardens planted with exotic fruit trees, flowering shrubs, and palms from around the world. Your adventure begins in Golfito, where the lodge's speedboat picks you up for the 45-minute boat ride to the lodge. Days are spent lounging in hammocks, swimming, sunning, and exploring the jungle, reading, bird and wild animal watching, and maybe a bit of fishing. But mostly you get to just do nothing, and not feel guilty about it.

Rooms in the main lodge, which is made almost completely of polished tropical hardwoods, are all decorated with antiques, stained glass, and Oriental carpets. The second-floor rooms are the least expensive and smallest rooms available. However, they still have plenty of room. For just a little more, you can have the penthouse, a large third-floor room with four open walls and tree-top views of the gulf. Only slightly more expensive are the spacious cabinas, which are built on stilts and have open living rooms and large bedrooms that can be divided into small rooms.

Meals are served family-style with a set menu each evening. However, the creativity of the chef and the quantities of food guarantee that everyone leaves the table satisfied. Though beer is available, you should bring your own liquor. Fishing trips (barracuda, roosterfish, snook, and red snapper are plentiful), boat charters ($35 per hour for a boat that can carry four passengers), and guided hikes can all be arranged. The lodge has several well-maintained trails through primary rain forest, with jungle waterfalls and wonderful swimming holes. A private beach provides protected swimming and, in the dry season, some good snorkeling (equipment available at no charge).

WHERE TO EAT

In addition to the restaurants listed below, **Tingo's** is a new pizza place worth trying and **Luis Brenes' Restaurant** (across from the gas station) is a popular hangout and a good place to gather information on trips and tours around the gulf.

Jardin Cervecero Alamedas. 100 meters south of the Depósito Libre. ☎ **506/775-0126.** Main courses $2.80–$10. AE, MC, V. Daily 7am–midnight (closed Sunday and Monday during the low season). COSTA RICAN/SEAFOOD.

If you are staying at the Hotel Sierra, Golfo Azul, or any of the other hotels near the Depósito Libre, this should be your first choice when deciding where to eat. The restaurant is located underneath an old house that is built on stilts. White chairs and dark green tablecloths provide a sort of fern-bar feel, while outside real tropical gardens surround the house. There are great deals on seafood here, including a long list of ceviches. The only drawback is that they tend to play the stereo too loud.

Soda La Cubana. 150 meters east of the gas station, on the upper road through downtown Golfito. No phone. Main courses $2.80–$7.50. No credit cards. Daily 6am–10 pm. COSTA RICAN.

This small, open-air restaurant commands a good view of the gulf and serves hearty meals at rock-bottom prices. The menu is pretty basic, but a fresh whole fish in garlic sauce will cost you just $4.

Samoa del Sur. 100 meters north of the public dock. ☎ **506/775-0233.** Main courses $2.80–$17.50. AE, MC, V. Daily 8am–2am. CONTINENTAL.

It's hard to miss the Samoa del Sur. It's that huge circular rancho just north of the public dock. This oversized jungle structure seems out of place in a town where cinderblocks are the preferred construction material, but its tropical atmosphere is certainly well appreciated. The restaurant's biggest surprise, however, is its extensive menu of familiar continental and French dishes such as onion soup, salade niçoise, filet-of-fish meuniere, and paella. There are also pizzas and spaghetti. There's a good view of the gulf, which makes this great spot for a sunset drink or dinner. In addition to the food, the giant rancho also houses a pool table, several high-quality dart boards, and a big-screen TV. The bar sometimes stays open all night.

4 Playa Zancudo

19 kilometers S of Golfito (by boat); 35 kilometers S of Golfito (by road)

Although the word is starting to get out, Playa Zancudo remains one of Costa Rica's main backpacker hangouts, which means that there are plenty of cheap rooms, some cheap places to eat, and lots of young gringos around. These factors alone are enough to keep Zancudo jumping through the winter months. The beach itself is long and flat, and because it is protected from the full force of Pacific waves, it's relatively good for swimming. However, it is certainly not one of the most beautiful beaches in the country. Behind the beach, which disappears at high tide, are piles of driftwood and plastic flotsam and jetsam that have washed up on the shore. There is a splendid view across the Golfo Dulce, though, and the sunsets are hard to beat. Because there is a mangrove swamp directly behind the beach, mosquitoes here can be a problem. Be sure to bring insect repellent.

ESSENTIALS
GETTING THERE

By Plane The nearest airport is in Golfito. See "Golfito: A Place for Sportfishing & Touring Botanical Gardens," above, for details.

By Boat Water taxis can be hired in Golfito to make the trip out to Playa Zancudo. However, trips depend on the tides and weather conditions. You're more likely to get a boat early in the morning before the winds pick up and make the waters choppy. Currently it costs around $7 per person for a water taxi, with a minimum charge of $20. If you can round up any sort of group, be sure to negotiate.

Alternatively, there is a passenger launch that leaves from the municipal dock in Golfito daily at 4:45 and 7:30am and noon. Beacause the schedule sometimes changes, be sure to ask in town for the current schedule. Trip duration is 45 minutes. Fare is $1.50.

By Bus   There is a daily bus from Golfito to Zancudo, at 1:30pm. The bus leaves from near the Free Port and picks up passengers all along the main road. Fare is $1.25. Duration is 3 to 4 hours. This bus sometimes stops running in the rainy season, so be sure to ask at your hotel or call the **Golfito Office of Tourist Services** (☎ **506/775-0131**).

By Car   If you've got a four-wheel-drive vehicle, you should be able to make it out to Zancudo even in the rainy season, but be sure to ask in Golfito before leaving the paved road. A four-wheel-drive taxi will cost around $20 from Golfito. It takes about 2 hours when the road is in good condition.

DEPARTING

The public launch to Golfito leaves daily at 6am and 1:30pm from the dock near the school in the center of Zancudo. If you're heading to Pavones or the Osa peninsula next, contact Zancudo Boat Tours, which is sometimes willing to make the trips to these two places. They charge $10 per person with a minimum charge of $20 for the Golfito trip; and $15 per person, with a $30 minimum for the Puerto Jiménez trip.

ORIENTATION

Zancudo is a long, narrow peninsula (sometimes only 100 yards or so wide) at the mouth of the Río Colorado. On one side is the beach, on the other is a mangrove swamp. There is only one road that runs the length of the beach, and it is along this road, spread out over several kilometers of long, flat beach, that you will find the hotels mentioned here. It's about a 30-minute walk from the public dock near the school to the popular Cabinas Sol y Mar.

WHAT TO SEE & DO

The main activity at Zancudo is relaxing, and folks take it seriously. There are hammocks at almost every lodge, and if you bring a few good books, you can spend quite a few hours swinging slowly in the tropical breezes. Sure, there's a bar that doubles as a disco, but people are more likely to spend their time just hanging out in restaurants meeting like-minded folks or playing board games. Depending on the season, you might be able to rustle up a volleyball or horseshoes game at Sol y Mar.

If you're feeling more energetic, you might consider a boat tour. Susan and Andrew Robertson, who rent out two small houses in Zancudo, also operate **Zancudo Boat Tours** (☎ **506/775-0353**, leave a message). Excursions they offer include a trip up the Río Coto to bird- and wildlife-watch, snorkeling trips, and trips to the Casa Orchidia botanical garden. Tour prices are $25 to $35 per person for half-day tours.

WHERE TO STAY
DOUBLES FOR LESS THAN $15

Cabinas Zancudo. Playa Zancudo, Golfito. ☎ **506/773-3027.** 20 rms (all with private bath). $5 single; $10 double; $15 triple. No credit cards.

This is your basic Tico weekend beach-getaway spot. The rooms are small, dark, and musty. There's no cross-ventilation, and half of the rooms are in a building facing the back wall of another building. Weekends are crowded and can be noisy, especially in the dry season. However, if you don't have much money to spend, this is a good choice. There is a *pulperia* (general store) on the premises, as well as a restaurant and bar.

DOUBLES FOR LESS THAN $25

✪ **Cabinas Sol y Mar.** Apdo. 87, Playa Zancudo, Golfito. ☎/fax **506/775-0353.** 4 rms (all with private bath). Dec 1–Apr 30 $23 single, $30 double; May 1–Nov 30 $17 single, $25 double. V (add 6% surcharge).

Although owners Bob and Monika Hara have only four rooms, they run the most popular lodging in Zancudo. Two of the rooms are modified geodesic domes with tile floors, verandahs, and tin roofs. The bathrooms have unusual showers that consist of a tiled platform surrounded by smooth river rocks. The bathrooms also have translucent roofs that flood the rooms with light. The other two rooms are larger and newer, but aren't as architecturally interesting. You'll have to decide between space and character. There is an adjacent open-air restaurant that is the best and most popular place to eat in Zancudo. Seafood dishes are the specialty here (the whole fried fish is good) and prices are very reasonable.

Hotel Los Almendros. Apdo. 41, Playa Zancudo, Golfito. ☎ **506/284-7759.** 14 rms (all with private bath). $20 single, $25 double, $30 triple; $40 single with A/C, $50 double with A/C. V.

Primarily a fishing lodge, this simple lodging at the north end of Zancudo is also one of the more comfortable and attractive places in town. All of the rooms look out onto a bright green lawn of soft grass, with the waves crashing on the beach a few steps beyond. They have hardwood floors, small, clean bathrooms, ceiling and floor fans, and small verandahs. There is a small restaurant that, of course, specializes in fresh fish. Meals run between $4 and $7 per person. The lodge offers many different types of fishing excursions.

DOUBLES FOR LESS THAN $35

Los Cocos. Apdo. 88, Golfito. ☎ **506/775-0353** (leave a message). 3 cabins. $30–$35 per night; $180–$210 per week. No credit cards.

Although owners Susan and Andrew Robertson prefer to rent their three small houses by the week or month, in a pinch they'll rent by the night. Set under the trees near Cabinas Sol y Mar (which is where you go to check in at Los Cocos), two of these houses served as banana-plantation housing in a former life, until the Robertsons salvaged them and placed them in their current location. The newest cabin is a thatched-roof affair with a sleeping loft. All have big verandahs and bedrooms, and large eat-in kitchens. Bathrooms are down a few steps in back and have hot water. If you plan to stay in Zancudo for a while, you'll appreciate the refrigerator and hot plate.

WHERE TO EAT

The best restaurant in Zancudo is at **Cabinas Sol y Mar.** The small open-air spot is also a popular hangout for resident gringos as well as travelers.

5 Playa Pavones: A Surfer's Mecca

40 kilometers S of Golfito

Touted as the world's longest rideable left wave, Pavones is a legendary surf spot. It takes around 6 feet of swell to get this wave cranking, but when the surf's up, you're in for a long, long ride. So long, in fact, that it's easier to walk back up the beach to where the wave is breaking than it is to paddle back. The swells are most consistent here during the rainy season, but you're likely to find surfers here year-round. Other than surfing, nothing much goes on here. However, the beach is quite nice, with some rocky areas that give Pavones a bit more visual appeal than Zancudo has. If you stick around for a while, you'll learn that the beach has been the site of a bitter land dispute. Various lodges are starting to sprout up, but as of yet, most accommodations here are very basic. Pavones is a tiny village with few amenities and no electricity.

Other than surfing when the surf is up and swimming when it's not, there isn't a whole lot to do. You can walk the beach, swing in your hammock, or if you feel energetic, go for a ride on horseback.

ESSENTIALS
GETTING THERE & DEPARTING

By Plane   The nearest airport is in Golfito. See "Golfito: A Place for Sportfishing & Touring Botanical Gardens," above, for details.

By Bus   There is a bus to Pavones from Golfito daily at 2pm. Duration is 3 to 4 hours. Fare is $1.80.

The bus to Golfito departs Pavones daily at 5am.

By Car   If you have a four-wheel-drive vehicle, you should be able to get to Pavones even in the rainy season, but be sure to ask in Golfito before leaving the paved road. A four-wheel-drive taxi from Golfito to Pavones will cost between $30 and $40. It takes around 3 hours from Golfito.

WHERE TO STAY & EAT

In Pavones, there are several very basic lodges renting rooms for between $10 and $20 per night for a double room. There are also a couple of sodas where you can get Tico meals. To make reservations at any of the lodges in Pavones, you can try calling the **Golfito Office of Tourist Services** (☎ **506/775-0131**).

DOUBLES FOR LESS THAN $25

Casa Impacto. Apdo. 133, Golfito. ☎ **506/775-0637.** 5 rms (all with private bath). $10 single; $20 double. No credit cards.

Casa Impacto is an octagonal house with four simple rooms plus a separate cabin. Most of its clients are surfers, and of course there are surfboards for rent. You can also rent horses, for $10 per hour, or a sea kayak. Meals will run you around $20 per person per day and include fresh juices, pizzas, and freshly baked breads and cakes. Electricity is provided by photovoltaic cells.

11 The Caribbean Coast

Although this was the coast Christopher Columbus discovered in 1502 and christened Costa Rica (Rich Coast), it has until recently remained *terra incognita*. It was not until 1987 that the Guápiles Highway opened between San José and Limón. Prior to that the only routes down to this region were the famous jungle train (which is no longer in operation) and the narrow winding road from Turrialba to Siquírres. More than half of this coastline is still inaccessible except by boat or small plane. This inaccessibility has helped preserve large tracts of virgin lowland rain forest, which are now set aside as Tortuguero National Park and Barra del Colorado National Wildlife Refuge. These two parks, on the northern reaches of this coast, together form one of Costa Rica's most popular destinations with ecotravelers. Of particular interest are the sea turtles that nest along this stretch of coast. Another intriguing national park in this area is in Cahuita, a beach town. The park was set up to preserve 500 acres of coral reef, but its palm-tree lined beaches are stunningly perfect.

So remote was the Caribbean coast from Costa Rica's population centers in the Central Valley that it developed a culture all its own. Until the 1870s, there were few non-Indians in this area. However, when Minor Keith built the railroad to San José and began planting bananas, he brought in black laborers from Jamaica and the Antilles to lay the track and work the plantations. These workers and their descendants established fishing and farming communities up and down the coast. Today dreadlocked Rastafarians, reggae music, Creole cooking, and the English-based patois of this Afro-Caribbean culture give this region a distinctly Jamaican flavor. Many visitors find fascinating this striking contrast with the Spanish-derived Costa Rican culture. However, in beach towns such as Cahuita and Puerto Viejo, some visitors see only a drug-and-surf culture—and there is no denying that surfing and partying are a way of life for many people, local and visitor alike, in these two towns. Although you need not participate in such activities, if this lifestyle is offensive to you, consider heading to one of the many beaches on the Pacific coast.

1 Tortuguero National Park

250 kilometers NE of San José

"Tortuguero" comes from the Spanish name for the giant sea turtles (*tortugas*) that nest on the beaches of this region every year from mid-February to mid-October. The chance to see nesting sea turtles is what attracts many people to this remote region. However, just as many come to explore the intricate network of jungle canals that serve as the main transportation arteries here. This stretch of coast is connected to Limón, the Caribbean coast's only port city, by way of a series of rivers and canals that parallel the sea, often only 100 yards or so from the beach. This aquatic highway is lined for much of its length with dense rain forest that is home to howler monkeys, three-toed sloths, toucans, and great green macaws. A trip up the canals is akin to cruising the Amazon, though on a much smaller scale.

North of Tortuguero is **Barra del Colorado National Wildlife Refuge.** This area is better known among anglers than naturalists and is even more remote. You can reach it by continuing up the canals from Tortuguero or by boat from Puerto Viejo de Sarapiquí along the Río Sarapiquí. The waters at the mouth of the Río Colorado offer some of the best tarpon and snook fishing in the world. See chapter 3 for listings of fishing lodges near Barra del Colorado.

Overall, remember the climate in this region: It rains a lot here—over 200 inches per year— so you can expect rain at any time of the year.

ESSENTIALS
GETTING THERE & DEPARTING

By Plane   Sansa (☎ **506/233-0397,** 506/233-3258, or 506/233-5330) has flights departing Tuesday, Thursday, and Saturday at 6am for Barra del Colorado from San José's Juan Santamaría International Airport. Duration is 30 minutes. Fare is $40 one way. From here you will have to take a water taxi, or arrange pickup with your hotel.

Travelair (☎ **506/220-3054** and 506/232-7883) has flights departing daily at 6am for Tortuguero, with an intermediate stop in Barra del Colorado, from San José's Pavas International Airport. Duration is 55 minutes (to Tortuguero). Fare is $72 one way, $110 round-trip.

In addition, many lodges in this area operate charter flights as part of their package trips.

If you are traveling independently, Sansa flights leave Barra del Colorado at 6:45am on Tuesday, Thursday, and Saturday for San José. Travelair flights depart Tortuguero daily at 7:05am and fly directly to San José.

By Boat   Although flying to Tortuguero is convenient if you have only a limited amount of time, a boat trip through the canals and rivers of this region is often the highlight of any visit to Tortuguero. All of the more expensive lodges here operate boats, and will make arrangements for you to travel by boat through the canals. However, if you are coming here on the cheap and plan to stay at one of the less expensive lodges or at a budget cabina in Tortuguero, you will have to arrange your own transportation. In this case, you have a couple of options.

The most direct method is to take a bus from San José to Limón and then on to the public docks in Moín (just north of Limón), and try to find a boat on your own. From Limón you can take one of the public buses that leave throughout the day from a stop 200 meters north of the central park. Fare is 25 cents. Alternatively, you can take a cab from Limón to Moín for around $2.50.

Once in Moín, you should be able to negotiate a fare between $35 and $60, depending on how many people you can round up to go with you. These boats tend to leave between 8 and 10am every morning. Usually, the fare you pay covers the return trip as well, and you can arrange with the captain to take you back across when you're ready to depart.

One boat captain to check with is **Modesto Wilson** (☎ **506/226-0986**), who owns a boat named *Francesca*. Wilson offers economical overnight packages to Tortuguero. The trip from Moín to Tortuguero takes between 3 and 4 hours. **Laura's Tropical Tours** (☎ **506/758-2410**) also offers boat tours to Tortuguero from Moín.

It is also possible—albeit expensive—to travel to Tortuguero by boat from Puerto Viejo de Sarapiquí (see chapter 8). Expect to pay $200 to $250 each way for a boat that will hold up to 10 people. Check at the public dock in Puerto Viejo de Sarapiquí or ask at the Hotel El Bambú if you're interested.

ORIENTATION

Tortuguero National Park is one of the most remote locations in Costa Rica. There are no roads into this area, so all transportation is by boat or plane. Most of the lodges are spread out over several kilometers to the north of the village of Tortuguero, and the small airstrip is at the north end.

EXPLORING THE PARK

According to existing records, Tortuguero National Park has hosted sea turtles since 1592, largely due to its extreme isolation. Even today, there are no roads into the park. Over the years since, turtles were captured and their eggs harvested by local settlers, but it wasn't until the 1950s that this practice became so widespread that the turtles faced extinction. Regulations controlling this mini-industry were passed in 1963; and in 1970, Tortuguero National Park was established. Today, four different species of sea turtles nest here: the green turtle, the hawksbill, the loggerhead, and the giant leatherback. The prime nesting period is from mid-June to mid-October (with August and September being the busiest months). The park's beaches are excellent places to watch sea turtles nest, especially at night. (Appealingly long and deserted, the beaches are not appropriate for swimming, however: The surf is usually very rough and the river mouths have a nasty habit of attracting sharks that feed on the many fish that live there.)

Green turtles are perhaps the most common turtle found in Tortuguero, so you are more likely to see one of them than any other species if you visit during the prime nesting season. Loggerheads are very rare here, so don't be disappointed if you don't see one. Perhaps the most spectacular sea turtle to watch laying eggs is the giant leatherback, however. The largest of all turtle species, the leatherback can grow to $6^{1}/_{2}$ feet long. From mid-February to mid-April it nests, predominately in the southern part of the park.

You can also explore the park's rain forest, either by foot or by boat, and look for some of the incredible varieties of wildlife that live here: jaguars, anteaters, howler monkeys, collared and white-lipped peccaries, some 350 species of birds, and countless butterflies, among others. There are several trails that branch out from the park entrance.

ENTRY POINT, FEES & REGULATIONS

The Tortuguero National Park entrance and ranger station is at the south end of Tortuguero Village. Admission to the park is $6. Flashlights and cameras are not permitted on the beach, since the lights can deter the turtles from nesting.

ORGANIZED NATIONAL PARK TOURS

Most visitors come to Tortuguero on an organized tour. If you'd like to see several national parks while you're in Costa Rica, you might want to join a tour run by one of the U.S.– or Costa Rican–based tour companies listed in chapter 3. Otherwise, most of the lodges listed below offer various hikes and night tours. See the individual

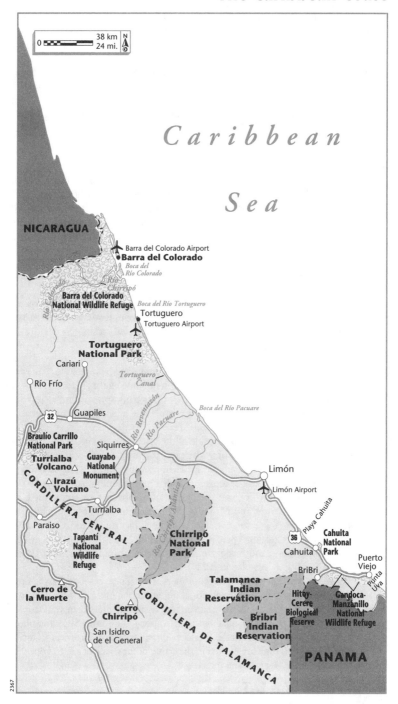

NICARAGUA

Caribbean

Sea

Barra del Colorado Airport
●**Barra del Colorado**
*Boca del
Río Colorado*

*Río
Chirripó*

**Barra del Colorado
National Wildlife Refuge** *Boca del Río Tortuguero*

Tortuguero
Tortuguero Airport

**Tortuguero
National Park**
Cariari

*Tortuguero
Canal*

Río Frío

Río Reventazón

32 Guapiles

Río Pacuare *Boca del Río Pacuare*

**Braulío Carrillo
National Park**

Siquirres

**Turrialba
Volcano**△ **Guayabo
National
Monument**

△ **Irazú
Volcano**

Limón

Limón Airport

*C
O
R
D
I
L
L
E
R
A
C
E
N
T
R
A
L*

Turrialba

Paraiso

Río Chirripó Atlántico

**Chirripó
National
Park**

Playa Cahuita

36

**Tapantí
National
Wildlife
Refuge**

**Cahuita
National
Park**

Cahuita

Puerto
Viejo

**Cerro de
la Muerte**

△ **Cerro
Chirripó**

*C
O
R
D
I
L
L
E
R
A
D
E
T
A
L
A
M
A
N
C
A*

BriBri

**Talamanca
Indian
Reservation**

**Hitoy-
Cerere
Biological
Reserve**

**Gandoca-
Manzanillo
National
Wildlife Refuge**

*Punta
Uva*

San Isidro
de el General

**Bribri
Indian
Reservation**

PANAMA

0 38 km
24 mi.
N

2367

lodge listings for rates. If you choose to stay at one of these lodgings, chances are you'll be on a package that includes a tour of Tortuguero, among other excursions. In addition, there are also several tour companies that offer budget 2-day/1-night excursions to Tortuguero, which include transportation, all meals, and limited tours around the region. Prices for these trips range between $55 and $80 per person, and guests are generally lodged in one of the basic hotels in Tortuguero village. These trips are good for travelers who like to be able to say, "been there, done that." Companies offering these excursions include **Ecole Travel** (☎ 506/223-2240), **Tortuguero Expeditions** (☎ 506/222-2175), and **Tortuguero Odyssey Tours** (☎ 506/758-0824).

BOAT CANAL TOURS

One of the most unique things you can do in Tortuguero is tour its canals by boat. Most of the lodges can arrange a canal tour for you, but you can also arrange a tour through one of the operators in Tortuguero Village. Ask around town, stop in at the local pulpería (☎ 506/710-6716), or look up Ernesto Castillo at Cabinas Sabina. Tours of the canals cost between $12 and $15 per person, plus the park entrance fee if you'll be going into the park. Night tours to watch turtles nest average between $5 and $10 per person.

FISHING TRIPS & PACKAGES

All of the lodges situated along this coast offer fishing trips and fishing packages. If you want to try your hand at reeling in a monster tarpon, it will generally cost you between $30 and $40 per hour, including boat, guide, and tackle.

EXPLORING THE TOWN

Tortuguero Village is a tiny collection of houses connected by footpaths. The village is spread out on a thin spit of land, bordered on one side by the Atlantic Ocean and on the other by the main canal. At most points, this spit of land is less than 300 meters wide. In the center of the village you'll find a kiosk that has information on the cultural and natural history of this area.

If you stay at a hotel on the ocean side of the canal, you will be able to walk into and explore the town at your leisure, whereas if you are across the canal you will be dependent on the lodge's transportation. However, many of the lodges across the canal have their own network of jungle trails that may appeal to naturalists.

The newest attraction in town is the small **Caribbean Conservation Corporation's Visitors' Center and Museum.** While the museum has information and exhibits on a whole range of native flora and fauna, its primary focus is on the life and history of the sea turtles. There is also a small gift shop here and all the proceeds go toward conservation and turtle protection. The museum is open daily 10am to noon and 2 to 5:30pm. Admission is $1.

In the village, you can also rent dugout canoes, known here in Costa Rica as *cayucos* or *pangas.* Be careful before renting and taking off in one of these. They tend to be heavy, slow, and hard to maneuver, and you may be getting more than you bargained for. There are a couple of souvenir shops in the village—the **Jungle Shop** (no phone), which donates 10% of its profits to local schools, and **Paraiso Tropical Gift Shop** (☎ 506/710-0323). Both are located in the center of the small village and open normal business hours, 7 days a week.

WHERE TO STAY & EAT

There are several basic lodges in the village of Tortuguero, offering budget lodgings for between $5 and $15 per person. **Cabinas Miss Junie** (☎ 506/710-0523) and

Cabinas Sabinas (no phone) are your best bets. If you choose one of these you will have to make your own arrangements for touring the canals or renting a canoe.

Although the room rates below appear quite high, keep in mind that most of them include round-trip transportation to and from San José (which amounts to approximately $100 per person) and all meals. When broken down into nightly room rates, most of the lodges charge between $40 and $60 for a double room.

When transportation is included in the prices below, it is for round-trip land and water transfers to and from San José. These trips drive through Braulio Carillo National Park and then usually stop for a brief tour of a banana plantation before continuing on to the lodge by river and canal. The river part of the trip provides a particularly good opportunity to spot crocodiles, monkeys, and sloths. All of the lodges will arrange a package price (slightly higher, of course) that features either one-way or round-trip air transportation.

DOUBLES FOR LESS THAN $35

El Manati Lodge. Tortuguero, Limón. ☎ **506/383-0330.** 6 cabins. $22 single; $28.50 double. No credit cards.

If you'd like to have a Tortuguero jungle lodge experience, but don't have the bucks to spend on the above places, this is your best choice. This lodge is located across the canal and about a kilometer north of Tortuguero Village. The young owners live here and have slowly built the lodge themselves over the years. The rooms are fairly basic, with cement floors and floor fans, but they have attractive curtains and new fixtures in the bathrooms. There's even warm water. Some rooms have two separate rooms, one of which has bunk beds. Breakfast ($5) and dinner ($8) are available. Canal tours and turtle-watching walks are $10 per person for 2 hours, and there are canoes that can be rented for $5 per hour.

Transportation up here and back can be arranged in Moín near Limón for $50 to $60 round-trip. Piece it all together and you come up with a 3-day, 2-night trip with tours, meals, and transportation from Limón for around $250 for two people!

WORTH A SPLURGE

Hotel Ilan-Ilan. Apdo. 91-1150, San José. ☎ **506/255-2262** or 506/255-2031. Fax 506/255-1946. 24 rms. $140 single, 2 days/1 night; $260.80 double, 2 days/1 night; $190 single, 3 days/2 nights; $350 double 3 days/2 nights. All rates include round-trip transportation and three meals daily. AE, DC, MC, V.

Named after a fragrant tropical flower that grows on the hotel grounds, the Ilan-Ilan is on the opposite side of the canal from the beach. Guest rooms are fairly basic, but large, and are all angled toward the canal so each gets a bit of a breeze. Screened windows in front and back and overhead fans also help keep the rooms cool. Be sure to ask for one of the rooms with a double bed if that's what you prefer; some rooms have only twin beds. Tico meals are served in the small screen-walled dining room, and there is a bar where you can chat with other guests. The lodge provides bilingual guides to point out wildlife and answer questions both during the trip to the lodge and during outings through the nearby canals and (in season) to the beach at night to watch sea turtles laying their eggs. The lodge also has several acres of forest land through which there are several kilometers of trails.

✪ **Jungle Lodge.** Apdo. 1818-1002, San José. ☎ **506/233-0133** or 506/233-0155. Fax 506/233-0778. 34 rms. $186 single, 2 days/1 night; $286 double, 2 days/1 night; $255 single, 3 days/2 nights; $389 double, 3 days/2 nights; $486.50 triple, 3 days/2 nights. All rates include transportation and three meals daily. AE, DC, MC, V.

Located just south of Ilan-Ilan on the same side of the river and about a kilometer from Tortuguero National Park, the Jungle Lodge offers rooms in wooden buildings raised up above the ground on pilings. There are long verandahs set with chairs where you can sit and bird watch or just relax and listen to the forest. Most rooms have windows on two sides to let the breezes through, plus ceiling fans. Wooden floors and walls give these rooms an attractive, tropical look. Simple-but-filling meals such as fried chicken or fish with rice and beans are served buffet-style at long tables in a screen-walled dining hall. Tours, led by bilingual guides, include boat tours through the canals to look for wildlife, a visit to Tortuguero Village, a hike through the forest, and (in season) trips over to the beach to watch the sea turtles lay their eggs. Optional canoe tours and night tours are also available for $10 and $15 respectively. Fishing trips cost around $35 per hour for two people. This is a big place and can seem crowded and impersonal at times.

✪ **Laguna Lodge.** Apdo. 344, San Pedro, San José. ☎/fax **506/225-3740.** 14 rms. $175 single, 2 days/1 night; $286 double, 2 days/1 night; $212 single, 3 days/2 nights; $382 double, 3 days/2 nights. All rates include transportation, tours, and three meals daily. MC, V.

This is one of the newest and smallest lodges in the area and is located 2 kilometers north of Tortuguero Village on the beach side of the canal. The rooms here are all very attractive, with wood walls, waxed hardwood floors, and tiled bathrooms with screened upper walls to let in air and light. Each room also has a little shared verandah. There's a small screen-walled dining room that serves tasty meals. A little covered deck has been built over the water, and there is even a tiny beach area on the river. Several covered palapa huts have also been built and strung with hammocks. The lodge owners live here year-round, which makes Laguna Lodge a bit more personal than other Tortuguero lodges. Like the Mawamba Lodge, this hotel has the added advantage of being on the beach side of the canal. Several different optional tours are available.

Mawamba Lodge. Apdo. 10050-1000, San José. ☎ **506/223-7490**, 506/223-2421, or 506/222-5463. Fax 506/255-4039. 36 rms. $164 single, 2 days/1 night; $328 double, 2 days/1 night; $205 single, 3 days/2 nights; $410 double, 3 days/2 nights. All rates include transportation and three meals daily. AE, MC, V.

Located about 500 meters north of Tortuguero Village on the beach side of the canal, Mawamba is a good choice for anyone who would like to be able to wander this isolated stretch of beach at will. Rooms have varnished wood floors, twin beds, cold-water showers, and table fans only. However, there are wide verandahs and plenty of hammocks around for anyone who wants to kick back. The gardens are lush and overgrown with flowering ginger, heliconia, and hibiscus. When I last visited, work was just being completed on a small swimming pool, and there were plans to add hot-water showers. Meals are above average for Tortuguero and might include pasta and lobster or chicken in béchamel sauce. Plus there is usually good, fresh bread. You can dine either in the screened-in dining room or out on the patio. Tours included in the rates include a 4-hour boat ride through the canals and a guided forest hike. There are also slide shows every other night that focus on the natural history of this area. Optional tours include a night hike ($17) and fishing trips ($40 per hour for two people).

2 Limón: Gateway to Tortuguero National Park & Southern Coastal Beaches

160 kilometers E of San José

It was just offshore from present-day Limón that Christopher Columbus is believed to have anchored in 1502, on his fourth and last voyage to the New World. Although he felt this was potentially a very rich land and named it Costa Rica, it never quite lived up to his expectations. However, the spot where he anchored has proved over the centuries to be the best port on the Caribbean coast. It was from here that the first shipments of bananas headed to North America in the late 19th century. Today, Limón is a busy port city that ships millions of pounds of bananas northward every year.

ESSENTIALS
GETTING THERE & DEPARTING

By Bus   Buses leave San José daily every hour between 5am and 7pm from the corner of Avenida 3 between calles 19 and 21. Duration is 2¹/₂ hours. Fare is $2.40. A slightly more comfortable direct bus leaves from the same block roughly every half-hour between 5:30am and 4:30pm; check in San José for current schedule. Fare is $2.95.

Buses leave Límon for San José roughly every half-hour between 5am and 7:30pm. The bus stop is one block east and half a block south of the municipal market. Buses to Cahuita and Puerto Viejo leave daily at 5 and 10am and 1 and 4pm. The Cahuita bus stop is at Radio Casino, which is one block north of the municipal market. Buses to Punta Uva and Manzanillo, both of which are south of Puerto Viejo, leave Limón daily at 6am and 2:30pm, from the same block.

By Car   The Guápiles Highway heads north out of San José on Calle 3 before turning east and passing close to Barva Volcano and through Braulio Carillo National Park en route to Limón. The drive takes about 2¹/₂ hours. Alternatively, you can take the old highway, which is equally scenic, though slower. This highway heads east out of San José on Avenida Central, and passes through San Pedro before reaching Cartago. From Cartago on, the road is narrow and winding, and passes through Paraiso and Turrialba before descending out of the mountains to Siquírres where the old highway meets the new. This route will take you 4 hours or more to get to Limón.

ORIENTATION

Nearly all addresses in Limón are measured from the market or from Parque Vargas, at the east end of town. The bus stop for buses out to Playa Bonita is just around the corner to the north of the Cahuita bus stop.

WHAT TO SEE & DO

Limón is not generally considered a tourist attraction. Most travelers use it primarily as a gateway to Tortuguero to the north and the beaches of Cahuita and Puerto Viejo to the south. If you do spend some time in Limón, you can take a seat in Parque Vargas along the sea wall and watch the city's citizens go about their business. There are even supposed to be some sloths living in trees here. Maybe you'll spot them. Take a walk around town if you're interested in architecture. When banana shipments built this port, many local merchants erected elaborately decorated buildings, several of which have survived the city's many earthquakes. Just be careful after dark, particularly outside of the city center. Limón has earned a reputation for frequent muggings and robberies.

The biggest event of the year in Limón, and one of the most fascinating festivals in Costa Rica, is the annual **Carnival,** which is held for a week around Columbus Day (October 12). For one week of the year, languid Limón shifts into high gear for a nonstop bacchanal orchestrated to the beat of reggae, soca, and calypso music. During the revelries, residents of the city don costumes and take to the streets in a dazzling parade of color. In recent years, however, the central government has tried to reign in on Carnival, citing health and safety concerns. If you want to experience this carnival, make hotel reservations early.

If you are planning on heading up to Tortuguero on your own, see "Tortuguero National Park," above, for details on how to get there from Limón.

A NEARBY BEACH

If you want to get in some beach time while you're here in Limón, hop in a taxi or a local bus and head north to **Playa Bonita,** a small public beach park. Although the water isn't very clean and usually too rough for swimming, the setting is much more attractive than downtown. This beach is very popular with surfers.

WHERE TO STAY & EAT
DOUBLES FOR LESS THAN $25

Hotel Acon. Avenida 3 and Calle 3 (Apdo. 528), Limón. ☎ **506/758-1010.** Fax 506/758-2924. 39 rms (all with bath). A/C TEL. $15 single; $20 double; $24 triple. AE, MC, V.

This older in-town choice is the best you can do in Limón. The rooms, all of which are air-conditioned (almost a necessity in this muggy climate), are clean and have two twin beds and a large bathroom. A television in your room will cost an extra $1.50 per day. The restaurant on the first floor just off the lobby is a cool, dark haven on steamy afternoons, highly recommended for lunch or as a place to beat the heat. Prices range from $2.75 to $10. The second-floor disco stays open late on weekends, so don't count on a quiet night.

Park Hotel. Avenida 3 between calles 1 and 3, Limón. ☎ **506/758-3476** or 506/798-0555. Fax 506/758-4364. 30 rms, 5 suites (all with bath). $12–$16 single; $18–$25 double; $22–$28 triple; $40–$50 suite. V.

You can't miss this tall pink, yellow, and turquoise building across the street from the fire station. It's certainly seen better years, but in Limón there aren't too many choices. What makes this place memorable is its aging tropical ambience, so don't expect clean and new. Be sure to ask for a room on the ocean side of the hotel because these are brighter, quieter, and cooler than those on the side of the hotel that faces the fire station. The suites are generally kept in much better condition and have private ocean-view balconies. The large, sunny dining room off the lobby serves standard Tico fare at very reasonable prices.

DOUBLES FOR LESS THAN $35

Cabinas Cocori. Playa Bonita (Apdo. 1093), Limón. ☎ **506/758-2930.** Fax 506/798-1670. 15 rms, 6 apts (all with bath). $16–$21 single; $32–$42 double; $41 apt (accommodates up to five people). AE, DC, MC, V.

Located on the water just before you reach Playa Bonita, this hotel and apartment complex commands a fine view of the cove and crashing surf. The grounds are in need of landscaping, but the rooms are quite nice. A two-story white building houses the apartments, each of which has a kitchenette with hot plate and refrigerator, two bedrooms, and a bathroom. A long verandah runs along both floors. The rooms are housed in a new adjacent building. The rooms are small and basic, but clean. The four rooms on the ground floor have air-conditioning; those above make do with a fan and sea breezes. Staying at this location is far preferable to staying in town. You can get here by bus or taxi.

WORTH A SPLURGE

Hotel Maribu Caribe. Apdo. 1306-2050, San Pedro. ☎ **506/758-4543** or 506/758-4010; 506/253-1838 in San José. Fax 506/758-3541, or 506/234-0193 in San José. 52 rms. A/C TEL. $68 single; $78 double; $88 triple. AE, DC, MC, V.

Located on top of a hill overlooking the Caribbean and built to resemble an Indian village, the Maribu Caribe is a pleasant, if not overly luxurious, choice if you are looking to spend some time in the sun. The hotel is popular with Tico families from San José because it is easy to get to for weekend trips. The guest rooms are in circular bungalows with white-tile floors and varnished wood ceilings. The furnishings are a bit old but are still comfortable.

The hotel's restaurant has the best view in Limón, or on the entire Atlantic coast, for that matter. It's built out over the edge of a steep hill with tide pools and the ocean almost directly below. In addition to the formal dining room, there are also tables outside on a curving verandah that makes the most of the view. Entree prices range from $5 to $16.50 and the emphasis is on seafood prepared in the continental style. There is a bar here, as well as a bar/snack bar by the pool. The Maribu Caribe can help you with tour arrangements, and has a gift shop.

✪ **Hotel Matama.** Apdo. 686, Limón. ☎ **506/758-1123** or 506/758-4409. Fax 506/758-4499. 16 rms. A/C. $60 single; $70 double; $85 triple; $100 quad. AE, MC, V.

Almost directly across the street from Cabinas Cocori, the Matama is in a class by itself. The hotel consists of several multiplex buildings set amid dense tropical vegetation across the road from the ocean. The strikingly modern design of the buildings, both inside and out, is a welcome surprise in an area of generally unmemorable accommodations. Each room is decorated with attractive matching drapes and bedspreads and has comfortable wicker furniture and, best of all, large bathrooms with solarium gardens that bring the jungle right into your bath. There are even some units with lofts. Splashing around in the small pool, you'll be surrounded by the sounds of the jungle, and if you want to explore nearby jungles further, you can arrange trips and car rentals here at the hotel. Seafood is the specialty of the large open-air restaurant, with prices ranging from $4.50 to $16.50. The meals are well-prepared and elegantly served, but the service can be a bit slow. Room service is also available.

3 Cahuita

200 kilometers E of San José; 42 kilometers S of Limón

The influx of tourists and an apparently robust drug trade have changed the face and feel of this quiet Caribbean town. A few notorious crimes against tourists have had a serious impact here, and it is highly recommended that you take every possible precaution against robbery and avoid walking alone outside of the "downtown" at night. Nevertheless, Cahuita is still one of the most laid-back villages you'll find anywhere in Costa Rica, and if you spend any time here, you'll likely find yourself slipping into a heat-induced torpor that affects anyone who ends up here. The gravel streets are almost always deserted, and the social heart of the village is on the front porches of Salon Vaz and Salon Sarafina, Cahuita's dueling bars and discos. The village traces its roots to Afro-Caribbean fishermen and laborers who settled in this region in the mid-1800s, and today the population is still primarily English-speaking blacks whose culture and language set them apart from other Costa Ricans.

The main reason people come to Cahuita, other than its laid-back atmosphere, are its miles of pristine beaches that stretch both north and south from town. The beaches to the south, as well as the forest behind them and one of Costa Rica's few coral reefs beneath the waters offshore, are all part of Cahuita National Park. Silt and pesticides washing down from nearby banana plantations have taken a heavy toll on the coral reefs, so don't expect the snorkeling to be fantastic. Still, the beaches inside the park are idyllic.

ESSENTIALS
GETTING THERE & DEPARTING

By Bus   Express buses leave San José daily at 10am and 3:30pm from Avenida 11 between Calle Central and Calle 1. Trip duration is 4 hours. Fare is $4.50. The Sixaola bus leaves from the same station at 6am and 1:30pm and will leave you on the highway at the entrance to Cahuita, about one kilometer from the town center.

Alternatively, you can take a bus to Limón (see above for details) and then take a Cahuita- or Puerto Viejo–bound bus from Limón. These latter buses leave Limón daily at 5, 8, and 10am and 1, 4, and 6pm from Radio Casino, which is one block north of the municipal market. Buses from Limón to Manzanillo depart daily at 6am and 2:30pm and stop in Cahuita. Duration is 1 hour. Fare is 85¢.

Buses departing Puerto Viejo and Sixaola (on the Panama border) stop in Cahuita at approximately 7, 10, and 11:15am and 4pm en route to San José. However, these buses are often full, particularly on weekends and throughout the high season. To avoid standing in the aisle all the way to San José, it is better to take a bus first to Limón, and then catch one of the frequent Limón–San José buses. Buses to Limón leave daily at 6:30 and 9am and 12, 3, 4:30, and 6pm. Another tactic I've used is to take a morning bus to Puerto Viejo, spend the day down there, and board a direct bus to San José at its point of origin, thereby snagging a seat.

By Car   Follow the directions above for getting to Limón, and, as you enter the outskirts of Limón, watch for a paved road to the right (it's just before the railroad tracks). Take this road south to Cahuita, passing the airstrip and the beach as you leave Limón.

ORIENTATION

There are only eight sand streets in Cahuita, so you shouldn't get lost. Three roads lead into town from the highway. Buses usually take the road that leads into the heart of town and drop their passengers at the Salon Vaz bar. An alternate route bypasses town and heads toward Playa Negra, which is just north of town. As you're coming from the north, the first road leads to the north end of Playa Negra. If you come in on the bus and are staying at a lodge on Playa Negra, head out of town on the street that runs between Salon Vaz and the small park. This road will curve to the left and continue a mile or so out to Playa Negra. The village's main street dead-ends at the entrance to the national park (a footbridge over a small stream). The bus stop is in front of Salon Vaz.

Fast Facts   You can wash your clothes at the self-service **laundromat** in front of Cabinas Vaz. One load in the washer or dryer will cost $1.50. The **police station** is located where the road from Playa Negra turns into town. The **post office,** next door to the police station, is open Monday through Friday from 8am to 5pm. In addition to tours and bicycle rentals, **Cahuita Tours & Adventure Centre** offers international fax service and allows travelers to exchange money. You'll find Cahuita Tours on the main road heading towards Playa Negra about 2¹/₂ blocks from Salon Vaz.

EXPLORING CAHUITA NATIONAL PARK

You'll immediately feel the call of the long scimitar of beach that stretches south from the edge of town. This beach is glimpsed through the trees from Cahuita's sun-baked main street, and extends a promise of relief from the heat. While the lush coastal forest and picture-perfect palm lines are a tremendous draw, the park was actually created to preserve the 600-acre coral reef that surrounds it. The reef contains 35 species of coral and provides a haven for hundreds of brightly colored tropical fish. You can walk on the beach itself or follow the trail that runs through the forest just behind the beach.

The best place to swim is beyond the Peresoso (Lazy river), a few hundred yards inside Cahuita National Park. The trail behind the beach is great for bird watching, and if you're lucky, you might see some monkeys or a sloth. The loud whooping sounds you hear off in the distance are the calls of howler monkeys, which can be heard from more than a mile away. Nearer at hand, you are likely to hear crabs scuttling about amid the dry leaves on the forest floor. There are half a dozen or so species of land crabs living in this region. My favorites are the bright orange-and-purple ones. The trail behind the beach stretches a little more than 4 miles to the southern end of the park at Puerto Vargas, where you will find a beautiful white-sand beach, the park headquarters, and a primitive campground with drinking water and outhouses. The reef is off the point just north of Puerto Vargas. If you don't dawdle, the hike should take no more than 3 hours.

ENTRY POINTS, FEES & REGULATIONS

The **in-town park entrance** is just over a footbridge at the end of the village's main street. The **main park entrance** is at the southern end of the park in Puerto Vargas. The road to Puerto Vargas is approximately 3 miles south of Cahuita on the left. Officially, admission is $6 per person per day but the last time I visited, the fee was only being collected at the Puerto Vargas entrance and it was possible to enter the park from the town of Cahuita with just a voluntary contribution. This situation is sure to change, and is probably occurring because of the confrontation last year's major increase in park admission fees sparked between the town of Cahuita and the government. The park is open daily from dawn to dusk and as stated above, a manned ranger station exists at the Puerto Vargas entrance where there are also campsites.

BEACHES & ACTIVE SPORTS OUTSIDE THE PARK

Outside the park, the best place for swimming is **Playa Negra.** Just keep an eye out for poisonous snakes. On my last visit, I was almost bitten by one on a path on Playa Negra. If you aren't a herpetologist, it's best to assume that all snakes here are poisonous.

If you want to find out where the best diving spots are (there is even a sunken ship you can visit), I suggest a snorkeling trip by boat. **Cahuita Tours & Adventure Centre** (☎ **506/755-0232**), on the village's main street heading out towards Playa Negra, has glass-bottomed boat and snorkling trips for $15 to $20 per person. They also arrange jungle tours ($25 to $35), white-water rafting trips ($65 to $85), and jeep tours to the Bribri reservation. Cahuita Tours also rents bicycles ($7.50 per day), boogie boards ($12.50 per day), and snorkeling equipment ($7.50 per day). **National Park Tours and Expeditions** (☎ **506/755-0024**), located on the left just before the town's park entrance, offers similar tours and rentals at similar prices, as well as 3-day boat trips to Bocas del Toro, Panama.

Brigitte (watch for the sign on Playa Negra) rents horses for $5 per hour (you must have prior experience) and also offers guided horseback tours for between $25 and $35.

BIRD WATCHING & CANOEING ALONG ESTRELLA ESTUARY

Bird watchers who have a car should head north 9 kilometers to the **Aviaros de Caribe bed-and-breakfast lodge** (☎ **506/382-1335**), where canoe tours of Estrella Estuary are available. Nearly 300 species of birds have been sighted in the immediate area. The tour costs $30 per person and leaves throughout the day, but it is best to leave very early or near dusk, and to make reservations in advance.

SHOPPING

At Restaurant Vaz and a couple of other places around the village, you can pick up a copy of Paula Palmer's *What Happen: A Folk-History of Costa Rica's Talamanca Coast* (Publications in English, 1993). The book is a history of the region based on interviews with many of the area's oldest residents. Much of it is in the traditional Creole language, from which the title is taken. It makes fun and interesting reading, and you just might bump into someone mentioned in the book.

You can pick up souvenirs and Caribbean beach clothing at either **Boutique Coco Miko** or **Boutique Bambata.** The latter is also a good place to have your hair wrapped in colorful threads and strung with beads.

CAHUITA AFTER DARK

The **Salon Vaz,** a classic Caribbean bar, has traditionally been the place to spend your nights (or days, for that matter) if you like cold beer and very loud reggae and soca music. Now, the **Salon Sarafina,** located just across the street, is giving Vaz a run for its money. There are usually local women hanging out on the front porches of each establishment selling local pati pies or bowls of run-down stew.

WHERE TO STAY
DOUBLES FOR LESS THAN $15

Cabinas Atlantic Surf. Cahuita, Limón. ☎ **506/755-0086.** 6 rms. $10 single; $15 double. No credit cards.

These small but attractive rooms are a great choice for budget travelers. In a town where all the newer hotels seem to be built of cement, the rustic, varnished wood walls, floors, and small porches of these rooms are a welcome sight. There are fans and tiled showers within, and Adirondack chairs on the porches. The upstairs rooms have high ceilings but still get pretty warm. The Atlantic surf is down the lane from the Cabinas Sol y Mar, only 100 yards from the park entrance.

Cabinas Rhode Island. Cahuita, Limón. ☎ **506/755-0264.** 11 rms (all with private bath). $7.50–$10 single; $10–$15 double. No credit cards.

These newer cinderblock rooms are down the lane beside the Cabinas Sol y Mar. The rooms are on the left, but the owners live in the house across the street. The rooms are very basic, but they're clean and have a tiled verandah. You're within 100 yards of the park entrance if you stay here.

Cabinas Sol y Mar. Cahuita, Limón. ☎ **506/755-0237.** 11 rms (all with private bath). $12.25 single or double; $15 triple. No credit cards.

The nicer rooms are the ones upstairs, facing the ocean. These have have more light and catch more of the breezes, an important factor in these hot, humid, and cloudy climes. However, all of the rooms are large, quite clean, and have fans. There isn't much decor, but you're only steps from the park entrance and the beach.

Surf Side Cabins. Apdo. 360, Limón. ☎ **506/755-0246.** 23 rms (all with bath). $10–$15 single or double. No credit cards.

Despite its name, most of the rooms are not right on the water; nonetheless, this remains a popular budget choice in Cahuita. All the rooms are clean and have jalousie windows that let in a lot of light and air. Only a few are close to the water, and they are always in high demand. The restaurant is popular with locals, who sit and play dominoes for hours, and it can get noisy at times. Prices for Tico meals range from $2.75 to $12.50. While I was eating here one night, a large sloth crawled into the open-air restaurant from an adjacent tree. With entertainment like that, it's hard not to recommend this place, although the hotel management can be rather unfriendly.

DOUBLES FOR LESS THAN $25

Cabinas Tito. 250 meters southeast of GAR, Cahuita, Limón. ☎ **506/755-0286.** 6 cabins (all with bath). Dec–Apr $25 single, $30 double; May–Nov $15–$20 single or double. All rates include continental breakfast. No credit cards.

Located down a grassy path just off the road to Playa Negra, these little cabins are quiet and comfortable. They're surrounded by a shady yard, and the owner's old Caribbean wood-frame house is to one side. The cabinas are made of cement block with tin roofs, but they have tile floors and small front porches with a couple of chairs. Two of the cabins have mini-refrigerators, and at least one has a tiled wall and wicker headboard for the bed. Good value, helpful owners, and pleasant surroundings have made this place an instant hit with budget travelers.

✪ **Seaside Jenny's.** Cahuita, Limón. ☎ **506/755-0256.** 8 rms (all with bath). $12.50–$20 single or double; rates slightly lower during off-season. No credit cards.

Located 200 yards straight ahead (toward the water) from the bus stop, Jenny's place has been popular for years, and her newer rooms are some of the best in town in this price range. Best of all, they're right on the water, so you can go to sleep to the sound of the waves. All of the rooms have shuttered windows, and on their porches there are sling chairs and hammocks. The more expensive rooms are on the second floor and have arguably the best views in Cahuita. There is one room in an older building, which, though it has a big porch and plenty of Caribbean atmosphere, is not quite as nice as the others.

DOUBLES FOR LESS THAN $35

✪ **Alby Lodge.** Apdo. 840, Cahuita, Limón. ☎/fax **506/755-0031.** 4 cabins (all with bath). $29 single or double; $33.50 triple; $37.50 quad. No credit cards.

Located about 150 yards down the winding lane to the right just before you reach the park entrance, the Alby Lodge is a fascinating little place hand-built by German owners Yvonne and Alfons Baumgartner. Though these four small cabins are close to the center of the village, they are surrounded by a large lawn and feel secluded. The cabins are all quintessentially tropical with thatched roofs, mosquito nets, hardwood floors and beams, big shuttered windows, tile bathrooms, and a hammock slung on the front porch. You won't find more appealing rooms in this price range.

WORTH A SPLURGE

✪ **Aviarios del Caribe.** Apdo. 569-7300, Limón. ☎ **506/382-1335.** Fax 506/755-0016. 6 rms (all with bath). $50 single; $60 double; $80 triple; $100 quad. All rates include full breakfast. MC, V.

If you prefer bird watching to lazing on the beach, this is the place to stay on this section of the Atlantic coast. As the name implies, birds are important here. A bed-and-breakfast located on the edge of a small river delta, the lodge's owners have spotted over 300 species of birds within the immediate area. You can work on your life list from the lawns, the second-floor, the open-air dining room, and the lounge, or from a canoe paddling around the nearby canals. This house is built up on stilts and is surrounded by a private wildlife sanctuary that also includes forest trails. The guest rooms are all large and comfortable and have fans, tile floors, potted plants, fresh flowers, and modern bathroom fixtures. Some rooms also have king beds. In the lounge area you'll find a fabulous mounted-insect collection, as well as terrariums that house live snakes and poison-arrow frogs. You'll also certainly make friends with Buttercup, the resident three-toed sloth. Only breakfast is served here, so you'll have to take your other meals in Cahuita (9 kilometers to the south), or at a roadside soda along the way.

Cabinas Atlantida. Cahuita, Limón. ☎ **506/755-0115.** Fax 506/755-0213. 30 rms (all with private bath). $42.80 single; $53.50 double; $64.20 triple; $74.90 quad. All rates include breakfast. AE, MC, V.

Set amid lush gardens and wide green lawns and run by French Canadians, the Atlantida is one of my favorite hotels in Cahuita. You'll find it beside the soccer field out by Playa Negra, about a mile out of town. The guest rooms are done in a style reminiscent of local Indian architecture, with thatched roofs, pale yellow stucco walls, and plenty of bamboo trim. All rooms have a patio with bamboo screen dividers for privacy, and when you sit there, you'll be gazing into a flourishing garden. Although only breakfast is included in the room rate, you can also order dinner for under $10. The meals are served in a rancho dining room. Breakfasts include fresh fruit and fresh juice, rolls, and homemade marmalade, and there is free coffee all day long. Continental-style dinners are some of the best in town, though they are only available to hotel guests. A host of different tours can be arranged here, from snorkeling, to horseback riding, to white-water rafting. The beach is right across the street, and the hotel also has a conference room, a small gym, and a nice tile pool.

✪ Chalet Hibiscus. Apdo. 943, Limón. ☎ **506/755-0021.** Fax 506/755-0015. 1 house, 2 cabins (all with bath). Dec–Apr $32–$40.75 cabin, $81.50 house (can accommodate up to six people); May–Nov $25–$32 cabin, $61 house. No credit cards.

If you're planning a long stay in Cahuita, I advise checking into this place. Although it is about 2 kilometers from town on the road along Playa Negra, it is well worth the journey. The house has two bedrooms and sleeps up to six people. There is hardwood paneling all around, a full kitchen, hot water, red-tile floors, a pila for doing your laundry, and even a garage. A spiral staircase leads to the second floor, where you'll find hammocks on a balcony that looks over a green lawn to the ocean. The attractive little cabinas have wicker furniture and walls of stone and wood. If you ever wanted to be marooned on the Mosquito Coast, this is the place to live out your fantasy. You're a kilometer north of Playa Negra here, but there is a tiny swimming pool for cooling off during the day. The chalet is both simple and elegant; the setting, serene and beautiful. Be sure to ring the bell outside the gate—there are guard dogs on the grounds. If the house and cabins here are full, the owner can also arrange rentals of similar accommodations nearby. When I last visited there were plans to add a simple kitchen, bar, and small recreation area with a billard table.

Hotel Jaguar Cahuita. Cahuita, Limón (Apdo. 7046-1000, San José). ☎ **506/226-3775** or 506/755-0238. Fax 506/226-4693. 45 rms. $24.50–$32.60 single; $45–$57 double. All rates include breakfast. MC, V.

Located directly across the sandy road from Playa Negra, the Jaguar is Cahuita's largest and most ambitious hotel to date. However, despite the fact that the rooms are the biggest in town and are close to the water, they leave a lot to be desired. When I last visited, there was an untended and run-down feel to the hotel, but I was assured a major sprucing up was in the works. Rooms were designed with solar principles in mind to stay cool and make the most of prevailing breezes. Unfortunately, sometimes the breezes aren't enough, and small table-top fans have had to be added to the rooms. Though half the rooms have views of the water, the rest face only the front rank of rooms. Surrounding the hotel are 17 acres of forest and brush through which a short nature trail has been cut. You're almost certain to see at least one sloth on a morning walk here. There's a small swimming pool here and the beach is just across the road. The open-air dining room serves very good, moderately priced meals. Many of the ingredients used in the meals come from trees on the hotel property.

✪ Magellan Inn. Plaza Víquez, Apdo. 1132, Cahuita, Limón. ☎ /fax **506/755-0035.** 6 rms. $55 single or double; $65 triple. All rates include continental breakfast. AE, DC, MC, V.

This small inn is out at the far end of Playa Negra (about 2 kilometers north of Cahuita) and is the most luxurious hotel in the area. The six large rooms are all carpeted and have French doors, vertical blinds, big tiled bathrooms with hardwood counters, and two joined single beds with attractive bedspreads. Each room has its own tiled verandah with an overhead fan and bamboo chairs. There is a casually sophisticated combination bar/lounge and sitting room that has Oriental-style rugs and wicker furniture. However, most memorable are the hotel's sunken pool and garden, both of which are built into a crevice in the ancient coral reef that underlies this entire region. There is often good birdwatching here in the hotel gardens. The owners, Jean-Paul Feuillatre and Elizabeth Newton, are from France and Canada, respectively. When I last visited, construction was about to be completed on an adjacent restaurant to be called Casa Creole, where the hotel's excellent chef will continue serving some of the best meals on the coast.

WHERE TO EAT

Coconut meat and milk figure in a lot of the regional cuisine. Most nights, local women cook up pots of various local specialties and sell them from the front porches of the two discos. A full meal will cost you about $2.50. For snacks, there is a tiny bakery on the left side of the main road as you head toward Playa Negra. The coconut pie, brownies, ginger snaps, banana bread, and corn pudding are all delicious. Prices range from 55¢ to $1.

MEALS FOR LESS THAN $12

Brigitte's Restaurante. Playa Negra Road, north of Cabinas Atlantida. ☎ **506/755-0053.** Reservations not accepted. Main courses $3.75–$7.25. No credit cards. Daily 10am–10pm. SWISS/CREOLE.

Brigitte is from Switzerland but she's been in Cahuita for quite a few years, so her menu includes an eclectic blend of cuisines. You can get a good Creole run-down stew, but you can also get a steak with mushroom sauce. There are good salads and home-baked breads as well. You never know what might show up as the daily special. Brigitte now also features a wide selection of ice creams for beating the midday heat. The restaurant is located at the back of a house just off the Playa Negra Road. Just follow the signs.

Margaritaville. Playa Negra Road, 2 kilometers north of Cahuita. ☎ **506/755-0038.** Reservations not accepted. Complete meals $5–$7.50. No credit cards. Mon–Sat 6–10pm. INTERNATIONAL.

There's only one dish served each night at this little restaurant, but if you drop by ahead of time and make a special request, the friendly owner may try to accommodate you. However, if you're an adventurous eater, I'm sure you'll enjoy whatever is coming from the kitchen, which might be a local Creole dish made with coconut milk or roasted chicken or eggplant lasagne. All the breads are home-baked, and if there's extra you may be able to take home a loaf. The tables here are set up on the open second floor of Moray's B&B. It's all very mellow, definitely not to be missed.

Pizzeria El Cactus. On the road from the south end of Playa Negra to the highway. ☎ **506/ 755-0276.** Reservations not accepted. Pizza or spaghetti $3–$8.50. No credit cards. Tues–Sun 4–10pm. ITALIAN.

There are only a few tables at this small open-air restaurant, so be sure to arrive early if you have your heart set on pizza. Try the pizza Cahuita, which is made with tomatoes, mozzarella, salami, red peppers, olives, and oregano. There's also one made with hearts of palm. The pizzas are just the right size for one hungry person. Also on the menu are seven types of spaghetti, salads, and ice cream.

Restaurant Edith. By the police station. ☎ **506/755-0248.** Reservations not accepted. Main courses $3.40–$11.50. No credit cards. Daily 7am–noon and 6–10pm; also often open for lunch. SEAFOOD.

Miss Edith is a local lady who decided to start serving up home-cooked meals to all the hungry tourists hanging around. If you want a taste of the local cuisine, in a homey sit-down environment, this is the place. While Miss Edith's daughters take the orders, Mom cooks up a storm out back. The menu, when you can get ahold of it, is long, with lots of local seafood dishes and Creole combinations such as yuca in coconut milk with meat or vegetables. The sauces here have spice and zest, and are a welcome change from the typically bland fare served up throughout the rest of Costa Rica. After you've ordered, it is usually no more than 45 minutes until your meal arrives. It's usually crowded here, so don't be bashful about sitting down with total strangers at the big table. Miss Edith's place is at the opposite end of town from the park entrance and is just around the corner from the main street.

4 Puerto Viejo

200 kilometers E of San José; 55 kilometers S of Limón

Though Puerto Viejo is even smaller than Cahuita, it has a slightly more lively atmosphere due to the many surfers who come here from around the country and around the world to ride the village's famous Salsa Brava wave. For nonsurfers, there are also some good swimming beaches close to town, and if you head still farther south, you will come to the most beautiful beaches on this coast. The waters down in this region are some of the clearest anywhere in the country and there is some good snorkeling among the coral reefs when the seas are calm.

You may notice, as you make your way into town from the highway, that there are cacao trees planted along the road. These trees are all suffering from a blight that has greatly reduced the cocoa-bean harvest in the area. However, you can still get delicious cocoa candies here in Puerto Viejo. Don't miss them.

ESSENTIALS
GETTING THERE & DEPARTING

By Bus Express buses to Puerto Viejo leave San José daily at 10am and 3:30pm from Avenida 11 between Calle Central and Calle 1. Duration is 5 hours. Fare is $5. Buses leave from the same station for Sixaola at 6am and 1:30pm and will leave you at the turnoff for Puerto Viejo about 5 kilometers outside of town.

Alternatively, you can catch a bus to Limón (see above for details), and then transfer to a Puerto Viejo–bound bus in Limón. These latter buses leave daily at 5, 8, and 10am and 1, 4, and 6pm from Radio Casino, one block north of the municipal market. Buses from Limón to Manzanillo also stop in Puerto Viejo and leave daily at 6am and 2:30pm. Trip duration is 1¹/₂ hours. Fare is $1.10.

Express buses leave Puerto Viejo for San José daily at 6:30 and 9am and 4pm. Buses for Limón leave daily at 6 and 8:40am and 1, 4, and 5pm. Buses to Punta Uva and Manzanillo leave Puerto Viejo daily around 7am and 4pm. These buses return from Manzanillo at 8:15am and 5:15pm.

By Car   To reach Puerto Viejo, continue south from Cahuita for another 16 kilometers. Watch for a dirt road that forks to the left from the paved highway (the right fork heads to Bribri and Sixaola). This road will take you into the village after another 5 kilometers.

ORIENTATION

Arriving   The dirt road in from the highway runs parallel to Playa Negra just before entering the village of Puerto Viejo, which has all of about six dirt streets. The sea will be on your left and forested hills on your right as you come into town.

Fast Facts   **Public phones** are located at Hotel Maritza, El Pizote Lodge, and the ATEC office, where you can also mail a postcard and obtain visitor information. The nearest **bank** is in Bribri, about 10 kilometers away. There is a Guardia Rural **police post** near the park on the beach. It's another 15 kilometers or so on a bad gravel road south to Manzanillo.

WHAT TO SEE & DO

Most people who show up in this remote village have only one thing on their mind— surfing. Just offshore from the village park is a shallow reef where powerful storm-generated waves sometimes reach 20 feet. These waves are the biggest and most powerful on the Atlantic coast. Even when the waves are small, this spot is recommended only for very experienced surfers because of the danger of the reef. There are also popular beach breaks south of town on Playa Cocles. For swimming, head out to Playa Negra, along the road into town, or to the beaches south of town, around Punta Uva, where the surf is much more manageable.

If you aren't a surfer, the same activities that prevail in Cahuita are the norm here as well. Read a book, take a nap, or go for a walk on the beach. However, if you have more energy, you can rent a bicycle or a horse (watch for signs) and head down the beach toward Punta Uva, which is a little less than 8 kilometers down a potholed gravel road.

You should be sure to stop in at the **Asociación Talamanqueña de Ecoturismo y Conservacion (ATEC)** (☎ **506/798-4244**) office across the street from the Soda Tamara. This local organization is concerned with preserving both the environment and the cultural heritage of this area and promoting ecologically sound development in the region. In addition to functioning as the local post office and information center, they have a little shop that sells t-shirts, maps, posters, and books. You can pick up Paula Palmer's oral history of the region *What Happen: A Folk-History of Costa Rica's Talamanca Coast* (Publications in English, 1993) here. They also publish and sell *Coastal Talamanca, A Cultural and Ecological Guide,* a small booklet packed with information about this area. They offer quite a few different tours, as well. There are half-day walks that focus on nature and either the local African-Caribbean culture or the indigenous Bribri culture. These walks pass through farms and forests and along the way you'll learn about local history, customs, medicinal plants, and Indian mythology as well as have an opportunity to see sloths, monkeys, iguanas, keel-billed toucans, and other wildlife. There are four different walks through the nearby Bribri Indians' KéköLdi Reserve. There are also more strenuous hikes through the primary rain forest. ATEC also offers snorkeling trips to the nearby coral reefs and snorkeling and fishing trips in dugout canoes. Bird walks and night walks will help you spot more of the area wildlife. There are even overnight treks. The local guides who lead these tours are a wealth of information and make a hike through the forest a truly educational experience; don't miss an opportunity to do a tour with ATEC. Half-day walks (and night walks) are $11 and full-day walks are $17. A half day of snorkeling or fishing will cost around $20 per person. The ATEC office is open Monday through Saturday from 8am to 8pm, and Sunday from 8am to noon and 4pm to 8pm. If you're looking to stay here for an extended period of time and would like to contribute to the community, ask about volunteering here.

If you continue south on the coast road from Puerto Viejo, you will come to a couple of even smaller villages. Punta Uva is 8 kilometers away, and Manzanillo is about 15 kilometers away. It is possible to walk along the beach from Punta Cocles to Manzanillo, a distance of about 10 kilometers. Another enjoyable hike is from Monkey Point (Punta Mono) to Manzanillo (about 5$^{1}/_{2}$ kilometers). There is a reef offshore from Manzanillo that is good for snorkeling. Still farther south is the **Manzanillo-Gandoca Wildlife Refuge,** which extends all the way to the Panamanian border. Within the boundaries of the reserve live manatees, crocodiles, and more than 350 species of birds. The reserve also includes the coral reef offshore. On one 5$^{1}/_{2}$-mile-long beach within the reserve, four species of sea turtles nest between March and July.

Color Caribe, across the street from Cabinas Grant, sells hand-painted t-shirts and coconut-shell jewelry. There are also a couple of *pulperías* (general stores) in the village.

If you'd like to learn more about the culture of the local Bribri Indians, look for a copy of *Taking Care of Sibö's Gifts*, written by Paula Palmer, Juanita Sánchez, and Gloria Mayorga.

If you're looking for nightlife, you'll find about all there is in Puerto Viejo at **Stanford's Restaurant and Bar** (no phone), which has a raging disco nightly on the ground floor and a nice open-air restaurant on the second floor. Stanford's is right on the water just in front of the Salsa Brava break.

As mentioned in the section on Cahuita above, Puerto Viejo is showing some troubling effects of the combined tourism and drug trades. An increase in robberies and a few violent crimes have made headlines in recent years. Be careful here, especially after dark.

WHERE TO STAY
DOUBLES FOR LESS THAN $15

✪ **Casa Verde.** Puerto Viejo, Limón. ☎ **506/798-4244** (leave message). 12 rms (4 with private bath). $10–$15 single with shared bath, $15–$20 double with shared bath; $30 single or double with bath. No credit cards.

This little hotel is located on a side street on the south side of town. The older rooms, with shared bath, are in an interesting building with a wide, covered breezeway between the rooms and the showers and toilets out in back. The front and back porches of this building are hung with hammocks. A quiet sense of tropical tranquility pervades this place. The newer rooms are behind the house next door and are a bit larger than the older rooms. These new rooms have high ceilings, tile floors, and a verandah. Everything is well maintained, and even the shared bathrooms are kept immaculate.

DOUBLES FOR LESS THAN $25

Cabinas Black Sands. Puerto Viejo, Limón. ☎ **506/798-4244** (leave message). 3 rms (none with bath). $15 single; $20 double; $50 for up to six people. No credit cards.

The owners of this rustic, beachside thatched house are refugees from chilly Wisconsin. They offer basic accommodations in a secluded spot near the end of the long black-sand beach. The three rooms are all in a single thatched-roof building, which has a communal kitchen and dining-room table. If you want, you can rent the entire house. If you don't have the whole place to yourself, remember that the folks next door can hear everything you say because the walls don't go all the way to the ceiling. It's wonderfully tranquil out here, and although it's a bit of a hike to the nearest restaurant, there is a general store nearby where you can buy groceries for doing your own cooking. If arriving by bus, be sure to get off at the Pulpería Violeta, just before the road reaches the beach. Otherwise it's a long walk back out from the bus stop in town.

✪ **Cabinas Chimuri.** Puerto Viejo, Limón. ☎ **506/798-4244** (leave message). 4 cabins (none with bath). $14 single; $20 double; $24.50 triple; $28.50 quad. No credit cards.

If you don't mind being a 15-minute walk from the beach and you're an inveterate camper, I'm sure that you'll enjoy this rustic lodge. It's built in traditional Bribri Indian–style with thatched-roof A-frame cabins in a forest setting. In fact, it's a short stroll up a trail from the parking lot to the lodge buildings, and there are other trails on the property as well. This lodge is definitely for nature lovers who are used to roughing it: Accommodations are very basic, but there is a kitchen for guests to use. The lodge also runs several different hiking trips into the rain forest and the adjacent Bribri Indian KéköLdi Reserve. If arriving by bus, be sure to get off at the trail to Cabinas Chimuri before the road reaches the beach.

Cabinas Jacaranda. Puerto Viejo, Limón. No phone. 4 rms (3 with bath). $9.50 single without bath, $12.20 double without bath; $12.50 single with bath, $16.90 double with bath; $20.30 triple with bath. No credit cards.

This basic backpackers' special has a few nice touches that set it apart from the others. The floors are cement, but there are mats. Japanese paper lanterns cover the lights and mosquito nets hang over the beds. The Guatemalan bedspreads add a dash of color and tropical flavor, as do the tables made from sliced tree trunks. If you are traveling in a group, you'll enjoy the space and atmosphere of the big room. If the hotel is full, the owners also rent a few nearby bungalows. The **Garden Restaurant,** adjacent to the rooms, serves the best food in town.

Hotel Pura Vida. Puerto Viejo, Limón. No phone. 10 rms (2 with bath). $12.20 single shared bath; $15.50 double shared bath; $20 single or double with bath. No credit cards.

You'll find the Pura Vida around the corner from Cabinas Jacaranda and facing the soccer field. This pink and pale green cement and wood building is a sprawling structure with several cool and breezy covered patios. The second floor, where most of the guest rooms are located, has a veranda on three sides. Guest rooms have high ceilings, fans, and sinks, though the clean tiled bathroom is down the hall. Walls are made of wood, so sounds carry. Down in the shade of the patios there are hammocks for those who want to laze away the days.

DOUBLES FOR LESS THAN $35

Escape Caribeño. Puerto Viejo, (Apdo. 704-7300, Limón). ☎/fax **506/382-2572.** 12 rms (all with bath). $32.50 single; $36.70 double; $45.80 triple; $54.70 quad. MC, V.

Located just outside of Puerto Viejo on the road to Punta Uva, Escape Caribeño consists of 12 little white cabins with brick pillars and tiled patios. Clerestory windows, vertical blinds, and rather fancy hardwood furniture give these cabins the aesthetic edge over nearby lodgings in this price range. There are reading lamps by the beds and small refrigerators in every room. The attractive gardens have been planted with bananas and palms. It's a 5-minute walk into town or out to a beautiful beach that has a small island just offshore.

WORTH A SPLURGE

✪ El Pizote. Apdo. 230-2200, Coronado. ☎ **506/798-1938** or 506/229-1428. Fax 506/229-1428. 8 rms (none with bath), 6 bungalows. $34 single without bath, $82.50 single with bath; $50 double without bath, $82.50 double with bath; $66 triple without bath, $97 triple with bath; $76 quad without bath, $108 quad with bath. MC, V.

Although it originally billed itself as a surf resort, this comfortably rustic little lodge is ideal for anyone who simply wants to get away from it all. Located about 500 meters outside of town, El Pizote is set back across the road from a long black-sand beach. The rooms are in two beautiful, unpainted wooden buildings that are completely hidden from the road or even from the parking lot. You have to walk through a dense grove of dracaena plants, which you might recognize as a common houseplant. The rooms are cool—with polished wood walls, double beds, and absolutely beautiful bathrooms that have wood-slat floors in the showers and huge screen windows looking out on dense jungle. There are unusual burlap-and-bamboo window shades, as well as ceiling fans and reading lamps. For activity, there are hiking trails in the adjacent forest and a volleyball court. You can also rent snorkeling equipment, as well as sea kayaks, and there is good bird watching here. The restaurant serves only breakfast ($8) and dinner ($14.50), but drinks are available all day. There is a set menu each evening, which might be lobster with broccoli or an equally delectable fish plate. If arriving by bus, ask the bus driver to let you off at the entrance to the lodge. It's on the stretch of road that runs along the beach just before entering town.

NEARBY PLACES TO STAY
DOUBLES FOR LESS THAN $15

Cabinas Selvyn. Punta Uva, Limón. No phone. 10 rms (all with shared bath), 2 apts. $7.50–$10 single or double; $150–$200 per month for an apartment. No credit cards.

The atmosphere here is friendly and funky. Rooms are located in two old wooden buildings, behind the small open-aired restaurant. There are no fans here, so try to get one of the second-floor rooms, which receive a bit of the sea breezes. All the rooms come with mosquito nets, but, beyond that, the accommodations are Spartan. Nevertheless, the hotel is located 100 meters down a dirt lane from one of the most isolated and beautiful stretches of beach in Costa Rica, and owner Selvyn Brown is a great cook.

DOUBLES FOR LESS THAN $35

Miraflores Lodge. Playa Chiquita, (Apdo. 6499-1000, San José) Puerto Viejo, Limón. ☎/fax **506/233-2822.** 10 rms (6 with bath). $12.50 single without bath, $25 double without bath; $32.50–$40 single with bath, $40–$50 double with bath. All rates include breakfast. No credit cards.

Located a few miles south of Puerto Viejo on the road to Punta Uva, Miraflores Lodge is a former private home and ornamental flower farm turned bed-and-breakfast. Because it was a private home, the decor is far more attractive than at other lodges in the area. The large second-floor porch, which is virtually an open-air living room, is decorated with wood carvings, masks, and Panamanian and Guatemalan textiles. Huge vases hold fresh flowers and there is a free-form table made from a slice of tree trunk. Surrounding the lodge is the flower farm where heliconias, ginger, banana, anthurium, and orchids are grown. The guest rooms with private bath are very large and can sleep up to six people in two sleeping areas. Walls and doors are faced with cane, and there are hardwood floors in the second-floor rooms. The hotel's restaurant now serves three meals a day, with an emphasis on fresh fruits, vegetables, and fish.

WORTH A SPLURGE

✪ **Playa Chiquita Lodge.** Avenida 2 between calles 17 and 19 (Apdo. 7043-1000), San José. ☎ **506/233-6613.** Fax 506/223-7479. 11 rms (all with bath). $35 single; $45 double; $65 triple. No credit cards.

This place just oozes jungle atmosphere and is sure to please anyone searching for a steamy retreat on the beach. Set amid the shade of large old trees a few miles south of Puerto Viejo toward Punta Uva (watch for the sign), the lodge consists of unpainted wooden buildings set on stilts and connected by wooden walkways. There are wide verandahs with rocking chairs and seashell mobiles hanging everywhere. Rooms are dark and cool with wide-board floors and paintings by local Indian artists. The top of the bathroom wall is screened so you can gaze out into the jungle as you shower. There is a short trail that leads down to a private little swimming beach with beautiful turquoise water, as well as tide pools. Meals here cost from $5 to $13 and choices range from spaghetti to lobster; since the management is German, you can expect a few German dishes as well. Throughout the day there are free bananas and coffee.

✪ **Villas del Caribe.** Puerto Viejo, Limón (Apdo. 8080-1000, San José). ☎ **506/233-2200.** Fax 506/221-2801. 12 apts. $69 single or double; $79 triple; $89 quad. AE, MC, V.

If you want to be right on the beach and have spacious, comfortable accommodations, there is not a better choice in this area. Villas del Caribe, built in a sort of contemporary Mediterranean style and set on a 100-acre nature reserve, offers two-story townhouse apartments with full kitchens and a choice of one or two bedrooms. The living rooms have built-in sofa beds, and just outside there is a large terrace complete with barbecue grill. The kitchens are attractively designed with blue-tile counters. Bathrooms are tropical fantasies with wooden-slat shower doors, potted plants on a platform by the window, louvered and screened walls that let in light and air, and more blue tile counters. Upstairs you'll find either a large single bedroom with a king bed, or two smaller bedrooms (one with bunk beds). Either way, there's a balcony, with hammock and ocean view. The water, which is usually fairly calm, is only steps away through the coconut palms and there is some coral just offshore that makes for good snorkeling. The hotel can arrange horseback rides, fishing trips, snorkeling and diving, even oxcart rides. When I last visited, there was talk of opening a restaurant on the grounds.

WHERE TO EAT

To really sample the local cuisine, you need to look up a few local ladies. Ask around for **Miss Dolly** and see if she has anything cooking. Her specialties are bread (especially banana) and ginger biscuits, but she will also fix a special Caribbean meal for you if you ask a day in advance and she has time. **Miss Daisy** makes pan bon, ginger cakes, patties (meat-filled turnovers), and coconut oil (for tanning). Both **Miss Sam** and **Miss Irma** serve up sit-down meals in their modest little sodas. Just ask around for these folks and someone will direct you to them. Be sure to try run-down soup, which is a spicy coconut-milk stew made with anything the cook can run down.

MEALS FOR LESS THAN $6

Soda Tamara. On the main road through the village. No phone. Main courses $2.50–$5. No credit cards. Wed–Mon 7am–9pm. COSTA RICAN.

This little Tico-style restaurant has long been popular with budget-conscious travelers and has an attractive setting for such an economical place. There's a small patio dining area in addition to the main dining room, which is a bit dark. The painted picket fence in front gives the restaurant a very homey feel. At the counter inside, you'll find homemade cocoa candies and unsweetened cocoa biscuits. These are made by several ladies in town, and are definitely worth a try.

MEALS FOR LESS THAN $12

Cafe Pizzeria Coral. On the road to the soccer field. No phone. Reservations not accepted. Pizza $3.65–$6.80; pasta $4.05–$4.75. No credit cards. Tues–Sun 7–11am and 5:30–9pm. ITALIAN/PIZZA.

Although this place bills itself as a pizzeria, your best bets are the breakfasts, desserts, and fresh breads. While the pizza is mediocre, the chocolate cake is a standout. You'll find the Cafe Pizzeria Coral about two blocks from the water in the center of the village. The open-air dining room is up a few steps from the street and has hardwood floors and wood railings. The whole place is walled in by flowering hibiscus that attract plenty of hummingbirds in the morning, which is why this is my favorite breakfast joint in town.

✪ **Garden Restaurant.** Cabinas Jacaranda. No phone. Reservations not accepted. Main courses $4–$8. No credit cards. Thurs–Mon 5:30–9pm. Closed May–June and September. CARIBBEAN/ASIAN.

Just up the block form Cafe Coral, this restaurant serves the best food in Puerto Viejo and some of the best in all of Costa Rica. The co-owner and chef is from Trinidad by way of Toronto and has created an eclectic menu that is guaranteed to please. You'll find such surprising offerings as chicken saté (a Thai dish), fresh garden salad with passion-fruit dressing, Jamaican jerk chicken, calypso curry fish, and chicken Bangkok. There are also daily specials and lots of delicious fresh juices. Many of the ambrosial desserts are made with local fruits, and there are also such delights as ginger spice cake and macadamia chocolate torte. Every dish is beautifully presented, usually with edible flowers for garnish.

A NEARBY PLACE TO EAT

El Duende Feliz. On the main road, Punta Uva. No phone. Reservations not accepted. Main courses $3.50–$10.50. No credit cards. Sat–Wed 11am–2pm and 6–9pm, Thurs–Fri 6–9pm. ITALIAN.

Isn't it reassuring to know that even in the middle of nowhere, you can get a decent plate of gnocchi? El Duende Feliz is on the outskirts of Punta Uva Village and serves a wide selection of authentic Italian dishes. Seafood shows up quite a bit, of course. Depending on the day's catch, you can get seafood spaghetti and pizza with clams, among other dishes. There are also steaks and plenty of pasta dishes. You can even finish off your meal with a scoop of gelati and an espresso.

Getting to Know Belize 12

Belize is a Central American anomaly: it's an English-speaking nation surrounded by Spanish-speaking neighbors. Until it was renamed in 1973, it was called British Honduras, after the British settlers who set up camp here and began to supply hardwoods and other wood products to the British empire. With only 200,000 people, it is the least-populated country in all of Central America. The importance of this statistic is only now becoming significant as environmentalists continue to discover the vast undisturbed wilderness of Belize, where jaguars still roam the jungle in search of tapirs, and macaws still screech in the treetops. Add to this the dozens of tiny islands set amid the world's second-longest barrier reef (which offers world-class diving and fishing), a population that is more than 60% black Creole and Garifuna (people of black and Indian ancestry), and you have what is ostensibly a Caribbean-island nation on the Central American mainland. The most important British legacy left to Belize, however, is a stable political environment in a region of constant turmoil.

1 The Natural Environment

Belize is situated on a narrow strip of land along Central America's Caribbean coast, due south of Mexico's Yucatán Peninsula. It covers an area of just under 9,000 square miles, about the same size as the state of Massachusetts, and is bordered on the west and south by Guatemala and on the east by the Caribbean Sea. Offshore are hundreds of tiny islands, known as cayes (pronounced "keys"), that rise up from the world's second-longest barrier reef, which extends for more than 185 miles along the Belizean coast. From the wide, flat coastal plains, Belize rises up to form the Maya Mountains, mountain peaks of more than 3,000 feet and the source of the many rivers that wind through the country. For centuries these rivers were the principal means of transportation within Belize.

Despite the fact that most of Belize's primary forest and tropical hardwoods were harvested throughout the past three centuries, population density has always been extremely low and the forest reclaims ground quickly. Though Belize lacks any true primary tropical rain forest, it does possess large expanses of tropical moist and lowland secondary rain forest, as well as mangrove, swamp, and even highland pine forests. In fact, nearly 65% of Belize is uninhabited. This low level of human population has been a boon for a wide range of flora and fauna. More than 500 species of migratory and resident birds have been identified in Belize, including the massive Jabiru stork, the scarlet macaw, and the keel-billed toucan. Belize is also home to the largest concentration of jaguars on the planet. Revered by the ancient Maya and feared by most jungle dwellers, the jaguar is the largest New World cat, and can reach more than 6 feet in length and weigh over 250 pounds. The Cockscomb Basin Wildlife Sanctuary was created as the world's only jaguar preserve.

In addition to the jaguar, Belizean forests are home to several other cats, including the puma, ocelot, margay, and jagarundi, as well as such quintessential jungle dwellers as howler monkeys, green iguanas, and boa constrictors. The tapir is the country's national animal. Also called a mountain cow, the tapir is docile, curious, and entirely vegetarian. Still, these wild creatures stand nearly 5 feet tall and can weigh over 500 pounds.

Off Belize's coast, the barrier reef is a world all its own. Though the cayes are little more than low, flat coral and limestone outcroppings, the myriad underwater flora and fauna here is truly astounding. Colorful angel, parrot, and trigger fish feed on the multi-colored coral. Giant sponges provide homes and feeding grounds for hundreds of smaller fish and delicate coral shrimp. Under the rocks and caverns dwell lobster, moray eels, and octopus. Larger predators, such as sharks and barracudas, cruise the reefs for their plentiful prey, while manta and tiger rays glide gracefully over the sand bottoms and conch thrive in the sea grass.

2 The Regions in Brief

Northern Belize   Anchored by Belize City in the south, this is the country's business and agricultural heartland. Belize City is the only major city to speak of in Belize, with under 80,000 inhabitants. Toward the north lies Orange Walk Town and Corozal Town. Both of these small cities have a strong Spanish feel and influence, having been settled largely by refugees from Mexico's Caste War. The Maya also lived here, and their memories live on at the ruins of Altun Ha, Lamanai, Cerros, and Santa Rita, all in this zone. This is a land that was once submerged and is still primarily swamp and mangrove. Where the land is cleared and settled, sugar cane is the main cash crop.

The Cayes & the Barrier Reef   Belize's offshore islands lie between the coast of the mainland and the protection of the 185-mile-long barrier reef. The reef, easily visible from many of the cayes, offers some of the world's most exciting snorkeling, diving (there's a visibility of up to 200 feet), and fishing. The more developed cayes have extensive lodging facilities, while numerous charter boats and dive operators offer various day and overnight trips to explore the more remote islands.

For those whose main sport is catching rays, not fish, it should be mentioned that the cayes, and Belize in particular, lack wide, sandy beaches. Although the water is as warm and clear blue as it's touted to be, most of your sunbathing will be on docks or on deck chairs.

The Cayo district   This mountainous district near the Guatemalan border has become Belize's second most popular destination. Here you'll find some of Belize's most beautiful countryside and most fascinating natural and man-made sights. The limestone mountains of this region are dotted with numerous caves, sinkholes, jagged

Belize

MEXICO

GUATEMALA

Chetumal
Santa Rita
Corozal Town

Orange Walk

San Pedro

Blue Creek

Crooked Tree Wildlife Sanctuary

Altun Ha

Northern Highway

Uaxactún

Rio Bravo

Community Baboon Sanctuary

International Airport

Tikal

Spanish Lookout

Ladyville
Belize City

Hattieville

Belize River

San Ignacio

Belmopan

Western Highway

Santa Elena

Northern Lagoon

Caracol

Mountain Pine Ridge

Hummingbird Highway

Southern Lagoon

Maya Mountains

Cockscomb Range

South Stann Creek

Gales Point

Cockscomb Basin Wildlife Sanctuary

Dangriga
Hopkins

San Antonio

Monkey River

Placencia

Blue Creek Village

Southern Highway

Punta Gorda

Mobo River

Barranco

Temash River

Sarstoon River

Gulf of Honduras

Caribbean

Sea

Livingston

Castillo de San Felipe

Fronteras

Puerto Barrios

Lake Izabal

Morales

Quiriguá

CA9

Rio Hondo

HONDURAS

2-0138

259

peaks, and waterfalls. There are clear flowing rivers that are excellent for swimming and canoeing, as well as mile after mile of unexplored forest full of wild animals and hundreds of bird species. This was also the site of several major Mayan settlements more than 1,000 years ago. Caracol is said to be one of the largest classical Mayan cities known, but it has not yet been fully excavated. Xunantunich and Cahal Pech are smaller, but still impressive, pyramid-and-temple complexes not far from the town of San Ignacio.

Southern Belize   Southern Belize encompasses two major districts, Stann Creek and Toledo. The former includes the Cockscomb Basin Wildlife Sanctuary and the coastal towns of Dangriga, Hopkins Village, and Placencia. Dangriga is the country's major center of Garifuna culture and Placencia boasts what is arguably the country's only true beach. Farther south, the Toledo District is Belize's final frontier. While the coast is settled primarily by Garifuna and black Creoles, the inland hills and jungles are home to numerous Kekchi and Mopan Mayan villages. The Toledo district is also emerging as an ecotourism destination, with the country's richest, wettest, and most undisturbed rain forests.

3 Belize Today

Belize is the youngest nation in the Western hemisphere, having been granted independence in 1981. Originally a major part of the ancient Mayan empire, Belize was next settled by pirates and then colonized by the British, using slave labor. The descendants of each of these groups are woven into the historical lore and cultural fabric of modern Belize. Add to the mix the independent and unique Garifuna people, who settled all along the remote southern shore in the early part of the 19th century, and more recent waves of Mexican, Chinese, and East Indian immigrants, and you have an idea of the cultural melting pot that constitutes this unique Central American country. Surprisingly, Belizeans of all cultural stripes tend to get along a lot better and with far fewer outward and untoward shows of racism than most other nations. This is a small country. A sense of community is strong and, even in the big city, people tend to know their neighbors and almost everyone is somehow related.

Belize is a developing nation, plagued with a small economy, a tiny industrial base, no oil or natural gas reserves, a huge trade deficit, and an historic dependence on foreign aid. These problems have been compounded by the British pullout and a universal diminishing in international largesse. Sugar and citrus are the principal cash crops, though banana and seafood exports also help. Tourism is perhaps the most promising emergent source of income.

Belize held its first parliamentary elections in 1984. Since then, power has pingponged back and forth between the United Democratic Party (UDP) and the People's United Party (PUP). The former is a more conservative, free-market oriented party, while the latter champions a more liberal, social-democratic agenda. All of the country's newspapers hold fierce party loyalties and the strident political slant and tenor of the news stories and editorials might shock visitors accustomed to a more passive press.

In general, the pace of life (and business) is slow in Belize. You won't find people rushing down the sidewalks or dirt streets. There are only three major highways in the country and traffic is never heavy on these. However, one of the oddest things visitors first notice is the abundance of older, gas-guzzling American cars and station wagons. Due to high import duties on newer, more economical cars, mostly what you'll see—and hear—on the road are big clunkers.

4 History 101

Before the arrival of the first Europeans (ship-wrecked English sailors), this was the land of the enigmatic Mayas. Although most people think of Mexico's Mayan cities in the Yucatán and Guatemala's Tikal when they hear the word "Mayas," recent discoveries show that what is to-day known as Belize was once a major part of the classic and post-classic Mayan Empire. River and coastal trade routes connected dozens of cities and small towns throughout this region to the now better-known and more frequently visited cities in Mexico and Guatemala. Caracol, a Mayan ruin in the Cayo district of western Belize, is a huge ceremonial city that apparently defeated Tikal in battle in A.D. 562. Unfortunately, very little of this amazing discovery has been excavated or is likely to be excavated soon. The funds for massive res-torations, such as those done at Tikal and Chichén Itzá, simply are not available.

Corozal Town, in northern Belize, is built on the site of the last Mayan city still occupied when this area was discovered by a Spanish expedition-ary force in the 1530s. By the time those first un-lucky sailors washed ashore, the Mayan civilization was a mere remnant of its former glory.

Belize likes to play up the fact that it was founded by pirates and buccaneers, and, indeed, these unsavory characters were some of the first to make this region their base of operations, but they were hardly a civilizing influence. By the mid-17th century, British loggers were settling along the coast and making their way up the rivers and streams in search of mahogany for shipbuilding and other types of wood for making dyes. When it formally became the colony of British Hondu-ras in 1862, it was firmly established as a major source of wood for the still-expanding British em-pire. The forests were exploited, but agriculture was never encouraged. The British wanted their colony to remain dependent on the mother country, so virtually all the necessities of life were imported. Few roads were built, and the country remained unexplored and undeveloped with a tiny population, mostly clustered along the coast.

During the 18th and 19th centuries, African slaves were brought to British Hon-duras, and black Caribs also migrated here from the Caribbean Islands. They estab-lished their own villages and culture along the coast. In the mid-19th century, many Mexican and Guatemalan refugees fled across the borders into British Honduras and founded such towns as Corozal Town and Benque Viejo.

Dateline

- **2000** B.C.–A.D. **1000** Mayan civilization flourishes.
- **1638** Shipwrecked English sailors establish the first European settlement.
- **1783** English settlement rights are recognized.
- **1786** Settlements become self-governing. British super-intendent takes up residence.
- **1798** The last Spanish attack is beaten off by the settlers with British support.
- **1859** The border between Guatemala and British Honduras is established.
- **1862** The area officially becomes the colony of British Honduras.
- **1931** Hurricane destroys Belize City.
- **1948** Guatemala, laying claim to British Honduras, closes border.
- **1957** First Mennonite farmers arrive from Mexico.
- **1964** The new constitution provides for self-government, but Guatemalan claims to the country delay independence.
- **1973** British Honduras renamed Belize.
- **1981** Belize becomes an independent nation.
- **1984** First parliamentary election.
- **1992** An agreement is reached wherein Guatemala acknowledges Belize's independence and territorial limits.
- **1996** Famed Mayan healer Don Elijio Panit dies at an estimated 104 years of age.

In the early 1960s, groundwork was laid for granting British Honduras independence. However, based on 16th-century Spanish claims to all Central America, Guatemala claimed that the territory belonged to them. Fearful of an invasion by Guatemalan forces, the British delayed granting independence until an agreement could be reached with Guatemala. Although the 1964 constitution granted self-government to the British colony, it was not until September 21, 1981, that Belize, which had changed its name in 1973, actually gained its independence. Thus Belize is Central America's newest nation.

The British legacy in Belize is a relatively stable government with a parliamentary system and regular elections that are contested by two major parties and several smaller parties.

5 Speaking of Tongues

English is the official language of Belize, but the traveler will most likely run across a wide range of languages. Three centuries of colonization have given the Queen's English some foothold here; however, a large percentage of the local population, particularly black Creoles, speak a *patois* or Creole English that is downright unintelligible to most English-speaking visitors. In recent years there have been moves to standardize and record Creole, and you may see it written out on billboards and in newspapers. *How fi Rite Bileez Kriol* ("How To Write Belize Creole") is a widely available pamphlet sold at local bookstores and gift shops, if you want to take a stab at communicating in Creole.

Moreover, this is still Central America and Spanish is widely spoken in Belize, especially in the northern and western regions near the borders with Mexico and Guatemala. If that's not enough, Belize has three relatively homogenous indigenous groups, the Garifunas, the Kekchi, and the Mopan Mayas, each of whom has a distinct language. Finally, rounding out this polyglot pastiche, you may also hear some Chinese, Arabic, Hindi, or even some archaic German (used by the country's small Mennonite community).

6 Belizean Food & Drink

Don't expect gourmet food during your visit to Belize. Since Belize is a coastal nation, seafood is common. Eat it as often as you can. It's fresh, delicious, and by far the best bargain to be had. Belize has little in the way of its own cuisine, so you'll find plenty of burgers, pizzas, fried fish, and Chinese food.

Because Belize only recently began to grow its own beef and crops, the country relied for a long time on wild game. A favorite is gibnut, a large forest rodent that looks like a cross between a rat and a deer. The gibnut is alleged to taste like rabbit. The Queen Mother tried some during her last visit here, earning this culinary oddity the title of "the Royal Rat."

Another popular wild animal found prepared in restaurants is the sea turtle, endangered all over the world, including in Belize. It's not yet illegal to sell sea turtle within Belize, but international agreements prohibit its export. Please don't order gibnut, turtle steak, or other wild game. Belize is struggling to preserve its natural environment, and as long as people order wild game, it will show up on menus.

Belize has also been a major exporter of lobster for many years, but overfishing has caused the population to decline. It is still available and quite inexpensive, but there is a season on lobster (which is subject to change). During the off-season (usually between Feb 15 and July 14), it should not be on any menus, but please do not order it if it is.

Most major brands of soft drinks are available, as are fresh lime juice (lime-aid) and orange juice. You're in the Tropics, so don't be surprised to find fresh shakes made with papaya, pineapple, or mango. Belikin beer and Belikin stout are the local beers, but a few other imported brands are available. Several commercially bottled fruit wines are produced in Belize using native fruits. These wines are very sweet and more of a novelty than anything else. In remote parts of the country, you'll find homemade fruit wines that are a bit like hard cider. Most restaurants serve mixed drinks, with a variety of domestic and imported liquors available.

A WORD ABOUT WATER

Much of the drinking water in Belize is rainwater. People use the roof of their house to collect water in a cistern which supplies them for the year. Tap water generally is not considered safe to drink, even in most major cities. The water in Belize City and San Ignacio is reputably safe to drink, but as most of us get a touch of diarrhea whenever we hit a foreign country, play it safe. Ask for bottled drinking water at your hotel, and whenever you can, pick up a bottle of spring or purified water to have handy (it's available in most markets).

13 Planning a Trip to Belize

More and more intrepid explorers are discovering Belize's natural and historic wonders: bird, monkey, and jaguar sanctuaries; Mayan ruins; mahogany forests; and huge limestone caves. Most visitors head straight for the cayes—to play in or on, or to simply marvel at all that beautiful Belizean blue water. While the interior doesn't give itself up easily (that's why it's remained so special and undeveloped), there are plenty of natural wonders and adventures for folks who head inland. Belize is expensive by Central American standards, but there are still bargains to be had. This chapter will tell you all you need to know to plan for your trip.

1 Visitor Information & Entry Requirements

VISITOR INFORMATION

The U.S. office of the **Belize Tourist Board,** 421 Seventh Ave., New York, NY 10001 (☎ **800/624-0686** or 212/563-6011; fax 212/563-6033), will send you a packet of information about the country in response to a phone call or faxed request.

Once you're in Belize, you can visit the **Belize Tourist Board** at 83 North Front St. in Belize City (☎ **501-2/77213** or 501-2/73255; fax 501-2/77490). The office is open Monday to Friday from 8am to noon and from 1 to 5pm, although they tend to close one half-hour earlier on Friday. You'll also find books and pamphlets about Belize in most gift shops and bookstores around the country.

ENTRY REQUIREMENTS

Documents If you are a citizen of the United States, Canada, or a Commonwealth country, you need only a valid passport to enter Belize. All other visitors must also have a visa, available from a Belizean consulate. Visas and entry stamps are issued for up to 30 days. To extend your visa, apply at the **Immigration Office** on Mahogany Street Extension, Belize City (☎ **501-2/24620**). For B$25 ($12.50), you can extend your visa for 30 days, provided you have proof of sufficient funds.

Belize Online

With the explosion of the Internet and World Wide Web, you'll be able to find quite a bit of information about Belize online. **The Belize Tourism Industry Association** has a web site (http://www.belize.com/). This is the most extensive Belize-related site and has the largest collection of hotel listings, as well as useful facts, descriptions of the various Mayan sites, and general and business information. You can also try the **"Belize Network"** (http://www2.belizenet.com/Bus/Rath/). Designed and maintained by photographer and artist Tony Rath, this is the most aesthetically pleasing Belizean web site, with a photo gallery, hotel listings, Angelus Press' online catalogue (with ordering information), and an online version of the weekly Belize Reporter. For a more down-home Belizean web site experience, visit **"You Better Belize It!"** (http://www.belizeit.com/). This site has historical, cultural and tourism information, but my favorite aspect is its "Shout Out" section, a public bulletin and message board for Belizeans and friends around the world.

The Belize Embassy in the United States is at 2535 Massachusetts Ave. NW, Washington, D.C. 20008 (☎ **202/332-9636**); in England, it's at 10 Harcourt House, 19A Cavendish Square, London W1M 9AD (☎ **71/499-9728**). In Canada, contact the Belize High Commission, 112 Kent St., Place de Ville, Tower B, Suite 2005, Ottawa, Ontario (☎ **613/232-7389**).

Customs   Visitors may bring 200 cigarettes and a fifth of liquor into Belize. Most personal items, including fishing and diving gear, as well as personal laptop computers and portable CD- and tape players, are also allowed in duty free.

2 Money

CASH/CURRENCY

The unit of currency in Belize is the Belizean dollar, abbreviated B$. Denominations of B$1, B$2, B$5, B$10, B$20, B$50, and B$100 are available. Coins come in 1B¢, 5B¢, 25B¢, 50B¢, and B$1 denominations. United States dollars are accepted at most major hotels and larger tourist attractions; however, the use of the national currency is preferred.

The Belize dollar is officially tied to the U.S. dollar at a 2-to-1 ratio ($1 U.S. equals B$2). Although it is officially illegal, the black or "grey" market is where everyone exchanges money because the banks charge a 2% to 3% commission. Never exchange money with someone who approaches you on the street. Always ask at your hotel where you can exchange money. If they can't make the transaction themselves, they'll tell you who will.

It's good to have at least $25 in U.S. dollars with you for emergencies (most places will take them if you don't have Belize dollars).

TRAVELER'S CHECKS

Traveler's checks are almost as readily convertible as cash dollars anywhere in Belize, so it pays to take the precaution of carrying your money in this more secure form.

What Things Cost In Belize	U.S. $
Taxi from the airport to the city center	$15.00
Local telephone call	.13
Double at Chaa Creek Cottages (expensive)	$115.00
Double at Barrier Reef Hotel (moderate)	$65.00
Double at Rubie's Hotel (inexpensive)	$25.00
Lunch for one at Elvi's Kitchen (moderate)	$10.00
Lunch for one at The Reality Cafe (inexpensive)	$6.00
Dinner for one, without wine, at the Lagoon Restaurant (expensive)	$20.00
Dinner for one, without wine, at Lily's (moderate)	$15.00
Dinner for one, without wine, at Ambergris Delight (inexpensive)	$7.00
Bottle of beer	$1.25
Coca-Cola	.65
Cup of coffee	.50
Roll of ASA 100 Kodacolor film, 36 exposures	$7.00
Admission to the Xunantunich ruins	$5.00

The Belizean Dollar, the U.S. Dollar & the British Pound

The Belize dollar is fixed to the U.S. dollar. However, the exchange rate for both fluctuates in relation to the British pound. Therefore the following table should be used only as a guide:

B$	U.S.$	U.K.£	B$	U.S.$	U.K.£
1	.50	.33	7	3.50	2.30
2	1.00	.65	8	4.00	2.60
3	1.50	1.00	9	4.50	2.90
4	2.00	1.30	10	5.00	3.20
5	2.50	1.60	50	25.00	16.00
6	3.00	2.00	100	50.00	32.00

Most hotels, restaurants, and gift shops will give you a straight 2-to-1 exchange, although some will take out a small percentage.

CREDIT CARDS

Credit cards are becoming more and more accepted in Belize; however, hotels, restaurants, and shops will sometimes add a 5 to 10% surcharge on credit card purchases. American Express, MasterCard, and VISA are the most readily accepted cards in Belize. In more remote destinations, you are less likely to be able to charge things.

ATMS

At present, you will not find any ATMs in Belize that will grant you access to your home bank accounts or give you a cash advance off of one of your credit cards.

3 When to Go

Most people plan their trips to Belize around the weather. The Belizean "dry" season corresponds well with northern winters, and that's when most visitors come to Belize. However, if you choose to come during the "rainy" season, you will find better bargains and far fewer fellow travelers. Diving is also outstanding during the months of June through August, when the seas outside the barrier reef calm down.

CLIMATE

Belize's climate is very similar to southern Florida. In the summer months, it is very hot (temperatures in the shade can approach 100°F); and from June to mid-November, it rains almost daily. Usually, this is just a dependable and short-lived afternoon shower. However, the amount of rainfall varies considerably from region to region. In the south, there may be more than 150 inches per year, while in the north there's rarely more than 50 inches per year. There's also a brief dry period in August, known as the *mauger*.

Most tourists come to Belize during the dry season, which extends from December to May. From time to time, during the dry season, a storm front—or "norther"—in the northern hemisphere will bring a few days of cooler temperatures, strong winds, and rain, especially to the cayes.

Daytime temperatures in Belize City average 80°F, although it gets considerably warmer between June and August. Temperatures on the coast can climb quite high in the summer, but the constant trade winds offer a bit of relief. During the northern winter months, temperatures can dip as low as 40°F at night in the mountains of the Cayo district, although it warms up during the day.

Average Monthly Temperatures & Rainfall in Belize

	Jan	Feb	Mar	Apr	May	June	July	Aug	Sept	Oct	Nov	Dec
Temp °F	73.4	76.1	77.9	79.7	81.5	81.5	81.5	81.5	80.6	78.8	75.2	74.3
Temp °C	23	24.5	25.5	26.5	27.5	27.5	27.5	27.5	27	26	24	23.5
Days of Rain	12	6	4	5	7	13	15	14	15	16	12	14

HOLIDAYS

Official holidays in Belize include January 1, New Year's Day; March 9, Baron Bliss Day; Good Friday; Holy Saturday; Easter Monday; May 1, Labor Day; May 24, Commonwealth Day; September 10, St. George's Caye Day; September 21, Independence Day; October 12, Columbus Day; November 19, Garifuna Settlement Day; December 25, Christmas; December 26, Boxing Day; December 31, New Year's Eve.

BELIZE CALENDAR OF EVENTS

February

- **Carnival,** San Pedro, Ambergris Caye. Traditional Caribbean Carnival or Mardi Gras celebration; watch out for painters. The weekend before Lent begins. For more information, call the Belize Tourist Board (☎ **501-2/77213** or 501-2/73255) or the San Pedro Town Board (☎ **501-26/2198**).

March

✪ **Baron Bliss Day.** Nationwide celebrations of the country's eccentric benefactor. In Belize City, there are horse, foot, and boat races. March 9.

May
- **Cashew Festival,** Crooked Tree Village. A weekend-long celebration of this small village's cashew harvest. It's a chance to sample cashew bread, cashew wine, and a wide range of dishes featuring this exotic nut. First weekend of May. For more information, call the Belize Tourist Board (☎ **501-2/77213** or 501-2/73255).

June
- **Dia de San Pedro,** San Pedro, Ambergris Caye. Three-day festival in honor of the town's patron saint. June 16 through 19.

September
- **St. George's Caye Day,** Belize City. Located just a few miles outside the harbor in Belize City, St. George's Caye was the site of a decisive victory over Spanish forces in 1798. Parades and street parties celebrate this early Belizean triumph over colonial forces. September 10.
- **Independence Day.** Nationwide independence day celebration, with parades, street fairs, outdoor concerts, and flag raisings. September 21.

November
- ✪ **Garifuna Settlement Day.** Celebrated throughout the coastal region, but the largest and most impressive celebration occurs in Dangriga, where Garifunas from across Belize gather to commemorate their arrival from St. Vincent in 1832. November 19.

4 Organized Tours & Packages

Belize is a user-friendly country for do-it-yourself frugal travelers. Travel within the country is cheap and reliable, both by bus and plane. In most towns (except perhaps Caye Caulker and San Pedro during the high season) you can usually rustle up a place to stay even if you arrive without a reservation, although it's always advisable to reserve a room in advance whenever possible.

Established tour operators and prepaid packages do have their advantages. First-time travelers might enjoy having a lot of the guesswork taken out of the trip. In addition, large operators can sometimes save you money by buying space in bulk and in advance. At the very least, most of the companies listed below will be more than happy to send you information packets, brochures, and price quotes.

Some international operators with a history of organizing trips to Belize include: **Belize International Travel Representatives,** P.O. Box 83-0818, Miami, FL 33283 (☎ **800/545-2510** or 305/385-6033); **Global Travel Club,** 1 Kiln Shaw Langdon Hills, Basildon, Essex SS16 6LE, England (☎ **44/268-541732** in England; Fax 44/268-542275); **International Expeditions Inc.,** One Environs Park, Helena, AL 35080 (☎ **800/633-4734** or 205/428-1700); Magnum Belize, P.O. Box 1560, Detroit Lakes, MN 56502 (☎ **800/447-2931;** Fax 218/847-0334); **Winter Escapes,** P.O. Box 429, Erickson, Manitoba, R0J 0P0, Canada (☎ **204/636-2968;** Fax 204/636-2557).

5 Health & Insurance

STAYING HEALTHY

Staying healthy while traveling is predominantly a matter of being a little cautious about what you eat and drink, and using common sense. Know your physical limits and don't overexert yourself in the ocean, on hikes, or in athletic activities. The most common health problems to mar a vacation in the Tropics are sunburn and a mild case of *turista*, or diarrhea. The former is easily guarded against with a good sunscreen. The latter is directly related to what you eat and drink. With a little precaution you should be fine.

The water in Belize is predominantly rainwater collected in cisterns. Although the water in major cities like Belize City and San Ignacio is treated and reputedly safe to drink, I recommend buying and drinking bottled water or soft drinks.

Vaccinations   No vaccinations are required for a visit to Belize. However, because sanitation is generally not as good as it is in developed countries, you may be exposed to diseases for which you may wish to get vaccinations: typhoid, polio, tetanus, and infectious hepatitis (gamma globulin). Your risk of encountering any of these diseases is minimal, but many travelers would rather be safe than sorry. Consult your physician a couple of months before your trip to see if you can be immunized, or if other precautions are advisable.

Tropical Diseases   Your chances of contracting any serious tropical disease in Belize are very slim. However, both malaria and dengue fever do exist in Belize, particularly in the more rural inland areas. Your best protection from these is a good mosquito repellent. Cholera is also known in Belize, but relatively uncommon. In more rural and off-the-beaten-track areas, avoid undercooked food, raw-fish ceviche, and garden salads. For more information on these diseases, and recommendations about avoiding mosquito bites, see chapter 5, "Planning a Trip to Costa Rica."

Snakes   Belizean jungles and forests are home to several species of venomous snakes, including the brightly banded and highly poisonous coral snake and the feared fer-de-lance. However, your chances of seeing one of these, much less being bitten, are minimal, especially if you refrain from sticking your hands under rocks and fallen logs in the forest.

INSURANCE

Before leaving on your trip, contact your health-insurance provider and find out whether your insurance will cover you while you are away. If not, contact a travel agent and ask about travel health-insurance policies. See "Health and Insurance," in chapter 5 for more information.

6 Tips for Travelers with Special Needs

FOR TRAVELERS WITH DISABILITIES

Few streets in Belize have sidewalks, and on the cayes there are really no streets at all, only sandy lanes and paths. There are currently no organizations in Belize to help disabled travelers and I've yet to come across a hotel designed with people with disabilities in mind. Consequently, disabled visitors to Belize have a very difficult time.

FOR SENIORS

Don't expect to find senior-citizen discounts here. The tourism industry is still a fledgling enterprise in Belize, and seniors are treated the same as anyone else. Still, many airlines now offer senior-citizen discounts, so be sure to ask about these when making reservations. If you don't think you have the energy required for a visit to a jungle lodge, think again. Many of the jungle lodges in Belize offer a wide variety of activities that people of all ages will find enjoyable. You're never too old to explore the jungles!

FOR SINGLES

As in most places, the single traveler is at a disadvantage in Belize. Some hotels do have single rooms and single-room rates. Unfortunately, single-room rates are usually higher than what each person would pay in a double room. In many hotels you may have to pay the rate for a double room, particularly if you want a private bath. It's always a good idea to find a fellow solo traveler to help cut costs. In San Ignacio, **Eva's Restaurant** serves as a meeting ground for lone travelers seeking other adventurers to share the cost of taxis, canoe rentals, and tour rates. Tell Bob behind the counter what you're interested in doing, and he'll put your name on a list with other people interested in the same activity.

If you are looking for someone to travel with before heading south, **Travel Companions Exchange,** P.O. Box 833, Amityville, NY 11701-0833 (☎ **516/454-0880**), provides listings of possible travel companions categorized under such headings as special interests, age, education, and location. It costs a minimum of $99 for an eight-month membership and subscription to the service. It's also possible to subscribe to the organization's bimonthly newsletter without becoming a member. The newsletter costs $24 for a six-month subscription.

FOR STUDENTS

Belize has no organized youth-hostel network or student rates. Check with the airlines when purchasing a ticket; there are sometimes special fares for students.

FOR GAY & LESBIAN TRAVELERS

Belize is a relatively conservative country and whatever gay and lesbian community exists is extremely low profile. Same-sex displays of affection are uncommon in public and would probably draw unwelcome attention and verbal comments. When I last visited, there were no well-known gay or lesbian bars in operation.

7 Getting There

BY PLANE

Now that Belize has hit the international map, fares have dropped considerably and are comparable to those to other cities in the region. Daily flights to Belize City run from New York, Los Angeles, Miami, Houston, and New Orleans, with additional flights originating in Mexico and most Central American nations. **Tropic Air** (☎ **800/422-3435**), a small Belizean airline, has daily flights from Flores (Tikal).

FINDING THE BEST AIRFARE

Airline prices fluctuate dramatically, especially international fares. Fare wars break out unexpectedly and usually the best deals are not loudly advertised. However, if one airline announces a cheap fare, its competitors usually rush in the next week to match it, or offer an even lower fare. Call around when you see a tantalizing advertisement or two. That said, truly inexpensive fares often come with an armload of restrictions and clauses. You'll probably have to stay over at least one Saturday night, pay for your ticket within 24 hours of booking it, and reserve it several weeks, if not months, in advance. One thing to keep in mind is that flights in the off-season (late spring through early fall) are frequently cheaper.

REGULAR AIRFARES

The aforementioned instability makes it very tricky to quote airline prices. If you want a rock-bottom ticket, your best bet is to do your homework and make lots of phone calls. **APEX (advance-purchase excursion) fares** are often similar from airline to airline, but the cost of a first-class ticket can vary greatly. At press time, an APEX or a coach ticket from Miami to Belize City was running between $396 and $550; from New York, between $440 and $660. First class from Miami starts at about $1,150; from New York, $1,410.

TICKET BROKERS/CONSOLIDATORS

You can shave a bit off the price you pay by purchasing an airline ticket from what is known as a ticket broker or consolidator. These ticketing agencies sell discounted airfares on major airlines; although the tickets have as many, and sometimes more, restrictions than an APEX ticket, they can help you save money. You'll find ticket brokers' listings—usually just a column of destinations with prices beside them—in the Sunday travel sections of major city newspapers. You'll almost never get the ticket for the advertised price, but you'll probably get it for less than the airline would sell it to you. If you'd like to shop around, try **Cheap Tickets, Inc.** (☎ **800/377-1000**) or **World Travel Consultants** (☎ **800-318-8802**).

THE MAJOR AIRLINES

At press time, there are no direct flights to Belize from Europe. From Canada, only charter flights fly direct. Otherwise, all international travelers (except those arriving from Central and South America) must make a connection in the United States. The following airlines currently serve Belize from the United States, using the gateway cities listed. **American Airlines** (☎ **800/433-7300**) has direct flights from Miami and Dallas/Fort Worth; **Continental** (☎ **800/231-0856**) offers a nonstop direct flight from Houston; **TACA** (☎ **800/535-8780**), El Salvador's national airline, has direct flights originating from Los Angeles, Houston, New Orleans, New York, Miami, and Washington.

BY BUS

There are only two land routes into Belize—from Chetumal, Mexico, and from Flores, Guatemala. Both routes offer daily bus service, although the road from Guatemala can become impassable in the rainy season. Buses from Chetumal cross the border throughout the day and proceed into Corozal Town. From Corozal Town, you can catch a bus to Belize City or fly to San Pedro on Ambergris Caye (see chapter 18 for more details).

Buses from Flores, Guatemala drop passengers in Melchor de Mencos at the bridge that separates Guatemala and Belize. From there, there are several buses a day heading directly into Belize City. However, you might have to cross the bridge by foot, pass through customs, and catch a local Belizean bus or take a taxi. The first town in Belize is Benque Viejo, which has few services or accommodations and is less than a mile from the border. Your best bet is to continue another 8 miles into San Ignacio by either bus or taxi. There is fairly regular service between the border and San Ignacio throughout the day. If you have a group of people together, you can share a taxi for around B$5 ($2.50) per person; otherwise, you'll have to pay about B$20 ($10) to hire a taxi to San Ignacio. The bus from the border to San Ignacio is B$1.50 (75¢). From San Ignacio, you can catch a bus to Belize City (see chapter 15).

See "By Car," below, for details on crossing the border.

BY CAR

It's possible to enter Belize by car from either Mexico or Guatemala, but very few travelers bring their own vehicles on the grueling overland route from Guatemala City to Petén and the Belizean border.

If you're entering Belize at Chetumal, you must hand in your Mexican Tourist Card (and/or car papers, if you have them) at the Mexican border station. You'll be issued new ones if you re-enter Mexico. If you have Mexican auto insurance, get the policy stamped by an official so that you can get a rebate for the days you're outside Mexican territory. Cross the bridge over the Río Hondo and you're in Belize.

All border stations are open 24 hours a day, with no breaks for lunch. However, it is always advisable to try to clear customs and handle paperwork during daylight hours.

Your entry permit is the rubber stamp put on your passport (other forms of identification are not accepted), and it will show how long you're allowed to stay. To be on the safe side, ask for a few more days than you think you'll need; the cayes can be very enticing.

Be sure to get a **Temporary Import Permit** for your car, even if no one tells you a thing about it. Ask for the Customs official if he's not there and get the permit, or you'll be held up at the border when you leave the country. Also required is Belizean auto insurance, which you can buy at several stands located just inside Belize, at either border crossing. Be careful: The insurance stands usually follow normal business hours, and may be closed on weekends and holidays (they're usually open Saturday). Without insurance, you will not be able to proceed, so try to cross during business hours on a weekday.

After they've stamped your passport, issued your auto permit, and inspected your car (a process that ranges from a glance through the window to a good search), you're on your way.

The money changers at the border will give the standard 2-to-1 ratio for your U.S. dollars. *However, if you try to change pesos or quetzals at the border you will probably do poorly.* Once inside Belize, a bank is your best bet for exchanging any foreign currency, except dollars.

8　Getting Around

BY PLANE

Because of the lack of decent roads in most of the country and thanks to very reasonable airfares, flying is a common and recommended means of getting around inside Belize. There are flights between Corozal Town and San Pedro and between Belize City and Corozal Town, San Pedro, Caye Caulker, Caye Chapel, Dangriga, Big Creek, Placencia, and Punta Gorda. The following small Belizean airlines have telephone numbers in the United States: **Island Air** (☎ **800/257-8802**) and **Tropic Air** (☎ **800/422-3435**). See the regional chapters for more information about flight schedules and fares to your particular destination.

BY BUS

Buses run between all the main towns (except the cayes) and tourist destinations in Belize, with Belize City acting as the hub for most routes. The fares are low, and buses are generally in good condition. However, bus service isn't always frequent. See the regional chapters for specific schedules and fares.

BY CAR

Driving, whether in your own car or a rental, does add a sense of freedom and flexibility to your travels. Nevertheless, most roads in Belize are not paved, so you must have a very sturdy vehicle, preferably with four-wheel drive (especially in the rainy season). Belize is not a particularly scenic country for car touring and most destinations are well served by bus, air, and tour services.

There are really only two paved highways—the **Northern Highway** and the **Western Highway.** The Hummingbird, or Southern, Highway was partially paved at one time, but is now a battlefield of potholes that's periodically repaired and then washed out in the next heavy rain. You'll be thankful for plain old dirt after driving this road. If you're driving your own car, install heavy-duty shocks. Also, keep your eyes peeled for "sleeping policemen"—speed bumps (usually unmarked)—that can be found as you enter any populated area.

Belize's rental fleet has been upgraded in recent years, and most agencies now only rent four-wheel-drive vehicles. All agencies are based in Belize City, with offices either at the airport or downtown, or both. International car-rental agencies with offices in Belize City include **Avis** (☎ **800/331-1212** in the U.S.), **Budget** (☎ **800/527-0700** in the U.S.), and **National** (☎ **800/328-4567** in the U.S.). You can often save quite a bit of money by booking your car rental in advance from the United States, or abroad.

Whether you're driving your own car or a rental, you will have to have insurance coverage. On rental cars, most credit-card and U.S. policies are invalid because the driving is considered "off-road" and the vehicles are usually four-wheel drive.

Despite its long history as a British colony and dependency, Belizeans drive on the right-hand side of the road. Gasoline currently costs around B$4.70 ($2.35) per gallon.

BY RV

There are a few campgrounds with RV hookups scattered around Belize. **Caribbean Village Resort** (☎ **501-4/222725**) in Corozal Town is one. You can also camp at the **Cockscomb Basin Jaguar Preserve.** You'll need an overnight permit, available at preserve headquarters.

BY FERRY

Boats make regular runs to Caye Caulker and Ambergris Caye from Belize City; others operate between Big Creek and Placencia, which is not an island but a long spit of land. See chapters 16 and 18, respectively, for more information.

HITCHHIKING

You can hitchhike in Belize, but buses are easier and safer and quite cheap. The only time you might wish to hitchhike is if you're trying to get to one of the remote parks or preserves on your own and you don't want to rent a car. You may have to wait a while for a ride, though; there's not much traffic on Belize's back roads. One more caveat: While Belize is safer than some other places, hitchhiking is always a risky proposition, especially for women traveling alone, or in pairs.

FAST FACTS: Belize

American Express   Belize's only American Express office is in Belize City. See "Fast Facts: Belize City," in chapter 14 for location and hours.

Business Hours   In general, banks are open Monday through Thursday from 8am to 1pm, and Friday 8am to 1pm and 3 to 6pm. However, in smaller towns, hours may vary. Most offices and stores are open Monday to Friday from 8am to noon and 1 to 5pm. Some stores are starting to open on Saturday. Restaurants are generally open daily from 11am to 2pm and again from 6 to 10pm.

Climate   See "When to Go," earlier in this chapter.

Currency   See "Money," earlier in this chapter.

Driving Rules   See "Getting Around," earlier in this chapter.

Drug Laws   Although marijuana is grown in Belize, it's illegal, and the penalties for its possession are stiff. The same goes for cocaine. Be sure to bring along copies of prescriptions for any medicines you regularly take; this can save you hassles going through Customs, and make it easy to fill prescriptions while you're here.

Drugstores   You'll find licensed pharmacies in most of the larger towns in Belize.

Electricity   The electrical current is 110 volts.

Embassies and Consulates   United States Embassy, 29 Gabourel Lane, Hutson Street, Belize City (☎ **501-2/77161**); Canadian Consulate, 83 North Front St., Belize City (☎ **501-2/31060**); British High Commission, Embassy Square, Belmopan (☎ **501-8/22146** or 501-8/22147); Guatemalan Embassy, 6A St. Mathews St., Belize City (☎ **501-2/33150** or 501-2/33314); Mexican Embassy, 20 North Park St., Belize City (☎ **501-2/30193**).

Emergencies   In case of fire, or to call an ambulance, dial 90; for the police, dial 911 anywhere or 72210 in Belize City, 22222 in Belmopan, 2022 in San Ignacio or San Pedro, 23129 in Placencia, 2120 in Caye Caulker, or 22022 in Dangriga, Punta Gorda, Orange Walk, or Corozal Town.

Holidays   See "When to Go," earlier in this chapter.

Language   English is the official language, although Spanish, several Mayan dialects, Garifuna, and Creole also are spoken.

Liquor Laws   You must be 18 years old to purchase alcoholic beverages in Belize.

Mail   Letters take about a week to reach the United States. A postcard to the United States costs 30B¢ (15¢), a letter, 60B¢ (30¢). It costs 40B¢ (20¢) to send a postcard to Europe, and 75B¢ (38¢) for a letter. You can usually buy stamps at hotels, shops that sell postcards, and the post office.

For those requiring faster service, **DHL Worldwide Express** has an office at 38 New Road, Belize City (☎ **501-2/34350**). Regardless of what the clerk may tell you, overnight packages tend to take 3 or 4 days to reach the U.S.

Maps   The Belize Tourist Bureau in Belize City has several different maps—some free, others for a few dollars. They sell a very good map of the entire country for B$14 ($7). Maps are also available at most bookstores and gift shops.

Newspapers/Magazines   The *Miami Herald* and *USA Today* are the most readily available international newspapers in Belize and can be found at larger hotels throughout the country. Belizean newspapers are profoundly lacking in hard news, being primarily mouthpieces for the many political parties in the country. There are four principal papers: the *Belize News,* the *Reporter, Amandala,* and the *Observer.* All are weeklies, appearing on Friday, but dated the subsequent Sunday.

Pets   If you want to bring your pet along, check with the Belizean consulate before traveling. At the very least, you will be required to produce a recent veterinarian's certificate of good health and proof that Fido or Morris has been inoculated against rabies sometime in the last year.

Police   See "Emergencies," above.

Radio/TV   There are several AM and FM radio stations in Belize. Programming consists of talk shows and plenty of soca and reggae music. TV offerings include two national TV stations, and widespread satellite- and cable TV.

Taxes   On April 15, 1996, the Belizean government instituted a 15% Value-Added Tax (VAT) on all goods and services. Hotel rooms are exempt, but all meals at hotels and independent restaurants are taxed. At press time, the hotel tax is 7%, although there's been talk of raising it to 15%, so that the nation enjoys a standardized rate. Many restaurants (and some hotels) add on a 10% to 15% service charge. This is intended to cover tipping. If you're unsure, ask what your hotel's policy is, and check your bill at restaurants. The prices quoted in this guidebook do not include the service charge, VAT, or the hotel tax, so please take them into consideration when planning your trip.

If you depart by air, you'll be charged a departure tax of B$22.50 ($11.25).

Telephones   Pay phones can be found sporadically on the streets of major cities and towns as well as in the lobbies of large hotels. They accept coins of different denominations but do not give change; a local phone call is B25¢ (13¢). The dial tone is similar to that in the United States.

The **country code** for Belize is 501, and this number must be used when dialing Belize from the U.S. Phone numbers in Belize differ in the number of digits they have, and each town has its own city code. When dialing long distance from within Belize, you must always dial a zero before the city code. When calling from outside Belize, you don't use the zero. When making local calls, do not use the city code.

The **city codes** are: Belize City, 2; Belmopan, 8; Benque Viejo, 9; Blue Creek, 3; Burrell Boom, 28; Caye Caulker, 22; Corozal, 4; Dangriga, 5; Independence, 6; Ladyville, 25; Orange Walk, 3; Placencia, 6; Punta Gorda, 7; San Ignacio, 92; San Pedro, 26; Spanish Lookout, 8.

Time   Belize is on central standard time, or 6 hours behind Greenwich mean time.

Tipping   It's customary to tip waiters and waitresses 10% to 15%, but only if a service charge is not included in the bill. Bellhops and porters expect B$1 per bag. It's not necessary to tip taxi drivers.

Water   On the cayes, avoid tap water, which is often from shallow wells. In Belize City and most major towns, tap water is heavily chlorinated and reputed to be safe to drink. Throughout the country, people rely on cisterns to collect rainwater for drinking. At your hotel, a pitcher of drinking water will generally be provided upon request; otherwise, bottled water is available and recommended.

14 Belize City

Belize City is no longer the capital of Belize, but as the largest city, it remains the business, transportation, and cultural hub of the country. Sooner or later you're going to have to spend some time here, unless you do all your intra-country traveling by air or have a very well-planned itinerary. Whether you are just passing through or spending a day or two here, this chapter will make Belize City a breeze for you.

Despite a reputation for crime and violence, periodic devastation from passing hurricanes, and the loss of its capital status, Belize City remains the urban heart and soul of Belize. Actually, it's the only urban center in Belize, with a population nearing 80,000. Surrounded on three sides by water, Belize City is a strange, yet fascinating mix of narrow streets and canals (the latter are little more than open sewers and pretty pungent in hot weather), modern stores, dilapidated shacks, and quaint wooden mansions. At high tide, it's nearly swamped.

Though founded by pirates (a historical point of fact its residents seem to relish), Belize City was actually settled by British loggers, with the aid of slave labor. Throughout its history, it's had a reputation as a rough-and-tumble kind of place. And while recent municipal efforts have led to reduced street crime, you should still stick pretty close to the well-trafficked parts of town. In addition, even though Belize City is eminently walkable, avoid walking its streets at night (taxis are inexpensive). During the day, do what the locals do: shop (this is a good place to buy handcrafts and other made-in-Belize products, such as sauces, chutneys, and inexpensive rums) and stock up on any supplies you might need before you head elsewhere. There are restaurants where you can eat a good meal, and there's a charming fleet of working wooden fish sloops near the swing bridge that connects the north and south sections of the city. You can watch the bridge being hand-cranked open twice daily, and admire the boats passing up and down Haulover Creek.

1 Deals & Discounts

Belize City is a tough nut to crack and it doesn't yield much fruit for frugal-minded travelers looking for unique, offbeat, and inexpensive (or free) experiences. There are currently no museums, active theaters, or movie houses, so forget about finding ticket bargains.

However, the best show in town is still the twice-daily opening and closing of the swing bridge, and it's free.

There is no public transportation to give you an unofficial tour of the city. Luckily, the city is small and most of the major attractions and shops are within a very concentrated area. Furthermore, taxis are inexpensive—around B$5 ($2.50) for a ride anywhere within the city limits—so don't hesitate to take a cab, especially at night.

Small-craft flights on the local commuter lines are a great choice for getting around in Belize—and always remember that the fares are substantially cheaper if you fly into and out of the municipal airport. What's more, a cab to or from the municipal airport is only B$5 ($2.50), compared to the going rate of B$30 ($15) one-way to or from the international airport.

In terms of lodgings, don't expect senior-citizen or student discounts. You can sometimes get discounts for children under 12, so be sure to ask. Your best bet for saving money on lodgings is to travel with a partner or in a small group. You can also opt for a room with a shared bath, which usually will save you.

The Fort Street Restaurant (☎ 2/77267) has my favorite lunch special. For B$9 ($4.50) you get a main course, rice or beans, salad, and a fresh fruit drink or limeade. And a seat in the shade on the wraparound verandah of this Victorian house is priceless. The lunch special changes daily and main courses include stewed chicken, spare ribs, chilemole (a Mayan stew), and fresh fish filets.

Supermarkets still seem to be the best place to shop for souvenirs and gifts to bring home. Here you'll find the best deals on Marie Sharp's sauces and local rums—my favorite take-home items. Aside from this, be sure to stop in at the **National Handicraft Center**, 3 Fort St. (☎ 2/33833) for a one-stop, and reasonably priced, selection of Belizean arts and crafts.

2 Orientation

ARRIVING & DEPARTING

By Plane   All international flights into Belize land at the **Philip S. W. Goldson International Airport**, which is located 10 miles northwest of the city on the Northern Highway. **Continental** (☎ 800/231-0856), **American** (☎ 800/433-7300), **TACA** (☎ 800/535-8780), and several local airlines serve Belize City's two airports. See chapter 13, "Planning a Trip to Belize," for details.

At the airport you'll find a bank, open daily from 8:30 to 11am and from 12:30 to 4:30pm, just outside the terminal entrance. Across the parking lot, you'll find car-rental and tour-agency desks, open 8am to 9:30pm daily. A taxi into town will cost B$30 ($15).

If you fly in from somewhere else in Belize, you'll probably land at the municipal airport on the edge of town. A taxi from here costs just B$5 ($2.50). Unfortunately, there's no direct bus service to either airport.

By Bus   If you arrive in town by bus, you'll be somewhere on the west side of town, depending on where you came from and which bus line you used. All of Belize City's bus stations are within 10 blocks of Albert Street and the swing bridge, which is an easy walk in the day, but is not recommended after dark. A taxi from any bus station to any lodging in town should cost no more than B$5 ($2.50).

The stations are named for the bus lines that operate from them. From Albert Street (between the swing bridge and the central park), walk up Orange Street, cross a canal, continue to the far side of the next canal, and turn left for **Novelos,** located on West Collet Canal Street (☎ 2/77372); **Batty Bros.**, on Mosul Street

(☎ **2/72025**), is situated one block to the right before you cross the second canal. The last two companies, **Venus** (☎ **2/73354**) and **Z-Line** (☎ **2/73937**), share a terminal just a bit farther away, off Orange Street; turn right onto Magazine Road to find it.

Batty Bros. runs daily buses to San Ignacio and Melchor de Mencos, Guatemala every half-hour from 5 to 10:15am. The trip takes 1¹/₂ hours to Belmopan, where there's a brief stop, another hour to San Ignacio, and then 20 minutes to the border. **Novelos** buses leave for San Ignacio at 11am and then every half-hour between noon and 9pm. Only the first two buses continue on to Melchor de Mencos; the others end at Benque de Viejo, on the Belizean side of the border. The schedule is pared down a bit on Sundays and holidays.

Venus and **Z-Line** serve Dangriga, Mango Creek, Placencia, and Punta Gorda. **Batty Bros.** and **Venus** split the northern route to **Chetumal;** between the two of them, a bus runs at least once every hour. Batty Bros.' first bus departs at 4am, with hourly departures through 11:15am. Venus commences its northern service at 11:45am, departing hourly through 7pm.

Typical fares from Belize City: Belmopan, $B3.50 ($1.75); San Ignacio, $B5 ($2.50); Melchor de Mencos, B$5.50 ($2.75); Dangriga, B$10 ($5); Punta Gorda, B$22 ($11); Orange Walk, $B4.50 ($2.25); Corozal, $B7.50 ($3.75); and Chetumal, $B10 ($5).

By Car   There are only two highways into Belize City—the Northern Highway, which leads to the Mexican border, and the Western Highway, which leads to the Guatemalan border. Both are well-marked and pretty straightforward. If you arrive by car from the north, keep on the road into town, paying close attention to one-way streets, and you'll end up at the swing bridge. If you're arriving on the Western Highway, stay on it after it becomes Cemetery Road, and you'll end up at the intersection with Albert Street, a block away from the swing bridge.

By Boat   Several boats ply routes between Belize City and Ambergris Caye and Caye Caulker. See chapter 16 for exact times.

VISITOR INFORMATION

The **Belize Tourist Board,** 83 North Front St. (☎ **501-2/77213** or 501-2/73255), is open Monday to Friday from 8am to noon and 1 to 5pm. Travel agencies are another good source of information.

CITY LAYOUT

Belize City is surrounded on three sides by water, with the murky waters of Haulover Creek dividing the city in two. The swing bridge, near the mouth of Haulover Creek, is the main route between the two halves of the city. At the southern end of the bridge is the market and the start of Regent and Albert streets, where you'll find most of Belize City's shops and offices. To the east of these two major roads is a grid of smaller roads lined with dilapidated wooden houses. On the north side of the bridge, you'll find a pleasant neighborhood of old mansions. This is where you'll find the U.S. Embassy, a couple of guest houses, and several expensive hotels. Cemetery Road heads out of town to the west and becomes the Western Highway, and Freetown Road becomes the Northern Highway.

3 Getting Around

Belize City has no urban transit system. The only way to get around town is on foot or by taxi, unless you have your own car. The downtown area is extremely compact and taxis are very reasonably priced.

Belize City

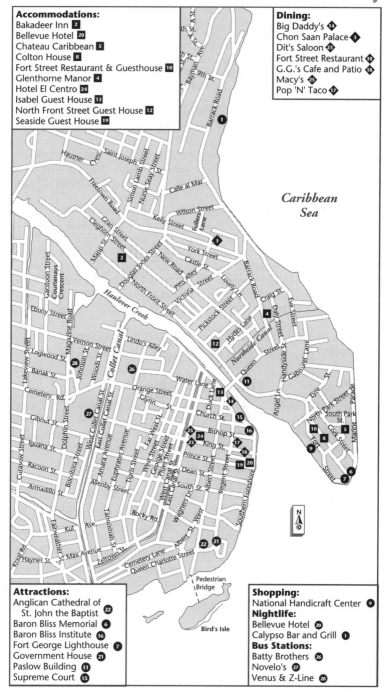

Accommodations:
Bakadeer Inn **2**
Bellevue Hotel **20**
Chateau Caribbean **5**
Colton House **8**
Fort Street Restaurant & Guesthouse **10**
Glenthorne Manor **4**
Hotel El Centro **24**
Isabel Guest House **13**
North Front Street Guest House **12**
Seaside Guest House **19**

Dining:
Big Daddy's **14**
Chon Saan Palace **3**
Dit's Saloon **23**
Fort Street Restaurant **10**
G.G.'s Cafe and Patio **18**
Macy's **25**
Pop 'N' Taco **17**

Attractions:
Anglican Cathedral of
   St. John the Baptist **22**
Baron Bliss Memorial **6**
Baron Bliss Institute **16**
Fort George Lighthouse **7**
Government House **21**
Paslow Building **11**
Supreme Court **15**

Shopping:
National Handicraft Center **9**
Nightlife:
Bellevue Hotel **20**
Calypso Bar and Grill **1**
Bus Stations:
Batty Brothers **26**
Novelo's **27**
Venus & Z-Line **28**

BY TAXI

A taxi ride should cost you B$5 ($2.50) between any two points in the city. For extremely short rides, you may be able to bargain the fare down to B$4 ($2), but you'll have to work at it. You'll find taxis waiting on the Market Square near the swing bridge, or you can call **Bizmark Plaza taxi stand** (☎ 2/7681), **Caribbean Taxi Garage** (☎ 2/72888), or **Cinderella Plaza Taxi** (☎ 2/33340).

BY CAR

Car Rentals Belize City's rental fleet has been transformed in recent years. Gone are the gas-guzzling Detroit monsters (most have been pressed into taxi service), and in their place are armies of small four-wheel-drive vehicles. However, they don't come cheap. Expect to pay between B$130 and B$170 ($65 to $85) per day, plus an optional B$20 to B$24 ($10 to $12) per day for insurance. You get a small break on the weekly rate, but not much.

International car-rental agencies with offices in Belize City include **Avis** (☎ 800/ 331-1212 in the U.S.), with offices at the **Philip S.W. Goldson International Airport** (☎ 25/2385) and the **municipal airport** (☎ 501-2/34619); **Budget** (☎ 800/527-0700 in the U.S.) at 771 Bella Vista (☎ 501-2/32435); and **National** (☎ 800/328-4567 in the U.S.) at 12 North Front Street (☎ 501-2/31650 or 501-2/31587). Local companies you might try are: **Jabiru Auto Rental,** 5576 Princess Margaret Drive (☎ 501-2/44680); **Jaguar Eco Tours,** Philip S.W. Goldson International Airport (☎ 25/2747); or **Safari Car Rental,** 73 Eve Street (☎ 501-2/30268).

Try to make a reservation several weeks in advance with one of the international companies. You'll be glad you did.

FAST FACTS: Belize City

American Express The office is located upstairs from **Belize Global Travel Services,** 41 Albert St. (☎ 2/77363). Open Monday to Friday from 8am to noon and 1 to 5pm, Saturday 8am to noon. For lost or stolen cards, phone **305/ 364-4800** (a collect call to the U.S).

Bookstores **Angelus Press LTD,** 10 Queen St.(☎ 2/35777), is a general stationary and office-supply outlet with a good selection of Belizean reference and fiction works. **The Book Center,** 4 Church Street (☎ 2/77592), sells a wide selection of newspapers and magazines, as well as Belizean and classic books. It's located on the second floor of a general grocery store and is open Monday to Friday from 8am to noon and 1 to 7pm; Saturday 8am to noon and 1 to 5pm.

Business Hours Most businesses and banks are open Monday through Friday from 8am until noon and 1 to 5pm, although some stay open through the lunch hour. Many businesses and banks close slightly earlier on Friday, while others open for restricted hours on Saturday.

Climate See "When to Go," in chapter 13.

Crime See "Safety," below.

Currency See "Money," in chapter 13.

Currency Exchange Most banks are located on Albert Street just south of the swing bridge, though few people use banks for exchanging money because they charge a commission. Ask your hotel manager about exchanging money. If the hotel can't help you, they can usually point you in the right direction. If you pay for any meal, room, or merchandise with traveler's checks, you will receive your change in Belize dollars.

Drugstores   **Brodie's Pharmacy,** Regent and Albert Streets. (☎ **2/77070**), is open Monday through Thursday 8:30am to 7pm, Friday 8:30am to 9pm, Saturday 8:30am to 5pm, and Sunday 9am until 12:30pm.

Embassies and Consulates   See "Fast Facts: Belize," in chapter 13.

Emergencies   In case of **fire** or to call an **ambulance,** dial 90; for the **police,** call 911 or 2/72210.

Holidays   See "When to Go," in chapter 13.

Hospitals   The two major medical-care facilities are **St. Michael's Clinic & Hospital** (☎ **2/35148**) and **Medical Associates** (☎ **2/30303**).

Laundry/Dry Cleaning   Your best bet is to ask at the front desk of your hotel. If the hotel doesn't offer a laundry service, the staff should be able to refer you to a laundromat nearby, or you can try **Belize Dry Cleaners & Laundromat** at 3 Dolphin St. (☎ **2/75153**).

Luggage Storage/Lockers   Ask at your hotel or try a bus station; otherwise, there's no place to leave luggage in Belize City.

Lost Property   The best you can do is contact the police.

Newspapers/Magazines   The *Miami Herald, USA Today, Time,* and *Newsweek* are available at the bookstores listed above and at some of the larger hotels, including the Ramada Reef Hotel and the Radisson Fort George Hotel. There are four local newspapers: the *Belize News,* the *Reporter, Amandala,* and the *Observer.* All are weeklies that hit the street each Friday.

Photographic Needs   Both **Spooner's,** 89 North Front St. (☎ **2/31043**) and **Belize Photo Lab,** 46 Bishop St. (☎ **2/74991**), sell film and photographic supplies and process film.

Police   Dial **911** or **2/72210** in case of emergency. To report a crime, call "Crimestoppers," at **2/44646.**

Post Office   The **main post office** is on North Front Street at the north end of the swing bridge (☎ **2/72201**). It's open Monday to Thursday 8am to 5pm, and Friday 8am to 4:30pm. The **parcel post office** next door is open Monday to Thursday 8am until noon and 1 to 5pm, Friday 8am until noon and 1 to 4:30pm.

Restrooms   You'll find restrooms in restaurants and hotels, but there are few public facilities.

Safety   Like any big city, Belize City has its share of street crime, although with a bit of caution and common sense, you shouldn't have any problems. You'll hear that you shouldn't go out alone at night in Belize City, but there's nothing that should prevent you from walking from a restaurant to your hotel in pairs, down well-lit main streets.

Taxes   See "Fast Facts: Belize," in chapter 13.

Taxis   See "Getting Around," earlier in this chapter.

Telephones   The **city code** for Belize City is 2. Public pay phones are rare in Belize City. As you can only make local and operator-assisted intra-country calls from them, it's best to head to the **Belize Telecommunications Ltd.** office at 1 Church St. (open Monday through Saturday 8am to 9pm, Sunday 8am to noon) to make an international phone call. You'll find direct-dial AT&T and Sprint phones here, as well as UK and Canada direct phones. Depending on your hotel, you may be able to make calling-card calls from your room or the front desk.

For **directory assistance,** dial 113; for a **local** or **regional** operator, dial 114; for an **international operator,** dial 115; for the **current time,** dial 121. See "Fast Facts: Belize," in chapter 13 for more information.

Water   See "Fast Facts: Belize," in chapter 13.

4   Where to Stay

It's tricky to find a comfortable place to stay in Belize City that's also affordable. I don't recommend the least expensive lodgings because their security is lax; and the most expensive properties, while safe, often charge too much for what you get. The lodgings listed here are both affordable and safe, and all are situated within a ten-block radius of the swing bridge.

Doubles for Less Than B$50 ($25)

Isabel Guest House. 3 Albert St., Belize City. ☎ **501-2/73139.** 3 rms (all with bath). B$35 ($17.50) single; B$46 ($23) double. No credit cards.

The three rooms of this small guesthouse are on the third floor of a prominent building, located above a drugstore just across the swing bridge on Albert Street. To enter the property, follow the signs through the winding alley behind the drugstore, and then climb a rickety flight of wooden stairs. Inside, the rooms are very clean and spacious, with painted wooden floors and angled ceilings from the numerous gables and dormers. Room number 2 is cavernous, with a good view over Belize City's busiest intersection and bridge.

North Front Street Guest House. 124 North Front St., Belize City. ☎ **501-2/77595.** 8 rms (all with shared bath). B$17 ($8.50) single; B$27 ($13.50) double; B$36 ($18) triple. No credit cards.

This old wooden guesthouse along the road into town from the airport is a safe and clean budget choice. The rooms are small and Spartan and the beds are ancient, but the price and location are right. There's a small sitting area that overlooks a well-groomed backyard. The guest house is just one block from the Caye Caulker ferry dock.

✪ **Seaside Guest House.** 3 Prince St., Belize City. ☎ **501-2/78339.** 5 rms (all with shared bath). B$18 ($9) single bed in dorm room; B$30 ($15) single; B$44 ($22) double; B$56 ($28) triple. No credit cards.

One of Belize City's most popular low-budget lodgings, the Seaside is located on a very quiet street just off Southern Foreshore. Two years ago, this small Caribbean wood-frame guest house was taken over by the Quakers. It's been a haven for the backpack crowd for years, and securing a room without a reservation is very difficult. If you want to stay here, call ahead and make a reservation. There are four private rooms and one dormitory that holds up to seven travelers. Breakfasts are served between 7 and 9am for a modest cost, and there's a small shop specializing in Garifuna crafts and literature. Don't believe any taxi driver who tells you the guest house is closed. The management has refused the common practice of paying cab drivers to bring guests here, and there is mutual animosity over this.

Doubles for Less Than B$90 ($45)

✪ **Colton House.** 9 Cork St., Belize. ☎ **501-2/44666.** Fax 501-2/30451. 5 rms (all with bath). B$75 ($37.50) single; B$90 ($45) double; B$105 ($52.50) triple; B$120 ($60) garden room; add B$10 ($5) for air-conditioning. No credit cards.

Located in Belize City's most attractive historical neighborhood, Colton House is directly across the street from the much pricier Radisson Fort George Hotel. A lushly planted yard, a wide wraparound verandah, hardwood floors, shuttered windows, and big rooms with high ceilings and overhead fans all add up to a tropical colonial atmosphere, with more than a touch of elegance. The garden room is located at ground level, under the main building. Equipped with a full kitchenette and TV, it's a good option for longer stays, but isn't nearly as charming as the other rooms. The owners are friendly, helpful, and knowledgeable. No meals are served, but there's complimentary coffee and fruit in the mornings. If you can afford to spend a bit more, you can't do much better than this. During a stay here, it's easy to forget you're in Belize City.

Glenthorne Manor. 27 Barrack Rd., Belize City. ☎ **501-2/44212.** 11 rms (9 with bath). B$60–B$70 ($30–$35) single; B$80–B$85 ($40–$42.50) double; B$95 ($47.50) triple. All rates include continental breakfast. No credit cards.

This colonial-style home overflows with a funky sense of Belizean charm and hospitality. Rooms are identified by their color schemes, not numbers. The white room, or honeymoon suite, has its own wraparound private balcony. Other rooms share common sitting areas, verandahs, a TV room, and a full-service kitchen. A filling continental breakfast, with daily Creole specialties such as fried jacks and johnny cakes, is served in an outdoor gazebo, beneath a large mango tree. The management is friendly and helpful. Before long, they'll have you feeling like part of the family.

Hotel El Centro. 4 Bishop St., P.O. Box 2267, Belize City. ☎ **501-2/72413,** 501-2/77739, or 501-2/78101. Fax 501-2/74553. 13 rms (all with bath). TV TEL. B$80 ($40) single; B$90 ($45) double; B$100 ($50) triple. AE, MC, V (with a 7% surcharge).

This is a bit of a splurge, but the rooms are fairly new, generally clean, and air-conditioned. Some are quite large; all are comfortable by Belize City standards. There is even a lawn in back, a rarity around here. Situated in the heart of the business and shopping district, there are several restaurants within a few blocks. At street level is an air-conditioned restaurant that serves breakfast, lunch, and dinner. If you plan on staying several days, ask for a discount.

WORTH A SPLURGE

Bakadeer Inn. 74 Cleghorn St., P.O. Box 512, Belize City. ☎ **501-2/31400.** Fax 501-2/31963. 12 rms (all with bath). A/C TV TEL. B$100 ($50) single; B$120 ($60) double. All rates include breakfast. Lower rates between May 1–October 31. AE, MC, V.

Built in 1990, this inn has a pleasant Tudor exterior. The rooms, although furnished in a chain-motel style, are clean, with air-conditioning, telephones, cable TV, and refrigerators. A restaurant is conveniently located downstairs. If you have a car, you'll appreciate the secure parking area.

Bellevue Hotel. 5 Southern Foreshore (P.O. Box 428), Belize City. ☎ **501-2/77051.** Fax 501-2/73253. 35 rms (all with bath). A/C TV TEL. B$110 ($55) single; B$130 ($65) double; B$150 ($75) triple. AE, MC, V.

This old family home on the southern-shore road, facing the harbor, is now a comfortable hotel. The owners were both born in this building, and their deep personal connection with the property, city, and region is evident. The rooms are comfortable and carpeted. There's an open courtyard, garden, and swimming pool in the back. The second-floor Harbour Room bar and restaurant serves well-prepared, reasonably priced meals, and is one of the livelier meeting places on weekend nights. There's also a separate restaurant and bar on the ground floor. The Finlayson family also runs the **Cottage Colony Fishing and Dive Resort** on St. George's Caye, and a shuttle launch to the sister property leaves from a nearby dock.

Chateau Caribbean. 6 Marine Parade (P.O. Box 947), Belize City. ☎ **501-2/32988** or 501-2/30800. Fax 501-2/30900. 21 rms (all with bath). A/C TV TEL. B$138 ($69) single; B$158 ($79) double; B$178 ($89) triple; B$190 ($95) deluxe. AE, MV, V.

This moderately sized and priced hotel fronts the sea in the Fort George section of Belize City. Standard rooms are newly carpeted, with comfortable double beds, modern furnishings, and cable TV. The third-floor deluxe rooms are somewhat misnamed. I find these a bit threadbare and barren, with too much empty space taken up by bright orange shag carpeting. The second-floor dining room serves good moderately priced meals with a wonderful view of the ocean.

✪ **Fort Street Restaurant & Guesthouse.** 4 Fort St. (P.O. Box 3), Belize City. ☎ **501-2/30116.** Fax 501-2/78808. 6 rms (none with bath). B$90 ($45) single; B$120 ($60) double; B$150 ($75) triple. All rates include a full breakfast. DISC, MC, V.

There aren't too many historic homes left in Belize City—repeated hurricanes have made sure of that—so it's a special treat to stay in this lodging, one of the city's old gems. Even though all six rooms share one bathroom (a definite drawback), the rooms are comfortable and clean, with four-poster beds and mosquito netting. Situated on a triangular corner lot with a grassy front yard, the lovely, restored 1928 house has a long flight of steps leading up to the first floor, where you'll find a gift shop selling many Guatemalan handcrafts and textiles. The guest rooms are located on the second floor, where you'll also find two wicker sitting areas. The table settings of crystal goblets and linen tablecloths set a very romantic mood in the first-floor dining room. The woodwork is dark and rich; it's right out of an old New England village, with a dash of the islands thrown in. You place your breakfast order the night before by leaving a note in a bottle outside the door of your room. Lunch, served from 11am to 2pm, is a good value, from B$9 ($4.50) to B$15 ($7.50). Dinner, from B$24 ($12) to $32 ($16), is pricey, however.

5 Where to Eat

In addition to the restaurants listed below, ask around for the new location of the **Sea Rock Indian Restaurant.** On my last visit, I discovered that this long-running establishment, a favorite among locals and visitors, burned down at its former home on Queen Street. The new operation should be open by the time of this guidebook's publication.

You'll almost never have to dress up for dinner in Belize, unless you're on business. You'll feel perfectly comfortable in casual wear at any of the restaurants listed here, but don't hesitate to wear a light sport jacket if you're feeling a little formal.

MEALS FOR LESS THAN B$20 ($10)

Big Daddy's. Second floor, Commercial Center. ☎ **2/70932.** Main dishes B$6–$B20 ($3–$10). No credit cards. Mon–Sat 7am–5pm. BELIZEAN.

Located in the new Belize City market, Big Daddy's is a clean and comfortable cafeteria-style restaurant. The menu varies from day to day, but there are always several salads, rice dishes, vegetables, and main courses to choose from, and portions are large. From the big windows, there are great views of sailboats plying the river. A full breakfast at Big Daddy's will run you about B$6 ($3).

Chon Saan Palace. 1 Kelly Street. ☎ **2/33008.** Main courses B$9–B$24 ($4.50–$12). MC, V. Daily 11am–3pm and 5–10pm. CHINESE.

If you're in the mood for Chinese food in Belize City, you can't do much better than this local favorite. The room and menu are immense. You'll find plenty of chow mein and Cantonese dishes, but there's also a substantial number of Szechuan specialties, and a show-stopping steak that you can hear before it arrives, sizzling hot at your table.

Dit's Saloon. 50 King St. ☎ **2/73330.** Slice of cake 75¢–B$1.50 (40¢–75¢); burgers, etc. B$2.50–B$8 ($1.25–$4). Mon–Sat 7am–9pm, Sun 8am–4pm. PASTRIES/BELIZEAN.

When a craving for cake comes on, search out this cafe. A tempting assortment of cakes, pastries, and pies is displayed in a glass case at the counter, including many Central American specialties you may never have encountered before—cow pie, raisin pie, three-milks cake, and coconut tart. Dit's also serves simple meals of Belizean rice and beans, fried chicken, and hamburgers. This place feels a lot more like a diner or cafe than a saloon, with bright fluorescent lighting, formica tables, and no hard liquor.

☻ G.G.'s Cafe and Patio. 2B King St. ☎ **2/74378.** Main courses B$6–B$15 ($3–$7.50). No credit cards. Reservations recommended for lunch. Mon–Sat 11:30am–2pm and 5:30–9pm. Closed holidays and first two weeks of July. BELIZEAN.

This pleasant cafe serves simple, well-prepared meals. The outdoor patio, lined with flowering heliconia, is a wonderful place for lunch beneath the shade of a large Belikin umbrella (set in the center of your wrought-iron table) with a leafy backdrop of banana, palm, and ficus trees. The Belizean plates of rice and beans with fresh fish, pork, beef, or chicken are excellent. If you want something lighter, the hamburgers are among the best available in Belize.

Macy's. 18 Bishop St. ☎ **2/73419.** Main courses B$9–B$15 ($4.50–$7.50). No credit cards. Mon–Sat 11:30am–9:30pm. BELIZEAN.

For authentic Belizean cooking, try this tiny local place. The food is consistent, the service is friendly, and the dining room is cool and cozy. Order a fish filet with rice and beans for B$9 ($4.50), or be more daring and try one of their daily chalkboard specials. You may want to skip the wild game to help preserve Belize's wildlife. A tall glass of cold, fresh-squeezed orange juice is a bargain in the Belizean heat at B$2.50 ($1.25).

Pop 'N' Taco. 24 Regent St. ☎ **2/73826.** Main courses B$2–B$19 ($1–$9.50). No credit cards. Mon–Sat 8am–3pm, 5–9:30pm. CHINESE.

Despite the Mexican name, the menu at this small local joint is heavy on Chinese standards like fried rice, chow mein, and low mein. The restaurant is popular with folks from the surrounding neighborhood (which happens to house several budget lodgings). There are only a few tables. If you can't find a seat, you can always order your food to go. Most dishes are between B$6–B$10 ($3–$5).

WORTH A SPLURGE

☻ Fort Street Restaurant. 4 Fort St. ☎ **2/30116.** Fax 2/78808. Main courses B$9–B$32 ($4.50–$16). DISC, MC, V. Mon–Sat 7–10am, 11am–2pm, and 6–10pm. BELIZEAN/INTERNATIONAL.

This remains, justifiably, one of the top dining choices in Belize City. Whether you choose a seat on the open wraparound verandah, or in the small, candle-lit dining room, a meal at the Fort Street is a quiet and enjoyable treat. The fixed-price dinners include salad and an appetizer. Fresh seafood dominates the changing chalkboard menu, but you can also get chicken and meat dishes. Creole shrimp (and Creole lobster, in season) comes in a spicy red sauce on a bed of white rice. The daily lunch special is always a good bargain at B$9 ($4.50).

6 Seeing the Sights

There are only a handful of sights and conventional tourist attractions in Belize City. There are no museums, no cinemas, and no active theaters. A walk around town is the principal form of entertainment in Belize City and the raised wooden houses, with gingerbread trim and white-washed picket fences, are the most interesting sights.

For a pleasant walking tour, begin at the **Fort George Lighthouse** and **Baron Bliss Memorial,** out on the northeastern tip of the city. A small slate stone marks the grave of Henry Edward Victor Bliss, who came to Belize on his yacht in 1926. British born, the baron derived his nobility from Portugal. Throughout his stay in Belizean waters, Bliss was gravely ill from food poisoning he picked up in the Lesser Antilles. Baron Bliss never actually stepped foot on the mainland. Nevertheless, he left Belize City most of his fortune (a few million dollars, in fact) when he died after living several months aboard ship in the harbor, and many of the city's public buildings derive from his bequest.

After soaking up the view of the Caribbean and some fresh sea air, head downtown on Fort Street. On your left, in an innocuous warehouse building, you'll find the **National Handicraft Center** (☎ 2/33833). Stop in and shop, or just browse the variety of local and regional arts and crafts. As you continue along Fort Street, it becomes North Front Street. Just after it does, and before you reach the swing bridge, you'll find the main post office, housed in the **Paslow Building,** on the right. Thomas Paslow was a well-to-do 19th century Bayman, who figured prominently in the 1878 Battle of St. George's Caye.

Now, cross the swing bridge and head south. In a few blocks, you'll reach the **Supreme Court building,** just off the central park. It's a real prize of English colonial architecture with the city's only (albeit undependable) clock tower. As you continue south, you can take either Albert Street, the city's principal commercial avenue, or the quieter, and parallel, Regent Street.

At the southern end of Regent Street, you'll find the **Government House** and the **Anglican Cathedral of St. John the Baptist.** Both of these buildings were constructed with slave labor in the early 19th century, and remain the most prominent reminders of Belize's British colonial past. Also along Regent Street are several buildings that were once slave quarters. Head toward the water, making your way back downtown via the Southern Shore Road.

7 Shopping

You won't be bowled over by the shopping in Belize City, but as very few people come to Belize to shop, perhaps you won't be overly disappointed. What you'll find is a modest handcrafts industry, with various regional specialties. Creoles from the coastal area and outer cayes specialize in coral and shell jewelry as well as wood carvings with maritime (dolphins, turtles, and ships) themes. (As coral is a very delicate, rapidly disappearing living organism that grows very slowly, you may want do your part to preserve the spectacular Belizean reefs and avoid purchasing goods made with it, however.) The Belizean Mayan population produces modern replicas of ancient petroglyphs on different-sized pieces of slate. And, lastly, the Garifuna peoples of the southern coastal villages are known for their small dolls.

Belize City happens to be a good place to pick up my favorite gift item in Belize, Marie Sharp's hot sauce, which comes in three heat gradations—mild, hot, and fiery hot. Its unique blend of habanero peppers, carrots, and vinegar is unbeatable. Marie Sharp also produces a mango chutney and an assortment of pepper jams. You can pick up these products at most gift shops and any supermarket (**Brodie's** and **Romac's** on Albert Street generally have a good selection), with supermarkets offering better value.

While at the supermarket, you can also stock up on Belizean rum. **Caribbean Rum** is a regional award winner and comes in light, dark, and anise–flavored varieties.

If you'd like to take a further foray into Belizean cooking, look for the **Genesis in the Jungle** line of spices. Produced on Ambergris Caye and sold at gift shops around the country, these spices come with complete instructions and spice mixtures to make jerk chicken, rice and beans, and other local favorites.

As mentioned above, one of your best bets is the **National Handicraft Center,** 3 Fort St. (☎ **2/33833**), which houses a wide selection of local and regional crafts and souvenirs all under one roof. You'll find Mayan stone carvings, coconut-shell jewelry, and wooden knickknacks. If you don't make it to southern Belize, you can pick up Garifuna dolls here. **Go-Tees,** 23 Regent Street (☎ **2/74082**), has a more than extensive collection of t-shirts and local textiles. This full-service gift shop also carries a wide range of handmade jewelry, Guatemalan textiles, Mexican hammocks, and Belizean spices, sauces, and herbal medicines.

8 Belize City After Dark

The numerous bars in Belize City can be rough places and are not recommended unless you have a local guide who can take you to places they know. If you just want to relax over a drink, try the second-floor bar at the **Bellevue Hotel** on Southern Foreshore. It looks over the water and occasionally has live bands or karaoke on the weekends.

Over at the Ramada Royal Reef Resort, the **Calypso Bar and Grill** (☎ **2/32670**) is a popular and lively nightspot. You can usually count on live music or karaoke here, but the drinks aren't cheap.

The **Baron Bliss Institute,** 1 Bliss Promenade. (☎ **2/72110**), named for and financed by Belize City's benefactor, is the city's public library and cultural center. Open Monday through Friday from 8am until noon and 1 to 5pm, the Bliss Institute also serves as the city's principal performing-arts space, with a modest theater that features the occasional dance performance, concert, or poetry reading. The institute also sponsors an annual arts festival each May. For more information, call the phone number above.

9 Side Trips from Belize City

In addition to the excursions listed below, organized and self-guided trips to the **Mayan ruins of Altun Ha and Lamanai,** as well as the **Crooked Tree Wildlife Sanctuary,** are popular and easy day trips out of Belize City. See chapter 14 for more information.

THE BELIZE ZOO

By the time you finally get around to visiting the **Belize Zoo,** you'll already be familiar with the zoo's most famous resident—April the tapir—because her picture appears on posters all over the country. April is just one of dozens of species of animals native to Belize that are housed in this zoo. Among the most popular are a variety of indigenous Belizean cats and other wild animals in natural surroundings. The animals here are some of the liveliest and happiest looking I've ever seen in a zoo. It's obvious that they're well cared for. All the exhibits have informative hand-painted signs accompanying them.

It's best to visit early in the morning or close to closing time, as that's when the animals are at their most active and the Belizean sun is at its least oppressive.

The entrance is a couple hundred yards from the Western Highway at mile 29. Any bus traveling between Belize City and Belmopan or San Ignacio will drop you off at the zoo entrance. Admission is B$13 ($6.50); open daily 9am to 4pm.

COMMUNITY BABOON SANCTUARY

No, there really aren't baboons in Belize—this is just the local name for the black howler monkeys who reside in this innovative sanctuary. The sanctuary is a voluntary program run by local landowners in eight villages to preserve the local population of these endangered and vociferous primates. There's a **visitors' center and natural history museum** in the village of **Bermudian Landing,** and it is here that you can pay your B$10 ($5) admission fee. The fee includes the services of a guide, so don't bother hiring one of the local guides. There are several trails through the preserve and as you walk along, you will undoubtedly hear the whooping and barking of the howler monkeys as they make their way through the treetops feeding on fruits, flowers, and leaves. With your guide's help, you should be able to spot the monkeys, though they are often quite high in the trees. Carry binoculars. Many other species, especially birds, make their homes in this preserve.

Bermudian Landing village, site of the preserve's visitor center, is about 20 miles west of Belize City. If you are driving, head north on the Northern Highway and watch for the Burrel Boom Road turnoff. Buses to Bermudian Landing leave Belize City Monday through Saturday at 12:30pm from the corner of Orange and Mosul streets, and at 12:30, 1, 3:30, and 5pm from the corner of Orange and George streets. Buses return to Belize City at 5:30 and 6am. The fare is around B$4 ($2). Accommodations are available with local families for around B$15 ($7.50) single and B$20 ($10) double. Three meals will cost an additional B$15 ($7.50) per person. For more information or to make a reservation for accommodations, contact the **Belize Audubon Society,** 12 Fort St. (P.O. Box 1001), Belize City (☎ **501-2/35004**).

Alternatively, you can stay at the **Jungle Drift Lodge** (P.O. Box 1442, Belize City, ☎ **501-2/32842**). This basic lodge and camping spot is located just 200 yards from the museum and trail entrance. A palmetto stick cabin with a thatched roof costs B$40 ($20) double. If you'd prefer to camp, a campsite is B$10 ($5) per person; bring your own tent. Be sure to bring mosquito repellent and/or mosquito coils if you plan to stay overnight.

Northern Belize

15

Northern Belize is almost a forgotten place, often overlooked by travelers who fly into the country and head directly to the cayes, the southern beaches, or the Maya mountains. Even those who enter by land from Mexico frequently make a beeline for Belize City and bypass this region of low, flat lands with wide swamps and lagoons and slow-running, steamy jungle rivers, where there are few people and even fewer population centers. Until the Northern Highway brought this region into contact with Belize City in the 1930s, its people had much more in common with Mexicans than Belizeans. Spanish is spoken as often as Creole here and there's a decidedly Latin tradition and spirit. Those who make their homes here are farmers raising sugarcane crops on the fertile lowlands. The sugarcane industry is thriving, and in recent years, some farms have begun to experiment with a wide range of other crops, but it remains to be seen how successful they will become.

It may not have spectacular diving or a gorgeous coastline, but northern Belize has its charms, not the least of which is its undiscovered feel. It's where you'll find some of the country's larger biological reserves and most impressive Mayan sites. With its strategic location as the meeting place of both land and sea trade routes, this region held significant importance to the Maya. One site puts a unique twist on exploring the world of the ancient Maya today. At Chan Chich Lodge, a nature lodge in the jungle just outside the town of Orange Walk, you'll be staying on top of what used to be the main plaza of a Mayan city.

1 Exploring Northern Belize

Belize's Northern Highway runs from Belize City in the south to the Mexican border in the north, a distance of a little more than 100 miles. The main road—indeed, in some parts, the only road—through this region, the Northern Highway, passes through a landscape that's not particularly scenic—flat and monotonous describes it well—but at least the potholes and treacherous patches of washed-out pavement of a few years back have been largely remedied. Even though it's possible to drive—or take a bus—here from Mexico, I've organized this chapter based on the assumption that you'll enter this area from the south, either by car or bus from Belize City. Along this route, you'll first encounter the largest of the area's ruins, Altun Ha, as well as Crooked Tree Wildlife Sanctuary, a wetland bird watcher's wonderland that's also the nesting site of the Jabiru stork, the largest bird in the Americas, before reaching the largest community in the north, Orange Walk. From here, you can easily reach the ruin of Lamanai, on the shores of the New River lagoon, notable for its remarkable pyramids. The other ruins I cover in this chapter, Cerros and Santa Rita, are situated near the most northern settlement, Corozal Town, just 15 minutes by car from the Mexican border.

2 En Route to Orange Walk

THE MAYAN RUIN OF ALTUN HA

Altun Ha flourished during the classic period of Mayan civilization, from about A.D. 250 up to the 800s. It was an important trading center linking the coastal and interior settlements. Only a few of the most imposing temples, tombs, and pyramids have been uncovered and rebuilt; hundreds more lie under the jungle foliage. The unique jade-head sculpture of Kinich Ahau (the Mayan sun god), the largest well-carved jade from the Mayan era, was discovered here. Today, it's kept in a bank vault in Belmopan, out of public view, although you may see replicas around Belize. The site was named after the village in which it's situated—Rockstone Pond, the literal Mayan translation meaning "stone water." The archeological work was done principally by the Royal Ontario Museum beginning in 1964, and although the restoration has resulted in some anachronistic juxtapositions, it's a beautiful ruined city, well worth the visit.

A soft-drink stand and **picnic area** are available. Don't wander too far off the beaten track in this area. Even if you're an intrepid explorer of lost ruins, get a guide. If you come on your own, you'll be able to hire a guide near the site entrance. A 1- to 2-hour tour of Altun Ha should cost around B$10 to B$20 ($5 to $10) per person. The site is open daily from 8am to 5pm; admission is B$10 ($5) per adult, free for children under 12.

Altun Ha is located about 30 miles north of Belize City on the Old Northern Highway. There is no public transportation to Altun Ha, so you'll need to take a tour (see below), or drive. Watch for signs to the Maruba Resort; the turnoff is to the right just past Sand Hill. Once you're on the Old Northern Highway, it's 10$^1/_2$ miles to the Altun Ha road. From the highway, it's another bumpy 2$^1/_4$ miles to the ruins. About 1$^1/_2$ miles in, the road forks; take the right fork.

Half-day tours to Altun Ha from Belize City cost between B$60 and B$70 ($30 to $35). Full-day tours can be combined with visits to Crooked Tree Wildlife Sanctuary (see below) or the Community Baboon Sanctuary (see chapter 14). Ask at your hotel, or try **Belize Travel Adventures LTD.** (☎ **501-2/33064**), **Discovery Expeditions** (☎ **501-2/30748**), or **S&L Guided Tours** (☎ **501-2/77593**).

CROOKED TREE WILDLIFE SANCTUARY

Crooked Tree Wildlife Sanctuary is a swampy lowland that serves as a resting spot for dozens of species of migratory birds, including kites, hawks, ducks, grebes, pelicans, ospreys, egrets, and herons. However, the preserve was established primarily to protect Belize's main nesting site of the endangered Jabiru stork, the largest bird in the western hemisphere. The Jabirus arrive each November and pass the winter in these warm lowland climes. Crooked Tree has rapidly become known as an excellent place to spot other endangered wildlife as well. Crocodiles, iguanas, coatimundi, and howler monkeys are all frequently sighted. The best way to explore the preserve's swamps, lagoons, and waterways is by dugout canoe. Ask around in the small village of Crooked Tree or at the sanctuary's visitor's center and administrative building for a local who will paddle you around in a dugout for a few hours. When I last visited, the going rate was B$10 to B$15 ($5 to $7.50) per person for a 2-hour paddle tour of the lagoons.

Crooked Tree is also home to a thriving cashew industry. Every year, on the first weekend of May, Crooked Tree Village hosts its annual cashew festival. Somewhat akin to the Gilroy garlic festival in California's Central Valley, this is an opportunity to taste any one of a plethora of concoctions made with raw and roasted cashews, including cashew wine, cashew jelly, and more.

Crooked Tree is located 33 miles northwest of Belize City. If you are driving, head up the Northern Highway and watch for the turnoff to Crooked Tree. Alternatively, buses leave for Crooked Tree Village from two bus terminals in Belize City. **Batty Bros.** on Mosul Street (one block before West Collet Canal) has buses departing Monday through Friday at 4pm, returning at 7am the following day; Saturday at noon, returning at 4pm the same day; and Sunday at 9am, returning at 4pm the same day.

Jex bus company leaves from the same terminal in Belize City Monday through Saturday at 10:55am and 5:15pm, returning from Crooked Tree at 5:30 and 7am and 2:15pm. The fare is B$4 ($2).

If you'd rather travel here on a guided tour, a few companies in Belize City can assist you. **Belize Travel Adventures LTD.** (☎ **501-2/33064**), **Discovery Expeditions** (☎ **501-2/30748**), and **S&L Guided Tours** (☎ **501-2/77593**) all run half-day tours to Crooked Tree for between B$60 to B$80 ($30 to $40) per person. A full-day trip combining Crooked Tree and Altun Ha, including transportation, guide, and lunch, should cost around B$200 ($100) per person.

If you'd like to spend the night, accommodations can be arranged with a local family for around B$15 ($7.50) single or B$20 ($10) double. Meals are an additional B$15 ($7.50) per person. Admission to the sanctuary is B$8 ($4). For more information or to make a room reservation, contact the **Belize Audubon Society,** 12 Fort St. (P.O. Box 1001), Belize City (☎ **501-2/35004**).

3 Orange Walk

55 miles N of Belize City; 31 miles S of Corozal

Between Belize City and Corozal Town, the only town of any size is Orange Walk. It is the center of Belize's sugarcane industry. There are no tourist attractions in Orange Walk proper, but it makes a good base for visiting nearby Mayan ruins, especially if you have your own car.

ESSENTIALS
GETTING THERE & DEPARTING
By Bus　Both **Batty Bros.** and **Venus** bus lines run buses throughout the day from Belize City. In both cases, you will be boarding a bus bound for Corozal Town and getting off in Orange Walk. Batty Bros. begins service at 4am, with buses leaving roughly every hour until 11:15am. Venus takes over at 11:45am, with a final bus at 7pm. Duration is 1¹/₂ hours. Fare is B$4.50 ($1.75).

Buses from Corozal en route to Belize City pick up passengers in Orange Walk throughout the day. The final bus is at 8:30pm. Alternatively, northbound buses heading to Corozal also stop in Orange Walk throughout the day.

By Car　Orange Walk is on the Northern Highway about 55 miles outside Belize City. Take Freetown Road out of Belize City to connect with the Northern Highway.

ORIENTATION

Orange Walk is an unspectacular agricultural town. The city of about 10,000 inhabitants is laid out north-south on the western bank of the New River.

Fast Facts The city code is 3. The police station (☎ 3/22022) and post office anchor the northern end of town. The Belize Telecommunications Limited (☎ 3/22196) office—the best place to make a phone call to the U.S.—several banks, and a bus depot are in the center of town.

EXPLORING THE NEARBY RUIN OF LAMANAI

Lamanai is one of the more adventurous and picturesque Mayan ruins to visit in Belize—although both time and money are required to rent a boat to take you down the New River from either Guinea Grass or Shipyard, two small villages south of Orange Walk. The trip downriver is an hour of naturalist heaven as you cruise between narrow and densely forested banks. Eventually, the river opens on to the New River Lagoon, with the former Mayan city perched strategically atop some modest limestone cliffs.

Lamanai (which means "submerged crocodile" in Mayan) is one of the largest Mayan sites in Belize. It was occupied from around 1500 B.C. until the Spanish arrived in the 16th century, and has supported non-Mayan populations on into the 19th century. In addition to the numerous pyramids and temples, you'll find the ruins of two churches built by the Spanish during the 16th century. Just next to these are the rusting remains of a more recently abandoned sugar mill, built and run by former U.S. Confederate soldiers who chose exile after the Civil War.

Lamanai was an important and powerful trading city during the pre-classic Mayan period. Its most striking feature is the 12-foot-high stone-and-mortar face set into the side of one of the temples. Most of Belize's ruins have not been cleared and are surrounded by dense rain forest, whereas here you have the sense of walking the paths of what was once a major city. The trails leading between temples offer excellent bird watching.

The most popular way to visit Lamanai is on an organized tour out of Belize City or Ambergris Caye. However, many do-it-yourselfers choose to get themselves to Orange Walk first and then hire a boat at Shipyard or Guinea Grass Village. Ask around in Orange Walk, or call **Herminio Novelo at Jungle River Tours** (☎ **501-3/22293**) or **New River Park Limited** (☎ **501-3/23987**) before heading south, and you should be able to arrange a tour straight from Orange Walk. Expect to pay around B$60 ($30) per person for a boat to take you upriver to the ruin. Most of the year it's possible to drive to Lamanai if you have a four-wheel-drive vehicle. During the heavy part of the rainy season, the road may become impassable, however. From Orange Walk, take the road to San Felipe. Lamanai is open daily from 8am until 4pm. Admission is B$10 ($5).

WHERE TO STAY

✪ **D'Victoria Hotel.** 40 Belize-Corozal Rd., Orange Walk. ☎ **501-3/22518.** Fax 501-3/22847. 31 rms (all with bath). B$45 ($22.50) single; B$50 ($25) double; B$75 ($37.50) double with A/C, TV. No credit cards.

Spacious, clean rooms with tile floors and hot and cold water await you here, a surprisingly nice lodging on an otherwise dreary section of road. It's a more than adequate place to stay if you're on your way either north or south, and just can't go any farther. You'll also find a cool swimming pool with a tiled patio around it. The restaurant serves Belizean and Chinese food at reasonable prices.

WORTH A SPLURGE

Chan Chich Lodge. (P.O. Box 37, Belize City), Gallon Jug, Orange Walk district. ☎ **800/ 343-8009** in the U.S. or 501-2/75634. Fax 501-2/76961. 12 rms (all with bath). B$230 ($115) single; B$260 ($130) double; B$350 ($175) triple. AE, MC, V.

This deluxe jungle lodge is beyond most frugal budgets, but if you've taken the trouble to travel north from Belize City and explore this region, it's worth a splurge. Each of the rooms is a spacious individual wooden bungalow with a thatched roof. The whole compound is set in the plaza of an ancient Mayan city dating back to around A.D. 500. Inside, each bungalow has a wealth of varnished wood, with high ceilings, an overhead fan, two double beds, and a desk and chair. The bird watching is excellent here, and all sorts of guided and independent tours are available, including jungle hikes, horseback riding, canoeing, and visits to other ruins. A meal package will run you B$80 ($40) per person per day. Chan Chich is accessible by a rugged road heading south and west out of Orange Walk (about 4 hours total from Belize City), or by a charter flight to Gallon Jug, which can be arranged by the lodge.

4 Corozal Town & The Northern Highway

86 miles N of Belize City; 31 miles N of Orange Walk; 8 miles S of the Mexican border

Just south of the Hondo river, which forms the border between Mexico and Belize, lies the town of Corozal. Set on a crystal-clear bay, Corozal was an important point on the early Mayan trading routes, and the evidence remains in the ruins of Cerros and Santa Rita. During the mid-1800s the modern town was settled with a large population of refugees from Mexico's Caste War. In 1955, Hurricane Janet paid a visit and left few of the town's wooden buildings standing. The rebuilding relied heavily on cement and cinderblock construction. Today, Corozal is a quiet town with a growing expatriate community that makes a great base for fishing excursions in the calm bay, shopping trips to nearby Chetumal, Mexico, and explorations of Mayan ruins.

ESSENTIALS
GETTING THERE & DEPARTING

By Plane   Both **Island Air** (☎ **501-26/2435** in San Pedro, or 501-2/31140 in Belize City) and **Tropic Air** (☎ **501-26/2012** in San Pedro) operate two flights daily from San Pedro. Duration is 20 minutes. Fare is B$60 ($30) one-way; B$110 ($55) round-trip. If you want to fly to or from Belize City, add another B$77 ($38.50) round-trip or B$43 ($21.50) each way.

By Bus   Both **Batty Bros.** and **Venus** bus lines run buses throughout the day from Belize City. Batty Bros. begins service at 4am, with buses leaving roughly every hour until 11:15am. Venus takes over at 11:45am, with a final bus at 7pm. Duration is 3 hours. Fare is B$7.50 ($3.75). Buses originating from Chetumal, Mexico, go into town daily every hour from 4am to 6pm.

Buses leave throughout the day for both Chetumal, Mexico and Belize City. The fare for the 8-mile trip to Chetumal is B$2.50 ($1.25). Expect to spend 30 to 45 minutes going through border formalities.

By Car   Corozal Town is the last town on the Northern Highway before you reach the Mexican border. Take Freetown Road out of Belize City to connect with the Northern Highway. If you want to visit the Altun Ha ruins (see "En Route to Orange Walk," above), take the Old Northern Highway. The turnoff is 22 miles from Belize City, on the right. If you're driving in from Mexico, you'll reach a fork in the road 3 miles from the border; bear left to reach Corozal Town.

ORIENTATION　The bay is a block and a half to the east, and the town's **market** is on the bay just south of the customs pier.

Fast Facts　The city code is 4. The **bus station** is located two blocks west of the town's **central park.** The **post office** is located near the bus station on First Street North.

WHAT TO SEE & DO

There isn't much to see or do in Corozal. It's mostly just a stopping point for weary travelers. However, it sits on the shores of the Bay of Chetumal, which has the most amazing turquoise-blue water. If you've just come from Mexico, swim in the bay, or walk around town and marvel at the difference between Mexican culture and Belizean culture. The countries are so close and yet worlds apart. While Spanish is spoken here, Corozal (and the rest of Belize) is truly Caribbean, with frame houses built on high stilts to provide coolness, protection from floods, and shade for sitting. Farming and growing sugarcane are what Corozal survives on, plus a little fishing.

If you haven't yet had your fill of Mayan ruins, there are a couple to visit in the area. If you look across the water from the shore in Corozal Town, you can see **Cerros** or **Cerro Maya** on the far side of the Bay of Chetumal. It's that little bump in the forest, but up close it seems much larger. Cerros was an important coastal trading center during the late pre-classic period. Some of the remains of this city are now under the waters of the bay, but there's still a 65-foot-tall pyramid that you can visit. By asking around town, you should be able to find someone willing to take you by boat to the ruins.

Right in town is another small ruin called **Santa Rita.** Corozal Town is actually built on the ruins of Santa Rita, which was an important late post-classic Mayan town and was still occupied at the time of the Spanish Conquest. The only excavated building is a small temple across the street from the Coca-Cola bottling plant. To reach it, head north past the bus station and, at the curve to the right, take the road straight ahead that leads up a hill. You'll see the building one block over to the right.

WHERE TO STAY & EAT

Three of the lodgings listed below are at the southern end of the town. If you've arrived here by bus, ask the driver to drop you off at your hotel, or take a taxi from the bus station. You'll find good and inexpensive food at the market, three blocks south of the central square.

Doubles for Less than B$25 ($12.50)

✪ **Caribbean Motel.** Cabins and trailer park, south end of town on Belize Highway, Corozal Town. ☎ **501-4/22725.** Fax 501-4/23414. 6 rms (all with bath). B$30 ($15) single; B$40 ($20) double; B$10 ($5) per person for a campsite; B$20 ($10) for an RV hookup. MC, V.

On the bay, in an idyllic location shaded by lofty palms and with a swimming dock across the street, this is where travelers to Corozal Town have stayed for years. Even though it has seen better days, the Caribbean is still a great deal. Quaint and primitive thatched bungalows are built according to traditional Mayan designs and are almost identical (from the outside) to the ones that you see all over the Yucatán.

The **restaurant** is open every day except Tuesday and serves three meals a day.

Nestor's Hotel. 123 Fifth Ave., Corozal Town. ☎/fax **501-4/22354.** 18 rms (all with bath). B$20 ($10) single; B$25–B$35 ($12.50-$17.50) double. No credit cards.

The cheapest rates in town are to be found here, on the corner of Fifth Avenue and Fourth Street. Rooms are basic, with solar-heated showers and fans, and the plumbing tends to act up now and then in the back rooms.

DOUBLES FOR LESS THAN B$60 ($30)

Hotel Maya. P.O. Box 112, Corozal Town. ☎ **501-4/22082.** Fax 501-4/22827. 15 rms (all with bath). B$38 ($19) single; B$60 ($30) double; B$64 ($32) triple. MC, V.

Located on the shore road south of town, the Maya is probably your best bet. The rooms are very clean and basic, and all have private showers with hot and cold running water. This place tends to be popular, so it pays to make a reservation, or you may find no rooms available. Unfortunately, it can also get a little bit noisy. You can get a big breakfast for B$9 ($4.50), including meat, beans, orange juice, coffee, and toast or johnnycakes. Dinner runs B$8 to B$15 ($4 to $7.50).

WORTH A SPLURGE

Tony's Inn & Beach Resort. South End (P.O. Box 12), Corozal Town.☎ **800/447-2931** in the U.S. or 501-4/22055. Fax 501-4/22829. 29 rms, all with bath. B$42.40–B$127.20 ($21.20–$63.60) single; B$53–B$148.40 ($26.50–$74.20) double. Lower rates in summer months; children under 12 stay free in parents' room. AE, MC, V (5% surcharge added).

The rooms are newer and larger than those in the above hostelries, and consequently this place is popular with group tours and conferences. Tony's is on the left just past the Caribbean Motel on the shore road heading south out of town. The grounds are nicely landscaped, with lawn chairs that overlook the ocean. There's even a little beach and private dock. The rooms come with mahogany furniture, tile floors, attractive floral-print bedspreads, and potted plants. Those with air-conditioning also have cable color TVs. Although the prices in the restaurant are high, especially when compared with Mexico, its cool, air-conditioned dining room is a welcome oasis in summer.

16 The Cayes & the Barrier Reef

When Belizeans talk about the "blues," they're usually not referring to an expressive musical form. They're talking about the crystal-clear, turquoise waters that surround the numerous cayes—or small islands—strung along the country's barrier reef. If you've done any research into Belize, you've probably seen them, since they've been a popular location shoot for travel magazines for several years now. If anything, the magazine covers are understatements. Flat approximations. Seen first hand, there's something truly mesmerizing and almost unbelievable about the clarity and color of the water that surrounds these islands just off the coast of Belize City. And, unlike Belize City, the cayes are hard to leave.

If the hundreds of idyllic cayes were not enough, Belize is also blessed with two major atolls. Much more common in the South Pacific, atolls are rings of reef and small islands that form and protect an ocean lagoon. The waters of these mid-ocean lagoons are typically very calm and clear. Belize's two atolls are the Turneffe Islands atoll and the Glover's Reef atoll. The former is a major diving mecca, with the prime dive spots of Lighthouse Reef and the Blue Hole nearby. While the Turneffe Islands atoll does have a few upscale dive and fishing resorts, most travelers visit these islands and their neighboring reef on live-aboard dive boats. Glover's Reef atoll, on the other hand, is less developed and geared towards the adventurous budget traveler.

From the bustling mini-resorts of Ambergris Caye to the deserted getaways on Glover's Reef atoll, it's hard to beat the incredible combination of sun and sea the cayes and atolls offer.

1 Exploring & Enjoying the Cayes

You've got two options for getting to the cayes: sea or air. The trip is usually beautiful by either means. When the weather's rough, it's bumpy both ways, although you're more likely to get wet in the boat. Once there, you probably won't get in or need a car (with the exception of the short taxi ride from the airport to town on Ambergris Caye) for the length of your stay. Most of the cayes are small enough to walk from one end to the other in under 20 minutes. On others, it won't take you nearly as long.

With the reef providing protection from the open ocean, the cayes become literal islands of tranquillity in a calm blue sea. Aside from sunbathing and slow strolling, fishing and diving are the main attractions in the cayes. On the plentiful flats found inside the reefs and up in nearby estuaries, anglers find action with tarpon, snook, permit, and feisty bonefish. There's more tarpon, as well as giant snapper and grouper, found along the reefs. Out on the open ocean, the tackle and game get bigger, with marlin, sailfish, tuna, and wahoo as the principal players.

The diving here is world-class. Jacques Cousteau put Belize on the diving map back in 1971, with his explorations of the Blue Hole. The country has almost 200 miles of continuous barrier reefs and visibility of up to 200 feet on some days. It's hard to open a diving magazine without finding an article on diving in Belize.

For more specific information on fishing or diving in the cayes, see the individual sections below, or chapter 3, "Bird Watching, Diving & Other Active Vacations in Costa Rica and Belize."

2 Ambergris Caye

36 miles N of Belize City; 40 miles SE of Corozal Town

Long before the British settled Belize, and long before sun-seeking vacationers and zealous reef divers discovered Ambergris Caye, the Maya were here. In fact, the Maya created Ambergris Caye when they cut a channel through the long, thin peninsula that extended south from what is now Mexico. The channel was cut to facilitate coastal trading and avoid the dangerous barrier reef that begins not too far north of San Pedro, the caye's principal (in fact, only) community. Today, Ambergris Caye is 25 miles long and only half a mile wide.

For some time now San Pedro has been Belize's sun-and-fun community, and it's here that you'll find the country's largest concentration of tourist developments. The compact "downtown" area is a jumble of souvenir shops, interesting eateries, dive shops, and tour agencies. Though San Pedro continues to attract primarily scuba divers and fishermen, today it's popular with a wide range of folks who like the slow-paced atmosphere. People compare it to the Florida Keys 30 or 40 years ago, though San Pedro is rapidly catching up. The town still has no paved streets, but golf carts and automobiles proliferate, constantly forcing pedestrians to the side of the road. In the wake of rapid construction, wooden Caribbean houses have given way to concrete and cinderblock buildings. Unfortunately, in the process, the town has lost almost all of its shade trees, so be sure to bring sunblock, a wide-brimmed hat, and sunglasses.

Development has reached both ends of Ambergris Caye and steady construction appears destined to fill in the blanks from north to south. Despite the fact that much of the island is seasonally flooded mangrove forest (and laws prohibit the cutting of mangroves), developers continue to clear this marginal land. Indiscriminate cutting of the mangroves is already having an adverse effect on the nearby barrier reef: Without the mangroves to filter the water and slow the impact of waves, silt is formed and carried out to the reef where it settles and kills the coral. There is still spectacular diving to be had just off the shore here, but local operators and long-term residents claim to have noticed a difference and are expressing concern.

ESSENTIALS
GETTING THERE & DEPARTING

By Plane   There are dozens of daily flights between Belize City and San Pedro on Ambergris Caye. Flights leave from both the Philip S. W. Goldson International Airport and the Belize City Municipal Airport nearly every half-hour. If you're coming in on an international flight and heading straight for San Pedro, you should book a flight from the international airport. If you're already in Belize City, it's cheaper to fly from the municipal airport, which is also cheaper to reach by taxi. During the high season, and whenever possible, it's best to have a reservation. However, you can usually just show up at the airport and get a seat on a flight within an hour.

Tropic Air (☎ 501-2/45671 in Belize City, 501-26/2012 in San Pedro), **Island Air** (☎ 501-2/31140 in Belize City, 501-26/2435 in San Pedro), and **Maya Airways** (☎ 501-2/44234 or 44032 in Belize City, 501-26/2611 in San Pedro) are the three main airlines flying to San Pedro. Flight duration is 20 to 30 minutes. Fare (from the municipal airport) is B$41 to B$43 ($20.50 to $21.50) one-way and B$73 ($31.50) round-trip. Fares from the international airport are B$77 ($36.50) one-way. Because a taxi into Belize City from the international airport costs B$30 ($15), and the boat to San Pedro costs B$20 ($10), it's only slightly more expensive to fly if you are heading directly to San Pedro after arriving on an international flight.

If you're already on Caye Caulker, many of the above flights stop here first to drop off and pick up passengers on their way to San Pedro. Duration is 15 minutes. Fare is B$38 ($18) one-way, B$70 ($35) round-trip. Check at the airport or with a Caye Caulker tour agency for seat availability.

There are two flights a day between Corozal Town and San Pedro on Tropic Air at 10:30am and 3:30pm. Duration is 20 minutes. Fare is B$60 ($30) one-way, B$110 ($55) round-trip.

By Boat   Several regularly scheduled boats ply the route between Belize City and Ambergris Caye. All post signs around Belize City and leave from somewhere near the swing bridge. New boats enter the field periodically and schedules change unexpectedly, so be sure to check when you're in Belize City.

The *Triple J* (☎ 501-2/44375) leaves from a pier near the swing bridge every morning at 9am. The *Andrea II* (☎ 501-2/74988 in Belize City; 501-26/2578 in San Pedro) departs daily from a pier in front of the Bellevue Hotel on Southern Foreshore at 3pm. The *Banana Boat* (☎ 501-26/2807) leaves from the same dock one hour later, at 4pm, daily. Trip duration is 75 minutes. Fare is B$20 ($10) each way. The *Thunderbolt* (no phone) leaves from a pier by the swing bridge every day at 1:30pm and charges B$25 ($12.50). Duration is one hour.

Most of these boats stop to drop off and pick up passengers in Caye Caulker on their way. If you're going to Ambergris from Caye Caulker, these boats will pick you up. Find out on Caye Caulker just where and when they stop. Fare is B$15 ($7.50) each way.

You can also sail to San Pedro from Caye Caulker on one of the sailboats that goes out to Hol Chan Marine Reserve. These boats usually stop for lunch on Ambergris Caye, and there is nothing to stop you from staying in San Pedro. Fare is around B$35 ($17.50). Daily departures from Caye Caulker are around 10am.

The *Andrea II* departs San Pedro daily at 7am. Its dock is toward the north end of San Pedro on the reef side of the town. The *Banana Boat* leaves every morning at 8am from a pier more or less in front of the Spindrift Hotel. The *Triple J,* which leaves from a dock on the reef side of the island toward the north end of town, departs daily at 3pm for Caye Caulker and Belize City. *Thunderbolt* makes its return trip every day at 4:30pm. Flights leave throughout the day for Belize City's two airports and Caye Caulker. Boat and plane reservations can be made at any of the travel agencies along Barrier Reef Drive. For plane reservations, you can also walk to the airport and make a reservation in person.

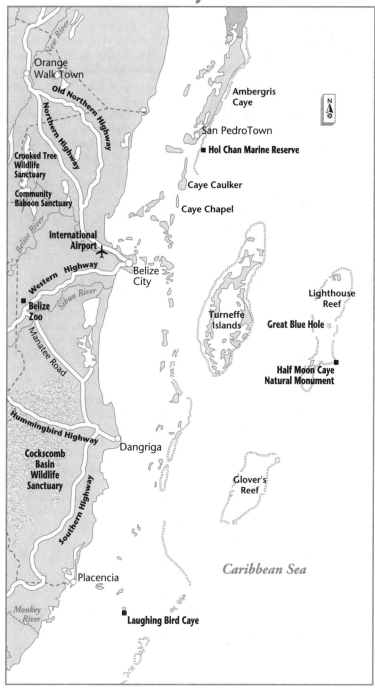

ORIENTATION

San Pedro is three streets wide. The streets, from seaside to lagoonside, are Barrier Reef Drive (Front Street), Pescador Drive (Middle Street), and Angel Coral Street (Back Street). The airport is at the south end of town. The island stretches on both north and south of San Pedro with higher-priced resorts dotting the seafront on each end.

Fast Facts **Belize Bank** (☎ 26/2482), across from the Spindrift Hotel on Barrier Reef Drive, is open Monday through Thursday from 8am until 1pm and Friday 8am to 1pm and 3 to 5pm. The **Atlantic Bank** (☎ 26/2195) is on the ocean side of Barrier Reef Drive, just south of the park. Its hours are Monday through Friday 8am to 2pm, Saturday 8:30am to noon. The **city code** for Ambergris Caye is 26. In case of an **emergency,** dial **911;** for the **police,** dial **26/2022;** in case of a **fire,** dial **26/2372;** to call an **ambulance,** dial **26/2234.**

Most hotels provide **laundry** service, but pricing varies widely, so ask first. If yours seems too pricey, there are two laundries on Pescador Drive toward the south end of town. Belize Laundromat (☎ 26/2545) charges B$9 ($4.50) per load (soap is included). J's Laundromat (☎ 26/2373) charges B$1.50 (75¢) per pound. They offer free pickup and delivery, but soap is extra. Lopez Drugs, a **pharmacy,** is in a shopping center on Barrier Reef Drive toward the north end of town, open daily 9am to 9pm.

The **post office** is located on a cross street near the Atlantic Bank, just around the corner from Barrier Reef Drive. It's open Monday through Thursday from 8am to noon and 1 to 4:30pm, Friday 8am to noon and 1 to 5pm. The **BTL telephone office** is on Pescador Drive at the north end of town, and is open Monday through Friday 8am until noon and 1 to 4pm, Saturday 8am until noon. If you have to make any long-distance phone calls, especially using an AT&T, Sprint, or MCI operator, this is your best bet, although it's always worth asking at your hotel first. You can also send and receive international telegrams and telexes from this office.

Special Events A small version of the pre-Lenten festival **Carnival**—with a twist—is celebrated in San Pedro over the weekend preceding Ash Wednesday. In addition to colorful and lively *comparsa* parades, with marching-drum bands and costumed dancers, locals armed with paintbrushes work the crowds, painting faces with home-made flour-based paints. In past years, tourists were usually asked before being painted, and their refusals respected. Recently, however, painting fever has reached a raucous all-time high, with fresh eggs and the occasional oil-based paint introduced as weapons; tourists are now often painted despite pleas to the contrary. My small daypack still proudly bears its mark. If you can shower relatively soon afterward, it'll wash off without much hassle. Still, if you go out during Carnival, expect to get painted and dress accordingly.

FUN ON, UNDER & OFF THE WATER

As an island resort, you can expect to find most major watersports available on Ambergris Caye—with scuba diving and fishing being the primary ones. There are no submarine rides, but you can rent a sailboard or jet ski; there are no sunset dinner-dance cruises, but you do get a rum punch when you go out on a glass-bottomed boat. Sorry, golfers: There are no golf courses here—yet.

The "Beaches" By any conventional definition, there are no beaches on Ambergris Caye. Instead, there's a narrow strip of sand where the land meets the sea, but even at low tide it isn't wide enough for unrolling a beach towel in most places. The widest section of sand happens to be right in the middle of town, where all the boats dock (not a pleasant place to hang out). Try walking north or south from town along the water to find a more secluded spot where you can sit and stare out to sea. Otherwise, the beachfront (read "expensive") hotels create their own beaches by building retaining walls and filling them in with sand.

Likewise, swimming is not what you might expect. For 100 yards or more out from shore, the bottom is covered with sea grass. In a move that placed the environment over tourism, the local and national government has decided to protect the sea grass, which supports a wealth of aquatic life. Beneath the grass is a layer of spongy roots and organic matter topped with a thin layer of white sand. Walking on this spongy sand is most unnerving—there's always the possibility of a sea urchin or stingray lurking, and it's easy to trip and stumble. Swimming is best off the piers at the **Paradise Resort Hotel** and **Ramon's Village,** where they have created swimming areas in the sea by scooping out a deep spot and clearing away all the grass. Ramon's Village also has one of the nicest "beaches" around. All the beaches on the caye are public, and you can probably use the hotel's lounge chairs if it's a slow day. The best swimming is from boats anchored out in the turquoise waters between the shore and the reef.

Biking & Motor Scootering   If you'd like to explore Ambergris Caye itself, you can rent a bike for around B$5 ($2.50) per hour, a motor scooter for around B$16 ($8) per hour, or even a golf cart for between B$20 ($10) and B$30 ($15) per hour at several places around town. You'll save if you rent by the half-day or full day. Check at **The Rental Center,** near the airport (☎ 501-26/2008 or 501-26/3188), **Ramon's Wheel Rental,** at the airport (☎ **501-26/2790**), or **Polo's EZ-Go,** at the north end of Barrier Reef Drive (☎ **501-6/2080**).

Catamaran and Sailboat Tours   The *Me Too* (☎ **501-26/2658**) is a 44-foot catamaran that makes daily trips to Caye Caulker. For B$80 ($40) per person, you get a pleasant sail, several stops for snorkeling (equipment is not included), and complimentary drinks (beer, rum punch, or soft drinks). The boat docks at Caye Caulker for lunch, but lunch is extra. Feel free to bring your own bag lunch; however, this is a good chance to walk around this small island and sample one of the fine restaurants here (see below for listings). The *Me Too* also does a sunset cruise every Tuesday and Thursday, leaving at 4:30pm. Cost is B$60 ($30) per person.

The *Winnie Estelle,* a 66-foot island trader operated by **Heritage Navigation** (☎ **501-26/3707**) does a similar trip for B$90 ($45) per person that leaves from the Paradise Hotel dock. The itinerary is the same as that of the *Me Too,* and includes the same snorkeling stops, complimentary beer, rum punch, and soft drinks, and the requisite lunch stop on Caye Caulker. This boat can also be chartered for longer trips to the outer atolls.

Diving   Within a 10- to 20-minute boat ride from the piers in San Pedro lie scores of world-class dive sites, including Mexico Rocks, Mata Rocks, Tackle Box, and Rocky Point. A day's diving will almost always feature a mix of steep wall drops and coral caverns and tunnels here.

There are scores of dive operators in San Pedro and almost every hotel can arrange a dive trip, either because they have their own dive shop or subcontract with one. For the most part, rates are standardized, but you may be able to get deals on multi-day, multi-dive packages. While it's often tempting to purchase all-inclusive dive packages before coming to Belize, this limits your flexibility, especially on days when the weather is less than appealing, and you'd rather take an inland tour to a Mayan ruin than head underwater again.

For reliable scuba-diving service and reasonable rates, contact **Adventures in Watersports/Dive Dreams,** P.O. Box 66, San Pedro, with offices on Barrier Reef Drive and at the **Seychelles's Guest House** (☎ **501-26/3223** or 501-26/3706);

Belize Dive Center, at the Belize Yacht Club Hotel, south of the airport (☎ 501-26/2797 or 800/938-0860 in the U.S.); **Hustler Tours,** Barrier Reef Drive (☎ 501-26/2693); **Out Island Divers,** P.O. Box 7, San Pedro (☎ 501-26/2151); or **Tortuga Dive Center,** on Barrier Reef Drive (☎ 501-26/2802 or 800/375-8842 in the U.S.).

Most of these companies charge between B$90 and B$100 ($45 to $50) for a two-tank dive, with equipment rental running around B$14 ($7) for a BC and regulator and B$7 ($3.50) for a mask and fins.

For more adventurous and truly world-class diving, you'll probably want to head out to the Turneffe Islands and Lighthouse Reef atolls or the Blue Hole. All of these are world-renowned dive spots, particularly the Blue Hole, a huge offshore sinkhole (collapsed cavern) made famous by Jacques Cousteau. You'll see postcards, photos, and t-shirts showing off aerial views of this perfectly round hole in the ocean all over town. At ocean level, the Blue Hole is almost 1,000 feet across, with straight wall drops of up to 400 feet. **The Blue Hole Dive Center,** Barrier Reef Drive (☎ 501-26/2982) offers a one-day trip to the Blue Hole for B$330 ($165), including all transportation, three dives, tanks/weights, and meals. However, since these atoll islands and reefs are 4 to 6 hours away by boat it is really best to do overnight and multi-day trips to these sites. In addition to the Blue Hole Dive Center, all the above-mentioned operators offer multi-day trips to the outer atoll islands. Prices average around B$500 ($250) for a 2-day trip; B$700 ($350) for a 3-day trip.

If you've always dreamed of learning to scuba dive and plan on spending any time in San Pedro, you should consider taking a course here. Resort courses will give you a great one-day introduction into the world of scuba diving, including a very controlled shallow-water boat dive. The average cost of a one-day course is usually B$200 to B$250 ($100 to $125) per person. If you've got 3 or 4 days, that's enough time to become fully certified as an open-water diver. The cost of a certification course, including four open-water and reef dives, is usually B$650 to B$700 ($325 to $350) per person.

Adventures in Watersports/Dive Dreams (☎ 501-26/3223 or 501-26/3706), **Belize Dive Center** (☎ 501-26/2797 or 800/938-0860 in the U.S.), **Hustler Tours** (☎ 501-26/2693), **Out Island Divers** (☎ 501-26/2151), and **Tortuga Dive Center** (☎ 501-26/2802 or 800/375-8842 in the U.S.) all offer the above courses.

Fishing The waters off Ambergris Caye and the barrier reef here offer some of the finest sportfishing in the world—over the years a few record tarpon and bonefish catches have been made. If you prefer deep-sea fishing, there's plenty of tuna, dolphin, and marlin to be had beyond the reefs. Contact **Hustler Tours** (☎ 501-26/2693 or 501-26/2538), **Tortuga Dive Center** (☎ 501-26/2802), or **Sea Boots** (☎ 501-26/2911) for information and reservations. They offer reef, deep-sea, protected-water, and mangrove/estuary trips. A half-day of reef trolling, casting, or fly-fishing for bonefish or tarpon runs around B$250 ($125); a full day costs around B$360 ($180). Deep-sea trolling for larger game runs around B$800 to B$1000 ($400 to $500) for a half-day, B$1500 to B$2000 ($750 to $1000) for a full day. The prices quoted here are per boat for up to four people and usually include drinks, tackle, and lunch.

Parasailing If you want a bird's-eye view of Ambergris Caye, try parasailing. **Caribe Parasail** (☎ 501-26/3233) and **Fido's Watersports** (☎ 501-26/2056) will both take you on a 15- to 20-minute ride for B$80 ($40).

Snorkeling If you're hesitant to take a tank plunge, don't miss a chance to at least snorkel. There's good snorkeling all along the protected side of the barrier reef, but some of the best is at **Shark-Ray Alley** and **Hol Chan Marine Reserve,** about 4 miles southeast of San Pedro. Shark-Ray Alley provides a nice adrenaline rush for all but the most nonchalant and experienced of divers. Here you'll be able to snorkel above and between schools of resting nurse sharks and stingrays. *Hol chan* is a Mayan term meaning "little channel," which is exactly what you'll find here—a narrow channel cutting through the shallow coral reef. The walls of the channel are popular with divers, and the shallower areas are frequented by snorkelers. Some of the more exciting residents of the area include several large green moray eels (friendly but dangerous), stingrays (don't touch), and nurse sharks (harmless). The reserve covers 5 square miles and is divided into three zones: the reef, the sea-grass beds, and the mangroves. There is a B$3 ($1.50) charge for diving at Hol Chan, which may or may not be included in the price of a boat excursion to the reserve.

Unfortunately, Hol Chan seems to be getting too many visitors and the coral seems to be dying, with fewer and fewer fish every year. You may want to consider visiting a different snorkeling site, such as Mexico Rocks, Coral Gardens, Tres Cocos, or Mata Rocks.

Most diving outfitters and several boat operators offer snorkeling excursions and equipment rental. The *Reef Seeker* glass-bottom boat tour to Hol Chan costs B$25 ($12.50), and offers an hour of snorkeling (gear is not included) after the tour is complete. The *Reef Seeker* leaves daily at 9am and 2pm. Reservations can be made through **Amigo Travel** (☎ **501-26/2180**) or **Tortuga Dive Shop.**

Trips to other sites range in price from B$25 ($12.50) to B$36 ($18). **Lil Alfonse** (☎ **501-26/2584**) charges B$50 ($25) for a full-day trip to Caye Caulker and back, with snorkeling at several sites.

Snorkeling gear is available from most of the above operators and at several other sites around town. A mask, a set of fins, and a snorkel will usually cost from B$6 to B$10 ($3 to $10) per person per day. If you're the independent type, you can just rent your own snorkeling gear and hop off one of the docks. However, you really need to go out to the reef to see much of anything other than sand and sea grass.

Snorkeling & Manatee-Watching A popular day trip from San Pedro combines a leisurely tour of manatee feeding sites with snorkeling off the coasts of the isolated Geoff's and Sergeants cayes, little more than picturesque patches of sand with a few palm trees. This tour includes all transportation, lunch on one of the cayes, and several snorkeling stops, and costs between B$100 and B$150 ($50 to $75) per person. Most hotels and tour agencies in Ambergris Caye offer these trips. Alternatively, check with **Hustler Tours** (☎ **501-26/2693**) or **Manatee Tour Center** (☎ **501-26/3235**).

Windsurfing & Jet Skiing The local windsurfing center is housed at **Ramon's Village resort.** Rental rates are B$30 ($15) for an hour's sail, B$80 ($40) for a half-day, and B$120 ($60) for a full day. Ramon's also has a few Hobie Cats that they rent for B$50 ($25) an hour, B$180 ($90) for a half-day rental, and B$240 ($120) for a full day.

Innovative Watersports (☎ **501-26/3337**), on a pier just north of Ramon's Village, rents jet skis and wave runners for B$100 to B$120 ($50 to $60) per hour.

SHOPPING

There's not much more to buy on Ambergris Caye than t-shirts and touristy souvenirs. Beyond the trinket category, the best buy on the island is handmade jewelry sold by local Belizean artisans from makeshift display stands along Barrier Reef Drive. I'd be wary of black-coral jewelry, though. While extremely beautiful, black coral is an endangered resource, and buying it just leads to increased harvesting of the slow-growing coral.

At **Fido's Courtyard** (on Barrier Reef Drive), Elizabeth (☎ **26/2811**), a hand-made jeweler with a specialty in amber, sells pieces that are a cut above street fare in terms of quality, but are also slightly more expensive; inside **Belizean Arts** (☎ **26/3019**), you'll find the island's best collection of original paintings and crafts. Of special note are the prints and paintings of co-owner Walter Castillo, a Nicaraguan-born artist whose simple but bold style captures the Caribbean colors and rhythms of Belize.

San Pedro is also home of **Genesis in the Jungle** (☎ **26/3780**), a micro-enterprise producing spice mixtures and local wines. Look for their wares on the shelves of gift shops.

If you're a diver, you might want to bring home a video reminder of those infamous Belizean blues. Mitch Ward (☎ **26/3643**) will create a 45-minute custom video of your vacation, splicing in shots of your dives (he'll accompany you on a two-tank dive) with stock footage for B$70 ($35).

Otherwise, you might check out the work of Joe Miller, on Middle Street (☎ **26/2577**). Miller's underwater and terrestrial work is frequently featured in travel magazines. He also rents underwater cameras, lights, and video cameras from his studio, starting at B$50 ($25) per day.

WHERE TO STAY
DOUBLES FOR LESS THAN B$30 ($15)

Milo's. P.O. Box 21, San Pedro, Ambergris Caye. ☎ **501-26/2033.** Fax 501-26/2196. 20 rms (5 with bath). B$21.20 ($10.60) single without bath; B$26.50 ($13.25) double without bath; B$37.10 ($18.55) triple without bath; B$42.80 ($21.40) single or double with bath. MC, V.

Milo's rooms are among the cheapest on the island for a few reasons: You'll share a bathroom with someone else, the rooms are rather dark, and there's no atmosphere to speak of. Despite these apparent drawbacks, some repeat guests swear by Milo's. If you don't plan on spending much time in your room, you may appreciate the good value as well. The shared bathrooms are clean. On my last visit, about half of the soft foam mattresses had just been replaced with newer, firmer foam mattresses—it's worth checking out a room or two before accepting yours. To register, enter the general store downstairs. Milo's is about a half-block south of the Paradise Hotel on Front Street.

○ **Rubie's Hotel.** Barrier Reef Drive (P.O. Box 56), San Pedro, Ambergris Caye. ☎ **501-26/2063.** Fax 501-26/2434. 21 rms (15 with bath). B$25 ($12.50) single or double without bath; B$53–B$55 ($26.50–$27.50) single or double with bath. No credit cards.

The least expensive lodging in town with a water view, Rubie's is also among the first places you'll encounter as you come into town from the airstrip. In addition to the public areas, most of the rooms in this three-story whitewashed building with red-gingerbread trim overlook the water; all have simple furnishings and hardwood floors. The showers in the rooms with baths are generally clean. You can't beat the location for the price in San Pedro. Downstairs is Rubie's Deli (open 6am until 5pm daily), a good place for breakfast or a casual midday meal.

DOUBLES FOR LESS THAN B$70 ($35)

Martha's. Pescador Drive (P.O. Box 27), San Pedro, Ambergris Caye. ☎ **501-26/2053.** Fax 501-26/2589. 14 rms (all with bath). Nov–Apr B$40 ($20) single; B$60 ($30) double; B$80 ($40) triple; May–Oct B$30 ($15) single; B$55 ($27.50) double; B$75 ($37.50) triple. AE.

It's hard to believe that a hotel located upstairs from a grocery store could be so expensive, but here in San Pedro, nothing is cheap. At least the new rooms here are larger than those at most other hotels. There are reading lights over the two double beds, ceiling fans, and big verandahs at either end of the building, so you can watch the sunrise or sunset. You'll find Martha's about halfway down Pescador Drive.

Hotel San Pedrano. Barrier Reef Drive, San Pedro, Ambergris Caye. ☎ **501-26/2054.** Fax 501-26/2093. 7 rms (all with bath). Nov–Apr B$50 ($25) single; B$60 ($30) double; B$75 ($37.50) triple; May–Oct B$40 ($20) single; B$50 ($25) double; B$60 ($30) triple; add B$20 ($10) for A/C. AE, MC, V.

Although few of the rooms have ocean views, all have nice wooden floors, well-maintained blue patio furniture, and clean baths with tubs. What views the San Pedrano has from the wide verandah are of the rooftops of adjacent buildings; while these hardly make for a spectacular vista, the verandah is still a great place for reading a book. The rooms are located above a small dive shop toward the northern end of Front Street.

Seychelles Guest House. San Pedro, Ambergris Caye. ☎ **501-26/3223.** 4 rooms (all with shared bath). B$60 ($20) single; B$70 ($35) double. No credit cards. All rates include full breakfast.

This older house on stilts is just south of the airport. The second floor is a clean and casual bed-and-breakfast. The rooms are small and quite Spartan, but all are airy and have fans. There's a combination living room and dining room where guests can hang out, and a kitchen available for their use. The fresh baked goods at breakfast receive raves from past guests. From the front porch, there's a view of the water, but you have to walk a hundred yards or so to actually get your feet wet. Downstairs you'll find the headquarters and dive shop of Adventures in Watersports.

Tomas Hotel. Barrier Reef Drive, San Pedro, Ambergris Caye. ☎ **501-26/2061.** 7 rms (all with bath). B$40 ($20) single; B$53 ($26.50) double; B$70 ($35) double with A/C. MC, V.

Heading toward the north end of Front Street, directly across the street from an old blue wooden house with flower designs on it, you'll spot the sign for the Tomas Hotel. While not particularly attractive, the modern cement building is one of the better budget lodgings on the island. All the rooms have tile floors, very clean bathrooms, and fans. There's a deck on the second floor where you can get a bit of sun.

DOUBLES FOR LESS THAN B$90 ($45)

Hide-A-Way Sports Lodge. P.O. Box 43, San Pedro, Ambergris Caye. ☎ **501-26/2141.** Fax 501-26/2269. 19 rms (all with bath). B$80–B$120 ($40–$60) single or double; B$90–B$180 ($45–$90) triple or quad. All rates include full breakfast. AE, DISC, MC, V.

Located just south of the airport, the Hide-A-Way is the cheapest lodging you'll find in San Pedro with a pool, and though it's a small pool, it's convenient for an early morning or late afternoon swim. The Hide-A-Way is fairly comfortable, yet relatively basic. It caters to divers and fishermen, not beach vacationers, which means that while relatively comfortable, its amenities are pretty basic. There's a bit too much cement and not much shade (walls in the downstairs rooms are cinderblock), which tends to make things a bit hot. However, if you spend your days in the water, it shouldn't matter too much. Five of the pricier rooms have air-conditioning. There's a nice second-floor restaurant, which is closed on Tuesday.

Oasis del Mar. P.O. Box 89, San Pedro Town, Ambergris Caye. ☎ **501-26/2695.** Fax 501-26/2254. 6 cabins (all with bath). B$78–B$130 ($39–$65) single, double, triple, or quad. Lower rates in the summer. MC, V.

Located just south of the airport on the outskirts of town, this collection of tropical cabins tries to live up to its name. Though the frequent planes overhead make this place noisy during the day, the shade trees, flowers, and shrubs make it a genuine oasis in barren San Pedro. The cabins sleep up to four people and are all quite spacious. High ceilings, louvered windows, and ceiling fans help keep the rooms cool, and there are kitchenettes. Though the price is high for one or two people, this is a deal for three or four, especially if you cook your own food. When I last visited, the place was actively for sale, and there was a sense of neglect to the grounds.

Worth a Splurge

Barrier Reef Hotel. Barrier Reef Drive (P.O. Box 34), San Pedro, Ambergris Caye. ☎ **501-26/2075.** Fax 501-26/2719. 11 rms (all with bath). A/C TV. B$96 ($48) single; B$130 ($65) double; B$150 ($75) triple. Lower rates during the off-season. AE, MC, V.

This hotel charges a bit too much for rather basic rooms, but is located in one of my favorite buildings in San Pedro—a blindingly white structure designed to resemble a traditional Caribbean wooden house that sits directly across from the town square. A long verandah wraps around the second floor, and a small balcony extends from the third floor. Three gables extend seaward from the roof to complete the picture. Each room has both a double and single bed with built-in headboards, tile floors, a fan, and air-conditioning. The nicest rooms are those facing the water, with views and access to the best section of verandah. Out back there's a small swimming pool. The restaurant and bar on the first floor is a casual place serving hot sandwiches and burgers for B$8 ($4), fresh fish dinners for B$14 ($7), and pizza for B$16 to B$38 ($8 to $19). Daily specials might include shrimp scampi and fish filet in lemon sauce.

✪ **Hotel Casablanca.** Pescador Drive, San Pedro, Ambergris Caye. ☎ **501-26/2327.** Fax 501-26/2992. 5 rms (all with bath). A/C. Nov–Apr B$180 ($90) single, double, or triple; May–Oct B$110 ($55) single, double, or triple. MC, V.

This hotel, owned and operated by a former nightclub designer from Britain, is a refreshingly contemporary lodging that diverges from the San Pedro norm. Instead of bamboo furnishings and tropical motifs, you get a combination of Miami Beach modern and Marrakech Moorish. There are bright, primary colors everywhere, unusual cement corner shelves, and contemporary furniture designs (even stylish steel chairs). The guest rooms have one king or two double beds and are comfortably stark. On the ground floor is one of the best restaurants on the island, the **Lagoon.** Up on the roof, there's the **Sunset Bar,** with a panoramic view of San Pedro and the water.

Lily's. On the beach, San Pedro, Ambergris Caye. ☎ **501-26/2059.** 10 rms (all with bath). Dec–Apr B$120 ($60) single, B$150 ($75) double; May–Nov B$1000 ($50) single, B$120 ($60) double. MC, V.

If you've stayed here before, take note of the room rates; they recently skyrocketed. Now, if you want a private bath and a water view, you'll have to pay for it. Situated right on the beach, Lily's is behind the Tomas Hotel. Rooms are large and have ceiling and table fans, wood paneling, and fluorescent lighting. Not all have a water view, although most do. There's pleasant seating for guests on the front verandah and free lounge chairs on the beach.

✪ **San Pedro Holiday Hotel.** Barrier Reef Drive (P.O. Box 61), San Pedro Town, Ambergris Caye. ☎ **501-26/2014.** Fax 501-26/2295. 18 rms (all with bath). A/C. B$168–B$188 ($84–$94) single or double. AE, MC, V.

You can't miss this brilliantly white three-building complex with purple and pink trim in the center of town. The first hotel to open on Ambergris Caye some 30 years ago, it's quite outside our price range; however, as every room has air-conditioning, and most have excellent ocean views and small refrigerators, you may want to splurge. Rooms on the second floor have wonderful balconies. The original owner, Celi McCorkle, still presides over the San Pedro, and it continues to keep pace with the times. Facilities include a full-service dive shop, a popular bar and restaurant, and a small gift shop.

WHERE TO EAT

Seafood is, of course, the most popular food on the island, and there's plenty of it available year-round. You'll get the most for your money if you order based on what's in season. The **lobster season** is from July 15 to February 14, and conch is available from October 1 to June 30. When lobster is in season, it's the best deal on the island, and you can order it three meals a day and still not go bankrupt. However, it's rock lobster, which lacks large claws and is not as flavorful as northern, cold-water lobster.

In addition to the restaurants listed below, **Rubie's Cafe** and **Celi's Deli,** on the ground floors of Rubie's Hotel and the Holiday Hotel, respectively, are good places to pick up a light meal. Both specialize in freshly baked breads and pastries, and sandwiches to go.

MEALS FOR LESS THAN B$10 ($5)

Ambergris Delight. Pescador Drive. ☎ **26/2464.** Main courses B$7–B$12 ($3.50–$6). MC, V. Daily 11am–2pm and 6–10pm. BELIZEAN.

Located a block north of Elvi's, Ambergris Delight is popular with locals and offers excellent and inexpensive burgers and seafood. A big blackboard serves as a menu and occasionally includes such specials as conch soup. The best deals are the combination dinners of rice and beans served with a fish filet, whole fried fish, broiled fish, or chicken for B$10 ($5). There are always a few cakes and pies on the counter.

The Pizza Place. At the Paradise Hotel, north end of Barrier Reef Drive ☎ **26/2444.** Main courses B$10–B$28 ($5–$14), whole pizza B$12–B$38 ($6–$19). MC, V. Daily 11am–9pm. PIZZA/ITALIAN.

For a quick and casual meal, try this popular restaurant, that recently relocated. The setting is now indoors, yet only slightly more formal, and you can still take your food out to a table under one of the small shady palapas. There's sometimes live music in the evenings. A large pizza is plenty for four people.

MEALS FOR LESS THAN B$20 ($10)

✪ **Elvi's Kitchen.** Halfway down Pescador Drive. ☎ **26/2359.** Reservations recommended during high season. Main courses B$10–B$36 ($5–$18). AE, MC, V. Mon–Sat 11am–2pm and 5:30–10pm. SEAFOOD/INTERNATIONAL.

Elvi's is the most popular restaurant on Ambergris Caye, with a strong word-of-mouth reputation. Despite an enlarged dining room, they still can't keep up with the dinner crowds that flock here for the substantial servings cooked to order and fair prices. The setting's pretty primitive, but that's part of Elvi's charm: a thatched-roofed hut with screens and picnic tables. The floor is made of crushed shells and sand, and a large tree grows through the roof. Fans keep diners cool, and the varnished wood tables, chairs, and walls add a touch of refinement. A typical dinner might include cream of vegetable soup, followed by a main dish of squid, scallops, and shrimp in red sauce with a side of okra. Thursday and Saturday are theme nights—Caribbean and Mexican, respectively.

Estel's Dine by the Sea. Oceanside behind Atlantic Bank. ☎ **26/2019.** Main dishes B$8–B$26 ($4–$13). No credit cards. Wed–Mon 6am–8pm. INTERNATIONAL.

If you want to dine right by the water, it's hard to get much closer than Estel's. This casual place has a sand floor and thatched roof and a sand terrace outside. The food, though pretty standard, gains from its proximity to the water. There's a Mexican plate, as well as barbecued chicken and grilled fish. In general, it's a mellow scene, with great music on the stereo and occasional live performances.

Jade Garden. 1¼ miles south of airstrip. ☎ **26/2126** or 26/2506. Main courses B$9–B$36 ($4.50–$18). AE, MC, V. Daily 11am–2pm and 6–10pm. CHINESE.

Located in a large contemporary house south of the airport, Jade Garden has long been popular. Wicker chairs, overhead fans, high ceilings, and a balcony overlooking the sea and garden create a pleasant atmosphere, and the kitchen serves up a long menu of well-prepared Chinese standards with an emphasis on seafood. There are also several non-Chinese specialties, such as surf-and-turf kebabs, broiled lobster, and T-bone steak.

MEALS FOR LESS THAN B$30 ($15)

✪ **Lagoon Restaurant.** Pescador Drive. ☎ **26/2327.** Reservations recommended during high season. Main courses B$18–B$40 ($9–$20). MC, V. Thur–Tue 7am–2pm and 6–10pm. INTERNATIONAL.

Located below the Hotel Casablanca, the Lagoon is an equally sophisticated place that brings contemporary haute cuisine and North American restaurant decor to Belize. Custom-made steel chairs and candelabras, track lighting, a deep blue ceiling painted with stars, and blue glass blocks in the bar spell out an urban chic that has never before been seen on Ambergris Caye. You can start your evening with a sunset cocktail up on the roof and then head downstairs for a culinary treat of a dinner. The menu changes regularly, but you might find such offerings as chicken and shrimp satay; orange, onion, and radish salad; chilled cucumber soup; black-bean lasagna; lobster anise; and cajun shrimp. Breakfasts feature fresh-baked bagels. Don't miss the watermelon granita with blackberry brandy.

Lily's. On the beach in the middle of town. ☎ **26/2059.** Reservations recommended. Main courses B$25–B$30 ($12.50–$15); lunch B$15–B$20 ($7.50–$10). MC, V. Daily 7am–2pm and 5:30–9pm. SEAFOOD.

Lily's Hotel, on the waterfront, is also home to one of the best restaurants in San Pedro. You don't get much choice here, but if you like seafood, you'll love this place. A fish, lobster, conch, or fish/shrimp combo dinner costs between B$25 and B$30 and is served family-style, so you can eat your fill. The delicious food is cooked to order and comes with french fries, cole slaw, and a vegetable. The restaurant itself is brightly lit, but candlelit tables and wicker chairs help create an attractive atmosphere.

Little Italy Restaurant. At the Spindrift Hotel, Barrier Reef Drive. ☎ **26/2866.** Main courses B$10–B$35 ($5–$17.50). AE, MC, V. Daily 11:30am–2pm; Thurs–Tues 5:30–9pm. ITALIAN.

At the back of the Spindrift Hotel, you'll find this Italian restaurant. It's located right on the water and has a covered terrace dining area as well as an indoor dining room. Though the decor is more tropical than Italian, the food is authentic. Regular menu items include the likes of manicotti and spaghetti with shrimp or snapper, while the daily special might be something slightly less familiar, such as fresh shrimp with linguine, sweet peppers, olives, and feta cheese. Desserts include ice cream with liqueur. There is a good wine list, as well as a full bar.

Reality Cafe. At Fido's Courtyard, Barrier Reef Drive. ☎ **26/3586.** Breakfast and lunch items B$9–B$13 ($4.50–$6.50); main courses B$25–B$35 ($12.50–$17.50). V. Daily 7am–10pm. SEAFOOD/INTERNATIONAL.

By day, this is a casual coffee shop, serving up hefty breakfasts and good nachos, burgers, and chili dogs. In the evening, more creative cooking is featured. The menu changes nightly, but you're bound to find some excellent seafood, such as lobster Creole, beer-battered shrimp, or sautéed grouper. The garden-fresh salads are a treat on this barren island, where a good head of lettuce is a prime commodity. You can sit upstairs in the small cafe, or at any of the tables spread around Fido's covered courtyard.

❍ **Vijay's at Pirate's Lantern.** South of the airport. ☎ **26/2146.** Main courses B$15–B$36 ($7.50–$18). AE, V. Tues–Sun 11:30am–2pm and 6–10pm. INDIAN.

This former budget inn and restaurant has been taken over by a local East Indian family and converted into one of the best Indian restaurants in the country. Tables are spread around a simple screened-in porch. There's not much ambience, but the food is authentic and spicy. Try the mutton biryani (B$24) or pannir masal. If you've got a real hot tooth, go for the chicken vindaloo (B$24). There's a wide selection of appetizers and Indian breads (B$3 to B$8) and a full bar.

AMBERGRIS CAYE AFTER DARK

There are really only three spots of note in San Pedro, and none outside.

Big Daddy's. Across from the Barrier Reef Hotel and behind the church. No phone.

Nowhere have I ever seen a bar or disco located so close to a church. The saints and the sinners seem to be in a competition to see who can play the loudest music. The church often throws its doors open and cranks up the volume on its organ, but there always seem to be more people in the disco. The dress is casual, and the drinks are not overpriced. Big Daddy's has an extensive happy hour from 5:30–10pm every night.

Tarzan's Club. Barrier Reef Drive, in front of the park. No phone.

Not far from—and certainly competing with—Big Daddy's, is this new entry into the local disco scene. The action starts around 8pm and continues into the early hours of the morning. On the ground floor there's a medium-sized raised dance floor set in the sand. Encircling this is a second- floor balcony, where you'll find the bar and some tables. It's loud and there's a mirrored ball and flashing lights—what more could you ask for?

The Tackle Box Bar. Off Barrier Reef Drive near the south end of town. No phone.

Drop in for a beer (B$4) or a piña colada (B$7) at San Pedro's most famous watering hole, and you'll have to fight with local fishermen and sailors for a seat at the bar. Situated at the end of a short pier, this is where seafaring types gather to exchange information. If you want a boat to another caye, the folks behind the bar will be able to set you up with a ride. The bar, some seating, a dart board, and video games are all indoors, but I suggest you grab one of the outdoor tables and watch the moon and stars rise.

SIDE TRIPS FROM AMBERGRIS CAYE

If you've been on the island for a while and want to see more of Belize, contact **Amigo Travel** (☎ 501-26/2180), **Freedom Tours** (☎ 501-26/3272), or **Hustler Tours** (☎ 501-26/2279), all of which have offices on Barrier Reef Drive. They offer day trips to various locations—including Altun Ha, Lamanai, Xunantunich,

Mountain Pine Ridge, and Tikal. While most are quite expensive, one of the most popular, the excursion to the Mayan ruins at Altun Ha, is almost within our price range. It begins with an early morning departure from San Pedro. You are quickly whisked by boat across protected waters and then up the Northern River to the small village of Bomba, where you dock and transfer to a taxi that takes you to the ruins. Lunch, and the return trip to San Pedro, are included in the price (B$116–B$120— $58–$60—per person).

3 Caye Caulker

20 miles N of Belize City; 10 miles S of Ambergris Caye

The word is definitely out about Caye Caulker. Room rates have edged up over recent years, hotels have been renovated in anticipation of better-heeled guests, and more gift shops have opened. If you walk its streets, you'll be practically bombarded with offers to go snorkeling. Yet resourceful types can still stay here and not break the bank. As yet, there are no resorts, the pace is still slow, and the atmosphere remains laid back. And, unlike neighboring San Pedro, you won't be constantly run off the road by golf carts.

There's one more thing you should know about Caye Caulker—it's home to the nasty sand flea, a tiny insect with a vicious bite that leaves an itchy welt. Sand fleas come out whenever the trade winds die down. When this happens, the best solution is to put on socks and long pants, since the fleas tend to target feet and ankles. Sitting out at the end of a long pier also offers some relief.

ESSENTIALS
GETTING THERE & DEPARTING

By Plane **Island Air** (☎ **501-2/31140** in Belize City or 501-26/2435 in San Pedro) has seven daily flights to Caye Caulker from both the international and municipal airports in Belize City. Duration is 15 minutes. Fare is B$38 ($19) one-way from the municipal airport, B$70 ($35) one-way from the international airport. Island Air also flies between Ambergris Caye and Caye Caulker. Duration is 15 minutes. Fare is B$38 ($19) one-way, B$60 ($30) round-trip. If you just flew into Belize from another country and are headed directly to Caye Caulker, you might consider flying, because the combination taxi/boat ride into Belize City and Caye Caulker, respectively, costs B$45 ($22.50)—only B$22 ($12.50) less than the plane.

Tropic Air (☎ **501-2/45671** in Belize City) has 11 daily flights (roughly every hour on the half-hour, beginning at 7:30am) to San Pedro from the municipal airport, and 10 daily flights from the international airport (every hour on the hour, between 7am and 4pm). These will stop on request at Caye Caulker. Duration is 15 minutes. Fare is B$38 ($19) one-way from the municipal airport; B$70 ($35) one-way from the international airport.

When you're ready to depart, there are daily flights to both Belize City airports and to Ambergris Caye. Sometimes they only stop in Caye Caulker if there is a reserved passenger waiting. Check directly at the airport, or with **Dolphin Bay Travel** (☎ 501-22/2214) to make reservations and buy tickets.

By Boat Most of the boats heading out to Ambergris Caye stop at Caye Caulker to pick up and discharge passengers. The *Triple J* (☎ 501-2/44375) leaves from a pier near the swing bridge every morning at 9am. The *Andrea II* (☎ 501-2/74988 in Belize City or 501-26/2578 in San Pedro) departs daily from a pier near the Bellevue Hotel on Southern Foreshore at 3pm. The *Banana Boat* (☎ 501-26/2807) leaves from the same dock at 4pm daily. Duration is 50 minutes. Fare is B$15

($7.50). The ***Thunderbolt*** leaves from a pier by the swing bridge everyday at 1:30pm and charges B$20 ($10). Duration is 50 minutes.

High-speed launches leave from behind the A&R Texaco station on North Front Street. You'll find the gas station about 50 yards west of the swing bridge, downtown Belize City's main reference point. Loosely organized as the **Caye Caulker Water Taxi Association** (☎ **501-2/22160** in Belize City), these boats leave periodically throughout the day as they fill up, between 8am and 4pm. One-way fare is B$15 ($7.50). You pay when you arrive at Caye Caulker. Unsavory street guides will offer to take you to the boat to Caye Caulker; these guides are not to be trusted, so don't wander off with one to negotiate any deals.

Boats to Belize City leave periodically throughout the day. **The Caye Caulker Water Taxi Association** (☎ **501-22/2073** on Caye Caulker) maintains a booth on Front Street near the Vega Inn. They can sell you advance tickets and give you up-to-date schedules. During the high season, it's a good idea to buy your ticket the day before you plan to leave.

Alternatively, you can hop on one of the water taxis heading out to Ambergris Caye. Most of these boats stop at the Texaco dock on the west side of the island, although some use a dock on the ocean side. Fare is B$15 ($7.50). Duration is 30 minutes. Ask at the Caye Caulker Water Taxi Association for current schedules or see "Getting There," under "Ambergris Caye" above. Boats pass through Caye Caulker about 50 minutes after leaving Belize City.

You can also sail over to Ambergris Caye on one of the sailboats that go out to the Hol Chan Marine Reserve; these boats usually leave Caye Caulker around 10am and stop for lunch in San Pedro in the afternoon. Instead of sailing back, you can just stay in San Pedro.

ORIENTATION

Most boats dock at a pier that juts out from Front Street; it's called **front bridge** (if you're facing the reef—east—this is the front side of the island). The town extends north and south from here. As you disembark, you'll be able to see the western side of the island and back bridge, the other dock in Caye Caulker. The island consists of two main north-south sand roads (Front and Back streets), a few cross streets, and numerous paths.

Fast Facts   You can exchange money and traveler's checks at the **Atlantic Bank** on Back Street (at the center of the island), open Monday through Friday from 8am until noon and 1 to 4pm, and Saturday 9am until noon; or at most hotels, where you'll probably get a better rate. The **city code** is 22. If you are calling from somewhere else in Belize, remember to dial "0" before the phone number and include the city code. Several women on the island take in **laundry;** watch for their signs around town.

Most **shops** on the island keep very informal store hours, but are generally open between 8am and 7pm, with a lunch break between 1 and 3pm. The **BTL telephone office** is about midway along Front Street, and is open Monday through Friday from 8am to noon and 1 to 4pm, Saturday 8am to noon. If you need to make a long-distance call, this is your best option, although some hotels may allow you to make a calling-card or collect call from their phone.

FUN ON & OFF THE WATER

The main activities on Caye Caulker are strolling up and down the sand streets, and swimming and sunbathing off the docks. The most popular spot is at the north end of the inhabited part of Caye Caulker, called the Split. The Split was formed in 1961 when Hurricane Hattie literally "split" the island in two. You'll find the water's edge rimmed with a nice wooden dock and there's even a roped-off swimming area that includes a tiny mangrove island. The water is very calm by the Split, making it a good place to practice if you're an inexperienced snorkeler.

Take care when swimming off the docks here. At least one swimmer was killed by a boat, so stick to designated swimming areas and out of obvious boat channels.

Biking Although it's possible to bike around Caye Caulker for the fun of it, bikes are rarely used by locals to get around since you can walk anywhere on the island in under 15 minutes. Bike rentals average B$5 ($2.50) an hour. Check at gift shops around town, such as **Traci's Island Wear** (☎ 501-22/2075), **Sea Horse Gift Shop** (☎ 501-22/2082), or **Mayan Secrets** (☎ 501-22/2060).

Diving There are two main dive shops on Caye Caulker. **Belize Diving Services** (☎ 501-22/2143), west of the soccer field, is Caye Caulker's best-equipped dive center. A two-tank dive will cost you B$80 ($40) per person. Trips to Hol Chan or St. George's Caye, with two-tank dives, run B$100 ($50) per person. They also offer cave diving to certified cave divers, scuba-diving courses, and equipment rental. **Frenchie's Diving Services** (☎ 501-22/2234), on the north end of the island a half block west of Front Street, offers similar services at comparable prices. Both of these outfitters can also arrange trips to Turneffe Islands atoll, Lighthouse Reef atoll, and the Blue Hole.

Golf Cart Rentals While you can't play golf here, golf carts are available for rent as a means of getting around. If you're interested, go to **Island Rentals** (☎ 501-22/2229), between Front and Back streets in the center of town. An electric golf cart rents for B$15 ($7.50) per hour, or B$80 ($40) per day.

Kayaking If you know how to kayak, it's a great way to orient yourself to the island—paddle around its circumference, poking into mangroves as you go. Kayaks are available for rent at **Daisy's hotel** (☎ 501-22/2150). A 4-hour rental of a one-person kayak costs B$30 ($15); for a double kayak, the cost is B$40 ($20). Hourly rates for the two types of kayaks are B$10 ($5) and B$15 ($7.50) per hour, respectively.

Snorkeling Several boats leave from the front bridge dock every morning on half-day snorkeling trips to the reef. Since the reef is so close, you might consider taking one of the local sailing sloops out. For safety's sake, the boat should be in good condition, with a working motor (even on sailboats), in case the seas become rough or in the rare event that a quick rescue is needed. Your guide should be attentive and aware of your level of experience.

Some of the more established snorkeling guides work with **Dolphin Bay Travel** (☎ 501-22/2214), **Driftwood Snorkeling** (☎ 501-22/2122), and **Hicaco Tours** (☎ 501-22/2073). Half-day trips usually cost around B$20 ($10) per person, and a set of gear will run you an extra B$5 ($2.50). These operators also offer full-day excursions to Hol Chan Marine Reserve off San Pedro (see "Side Trips from Ambergris Caye," above). These trips usually cost around B$35 to B$40 ($17.50 to $20) per person, and include lunch (you'll stop to eat it in San Pedro) as well as the entrance fee to Hol Chan. Gear is extra.

One of the most popular guides is **Chocolate,** with whom you can book a snorkeling tour directly (☎ 501-22/2151). He's well-liked mostly because he's such a warm and personable character, but also because he's got a nice boat. Chocolate runs a variety of tours, usually full-day tours, including trips to Hol Chan and Geoff's Caye. Fares usually run between B$40 and B$50 ($20 to $25) per person and include gear, but not lunch. Inquire the day before at Chocolate's home and boutique at the north end of Front Street.

EXCURSIONS TO ALTUN HA

Dolphin Bay Travel (☎ 501-22/2214), **Driftwood Snorkeling** (☎ 501-22/2122), and **Hicaco Tours** (☎ 501-22/2073) all offer trips to Altun Ha for around B$100 ($50) per person, not including lunch. For a description of this trip, see "Side Trips from Ambergris Caye," above.

SHOPPING

You'll be overwhelmed by the number of small gift shops and makeshift souvenir stands lining the few streets here. Mostly what you'll be able to buy are t-shirts and jewelry made by local artisans. **Chocolate's Boutique** (☎ 22/2151) has slightly higher quality goods, including reasonably priced Guatemalan and Indonesian textiles. **Sea-ing is Belizing** (☎ 22/2189), open daily from 9am to 5pm) is a gallery that specializes in underwater and nature photography by co-owner James Beveridge, who has been photographing Belize since 1969. Besides selling photographic postcards, slides, and framed and unframed prints, the gallery offers slide shows illustrating the reefs and cayes. Programs are held regularly at 7pm and cost B$5 ($2.50) per person. They also offer guided sailboat trips that explore the barrier reef ecosystem, as well as t-shirts, books about Belize, and film processing.

Jan's Deli, (on Front Street; ☎ 22/2188) a good place to pick up bread, cheese, yogurt, drinks, and other staples, is open Monday to Saturday from 7am to 1pm and 3 to 7pm, and Sunday from 8am to noon.

WHERE TO STAY

Accommodations on Caye Caulker have improved in recent years. While most offerings are far from luxurious (even if the room rates might indicate otherwise), there are no resorts yet, and inexpensive lodgings can still be found. In the off-season between May and August, it's possible to get substantial discounts. However, you'll have to put up with biting fleas when the winds die down, and mosquitoes in June, July, and August.

If you plan on staying any length of time, look into renting a small cottage or apartment. Keep your eyes posted for signs or bulletin boards advertising places for rent, or check with **Heredia's House Rental** (☎ 501-22/2132) or **M&N Apartments** (☎ 501-22/2111). Rates for a beachfront apartment start at around B$400 ($200) per week.

Camping is allowed at Vega Inn (☎ 501-22/2142), but over the years I've heard several accounts of tents and backpackers being robbed here.

DOUBLES FOR LESS THAN B$50 ($25)

The Anchorage. South of the front bridge, Caye Caulker. ☎ **501-22/2002.** 3 rms (all with bath). B$30 ($15) single or double; B$45 ($22.50) triple. No credit cards.

A 10-minute walk south of the front bridge, for years the Anchorage was the sort of place tropical travelers on a very low budget dream about—white sand, coconut palms rustling in the trade winds, turquoise water, and the distant murmur of waves crashing on the barrier reef. Composed of three whitewashed adobe huts with palm-thatched roofs, each with its own bath (cold-water showers only), it's hard to imagine a more idyllic setting. However, on my last visit, the Anchorage was actively for sale and quite run down. Perhaps a new owner will restore it to its former glory.

Daisy's. Front Street, west of the cemetery and Tropical Paradise Restaurant (P.O. Box 996, Belize City), Caye Caulker. ☎ **501-22/2150.** 13 rms (1 with bath). B$15 ($7.50) single with shared bath; B$26.50 ($13.25) double with shared bath, B$40 ($20) double with bath; B$35 ($17.50) triple with shared bath. No credit cards.

Daisy's is located on Front Street in a long two-story wooden building that's part of a small family compound and courtyard. Even though the rooms have fans, the ones on the first floor are stuffy and have little air circulation. The larger rooms upstairs are much roomier and, because they catch the ocean breezes, cooler. Get one of these if you can. Furnishings are rather stark, with a single fluorescent light in the middle of the ceiling. The bathrooms have cold water only.

Ignacio's Beach Cabañas. South of front bridge, Caye Caulker. ☎ **501-22/2212.** 21 rms (all with bath). B$30 ($15) single, double, or triple old cabaña; B$45 ($22.50) single, double, or triple new cabaña. No credit cards.

Located just south of the Anchorage, these cabañas are brightly painted little wooden boxes sitting either directly on the sand or on stilts. At first, it may give the appearance of a shanty town, but the groups of young travelers relaxing in hammocks strung between the palm trees indicate that this is a low–budget tropical paradise. The more expensive cabañas are closest to the water and have small ocean view verandahs. The owner, Ignacio, is one of the island's more colorful characters.

✪ Jiménez Cabañas. Caye Caulker. ☎ **501-22/2175.** 8 cabañas (all with bath). B$48 ($24) single or double; B$58 ($29) triple; B$64 ($32) quad. AE, MC, V.

Down the road from the Tropical Paradise Hotel (see below), on the western side of the island, is this very attractive little grouping of cabañas set in a sunny garden with a conch shell-lined walkway. Peaceful and secluded, each has palmetto-trunk walls, a thatched roof, and a small porch, and a simple bath with hot water. The owner is a former lobsterman, who left the business when the population began to decline.

Lena's Hotel. On the water near the Tropical Paradise Hotel, Caye Caulker. ☎ **501-22/2106.** 18 rms (10 with bath). B$30 ($15) single or double without bath; B$50–B$60 ($25–$30) single or double with bath; B$74 ($37) triple with bath. No credit cards.

Lena's is right on the water, and if you have an ocean-front room, you will also have a verandah that's perfect for sitting and gazing out at the Caribbean. Unfortunately, the other rooms aren't nearly as pleasant. While all are clean and well-kept, with firm foam mattresses, newish sheets, and fans, that's about all they offer. Rooms with a private hot-water bath are preferable to those with a shared bath and are within a frugal traveler's price range. The owners are friendly and can help arrange a variety of tours for guests.

Tom's Hotel. On the beach, south of front bridge. ☎ **501-22/2102.** 31 rms (none with bath), 5 cabañas (all with bath). B$20–B$35 ($10–$17.50) single or double without bath; B$55 ($27.50) single, double, or triple cabaña with bath. No credit cards.

If one were to rank the accommodations at this beachfront lodging, the roomy cabañas, with private baths, would take first place, hands down. Second place belongs to the newer, and more expensive, rooms, which are clean and bright and have cool tile floors. Third place goes to the older rooms, some of which are tiny and can get hot and stuffy; but if you spend all your time snorkeling or hanging out elsewhere, perhaps you won't mind very much. A second floor verandah overlooking the water is open to all guests for reading or just lounging, and there's a private dock for tanning.

DOUBLES FOR LESS THAN B$70 ($35)

Rainbow Hotel. North of front bridge on the ocean, Caye Caulker. ☎ **501-22/2123.** Fax 501-22/2172. 17 rms (all with bath). B$45–B$55 ($22.50–$27.50) single; B$55–B$65 ($27.50–$32.50) double; B$70–B$80 ($35–$40) triple; lower rates May–Oct. MC, V.

You can't miss this brightly painted lodging on Front Street. Only a few feet from the water, the Rainbow has a nice ocean view and a private dock for guests. The rooms are clean, with tiled showers, ceiling fans, and louvered windows that let in the breezes; double and twin beds are available.

Upstairs rooms are only slightly more expensive and have cable TV, better furniture, and private verandahs. If you can't find the manager, ask at the restaurant in front of the hotel, just past the volleyball court. The restaurant serves good, inexpensive meals; it's closed Monday.

Tree Tops Hotel. On the waterfront south of front bridge, Caye Caulker (P.O. Box 1648, Belize City). ☎ **501-22/2008.** Fax 501-22/2115. 4 rms (1 with bath). TV. B$50–B$55 ($25–$27.50) single or double with shared bath; B$65 ($35) single or double with private bath. MC, V.

Located between Tom's Hotel and the Sea Beezzz, this new lodging offers clean, spacious, and cool rooms in the lower half of a two-story home. Each room has tile floors, high ceilings, a standing fan, and a small refrigerator. Though set back about 50 yards from the shore, the only thing between you and the ocean are some shady coconut palms. There's no restaurant on the premises, but it's just a short walk to any number of eateries.

Tropical Paradise Hotel. (P.O. Box 1573, Belize City), Caye Caulker. ☎ **501-22/2124** or 501-22/2063. Fax 501/22-2225. 5 rms, 6 cabañas, 5 air-conditioned suites (all with bath). Rooms B$60 ($30) single, B$70 ($35) double; cabañas B$75–B$90 ($37.50–$45) single, B$80–B$100 ($40–$50) double; suites B$140 ($70) double. Add a 5% surcharge. MC, V.

Proprietor Ramon Reyes runs a tight ship: The rooms are very clean and paneled, with a little bit of storage space for your things, and a narrow front porch for catching the breeze. The hot water is a bit finicky, however. The cabañas and suites, with full baths, are more expensive and are quite a bit larger than the rooms. Nevertheless, with their location at the back of the complex behind the restaurant, they lack breezes and a view.

WORTH A SPLURGE

Sea Beezzz. On the waterfront south of Front Bridge, Caye Caulker. ☎ **501-22/2176** or 516/668-9212 in the U.S. 6 rms (all with bath). B$80 ($40) single or double. Add 5% surcharge. V. Open Nov–Apr only.

These gray buildings with white trim may remind you of Cape Cod, but the iron bars on the windows make it clear you're in Central America. Although the guest rooms are modern and clean and have ceiling fans and hot water, they are situated in such a way that they don't catch the breezes. To make up for this, there's a pretty garden with tables in the sand only steps from the water. Sea Beezzz also has its own small restaurant and bar that serves excellent margaritas.

✪ Shirley's Guest House. Close to the airstrip (P.O. Box 1174, Belize City), Caye Caulker. ☎ **501-22/2145.** Fax 501-22/2264. 8 rms (3 with bath). B$85 ($42.50) double without bath; B$110–B$125 ($55–$62.50) double with bath. MC, V.

These picturesque white cabins with green trim are just about the first accommodations you'll see as you walk north along the water from the airstrip. Set on stilts and shaded by coconut palms, they're hard to miss. The setting is idyllic, safe, and quiet. The rooms have varnished floors, quilted bedspreads, and some come with a small refrigerator. Although a little on the expensive side, the location and large, comfortable rooms make Shirley's worth every penny.

WHERE TO EAT

As on Ambergris Caye, seafood is popular and plentiful all year, and it's even a little cheaper here. Do remember to abide by the seasons on lobster, conch, and shrimp, and don't order turtle soup or steaks (sea turtles are endangered). Restaurants are not supposed to serve lobster in the off-season, when the lobsters are breeding. If it's on the menu during off-season, please don't order it.

Caye Caulker has a thriving cottage industry of snack bakers and informal eateries. Wander the streets and you're sure to see signs offering yogurt and granola, freshly squeezed juices, hot lobster pie, sweet rolls, and chocolate or cheese pie—each B$1 to B$2 (50¢ to $1). Don't be bashful: Just step right up and knock on the door for a homemade treat. You won't be disappointed. (It's also a chance to get a glimpse into a few Belizean homes.) You can get your ice-cream fix at **Scoops Ice Cream** (one block south of the soccer field). For more substantial meals, try one of the places listed below.

MEALS FOR LESS THAN B$20 ($10)

Castaways Restaurant. On Front Street, north of front bridge, Caye Caulker. ☎ **22/2294.** Main courses B$9–B$30 ($4.50–$15). MC, V (add 5% surcharge). Wed–Mon 6:30am–9pm. BELIZEAN/INTERNATIONAL.

Inside this traditional red-trimmed white Belizean cottage, you'll find such international favorites as Thai chicken, chicken Korma, lasagna, curries, chow mein, and delicious stone crab, when it's available. The British owner (who also rents rooms) has lived in Belize for many years and is a good person to search out for a convivial chat. If you're looking for an early breakfast, this is the place. There's a B$25 ($12.50) breakfast special that includes your water taxi ride back to Belize City.

✪ **Glenda's.** In back of Atlantic Bank, Caye Caulker. ☎ **22/2148.** Breakfast B$6 ($3); lunch B$1–B$5 (50¢–$2.50). No credit cards. Daily 7am–3pm. BELIZEAN.

Run by Glenda and her daughter, this establishment is one of Caye Caulker's little home bakeries gone upscale. It's also *the* breakfast spot on the island. They specialize in fresh cinnamon rolls, pastries, *garnaches*, and fresh juices. Locals and tourists alike say the burritos and other lunch items are great home cookin'.

Marin's Restaurant & Bar. Located a block west of the Tropical Paradise. ☎ **22/2110.** Main courses B$6–B$18 ($3–$9). MC, V. Daily 8am–2pm and 5:30–10pm. BELIZEAN/INTERNATIONAL.

There's plenty of local atmosphere here, with soca music or reggae playing all day long. Marin's serves fresh seafood in its outdoor garden or in its mosquito-proof dining room. In lobster or shrimp season, try the shrimp or lobster with pineapple (Belizean style, sweet-and-sour) for B$16–B$18 ($8–$9) or jerk or barbecued lobster. Vegetarians can order a pile of vegetables with rice. If you're starving, go for the Marin's special, a platter of fried shrimp, conch, and fish.

Rainbow Restaurant. On Front Street. ☎ **22/2123.** Main courses B$2.50–B$18 ($1.25–$9). Tues–Sun 8am–3pm and 6–10pm. MC, V. MEXICAN/SEAFOOD.

Part of the Rainbow Hotel, this restaurant was built out over the water. Diners sit either on an open deck or inside in a screened-in dining room. Either place, you'll hear the peaceful sound of water lapping against the pilings. You can get an assortment of filling burritos for under B$5 ($2.50), or one of three varieties of fajitas:

chicken B$10 ($5), conch B$13 ($6.50), or lobster B$18 ($9). A full plate of rice and beans with steak runs B$16 ($8).

✪ **Sand Box Restaurant.** On Front Street. ☎ **22/2200.** Lunch B$4–B$9 ($2–$4.50); main courses B$9–B$24 ($4.50–$12). V. Thurs–Tues noon–10pm. SEAFOOD/INTERNATIONAL.

By the time you read this, the Sand Box should be well settled into its new digs on Front Street, several blocks south of the former site. If the restaurant's past reputation is any guide, the quality of the food should be consistently good. The menu is rather eclectic, and is posted on a bulletin board the waitstaff brings to your table. For appetizers, there are crunchy conch fritters and nachos. Shrimp shows up in curried shrimp, jambalaya, and shrimp salad; other dishes include jerk chicken, snapper almondine, a delicious vegetarian lasagna, and seafood chowder rich with fish, shrimp, and potatoes. The awesome chocolate cake topped with coconut ice cream is worth a nightly pilgrimage. Aside from the move, there was talk of adding breakfast to the restaurant's repertoire.

Tropical Paradise Hotel Restaurant. South of front bridge, by the cemetery. ☎ **22/2124.** Breakfast B$4–B$8 ($2–$4); main courses B$6–B$24 ($3–$12). MC, V. Mon–Sat 8am–2pm and 6–9pm; Sun 8am–2pm. BELIZEAN.

The Tropical Paradise stays packed all day long because it serves consistent food at good prices. Inside, it has the feel of a small-town diner. Try one of the dinner specials, such as curried lobster or fried chicken. In front of the restaurant, there's a coffee shop/bar that's open for most of the day.

CAYE CAULKER AFTER DARK

For evening entertainment, you can stargaze, go for a night dive, or have a drink in one of the island's handful of bars. Periodically, one of the bars will crank up the music, and voila...a disco. **I&I Bar and Cafe** (just west of Tropical Paradise) has a nice third-floor open-air bar, with wooden plank swings for seats; **Mike's Movie House** (in a green house on the ocean near the Health Center) shows popular videos on a large-screen TV at 8pm most nights. Admission is B$4 ($2). That's about it for nightlife on Caye Caulker.

4 The Southern Cayes & Atolls

If t-shirt stands and golf carts aren't exactly your cup of tea, take heart: It's possible to get a taste of untouched Belize along the barrier reef south of Belize City. On Tobacco Caye, South Water Caye, and the assorted small islands of Glover's Reef atoll, there's far less development and far more tranquillity. To reach most of these places, you'll need to head south to the coastal towns of Dangriga or Placencia, so information on getting there, as well as recommended lodgings and restaurants, is in chapter 18, "Southern Belize." If you make it to one of these isolated little islands, you'll feel like a cross between Robinson Crusoe and Robin Leach: Accommodations are most often basic, but the settings are priceless. Divers will delight in the hundreds of miles of crystal-clear waters, steep walls, and intricate coral canyons (not to mention the far fewer divers than in the more popular northern cayes of Ambergris and Caulker), and have the opportunity to dive virgin sites. Adventurous travelers who appreciate value will enjoy the peaceful, yet affordable, beach vacation that awaits them here.

17

Western Belize & the Cayo District

The western region of Belize, from the capital city of Belmopan to the Guatemalan border, is a land of rolling hills, dense jungles, abundant waterfalls, clear rivers, extensive caves, and numerous Mayan ruins. This area was the heart of the Belizean Mayan world, and today is where the major ruins of Caracol, Xunantunich, and El Pilar, as well as the less extensive settlements of Cahal Pech, Pacbitun, Tipu, and Baking Pot can be found. At the height of the classic Mayan period, there were more residents here than in all of modern Belize. Today, the area directly around Belmopan, extending through the Cayo district, is the heart of Belize's ecotourism industry. New eco-lodges are built at a steady rate, and several are within the range of the frugal traveler. The area's jungles are great for hiking and birdwatching, the rivers for canoeing and inner-tubing, and the dirt roads for horseback riding and mountain biking.

1 Belmopan

52 miles W of Belize City; 20 miles E of San Ignacio; 90 miles N of Placencia

After yet another hurricane—Hattie, this time—devastated Belize City in 1961, government officials figured enough was enough and decided to move the country's capital safely inland. Conceived as the dynamic center of a growing Belize, the now middle-aged Belmopan (pop. 4,000) is actually a sleepy place 2 miles in from the Western Highway.

While in many respects a model city, designed and built from scratch in the jungle at the geographical center of the country, it has yet to attract Belizeans in any great numbers. The initial growth it had has stagnated, and the modest government buildings and small residential areas, enclosed by a ring road, are almost all there is to the city. Local industry seems limited to a gas station, a few food shops, and a handful of modest hostelries. For travelers passing through on the bus (very few tourists choose to come here), useful facilities include a bank, post office, and hospital.

Nevertheless, with its close proximity to Guanacaste and Blue Hole national parks, Belmopan is a convenient place to spend the night—before or after a day spent exploring the natural wonders of these two great outdoor spaces.

ESSENTIALS
GETTING THERE & DEPARTING

By Bus   **Batty Bros., Novelos, Z-Line,** and **Venus** all run buses to Belmopan frequently throughout the day. From Belize City, Batty Bros. (☎ **501-2/72025**) begins its daily service at 5am, running buses every half-hour until 10:15am. Novelos (☎ **501-2/77372**) begins its service to Belmopan at 11am and follows a similar schedule, with a final bus at 9pm. Z-Line (☎ **501-2/73937**) and Venus (☎ **501-2/73354**) buses to Dangriga, Placencia, and Punta Gorda leave throughout the day and stop at Belmopan en route. Trip duration is 1¹/₂ hours. Fare is B$3–B$4 ($1.50–$2).

When you're ready to depart, buses run frequently to San Ignacio, Belize City, and Dangriga. From Dangriga you can get a bus to Placencia if you arrive before 3pm on Monday, Wednesday, Friday, or Saturday. It's about 1¹/₂ hours to either Belize City or San Ignacio and 3 hours to Dangriga.

By Car   From Belize City, take Cemetery Road to the Western Highway. At mile 50 you'll see the well-marked turnoff for the Hummingbird Highway and Belmopan. Turn left here and follow the signs to Belmopan, about 2 miles beyond the turnoff.

City Layout   Belmopan is a planned city with a ring road and wide, deserted streets. There is only one road in or out. It branches off the Hummingbird (Southern) Highway 2 miles south of the Western Highway. When you first enter town, you'll see the combined bus stations and a small central market on your left. Just to the north are a couple of banks and a collection of government buildings.

FAST FACTS

Belmopan's **city code** is 8. The public **hospital** (☎ **8/22263**) is located on the North Ring Road. The **police** can be reached by calling **8/22221.**

EXPLORING GUANACASTE & BLUE HOLE NATIONAL PARKS

Guanacaste Park, a 50-acre protected area situated about 2 miles north of Belmopan (where the Hummingbird Highway intersects the Western Highway), is an excellent introduction to tropical forests. The park is named for a huge old guanacaste tree found within. Guanacaste trees were traditionally preferred for building dugout canoes, but this particular tree, which is about 100 years old, was spared the boatbuilders' ax because it has a crooked and divided trunk that makes it unsuitable for canoe building. More than 35 species of epiphytes (plants that grow on other plants), including orchids, bromeliads, ferns, mosses, lichens, and philodendrons, cover its trunk and branches.

There are nearly 2 miles of trails in the park, with several benches for sitting and observing wildlife. The park is bordered on the west by Roaring Creek and on the north by the Belize River. Among the animals you might see are more than 100 species of birds, large iguanas, armadillos, kinkajous, deer, agoutis (large rodents that are a favorite game meat in Belize), and jaguarundis (small jungle cats). Bring along a swimsuit, in case you want to take a refreshing dip in the Belize River.

A map and a brochure about the park are available from the Belize Audubon Society's offices in Belize City and from the small visitor's center in the park; open daily 8am to 4pm, admission is B$5 ($2.50). For more information, contact the **Belize Audubon Society,** 12 Fort St. (P.O. Box 1001), Belize City (☎ **501-2/35004**).

The Maya mountains are primarily limestone and consequently laced with caves—that's why this region of Belize is known as Cave Branch. About 12 miles from

Belmopan on the Hummingbird Highway, you'll find Blue Hole National Park. You'll know you're almost there when you see the parking area and trail entrance to St. Herman's Cave. From here, it's just a half-mile hike to one of the largest and most easily accessible caves in Belize. You'll need a good flashlight and sturdy shoes to explore this undeveloped half-mile-long cave.

Farther along the Hummingbird Highway, you'll come to the main entrance to **Blue Hole National Park.** The park gets its name from a crystal-clear pool that formed in a collapsed cavern. After locking your car and placing any valuables in the trunk, walk down the cement steps. Dense jungle surrounds a small natural pool of deep turquoise. A limestone cliff rises up from the edge of the pool on two sides. The water flows for only about 100 feet on the surface before disappearing into a cave and flowing underground to the Sibun River. This is a great place for a quick dip on a hot day because the water is refreshingly cool and clear. It can get crowded on weekends, but early in the morning during the week, you may have the place almost to yourself. You can clearly see fish swimming around the edges of the Blue Hole. A 1½-mile-long trail connects the Blue Hole pool with St. Herman's Cave. The park is open daily from 8am to 4pm; admission is B$8 ($4).

FOR THE ARCHEOLOGY BUFF

Since Belize doesn't yet have a museum, the many Mayan artifacts that have been found at sites around the country are stored in the basement of the government's **archeology department** (☎ 501-8/22106), which is housed in one of the central government buildings just off the National Assembly on the eastern edge of the quadrangle formed by the market/bus depot. The collection is open Monday, Wednesday, and Friday from 1:30 to 4pm. Admission is free, but you must make an appointment at least one day in advance of your visit.

WHERE TO STAY & EAT

Accommodations in Belmopan are limited, restaurants even more so. If you stay here, you'll most likely take your meals in your lodging's dining room. And since Belmopan is a governmental and diplomatic center, most places are not geared toward the frugal traveler.

IN BELMOPAN

El-Rey Inn. 23 Moho St., Belmopan. ☎ **501-8/23438.** Fax 501-8/22682. 12 rms (all with bath). B$40 ($20) single; B$50 ($25) double. No credit cards.

This small lodging is located in a residential neighborhood that's just a short walk, drive, or taxi ride from the bus station. The rooms are fairly basic, but the rates are quite reasonable for Belmopan. There's a restaurant serving reasonably priced meals, and tours and horseback riding can be arranged.

OUTSIDE BELMOPAN

✪ **Banana Bank Ranch.** Box 48, Belmopan. ☎ **501-81/2020** or 501-81/23180. Fax 501-81/2020. 4 rooms (2 with bath), 5 cabañas (all with bath). B$94 ($47) single without bath, B$140 ($70) single with bath; B$130 ($65) double without bath, B$195 ($97.50) double with bath; B$230 ($115) triple with bath. MC, V. All rates include breakfast.

The turnoff for this fascinating lodge is at Mile 47 on the Western Highway, just before you reach Belmopan. From the highway, it's about 1¼ miles to the ranch. Owners John and Carolyn Carr moved to Belize from the United States about 17 years ago. Carolyn is an artist and John is a cowboy from Montana. Together, they operate one of the oldest cattle ranches in Belize; for several years, they've been taking in satisfied paying guests. The guest quarters are on the banks of the Belize River. Each of the cabins is large enough for six people, and comes complete with a sleeping loft, private bathroom, two bedrooms with queen-size beds, and a private patio overlooking the river. Added benefits of a stay at the ranch include exploring a Mayan ruin on the property and meeting the Carrs' jaguar, Tika. Horseback riding, canoeing, excursions to nearby Maya ruins, and other day and overnight trips can be arranged at additional cost. Meals are served family-style in a small dining room.

CAMPING

Monkey Bay Wildlife Sanctuary. Mile 32 Western Highway, P.O. Box 187, Belmopan. ☎ **501-8/23180.** Fax 501-8/23235. B$10 ($5) per person per night.

About 1^1/$_2$ miles down a dirt road off the Western Highway, 4 miles west of the Belize Zoo, is a tranquil spot where you can park your RV or pitch a tent. There are no monkeys and no bay, but there are beautiful big trees, acres of pasture, a creek, the Sibun River nearby, and plenty of solitude. The privately owned sanctuary is only just being developed, so the facilities are primitive. Shared bathrooms and cold-water showers are available in the main lodge. There are several raised platforms, if you'd prefer to pitch your tent off the ground. Meals are available for around B$5 to B$10 ($2.50 to $5). Register with the caretaker, Pedro Reyes, who lives in the small house on the other side of the fence.

2 San Ignacio & the Cayo District

72 miles W of Belize City; 20 miles W of Belmopan; 9 miles E of the Guatemalan border

In the foothills of the mountains, close to the Guatemalan border, lie the twin towns of Santa Elena and San Ignacio (combined pop. 9,701) on either side of the beautiful, clear Macal River (good for a swim). Just north of town, the Macal and Mopan rivers converge to form the Belize River. San Ignacio is the business and administrative center for the Cayo district, a region of cattle ranches and dense forests, clear rivers and Mayan ruins. It is also the third largest metropolitan center in the country. But you won't find any urban blight here. If you've come from Guatemala, you'll sense immediately that you are now in a Caribbean country. If you've come from the coast, you might be surprised by how cool it can get up here in the mountains. Cayo and the cayes are worlds apart. While the cayes cater to those looking for fun in the sun, Cayo caters to those interested in nature and classic Mayan ruins. This area makes a good first stop in Belize; you can get in a lot of activity before heading to the beach to relax.

ESSENTIALS

GETTING THERE & DEPARTING

By Plane   There is no regularly scheduled air service to San Ignacio or the Cayo district, but flights can be chartered to the airstrip in front of Blancaneaux Lodge in Mountain Pine Ridge.

By Bus   **Novelos** and **Batty Bros.** buses leave frequently from their Collet Canal stations in Belize City (the Batty Bros. station is actually one block before the canal, down a side street to the right). Batty Bros. service begins at 5am and runs roughly every half-hour until 10:15am. Novelos takes over at 11am, with the same frequency. The final bus of the day leaves Belize City at 9pm (6pm on Sunday and holidays). Duration is 3 hours. Fare is B$5 ($2.50). There's also frequent daily service from Belmopan. Duration is 1^1/$_2$ hours. Fare is B$2 ($1).

When you're ready to depart, Novelos and Batty Bros. operate buses to Belmopan and Belize City daily between 4am and 4pm.

By Car   Take the Western Highway from Belize City.

ORIENTATION

San Ignacio sits on the western bank of the Macal River, just across from its sister city of Santa Elena. Once you've crossed the single-lane Hawksworth Bridge (an old metal bridge that separates the two cities), you'll hit a traffic circle. Downtown San Ignacio is to the right on Burns Avenue, and the San Ignacio Hotel is to the left up a hill on Buena Vista Road. Most of the city's lodgings and restaurants are on or within a block of Burns Avenue.

Visitor Information   If you can't find the information you need on the walls of **Eva's Restaurant** on Burns Avenue, ask Bob Jones behind the counter. He can help you arrange tours and accommodations, and will put you in touch with fellow travelers with similar interests and budgets.

Getting Around   As in the rest of Belize, there are few roads and almost everything is on or just off the Western Highway. Numerous buses ply the main road between Belmopan and San Ignacio, continuing on to the border town of Benque Viejo. If you want to drive yourself, particularly anywhere off the main highway, a four-wheel-drive vehicle is nearly essential.

Fast Facts   The **Belize Bank** is open Monday through Thursday from 8am to 1pm and Friday from 8am until 4:30pm. The **Atlantic Bank** is open Monday through Friday from 8am until 2pm and Saturday 8:30am to noon. San Ignacio's **city code** is 92. To reach the **police**, dial **2022.**

You can have your **laundry** done, or do it yourself, at August Laundromat, 10 West St. (☎ **92/3647**). This is run by Martha August, of Martha's Guest House and Kitchen. A combination **pharmacy and general store** is underneath the Venus Hotel at 29 Burns Ave. (☎ **92/2186**), open from 7am to 9pm. The **post office** is located on the traffic circle just above the police station. It's open Monday through Thursday 8:30am to noon and 1 to 4:30pm, Friday from 8:30am to noon and 1 to 4pm. The **BTL telephone office** is across from the Venus Hotel on Burns Avenue. It's open Monday through Friday 8am to noon and 1 to 4pm, Saturday 8am until noon. This is the place to go to make any long-distance or calling-card telephone calls to the U.S. Alternatively, you can usually make long-distance calls from Eva's Restaurant (☎ **92/2267**) and pay in cash. Bob may even let you receive a fax here.

EXPLORING THE MAYAN RUIN OF CAHAL PECH

High on a hill to the southwest of downtown San Ignacio is the Mayan ruin of **Cahal Pech.** This former royal residence was recently restored with the help of the United States Agency for International Development and San Diego State University. The restoration created a bit of controversy in San Ignacio because parts of the ruin were restored to the way they looked when the castle was first built, which is a bit more polished and modern-looking than most people like their ruins. However, the setting is beautiful, with tall old trees shading the site's main plaza and pyramid. The name Cahal Pech translates as "Place of the Family of Pech," and was given to the site in the 1950s—not to honor a great Mayan family, but because the area was infested with ticks at the time and the word pech means "tick" in Mayan. The ruin dates back to between A.D. 650 and 900, though there are indications that the site was used prior to this time as well.

A **museum** displays a collection of artifacts recovered from the site and provides insight into the Cahal Pech social structure. Admission to the museum and ruin is B$10 ($5), and the site is open 8am to 5pm daily. Be sure to ask for a copy of the very informative guide. To reach Cahal Pech, walk toward the San Ignacio Hotel. Continue around the curve for a few hundred yards until you pass the soccer field.

Turn left and climb the hill toward the ruin and the Cahal Pech disco. The entrance is just beyond the large thatched building that houses the disco. Be sure to walk beyond the soccer field and then turn left. The last time I visited there were signs pointing to an earlier turnoff, but most people get lost following this alternate route. It's about a 20-minute walk from town.

ENJOYING THE RIVERS OF SAN IGNACIO & THE CAYO DISTRICT

For much of Belize's history, rivers were the main highways. The Mayans used them for trading, and British loggers used them to transport mahogany and logwood. If you're interested, you can explore the Cayo district's two rivers by canoe. In fact, you can paddle as far as the coast if you're so inclined. Throughout most of the year, the waters in these rivers are easily navigable both up- and downstream. However, during the rainy season, things can change drastically—and fast. I've heard of a few flash floods, including one in which the water rose so high it nearly reached the deck of Hawksworth Bridge. Most of the time, you should find the waters calm, however— just fine for a leisurely paddle or swim.

Canoeing   Canoe rentals are available from **Tony's Adventure Tours** (☎ 501-92/ 2267) and **David's Adventure Tours** (inquire at Martha's Restaurant; ☎ 501-92/ 3647). David's also offers day-long guided canoe trips up the Macal River as far as Chaa Creek Cottages and the Panti Medicine Trail, which cost B$25 ($12.50) per person. Along the way, you're likely to see iguanas, snakes, toucans, and other wildlife. There are always plenty of stops to cool off in the water, and you can have lunch at Chaa Creek and then tour the Panti Medicine Trail (but both of these cost extra).

If the water's a bit high, or you're just plain lazy, you might prefer putting in upstream at either Chaa Creek or duPlooy's and then floating leisurely downstream. Both lodgings rent canoes, and the previously mentioned rental outfits can be persuaded to haul you and the canoes upriver for an additional fee.

Kayaking   If you prefer kayaking, **Toucanoe Kayak Rental** (☎ 501-92/2823) will put you on the water for a full day and provide a bag lunch for B$50 ($25) per person. During the rainy season (July through September), a day-long white-water kayaking excursion is available for B$115 ($57.50) per person.

Swimming   Both of Cayo's principal rivers are great for swimming. On the Macal River, you can join the locals in town where the river is treated as a free laundry, car wash, horse and dog wash, and swimming hole. However, you'll do better to head upstream at least a few hundred yards to a swimming hole complete with a rope swing and cliffs for high divers.

Another alternative is to head downriver about 1 1/2 miles to a spot called Branch Mouth, where the different-colored waters of the Macal and Mopan rivers converge. Branch Mouth is a favorite picnic spot, with shady old trees clinging to the river banks. There's even a rope swing from one of the trees. The road is dusty, so you'll be especially happy to go for a swim here. Farther upstream, on both the Macal and Mopan rivers, are numerous swimming holes. One of my favorites is at Clarissa Falls Cottages (☎ 92/3916), where you can rent an inner tube for B$3 ($1.50).

OTHER ACTIVE SPORTS

Horseback Riding   If you enjoy horseback riding, **Easy Rider** (☎ 501-92/3310) offers guided jungle, valley, and ruin rides for around B$80 ($40) per person per day. Call them to arrange a free pickup in San Ignacio. **Macal Adventures,** based out of the Belizean Handicraft Center on West Street (☎ 501-92/3907), offers similar trips at B$70 ($35) per day; B$40 ($20) half-day; and B$10 ($5) per hour, with a 2-hour minimum.

You might also try **Mountain Equestrian Trails,** Mile 8 Mountain Pine Ridge Road, Central Farm P.O., Cayo (☎ **501-92/3310**). This basic campsite and lodge is a pioneer in local ecotourism and conservation efforts. The owners helped create the private Slate Creek Preserve, a 3,000-acre tract of land bordering the Mountain Pine Ridge Preserve. Although not cheap, they provide excellent horseback tours of the area, including visits to caves and waterfalls. A half-day trip including lunch costs B$120 ($60) per person; a full-day trip costs B$160 ($80).

Also, keep in mind that most lodges in the area offer horseback riding, so ask around if you're bargain hunting.

Mountain Biking   If your preferred activity is mountain biking, you can rent bikes at **B&M Mountain Bike Hire** (☎ **501-92/2457**), 119 George Price Avenue, Santa Elena; **Chaa Creek Inland Expeditions** (☎ **501-92/2037**), or **Tropical Adventures** (☎ **501-92/2428**). Rentals should run around B$5 ($2.50) per hour, or between B$30 and B$50 ($15 to $25) per day. Be advised that the hills in this region are steep and the heat and humidity can be overwhelming. Take (and drink) lots of water, and try to avoid pedaling at the height of the day.

AN INTERESTING MUSEUM & SHOP

Throughout Belize, and especially in Cayo, you'll see slate carvings of Mayan hieroglyphs. If you're in the area, it's worth a visit to one of the sources, the Garcia sisters. This family of artisans runs an interesting museum-cum-craft shop located outside of San Antonio village, a small Mayan community located along the road leading from Santa Elena to Mountain Pine Ridge (the former home of Don Elijio Panti and his clinic). Called the **Tanah Mayan Art Museum** (☎ **501-92/3310**), it contains a nice collection of the Garcia sisters' carvings, as well as other Mayan artifacts, tools, and handcrafts, and is open daily from 8am to 5pm.

WHERE TO STAY

Inexpensive rooms are abundant in San Ignacio and several of the nearby nature lodges offer excellent accommodations for a reasonable price.

DOUBLES FOR LESS THAN B$30 ($15)

Hi-Et. 12 West St., San Ignacio, Cayo. ☎ **501-92/2828.** 5 rms (none with bath). B$10 ($5) single; B$15 ($7.50) double. No credit cards.

Beyond the obvious, but playful, name, this lodging has a funky, run-down charm. The water is cold and you have to share a bathroom, but the Hi-Et is family-run, clean, and secure. This is one of the best cheap hotels in San Ignacio. Unfortunately, it's almost always full, and making a reservation can be a challenge (you'd better speak good Spanish).

Princesa Hotel. 3 Burns Avenue, San Ignacio, Cayo. ☎ **501-92/2256.** 7 rms (all with bath). B$28 ($14) single or double. No credit cards.

This new budget hotel is located above a general store just across the Hawksworth Bridge on the San Ignacio side. The rooms are new, neat, and tidy. Those on the south side of the building face the police station and the traffic circle, while those across the hall are a little quieter. There's a small balcony on the back of the building, which overlooks the Macal River.

DOUBLES FOR LESS THAN B$50 ($25)

The New Belmoral Hotel. 17 Burns Ave., San Ignacio, Cayo. ☎ **501-92/2024.** 11 rms (all with bath). TV. B$25–B$75 ($12.50–$37.50) single; B$37.50–B$80 ($18.75–$40) double; B$53.50 ($26.75) triple. AE, MC, V.

Located right beside the bus station, the Belmoral is one of San Ignacio's better deals (and most outlandish hotels). The "new" in the name refers to a recent renovation that has spruced things up. Walls throughout the hotel are covered with one-inch square mirrors and have painted patterns of combed plaster. You have to see it to believe it. Three of the rooms have air-conditioning, which is reflected in the prices above, but you probably won't need it. The rooms vary considerably in size and comfort, but most are acceptable. There is morning coffee available, and a continental breakfast can also be arranged.

✪ **Martha's Guest House.** 10 West St., San Ignacio. ☎ **501-92/3647.** 3 rms (all with shared bath). B$26 ($13) single; B$30 ($15) double. MC, V.

Staying at this small guest house is a bit like living with a Belizean family. The rooms are in a modern apartment above the inn's restaurant. Guests can hang out in the high-ceilinged living room, which has couches and plaited mats for rugs, in their rooms, or on the large balcony. There's also a kitchen available for guests' use. The restaurant serves breakfast (B$5 to B$7/$2.50 to $3.50), lunch, and dinner (B$8 to B$20/$4 to $10). Tours and a laundry service are available. This is one of San Ignacio's newest and cleanest budget hostelries and as such is a very good deal.

Plaza Hotel. 4A Burns Ave., San Ignacio, Cayo District. ☎ **501-92/3332.** 12 rms (all with bath). TV. B$36–B$60 ($18–$30) single; B$45–B$83 ($22.50–$41.50) double. V.

The Plaza, located right on San Ignacio's main street about a block from the bus station, is a basic Belizean business hotel. Though it's fairly modern, there's no character. There are, however, TVs and ceiling fans in all rooms, as well as air conditioners in the more expensive rooms. Bathrooms are small and the housekeeping isn't always perfect, but in Belize, you don't ask too much of a budget hotel.

WORTH A SPLURGE

Rose's Guest House. 1178 Cahal Pech Hill, San Ignacio. ☎/fax **501-92/2282.** 5 rms (all with shared bath). B$65 ($32.50) single; B$80 ($40) double. All rates include full breakfast; lower rates in off-season. No credit cards.

Located on a hill above San Ignacio and adjacent to the Cahal Pech ruin, Rose's is an attractive house with stucco walls and a red-tile roof. The guest rooms are large, modern, and comfortable and some have good views of San Ignacio in the valley below. There always seem to be cooling breezes and the lawn is a great place for reading and enjoying the views.

✪ **San Ignacio Hotel.** 18 Buena Vista Street (P.O. Box 33), San Ignacio, Cayo. ☎ **501-92/ 2034** or 501-92/2125. Fax 501-92/2134. 26 rms (all with bath). B$50–B$130 ($25–$65) single; B$60–B$150 ($30–$75) double; B$70–B$170 ($35–$85) triple. AE, MC, V.

The San Ignacio Hotel is located on the top of a steep hill just past the police station, at the west end of town. Because it's situated on Buena Vista Road, it has magnificent views of the jungle. The hotel is a welcome oasis in this country of generally substandard accommodations, but it's often full by sundown. Although it's a bit expensive, it's clean and comfortable.

There's a modest gift shop and a good restaurant and bar with great views from its terrace. A full breakfast costs B$9 ($4.50); dinner will run you between B$15 to B$30 ($7.50 to $15). Other amenities include a swimming pool and basketball court, convention and conference facilities, nearby jungle trails, a small iguana farm, and a riverside beach and swimming hole. A bird-watching walk leaves the lobby at 6:30am daily and costs B$5 ($2.50) per person.

CAMPING

There are a couple good camping options in and around San Ignacio. My favorite is **Clarissa Falls Cottages** (☎ **92/3916**), on the Mopan River below a gentle waterfall. A site costs B$7.50 ($3.75) per person per night. There are bathroom and shower facilities and a good local restaurant serves reasonably priced meals. **Cosmos Camping,** just off the road to Branch Mouth and Las Casitas, is a cheaper alternative. You can park your van or pitch your tent for B$10 ($5) per day. There's a cold-water shower and an outhouse, but not much else. However, the setting—in a field near the river—is rather peaceful.

WHERE TO EAT

Eva's Restaurant & Bar. 22 Burns Ave. ☎ **92/2267.** Main courses B$6–B$9 ($3–$4.50). MC, V. Daily 7am–midnight. BELIZEAN/INTERNATIONAL.

Above and beyond dishing up good economical meals, Eva's serves as San Ignacio's central meeting place and unofficial tourist bureau. Hotel and tour advertisements fill two whole walls here and brochures are abundant. Owner Bob Jones is a wealth of information about the area, in case what you're looking for is not listed. If you want to get a group of people together to rent a taxi or canoe, or to defray the costs of a tour, let Bob know—he'll try to put you in touch with other like-minded folks. Rice, beans, and chicken costs B$8 ($4); fish and fries costs B$14 ($7). There are daily specials (usually local dishes) such as escabeche or chilemole for B$9 ($4.50), that are always good choices.

Maxim's Chinese Restaurant. 23 Far West St. ☎ **92/2283.** Most items B$5.50–B$16 ($2.75–$8). No credit cards. Daily 11am–3pm and 5:30–10pm. CHINESE.

For good Chinese food in San Ignacio, try this casual place. Various plates of fried rice range from B$5 ($2.50) to B$10 ($5), and sweet-and-sour dishes cost B$8 ($4) to B$10 ($5). There's also a host of vegetarian dishes. Try the Belikin Stout if you like dark beer with a bite. The owner goes into Belize City once a week to secure fish and other ingredients (and will also change traveler's checks if you're in a bind). Take-out is available.

✪ **Running W Steak House & Restaurant.** 18 Buena Vista Street. ☎ **92/2034.** Main courses B$8–B$30 ($4–$15). AE, MC, V. Daily 7am–11pm. BELIZEAN.

Located in the San Ignacio Hotel, this restaurant is affiliated with Belize's largest beef-and-cattle operation, its namesake. Try the Mayan steak (B$15), marinated strips of tenderloin, grilled and served with fresh tortillas. If you want something more traditional, order the 16-ounce porterhouse (B$22), or try one of the several fish and chicken dishes. The dining room is large and comfortable, with plenty of varnished wood. A few wrought-iron tables line an outdoor patio, and make a great place to have lunch with a jungle view, or dinner under the stars.

✪ **Serendib Restaurant.** 27 Burns Ave. ☎ **92/2302.** Main courses B$5.50–B$20 ($2.75–$10). V. Mon–Sat 9:30am–3pm and 6:30–11pm. BELIZEAN/SRI LANKAN/CHINESE.

This pleasant little restaurant is an unexpected surprise in the tiny town of San Ignacio. Owner Hantley Pieris is from Sri Lanka and came to Belize years ago with the British army. He now runs a restaurant serving excellent curries in the style of his native country. You can get beef or chicken curry with yellow or fried rice and potato salad for B$9.50 ($4.75). In addition, there are sandwiches, burgers, chow mein, and fried fish that range in price from B$3 to B$15 ($1.50 to $7.50). Mr. Pieris also operates a coffee shop, serving ice cream and pastry, to the left of the restaurant.

Shal's Diner. Mile 67¹/₂ Western Highway, Santa Elena. ☎ **92/23856.** Most items B$5–B$12 ($2.50–$6). No credit cards. Daily 6am–10pm. BELIZEAN.

For some good Belizean cooking, take a 10-minute walk from the metal bridge through Santa Elena to Shal's Diner. There are tables both inside and on the porch. A breakfast of corn tortillas, refried beans, and eggs costs B$6 ($3); rice and beans with chicken, salad, and fried plantain is B$6.50 ($3.25); and a large glass of fresh-squeezed orange or grapefruit juice is B$1.50 (75¢). The diner (as well as its bathrooms) is spotlessly clean. You'll find Shal's on the south side of the highway, just before the Hawksworth Bridge.

NEARBY PLACES TO STAY & EAT

While San Ignacio is the regional hub and does make a good base for side trips, the real attractions in the Cayo district are up the rivers and in the forests. Within a few miles of San Ignacio are several jungle lodges where you can canoe clear rivers past 4-foot iguanas sunning themselves on the rocks, ride horses to Mayan ruins, hike jungle trails, and spot dozens of beautiful birds and, occasionally, other wild animals. I highly recommend that you stay at one of the jungle lodges listed below while you're in the area. A few of the lodges can be reached by public bus from San Ignacio though you may have to walk up to 20 minutes after getting off the bus. Consider taking a taxi, or arranging a pick-up in town with your lodge. All lodges will arrange trips to various sites in the area, including Mountain Pine Ridge, Xunantunich, and Tikal across the border in Guatemala.

DOUBLES FOR LESS THAN B$50 ($25)

Clarissa Falls Cottages. P.O. Box 44, San Ignacio, Cayo. ☎ **501-92/3916.** 7 cabins (4 with bath). B$25 ($12.50) single with shared bath, B$40 ($20) single with private bath; B$40 ($20) double with shared bath, B$60 ($30) double with private bath; B$7.50 ($3.75) per person to camp. MC, V.

Clarissa Falls, hilly pastures, and the jade green waters of the Mopan River are the backdrop for this, my favorite budget lodging in Cayo. Situated on an 800-acre work-ing cattle ranch, these cottages are quite basic, with cement floors, bamboo walls, simple beds, and little else. However, the beautiful surroundings more than compen-sate for the Spartan decor.

An open-air restaurant serving excellent Belizean/Creole-style meals for B$10 ($5) to B$15 ($7.50) sits atop a small Mayan ruin. Boats and inner tubes can be rented and horseback riding is available. If you'd like to visit for the day, you can swim in the river and picnic for B$2 ($1), a very popular activity on weekends (if you crave peace and tranquillity, visit on a weekday). Clarissa Falls Cottages is about one mile down a dirt road, off the Western Highway about 4 miles west of San Ignacio. The bus to Benque Viejo will drop you at the turnoff.

Mida's Resort. Branch Mouth Road, San Ignacio. ☎ **501-92/3172,** 501-92/2101, or 501-92/2737. Fax 501-92/3172. 4 cabins (2 with bath). B$30 ($15) single without bath, B$40 ($20) single with bath; B$40 ($20) double without bath, B$45 ($22.50) double with bath; B$7 ($3.50) per person to camp. MC, V.

Though Mida's is just a short walk from downtown San Ignacio, it feels a world away. The round Mayan-style cottages are set in a sunny garden but have thatched roofs and screen walls so they stay cool, and there's lawn space for camping. The Macal River is only a stroll away down a grassy lane, and you can easily spend the day loung-ing on the little beach on the river bank. Breakfast here costs B$10 ($5); lunch and dinner will run you between B$10 and B$15 ($5 and $7.50) each. To reach Mida's, walk out of town across the fields behind San Ignacio's combination bus terminal and public park. A dirt road leads past Mida's toward Branch Mouth.

Parrot's Nest. Bullet Tree Falls, San Ignacio, Cayo. ☎ **501-92/3702.** 4 rms (all with shared bath). B$40 ($20) single or double. No credit cards.

Located 3 miles from San Ignacio and operated by Fred Prost, who once ran the popular Seaside Guest House in Belize City, the Parrot's Nest is a unique accommodation for backpackers. Set on a 5-acre tropical-plant farm on the banks of the river, the rustic lodge consists of four very basic treehouses. Though there is a bit of noise from traffic passing by on the adjacent road, this is otherwise a great place to spend a few days. Meals are available, but alcoholic beverages are not, so bring your own. Guided hikes and horseback rides are also available.

Doubles for Less than B$90 ($45)

Black Rock Jungle River Lodge. P.O. Box 48, San Ignacio, Cayo district. ☎ **501/92-2341** or 501/92-3296. Fax 501-92/3449. 6 cabanas (3 with bath). B$72 ($36) single without bath, B$110 ($55) single with bath; B$84 ($42) double without bath, B$130 ($65) double with bath. MC, V.

So, you *really* want to get away from it all? Well, this is the place. To reach Black Rock, you must travel 6 miles down a dirt road and then hike for a mile along the Macal River. What do you do at Black Rock? Why, nothing of course! Just enjoy the river, with its rapids, waterfalls, and cliffs. The only electricity out here is from photovoltaic cells, so at night it's just you and the stars and all those strange noises. Three meals a day will run you B$50 ($25) per day. This lodge is owned by the same folks who run Caesar's Place at Mile 62 on the Western Highway. You can just get yourself dropped off there, before continuing on to Black Rock, if you wish.

Cahal Pech Village. Cahal Pech Hill, San Ignacio, Cayo district. ☎ **501-92/3203** or 501-92/2186. Fax 501-92/2225. 18 rms (all with bath). B$70 ($35) single or double; B$80 ($40) triple; B$90 ($45) quad. AE, MC, V.

This new lodging has a spectacular view of San Ignacio and is just a stone's throw away from the Cahal Pech Mayan ruin. Accommodations are in the main building or in one of the thatched-roof individual bungalows. I'd opt for the latter. Both come with two double beds, tiled modern bathrooms, carved Mayan wall hangings, and colorful Guatamalan bedspreads, but the bungalows give a wonderful sense of privacy and luxury at very reasonable rate. There are plans to add a swimming pool soon, as well as four more rooms. The hotel is located just next to the Cahal Pech disco, and this can be a bit of a problem if you want to go to bed early on the weekend.

Worth a Splurge

✪ **Chaa Creek Cottages.** P.O. Box 53, San Ignacio, Cayo. ☎ **501-92/2037.** Fax 501-92/2501. 20 rms (all with bath). B$190 ($95) single; B$230 ($115) double. Meals are an additional B$80 ($40) per person per day. AE, MC, V.

Much loving care has gone into creating the beautiful grounds and cottages here; if you decide to spend the extra money, you'll be glad you did. Located on a high, steep bank of the Macal River, this is one of the oldest jungle lodges in the Cayo district and one of the better-run eco-resorts in the country. All of the thatched-roof cottages are artistically decorated with Guatemalan textiles and handcrafts and have private baths with hot water. Each also has a quiet porch or balcony area set amid the flowering gardens. There is no electricity in the cottages and the thatched roofs are open at the peaks, but your oil lanterns are lit each night at sunset and biting bugs never seem to be a problem.

The Panti Medicine Trail is just next door, as are a Blue Morpho butterfly breeding farm and a natural history center. There are canoes and mountain bikes available for an additional charge, and horseback rides can always be arranged. For those seeking a real jungle experience, several-day hiking trips through the jungle can also be arranged. A separate bar and dining area provide plenty of space for socializing, and Mick and Lucy Fleming, who originally began farming this land in 1977, are the engaging hosts.

To reach the cottages, drive 5 miles west from San Ignacio and watch for the sign on your left. It's another couple of miles down a rough dirt road from the main highway.

✪ **duPlooy's.** San Ignacio, Cayo district. ☎ **501-92/3101.** Fax 501-92/3301. 19 rms (12 with bath). B$80 ($40) double without bath, B$190–B$280 ($95–$140) double with bath. MC, V (with a 3.75% surcharge).

You'll certainly think that you're lost long before you reach this remote lodge, but keep following the rutted road. When you finally reach the top of a very steep hill and gaze down into the pastured valley below, you won't ever want to leave. The lodge overlooks the Macal River, with jungle-covered limestone cliffs opposite. Jungle covers the surrounding hills. Ken and Judy duPlooy, who moved here from South Carolina, are your hosts. Their lodge has everything from clean, inexpensive rooms with shared baths to luxurious new bungalows with functional kitchenettes. These accommodation choices, combined with a stunning location, make duPlooy's one of my favorite jungle lodges in Cayo. The nine rooms are in three stone-and-stucco buildings with tile roofs. Each has a screened porch and private bath. The open-air bar features a spacious deck overlooking the river. Breakfast should cost no more than B$10 ($5); lunch and dinner will run you between B$10 ($5) and B$25 ($12.50).

There's a beach on the river, as well as a riverside trail that's great for birdwatching. Horses, canoes, and fishing equipment are all available for rent. To get here, follow the directions for Chaa Creek Cottages. DuPlooy's is a bit farther down the same dirt road, but be sure to take the right fork and follow the signs.

Five Sisters Falls & Lodge. Mountain Pine Ridge (Office #29, Teodocio Ochoa St., San Ignacio), Cayo district. ☎ **501-92/2985.** 11 rms (6 with bath). B$80–B$100 ($40–$50) single with shared bath, B$160 ($80) single with private bath; B$100–B$120 ($50–$60) double with shared bath, B$190 ($95) double with private bath. AE, MC, V.

This lodging is located in the heart of the Mountain Pine Ridge Reserve about 200 feet above a rambling series of waterfalls and swimming holes. The cottages have palmetto-stick walls, thatched roofs and two double beds with mosquito netting. The rooms are new and clean, and located in the main building below the restaurant. Whether you choose a room or a cottage, ask for a balcony. The Toledo and Orange Walk cottages have wonderful views of the falls below. It's 290 steps, almost straight down, to the water, but worth the journey. Once you're there, you'll find a snack bar, a small riverside beach, and countless secluded swimming holes just a short walk up or down the river. The restaurant serves Belizean and international fare at reasonable rates.

Log Cab-Inns. Benque Viejo Road, Cayo district. ☎ **501-92/2289** or 501-92/3367; 800/783-4400 in the U.S. Fax 501-92/2289. 6 rms (all with bath). TV. B$84 ($42) single; B$110 ($55) double. V.

These new log-cabin bungalows are located about one mile outside San Ignacio on the road to Xunantunich. All are clean and spacious, with two double beds, a plywood table, plastic chairs, and a small black-and-white television. The cabins are separated by neat cement paths through the former cattle land that is currently being planted with a wealth of fruit trees and tropical flowers. There's a small screened-in dining room, bar, lounge, and gift shop. The local family who runs these cabins is very friendly and will help arrange a variety of tours. They may even give you a free ride into town.

Macal River Tent Camp. P.O. Box 53, San Ignacio, Cayo district. ☎ **501-92/2037.** Fax 501-92/2501. 10 tents. B$84 ($42) per person. Rate includes three meals daily. AE, MC, V.

Run by Mick and Lucy Fleming of Chaa Creek Cottages, this deluxe campsite is a great choice for those who want to be close to nature, but like to have a few frills and easy accessibility. There are ten spacious platform tents nestled among the forest trees. Each comes with two single cots and air mattresses. There's a small sitting area, with an oil lamp and a couple of chairs. Meals are served in a central open-air thatched-roof hut, which also has some hammocks for hanging out. The communal bath and shower areas are clean and well maintained. The river is down a short path from the campsite, and Ix Chel Farm and Chaa Creek are nearby. Guests at the tent camp can rent canoes or sign up for any tours offered at Chaa Creek. Overall, this is a pretty plush camping experience, but you may be asked to help wash your own dishes.

Nabitunich Stone Cottages. San Lorenzo Farm, Cayo district. ☎ **501-93/2096.** Fax 501-93/3096. 7 rms (all with bath). B$100 ($50) double. V.

Set amid flowering gardens on a working cattle farm, these bungalows have a commanding view of the nearby Xunantunich Mayan ruin. All around you will see signs of the ongoing archeological excavation of this area. The accommodations are clean and modern, but some of the doubles can feel a bit claustrophobic, with low ceilings. My favorite is the redwood cabin, which has a spacious private porch and a fantastic view of the ruins. Plentiful meals will cost you B$70 ($35) per day. The lodge will pick up guests in San Ignacio by prior arrangement.

Rancho Los Amigos. San José Succotz Village. ☎ **501-93/2483.** 4 cabins (none with bath). B$50 ($25) single; B$100 ($50) double; B$150 ($75) triple; B$30 ($15) per person to camp. All rates include breakfast and dinner. No credit cards.

If you don't mind using an outhouse and bathing in a spring-fed pool, Rancho Los Amigos may just be your idea of paradise. This rustic retreat is an economical place to experience all the best of the Cayo district. The Xunantunich ruin and the Mopan River are only a mile or so away, and if you have more energy, you can walk to Black Rock on the Macal River. The cabins are rustic but comfortable, and your hosts, the Jenkins family (refugees from Southern California), will make you feel right at home. Excellent meals (including vegetarian dishes) are cooked in an open-air kitchen atop a Mayan ruin. The lack of electricity here just adds to the rustic appeal. If you happen to have any aches or pains, you might even get Ed Jenkins to perform a bit of acupuncture on you. Keep in mind that prices include two full meals per day.

SAN IGNACIO AFTER DARK

San Ignacio is a pretty sleepy town. Most travelers chose to spend quiet evenings at **Eva's** (☎ **92/2267**), trading tales and planning adventures with new friends. There are several bars around the downtown area, however. By far the liveliest during the week is the **Western Bar & Grill** (☎ **92/2553**), by the banks of the Macal River near the New Balmoral Hotel. On the weekend, everyone moves uphill to the **Cahal Pech Disco** (☎ **92/3380**), which rocks the town and perhaps even a few Mayan spirits, to a loud mix of reggae, soca, and Punta rock.

3 Side Trips to the Mayan World

XUNANTUNICH

Although you may not be able to pronounce it (say "Shoo-nahn-too-nitch"), you can visit it. Xunantunich is a Mayan ruin 6¹/₂ miles past San Ignacio on the road to Benque Viejo. The name translates as "maiden of the rocks."

The main pyramid here, **El Castillo,** rises to 127 feet and is clearly visible from the Western Highway as you approach. The view from the top is amazing—don't miss it. You'll be able to make out the twin border towns of Benque Viejo, Belize and Melchor de Menchos, Guatemala. On the east side of the pyramid, near the top, is a remarkably well-preserved stucco frieze.

Down below in the temple forecourt, archeologists found three magnificent stelae portraying rulers of the region. These have been moved to the protection of a small, onsite museum, yet the years and ravages of weather have made the carvings difficult to decipher. Xunantunich was a thriving Mayan city about the same time as Altun Ha, during the classic period, from about A.D. 600 to 900.

Open daily from 8am to 5pm, admission to the site is B$10 ($5). To get there, take a bus bound for Benque Viejo and get off in San José Succotz. To reach the ruin, you must cross the Mopan river aboard a tiny hand-cranked car-ferry in the village of San José Succotz. You may be able to watch colorfully dressed women washing clothes in the river as you are cranked across by the ferryman. After crossing the river, it is a short, but dusty and vigorous, uphill walk to the ruins. If you've got your own vehicle, you can take it across on the ferry and drive right to the ruins. You can also take a taxi to the border, but it's very expensive—unless you share one for about B$4 ($2) per person. Ask the driver to drop you off at the ferry.

IX CHEL FARM & THE PANTI MAYAN MEDICINE TRAIL

Ix Chel is the Mayan goddess of healing. Located adjacent to Chaa Creek Cottages, **Ix Chel Farm** (fax **501-92/3870**) is a tropical-plant research center operated by Drs. Rosita Arvigo and Greg Shropshire. Rosita studied traditional herbal medicine with Don Eligio Panti, a local Mayan medicine man. Panti is a bit of a folk hero in Belize. He died in February 1996 at the estimated age of 104. Here on the farm, they have built a trail through the forest to share with visitors the fascinating medicinal values of many of the tropical forest's plants. At the end, there is a full-scale replica of Don Panti's thatch and bamboo hut-cum-clinic. You can tour the trail with a guide for B$15 ($7.50) per person or use Rosita's very informative guidebook to the trail for B$10 ($5). Contact your lodge owner or Bob at Eva's Restaurant for information on scheduling a visit.

There's a small **gift shop** at the farm that features local crafts, t-shirts, and several relevant books, including Arvigo's *Sastun: My Apprenticeship with a Mayan Healer.* You'll also find Ix Chel's line of herbal concentrates, salves, and teas called Rainforest Remedies. Arvigo has organized the Belize Association of Traditional Healers, which in turn has helped to create Terra Nova, an old-growth forest reserve to be managed for the preservation and study of medicinal plants. If you are interested in supporting this project, or would like information on some of the traditional healing seminars hosted here, you can speak with someone at the farm or write to the **Belize Association of Traditional Healers,** c/o Dr. Rosita Arvigo, Ix Chel Farm, San Ignacio, Cayo, Belize, C.A.

MOUNTAIN PINE RIDGE & CARACOL

Few people think of pine trees as being a tropical species, but you'll see plenty of them in Belize, especially in these rugged mountains. This 3,400-foot-high ridge is a natural wonderland of spectacular waterfalls, wild orchids, parrots, keel-billed toucans, and other exotic flora and fauna. Mountain Pine Ridge, Hidden Valley Falls (also called Thousand Foot Falls), Five Sisters Falls, and the Río On and Río Frío Caves are all located where the Western Highway intersects with the town of Georgeville. Alternatively, you can reach Mountain Pine Ridge by taking the well-marked turnoff toward Cristo Rey in Santa Elena, about a mile before the Hawksworth Bridge.

Continuing on through the Mountain Pine Ridge, you'll eventually come to Caracol, which is the largest of the Belizean Mayan ruins. It's not really set up as a tourist site yet, and excavations have only barely begun. But if you have the interest, stamina, and vehicle to make it, you can visit. At nearly 140 feet, the main pyramid at Caracol remains the tallest man-made structure in Belize. Caracol was a major classic Mayan center, rivaling and frequently battling nearby Tikal.

These roads are nearly impassable in the wet season and are pretty bad even in the dry season, so don't even think about attempting the trip in anything less than a four-wheel-drive vehicle.

The easiest way to visit either Mountain Pine Ridge or Caracol is on a guided tour out of San Ignacio, or through one of the nearby lodges. These tours average from B$40 ($20) per person for a half-day tour of Mountain Pine Ridge and a visit to one of the waterfalls, to B$80 ($40) for a full-day guided trip, including lunch, to Caracol. Prices drop dramatically as the size of your group increases. Find out what your lodge or hotel has to offer, and then check with Bob down at Eva's.

CHECHEM HAH

Ten miles south of Benque Viejo, on a dirt road that is recommended only for four-wheel-drive vehicles, is the cave of Chechem Hah, which was only rediscovered a few years ago. When the cave was explored, a cache of Mayan artifacts, including large fully preserved pots, was discovered within. Archeologists estimate the relics could have been placed here over 2,000 years ago. The Mayas believed that caves were a direct avenue to the underworld gods; caves filled with offerings have been found throughout Mayan territory. Chechem Hah is privately owned and there is an admission charge of B$50 ($25) per group for a tour of the cave, where you can see many of the Mayan relics just as they were found. It is also possible to stay on a farm near the cave. In the vicinity is Vaca Fall, a beautiful and remote waterfall that's a popular day trip with horseback riders. As with most attractions and adventures in this area, it's best to check at Eva's for more information or to round up a group to cut costs.

Southern Belize

18

Southern Belize is the least-developed region of Belize; in many places, you'll feel as if the 20th century has yet to roll around. Its two major towns, Dangriga and Punta Gorda, and its one beach village, Placencia, draw visitors because of their close proximity to the more remote southern cayes and atolls. Chances are if you're heading out to South Water Caye or Glover's Reef atoll, you'll have to pass through either Dangriga or Placencia first. Yet the region has another feature to recommend it: It's one of the few places on earth where you can participate in a homestay in a traditional Mayan village, making new friends and experiencing life without the gadgets and speed of the modern Western world. Wildlife-watching devotees know it also as an excellent place to observe manatees, particularly in Gales Point, a small Creole village on the shores of the Southern Lagoon, as well as for being the home of the world's only jaguar preserve, Cockscomb Basin Wildlife Sanctuary, outside of Placencia.

The pleasures to be had here are simple ones; by conventional standards, there's a low quality of service, and luxury is nonexistent. But those who are willing to rough it are richly rewarded with a truly off-the-beaten-path vacation.

1 Exploring Southern Belize

Heading south from Belmopan along the Hummingbird Highway, you'll pass through some of Belize's most picturesque countryside. The road weaves through jungle mountains and crosses clear streams and small rivers—and though achingly beautiful, it's slow. Alternatively, you can take the Manatee Road, which branches off from the Western Highway just past the Belize Zoo; it's faster, but less scenic. A red-dirt affair, the Manatee Road passes through a lot of lowland swamps and mangroves bordering Belize's large southern lagoon. In many places you'll have to cross single-lane, rail-less wooden-plank bridges that give some drivers vertigo, even though they're not very high.

If you plan on exploring this region by car, you'd best reserve a four-wheel-drive vehicle. Buses are regular and dependable, but if you're heading all the way down to Punta Gorda, you might consider flying—it's a long way.

2 Dangriga

72 miles S of Belize City; 64 miles SE of Belmopan; 48 miles N of Placencia

Dangriga is the largest city in southern Belize and the seat of the country's Garifuna culture. The Garifunas, descended from free Africans and Carib Indians, are a proud and independent people who have managed to maintain their unique language and culture since the 16th century.

Dangriga, which means "standing waters" in the Garifuna language, was originally called Stann Creek, and you may still hear it referred to as such. It's the capital of the Stann Creek district, one of the main citrus-growing regions of Belize, and as such, is a bustling agricultural community. Despite its boomtown air, it lacks the seaminess that characterizes Belize City. It's generally safe to walk around Dangriga, even at night, although caution should be exercised when wandering far from the center of town. The town fronts the Caribbean and has several waterfront parks, which are surrounded by attractive residential neighborhoods.

Dangriga is also the main transportation hub to the southern cayes—Tobacco Caye, Glover's Reef atoll, and South Water Caye.

ESSENTIALS
GETTING THERE & DEPARTING

By Plane   Maya Airways (☎ 501-2/44234 or 501-2/44032) has three flights daily from Belize City to Dangriga and one extra flight Monday through Saturday. Duration is 20 minutes. Fare is B$52 ($26) each way from the municipal airport, B$77 ($38.50) each way from the international airport.

There are daily flights from Dangriga's airport at the north end of town to Belize City, Big Creek (Placencia), and Punta Gorda.

By Bus   Z-Line (☎ 501-2/73937) buses leave from the Belize City's Magazine Road bus station at 8, 9, and 10am and noon, 2, and 3pm. Duration is 4 hours. Fare is B$10 ($5).

Buses leave periodically throughout the day for Belize City, Belmopan, and Punta Gorda. There are also three daily buses to Placencia at 12:15, 2:05, and 4:15pm. You can purchase tickets from two places: the ticket office at the north end of St. Vincent Street near the new bridge that crosses the Gumaragu River (also called Stann Creek), and the bus station at the south end of St. Vincent Street. Each location provides current bus schedules.

By Car   From Belize City, head west on Cemetery Road, which becomes the Western Highway. Just past the Belize Zoo, at around Milepost 30, turn left (south) onto the New Belize, or Manatee Road. This road is shorter, faster, and smoother than the old Hummingbird Highway route through Belmopan. Follow this road, which rejoins the Hummingbird Highway about $8^{1}/_{2}$ miles from Dangriga. Just after you are back on the Hummingbird, there's a turnoff for Dangriga. Turn left and head into town. You'll enter Dangriga from the south end of town.

By Boat   Boats bound for Tobacco Caye depart Dangriga from Southern Foreshore (around the corner from the Z-Line ticket office of St. Vincent Street). The going round-trip rate is around B$250 to B$275 ($125 to $137.50) for up to eight people, so it's definitely advisable to round up a group before heading out. There is also a small boat that runs from Dangriga to Puerto Cortez, Honduras, every Saturday. The trip takes between 3 to 5 hours and costs B$80 ($40) each way. For more information, call **501-5/23227.**

ORIENTATION

Dangriga's main street, St. Vincent Street, runs south–north from the new bridge to Commerce Street.

Fast Facts   You'll find a branch of the **Scotia Bank** on Commerce Street just north of the new bridge, and the **Belize Bank** on St. Vincent Street one block south of the Z-Line ticket office. Both are open Monday through Thursday from 8am to 1pm; on Friday, the Scotia Bank extends its hours from 8am to 4:30pm, and the Belize Bank stays open from 8:30am to 4pm. The **BTL telephone office,** across from the police station about halfway up Commerce Street, is open Monday through Friday 8am to noon and 1 to 4pm; Saturday 8am to noon. If your hotel is unable to help you, this is the place to go to make any phone call—local, intra-country, or international.

Special Events   Each year on November 19, **Garifuna Settlement Day** is celebrated in Dangriga, with Garifunas coming from around Belize, and as far away as Honduras and Nicaragua. The celebration is a riot of street music and colorful parades. There's a grand carnival air to the festivities. Eating, drinking, and dancing go on well into the night. The Garifuna have their own traditional music, based on wooden drums and choral singing. The rhythms and songs have strong African roots, and have given birth to a hybrid pop music called Punta rock, which has become quite popular throughout Belize in recent years.

WHAT TO SEE & DO

The main activity in Dangriga is walking, slowly, up and down St. Vincent Street. If you tire of watching the endless procession of people and listening to the colorful mix of English, Creole, and Garifuna, head a block or two over toward the sea and take a seat in one of the town's oceanfront parks.

SHOPPING

As the cultural seat of the Garifuna people, Dangriga is a great place to pick up, or just admire, some local arts and crafts. If the beat really gets to you, you can buy a **handmade wooden drum** from Austin Rodriguez, 32 Tubroose St (☎ **5/22308**). Drums vary in size and cost between B$75 to B$200 ($37.50–$100).

If you'd like to have a look at some **Garifuna paintings,** visit the studio of Benjamin Nicholas, 25 Howard Street (☎ **5/22785**). Using a naive Caribbean style, Nicholas paints scenes of traditional Garifuna village life. You'll find the studio a couple of blocks south of the Gumaragu River and a block east of St. Vincent Street.

Finally, Mercy Sabal, 22 Magoon St. (no phone), has become quite famous for her **hand-crafted Garifuna dolls.** These small dolls are mostly female figures in traditional dress, and cost between B$30 to B$60 ($15–$30).

WHERE TO STAY

DOUBLES FOR LESS THAN B$40 ($20)

Pal's Guest House. 868A Magoon St., Dangriga. ☎ **501-5/22095.** 14 rms (11 with bath). B$15 ($7.50) single without bath, B$30–B$40 ($15–$20) single with bath; B$25–B$30 ($12.50–$15) double without bath, B$40–B$60 ($20–$30) double with bath. No credit cards.

This lodging is situated at the south end of town near the bus station (at the mouth of Havana Creek), and is clean and quiet. The rooms with shared bath are small and basic, but otherwise fine. If you have a bit more money to spend, you should opt for one of the beachfront rooms in the new building, which have air conditioning, hot water, cable TVs, and small balconies overlooking the sea. The owner, Austin Flores, is friendly, knowledgeable, and an active member of the local Garifuna community.

Rio Mar Hotel. 977 Southern Foreshore, Dangriga. ☎ **501-5/22201.** 7 rms (all with bath). B$25 ($12.50) single; B$35 ($17.50) double. No credit cards.

This small, basic hotel takes its name from its location, where the mouth of the Gumaragu River (*río*) flows into the sea (*mar*). The rooms are a bit run-down and starkly furnished, but the setting is pleasant. There's a restaurant and bar on the ground floor, which can sometimes get noisy at night.

DOUBLES FOR LESS THAN B$90 ($45)

Bonefish Hotel. 15 Mahogany St. (P.O. Box 21), Dangriga. ☎ **501-5/22165** or 800/798-1558 in the U.S. Fax 501-5/22296. 10 rms (all with bath). A/C TV. B$70–B$90 ($35–$45) single; B$90–B$120 ($45–$60) double. MC, V.

Located a block from the water and across the street from a park, the Bonefish provides one of the best all-around values in Dangriga. Though it is out of our price range, it is significantly more comfortable than the other lodgings listed here. The guest rooms are generally quite large and carpeted. If you'd prefer to leave the air conditioner off, there are jalousie windows to let in the breezes. All baths have full-size tubs, and there's a TV lounge in the lobby, as well as a small bar. Owned and operated by the same folks who maintain the Blue Marlin Lodge on South Water Caye, this is a convenient place to stay if you are headed out to Tobacco or South Water Caye.

WORTH A SPLURGE

✪ **Pelican Beach Resort.** P.O. Box 14, Dangriga. ☎ **501-5/22044.** Fax 501-5/22570. 20 rms (all with bath). B$90–B$128 ($45–$64) single; B$120–B$160 ($60–$80) double; B$140–B$186 ($70–$93) triple. AE, MC, V.

Located at the northern end of town near the airstrip, this is one of Belize's first lodges. Over the past 25 years, the folks here have built up a comfortable and spacious Caribbean resort. Room rates differ depending on location. The most frugal rooms are in a separate building set in from the ocean. The most expensive rooms have second-floor ocean views with wonderful balconies. Some of the furnishings show their age, not so much in wear and tear, but in their design—1970s vinyl chairs just seem anachronistic these days. There's no real beach here, but there are plenty of palm trees, lounge chairs, and hammocks spread around. There's a small gift shop featuring Garifuna crafts, Belizean books, and Tony Rath's popular wildlife photography. The restaurant serves up excellent Belizean and Garifuna meals at reasonable rates. A variety of fishing, diving, and inland tours are available.

WHERE TO EAT

Up and down St. Vincent and Commerce streets, you'll find numerous very basic (and usually very noisy) restaurants. In addition to the place recommended below, **The Burger King Restaurant** (not affiliated with the fast-food chain) is a local favorite serving simple Belizean meals heavy on the grease. There are also several Chinese restaurants.

MEALS FOR LESS THAN B$10 ($5)

River Cafe & Tourist Information Center. South Riverside Drive, Dangriga. ☎ **5/39908.** Most items B$3–B$10 ($1.50–$5). No credit cards. Daily 6am–10pm. BELIZEAN.

This simple cafe and bar is popular with local boatmen. It opens early and serves food throughout the day. You can get a full meal of fried chicken, beans, and rice for B$8 ($4) or a hearty and equally inexpensive breakfast. This is a good place to ask about rides out to one of the nearby cayes, or to pick up activity and tour brochures from the wall-mounted racks. Just east of St. Vincent Street on the south side of the Gumaragu river.

MEALS FOR LESS THAN B$20 ($10)

Pola's Kitchen. 25A Tubroose Street, Dangriga. ☎ **5/22675.** Main courses B$12–B$18 ($6–$9). No credit cards. Mon–Sat 8am–2pm and 6–9pm. BELIZEAN/GARIFUNA.

You'll be surprised to find this unassuming restaurant specializing in down-home local cooking housed in the lower floor of a two-story building, around the corner from Pal's Guesthouse. The room is new, tiled, and sprinkled with ceiling fans as well as an air conditioner. There's a small Garifuna display in one corner, and posters honoring Rosa Parks, Martin Luther King Jr., and Malcolm X on the walls. Pola lives upstairs and cooks a fresh batch of *hudut* (a Garifuna specialty of fresh fish cooked in coconut milk and served with mashed plantains) every day. It often goes quick, so come for lunch if you want to try some. There's always some stewed fish, chicken, and beef on the menu, as well as cow-feet soup. Breakfast is a treat, with freshly baked bread and johnnycakes.

3 Side Trips from Dangriga

GALES POINT

Gales Point is a small Creole fishing village about 25 miles north of Dangriga. It's a peaceful place for getting to know one of Belize's traditional cultures and its slower pace of life. However, what brings most people to Gales Point are the manatees that inhabit the water of the lagoon that surrounds the village. For B$60 ($30), you can hire a dory to take you out to where the manatees are usually seen. A dory will hold up to eight people, so the more people you can line up, the less it will cost each of you. You can also ask around in the village about renting a dugout canoe to paddle yourself out to where the manatees feed. Although previously encouraged, swimming with the manatees is no longer allowed. The contact is potentially dangerous for both species and it's best to just enjoy a pleasant sighting of these gentle water mammals.

Other possible trips from Gales Point include visits to the beach or the caves and nighttime turtle walks. All of these trips cost between B$60 to B$100 ($30–$50) for a boat.

Gales Point is one of several villages in Belize to have a community-based ecotourism homestay program. Rooms in local villagers' homes are very basic and usually do not have running water or flush toilets. The rates are B$10 ($5) for a single and B$15 ($7.50) for a double. Breakfast is B$5 ($2.50) and lunch and dinner cost B$8 ($4) each. You can also camp in Gales Point for B$5 ($2.50) per person. To arrange a homestay in Gales Point, call the **community phone** (☎ **501-5/22087**) and ask for Mr. Walter Goff or Ms. Hortense Welch. If you should arrive in the village without a reservation, go to the homestay coordinator's home and arrange your night's lodging.

GETTING THERE & DEPARTING

There is no regular bus service to Gales Point, so from Dangriga you will have to take a Belize City–bound bus using the Manatee Road and get off at the Gales Point Road. From here, you will have to hitchhike, or walk 1¹/₂ miles. From Belize City, you can take a boat from the Bolton Bridge pier. These boats travel down the inland waterway to the southern lagoon and usually leave Wednesday and Saturday at 10am, but it's always best to ask a boatman at the pier first. The trip takes between 3 and 4 hours and the fare is B$20 ($10). Boats usually return to Belize City Wednesday and Friday. Ask around in Gales Point for current schedules.

TOBACCO CAYE

Located 12 miles east of the town of Dangriga, Tobacco Caye sits right on the edge of the barrier reef and is surrounded by a shallow lagoon, so the snorkeling is always good. Legend has it that the early British settlers grew tobacco on the island, but it's hard to imagine. The island is only about 200 yards by 350 yards, so you'd better bring a few good books if you head out here. There's not much to do other than lie in the sun, snorkel the nearby reefs, or, if you're ambitious, organize a volleyball game. Despite the island's small size, it manages to support several modest lodges. In fact, the whole island is little more than a collection of small lodges. When I last visited, both of the island's dive shops had closed down due to compressor problems, and there was no indication they would open anytime soon. If you're a scuba diver, check first before heading out here.

GETTING THERE

To get out to Tobacco Caye, you'll have to pick up a boat in Dangriga, which costs around B$30 ($15) per person. In addition, you'll usually need to round up at least two or three people before a boatman will even consider making the trip. To find a boat, ask at a hotel in Dangriga, or head to the **River Cafe & Tourist Information Center** on the south side of the new bridge over the Gumaragu River. The ride out to Tobacco Caye takes about 30 to 40 minutes.

WHERE TO STAY

Island Camps. (P.O. Box 174, Belize City), Tobacco Caye. ☎/fax **501-5/23433.** 9 cabins (1 with bath). B$110 ($55) double with shared bath; B$130 ($65) double with private bath. All rates include three meals daily. No credit cards.

These small squat cottages occupy most of the north end of Tobacco Caye. The one cottage with a private bath is substantially larger, but the others are all suitable. There's a real "camp" feel to this place, and several times a year they host research and conservation groups. In addition to the small restaurant and bar, you'll find a central open-sided thatched hut with several hammocks, where many of the guests like to pass the hot hours of the day.

Ocean's Edge. (P.O. Box 265, Belize City), Tobacco Caye. ☎ **713/894-0548** in the U.S. 1 rm, 4 cabins (all with bath). B$70 ($35) per person. No credit cards.

Ocean's Edge offers some of the most interesting accommodations on the island. The four cabins are all about 7 feet off the ground and are attached to one another by an elevated walkway. There are fans to keep you cool and screens to keep out the insects. Things are a bit run down, but it's clean. Water for showers is provided by a rainwater cistern. Meals will run you an extra B$36 ($18) per person per day.

Reef's End Lodge. Tobacco Caye, P.O. Box 10, Dangriga. ☎ **501-5/22419.** 4 rms (all with bath); 2 cabins. B$80 ($40) single; B$130 ($65) double room; B$150 ($75) double cabin. All rates include three meals daily. No credit cards.

Operated by a former lobsterman, the Reef's End Lodge is a small place with a Caribbean feel that occupies the southeastern tip of Tobacco Caye. The rooms are in a wooden building with a long verandah across the front. Electricity is provided by photovoltaic cells. There are some newer separate cabins off the main building. All the beds come with mosquito nets. The lodge's dining room is built on a pier on the lagoon side of the island, and there's even a ladder leading down from the kitchen into the water. Given the location and the fact that all your meals are included, this is your best bet on the island.

SOUTH WATER CAYE

Located 14 miles southeast of Dangriga and just a few miles south of Tobacco Caye, South Water Caye is another tiny little island supporting a few lodges. The accommodations here are a bit more luxurious than those on Tobacco Caye, and there are more opportunities to scuba dive and fish. The snorkeling is also excellent. In addition, you can arrange to visit nearby Carrie Bow Caye, where the Smithsonian Institute maintains a biological research station. South Water Caye also has a delectable, albeit tiny, section of white-sand beach on its southern end.

GETTING THERE

In order to get here, you'll need to hire a boat out of Dangriga (see "Getting There," under "Tobacco Caye," above), although if you book a room at a lodge here, the lodge will arrange your transportation for you.

WHERE TO STAY

Pelican Beach at South Water Caye. P.O. Box 14, Dangriga. ☎ **501-5/22044.** Fax 501-5/22570. 10 rms, 3 cabins (all with private half-bath, and shared showers). B$120 ($60) per person per day in University building; B$208–B$272 ($104–$136) single; B$300–B$342 ($150–$171) double. All rates include three meals daily. AE, MC, V.

Run by the same folks who run the Pelican Beach Resort in Dangriga, this collection of older colonial-era buildings and new cabins provides an excellent resortlike vacation, with a variety of accommodation options. The five most inexpensive rooms here are in the Pelican University building. These all have bunk beds and are geared towards student groups. A little ways across this tiny island is a former Roman Catholic convent. The rooms here are all on the second floor and come with private oceanview balconies. On the first floor, you'll find this resort's restaurant and bar. Several separate cabins and cottages are set around the edges of the island nestled among mangroves and overlooking the sea. The older Frangipani and Osprey's Nest cottages each have three bedrooms, and there's a brand new individual cabin perfect for couples. Pelican Beach can arrange snorkel, scuba, and fishing expeditions and has the best (and only) beach on South Water Caye.

MAN-OF-WAR CAYE

Just a short boat ride away from Tobacco Caye and an easy day trip from South Water Caye or Dangriga is the small mangrove island known as Man-of-War Caye. This tiny mangrove outcropping is a major roosting site for magnificent frigate birds, which are also called Man-of-War birds. There's no real land to speak of here, so you must enjoy the bird watching from a boat. Throughout the day, the sky is marked by a large black whorl, as hundreds of these large sea birds circle the small caye. Meanwhile, an equal number of their kin roost quietly in the higher branches of the mangroves. As part of their mating ritual, the male frigates inflate a brilliant red throat sac that can reach the size of a basketball. Female frigates apparently find this very sexy. If you're staying at either Tobacco or Southwater Caye, ask if your lodge offers a bird-watching trip here. Depending on the size of your group, it should run you between B$30 and B$60 ($15 to $30) per person. If you want to do this trip out of Dangriga, you'll have to hire a boat, which should run you around B$60 and B$80 ($30 to $40) per person depending on the size of your group (see "Getting There," under "Tobacco Caye," above).

GLOVER'S REEF ATOLL

Located about 70 miles southeast of Belize City, Glover's Reef atoll is a trapezoidal ring of coral and small cayes surrounding a massive salt-water lagoon. The lagoon is home to coral heads and abundant marine life. The atoll is named after the pirate John Glover, who used these small islands as a temporary camp and base. The principal cayes here include Northeast Caye, Long Caye, and Middle Caye. On the ocean side of the atoll lie several shipwrecks. There's really only one place to stay here, and the listing for this lodging below provides information on getting to this atoll.

WHERE TO STAY

Glover's Atoll Resort. P.O. Box 563, Belize City. ☎ **501-5/23048.** 8 cabins (all with shared bath). One week package, including round-trip transportation: B$190 ($95) per person in cabin; B$140 ($70) camping. Meals about B$30 ($15) per person per day. MC, V (10% surcharge).

Located on Long Caye, off the central coast southeast of Dangriga, Glover's Atoll Resort is a very rustic sort of place that should appeal to hardy travelers accustomed to camping. Each of the cabins sleeps two and has its own kitchenette. You can either buy meals or bring your own food for the duration of your stay (a small store stocks only the basics), although you should be able to catch or buy fish while you are here. You'll also have to carry water from a well. The cabins have their own showers and outhouses.

Despite its rusticity, Glover's Atoll Resort offers a wide range of activities to guests. Canoes, kayaks, and sailboards can be rented, and there's a full-service dive shop. The reef is within swimming distance of the shore, the snorkeling is excellent, and the diving is said to be some of the best in Belize—you can swim to excellent wall dives from the shore.

Glover's Atoll Resort is reached by a private boat that leaves from Sittee River Village every Sunday at 8am; the boat ride takes about 4 hours. The best way to catch the boat is to spend the night in Sittee River Village at the Glover's Atoll Guest House, where a bed is only B$5 ($2.50). To get to Sittee River Village from Dangriga, take any bus heading for Punta Gorda or Placencia and be sure to tell the driver that you want to get off in Sittee River Village. The stop is in front of Kendal's G&G Cool Spot. From here a hitchhike or taxi (B$20/$10) will take you the rest of the way to Sittee River Village.

4 En Route to Placencia

Just 14 miles south of Dangriga, is **Hopkins,** a large Garifuna village. It's a picturesque place with lots of colorfully painted clapboard houses. There isn't much to do here but wander around the village talking with children, fishermen, and elderly folks hanging out in front of their homes. If you stick around long enough, you may be able to learn a bit about traditional Garifuna lifestyles. Fishing is still the main employment of many of the villagers, who head out to the barrier reef in large dugout canoes. From this large boat, smaller, one-man canoes are launched, and the fishermen spread out in search of the day's catch.

Hopkins is on a long, curving swath of beach, and because of its isolation, is rarely visited by tourists. Unfortunately, the beach right in the village is too polluted with garbage and human waste for swimming, but if you head north or south, you'll find cleaner sand and water. There are a couple of small restaurants around the village. My favorite is **Over the Waves,** which is built on a pier over the water.

Buses to Hopkins leave Dangriga Monday, Wednesday, Friday, and Saturday at 7am, returning the same days at noon. There is also a truck that carries passengers between Dangriga and Hopkins. Ask at the Z-Line bus station in Dangriga to find out about this alternative. If you are heading south, you can take the bus, truck, or hitchhike out to the Southern Highway and wait for a south-bound bus. If you choose the latter option, you will most likely end up walking the final 4¹/₂ miles into Hopkins.

Sittee River Village is a few miles south of Hopkins and is the staging site for trips out to Glover's Atoll Resort on Long Caye. This caye has only one accommodation on it, and consequently is one of the most remote budget accommodations in Belize. Sittee is tiny and generally only an overnight stop for folks heading out to Glover's Atoll Resort. For more information, see the listing for Glover's Atoll Resort, above.

WHERE TO STAY

Sandy Beach Lodge. Hopkins. ☎ **501-5/22033.** 10 rms (4 with bath). B$15 ($7.50) single without bath, B$20 ($10) single with bath; B$20–B$30 ($10–$15) double without bath, B$30 ($15) double with bath. No credit cards.

This small lodge is located right on the beach at the south end of Hopkins and is operated by a local women's cooperative. The cooperative was formed and the lodging opened to provide employment for local women, the only alternative to the back-breaking work on nearby orange plantations. The rooms are very basic, but the setting is great. There's a big, screened-in dining room serving inexpensive meals.

5 Placencia

150 miles S of Belize City (120 miles by New Belize Road); 100 miles SE of Belmopan; 55 miles NE of Punta Gorda

Located at the southern tip of a long, sandy peninsula that is separated from the mainland by a narrow lagoon, Placencia is a tiny Creole village of colorful clapboard houses on stilts. This is the only "real" beach in Belize—16 miles of white sand backed with palm trees and dense vegetation. There are an abundance of simple budget rooms to be had and camping is common here. Once you settle into the slow pace and relaxed atmosphere, it's hard to move on. Placencia is *the* definition of laid-back. The town's main thoroughfare is a sidewalk, which will give you some idea of how quiet this place is. If you're looking for lots to see and do, you're better off going to Ambergris Caye. Still, there are caveats. Placencia's beach is calm and protected, but it is also fairly dirty. The last time I visited, plastic bags, six-pack rings, cigarette butts, aluminum cans, and other assorted debris—both in the water and lining the beach—seriously spoiled the inherent natural beauty.

ESSENTIALS

GETTING THERE & DEPARTING

By Plane   Maya Airways (☎ **501-2/44234** or 501-2/44032) has daily flights from Belize City to Placencia at 8:30am and 1:30pm, as well as an additional 10:30am flight Monday through Saturday. Fare is B$97 ($48.50) each way from the municipal airport; B$115 ($57.50) from the international airport. **Tropic Air** (☎ **501-2/45671**) has three flights daily from the municipal airport, at 8:30am and 1:30 and 4:30pm. Fare is B$98 ($49) each way.

There are several daily flights from Placencia to Belize City and Punta Gorda.

By Bus   On Monday, Wednesday, Friday, and Saturday there is bus service between Dangriga and Placencia. Buses depart Dangriga around 2:30pm and from Placencia at 6am. Fare is B$8 ($4). Alternatively, there are several buses daily that operate between Dangriga and Mango Creek (Z-Line and Williams Bus) and between Belize City and Punta Gorda (Williams Bus Service from the Pound Yard Bridge and Z-Line from Magazine Road). In both cases you must get off in Mango Creek (also called Independence) and then take a water taxi across to Placencia, see "By Boat," below, for details. Bus fares: from Belize City B$15 ($7.50); from Dangriga B$6 ($3).

Four buses for Dangriga leave Placencia every morning between 5 and 6am. Two of these continue on to Belize City. Alternatively, you'll have to get off in Dangriga and catch one of the several city-bound buses there. Buses also leave from Mango Creek several times daily for Dangriga, Belize City, and Punta Gorda.

By Car Take the Western Highway from Belize City. Around Mile 30, watch for the Manatee Road turnoff for Democracia and points south. This good dirt road now has a bridge where it was once necessary to ford a river, which was possible only in the dry season. The road cuts 30 miles off the drive to Placencia but bypasses Belmopan, the Blue Hole, St. Herman's Cave, and Guanacaste Park. At the end of Manatee Road, turn left onto the Hummingbird Highway. In 1^1/$_2$ miles, you'll come to the turnoff for the Southern Highway (Dangriga is 6 miles farther). After 22^1/$_2$ miles on the Southern Highway, turn left onto the road to Riversdale and Placencia. From this turnoff it's another 20 miles to Placencia. Be sure to fill your tank in Dangriga.

By Boat Outboard-powered skiffs, which can carry up to six people, can be hired for the trip across Placencia Lagoon from Big Creek or Mango Creek for B$25 to B$40 ($12.50 to $20), one-way, for one or two people. For three or more persons, the fare is about B$10 ($5) per person.

ORIENTATION

There's only one road in Placencia, and it ends at the dock and gas station at the south end of town. The town's main thoroughfare is the Sidewalk, a narrow cement path that parallels the beach beginning near Mr. Clyde's Campground at the north end of town and ending at the Fishermen's Co-op by the dock.

Fast Facts The **post office** is located at Sonny's Resort near the south end of town; it's open Monday to Friday from 8am until noon and 1 to 5pm. The village's **public phone** is at the south end of town near the **gas station** and **Fishermen's Co-op.** There's no bank in Placencia, so finding a business that will take traveler's checks is about the only way to obtain Belize dollars.

FUN ON & OFF THE BEACH

There isn't much to do in Placencia, which is exactly why people come here. You just can't help slowing down and relaxing. Sit back, sip a seaweed punch, and forget your cares. Nobody ever seems to get up early (except maybe the fishermen), and most people spend their days camped in the sand reading books and eating seafood. The beach, although narrow, is arguably the best in Belize. You can walk for miles and hardly see a soul.

Biking It's generally flat, hot, and dusty riding, but a bike is a good means of getting around and exploring the nearby village of Seine Bight (see below). You can rent a bike for the whole day for B$15 ($7.50) from **Sonny's Resort** (☎ **501-6/23103**).

Diving If you're serious about diving, you'll want to get out to the barrier reef and its dozens of little offshore cayes. The diving here is as spectacular as at other more popular spots in Belize, and not as crowded. You may even be able to dive where no one else has before. The reef is between 10 and 25 miles from the shore, so just getting to it can be expensive. Most boats and dive shops offer a flat, per person fee, but it's always worthwhile to round up a group and try to bargain a little.

Sea Horse Guides (☎ **501-6/23166**), on its own pier on the south end of town, offers two-tank dives with lunch for B$100 ($50) per person. Equipment rental costs an extra B$40 ($20). A full-day snorkel trip will run you B$70 ($35), including lunch.

At **Placencia Dive Shop** (☎ **501-6/23313**), just off the boat pier at the south end of town, scuba divers pay B$130 ($65) each for two-tank dives; equipment rental costs an extra B$30 ($15). These trips include a lunch and snorkeling stop at Laughingbird Caye.

Local hotels specializing in diving include **Kitty's Place** (☎ **501-6/23227**), **Rum Point Divers** (☎ **501-6/23239**), **Sonny's Resort** (☎ **501-6/23103**), and **Turtle Inn** (☎ **501-6/23244**). Prices are pretty comparable, but if you're trying to save here and there, shop around.

Fishing   The fishing around here is superlative—among the best in Belize. A day's fishing expedition will cost between B$400 and B$450 ($200 to $225) for a boat holding up to four people. **Westby Sportfishing** (☎ **501-6/23234**) specializes in fly-fishing for bonefish, tarpon, and permit. If you prefer open-ocean trolling, this area is good for grouper, tuna, king mackerel, wahoo, and dolphin (mahi-mahi) catches.

Sea Kayaking   You can rent sea kayaks at **Kitty's Place** (☎ **501-6/23227**) and **Turtle Inn** (☎ **501-6/23244**). Both one- and two-person kayaks are available. Rates run from B$10 to B$15 ($5 to $7.50) per hour to B$50 to B$80 ($25 to $40) for a full day. The waters are calm, both on the ocean side and inside the mangrove lagoon.

Snorkeling   North of town a mile or two, there's good snorkeling right off the beach; the water's clear and you'll see plenty of fish and other forms of marine life along the seagrass and sand bottom. If you're feeling more adventurous, head for the reef. Ask at the dive shops and lodgings mentioned under "Diving," above, or check out: **Placencia Dive Shop** (☎ **501-6/23313**), which offers a snorkel trip to Laughingbird Caye along the reef, including equipment, lunch, and a guide, for B$90 ($45) per person; and **Sea Horse Guides** (☎ **501-6/23166**), which offers a full-day snorkeling trip that costs B$70 ($35) per person, including lunch. Other reputable snorkeling outfits include **Natural Mystic** (☎ **501-6/23278**) and **Ocean Motion** (☎ **501-6/23363**). Expect to pay about B$60 to B$80 ($30 to $40) per person for a day trip.

If you want to go it alone (or preferably with a group of friends), try to negotiate a reasonable flat, per-person fee with one of the boats or dive shops. The larger the group, the more you'll save.

GUIDED TOURS

Tours are available to the Cockscomb Basin Wildlife Sanctuary (see below), the Mayan ruins of Lubaatun and Nimli Punit (see "Punta Gorda," also below) and up the Monkey River. **Belize Eco Adventures** (☎ **501-6/23250**) or **Southern Guide** (☎ **501-6/23277**), as well as most of the lodgings and dive shops, can provide all these tours. These day trips generally cost between B$80 and B$100 ($40 to $50) per-person. More adventurous types can take an overnight boat trip up the Monkey River, where the wildlife watching is spectacular. Check around for pricing.

SHOPPING

Aside from the standard t-shirt and souvenir fare, shopping options are pretty thin in Placencia. However, it's definitely worth stopping in at **Sierra Design Studio** (☎ **6/23279**), in front of the octagonal Anglican Church on the west side of the Sidewalk. Delso Sierra, the resident artist, is a Belizean who creates excellent jewelry work in gold, silver, and coral. Prices range from B$70 to B$500 ($35 to $250).

EXPLORING COCKSCOMB BASIN WILDLIFE SANCTUARY

Weighing up to 200 pounds and measuring more than 6 feet from nose to tip of tail, jaguars are the kings of the New World jungle. Nocturnal predators, jaguars hunt peccaries (wild piglike animals), deer, and other small mammals. The Cockscomb Basin, a wildlife sanctuary established in 1986 as the world's first jaguar reserve, covers nearly 150 square miles of rugged forested mountains and has the greatest density of jaguars in the world. It is part of the even larger Cockscomb Basin Forest Reserve, which was created in 1984.

The forests within the preserve are home to other wild cats as well, including pumas, ocelots, and margays, all of which are very elusive, so don't get your hopes of seeing them too high. Few people do; however, a good guide may be able to find you some tracks. Other mammals that you might spot if you're lucky include otters, coatimundis, kinkajous, deer, peccaries, anteaters, and armadillos.

The largest land mammal native to Central America—the tapir—is also resident. Locally known as a "mountain cow," the tapir is the national animal of Belize. A tapir can weigh up to 600 pounds and is related to the horse, although its protruding upper lip is more like an elephant's trunk.

Much more easily spotted in the dense vegetation surrounding the preserve's trails are nearly 300 species of birds, including the scarlet macaw, the keel-billed toucan, the king vulture, and the great curassow.

Great caution should be exercised when visiting the preserve—in addition to jaguars, which can be dangerous, there are also poisonous snakes, including the deadly fer-de-lance. Always wear shoes, preferably boots, when hiking the trails here.

Ellis Burgess (☎ **501-6/23186**) is an excellent naturalist (formerly a bush guide for the British army) who offers guided trips to the Cockscomb Basin for about B$50 ($25) per person. Many mornings he can be found at BJ's Restaurant in Placencia (see "Where to Eat," below).

Admission to the reserve is B$10 ($5) per person. Visitor's facilities include an information center, picnic area, campground—B$3 ($1.50) per person, bring your own tent—and a few primitive cabins costing B$15 ($7.50) per person per night. Drinking water is available. For more information on the preserve, contact the **Belize Audubon Society,** P.O. Box 1001, 12 Fort St., Belize City (☎ **501-2/77369**).

WHERE TO STAY

In addition to the hotels and inns listed here, there's an idyllic **beachfront campground** at the north end of town, where the Sidewalk ends. Mr. Clyde (no phone) charges B$3 ($1.50) per person for the privilege of putting up a tent and using the showers and toilets. It's nice to set up shop in the soft sand, under the shade of the many coconut palms. But it's also a little nerve-racking sleeping under all those hefty nuts—be careful where you set up your tent.

DOUBLES FOR LESS THAN B$50 ($25)

Julia's Rooms. South of the Flamboyant, on the east side of the Sidewalk, Placencia. ☎ **501-6/23185.** 4 rms (all with shared bath). B$15 ($7.50) single; B$20 ($10) double. No credit cards.

There's nothing fancy about these basic, budget rooms in a wooden clapboard house. Still, they are clean and close to the beach. Julia Mayen runs a tight ship and is a pleasant host.

Paradise Vacation Hotel. Placencia. ☎ **501-6/23179.** 16 rms (8 with bath). B$25 ($12.50) single or double without bath; B$40–B$45 ($20–$22.50) single or double with bath. MC, V.

Although it hardly lives up to its glorious name, the Paradise Vacation Hotel is Placencia's best and most popular true budget hotel. You'll find everyone from backpackers to vacationing lodge-owners here. The rooms that have private baths are slightly more spacious than those without. The rooms on the second floor get more breezes and are close to the inviting sea-view verandah. The calm waters of the bay lap at your doorstep, and there's a pier that's great for sunning and swimming. You can rent fins and masks here for B$10 ($5) or a sailfish for B$10 ($5) per hour.

There's a new bar built out over the water on the end of the pier. **Tentacles** next door serves good seafood and is a popular place to hang out and meet interesting people. Meals range from B$6 to B$40 ($3 to $20).

Seaspray. Placencia. ☎ **501-6/23148.** 13 rms, 1 cabin (all with bath). B$25–B$40 ($12.50–$20) single; B$35–B$50 ($17.50–$25) double; B$70 ($35) cabin for up to four. MC, V.

The older rooms here are small and lack any semblance of style, but they're inexpensive and conveniently located in the middle of town. Fans help you stay cool at night. There are five newer rooms in a building closer to the water, as well as one separate cabin. These are generally in a little better shape, with cool tile floors and more space.

DOUBLES FOR LESS THAN B$90 ($45)

Sonny's Resort. Placencia. ☎/fax **501-6/23103.** 6 rms, 8 cabins (all with bath). B$66 ($33) single; B$88 ($44) double; B$117 ($58.50) single or double cabaña. MC, V.

One of the older lodgings in Placencia, Sonny's started out as a couple of mobile homes divided into three guest rooms each. Over the years, screened porches were added, giving the mobile homes a more permanent feel. Although they've seen better days, they're kept clean. Better and more comfortable, though, are the eight spacious wooden cabins on stilts that have been added since. Closer to the water, each has a large porch and is situated to make the most of the prevailing trade winds. They also have small refrigerators, coffee makers, reading lamps, and high ceilings with fans.

Sonny's Restaurant is a casual diner-style place with a small bar where fishermen swap stories in the evening. It's open 7am to 10pm daily. Prices range from B$6 to B$22 ($3 to $11).

WORTH A SPLURGE

✪ **Kitty's Place.** Placencia. ☎ **501-6/23277.** Fax 501-6/23226. 9 rms, 2 apts (2 with shared bath). B$66–B$186 ($33–$93) single; B$86–B$216 ($43–$108) double. AE, MC, V.

This spread-out collection of beach cabañas and colonial-styled clapboard buildings all adds up to a relaxed vacation spot north of Placencia proper. The whole thing has a resort feel, without the hype. Accommodations range from cement-floor garden rooms with shared baths to spacious beach cabañas with high ceilings, Guatemalan bedspreads, full-size bathtubs, mini-fridges, coffee makers, and private porches with hammocks. The apartments have full kitchens. There's a wealth of activities and tours available, including scuba diving and sea kayaking expeditions, bike rentals, and tours of nearby Mayan ruins, French Louis Caye, and the Cockscomb Basin Wildlife Sanctuary. The restaurant serves classy meals with daily Creole specialties. Breakfast or lunch will run you between B$6 and B$10 ($3 to $5), while dinner will cost you between B$15 and B$40 ($7.50 to $20).

Ranguana Lodge. Placencia. ☎/fax **501-6/23112.** 5 cabins (all with bath). B$120 ($60) per cabaña (triple). MC, V.

Although the five cabins here are packed together on a tiny piece of sand in the middle of town, they're still very attractive inside. The water is only a few steps away. Nearly everything in these cozy cabins is made of hardwood—the walls, floors, ceilings, even the louvered windows. Each has a little refrigerator and coffee maker, porch, tub, and table. If possible, get one of the three front cabins, and you'll have an unblocked view of the beach and bay.

The nearby **Kingfisher** serves as the unofficial restaurant for the Ranguana Lodge. It's a big screened-in room right on the water, where a meal will cost anywhere from B$8 to B$20 ($4 to $10).

✪ **Turtle Inn.** Placencia. ☎ **501-6/23244.** Fax 501-6/23245. 7 cabañas (all with bath). B$135 ($67.50) single; B$188 ($94) double; B$220 ($110) triple. All rates include full breakfast.

This is one of the early dive resorts in Placencia and it's breaking in nicely with age. The grounds are lush by Belizean standards, with lots of flowering plants, coconut palms, and bromeliad-covered hardwoods. The bamboo-and-thatch cabins are rustic, yet surprisingly comfortable. I prefer the older ones, which are closer to the beach. All have varnished interior walls, wood floors, and good-sized porches, with a hammock. The restaurant has a good reputation for its local Creole cuisine, and an extensive wine selection (for these parts). There's a full-service dive-shop here, as well as sea kayaks for rent and a variety of tour options.

A NEARBY PLACE TO STAY

Ranguana Reef Resort. Ranguana Caye. ☎ **501-6/23112.** 3 cabanas (all with shared bath). B$60 ($30) single; B$90 ($45) double; B$120 ($60) triple or quad. MC, V.

Ranguana Caye is located 22 miles offshore from Placencia, and everything you ever wished for on a remote island retreat is here: peace, quiet, good snorkeling, fishing, a sand beach, sunrise on one side of your cabaña, and sunset on the other. The charming wood cabañas are beautifully maintained. Showers and drinking water are supplied by rainwater, and electricity by wind and solar power. Bring your own groceries, as no meals are included. Camping is possible for B$14 ($7) per person. Unfortunately, a big expense here is a water taxi from Placencia, which will cost you about B$150 to B$160 ($75 to $80) one-way for up to four people.

WHERE TO EAT

Placencia offers a wealth of excellent budget-dining options. In addition to the restaurants listed below, be sure to stop in at **Daisy's Ice Cream Parlour** (near the Flamboyant) for some homemade ice cream, good sandwiches, and snacks. Also, follow the signs to **John the Bakerman's** shop for fresh breads and cinnamon rolls.

MEALS FOR LESS THAN B$10 ($5)

✪ **Cozy Corner.** On the beach, south of the Flamboyant, Placencia. No phone. Main courses B$4–B$12 ($2–$6). No credit cards. Daily 11am–3pm and 6pm–midnight. BELIZEAN/INTERNATIONAL.

A small beachfront thatched-roof structure houses this bar and basic restaurant. The tables are scattered in the sand under shady coconut palms. The burgers, steak sandwiches, and nachos are all excellent and none cost over B$8 ($4). In the evening, they do beach barbecues (B$10) and the nearby disco (same ownership) frequently has live music on the weekends.

Da Tatch. Next to the Seaspray, east of the Sidewalk, Placencia. No phone. Main courses B$3–B$18 ($1.50–$9). No credit cards. Daily 7am–11pm. BELIZEAN/INTERNATIONAL.

This unassuming screened, thatched, and rough-hewn board structure serves hearty, inexpensive meals all day long. Try the massive omelets (B$6) or fresh pancakes (B$4) for breakfast, or stop in for a fish burrito (B$6) for lunch or dinner. Simple wooden tables are set in a thin layer of sand over a concrete slab or you can eat at one of the outdoor tables. The walls are covered with graffiti and signed t-shirts left by past travelers. They play classic rock and reggae here.

Omar's Fast Food Stop. South of The Flamboyant, east of the Sidewalk, Placencia. No phone. Main courses B$4–B$25 ($2–$12.50). No credit cards. Daily 7am–10pm. BELIZEAN/ INTERNATIONAL.

Fast food it isn't, but the shrimp, chicken, vegetable, or fish burritos, chow mein of shrimp or conch, and garnaches—tiny crisp tortillas with beans, cheese, cabbage, and tomato—are tasty, and come relatively soon after you've ordered them, considering there's only one cook in the kitchen. Order at the window and eat on the screened-in porch or at one of tables set in the sand outside, just across the Sidewalk.

MEALS FOR LESS THAN B$20 ($10)

BJ's Restaurant. On main road at north end of town, Placencia. ☎ **6/23108.** Breakfast B$4– $10 ($2–$5), dinner B$8–$25 ($4–$12.50). No credit cards. Daily 7am–10pm. BELIZEAN.

As you sit on a bench on the thatched porch, sip some fresh-squeezed orange juice or try a seaweed shake—BJ's makes one of the best around. For breakfast, try the fry cakes. The service is on Belizean time, so don't be in a hurry. If you want to go on a trip to Cockscomb Wildlife Preserve, ask for Ellis Burgess, a naturalist tour guide who frequently hangs out here.

Brenda's. At the southern end of town, Placencia. No phone. Main courses B$12–B$35 ($6– $17.50). Daily 6am–10pm. No credit cards. BELIZEAN/SEAFOOD.

At the southern end of town, facing the small boat anchorage, Brenda serves up authentic Creole cooking in a funky, down-home setting. Crude wood tables, with bench seats and plastic tablecloths, are set in the small dining room and on the sand out front. Try the fresh conch platter (B$18) or some spicy shrimp (B$20). A full breakfast costs B$10. Brenda can be heartwarming or harried, depending on her mood—either way, expect some banter and conversation with your service.

The Flamboyant. (Formerly Jene's Restaurant), across from Seaspray Hotel. ☎ **6/23174.** Main courses B$8–B$30 ($4–$15). MC, V. Tues–Sun 7:30am–11pm. BELIZEAN/INTERNATIONAL.

This is a long-time local favorite in Placencia; it's a place for meeting friends and escaping the midday heat. The small dining room has hardwood paneling, floors, and ceiling, as well as a popular dart board. There's a large "Flamboyant" tree outside, next to the pleasant seating area, where you can enjoy conch fritters, barbecued chicken, and shrimp or veggie burgers, while you plan your upcoming jungle expedition. Refreshing fresh juices are available and there's usually live Garifuna drumming and dancing on Sundays.

The Galley. Across the soccer field from the main road, Placencia. ☎ **6/23133.** B$8–$20 ($4–$10). No credit cards. Daily 7:30am–10pm. BELIZEAN/SEAFOOD.

The owner of this restaurant is a retired musician and usually has good jazz and Calypso playing on the stereo. Menu offerings include burgers and sandwiches, a full range of local seafood, and an exotic shake called *craboo*, made with a slightly bitter berry that looks like a miniature apple. Though the four-table atmosphere is slightly austere, as in all the restaurants in Placencia, shoes are optional. Beware of the habanero sauce here. It's made with fresh homegrown habanero chiles and is hot enough to peel paint.

Kingfisher Restaurant. Behind Ranguana Lodge. ☎ **6/23323.** Main courses B$8–B$20 ($4– $10). MC, V. Daily 3–10pm. BELIZEAN/SEAFOOD.

Situated on the beach, the Kingfisher is a large, open room with screen walls that let in the sea breezes. Inside, the decor is typically rustic, with a sportfish nailed to the wall. Fish, shrimp, conch, and lobster make up the bulk of the short menu, with pork chops, fried chicken, and steaks also available. There are daily seafood specials for around B$15 to B$18 ($7.50 to $9), which make this a good place to find inexpensive seafood.

Tentacles. Next door to Paradise Vacation Hotel. ☎ **6/23156.** B$6–B$40 ($3–$20). MC, V. Tues–Sun 11am–11pm. BELIZEAN/SEAFOOD.

It's hard to beat the view from the second-floor deck of this restaurant at the very southern end of Placencia. There are more tables outside than there are inside, but no matter where you sit, you'll be among friendly locals, tourists, businesspeople, and boaters who've come in from their sailboats anchored just offshore. The conversation is usually lively. You'll find all the Belizean standards on the menu. If the food isn't memorable, the setting certainly is: The mangrove swamps begin a few steps away, several little islands dot the far horizon, and sailboats rock gently at anchor while skiffs race back and forth to the mainland. It's positively bewitching when the moon sparkles on the waves.

A NEARBY PLACE TO EAT

Kulcha Shack. Seine Bight Village. ☎ **6/22015** (community telephone). Main dishes B$8–B$30 ($4–$15). No credit cards. Daily 8am–10pm. GARIFUNA/CREOLE

The name is a play on words and conjures up images of Belizean culture shock, but what you'll find here is actually some of the best down-home cooking and traditional entertainment in Belize. Seine Bight is a Garifuna village and the menu here includes several local specialties such as *hudut*, fish stewed in coconut milk and herbs and served with mashed plantains; *tapow*, a similar stew made with vegetables and served with rice and cassava bread; and *bundegah*, which is similar to tapow but is made with patties made from grated bananas. The Kulcha Shack also does traditional Garifuna drumming and dance performances if enough people are interested, though the charge for this entertainment is a rather steep B$20 ($10) per person.

6 Punta Gorda

205 miles S of Belize City; 100 miles S of Dangriga

Punta Gorda, or simply "P.G.," is Belize's southernmost town. It's the end of the road, and feels a bit like the end of the world. P.G. is a quiet place with clean paved streets, few cars, lush vegetation, and a very slow pace. Although it is right on the Caribbean, there is no beach and the water is rather murky. However, the surrounding scenery is as verdant as you'll find anywhere in Belize (due to nearly 200 inches of rain a year). Just offshore you'll find some small undeveloped cayes that form the southern limit of the great Belizean barrier reef. The surrounding Toledo district is home to several Mayan ruins and numerous villages that are still peopled by Maya Indians, who have been migrating here from Guatemala over the last century.

Settled by Garifunas in 1823, Punta Gorda was only accessible by boat for many years, and even though the Southern Highway now connects the town with points north, the 100 miles of bad gravel road ensure that the town is still isolated. As the administrative center for the Toledo district, Punta Gorda has an active market and bus services to the many surrounding Mayan villages, although connections are not very good. Most travelers do little more than pass through Punta Gorda on their way to or from Guatemala by way of the Puerto Barrios ferry. However, there is plenty to keep the adventurous traveler busy for several days.

ESSENTIALS
GETTING THERE & DEPARTING

By Plane   Maya Airways (☎ **501-2/44234** or 501-2/44032) flies twice a day from Belize City to Punta Gorda at 8:30am and 1:30pm. Trip duration is 1 hour and 20 minutes. Fare is B$125 ($62.50) one-way. **Tropic Air** (☎ **501-2/45671** in Belize City; 501-7/22008 in Punta Gorda) flies to Punta Gorda three times daily, at 8:30am and 1:30 and 4:30pm. Duration is 1 hour. Fare is B$227 ($113.50) round-trip; B$126 ($63) one-way.

The Punta Gorda airport is on the west edge of town within walking distance of the town's hotels and guest houses, although if your pack or bags are heavy you might want to grab a cab for B$4 ($2).

Planes depart daily for Mango Creek, Dangriga, and Belize.

By Bus   Z-Line buses leave from the Magazine Road bus terminal in Belize City Monday to Saturday at 8 and 10am and 3pm; and Sunday at 10am and 3pm. Duration is 8 hours. Fare is B$22 ($11).

Buses for Mango Creek (Placencia), Dangriga, Belmopan, and Belize City leave daily at 5 and 9am and noon, with an extra bus on Tuesday and Friday at 11am.

By Car   It's a long and grueling road to Punta Gorda. The Southern Highway, which starts in Dangriga, is unpaved for 100 miles and, though fairly good in the dry season, can get very muddy in the wet season. Any time of year you'll have to take it slowly. Coming from Belize City, you can take the Manatee Road turnoff just past the Belize Zoo or continue on to Belmopan and turn south on the Hummingbird Highway. Neither road is very good. The Hummingbird Highway is more scenic, but adds several hours to your trip.

By Boat   There is a ferry between Puerto Barrios, Guatemala, and Punta Gorda, Belize, every Tuesday and Friday, leaving Puerto Barrios at 7am. Buy your ticket the day before departure at the green ferry ticket office. Duration is 2 to 3 hours. Fare is $5.50. You can also catch a ride with one of the many small launches that ply the routes between Puerto Barrios and Livingston, Guatemala and Punta Gorda. Expect to pay between $10 and $20 per person. When you arrive, be sure to get your passport stamped at the immigration office just up from the dock.

The ferry to Puerto Barrios, Guatemala, leaves Tuesday and Friday at noon. Be sure to buy your ticket the day before at the office next to the Maya de Indita store half a block north from the northwest corner of the central park. Trip duration is 2 to 3 hours. Fare is B$13 ($6.50). Several launches also make the trip across to Puerto Barrios on a daily basis. They usually leave between 8am and noon from the main wharf and charge around B$20 to B$25 ($10 to $12.50). Ask around at the wharf for a boat.

ORIENTATION

Punta Gorda is a small coastal town, and the road into town runs right along the water before angling a bit inland.

Fast Facts   There is a **Belize Bank** on the northeastern corner of the town's central park; it's open Monday to Thursday 8am to 1pm, Friday 8am to 4:30pm. The **post office** is on Front Street across from Immigration and is open Monday through Thursday 8:30am until noon and 1 to 5pm, and Friday 8:30am to noon and 1 to 4:30pm. The small **central park** is where you can catch buses to nearby Mayan villages. Schedules change frequently, so ask first.

WHAT TO SEE & DO

A stroll through Punta Gorda is the best way to enjoy the Caribbean atmosphere. If you've come down from the north, you'll likely be surprised at what a clean and quiet town Punta Gorda is compared with Dangriga or Belize City. It's a welcome relief and worth savoring for a day or two.

If you get a little antsy at the slow pace, there are plenty of natural and cultural wonders within easy reach of P.G.

VISITING MAYAN RUINS & VILLAGES

None of the southern ruins are as spectacular or actively restored as the more famous sites in northern and western Belize. Still, the ancient Maya did have substantial cities and trading posts all up and down the Belizean coast and several impressive reminders can be found near Punta Gorda. Those interested in the ongoing Mayan tradition will find themselves in a region of numerous small Kekchi and Mopan Maya villages, many of which have taken tentative steps to enter the tourism industry with homestay programs or basic guest houses.

The largest of the nearby Mayan ruins is **Lubaantun** (Place of Fallen Rock), which is about 20 miles from Punta Gorda and about 1 mile from the village of San Pedro Columbia. From the main road it is a 20-minute walk to the ruin. This late-classic Maya ruin is unusual in that the structures were built using a technique of cut-and-fitted stones rather than the usual limestone-and-rock construction technique used elsewhere by the Mayans. Lubaantun is perhaps most famous as the site where a crystal skull was discovered by a Canadian woman in 1926. Kept in a vault in Canada, the skull has been surrounded with controversy. What was it used for? How could such a hard stone have been carved in such a detailed manner? Where did it come from? Some stories claim a light emanates from the skull; others attribute magical powers to it.

Nim Li Punit (Big Hat), off the Southern Highway 25 miles north of Punta Gorda, is the site of the largest Maya stela (carved record stone) known in Belize. It measures almost 30 feet tall and is one of more than two dozen stelae found here.

Other ruins in the area include **Uxbenka** near Santa Cruz and **Pusilha** near Aguacate. When I last visited, entrance fees were not being charged. However, the Belizean government has officially instituted a B$10 ($5) entrance fee for Lubaantun and Nim Li Punit and they may be collected by the time you visit.

Many people who make it as far as Punta Gorda are interested in learning more about Mayan village life. Though the ruins were abandoned centuries ago, Maya Indians still live in this region. The villages of the Toledo District are populated by two main groups of Maya Indians—the Kekchi and the Mopan—who have different languages and agricultural practices. The Mopan are upland farmers, while the Kekchi farm the lowlands. Both groups are thought to have migrated into southern Belize from Guatemala less than 100 years ago. The past four decades of political violence and genocide in neighboring Guatemala have bolstered this migration. San Antonio, the largest Mopan Maya village, is in a beautiful setting on top of a hill, with an old stone church in the center of the village. Steep streets wind through the village, and there are both clapboard houses and traditional Mayan thatched huts. San Antonio is known for its annual month-long festivities, which begin in late August and culminate on September 25. The celebrations include masked dances similar to those performed in the Guatemalan highlands. If you need a place to stay in San Antonio, I recommend **Bol's Hilltop Hotel** (no phone), a very basic place with great views that charges B$15 ($7.50) for a single and B$30 ($15) for a double.

Mayan culture may be the main attraction of Punta Gorda, but it also boasts natural attractions. About 2^1/$_2$ miles before the village of San Antonio is one of the most beautiful swimming holes in all of Belize. Flowing out of a cave in a limestone mountain, the aptly named **Blue Creek** is a cool stream with strikingly deep turquoise water. Lush rain forest shades the creek, creating an idyllic place to spend an afternoon. You can cool off by swimming up into the mouth of the cave from which the stream flows. Blue Creek is a privately owned park charging a B$4 ($2) admission.

Near the village of Big Falls, near a waterfall on the Rio Grande, there is a **natural hot spring** that's a popular weekend picnic spot. You can have a refreshing swim in the river at the falls and then warm your muscles in the hot spring. There are also some attractive small **waterfalls** near the village of San Antonio.

There are buses from Punta Gorda to San Antonio, Big Falls, and Blue Creek, and buses headed north to Belize City pass by Nim Li Punit. However, these buses run very infrequently and the schedules are subject to change, so making connections can be tricky. Check at **Nature's Way Guest House** (☎ **501-7/22119**) or with the **Toledo Visitor's Information Center** (☎ **501-7/22470**) at the wharf in Punta Gorda to find out about current bus schedules.

Many tourists opt to hire a taxi or go on an organized trip. In addition to Nature's Way and the Visitor's Information Center, you can check out **Requena's Charter Service** (☎ **501-7/22070**) or **Galvez Taxi & Tour Service** (☎ **501-7/22402**). However, this can be expensive, with most drivers charging between B$250 and B$300 ($125 to $150) for a day tour to the site or village of your choice. Still, this set price will usually cover a group of four.

Another option for getting around is to rent a bike. The **Belize Tourism Center,** 11 Front St. (☎ **501-7/22834**) rents mountain bikes for B$10 ($5) per day, and B$52.50 ($26.25) per week. You can reach most of the above sites and villages in an athletic couple hours of riding. Leave early to avoid the oppressive midday heat, and expect slow going and lots of mud in the rainy season.

WHERE TO STAY
DOUBLES FOR LESS THAN B$40 ($20)

Toledo Botanical Arboretum. P.O. Box 73, Punta Gorda. ☎ **501-7/22470.** 1 rm. B$30 ($15) single; B$40 ($20) double. No credit cards.

Formerly Dem Dats Doin, this local organic farm bills itself as an energy-sufficient low-input organic minibiosphere. As part of the farm, owners Alfredo and Yvonne Villoria have a single bedroom available as a bed-and-breakfast (lunch and dinner are also available for B$10 to B$12 ($5 to $6) per person per meal). The farm is primarily visited by people fascinated by sustainable agriculture (permaculture). Electricity and cooking fuel come from the sun and biogas, and there are more than 1,000 varieties of tropical plants, as well as a collection of butterflies and insects, on the farm. The farm is within walking distance of the Kekchi Maya village of San Pedro Columbia and Lubaantun ruins.

If you'd just like to visit and see what's doing, 2-hour tours are available for B$10 ($5). The Villorias also run the Toledo Visitor's Information Center on Front Street at the main wharf (where the Puerto Barrios ferry docks). The information center is open Monday through Wednesday and Friday and Saturday from 8am to noon. If you're interested in visiting their garden, finding out about local tours and transportation, or staying with a Mayan family in one of the nearby villages, ask here.

Staying in a Traditional Mayan Village

While it's possible to find modest hostelries in and around Punta Gorda, why not enrich your experience of Mayan life, past and present, by staying directly in a Mayan village, either on your own or as the guest of a Mayan family?

Two programs are actively working to allow tourists a chance to experience life in a traditional Mayan village, while providing the Maya with an ecologically friendly means of income. The two programs currently in operation take a markedly different approach. One has constructed separate, basic guest houses in the villages for the tourists; the other arranges direct homestays with the actual villagers. The former claims to offer a much more predictable and sanitary experience that spreads the income around more equitably, while the latter claims to be entirely run by local Maya, with all the income going directly to the local families. The verdict is still out, and I know quite a few traditionalists who claim that any contact with Western mores and material goods is a threat to the continuation of the traditional indigenous way of life.

The Toledo Ecotourism Association (TEA), which is headquartered at Nature's Way Guest House (☎ 501-7/22119) in Punta Gorda, has 11 guest houses in different villages around the region. Rates at the 10-member guest houses are B$18.50 ($9.25) per person per night and meals are an additional B$22 ($11) per person per day. The guest houses are all maintained by the TEA, and come with fresh sheets, foam mattresses, mosquito nets, indoor showers, and ventilated pit latrine outhouses. You can also arrange guided hikes through the forest; visits to ruins, waterfalls, and caves; and traditional music, dancing, and storytelling performances for between B$7 and B$10 ($3.50 to $5) per hour, although a full-evening's music and dance will cost B$75 ($32.50).

Alternatively, **The Maya Homestay Network,** which can be reached through the Toledo Visitor's Information Center (☎ 501-7/22470), provides accommodations directly with families in the Mayan villages. There's a B$10 ($5) registration fee for any stay and then accommodations cost B$10 ($5) per person per night; meals cost B$6 ($3) per person per day. These fees are paid directly to your host family. Accommodations during a homestay can range from a hammock to a simple bed, and almost all families have some sort of bathroom or latrine. Currently, the villages involved in the homestay program include San Antonio, Santa Cruz, Santa Elena, San Jose, Na Luum Ca, San Pedro Columbia, and Silver Creek.

In both programs you can expect to be eating what the local villagers eat, which in most cases means plenty of beans and tortillas, as well as the occasional chicken soup or meat dish. One of the highlights for many guests is being able to participate in the cooking chores, and learning the simple art of tortilla making.

Rokagus Inn. 49 Main Middle St., Punta Gorda. ☎ **501-7/22086.** 9 rms (all with bath). B$30 ($15) single; B$38 ($19) double. No credit cards.

Located right on the central park, the Rokagus is the former G&G Inn (and, briefly, Goyo's Inn). This is a convenient place to stay if you arrive in town after dark and don't want to wander around an unfamiliar town looking for a room. Light sleepers beware: There's an often rowdy restaurant and bar on the first floor, and behind this is the TV lounge. All rooms have hot water and cable TV, but otherwise vary considerably; some are large and clean, while others are smaller, darker, and not as clean.

Nature's Way Guest House. 65 Front St., Punta Gorda. ☎ **501-7/22119.** Fax 501-7/22199. 12 rms (2 with bath). B$16 ($8) single with shared bath; B$25 (12.50) single with private bath; B$26 ($13) double with shared bath; B$35 ($17.50) double with private bath; B$35 ($17.50) triple with shared bath. No credit cards.

Located three blocks south of the central park and across the street from the water, Nature's Way is a longtime favorite of budget travelers and should be your first choice in Punta Gorda. Even though most rooms do not have private bathrooms, the shared baths are large, clean, and modern. The guest house is operated by an American, William "Chet" Smith, who moved down here more than 20 years ago to promote sustainable agricultural and tourism practices. Chet is a wealth of information about the area and helped start a village guest-house program which allows visitors to stay in the nearby Mayan villages. Nature's Way is also the home of Belize Adventure Travel, which can arrange a wide variety of tours and adventures, including mangrove kayak paddles and overnight jungle camping.

St. Charles Inn. 23 King St., Punta Gorda. ☎ **501-7/22149.** 13 rms (11 with bath). TV. B$30 ($15) single; B$40 ($20) double. No credit cards.

Located two blocks north of the central park, the St. Charles is part of a small general store, which is where you should go to ask about a room. The guest rooms are in two buildings, and the second floor is a bit nicer since it has a verandah and overlooks a small green yard. The small rooms have louvered windows, fans for cooling, hot water, and cable TV.

DOUBLES FOR LESS THAN B$60 ($30)

Mira Mar Hotel. 95 Front St. (P.O. Box 2), Punta Gorda. ☎ **501-7/22033.** 10 rms (all with bath). TV. B$25 ($12.50) single; B$75 ($37.50) deluxe single; B$45 ($22.50) double; B$100 ($50) deluxe double. No credit cards.

This two-story hotel is located near the center of town by the water. The standard rooms are on the ground floor. They are cement-block affairs, but the walls are painted red, with yellow outlines in the seams. The deluxe rooms are all on the second floor and have air-conditioning and small balconies. All the rooms are clean and well maintained, and come with cable TV. Downstairs is a popular bar, with three pool tables that are apparently active all day and most of the night. The tidy adjoining restaurant serves Belizean and Chinese standards for B$10 to B22 ($5 to $11).

○ **Punta Caliente Hotel & Restaurant.** 108 José María Nunez St., Punta Gorda. ☎ **501-7/22561.** 8 rms (all with bath). B$43 ($21.50) single; B$53 ($26.50) double; B$15 ($7.50) for extra bed. No credit cards.

Inexpensive for Belize, this place has some nice features, such as plants in the hallway and an excellent restaurant serving Creole and Garifuna meals on the ground floor. Located next to the Z-Line bus station, the building is of modern cinderblock construction. There are, surprisingly, no doors on the bathrooms; they are separated by a partition only. Rooms have fans, and some even have a queen-size bed. The owner, Alex Arzu, is extremely friendly, informative, and helpful.

A SPLURGE CHOICE NEARBY

International Zoological Expeditions Lodge at Blue Creek. 35 Lemon St., Dangriga. ☎ **501-5/22119.** Fax 501-5/23152. ☎ 508/655-1461 and fax 508/655-4445 in the U.S. 6 cabins (all with shared bath). B$120 ($60) per person including all meals. No credit cards.

This lodge is located in the jungle near the Mayan village of Blue Creek, about 22 kilometers northwest of Punta Gorda. The comfortable cabins overlook the beautiful Blue Creek River, while the lodge, which is a meeting place for scientists performing ecological studies in the forest, houses the bathrooms and dining area.

Guided trips to nearby caves and other natural sites will cost around B$70 ($35) per day for a local guide, who can usually handle groups of up to six people. The IZE's tree-canopy observation platforms are located across the river, and although access is limited, it's interesting to watch the activity from below.

WHERE TO EAT

Dining options are far from extensive in P.G. In addition to the restaurants listed below, check out the **Punta Caliente** (see "Where to Stay," above) for authentic Garifuna cooking, and **Angie's Bar & Restaurant,** on Back Street about 5 blocks from the central park (☎ 7/22668), for casual dining.

MEALS FOR LESS THAN B$10 ($5)

✪ **Lucille's Kitchen.** 3 North Street, Punta Gorda. ☎ **7/22256.** Main courses B$6–B$12 ($3–$6). No credit cards. Daily 8am–11pm. BELIZEAN/CREOLE.

This place is charming, in a funky Caribbean sort of way. The white walls are covered with a hand-painted speckled pattern and the yellow posts feature red dots and zigzags. There are shell and driftwood mobiles scattered around. You can dine inside, but I'd recommend one of the outdoor tables, which are set amid a small garden of flowering hibiscus, bougainvillea, and orchids, with conch-shell borders. Lucille serves up tasty Belizean stew chicken, pork, and fish dinners (B$8, U.S. $4) with excellent rice and beans cooked in coconut milk. If the place looks closed or deserted, give a yell and Lucille will usually open up for you.

MEALS FOR LESS THAN B$20 ($10)

Kowloon Restaurant. 35 Main Middle St., Punta Gorda. ☎ **7/22692.** B$8–B$18 ($4–$9). No credit cards. Mon–Sat 11am–2pm and 6:30–11pm; Sun 6–11pm. CHINESE/AMERICAN.

There are several Chinese restaurants in Punta Gorda, but currently this is the best one. You can get all the regular Chinese dishes, such as chow mein, chop suey, and fried rice, but fixed with Belizean conch, fish, shrimp, and lobster. It's located a block off the square and three blocks over from the water.

Index

COSTA RICA

Accommodations. *See also* Camping; *and specific accommodations*
  apartotels, 98, 203
  best of, 13–15
  money-saving tips, 19–20
  tent camps, 209, 224–25
  wilderness lodges, 2, 14–15, 27, 218, 224
Activities. *See* Recreational activities; *and specific activities*
Addresses, locating, 81
Adventure travel tour operators, 28–30, 121, 191
Aerial Tram (near San José), 35, 123
Air plants (epiphytes), 54, 55
Airport, Juan Santamaría International (San José), 85, 88, 101
Air travel
  money-saving tips, 19
  to Costa Rica, 77–78
  within Costa Rica, 79
Alajuela, 126
  accommodations, 133–34
  Juan Santamaría Day, 70
Albergue De Montaña Savegre, 32, 212
Albergue de Montaña Tapantí, 7, 32, 212
Almost Paradise (Playa Nosara), 13, 155
American Express, 81, 91
Amor de Mar (Playa Montezuma), 13, 159
Annemarie Souvenir Shop (San José), 12, 115
Anteaters, 216, 236
Apartotels, 98, 203
Archeological museums, in San José
  Museo de Jade Marco Fidel Tristan, 107
  Museo de Oro Blanco Central, 108
Archeological sites, 11
  Guayabo National Monument, 11, 45, 122, 126
Archeology, historical overview, 58–59, 217

Arenal, Lake, 171, 172
  boating, 172
  fishing, 171, 172
  horseback riding, 172
  mountain biking, 3–4, 31
  swimming, 172
  windsurfing, 4, 40, 172
Arenal Botanical Gardens, 172
Arenal National Park, 44, 166, 167
Arenal Observatory Lodge (Escazú), 170
Arenal Volcano, 2, 55, 57, 123, 166, 167
Art museums, in San José
  Centro Nacional de Arte y Cultura, 22, 107
  Museo de Arte Costarricense, 107
Aserri, restaurants, 118
Asociación Talamanqueña de Ecoturismo y Conservación (ATEC), 251–52
ATM machines, 68
Aviarios del Caribe (Cahuita), 7, 15, 32, 245–46, 247–48

Bajo Tigre Trail (Monteverde), 177
Ballena Maritime National Park, 5, 207–8
Barra del Colorado National Wildlife Refuge, 164, 234
  fishing lodges, 38
Barra Honda National Park, 44, 152
Basilica de Nuestra Señora de los Angeles (Cartago), 10, 61, 123–24
Bat Island, 36
Beaches
  best of, 4–7
  riptides at, 74
  Corcovado National Park, 222
  Guanacaste, 5, 128
  Manuel Antonio National Park, 5, 199–200
  Playa Bonita, 242
  Playa Brasilito, 140–41
  Playa Carillo, 152
  Playa Chiquita, 254, 255
  Playa Cocles, 251
  Playa Conchal, 5, 140–41
  Playa de Jacó, 190

  Playa del Coco, 137–38
  Playa Dominical, 207–8
  Playa Escondido, 190
  Playa Espadilla, 199
  Playa Esterillos, 190
  Playa Flamingo, 140–42
  Playa Grande, 144, 146
  Playa Guiones, 154
  Playa Hermosa, 135–36
  Playa Hermosa de Jacó, 190, 193
  Playa Junquillal, 149–50
  Playa Matapalo, 206
  Playa Montezuma, 5, 157
  Playa Nancite, 5, 8, 40, 132
  Playa Naranjo, 132, 161
  Playa Negra, 245
  Playa Nosara, 154, 155
  Playa Ocotal, 137–38
  Playa Ostional, 40, 155
  Playa Panamá, 135–36
  Playa Pavones, 4, 232–33
  Playa Potrero, 140–42
  Playa Tamarindo, 5, 146
  Playa Zancudo, 230–31
  Punta Uva, 5–6, 252
  Punta Uvita, 5, 207–8
  Santa Rosa National Park, 5, 130, 132
  Sugar Beach, 141, 143
Bebedero River, cruises, 130
Bed-and-breakfasts, 13–14, 174
Beverages, 63–64
Bicycling, 31–32, 121. *See also* Mountain biking
  Playa de Jacó, 190
  Playa Grande, 146
  Vuelta de Costa Rica, 112
Bijahua (San José), 16, 106
Biodiversity, 54–56
Bioreserves. *See* National parks and bioreserves
Bird watching, 7, 32–34. *See also* Macaws; Quetzals
  Aviarios del Caribe (Cahuita), 7, 15, 32, 245–46, 247–48
  Cabo Blanco Absolute Nature Reserve, 158
  Caño Negro National Wildlife Refuge, 32, 45, 168
  Estrella Estuary, 245–46, 247–48

BELIZE

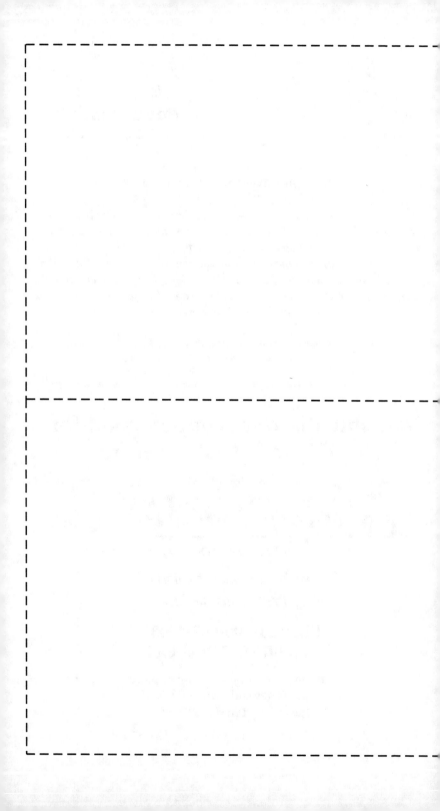

Comments from our customers:

* The hotels & lodges were superb! S.J.
* The trip met or exceeded our expectations! E. P.
* Mariah services were terrific & responsive-always! R.S.
* I would definetely recommend the trip to others and would especially recommend MARIAH! R.S.
* Efficiency of service in Costa Rica was excellent! R.G.
* We saw a pod of humpback whales near Corcovado! R.G.
* The trip exceeded my expectations! All Mariah's recommen dations were right on target! K.B.
* Excellent trip! Great accommodations, good food & beautiful country! The variety & beauty of the country & the great people made for a terrific trip! T.Z.
* Fabulous! Exceeded expectations! A real vacation because it is so different from our regular lives. H.B.

$50 Per Person Discount for any of our Costa Rica Programs

Valid for: Itineraries of 6 or more nights, direct reservations from clients.

Expires 12/31/98

"Touch The Wild"

COSTA RICA SPECIALISTS

Latin American Eco-Tours
Wildlife Adventures Worldwide

Experience makes the difference

Individual & special interest group travel

Preferred Adventures Ltd

Phone (800) 840-8687   Fax (612) 222-4221
e-mail: paltours @aol.com

{Over for Special Offer}

WHEREVER YOU TRAVEL, *H*ELP IS NEVER FAR AWAY.

From planning your trip to providing travel assistance along the way, American Express® Travel Service Offices are always there to help.

Costa Rica

Agencia Super Viajes (R)
Oficentro Ejecutivo La Sabana
Edificio #1, Sabana Sur
Costa Rica
506/220-0400

Banco de San José (R)
Between 3rd and 5th Avenues
Central Street
Costa Rica
506/223-3644

Banco Del Cafe, S.A. (R)
Avenida Reforma 9-30, Zona 9
1er Nivel-Torre Del Pais
Guatemala City
502-2/613-680

Clark Tours (R)
Torre 11, 1er Nivel-107
Diagonal 6, 10-65, Zona 10
Guatemala City
502-2/392-877

Belize Global Travel Services Ltd. (R)
41 Albert Street
Belize City
501-2/77185

Travel

http://www.americanexpress.com/travel